★ **British Museum** ④
See pages 126–9

★ **Tower of London** ⑫
See pages 154–7

★ **St Paul's** ⑩
See pages 148–51

Smithfield and
Spitalfields

⑪

⑩

The City

T H A M E S

⑫

Southwark
and
Bankside

★ **Houses of Parliament** ⑧
See pages 72–3

0 kilometres   1

0 miles   0.5

N

Greenwich
and
Blackheath

★ **Museum of London** ⑪
See pages 166–7

★ **Westminst**
See pages 76–9

D0377748

EYEWITNESS *TRAVEL GUIDES*

LONDON

EYEWITNESS *TRAVEL GUIDES*

LONDON

Main Contributor: MICHAEL LEAPMAN

DORLING KINDERSLEY
LONDON • NEW YORK • STUTTGART

A DORLING KINDERSLEY BOOK

PROJECT EDITOR Jane Shaw
ART EDITOR Sally Ann Hibbard
EDITOR Tom Fraser
DESIGNERS Pippa Hurst, Robyn Tomlinson
DESIGN ASSISTANT Clare Sullivan

MANAGING EDITOR Douglas Amrine
MANAGING ART EDITOR Geoff Manders
SENIOR EDITOR Georgina Matthews
SERIES DESIGN CONSULTANT Peter Luff
EDITORIAL DIRECTOR David Lamb
ART DIRECTOR Anne-Marie Bulat

PRODUCTION CONTROLLER Hilary Stephens
PICTURE RESEARCH Ellen Root
DTP EDITOR Siri Lowe

CONTRIBUTORS
Christopher Pick, Lindsay Hunt

MAPS
Andrew Heritage, James Mills-Hicks, Chez Picthall,
John Plumer (Dorling Kindersley Cartography)

PHOTOGRAPHERS
Philip Enticknap, John Heseltine,
Stephen Oliver

ILLUSTRATORS
Brian Delf, Trevor Hill, Robbie Polley

•

This book was produced with the assistance of
Websters International Publishers.

Film outputting bureau PLS (London)
Reproduced by Colourscan (Singapore)
Printed and bound by Graphicom (Italy)

First published in Great Britain in 1993
by Dorling Kindersley Limited
9 Henrietta Street, London WC2E 8PS
Reprinted with revisions 1994, 1995, 1996

Copyright 1993, 1996 © Dorling Kindersley Limited, London

ALL RIGHTS RESERVED. NO PART OF THIS PUBLICATION MAY BE
REPRODUCED, STORED IN A RETRIEVAL SYSTEM, OR TRANSMITTED IN ANY
FORM OR BY ANY MEANS, ELECTRONIC, MECHANICAL, PHOTOCOPYING,
RECORDING OR OTHERWISE, WITHOUT THE PRIOR WRITTEN PERMISSION
OF THE COPYRIGHT OWNER.

A CIP CATALOGUE RECORD IS AVAILABLE FROM THE BRITISH LIBRARY.

ISBN 0-75130-009-8

•

Every effort has been made to ensure that the information in this
book is as up-to-date as possible at the time of going to press.
However, details such as telephone numbers, opening hours,
prices, gallery hanging arrangements and travel information are
liable to change. The publishers cannot accept responsibility for
any consequences arising from the use of this book.

We would be delighted to receive any corrections and
suggestions for incorporation in the next edition. Please write to
the Managing Editor, Eyewitness Travel Guides
Dorling Kindersley
9 Henrietta Street, London WC2E 8PS.

CONTENTS

Portrait of Sir Walter Raleigh (1585)

INTRODUCING LONDON

Bedford Square doorway (1775)

The Broadwalk at Hampton Court (c.1720)

Beefeater at the Tower of London

Bandstand in St James's Park

Houses of Parliament

SURVIVAL GUIDE

St Paul's Church: Covent Garden

TRAVELLERS' NEEDS

HOW TO USE THIS GUIDE

THIS EYEWITNESS TRAVEL GUIDE helps you get the most from your stay in London with the minimum of practical difficulty. The opening section, *Introducing London,* locates the city geographically, sets modern London in its historical context and describes the regular highlights of the London year. *London at a Glance* is an overview of the city's specialities. *London Area by Area* takes you round the city's areas of interest. It

describes all the main sights with maps, photographs and detailed illustrations. In addition, five planned walk routes take you to parts of London you might otherwise miss.

Well-researched tips on where to stay, eat, shop, and on entertainments are in *Travellers' Needs. Children's London* lists highlights for young visitors, and *Survival Guide* tells you how to do anything from posting a letter to using the Underground.

LONDON AREA BY AREA
The city has been divided into 17 sightseeing areas, each with its own section in the guide. Each section opens with a portrait of the area, summing up its character and history and listing all the sights to be covered. Sights are numbered and clearly located on an *Area Map.* After this comes a largescale *Street-by-Street Map* focusing on the most interesting part of the area. Finding your way about the area section is made simple by the numbering system. This refers to the order in which sights are described on the pages that complete the section.

1 The Area Map
For easy reference, the sights in each area are numbered and located on an Area Map. *To help the visitor, the map also shows Underground and mainline stations and car parks.*

2 The Street-by-Street Map
This gives a bird's eye view of the heart of each sightseeing area. The most important buildings are picked out in stronger colour, to help you spot them as you walk around.

Photographs of facades and distinctive details of buildings help you to locate the sights.

A locator map shows you where you are in relation to surrounding areas. The area of the *Street-by-Street Map* is shown in red.

Colour-coding on each page makes the area easy to find in the book.

Sights at a Glance lists the sights in the area by category: Historic Streets and Buildings, Churches, Museums and Galleries, Monuments, Parks and Gardens.

The area covered in greater detail on the *Street-by-Street Map* is shaded red.

Numbered circles pinpoint all the listed sights on the area map. St Margaret's Church, for example, is ➏

Travel tips help you reach the area quickly by public transport.

A suggested route for a walk takes in the most attractive and interesting streets in the area.

St Margaret's Church is shown on this map as well.

Red stars indicate the sights that no visitor should miss.

LONDON AT A GLANCE
Each map in this section
concentrates on a specific
theme: *Celebrated Londoners,
Museums and Galleries,
Churches, Parks and Gardens,
Ceremonies.* The top sights are
shown on the map; others are
described on the following
two pages and cross-
referenced to their full entries
in the *Area by Area* section.

Each sightseeing area
is colour-coded.

The theme is explored in
greater detail on the pages
following the map.

3 Detailed information on each sight
*All important sights in each area are
described in depth in this section. They
are listed in order, following the
numbering on the* Area Map. *Practical
information is also provided.*

4 London's major sights
*These are given two or more full pages in
the sightseeing area in which they are
found. Historic buildings are dissected to
reveal their interiors; museums and
galleries have colour-coded floor plans to
help you find important exhibits.*

PRACTICAL INFORMATION
Each entry provides all the information
needed to plan a visit to the sight. The
key to the symbols is inside the back
cover.

Telephone number

Address

Map reference
to Streetfinder at
back of book

St Margaret's
Church ➏ — Sight Number

Parliament Sq SW1. **Map** 13 B5.
📞 *071-222 5152.* ⊖ *Westminster.*
Open *9.30am–5.30pm Mon–Sat,
1–5.30pm Sun.* 🕂 *11am Sun.*
Ⓜ ♿ 🎵 *Concerts.*

Opening hours

**Services and
facilities available**

Nearest Underground station

The Visitors' Checklist
provides the practical
information you will need
to plan your visit.

The facade of each major
sight is shown to help you
spot it quickly.

Red stars indicate the most
interesting architectural details
of the building, and the most
important works of art or
exhibits on view inside.

A timeline
charts the key
events in the
history of the
sight.

INTRODUCING
LONDON

Putting London on the Map

Lofndon, the capital of the United
Kingdom, is a city of seven million
people covering 601 sq miles (1,580 sq
km) of southeast England. It is built on
the River Thames at the centre of the
UK road and rail networks. From
London visitors can easily reach the
country's other main tourist attractions.

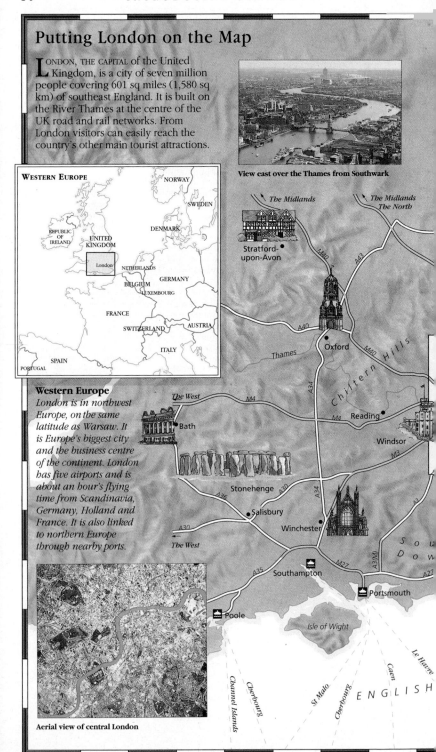

View east over the Thames from Southwark

WESTERN EUROPE

NORWAY
SWEDEN
DENMARK
REPUBLIC OF IRELAND
UNITED KINGDOM
London
NETHERLANDS
GERMANY
BELGIUM
LUXEMBOURG
FRANCE
SWITZERLAND
AUSTRIA
ITALY
SPAIN
PORTUGAL

Western Europe
*London is in northwest
Europe, on the same
latitude as Warsaw. It
is Europe's biggest city
and the business centre
of the continent. London
has five airports and is
about an hour's flying
time from Scandinavia,
Germany, Holland and
France. It is also linked
to northern Europe
through nearby ports.*

↖ The Midlands   ↖ The Midlands
The North

Stratford-
upon-Avon

Oxford

Chiltern Hills

Thames

The West

Bath   Reading

Windsor

Stonehenge

Salisbury

Winchester

*S o u
D o w*

The West

Southampton

Portsmouth

Poole

Isle of Wight

Le Havre
Caen
St Malo
Cherbourg
Cherbourg
Channel Islands

ENGLISH

Aerial view of central London

Greater London
*London has gradually
swallowed up many of the
towns and villages that once
surrounded it. Now it is an
urban sprawl bounded by
the M25 ring road. Details
of important sights outside
central London but within
the M25 are on
pages 240–57.*

GREATER LONDON

Watford
Enfield
Barnet
Edgware
Finchley
Ruislip
Walthamstow
Barking
Uxbridge
Dagenham
Ealing
London City
Greenwich
Dartford
Heathrow
Richmond
Bexley
Staines
Wandsworth
Dulwich
Kingston-
Upon-
Thames
Wimbledon
Beckenham
Bromley
Orpington
Epsom

see next page

0 kilometres   10

0 miles   5

The
Midlands   The North

Cambridge

Felixstowe
Hook of Holland
(Hoek van Holland)
Harwich
Zeebrugge

Luton
Stansted

London City
Heathrow
Southend-on-Sea
Flushing (Vlissingen)
Sheerness

N

North   Downs
Ramsgate
Dunkirk (Dunkerque)
Ostend
(Oostende)
Canterbury
Folkestone   Dover
Calais
Gatwick
Channel Tunnel
Tunbridge
Wells
Boulogne
Calais
Strait of Dover
Boulogne
Brighton   Newhaven
Boulogne

FRANCE

KEY

	Greater London
	Ferry port
	Airport
	Motorway
	A road

0 kilometres   25

0 miles   15

CHANNEL

Dieppe

Central London

MOST OF THE SIGHTS described in this book lie within 14 areas of central London plus two outlying districts of Hampstead and Greenwich. Each of these has its own chapter. If you're short of time you may decide to restrict yourself to the five areas that are packed with most of London's famous sights: Whitehall and Westminster, The City, Bloomsbury and Fitzrovia, Soho and Trafalgar Square, and South Kensington and Knightsbridge.

PAGES 216–23
Street Finder maps
3–4, 11–12

PAGES 232–9
Street Finder maps
23–24

PAGES 224–31
Street Finder maps
1–2

Hampstead

Regent's Park and Marylebone

Greenwich and Blackheath

PAGES 210–15
Street Finder maps
9–10, 17

Kensington and Holland Park

South Kensington and Knightsbridge

Piccadilly and St James's

Chelsea

PAGES 194–209
Street Finder maps
10–11, 18–19

PAGES 188–93
Street Finder maps
18–19

0 kilometres   1

0 miles   0.5

N

Bloomsbury and Fitzrovia

Smithfield and Spitalfields

Soho and Trafalgar Square

Holborn and the Inns of Court

Covent Garden and the Strand

The City

R I V E R   T H A M E S

Southwark and Bankside

South Bank

Whitehall and Westminster

THE HISTORY OF LONDON

IN 55 BC, JULIUS CAESAR'S Roman army invaded England, landed in Kent and marched north-west until it reached the broad River Thames at what is now Southwark. There were a few tribes-men living on the oppo-site bank but no major settlement. However, by the time of the second Roman invasion 88 years later, a small port and mercantile community had been established there. The Romans bridged the river and built their administrative headquarters on the north bank, calling it Londinium – a version of its old Celtic name.

The griffon: the City of London's symbol

LONDON AS CAPITAL
London was soon the largest city in England and, by the time of the Norman Conquest in 1066, it was the obvious choice for national capital.

Settlement slowly spread beyond the original walled city, which was virtually wiped out by the Great Fire of 1666. The post-Fire rebuilding formed the basis of the area we know today as the City but, by the 18th century, London enveloped the settlements around it. These included the royal city of Westminster which had long been London's religious and political centre. The explosive growth of commerce and industry during the 18th and 19th centuries made London the biggest and wealthiest city in the world, creating a prosperous middle class who built the fine houses that still grace parts of the capital. The prospect of riches also lured millions of the dispossessed from the countryside and from abroad. They crowded into insanitary dwellings, many just east of the City, where docks provided employment.

By the end of the 19th century, 4.5 million people lived in inner London and another 4 million in its immedi-ate vicinity. Bombing in World War II devastated many central areas and led to substantial rebuilding in the second half of the 20th century, when the docks and other Victorian industries disappeared.

The following pages illustrate London's history by giving snapshots of significant periods in its evolution.

A map of 1580 showing the City of London and, towards the lower left corner, the City of Westminster

A 15th-century manuscript showing the Tower of London with London Bridge in the background

Roman London

WHEN THE ROMANS invaded Britain in the 1st century AD, they already controlled vast areas of the Mediterranean, but fierce opposition from local tribes (such as Queen Boadicea's Iceni) made Britain difficult to control. The Romans persevered however, and had consolidated their power by the end of the century. Londinium, with its port, developed into a capital city; by the 3rd century, there were some 50,000 people living there. But, as the Roman Empire crumbled in the 5th century, the garrison pulled out, leaving the city to the Saxons.

1st-century Roman coin

EXTENT OF THE CITY

☐ *125 AD*   ☐ *Today*

Public Baths
Bathing was an important part of Roman life. This pocket-sized personal hygiene kit (including a nail pick) and bronze pouring dish date from the 1st century.

Site of present-day
Museum of London

Roman fort

Site of present-day St Paul's

Temple of Mithras
Mithras protected the good from evil. This 2nd-century head was in his temple.

Forum

Basilica

LONDINIUM
Roman London was an important centre on the site of the present-day City (see pp142–159). On the Thames, it was in a good position to trade with the rest of the Empire.

Forum and Basilica
About 200 m (600 ft) from London Bridge was the forum (the chief market and meeting place) and the basilica (the town hall and court of justice).

TIMELINE

55 BC Julius Caesar invades Britain

AD 61 Boadicea attacks

AD 43 Claudius establishes Roman London and builds the first bridge

200 City wall built

410 Roman troops begin to leave

100	200	300	400	5

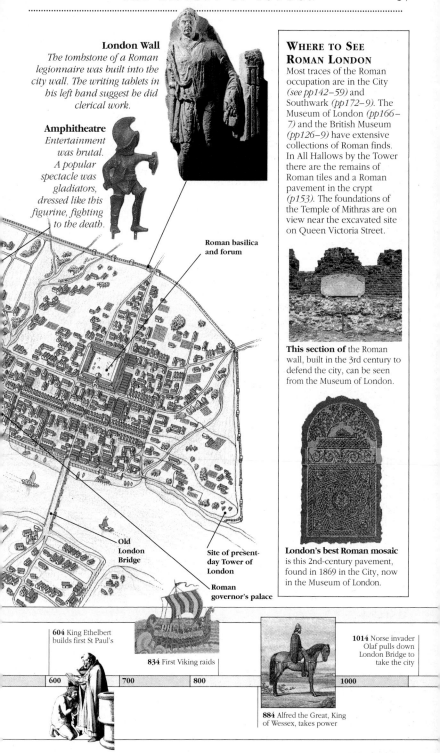

London Wall
The tombstone of a Roman legionnaire was built into the city wall. The writing tablets in his left hand suggest he did clerical work.

Amphitheatre
Entertainment was brutal. A popular spectacle was gladiators, dressed like this figurine, fighting to the death.

Roman basilica and forum

Old London Bridge

Site of present-day Tower of London

Roman governor's palace

WHERE TO SEE ROMAN LONDON

Most traces of the Roman occupation are in the City (*see pp142–59*) and Southwark (*pp172–9*). The Museum of London (*pp166–7*) and the British Museum (*pp126–9*) have extensive collections of Roman finds. In All Hallows by the Tower there are the remains of Roman tiles and a Roman pavement in the crypt (*p153*). The foundations of the Temple of Mithras are on view near the excavated site on Queen Victoria Street.

This section of the Roman wall, built in the 3rd century to defend the city, can be seen from the Museum of London.

London's best Roman mosaic is this 2nd-century pavement, found in 1869 in the City, now in the Museum of London.

604 King Ethelbert builds first St Paul's

834 First Viking raids

884 Alfred the Great, King of Wessex, takes power

1014 Norse invader Olaf pulls down London Bridge to take the city

600 700 800 1000

Medieval London

THE HISTORIC DIVISION between London's centres of commerce (the City) and government (Westminster) started in the mid-11th century when Edward the Confessor established his court and sited his abbey *(see pp76–9)* at Westminster. Meanwhile, in the City, tradesmen set up their own institutions and guilds, and London appointed its first mayor. Disease was rife, however, and the population never rose much above its Roman peak of 50,000. The Black Death (1348) reduced the population by half.

EXTENT OF THE CITY
▨ *1200*   ☐ *Today*

St Thomas à Becket
As Archbishop of Canterbury he was murdered in 1170, at the request of Henry II with whom he was quarrelling. Thomas was made a saint and pilgrims visited his Canterbury shrine.

LONDON BRIDGE
The first stone bridge was built in 1209 and lasted 600 years. It was the only bridge across the Thames in London until Westminster Bridge (1750).

The Chapel of St Thomas, erected the year the bridge was completed, was one of its first buildings.

Iron railings

Houses and shops projected over both sides of the bridge. Shopkeepers made their own merchandise on the premises and lived above their shops. Apprentices did the selling.

The piers were made from wooden stakes rammed into the river bed and filled with rubble.

Dick Whittington
The 15th-century trader was thrice mayor of London (see p39).

Stag Hunting
Such sports were the chief recreation of wealthy landowners.

The arches ranged from 4.5 m (15 ft) to 10 m (35 ft) in width.

TIMELINE

1042 Edward the Confessor becomes king	**1086** Domesday Book, England's first survey, published		**1191** Henry Fitzalwin becomes London's first mayor	**1215** King John's Magna Carta gives City more powers
1050	**1100**	**1150**	**1200**	**1250**
1066 William I crowned in Abbey		**1176** Work starts on the first stone London Bridge	**1240** First parliament sits at Westminster	
1065 Westminster Abbey completed				

☐ **Medieval London**

Chivalry
Medieval knights were idealized for their courage and honour. Edward Burne-Jones (1833–98) painted George, patron saint of England, rescuing a maiden from this dragon.

Geoffrey Chaucer
The poet and customs controller (see p39), *is best remembered for* Canterbury Tales *which creates a rich picture of 14th-century England.*

WHERE TO SEE MEDIEVAL LONDON
There were only a few survivors of the Great Fire of 1666 *(see pp22–3)* – the Tower *(pp154–7)*, Westminster Hall *(p72)* and Abbey *(pp76–9)*, and a few churches *(p46)*. The Museum of London *(pp166–7)* has artefacts while the Tate *(pp82–5)* and National Gallery *(pp104–7)* have paintings. Manuscripts, including the Domesday Book, are at the British Library *(p129)* and the Public Record Office *(p137)*.

The Tower of London was started in 1078 and became one of the few centres of royal power in the largely self-governing City.

A 14th-century rose window is all that remains of Winchester Palace near the Clink *(see p177)*.

Plan of the Bridge
The bridge had 19 arches to span the river making it, for many years, the longest stone bridge in England.

Many 13th-century pilgrims went to Canterbury.

	1348 Black Death kills thousands	**1394** Westminster Hall remodelled by Henry Yevele	*The Great Seal of Richard I shows us what medieval kings looked like.*
1350		**1400**	**1450**
	1381 Peasant's Revolt defeated	**1397** Richard Whittington becomes mayor	**1476** William Caxton sets up first printing press at Westminster

Elizabethan London

IN THE 16TH CENTURY the monarchy was stronger than ever before. The Tudors established peace throughout England, allowing art and commerce to flourish. This renaissance reached its zenith under Elizabeth I as explorers opened up the New World, and English theatre, the nation's most lasting contribution to world culture, was born.

EXTENT OF THE CITY
▢ *1561*   ▢ *Today*

Curtain

SHAKESPEARE'S GLOBE

Elizabethan theatres were built of wood and only half covered, so plays had to be cancelled in bad weather.

A balcony on the stage was part of the scenery.

The apron stage had a trap door for special effects.

Death at the Stake
The Tudors dealt harshly with social and religious dissent. Here Bishops Latimer and Ridley die for so-called heresy in 1555, when Elizabeth's sister, Mary I, was queen. Traitors could expect to be hung, drawn and quartered.

In the pit, below the level of the stage, commoners stood to watch the play.

Hunting and Hawking
Popular 16th-century pastimes are shown on this cushion cover.

TIMELINE

1535 Sir Thomas More executed for treason

1536 Henry VIII's second wife, Anne Boleyn, executed

1530

Rat catchers, and other pest controllers, could not prevent epidemics of plague.

1534 Henry VIII breaks with the Roman Catholic church

1553 Edward dies, succeeded by his sister Mary I

1550

1547 Henry dies, succeeded by his son Edward VI

▢ **Elizabethan London**

The galleries were for rich theatre-goers who could watch from the comfort of seats.

Elizabeth I
The "Virgin Queen" sat for this portrait to celebrate victory over the Spanish in 1588.

Tilting Spurs
The aim of this high-speed sport, popular among noblemen, was to knock opponents off their horses.

Steps allowed tiered seating.

Astronomical Clock
Made in 1540 at Hampton Court, it shows the sun moving round the earth.

Audience entrance

WHERE TO SEE ELIZABETHAN LONDON

The Great Fire of 1666 wiped out the City. Fortunately, Middle Temple Hall *(see p139)*, Staple Inn *(p141)* and the Lady Chapel inside Westminster Abbey *(pp76–9)* were beyond its reach. The Museum of London *(pp166–7)*, Victoria and Albert *(pp198–201)*, and Geffrye Museums *(p244)* have fine furniture and artefacts. Out of town are Hampton Court *(pp250–3)* and Sutton House *(p244)*.

Elizabeth I watched *Twelfth Night* by Shakespeare under the hammerbeam roof of Middle Temple Hall in 1603.

The Parr Pot, now in the Museum of London, was made by Venetian craftsmen in London in 1547.

1563 Plague sweeps Europe

1570 Francis Drake makes first voyage to the West Indies

1584 Walter Raleigh's first attempt to colonize America

1588 Drake defeats Spanish Armada

1591 First play by Shakespeare produced

| 1560 | 1570 | 1580 | 1590 |

1558 Mary I's death makes Elizabeth queen

Gloves made from imported silk and velvet

1603 Elizabeth dies, James I accedes

Restoration London

CIVIL WAR HAD BROKEN out in 1642 when the mercantile class demanded that some of the monarch's power be passed to Parliament. The subsequent Commonwealth was dominated by Puritans under Oliver Cromwell. The Puritans outlawed simple pleasures, such as dancing and theatre, so it was small wonder that the restoration of the monarchy under Charles II in 1660 was greeted with rejoicing and the release of pent-up creative energies. The period was, however, also marked with two major tragedies: the Plague (1665) and the Great Fire (1666).

EXTENT OF THE CITY

■ *1680*   □ *Today*

St Paul's was destroyed in the fire that raged as far east as Fetter Lane *(map 14 E1)*.

London Bridge itself survived, but many of the buildings on it were burned down.

Oliver Cromwell
He led the Parliamentarian army and was Lord Protector of the Realm from 1653 until his death in 1658. At the Restoration, his body was dug up and hung from the gallows at Tyburn, (near Hyde Park see p207).

Charles I's Death
The king was beheaded for tyranny on a freezing day (30 January 1649) outside Banqueting House (see p80).

Charles I
His belief in the Divine Right of Kings angered Parliament and was one of the causes of civil war.

TIMELINE

1605 Guy Fawkes leads failed attempt to blow up the King and Parliament

1623 Shakespeare's first folio published

1625 James I dies, succeeded by his son Charles I

1642 Civil war starts when Parliament defies king

1620   1640   1650

Feathered helmet worn by Royalist cavaliers

1649 Charles I executed, Commonwealth established

□ **Restoration London**

Newton's Telescope
Physicist and astronomer Sir Isaac Newton (1642–1727) discovered the law of gravity.

Samuel Pepys
His exuberant diaries tell us much about courtly life of the time.

The Tower of London was just out of the fire's reach.

WHERE TO SEE RESTORATION LONDON
Wren's churches and his St Paul's Cathedral *(see p47 and pp148–51)* are, with Inigo Jones's Banqueting House *(p80)*, London's most famous 17th-century buildings. On a more modest scale are Lincoln's Inn *(p136)* and Cloth Fair *(p165)*. There is a fine period interior at the Museum of London *(pp166–7)*. The British Museum *(pp126–9)* and the Victoria and Albert *(pp198–201)* have pottery, silver and textile collections.

Ham House *(p248)* was built in 1610 but much enlarged later in the century. It has the finest interior of its time in England.

THE GREAT FIRE OF 1666
An unidentified Dutch artist painted this view of the fire that burned for 5 days, destroying 13,000 houses.

Carts full of dead to bury.

The Plague
During 1665, carts collected the dead and took them to communal graves outside the city.

Peter Paul Rubens painted the ceiling in 1636 for Inigo Jones's Banqueting House *(p80)*. This is one of its panels.

1664–5 Plague kills 100,000

1666 Great Fire

1685 Charles II dies, Catholic James II becomes king

1692 First insurance market opens at Lloyd's

| 1660 | 1670 | | 1690 | |

1660 Monarchy restored under Charles II

A barber's bowl made by London potters in 1681

1688 James ousted in favour of Protestant William of Orange

1694 First Bank of England set up by William Paterson

Georgian London

THE FOUNDATION of the Bank of England in 1694 spurred the growth of London and, by the time George I came to the throne in 1714, it had become an important financial and commercial centre. Aristocrats with West End estates began laying out elegant squares and terraces to house newly-rich merchants. Architects such as the Adam brothers, John Soane and John Nash developed stylish medium-scale housing. They drew inspiration from the great European capitals, as did English painters, sculptors, composers and craftsmen.

George I (reigned 1714–27)

EXTENT OF THE CITY

▨ 1810	☐ Today

Manchester Square was laid out in 1776–8.

Portman Square was on the town's outskirts when it was started in 1764.

Great Cumberland Place
Built in 1790, it was named after a royal duke and military commander.

Grosvenor Square
Few of the original houses remain on one of the oldest and largest Mayfair squares (1720).

Docks
Purpose-built docks handled the growth in world trade.

TIMELINE

1714 George I becomes king

1727 George II becomes king

1717 Hanover Square built, start of West End development

1729 John Wesley (1703–91) founds the Methodist Church

1759 Kew Gardens established

1768 Royal Academy of Art established

1760 George III becomes king

1720	1740	1760	17

John Nash
Stylish Nash shaped 18th-century London with variations on Classical themes, such as this archway in Cumberland Terrace, near Regent's Park.

WHERE TO SEE GEORGIAN LONDON

The portico of the Theatre Royal, Haymarket *(see pp326–7)* gives a taste of the style of fashionable London in the 1820s. In Pall Mall *(p92)* Charles Barry's Reform and Travellers' Clubs are equally evocative. Most West End squares have some Georgian buildings, while Fournier Street *(p170)* has good small-scale domestic architecture. The Victoria and Albert Museum (V&A *pp198–201*) has silver, as do the London Silver Vaults *(p141)* where it is for sale. Hogarth's pictures, at the Tate *(pp82–5)* and Sir John Soane's Museum *(pp136–7)*, show the social conditions.

This English long case clock
(1725), made of oak and pine with Chinese designs, is in the V&A.

GEORGIAN LONDON
The layout of much of London's West End has remained very similar to how it was in 1828, when this map was published.

Captain Cook
This Yorkshire-born explorer discovered Australia during a voyage round the world in 1768–71.

Berkeley Square
Built in the 1730s and 1740s in the grounds of the former Berkeley House, several characteristic original houses remain on its west side.

Ironwork
Crafts flourished. This ornate railing is on Manchester Square.

Signatories of the American Declaration of Independence

1811 George III goes mad, his son George is made Regent

1820 George III dies, Prince Regent becomes George IV

1830 George IV dies, brother William IV is king

| 1800 | 1810 | 1820 | 1830 |

1776 Britain loses American colonies with Declaration of Independence

1802 Stock Exchange formally established

1829 London's first horse bus

Victorian London

MUCH OF LONDON TODAY is Victorian. Until the early 19th century, the capital had been confined to the original Roman city, plus Westminster and Mayfair to the west, ringed by fields and villages such as Brompton, Islington and Battersea. From the 1820s these green spaces filled rapidly with terraces of houses for the growing numbers attracted to London by industrialization. Rapid expansion brought challenges to the city. The first cholera epidemic broke out in 1832, and in 1858 came the Great Stink, when the smell from the Thames became so bad that Parliament had to go into recess. But Joseph Bazalgette's sewerage system (1875), involving banking both sides of the Thames, eased the problem.

Queen Victoria in her coronation year (1838)

EXTENT OF THE CITY

☐ *1900*   ☐ *Today*

The building was 560 m (1,850 ft) long and 33 m (110 ft) high.

Nearly 14,000 exhibitors came from all over the world, bringing more than 100,000 exhibits.

Pantomime
The traditional family Christmas entertainment (still popular today – see p326) started in the 19th century.

Soldiers marched and jumped on the floor to test its strength before the exhibition opened.

Massive elm trees growing in Hyde Park were left standing and the exhibition was erected around them.

The Crystal Fountain was 8 m (27 ft) high.

Carpets and stained glass were hung from the galleries.

TIMELINE

1837 Victoria becomes queen

1836 First London rail terminus opens at London Bridge

1840 Rowland Hill introduces Penny Post

1851 Great Exhibition

Season ticket for Great Exhibition

A Wedgwood plate in typical florid Victorian style

1861 Prince Albert dies

1860

1863 Metropolitan Railway, world's first Underground system, is opened

1870 First Peabody Buildings, to house the poor, built in Blackfriars Road

☐ **Victoria's reign**

Railways
By 1900 fast trains, such as this Scotch Express, *were crossing the country.*

WHERE TO SEE VICTORIAN LONDON

Grandiose buildings best reflect the spirit of the age, notably the rail termini, the Kensington Museums (*see pp194–209*) and the Royal Albert Hall (*p203*). Leighton House (*p214*) has a well-preserved interior. Pottery and fabrics are in the Victoria and Albert Museum, and the London Transport Museum (*p114*) has buses, trams and trains.

The Victorian Gothic style suited buildings like the Public Record Office (*p137*).

Telegraph
Newly-invented communications technology, like this telegraph from 1840, made business expansion easier.

Crystal Palace
Between May and October 1851, six million people visited Joseph Paxton's superb feat of engineering. In 1852 it was dismantled and reassembled in south London where it remained until destroyed by fire in 1936.

GREAT EXHIBITION OF 1851
The exhibition, held in the Crystal Palace in Hyde Park, celebrated industry, technology and the expanding British Empire.

Formal Dress
Under Victoria, elaborate men's attire was replaced by more restrained evening wear.

A special box for carrying top hats

1889 London County Council (LCC) established

1891 First LCC public housing built, in Shoreditch

1899 First motor buses introduced

1901 Queen Victoria dies, Edward VII accedes

1880

1890

1900

1890 First electric Underground line, from Bank to Stockwell, opens

Commemorative fan for the Boer War, which ended in 1903

London Between the World Wars

Art Deco china by Clarice Cliff

THE SOCIETY THAT emerged from World War I grasped eagerly at the innovations of early 20th-century London – the motor car, the telephone, commuter transport. The cinema brought transatlantic culture, especially jazz and swing music. Victorian social restraints were discarded as people flocked to dance in restaurants, clubs and dance halls. Many left the crowded inner city for new suburban estates. Then came the 1930s global Depression, whose effects had barely worn off when World War II began.

EXTENT OF THE CITY

☐ 1938   ☐ Today

METRO-LAND

Commuting
London's new outer suburbs were made popular by the underground railway. In the north was "Metroland", named after the Metropolitan line which penetrated Hertfordshire.

High Fashion
The sleek flowing new styles contrasted with the fussy elaboration of the Victorians and Edwardians. This tea gown is from the 1920s.

Formal evening wear, including hats for both sexes, was still compulsory when going to smart West End night spots.

A LONDON STREET SCENE
Maurice Greiflenhagen's painting (1926) captures the bustle of London after dark.

TIMELINE

Medals, like this from 1914, were struck during the campaign for women's votes.

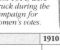

1910 George V succeeds Edward VII

1910

Cavalry was still used in the Middle Eastern battles of World War I (1914–18).

1921 North Circular Road links northern suburbs

1922 First BBC national radio broadcast

1920

☐ **Interwar period**

Early Cinema
London-born Charlie Chaplin (1889–1977), seen here in City Lights, *was a popular star of both silent and talking pictures.*

Seven new theatres were built in central London from 1924 to 1931.

George VI
Oswald Birley painted this portrait of the king who became a model for wartime resistance and unity.

Early motor buses had open tops, like the old horse-drawn buses.

Communications
The radio provided home entertainment and information. This is a 1933 model.

Throughout the period newspaper circulations increased massively. In 1930 *The Daily Herald* sold 2 million copies a day.

WORLD WAR II AND THE BLITZ

World War II saw large-scale civilian bombing for the first time, bringing the horror of war to Londoners' doorsteps. Thousands were killed in their homes. Many people took refuge in underground stations and children were evacuated to the safety of the country.

WOMEN OF BRITAIN
COME INTO
THE FACTORIES

As in World War I, women were recruited for factory work formerly done by men who were away fighting.

Bombing raids in 1940 and 1941 (the Blitz) caused devastation all over the city.

1929 US stock market crash brings world Depression

1939 World War II begins

1930

1927 First talking pictures

1936 Edward VIII abdicates to marry US divorcée Wallis Simpson. George VI accedes

1940 Winston Churchill becomes Prime Minister

Postwar London

MUCH OF LONDON was flattened by World War II bombs. Afterwards, the chance for imaginative rebuilding was missed – some badly designed postwar developments are already being razed. But, by the 1960s, London was such a dynamic world leader in fashion and popular music that *Time* magazine dubbed it "swinging London". Skyscrapers sprang up, but some stayed empty as 1980s boom gave way to 1990s recession.

EXTENT OF THE CITY

▨ *1959*   ▢ *Today*

The Beatles
The Liverpool pop group, pictured in 1965, had rocketed to stardom two years earlier with songs of appealing freshness and directness. The group symbolized carefree 1960s London.

Festival of Britain
After wartime, the city's morale was lifted by the Festival, marking the 1851 Great Exhibition's centenary (see pp26–7).

Margaret Thatcher
Britain's first woman Prime Minister (1979–90) promoted the market-led policies that fuelled the 1980s boom.

The Royal Festival Hall (1951) was the Festival's centrepiece and is still a landmark *(see pp184–5).*

Telecom Tower (1964), at 180 m (580 ft) high, dominates the Fitzrovia skyline.

The Lloyd's Building (1986) is Richard Rogers's Post-Modernist emblem *(see p159).*

TIMELINE

OLYMPIC GAMES
LONDON
1948

OFFICIAL SOUVENIR

1948 Olympic Games held in London

1951 Festival of Britain

1945 End of World War II

1952 George VI dies; his daughter Elizabeth II accedes

1954 Food rationing, introduced during World War II, abolished

RATION BOOK

Minis became a symbol of the 1960s; small and manoeuvrable, they typified the go-as-you-please mood of the decade.

1963 National Theatre founded at the Old Vic

1945	1950	1955	1960	1965

▢ **Postwar London**

Canada Tower (1991) is London's tallest building, and was designed by César Pelli *(see p245)*.

Docklands Light Railway
In the 1980s, new, driver-less trains started to transport people to the developing Docklands.

POST-MODERN ARCHITECTURE

The new wave of architects since the 1980s are reacting against the bleak and stark shapes of the Modernists. Some, like Richard Rogers, are masters of high-tech, emphasizing structural features in their designs. Others, Terry Farrell for example, adopt a more playful approach using pastiches of Classical features such as columns.

Charing Cross (1991) has Terry Farrell's glasshouse on top of the Victorian station *(see p119)*.

YOUTH CULTURE

With their new-found mobility and spending power, young people assumed an influence in the development of British popular culture in the years after World War II. Music, fashion and design were increasingly geared to their rapidly changing tastes.

Punks were a phenomenon of the 1970s and 1980s. Their clothes, music, hair and habits were designed to shock.

The Prince of Wales
As heir to the throne, he is outspokenly critical of much of London's recent architecture. He prefers Classical styles.

1977 Queen's silver jubilee; work starts on Jubilee line underground route

1971 New London Bridge built

1982 Last of the London docks closes

1984 Thames Barrier completed

Vivienne Westwood's clothes won prizes in the 1980s and 1990s.

1986 Greater London Council abolished

1985 Ethiopian famine led to the massive Live Aid relief campaign

1992 Canary Wharf development opens

| 1970 | 1975 | 1980 | 1985 | 1990 | |

Kings and Queens in London

LONDON HAS BEEN the royal capital of England since 1066, when William the Conqueror began a tradition of holding coronations in Westminster Abbey. Since then, successive kings and queens have left their mark on London and many of the places described in this book have royal associations: Henry VIII hunted at Richmond, Charles I was executed on Whitehall and the young Queen Victoria rode on Queensway. Royalty is also celebrated in many of London's traditional ceremonies – for more details on these turn to pages 52–5.

1413–22 Henry V

1509–47 Henry VIII

1399–1413 Henry IV

1485–1509 Henry VII

1066–87 William the Conqueror

1087–1100 William II

1100–35 Henry I

1135–54 Stephen

1327–77 Edward III

1483–5 Richard III

1050	1100	1150	1200	1250	1300	1350	1400	1450	1500
NORMAN		PLANTAGENET					LANCASTER	YORK	TUDOR
1050	1100	1150	1200	1250	1300	1350	1400	1450	1500

1154–89 Henry II

1189–99 Richard I

1199–1216 John

1216–72 Henry III

1307–27 Edward II

1272–1307 Edward I

1461–70 and 1471–83 Edward IV

1422–61 and 1470–1 Henry VI

1377–99 Richard II

Matthew Paris's 13th-century chronicle showing Kings Richard I, Henry II, John and Henry III

1483 Edward V

1553–8 Mary I

1660–85 Charles II

1685–8 James II

1689–1702
William and Mary

1702–14
Anne

1714–27
George I

1603–25
James I

1837–1901 Victoria

1901–10
Edward VII

1727–60 George II

1936 Edward VIII

1952– Elizabeth II

550	1600	1650	1700	1750	1800	1850	1900	1950	2000
	STUART		HANOVER				WINDSOR		
550	1600	1650	1700	1750	1800	1850	1900	1950	2000

1830–37
William IV

1649–60 The Common-
wealth under Oliver
Cromwell

1936–52 George VI shown
on the George Cross medal

1820–30
George IV

1910–36
George V

1625–49 Charles I

1558–1603 Elizabeth I

547–53 Edward VI

1760–1820 George III

LONDON AT A GLANCE

THERE ARE NEARLY 300 places of interest described in the Area by Area section of this book. These range from the cheerful Museum of the Moving Image *(see p184)* to gruesome Old St Thomas's Operating Theatre *(p176),* and from ancient Charterhouse *(p164)* to modern Canary Wharf *(p245).* To help you make the most of your stay, the following 20 pages are a time-saving guide to the best London has to offer. Museums and galleries, churches, and parks and gardens each have a section, and there are guides to famous Londoners and ceremonies in London. Each sight mentioned is cross-referenced to its own full entry. Below are the ten top tourist attractions to start you off.

LONDON'S TOP TEN TOURIST ATTRACTIONS

St Paul's
See pp148–51.

Hampton Court
See pp250–3.

Changing the Guard
Buckingham Palace, see pp94–5.

British Museum
See pp126–9.

National Gallery
See pp104–7.

Westminster Abbey
See pp76–9.

Madame Tussaud's
See p220.

Houses of Parliament
See pp72–3.

Tower of London
See pp154–7.

Victoria and Albert Museum
See pp198–201.

Westminster Bridge and the Houses of Parliament

Celebrated Visitors and Residents

MANY FAMOUS LONDONERS are famous for *being* Londoners – Samuel Pepys, Christopher Wren, Dr Samuel Johnson, Charles Dickens and count-less others *(see pp38–9)*. However, as a centre of international culture, commerce and politics, the English capital has also always attracted celebrated people from overseas. Some famous visitors were escaping war or persecution at home, others came to work or study, or as tourists. In some cases, their association with London is little-known and surprising.

Mary Seacole *(1805–81)*
The Jamaican-born writer and nurse in the Crimean War lodged first in Tavistock Street, then Cambridge Street, Paddington.

Regent's Park and Marylebone

Richard Wagner
(1813–83)
In 1877 the German opera composer lived at No. 12 Orme Square, Bayswater, from where he would walk across the park to conduct at the Royal Albert Hall (see p203).

South Kensington and Knightsbridge

Kensington and Holland Park

Henry James *(1811–1916)*
The American novelist lived at No. 3 Bolton Street, Mayfair, then at No. 34 de Vere Gardens, Kensington (1886–92). He died at Carlyle Mansions, Cheyne Walk.

Dwight Eisenhower
(1890–1969)
During World War II he planned the North African invasion in a house on Grosvenor Square, Mayfair.

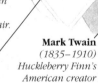

Chelsea

Mark Twain
(1835–1910)
Huckleberry Finn's American creator lived from 1896 until 1897 at No. 23 Tedworth Square.

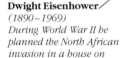

Jenny Lind
(1827–87)
The "Swedish Nightingale" lived for a time at No. 189 Old Brompton Road, Kensington.

DIO POPOLO PENSIERO
1805 1872
IN THIS COUNTRY

GIUSEPPE MAZZINI
THE APOSTLE OF MODERN
DEMOCRACY INSPIRED
YOUNG ITALY WITH THE
IDEAL OF THE INDEPENDENCE.
UNITY AND REGENERATION
OF HIS COUNTRY
1922

Giuseppe Mazzini
(1805–72)
The architect of Italian unity was exiled to London in 1837 and lived at No. 183 Gower Street until 1840. He founded a school for Italian immigrants at No. 5 Hatton Garden.

Karl Marx *(1818–83)*
The German philosopher lived at No. 28 Dean Street, and wrote Das Kapital *in the British Library Reading Room (see p129).*

Bloomsbury and
Fitzrovia

Smithfield and
Spitalfields

Holborn and
the Inns of
Court

The City

Soho
and
Trafalgar
Square

Covent
Garden and
the Strand

RIVER THAMES

South Bank

Southwark and
Bankside

ccadilly
nd St
mes's

Whitehall and
Westminster

0 kilometres 1

0 miles 0.5

GREATER LONDON COUNCIL
GENERAL
CHARLES DE GAULLE
President of the
French National Committee
set up
the Headquarters of the
Free French Forces
here in
1940

Mahatma Gandhi
(1869–1948) Founder of independent India, he studied law at Inner Temple (see p139) in 1889 and ate at the Central, a vegetarian restaurant in St Bride's Lane.

**Charles
de Gaulle** *(1890–1970)*
In World War II he organized the French resistance from Carlton House Terrace.

Charlie Chaplin *(1889–1977)*
America's greatest screen comedian was born in south London and lived at No. 287 Kennington Road. He began his career in London's music halls.

Remarkable Londoners

L ONDON HAS ALWAYS been a gathering place for the most prominent and influential people of their times. Some of these figures have come to London from other parts of Britain or from countries further afield; others have been Londoners, born and bred. All of them have left their mark on London, by designing great and lasting buildings, establishing institutions and traditions, and by writing about or painting the city they knew. Most of them have also had an influence on their times that spread out from London to the rest of the world.

Caricature of the Duke of Wellington

Venus Venticordia **by Dante Gabriel Rossetti**

ARCHITECTS AND ENGINEERS

John Nash's Theatre Royal Haymarket (1821)

A NUMBER OF people who built London still have works standing. Inigo Jones (1573–1652), London-born, was the father of English Renaissance architecture. He was also a landscape painter and a stage designer. Jones lived and worked at Great Scotland Yard, Whitehall, then the residence of the royal architect – the post in which he was later succeeded by Sir Christopher Wren (1632–1723).

Wren's successors as the prime architects of London were his protégé Nicholas Hawksmoor (1661–1736) and James Gibbs (1682–1754). Succeeding generations each produced architects who were to stamp their genius on the city: in the 18th century the brothers Robert (1728–92) and James Adam (1730–94), then John Nash (1752–1835), Sir Charles Barry (1795–1860), Decimus Burton (1800–81), and the Victorians Alfred Waterhouse (1830–1905),

Norman Shaw (1831–1912) and Sir George Gilbert Scott (1811–78). The engineer Sir Joseph Bazalgette (1819–91) built London's sewer system and the Thames Embankment.

ARTISTS

P AINTERS IN LONDON, as elsewhere, often lived in enclaves, for mutual support and because they shared common priorities. During the 18th century, artists clustered around the court at St James's

to be near their patrons. Thus both William Hogarth (1697–1764) and Sir Joshua Reynolds (1723–92) lived and worked in Leicester Square, while Thomas Gainsborough (1727–88) lived in Pall Mall. (Hogarth's Chiswick house was his place in the country.)

Later, Cheyne Walk in Chelsea, with its river views, became popular with artists, including the masters J M W Turner (1775–1851), James McNeill Whistler (1834–1903), Dante Gabriel Rossetti (1828–82), Philip Wilson Steer (1860–1942) and the sculptor

HISTORIC LONDON HOMES

Four writers' homes that have been recreated and are open to visitors are those of the romantic poet **John Keats** (1795–1821), where he fell in love with Fanny Brawne; the historian **Thomas Carlyle** (1795–1881); the lexicographer **Dr Samuel Johnson** (1709–84); and the prolific and popular novelist **Charles Dickens** (1812–70). The house that the architect **Sir John Soane** (1753–1837) designed for himself remains largely as it was when he died, as does the house where the psychiatrist **Sigmund Freud** (1856–1939) settled after fleeing from the Nazis before the outbreak of World War II.

The Hyde Park Corner house of the **Duke of Wellington** (1769–1852), hero of the Battle of Waterloo, is now being refurbished. Finally, the rooms of Sir Arthur Conan Doyle's fictional detective **Sherlock Holmes** have been created in Baker Street.

Dickens House

Carlyle's House

PLAQUES

All over London the former homes of well-known figures are marked by plaques. Look out for these, especially in Chelsea, Kensington and May-fair, and see how many names you recognize.

No. 3 Sussex Square, Kensington

No. 50 Lawford Road, Islington

No. 56 Oakley Street, Chelsea

Sir Jacob Epstein (1880–1959), Augustus John (1879–1961) and John Singer Sargent (1856–1925) had studios in Tite Street. John Constable (1776–1837) is best known as a Suffolk painter but lived for a while at Hampstead, from where he painted many fine views of the heath.

WRITERS

Geoffrey Chaucer (c.1345–1400), author of *The Canterbury Tales*, was born in Upper Thames Street, the son of an innkeeper. Both the playwrights William Shakespeare (1564–1616) and Christopher Marlowe (1564–93) were associated with the theatres in Southwark, and may have lived nearby.

The poets John Donne (1572–1631) and John Milton (1608–74) were both born in Bread Street in the City. Donne, after a profligate youth, became Dean of St Paul's. The diarist Samuel Pepys (1633–1703) was born off Fleet Street.

The young novelist Jane Austen (1775–1817) lived briefly off Sloane Street, near the Cadogan Hotel, where the flamboyant Oscar Wilde (1854–1900) was arrested in 1895 for homosexuality. Playwright George Bernard Shaw (1856–1950) lived at No. 29 Fitzroy Square in Bloomsbury. Later the same house was home to Virginia Woolf (1882–1941) and

George Bernard Shaw

became a meeting place for the Bloomsbury Group of writers and artists, which included Vanessa Bell, John Maynard Keynes, E M Forster, Roger Fry and Duncan Grant.

LEADERS

In legend, a penniless boy named Dick Whittington came to London with his cat seeking streets paved with gold, and later became Lord Mayor. In fact, Richard Whittington (1360?–1423), Lord Mayor three times between 1397 and 1420 and one of London's most celebrated early politicians, was the son of a noble. Sir Thomas More (1478–1535), a Chelsea resident, was Henry VIII's chancellor until they quarrelled over the king's break with the Catholic church and Henry ordered More's execution. More was canonized in 1935. Sir Thomas Gresham (1519?–79) founded the Royal Exchange. Sir Robert Peel (1788–1850) started the London police force, who were known as "bobbies" after him.

ACTORS

Nell Gwynne (1650–87) won more fame as King Charles II's mistress than as an actress. However, she did appear on stage at Drury Lane Theatre; she also sold oranges there. The Shakespearean actor Edmund Kean (1789–1833) and the great

tragic actress Sarah Siddons (1755–1831) were more distinguished players at Drury Lane. So were Henry Irving (1838–1905) and Ellen Terry (1847–1928), whose stage partnership lasted 24 years. Charlie Chaplin (1889–1977), born in Kennington, had a poverty-stricken childhood in the slums of London.

In the 20th century, a school of fine actors blossomed at the Old Vic, including Sir John Gielgud (1904–), Sir Ralph Richardson (1902–83), Dame Peggy Ashcroft (1907–91) and Laurence (later Lord) Olivier (1907–89), who was appointed the first director of the National Theatre.

Laurence Olivier

London's Best: Museums and Galleries

L ONDON'S MUSEUMS ARE FILLED with an astonishing diversity of treasures from all over the world. This map highlights 15 of the city's most important galleries and museums whose exhibits cater to most interests. Some of these collections started from the legacies of 18th- and 19th-century explorers, traders and collectors. Others specialize in one aspect of art, history, science or technology. A more detailed overview of London's museums and galleries is on pages 42–3.

British Museum
This Anglo-Saxon helmet is part of a massive collection of antiquities.

Wallace Collection
Frans Hals's Laughing Cavalier *is a star attraction in this museum of art, furniture, armour and* objets d'art.

Regent's Park and Marylebone

Royal Academy of Arts
Major international art exhibitions are held here, and the renowned Summer Exhibition, when works are on sale, takes place every year.

Kensington and Holland Park

South Kensington and Knightsbridge

Piccadill and St James

Science Museum
Newcomen's steam engine of 1712 is just one of many exhibits that cater for both novice and expert.

Chelsea

Natural History Museum
All of life is here, with vivid displays on everything from dinosaurs (like this Triceratops skull) to butterflies.

Victoria and Albert
It is the world's largest museum of decorative arts. This Indian vase is 18th-century.

0 kilometres	1
0 miles	0.5

National Portrait Gallery
Important British figures are documented in paintings and photographs. This is Vivien Leigh, by Angus McBean (1954).

National Gallery
The world-famous paintings in its collection are mainly European and date from the 15th to the 19th centuries.

Museum of London
London's history since prehistoric times is told with exhibits like this 1920s lift door.

Tower of London
Crown Jewels and the Royal Armouries are here. This armour was worn by a 14th-century Italian knight.

Bloomsbury and Fitzrovia

Smithfield and Spitalfields

Holborn and the Inns of Court

The City

Design Museum
New inventions and prototypes sit next to familiar, everyday objects from past and present.

Soho and Trafalgar Square

Covent Garden and the Strand

Southwark and Bankside

South Bank

Whitehall and Westminster

Courtauld Institute
Well-known works, such as Manet's Bar at the Folies Bergère, *line its galleries.*

Tate Gallery
Two outstanding national collections, of British art from 1550 and of international modern art, are housed here.

Imperial War Museum
It uses displays, film and special effects to recreate 20th-century battles. This is one of the earliest tanks.

Museum of the Moving Image
Actors and life-sized models, like this film director, bring the cinema to life.

Exploring Museums and Galleries

Austin Mini, exhibited at the Design Museum

Lᴏɴᴅᴏɴ ʙᴏᴀꜱᴛꜱ astonishingly rich and diverse museums, the product, in part, of centuries at the hub of world-wide trade and a far-flung Empire. The world-renowned collections cannot be missed, but do not neglect the city's range of smaller museums. From buses to fans, these cover every imaginable speciality and are often more peaceful than their grander counterparts.

Geffrye Museum: Art Nouveau Room

ANTIQUITIES AND ARCHAEOLOGY

Sᴏᴍᴇ ᴏꜰ ᴛʜᴇ most celebrated artefacts of ancient Asia, Egypt, Greece and Rome are housed in the **British Museum**. Other antiquities, including books, manuscripts, paintings, busts and gems, are displayed in **Sir John Soane's Museum**, which is one of the most idiosyncratic to be found in London.

The **Museum of London** contains much of archae-ological interest from all periods of the city's history.

FURNITURE AND INTERIORS

Tʜᴇ ᴍᴜꜱᴇᴜᴍ ᴏꜰ ʟᴏɴᴅᴏɴ recreates typical domestic and commercial interiors from the Roman period right up to the present day. The **Victoria and Albert Museum** (or V&A) contains complete rooms rescued from now vanished buildings, plus a magnificent collection of furniture ranging from the 16th century to work by contemporary designers.

Eclectic collection at Sir John Soane's Museum

On a more modest scale, the **Geffrye Museum** consists of fully-furnished period rooms dating from 1600 to the 1930s. Writers' houses *(see p38)* such as the **Freud Museum** give insights into the furniture of specific periods, while the **Linley Sambourne House** offers visitors a perfectly preserved example of a late Victorian interior.

COSTUME AND JEWELLERY

Tʜᴇ ᴠ&ᴀ'ꜱ ᴠᴀꜱᴛ collections include English and European clothes of the last 400 years, and some stunning jewellery from China, India and Japan. The priceless Crown Jewels, at the **Tower of London**, should also not be missed. **Kensington Palace** Court Dress Collection opens a window on Court uniforms and protocol from about 1750. The **Theatre Museum** has displays of costumes, props and other memorabilia, while the **Museum of Mankind** displays Aztec, Mayan and African costume.

CRAFTS AND DESIGN

Oɴᴄᴇ ᴀɢᴀɪɴ, the **V&A** is the essential first port of call; its collections in these fields remain unrivalled. The more specialized **William Morris Gallery** shows every aspect of this designer's work within the Arts and Crafts movement. For more modern craft and design, the **Design Museum** focuses on mass-produced goods, while the **Crafts Council Gallery** and **Contemporary Applied Arts** display (and sometimes sell) contemporary British craftwork.

MILITARY ARTIFACTS

Tʜᴇ ɴᴀᴛɪᴏɴᴀʟ ᴀʀᴍʏ ᴍᴜꜱᴇᴜᴍ uses vivid models and displays to narrate the history of the British Army from the reign of Henry VII to to the present. The crack regiments of Foot Guards, who are the elite of the British Army, are the main focus of the **Guards' Museum**. The Royal Armouries in the **Tower of London**, Britain's oldest

Design Museum display of chairs

public museum, hold the national collection of arms and armour; the **Wallace Collection** also has a display. In the **Imperial War Museum** re-creations of World War I trenches and the 1940 Blitz show war as it really was. The **Florence Nightingale Museum** illustrates the hardships of 19th-century warfare.

TOYS AND CHILDHOOD

TEDDY BEARS, toy soldiers, dolls' houses and Dinky cars are just some of the toys in the **London Toy and Model Museum**. **Pollock's Toy Museum** offers a similar collection, including Eric, "the oldest known teddy-bear". The **Bethnal Green Museum of Childhood** and the **Museum of London** are slightly more formal, but still fun, and illustrate aspects of the social history of childhood.

SCIENCE AND NATURAL HISTORY

COMPUTERS, ELECTRICITY, space exploration, industrial processes, and transport are all featured at the **Science Museum**. Transport enthusiasts are also catered for at the **London Transport Museum**, where visitors can clamber on underground trains, buses and trams. There are more specialized museums, such as the **Faraday Museum**, of the development of electricity; the **Kew Bridge Steam Museum**; the **National Maritime Museum**; and the **Museum of the Moving Image**.

The **Natural History Museum** mixes displays of

Samson and Delilah (1620) by Van Dyck at the Dulwich Picture Gallery

animal and bird life with innovative ecological exhibits. The **Museum of Garden History** is devoted to what is said to be the British people's favourite pastime.

Imperial War Museum

VISUAL ARTS

THE PARTICULAR STRENGTHS of the **National Gallery** are early Renaissance Italian and 17th-century Spanish painting and a wonderful collection of Dutch masters. The **Tate Gallery** specializes in 20th-century art from both Europe and America, and British paintings of all periods; the Clore Gallery is devoted to the work of Turner. The **V&A** is strong on European art of 1500–1900 and British art of 1700–1900. The **Royal Academy** and the **Hayward**

Stone Dancer (1913) by Gaudier-Brzeska at the Tate Gallery

Gallery specialize in major temporary exhibitions. The **Courtauld Institute** contains Impressionist and Post-Impressionist works, while the **Wallace Collection** has 17th-century Dutch and 18th-century French paintings. The **Dulwich Picture Gallery** includes works by Rembrandt, Rubens, Poussin and Gainsborough. **Kenwood House** is home to paintings by Reynolds, Gainsborough and Rubens in fine Adam interiors. Details of temporary exhibitions are in listings magazines *(see p324).*

London's Best: Churches

IT IS WORTH stopping to look at London's churches
and going in, if they're open. They have a special
atmosphere unmatched elsewhere in the city, and
they can often yield an intimate glimpse of the
past. Many churches have replaced earlier buildings
in a steady succession, dating back to pre-Christian
times. Some began life in outlying villages beyond
London's fortified centre, and were absorbed into
suburbs when the city expanded in the 18th century.
The memorials in the capital's churches and churchyards are a fascinating record of local life, liberally
peppered with famous names. A more detailed
overview of London churches is on pages 46–7.

All Souls
*This plaque comes from a
tomb in John Nash's Regency
church of 1824.*

Bloomsbury
and Fitzrovia

Regent's Park
and Marylebone

Soho and
Trafalgar
Square

St Paul's Covent Garden
*Inigo Jones's Classical church
was known as "the handsomest
barn in England".*

St Martin-in-the Fields
*James Gibbs's church
of 1722–6 was
originally thought
"too gay" for
Protestant worship.*

South Kensington
and Knightsbridge

Piccadilly
and St James's

0 kilometres   1

0 miles   0.5

Whitehall and
Westminster

Brompton Oratory
*This sumptuous Baroque
church was decorated with
works by Italian artists.*

Westminster Cathedral
*The Italian-Byzantine
Catholic cathedral's red-
and-white brick exterior
conceals a rich interior of
multicoloured marbles.*

Westminster Abbey
*The famous abbey has the
most glorious medieval
architecture in London,
and highly impressive
tombs and monuments.*

St Mary-le-Strand
Now on a traffic island, this ship-like church was built by James Gibbs in 1714–17 to a lively Baroque design. Featuring high windows and rich interior detailing, it was made solid enough to keep out the noise from the street.

St Mary Woolnoth
The jewel-like interior of Nicholas Hawksmoor's small Baroque church (1716–27) appears larger than the outside.

Holborn and the Inns of Court

Smithfield and Spitalfields

Covent Garden and the Strand

The City

South Bank

Southwark and Bankside

St Stephen Walbrook
Wren was at his best with this domed interior of 1672–7. Its carvings include Henry Moore's austere modern altar.

St Paul's
At 110 m (360 ft) high, the dome of Wren's cathedral is the world's second largest after St Peter's in Rome.

Southwark Cathedral
This largely 13th-century priory church was not designated a cathedral until 1905. It has a fine medieval choir.

Temple Church
Built in the 12th and 13th centuries for the Knights Templar, it is one of the few circular churches to survive in England.

Exploring Churches

THE CHURCH SPIRES that puncture London's skyline span nearly a thousand years of the city's history. They form an index to many of the events that have shaped the city – the Norman Conquest (1066); the Great Fire of London (1666); the great restoration, led by Wren, that followed it; the Regency period; the confidence of the Victorian era; and the devastation of World War II. Each has had its effect on the churches, many designed by the most influential architects of their times.

St Paul's, Covent Garden

MEDIEVAL CHURCHES

THE MOST FAMOUS old church to survive the Great Fire of 1666 is the superb 13th-century **Westminster Abbey**, the church of the Coronation, with its tombs of British monarchs and heroes. Less well known are the well-hidden Norman church of **St Bartholomew-the-Great**, London's oldest church, (1123), the circular **Temple Church** founded in 1160 by the Knights Templars and **Southwark Cathedral**, set amid Victorian railway lines and warehouses. **Chelsea Old Church** is a charming village church near the river.

CHURCHES BY JONES

INIGO JONES (1573–1652) was Shakespeare's contemporary, and his works were almost as revolutionary as the great dramatist's. Jones's Classical churches of the 1620s and 1630s shocked a public used to conservative Gothic finery. By far the best-known is **St Paul's Church** of the 1630s, the centrepiece of Jones's Italian-style piazza in Covent Garden. **Queen's Chapel, St James** was built in 1623 for Queen Henrietta Maria, the Catholic wife of Charles I. It was the first Classical church in England and has a magnificent interior but is, unfortunately, usually closed to the public.

CHURCHES BY HAWKSMOOR

NICHOLAS HAWKSMOOR (1661–1736) was Wren's most talented pupil, and his churches are among the finest

SPIRES

Look out for London's richly-decorated church steeples. Here are four of the city's most distinctive to get you started.

St Martin-in-the-Fields, by James Gibbs, is in a prominent position grandly overlooking Trafalgar Square.

Clock dating from 1758

St Mary-le-Bow, by Christopher, Wren has a copper dragon weathervane on top of its fine steeple.

Graceful bow arches

St Bride's has Wren's tallest steeple. Originally 234 ft (71m) high, 8 ft (2.5 m) were lost in a thunder storm in 1764.

Four octagonal tiers

St George's Bloomsbury, by Nicholas Hawksmoor, is topped by George I in a Roman toga.

Steeple rising in steps

Baroque buildings to be found in Britain.

St George's, Bloomsbury (1716–31) has an unusual centralized plan and a pyramid steeple topped by a statue of King George I. **St Mary Woolnoth** is a tiny jewel of 1716–27, and further east **Christ Church, Spitalfields** is a Baroque tour-de-force of 1714–29, now being restored.

Among Hawksmoor's East End churches are the stunning **St Anne's, Limehouse** and **St Alfege**, of 1714–17, which is across the river in Greenwich. The tower on this temple-like church was added later by John James in 1730.

St Anne's, Limehouse

CHURCHES BY GIBBS

JAMES GIBBS (1682–1754) more conservative than his Baroque contemporaries such as Hawksmoor, and he also kept his distance from the Neo-Classical trend so popular after 1720. His idiosyncratic London churches were enormously influential. **St Mary-le-Strand** (1714–17) is an island church which appears to be sailing down the Strand. The radical design of **St Martin-in-the-Fields** (1722–6) predates its setting, Trafalgar Square, by a hundred years.

REGENCY CHURCHES

THE END OF the Napoleonic Wars in 1815 brought a flurry of church building. The need for churches in London's new suburbs fused with a Greek Revival. The

CHRISTOPHER WREN

Sir Christopher Wren (1632–1723) was leader among the many architects who helped restore London after the Great Fire of London. He devised a new city plan, replacing the narrow streets with wide avenues radiating from piazzas. His plan was rejected, but he was commissioned to build 52 new churches; 31 have survived various threats of demolition and the bombs of World War II, although six are shells. Wren's great masterpiece is the massive St Paul's, while nearby is splendid **St Stephen Walbrook**, his domed church of 1672–77. Other landmarks are **St Bride's**, off Fleet Street, said to have inspired the traditional shape of wedding cakes, **St Mary-le-Bow** in Cheapside and **St Magnus Martyr** in Lower Thames Street. Wren's own favourite was **St James's, Piccadilly** (1683–4). Smaller gems are **St Clement Danes**, Strand (1680–82) and **St James, Garlickhythe** (1674–87).

results may lack the exuberance of Hawksmoor, but they have an austere elegance of their own. **All Souls, Langham Place** (1822–4), at the north end of Regent Street, was built by the Prince Regent's favourite, John Nash, who was ridiculed at the time for its unusual combination of design styles. Also worth visiting is **St Pancras,** a Greek Revival church of 1819–22, which is typical of the period.

VICTORIAN CHURCHES

LONDON HAS SOME of the finest 19th-century churches in Europe. Grand and colourful, their riotous decoration is in marked contrast to the chaste Neo-Classicism of the preceding Regency era. Perhaps the best of the capital's late Victorian churches is **Westminster Cathedral**, a stunningly rich, Italianate Catholic cathedral built in 1895–1903, with architecture by J F Bentley and *Stations of the Cross* reliefs by Eric Gill. **Brompton Oratory** is a grand Baroque revival, based on a church in Rome and filled with magnificent furnishings from all over Catholic Europe.

Brompton Oratory

London's Best: Parks and Gardens

SINCE MEDIEVAL TIMES London has had large expanses of green. Some of these, such as Hampstead Heath, were originally common land, where small-holders could graze their animals. Others, such as Richmond Park and Holland Park, were royal hunting grounds or the gardens of large houses; several still have formal features dating from those times. Today you can cross much of central London by walking from St James's Park in the east to Kensington Gardens in the west. Purpose-built parks, like Battersea, and botanical gardens, like Kew, appeared later.

Hampstead Heath
This breezy, open space is located in the midst of north London. Nearby Parliament Hill offers views of St Paul's, the City and the West End.

Hampstea

Kensington Gardens
This plaque is from the Italian Garden, one of the features of this elegant park.

Holland Park
The former grounds of one of London's grandest homes are now its most romantic park.

Kensington and Holland Park

South Kensington Knightsbi

Kew Gardens
The world's premier botanic garden is a must for anyone with an interest in plants, exotic or mundane.

0 kilometres   1

0 miles   0.5

Richmond Park
The biggest royal park in London remains largely unspoiled, with deer and magnificent river views.

Regent's Park
In this civilized park surrounded by fine Regency buildings, you can stroll around the rose garden, visit the open-air theatre, or simply sit and admire the view.

Greenwich Park
Its focal point is the National Maritime Museum, well worth a visit for its architecture as well as its exhibits. There are also fine views.

Hyde Park
The Serpentine is one of the highlights of a park which also boasts restaurants, an art gallery and Speakers' Corner.

Regent's Park and Marylebone

Bloomsbury and Fitzrovia

Holborn and the Inns of Court

Smithfield and Spitalfields

Soho and Trafalgar Square

The City

Piccadilly

RIVER THAMES

The South-bank

Southwark and Bankside

Whitehall and Westminster

N

Greenwich and Blackheath

Green Park
Its leafy paths are favoured by early-morning joggers from the Mayfair hotels.

Battersea Park
Visitors can hire a rowing boat for the best view of the Victorian landscaping around the lake.

St James's Park
People come here to feed the ducks, or watch the pelicans. A band plays throughout the summer.

Exploring Parks and Gardens

L ONDON HAS ONE of the the world's greenest city centres, full of tree-filled squares and grassy parks. From the intimacy of the Chelsea Physic Garden, to the wild, open spaces of Hampstead **Camilla** Heath, every London park has its own charm **japonica** and character. For those looking for a specific outdoor attraction – such as sports, wildlife or flowers – here is a list of the most interesting London parks.

Embankment Gardens

FLOWER GARDENS

T HE BRITISH are famed for their gardens and love of flowers and this is reflected in several of London's parks. Really keen gardeners will find all they ever wanted to know at **Kew Gardens** and the **Chelsea Physic Garden**, which is especially strong on herbs. Closer to the centre of town, **St James's Park** boasts some spectacular flower beds, filled with bulbs and bedding plants, which are changed every season. **Hyde Park** sports a magnificent show of daffodils and crocuses in the spring and London's best rose garden is Queen Mary's in

Regent's Park. **Kensington Gardens'** flower walk has an exemplary English mixed border, and there is also a delightful small 17th-century garden at the **Museum of Garden History**.

Battersea Park also has a charming flower garden, and indoor gardeners should head to the **Barbican Centre's** well-stocked conservatory.

FORMAL GARDENS

T HE MOST SPECTACULAR formal garden is at **Hampton Court**, which has a network of gardens from different periods, starting with Tudor. The gardens at **Chiswick**

House remain dotted with their 18th-century statuary and pavilions. Other restored gardens include 17th-century **Ham House**, and **Osterley Park**, whose 18th-century layout was retraced through the art of dowsing. **Fenton House** has a really fine walled garden; **Kenwood** is less formal, with its woodland area. **The Hill** is great in summer. The sunken garden at **Kensington Palace** has a formal layout and **Holland Park** has flowers around its statues.

RESTFUL CORNERS

L ONDON'S SQUARES are cool, shady retreats but, sadly, many are reserved for key-holders, usually residents of the surrounding houses. Of those open to all, **Russell Square** is the largest and most secluded. **Berkeley Square** is open but barren. **Green Park**, with its shady trees and deck chairs, offers a cool picnic spot right in central London. The Inns of Court provide some really pleasant havens: **Gray's Inn** gardens, **Middle Temple**

Sunken garden at Kensington Palace

GREEN LONDON

In Greater London there are 1,700 parks covering a total of 67 sq miles (174 sq km). This land is home to some 2,000 types of plant and 100 bird species who breed in the trees. Trees help the city to breathe, manu-facturing oxygen from the polluted air. Here are some of the species you are most likely to see in London.

The London plane, now the most common tree in London, grows along many streets.

The English oak grows all over Europe. The Royal Navy used to build ships from it.

gardens and **Lincoln's Inn Fields**. **Soho Square**, which is surrounded by streets, is more urban and animated.

MUSIC IN SUMMER

STRETCHING OUT on the grass or in a deck chair to listen to a band is a British tradition. Military and other bands give regular concerts throughout the summer at **St James's** and **Regent's Parks** and also at **Parliament Hill Fields**. The concert schedule will usually be found posted up close to the bandstand in the park.

Open-air festivals of classical music are held in the summer in several parks (see p331).

WILDLIFE

THERE IS A LARGE and well-fed collection of ducks and other water birds, even including a few pelicans, in **St James's Park**. Duck lovers will also appreciate **Regent's**, **Hyde** and **Battersea Parks**, as well as **Hampstead Heath**. Deer roam in **Richmond** and **Greenwich Parks**. For a wide variety of captive animals, **London Zoo** is in **Regent's Park** and there are aviaries or aquariums at several parks and gardens, including **Kew Gardens** and **Syon House**.

Geese in St James's Park

HISTORIC CEMETERIES

In the late 1830s a ring of private cemeteries was established around London to ease the pressure on the monstrously overcrowded and unhealthy burial grounds of the inner city. Today some of these (notably **Highgate Cemetery** and Kensal Green – Harrow Road W10) are worth visiting for their air of repose and their Victorian monuments. **Bunhill Fields** is earlier; it was first used during the plague of 1665.

Kensal Green cemetery

Boating pond at Regent's Park

SPORTS

CYCLING IS NOT universally encouraged in London's parks, and footpaths tend to be too bumpy to allow much rollerskating. However, most parks have tennis courts, which normally have to be reserved in advance with the attendant. Rowing boats may be hired at **Hyde**, **Regent's** and **Battersea Parks**, among others. Athletics tracks are at both Battersea Park and also **Parliament Hill**. The public may swim at the ponds on **Hampstead Heath** and in the Serpentine in Hyde Park. Hampstead Heath is also ideal kite-flying territory.

WHERE TO FIND THE PARKS

The common beech has a close relation, the copper beech, with reddish purple leaves.

The horse chestnut's hard round fruits are used by children for a game called conkers.

London's Best: Ceremonies

MUCH OF LONDON'S rich inheritance of tradition and ceremony centres on royalty. Faithfully enacted today, some of these ceremonies date back to the Middle Ages, when the ruling monarch had absolute power and had to be protected from opponents. This map shows the venues for some of the most important ceremonies in London. For more details on these and other ceremonies please turn to pages 54–5; information on all sorts of events taking place in London throughout the year can be found on pages 56–9.

St James's Palace and Buckingham Palace
Members of the Queen's Life Guard stand in front of the two royal palaces. The Guard is changed daily in summer.

Bloomsbury and Fitzrovia

Soho and Trafalgar Square

South Kensington and Knightsbridge

Piccadilly and St James's

Hyde Park
A Royal Salute is fired from a cannon in the park on six royal anniversaries each year, and also on other special occasions.

Whitehall and Westminster

Chelsea

Chelsea Hospital
In 1651 Charles II hid from parliamentary forces in an oak tree. On Oak Apple Day, Chelsea Pensioners decorate his statue with oak leaves and branches.

Horse Guards
At Trooping the Colour, the most elaborate of London's royal ceremonies, the Queen salutes as a battalion of Foot Guards parades its colours before her.

The City and Embankment

At the Lord Mayor's Show, pikemen and musketeers escort the newly elected Lord Mayor through the City in a gold state coach.

The Cenotaph

On Remembrance Sunday the Queen pays homage to the nation's war dead.

Holborn and the
Inns of Court

Covent
rden and
e Strand

The City

R I V E R   T H A M E S

South Bank

Southwark and
Bankside

0 kilometres   1

0 miles   0.5

Tower of London

In the nightly Ceremony of the Keys, a Yeoman Warder locks the gates. A military escort ensures the keys are not stolen.

Houses of Parliament

Each autumn the Queen goes to Parliament in the Irish State Coach, to open the new parliamentary session.

Attending London's Ceremonies

ROYALTY AND COMMERCE provide the two principal sources of London's rich calendar of ceremonial events. Quaint and old-fashioned these events may be, but what may seem arcane ritual has real historical meaning – many of the capital's ceremonies originated in the the Middle Ages.

ROYAL CEREMONIES

ALTHOUGH THE Queen's role is now largely symbolic, the Guard at Buckingham Palace still actively patrols the palace grounds. The impressive ceremony of **Changing the Guard** – dazzling uniforms, shouted commands, martial music – consists of the Old Guard, which forms up in the palace forecourt, going off duty and handing over to the New Guard. The Guard consists of three officers and 40 men when the Queen is in residence, but only three officers and 31 men when she is away. The ceremony takes place in full public view, right in front of the palace. The Guard is also changed at Horse Guards and on Tower Green, at the Tower of London.

The **Ceremony of the Keys** at the Tower of London is one of the capital's most timeless ceremonies. After each of the Tower gates has been locked, the last post is sounded by a trumpeter before the keys are secured in the Queen's House.

The Tower of London and Hyde Park are also the scene of **Royal Salutes** which take place on birthdays and other occasions throughout the year. At such times 41 rounds are fired in Hyde Park at noon, and 62 rounds at the Tower at 1pm. The spectacle in Hyde Park is a stirring one as 71 horses and six 13-pounder cannons swirl into place and the roar of the guns begins.

The combination of pageantry, colour and music makes the annual **Trooping the Colour** the high point of London's ceremonial year. The Queen takes the Royal Salute, and after her troops have marched past, she leads them to Buckingham Palace where a second march past takes place. The best place to watch this spectacle is from the Horse Guards Parade side of St James's Park.

Bands of the Household Cavalry and the Foot Guards stage the ceremony of **Beating the Retreat** at Horse Guards Parade. This takes place three or four evenings a week in the fortnight leading up to **Trooping the Colour** The spectacular **State Opening of Parliament**, when the Queen opens the annual parliamentary session in the House of Lords – usually in November – is not open to the general public, although it is now televised. The huge royal procession, which moves from Buckingham Palace to Westminster is, however, a magnificent sight, with the Queen travelling in the highly ornate Irish State Coach drawn by four horses.

A Queen's Guard in winter

MILITARY CEREMONIES

THE CENOTAPH in Whitehall is the setting for a ceremony held on **Remembrance Sunday**, to give thanks to those who died fighting in the two World Wars.

National **Navy Day** is commemorated by a parade down the Mall, followed by a service held at Nelson's Column in Trafalgar Square.

Royal salute, Tower of London

One of the Queen's Life Guards

Changing the Guard, Tower of London

Silent Change Ceremony at Guildhall for the new Lord Mayor

CEREMONIES IN THE CITY

NOVEMBER IS THE focus of the City of London's ceremonial year. At the **Silent Change** in Guildhall, the outgoing Lord Mayor hands over symbols of office to the new Mayor in a virtually wordless ceremony. The following day sees the rumbustious **Lord Mayor's Show**. Accompanying the Lord Mayor in his gold state coach a procession of bands, decorated floats and military detachments makes its way through the City from Guildhall past the Mansion House to the Law Courts, and back again along the Embankment.

Lord Mayor's chain of office

Many of the ceremonies that take place in the City are linked to the activities of the Livery Companies *(see p152)*. These include the Worshipful Companies of **Vintners' and Distillers'** annual celebration of the wine harvest and the Stationers' **Cakes and Ale Sermon**, held in St Paul's. Cakes and ale are provided according to the will of a 17th-century stationer.

NAME-DAY CEREMONIES

EVERY 21 MAY **King Henry VI**, who was murdered in the Tower of London in 1471, is still remembered by the members of his two famous foundations, Eton College and King's College, Cambridge,

who meet for a ceremony at the Wakefield Tower where he was killed. **Oak Apple Day** commemorates King Charles II's lucky escape from the Parliamentary forces of Oliver Cromwell in 1651. The King managed to conceal himself in a hollow oak tree, and today Chelsea Pensioners honour his memory by decorating his statue at Chelsea Hospital with oak leaves and branches. On 18 December, the diarist **Dr Johnson** is commemorated in an annual service held at Westminster Abbey.

INFORMAL CEREMONIES

EACH JULY, six guildsmen from the Company of Watermen compete for the prize in **Doggett's Coat and Badge Race**. In autumn, the **Pearly Kings and Queens**, representatives of east London's traders, meet at St Martin-in-the-Fields. In March children are given oranges and lemons at the **Oranges and Lemons service** at St Clement Danes Church. In February, clowns take part in a service for **Joseph Grimaldi** (1779–1837) at the Holy Trinity Church in Dalston E8.

Pearly Queen

WHERE TO FIND THE CEREMONIES

Beating the Retreat
Horse Guards *p80*, date arranged during first two weeks of June.
Cakes and Ale Sermon
St Paul's *pp148–51*, Ash Wed.
Ceremony of the Keys
Tower of London *pp154–7*, 9.30pm daily. Tickets from the Tower, but book well in advance.
Changing the Guard
Buckingham Palace *pp94–5*, Apr–Jul: 11.30am daily; Aug–Mar: alternate days. Horse Guards *p80*, 1pm daily. Tower of London *pp154–7*, noon daily.
Doggett's Coat and Badge Race
From London Bridge to Cadogan Pier, Chelsea *pp189–93*, July.
Dr Johnson Memorial
Westminster Abbey *pp76–9*, 18 Dec.
Joseph Grimaldi Memorial
Holy Trinity Church, Dalston E8, 7 Feb.
King Henry VI Memorial
Wakefield Tower, Tower of London *pp154–7*, 21 May.
Lord Mayor's Show
The City *pp143–53*, second Sat Nov.
Navy Day
Trafalgar Sq *p102*, 21 Oct.
Oak Apple Day
Royal Hospital *p193*, Thu after 29 May.
Oranges and Lemons Service
St Clement Danes *p138*, March.
Pearly Kings and Queens Harvest Festival
St Martin-in-the-Fields *p102*, autumn.
Remembrance Sunday
Cenotaph *p74*, Sun nearest 11 Nov.
Royal Salutes
Hyde Park *p207*, royal anniversaries and other state occasions.
Silent Change
Guildhall *p159*, second Fri Nov.
State Opening of Parliament, Houses of Parliament *pp72–3*, Oct–Nov. Procession from Buckingham Palace *pp94–5* to Westminster.
Trooping the Colour
Horse Guards *p80*, 2nd Sat Jun (rehearsals on previous two Sats). Limited tickets from headquarters Household Division, Horse Guards.
Vintners' and Distillers' Wine Harvest
St Olave's Church, Hart St EC3, second Tue Oct.

LONDON THROUGH THE YEAR

SPRINGTIME IN London carries an almost tangible air of a city waking up to longer days and outdoor pursuits. The cheerful yellow of daffodils studs the parks, and less-hardy Londoners turn out for their first jog of the year to find themselves puffing in the wake of serious runners in training for the Marathon. As spring turns into summer, the royal parks reach their full glory, and in Kensington Gardens nannies gather to chat under venerable chestnut trees. As autumn takes hold, those same trees are ablaze with red and gold and Londoners' thoughts turn to afternoons in museums and art galleries, followed by tea in a café. The year draws to a close with Guy Fawkes parties and shopping in the West End. Contact the London Tourist Board *(see p345)* or check the listings magazines *(p325)* for details of seasonal events.

SPRING

THE WEATHER during the spring months may be raw, and an umbrella is a necessary precaution. Druids celebrate the Spring Equinox in a subdued ceremony on Tower Hill. Painters compete to have their works accepted by the Royal Academy. Footballers close their season with the FA Cup Final at Wembley, while cricketers don their sweaters to begin theirs. Oxford and Cambridge Universities row their annual boat race along the Thames, and Marathon runners pound the streets.

Runners in the London Marathon passing Tower Bridge

MARCH

Chelsea Antiques Fair
(second week), Chelsea Old Town Hall, King's Rd SW3.
Ideal Home Exhibition
(second week), Earl's Court, Warwick Rd SW5. It is a long-established show with the latest in domestic gadgetry and state-of-the-art technology.
Oranges and Lemons Service, St Clement Danes *(p55)*. Service for schoolchildren; each child is given an orange and a lemon.
Oxford v Cambridge boat race *(Sat before Easter, or Easter)*, Putney to Mortlake *(p337)*.
Spring Equinox celebration *(21 Mar)*, Tower Hill EC3. Subdued pagan ceremony with modern-day druids.

EASTER

Good Fri and following Mon are public holidays. **Easter parades**, Covent Garden *(p114)*, Battersea Park *(p247)*.

Kite flying, Blackheath *(p239)* and Hampstead Heath *(p230)*.
Easter procession and hymns *(Easter Mon)*, Westminster Abbey *(pp76–9)*. One of London's most evocative religious celebrations.
International Model Railway Exhibition *(Easter weekend)*, Royal Horticultural Hall, Vincent Sq SW1. Of real interest to everyone, not just railway enthusiasts.

A London park in the spring

APRIL

Queen's Birthday gun salutes *(21 Apr)*, Hyde Park, Tower of London *(p54)*.
London Marathon *(Sun in Apr or May)*, Greenwich to Westminster *(p337)*.

MAY

First and last Mon are public holidays.
FA Cup Final, Wembley. Football season's climax *(p336)*.
Henry VI Memorial *(p55)*.
Beating the Bounds *(Ascension Day)*, throughout the City. Young boys selected from the City parish beat certain buildings, marking the parish boundaries.
Oak Apple Day, at the Royal Hospital, Chelsea *(p55)*.
Funfairs *(late May public hol weekend)*, various commons.
Chelsea Flower Show *(late May)*, Royal Hospital, Chelsea.
Beating the Retreat *(p54)*.
Royal Academy Summer Exhibition *(May–Jul)*, Piccadilly *(p90)*.

AVERAGE DAILY HOURS OF SUNSHINE

Hours

Jan Feb Mar Apr May Jun Jul Aug Sep Oct Nov Dec

Sunshine Chart
London's longest and hottest days fall between May and August. In the height of summer, daylight hours can extend from well before 5am to after 9pm. Daytime is much shorter in the winter, but London can be stunning in the winter sunshine.

SUMMER

L ONDON'S SUMMER season is packed full of indoor and outdoor events. The weather is very unreliable, even at the height of summer, but unless you are notably unlucky there should be enough fine days to sample what is on offer.

The selection includes many traditional events, such as the Wimbledon tennis championships and the many cricket test matches at Lord's and the Oval. Well out of view from the general public and prying photographers, the Queen holds garden parties for favoured subjects in the splendid grounds of Buckingham Palace. Summertime public holidays are also studded with funfairs in most of London's parks.

JUNE

Morris dancing *(Wed eves, all summer)*, Westminster Abbey *(pp76–9)*. Traditional English folk-dancing.
Coronation Day gun salutes *(2 Jun)*, Hyde Park and Tower of London *(p54)*.
Ceramics fair, Dorchester Hotel, Park Lane W1.
Fine Art and Antiques fair, Olympia, Olympia Way W14.
Trooping the Colour, Horse Guards *(p54)*.
Charles Dickens memorial service *(9 Jun)*, Westminster Abbey *(pp76–9)*. Celebration of London's famous author.
Duke of Edinburgh's Birthday gun salutes *(10 Jun)*, Hyde Park and Tower of London *(p54)*.
Wimbledon Lawn Tennis Championships *(two weeks in late Jun; p336)*.

Revellers at Notting Hill Carnival

Cricket test match, Lord's *(p336)*.
Open-air theatre Shakespeare season *(throughout the summer)*, Regent's Park and Holland Park. The perfect opportunity for a picnic *(p326)*.
Open-air concerts, Kenwood, Hampstead Heath, Crystal Palace, Marble Hill, St James's Park *(p331)*.
Street theatre festival *(Jun–Jul)*, Covent Garden *(p114)*. Street performers of every kind gather to flaunt their various talents.
Summer festivals *(late Jun)*, Greenwich, Spitalfields and Primrose Hill. Contact the London Tourist Board *(p345)* or see the listings magazines *(p325)* for times and venues of all these events.

JULY

Summer festivals, City of London and Richmond.
Sales. Price reductions across London's shops *(p311)*.

Doggett's Coat and Badge Race *(p55)*.
Hampton Court Flower Show, Hampton Court Palace *(pp250–3)*.
Royal Tournament *(mid-Jul)*, Earl's Court, Warwick Rd SW5. Impressive military spectacle put on by members of the combined armed forces.
Capital Radio Jazz Festival, Royal Festival Hall *(p184)*.
Henry Wood Promenade Concerts *(late Jul–Sep)*, Royal Albert Hall *(p203)*.

AUGUST

Last Mon is a public holiday.
Queen Mother's Birthday gun salutes *(4 Aug)*, Hyde Park and Tower of London *(p54)*.
Notting Hill Carnival *(late Aug holiday weekend)*. A celebration organized mainly by the area's various ethnic communities *(p215)*.
Funfairs *(Aug holiday)*, throughout London's parks.

Regimental band, St James's Park

AVERAGE MONTHLY RAINFALL

MM   Inches

Jan Feb Mar Apr May Jun Jul Aug Sep Oct Nov Dec

Rainfall Chart

London's average monthly rainfall remains much the same throughout the year. July and August, the capital's warmest months, are also two of its wettest. Rain is less likely in spring, but visitors should be prepared for a shower at any time of year.

AUTUMN

THERE IS A SENSE of purpose about London in autumn. The build-up to the busiest shopping season, the start of the academic year, and the new parliamentary session, opened by the Queen, inject some life into the colder months. The cricket season comes to an end in mid-September, while food-lovers may be interested in the spectacular displays of fresh fish that are laid out in the vestry of St Mary-at-the-Hill, celebrating the harvest of this island nation.

Memories of a more turbulent opening of Parliament are revived on 5 November, when there are bonfires and firework to commemorate the failure of a conspiracy led by Guy Fawkes to blow up the Palace of Westminster in 1605. A few days later the dead of two World Wars are commemorated at a ceremony held in Whitehall.

Pearly Kings gathering for the harvest festival at St Martin-in-the-Fields

London-to-Brighton veteran car run

SEPTEMBER

National Rose Society Annual Show, Royal Horticultural Hall, Vincent Sq W1.
Chelsea Antiques Fair *(third week)*, Chelsea Old Town Hall, King's Road SW3.
Last Night of the Proms *(late Sep)*, Royal Albert Hall *(p203)*.

OCTOBER

Pearly Harvest Festival *(3 Oct)*, St Martin-in-the-Fields *(p55)*.
Punch and Judy Festival *(3 Oct)*, Covent Garden WC2. Celebration of puppet duo.
Horse of the Year Show *(early Oct)*, Wembley *(p337)*. London's equestrian showpiece.
Harvest of the Sea *(second Sun)*, St Mary-at-Hill Church *(p152)*.
Vintners' and Distillers' Wine Harvest *(p55)*.
Navy Day *(p54)*.

State Opening of Parliament *(p54)*.

NOVEMBER

Guy Fawkes Night *(5 Nov)*. Listings magazines give details of firework displays *(p324)*.
Remembrance Day Service *(p54)*.
Silent Change *(p55)*.
Lord Mayor's Show *(p55)*.
London to Brighton veteran car run *(first Sun)*. Starts in Hyde Park *(p207)*.
Christmas lights *(late Nov–6 Jan)*, West End *(p313)*.

Autumn colours in a London park

Average Monthly Temperature

Temperature Chart
The chart shows the average minimum and maximum temperatures for each month. Top temperatures averaging 22° C (75° F) belie London's reputation for year-round chilliness, although November through to February sees icy conditions.

WINTER

SOME OF THE most striking images of London are drawn from winter: paintings of frost fairs in the 17th and 18th centuries, when the River Thames froze over completely; and Claude Monet's views of the river and its bridges.

For centuries thick "pea-souper" fogs were an inevitable part of winter, until the Clean Air Act of 1956 barred coal-burning in open grates.

Christmas trees and lights twinkle everywhere – from the West End shopping streets to construction sites. The scent of roasting chestnuts pervades as street pedlars sell them from glowing mobile braziers.

Seasonal menus feature roast turkey, mince pies and rich, dark Christmas pudding. Traditional fare in theatres includes colourful family pantomimes (where the customary cross-dressing between the sexes baffles many visitors – *p326*) and popular ballets such as *Swan Lake* or *The Nutcracker*.

Skaters use the open-air rink at the Broadgate Centre in the City, and sometimes it is safe to venture on to the frozen lakes in the parks.

Winter in Kensington Gardens

DECEMBER

Oxford v Cambridge rugby union match *(mid-Dec)*, Twickenham *(p337)*.
Dr Johnson memorial service *(18 Dec)*, Westminster Abbey *(p55)*.

CHRISTMAS AND NEW YEAR

25–26 Dec and 1 Jan are public hols. There is no train service on Christmas Day.
Carol services *(each*

evening on the lead up to *Christmas)*, Trafalgar Square *(p102)*, St Paul's *(pp148–51)*, Westminster Abbey *(pp76–9)* and other churches.
Turkey auction *(24 Dec)*, Smithfield Market *(p164)*.
Christmas Day swim Serpentine, Hyde Park *(p207)*.
New Year's Eve celebrations *(31 Dec)*, Trafalgar Square, St Paul's.

JANUARY

Sales *(p311)*.
International Boat Show, Earl's Court, Warwick Rd SW5.
International Mime Festival *(mid Jan – early Feb)*, various venues.
Charles I Commemoration *(last Sun)*, procession from St James's Palace *(p91)* to Banqueting House *(p80)*.
Chinese New Year *(late Jan–early Feb)*, Chinatown *(p108)* and Soho *(p109)*.

FEBRUARY

Clowns' Service *(first Sun)*, Dalston *(p55)*.
Queen's Accession gun salutes *(6 Feb)*, 41-gun salute Hyde Park; 62-gun salute Tower of London *(p54)*.
Pancake races *(Shrove Tue)*, Lincoln's Inn Fields *(p137)* and Covent Garden *(p114)*.

PUBLIC HOLIDAYS
New Year's Day (1 Jan); **Good Friday; Easter Monday; May Day** (first Monday in May); **Whit Monday** (last Monday in May); **August Bank Holiday** (last Monday in August); **Christmas** (25– 26 December).

Christmas illuminations in Trafalgar Square

A RIVER VIEW OF LONDON

IN OLD Celtic the word for river was *teme*, and the Romans adopted this as the name for the great waterway upon which they founded the city of *Londinium (see pp16–17)* nearly 2,000 years ago. The Roman settlers built their new city along the most easterly point at which the river could be bridged using the technology of the time. Since then, the Thames has continued to play a critical role in London's history. It was the route taken by the Viking invaders of the 8th and 9th centuries, the birthplace of the Royal Navy in Tudor times, and the artery for much of the country's commerce until well into the 1950s.

Now changing trade patterns have moved the big ships elsewhere, and the river has become the capital's foremost leisure

Decoration on Southwark Bridge

amenity instead. Where once stood wharves and warehouses, today there are riverside walks, marinas, bars and restaurants.

One of the most interesting ways of seeing the capital is by boat, and several companies offer sightseeing cruises from central London. These vary in length from 30 minutes to four hours. The most popular section of the river to travel runs downstream from the Houses of Parliament to Tower Bridge. A river view gives you a very different perspective of London's major sites, including Traitors' Gate, the infamous river entrance to the Tower of London, which was used for prisoners brought from trial in Westminster Hall *(see pp72–3)*. You can also take longer journeys past the varied architectural styles found between Hampton Court and the Thames Barrier.

The Thames in London
Passenger boat services cover about 30 miles (50 km) of the Thames, from Hampton Court in the west to the Thames Barrier in the former Docklands of the east.

Houseboats at Chelsea

TOUR OPERATORS

Most of these services run from 6 May until the end of October, when they revert to winter schedules, but phone first because some change earlier. During the winter there are no upriver services.

A circular cruise on *Mercedes*

Westminster Pier
Map 13 C5.
Westminster.

Downriver to Tower Pier
0171-515 1415.

Departures
10.20am, 10.40am, 11am, 11.30am and noon. Then every 20 minutes until 3pm. Then every 30 minutes until 5pm (every 30 minutes until 6pm during peak season).
Duration 30 minutes.

Downriver to Greenwich
0171-930 4097.
Departures every 30 minutes, 10.30am–4pm (5pm peak season).
Duration 40–50 minutes.

Downriver to the Thames Barrier
0171-930 3373.
Departures 10.15am, 11.15am, 12.45pm, 1.45pm and 3.15pm.
Duration 75 mins each way.

Private party on a chartered boat

Upriver to Kew
0171-930 4721.
Departures 10.30am, 11.15am, noon, 2pm and 2.30pm.
Duration about 90 minutes.

Upriver to Richmond
0171-930 4721.
Departures 10.30am and noon.
Duration about 3 hours.

Upriver to Hampton Court
0171-930 4721.
Departures 11.15am and noon.

The River Thames is at its most romantic at dusk. The view east from Waterloo Bridge shows St Paul's and the City on the north bank and the Oxo Tower on the south.

See pp62–3

See pp64–5

Rotherhithe Tunnel

Blackwall Tunnel

Thames Barrier

Thames

ISLE OF DOGS

Charlton

Greenwich Foot Tunnel Greenwich

Hammersmith Bridge

Chelsea Bridge

Lambeth Bridge

Vauxhall Bridge

Battersea Bridge

Albert Bridge

Grosvenor Rail Bridge

Battersea

Putney Bridge

Barnes Rail Bridge

Putney Rail Bridge

Wandsworth Bridge

Putney

0 kilometres   4

0 miles   2

KEY

Underground station

British Rail station

River boat stop

The river at Twickenham

The view from Richmond Hill

Open-decked boat

Duration 3–4½ hours.
Circular lunchtime cruise
📞 0171-839 3572.
12.45pm Sun.
Duration 2 hours.
Circular supper cruise
📞 0171-839 3572.
9pm Wed, Fri, Sun.
Duration 90 minutes.
Circular evening cruise
📞 0171-930 2062.
7.30 and 8.30pm.
Duration 45 minutes.

Charing Cross Pier
Map 13 C3.
Charing Cross, Embankment.

Downriver to Tower Pier
📞 0171-839 3572.
Departures every 30 minutes, 10.30am–4pm.
Duration 20 minutes.

Downriver to Greenwich
📞 0171-839 3572.
Departures every 30 minutes, 10.30am–4pm.
Duration 45-60 minutes.

Circular evening cruise
📞 0171-839 3572.
6.30, 7.30 and 8.30pm.
Duration 45 minutes.

Tower Pier
Map 16 D3. Tower Hill.

Upriver to HMS Belfast
📞 0181-468 7201.
Departures every 15 minutes, 11am–6pm.

Downriver to Greenwich
📞 0171-839 3572.
Departures every 30 minutes, 10.30am–4.30pm.
Duration 35 minutes.

Sightseeing boat

Westminster Bridge to Blackfriars Bridge

UNTIL WORLD WAR II, this stretch of the Thames marked the division between rich and poor London. On the north bank were the offices, shops, luxury hotels and apartments of Whitehall and the Strand, the Inns of Court and the newspaper district. To the south were smoky factories and slum dwellings. After the war, the Festival of Britain in 1951 started the revival of the South Bank *(see pp181–7)* which now has some of the capital's most interesting modern buildings.

Savoy Hotel
This hotel is on the site of a medieval palace (p116).

Shell Mex House
Offices for the oil company were built in 1931 on the site of the vast Cecil Hotel.

Somerset House is an office complex built in 1786 *(p117).*

Cleopatra's Needle was made in ancient Egypt and given to London in 1819 *(p118).*

Embankment Gardens is the site of many open-air concerts held in the bandstand during the summer months *(p118).*

Waterloo Bridge

Charing Cross

Embankment

Festival Pier

Charing Cross Pier

Hungerford Railway Bridge

The South Bank Centre was the site of the 1951 Festival of Britain and is London's most important arts complex. It is dominated by the Festival Hall, the National Theatre and the Hayward Gallery *(pp181–7).*

Charing Cross
The rail terminus is encased in a Post-Modernist office complex with many shops (p119).

The Banqueting House is one of Inigo Jones's finest works, built as part of Whitehall Palace *(p80).*

The Ministry of Defence is a bulky white fortress completed in the 1950s.

Westminster

Westminster Bridge

County Hall
Built early this century as the seat of London's government, the hall is now being turned into a hotel (p185).

Temple and the Inns of Court
*These historic buildings have been
the offices of
lawyers and
barristers for
over 500 years
(pp136–9).*

St Paul's
*Christopher Wren's masterwork,
finished in 1708, formerly dominated
the London skyline (pp148–51).*

Blackfriars

**Blackfriars
Bridge**

**Gabriel's
Wharf**

**Doggett's Coat
and Badge**
*The modern
pub here is
named after a
river race in
which boatmen
compete for this
huge badge
(p187).*

Cardinal's Wharf
afforded Wren a
good view of the
building of St
Paul's *(p178)*.

OXO Tower
*The windows were designed to
spell the brand name of a
popular meat extract.*

Blackfriars Bridge
*The logo of a former railway
company adorns the bridge.*

Gabriel's Wharf
*A lively craft market operates where
once there were warehouses (p187).*

St Paul's
The cathedral dominates views from the South Bank.

KEY

⊖ Underground station

⇌ British Rail station

▬ River boat boarding point

Southwark Bridge to St Katharine's Dock

FOR CENTURIES THE STRETCH just east of London Bridge was the busiest part of the Thames, with ships of all sizes jostling for position to unload at the wharves on both banks. Then, in the 19th century, the construction of the docks to the east eased congestion. Today most landmarks on this section hark back to that commercial past.

Old Billingsgate
Notice the flying fish weather vanes on what was London's main fish market (p152).

Fishmongers' Hall
The hall (1834) of this ancient City guild dominates the view north from London Bridge (p152).

Monument
The Great Fire of 1666 started near this spot (p152).

A Custom House has been here since 1272. This version dates from 1825.

Cannon Street

Monument

Southwark Bridge

Cannon Street Railway Bridge

Swan Lane Pier

London Bridge

London City Pier

London Bridge

St Olave's House
A fine Art Deco building shows its best face to the river (p177).

The Anchor
This pub is near the site of Shakespeare's Globe Theatre (p178).

Southwark Cathedral
Parts of this building date from the 12th century. It contains memorials to Shakespeare (p176).

Hay's Galleria
Once a wharf for unloading food, it has been covered to house shops and restaurants (p177).

Southwark Wharves
Now there are walkways with river views where ships used to dock.

Tower Bridge
It still opens to let tall ships pass, but not as often as it did when cargo vessels came through (p153).

Tower of London
Look out for Traitors' Gate, where prisoners would be taken into the Tower by boat (pp154–7).

St Katharine's Dock
The former dock is now a lively attraction for visitors. Its yacht marina is a highlight (p158).

Tower Pier

Tower Bridge

Victorian warehouses on Butlers Wharf have been converted into apartments.

HMS Belfast
The World War II cruiser has been a museum since 1971 (p179).

Design Museum
Opened in 1989, this ship-like building is a shining example of Docklands' renaissance (p179).

LONDON AREA BY AREA

WHITEHALL AND WESTMINSTER

W HITEHALL AND WESTMINSTER have been at the centre of political and religious power in England for a thousand years. King Canute, who ruled at the beginning of the 11th century, was the first monarch to have a palace on what was then an island in the swampy meeting point of the Thames and its vanished tributary, the Tyburn. Canute built his palace beside the church that, some 50 years later, Edward the Confessor would enlarge into England's greatest abbey, giving the area its name. (A minster is an abbey church.) Over the following centuries the offices of state were established in the vicinity. All this is still reflected in Whitehall's heroic statues and massive government buildings. But, to its north, Trafalgar Square marks the start of the West End entertainment district.

Horse Guard on Whitehall

SIGHTS AT A GLANCE

Historic Streets and Buildings
Houses of Parliament pp72–3 ❶
Big Ben ❷
Jewel Tower ❸
Dean's Yard ❺
Parliament Square ❼
Downing Street ❾
Cabinet War Rooms ❿
Banqueting House ⓫
Horse Guards ⓬
Queen Anne's Gate ⓮
St James's Park Station ⓰
Blewcoat School ⓱

Churches, Abbeys and Cathedrals
Westminster Abbey pp76–9 ❹
St Margaret's Church ❻
Westminster Cathedral ⓲
St John's, Smith Square ⓳

Museums and Galleries
Guards' Museum ⓯
Tate Gallery pp82–5 ⓴

Theatres
Whitehall Theatre ⓭

Monuments
Cenotaph ❽

GETTING THERE
British Rail and the Victoria, District and Circle lines all serve the area. Bus numbers 3, 11, 12, 24, 29, 53, 77, 77A, 88, 109, 159, 170 and 184 go to Whitehall; 2, 2B, 16, 25, 36A, 38, 39, 52, 52A, 73, 76, 135, 507 and 510 serve Victoria.

KEY

▢ Street-by-Street map
🔵 Underground station
🚆 British Rail station
🅿 Parking

SEE ALSO
• *Street Finder,* maps 13, 20, 21
• *Where to stay* pp276–7
• *Restaurants* pp292–4

0 metres 500
0 yards 500

Looking down Whitehall towards Big Ben

Street-by-Street: Whitehall and Westminster

COMPARED WITH MANY capital cities, London has little monumental architecture designed to overawe with pomp. Here, at the historic seat both of the government and of the established church, it most closely approaches the broad, stately avenues of Paris, Rome and Madrid. On weekdays the streets are crowded with members of the civil service, as most of their work is based in this area. At weekends, however, it is deserted, apart from tourists visiting some of London's most famous sights.

Earl Haig, the British World War I chief, was sculpted by Alfred Hardiman in 1936.

Downing Street
British Prime Ministers have lived here since 1732 ❾

Central Hall is a florid example of the Beaux Arts style, built in 1911 as a Methodist meeting hall. In 1946 the first General Assembly of the United Nations was held here.

★ Cabinet War Rooms
Now open to the public, these were Winston Churchill's World War II headquarters ❿

★ Westminster Abbey
The Abbey is London's oldest and most important church ❹

The Sanctuary
was a medieval safe-place for those escaping the law.

Dean's Yard
Westminster School was founded here in 1540 ❺

Richard I's Statue, by Carlo Marochetti (1860), depicts the 12th-century *Coeur de Lion* (Lionheart).

Jewel Tower
Kings once stored their most valuable possessions here ❸

The Burghers of Calais
is a cast of Auguste Rodin's original in Paris.

KING CHARLES ST

STOREY'S GATE

GREAT GEORGE STREET

BROAD SANCTUARY

PARLIAMENT SQUARE

GREAT COLLEGE STREET

ST MARGARET STREET

ABINGDON STREET

★ **Horse Guards**
*A mounted guard is
ceremonially changed
here twice a day* ⑫

**To Trafalgar
Square**

Dover House,
a stately mansion
dating from 1787,
now houses the
Scottish Office.

LOCATOR MAP
See Central London Map pp12–13

★ **Banqueting House**
*Inigo Jones designed
this elegant building,
which has a Rubens
ceiling, in 1622* ⑪

Cenotaph
*Edward Lutyens's
war memorial dates
from 1920* ⑧

Richmond House
is William Whitfield's prize-
winning 1980s building for
the Department of Health.

The Treasury
is where the
nation's
finances are
administered.

Norman Shaw Buildings
were the Victorian site of New
Scotland Yard, the Metropolitan
Police HQ.

Westminster Pier
is a starting point
for river excursions.

Boadicea,
the English queen who
resisted the Romans,
was portrayed by
Thomas Thornycroft in
the 1850s.

**Westminster
station**

★ **Houses of
Parliament and
Big Ben**
*These were designed by
Barry in 1834 when the
Palace of Westminster
burned down* ❶ ❷

**Parliament
Square**
*Statues of famous
statesmen, such
as Benjamin
Disraeli and
Winston Churchill,
stand here* ❼

St Margaret's Church
*Society weddings often
take place here, in
Parliament's church* ❻

STAR SIGHTS

★ **Westminster Abbey**

★ **Houses of
Parliament and
Big Ben**

★ **Banqueting House**

★ **Cabinet War Rooms**

★ **Horse Guards**

KEY

— — — Suggested route

| 0 metres | 100 |
| 0 yards | 100 |

Houses of Parliament ●

Since 1512 the Palace of Westminster has been the seat of the two Houses of Parliament, called the Lords and the Commons. The Commons is made up of elected Members of Parliament (MPs) of different political parties; the party with the most MPs forms the Government, and its leader becomes Prime Minister. MPs from other parties make up the Opposition. Commons' debates can become heated and are impartially chaired by an MP designated as Speaker. The Commons formulates legislation which is first debated in both Houses before becoming law.

The mock-Gothic building was designed by Victorian architect Sir Charles Barry. Victoria Tower, on the left, contains 1.5 million Acts of Parliament passed since 1497.

★ **Commons' Chamber**
The room is upholstered in green. The Government sits on the left, the Opposition on the right, and the Speaker presides from a chair between them.

Big Ben
The vast bell was hung in 1858 and chimes on the hour; four smaller ones ring on the quarter hours (see p74).

Members' entrance

Star Features

★ Westminster Hall

★ Lords' Chamber

★ Commons' Chamber

★ **Westminster Hall**
The only surviving part of the original Palace of Westminster, it dates from 1097; its hammerbeam roof is from the 14th century.

Central Lobby
*People who come to meet
their MP wait here under
a ceiling of rich mosaics.*

Peers are members of the
House of Lords – many of
them inherit their titles. This
is their lobby.

VISITORS' CHECKLIST

London SW1. **Map** 13 C5.
[0171-219 3000.
Westminster. 3, 11, 12,
24, 29, 53, 70, 77, 77a.
Victoria. Westminster Pier.
**House of Commons Visitors'
Galleries open** 2.30–10pm
Mon–Thu, 9.30am–3pm Fri (St
Stephen's entrance). **Question
time** 2.30–3.30pm Mon–Thu; UK
residents apply in advance to
local MP, others apply to Public
Information Office or their
national embassy. **Closed** Easter
week, May public hol, end
Jul–mid-Oct, 3 weeks over
Christmas. **House of Lords
Visitors' Galleries open** 2.30pm
onwards Mon–Thu, some Fri (St
Stephen's entrance). **Closed** (see
House of Commons).
by arrangement only, apply
well in advance to local MP or
Public Information Office.

Royal Gallery
*The Queen passes through
here at the State Opening.
It is lined with peers' desks.*

**St Stephen's
entrance**

★ Lords' Chamber
*At the State Opening of
Parliament (see pp54–5) the
Queen delivers a speech from the
throne of the House of Lords, which
outlines the Government's plans.*

TIMELINE

1042 Work starts on
first palace for Edward
the Confessor

1547 St Stephen's
chapel becomes first
Chamber of the House
of Commons

1642 Charles I
tries to arrest five
MPs but is forced
to withdraw by
the Speaker

1941 Chamber of
House of Commons
destroyed by World
War II bomb

1000	1200	1400	1600	1800	2000

1087–1100
Westminster
Hall built

*The Mace: symbol of royal authority
in the Commons*

1512 After a fire, palace
stops being a royal
residence

1605 Guy Fawkes and others
try to blow up the king
and Houses of Parliament

1834 Palace
destroyed by fire;
only Westminster
Hall and the Jewel
Tower survive

1870
Present
building
completed

Houses of Parliament ❶

See pp72–3.

Big Ben ❷

Bridge St SW1. **Map** 13 C5.
📞 0171-222 2219. 🚇 *Westminster.*
Not open to the public.

T O BE PEDANTIC, Big Ben is
not the name of the world-
famous four-faced clock in
the 106-m (320-ft) tower
that rises above the
Houses of Parliament, but
of the resonant 14-tonne
bell on which the hours
are struck. It was named
after Sir Benjamin Hall,
Chief Commissioner of
Works when the bell
was hung in 1858.
Cast at White-
chapel, it was the
second giant bell
made for the clock,
the first having
become cracked
during a test
ringing. (The
present bell also
has a slight crack.)
The clock is the
largest in Britain, its
four dials 7.5 m
(23 ft) in diameter and the
minute hand 4.25 m (14 ft)
long, made in hollow copper
for lightness. It has kept exact
time for the nation more or
less continuously since it was
first set in motion in May
1859. The deep chimes have
become a symbol of Britain
all over the world and are
broadcast daily on BBC radio.

Jewel Tower ❸

Abingdon St SW1. **Map** 13 B5.
📞 0171-222 2219. 🚇 *Westminster.*
Open Apr–Sept: 10am–6pm
daily; Oct–Mar: 10am–4pm daily.
Closed 1–2pm daily, 24–26 Dec,
1 Jan, for state occasions. **Adm
charge.**

T HIS AND WESTMINSTER HALL
(see p72) are the only
vestiges of the old Palace of
Westminster. The tower was
built in 1366 as a stronghold
for Edward III's treasure and

is today a small museum
containing relics relating to
the palace, pottery dug from
the moat, and fascinating
drawings of some of the best
losing designs for rebuilding
the Houses of Parliament after
the fire of 1834. The tower
served as the weights and
measures office from 1869
until 1938 and another display
relates to that. Alongside are
the remains of the moat and a
medieval quay.

Westminster Abbey ❹

See pp76–9.

Dean's Yard ❺

Broad Sanctuary SW1. **Map** 13 B5.
🚇 *Westminster.* **Buildings not open**
to the public.

**Entrance to the Abbey and
cloisters from Dean's Yard**

A N ARCH NEAR the west door
of the Abbey leads into
this secluded grassy square,
surrounded by a jumble of
buildings from many different
periods. A medieval house on
the east side has a distinctive
dormer window and backs on
to Little Dean's Yard, where
the monks' living quarters
used to be. Dean's Yard is
private property. It belongs to
the Dean and Chapter of
Westminster and is close to
Westminster School, whose
famous former pupils include
poet John Dryden and playwright Ben Jonson. Scholars
are, by tradition, the first to
acknowledge a new monarch.

St Margaret's Church ❻

Parliament Sq SW1. **Map** 13 B5.
📞 0171-222 5152. 🚇 *Westminster.*
Open 9.30am–5pm daily, .
1–5.30pm Sun. 🕐 11am Sun.
🚫 ♿ 🎵 **Concerts.**

**Statue of Charles I overlooking
St Margaret's doorway**

O VERSHADOWED by the
Abbey, this early-15th-
century church has long been
a favoured venue for political
and society weddings, such as
Winston and Clementine
Churchill's. Although much
restored, the church retains
some Tudor features, notably a
stained-glass window that
celebrates the engagement of
Catherine of Aragon to Arthur,
Henry VIII's eldest brother.

Parliament Square ❼

SW1. **Map** 13 B5. 🚇 *Westminster.*

L AID OUT IN THE 1840s to
provide a more open
aspect for the new Houses of
Parliament, the square
became Britain's first official
roundabout in 1926. Today it
is hemmed in by heavy
traffic. Statues of statesmen
and soldiers are dominated
by Winston Churchill in his
greatcoat, glowering at the
House of Commons. On the
north side Abraham Lincoln
sits in front of the mock-
Gothic Middlesex Guildhall,
completed in 1913.

Cenotaph ❽

Whitehall SW1. **Map** 13 B4.
🚇 *Westminster.*

T HIS SUITABLY BLEAK and pale
monument, completed in
1920 by Sir Edwin Lutyens to
commemorate the dead of
World War I, stands in the

middle of Whitehall. On Remembrance Day every year – the Sunday nearest 11 November – the monarch and other dignitaries place wreaths of red poppies on the Cenotaph. This solemn ceremony, commemorating the 1918 armistice, honours the victims of World Wars I and II *(see pp54–5)*.

The Cenotaph

Cabinet War Rooms ⑩

Clive Steps, King Charles St SW1. **Map** 13 B5. **☎** 0171-930 6961. **⊖** *Westminster.* **Open** 10am–6pm daily. **Closed** 24–26 Dec, 1 Jan. **Adm charge**.

THIS INTRIGUING slice of 20th-century history is a warren of cellar rooms below the Government Office Building north of Parliament Square. It is where the War Cabinet – first under Neville Chamberlain, then Winston Churchill – met during World War II when German bombs were falling on London. The War Rooms include living quarters for key ministers and military leaders and a sound-proofed Cabinet Room, where

Telephones in the Map Room of the Cabinet War Rooms

many strategic decisions were taken. All rooms are protected by a layer of concrete about a metre (3 ft) thick. They are laid out as they were when the war ended, complete with period furniture, including Churchill's desk, some old-fashioned communications equipment and maps with markers for plotting complex military strategy.

Downing Street ⑨

SW1. **Map** 13 B4. **⊖** *Westminster.* **Not open** to the public.

SIR GEORGE DOWNING (1623– 84) spent part of his youth in the American colonies. He was the second graduate from the nascent Harvard College before returning to fight for the Parliamentarians in the English Civil War. In 1680 he

No. 12, the Whips' Office, is where Party campaigns are organized.

bought some land near Whitehall Palace and built a street of houses. Four of these survive, though much altered. George II gave No. 10 to Sir Robert Walpole in 1732. Since then it has been the official residence of the Prime Minister and contains offices as well as a private apartment. In 1989, for security reasons, iron gates were erected at the Whitehall end.

Government policy is decided in the Cabinet Room at No. 10.

The famous front door of No. 10

No. 11 is the Chancellor of the Exchequer's official residence.

No. 10 is the official home of the Prime Minister.

The Prime Minister entertains official guests in the State Dining Room.

Westminster Abbey ❹

T HE ABBEY is world-famous as the resting-place of Britain's monarchs, and as the setting for coronations and other great pageants. Within its walls can be seen some of the most glorious examples of medieval architecture in London. It also contains one of the most impressive collections of tombs and monuments in the world. Half national church, half national museum, the abbey occupies a unique place in the British national consciousness.

★ Flying Buttresses
The massive flying butt-resses help transfer the great weight of the 31-m (102-ft) high nave.

North Entrance
The stonework here, like this carving of a dragon, is Victorian.

The North Transept has three chapels on the east side containing some of the Abbey's finest monuments.

★ West Front Towers
These towers, built in 1734–45, were designed by Nicholas Hawksmoor.

STAR FEATURES

★ **West Front Towers**

★ **Flying Buttresses**

★ **The Nave viewed from the West End**

★ **Henry VII Chapel**

★ **Chapter House**

Main entrance

★ The Nave viewed from the West End
At 10 m (35 ft) wide, the nave is comparatively narrow, but it is the highest in England.

The Cloisters, built mainly in the 13th and 14th centuries, used to link the Abbey church with the other buildings.

St Edward's Chapel
houses not only the royal Coronation Chair and Edward the Confessor's shrine, but also the tombs of many of England's medieval monarchs.

★ **Henry VII Chapel**
The chapel, built in 1503–12, has a superb vaulted ceiling and choir stalls dating from 1512.

VISITORS' CHECKLIST

Broad Sanctuary SW1. **Map** 13 B5. 0171-222 5152. *St James's Park, Westminster.* 3, 11, 12, 24, 29, 53, 70, 77, 77a, 88, 109, 159, 170. *Victoria, Waterloo.* *Westminster Pier.* **Adm charge** for Royal Chapels, Poets' Corner, Choir, Statesmen's Aisle (exc 6–7.45pm Wed), Chapter House, Pyx Chamber, Museum. **Nave & cloisters open** 8am–6pm Mon–Sat, between services on Sun. **Royal Chapels, Poets' Corner, Choir, Statesmen's Aisle open** 9am–4.45pm Mon–Fri, 9am–2.45pm, 3.45–5.45pm Sat. **Chapter House open** Apr–Sep: 10am–5.45pm daily; Oct–Mar: 10am–4pm daily. **Pyx Chamber & Museum open** 10.30am–4pm daily. **Brass rubbing centre open** 9am–5pm Mon–Sat. **Garden open** Thu. Concerts.

★ **Chapter House**
This octagonal structure is worth seeing for its 13th-century tiles.

The South Transept
contains "Poets' Corner", where memorials to famous literary figures can be seen.

Museum

TIMELINE

13th-century tile from the Chapter House

1000	1200	1400	1600	1800	2000

1050 New Benedictine abbey church begun by Edward the Confessor

1376 Henry Yevele begins rebuilding the nave

1838 Queen Victoria's coronation

1245 New abbey begun to the designs of Henry of Rheims

1269 Body of Edward the Confessor moved to new shrine in the abbey

1734 West towers begun

1540 Monastery dissolved

1953 Most recent coronation in the abbey: Elizabeth II's

A Guided Tour of Westminster Abbey

THE ABBEY'S INTERIOR presents an exceptionally diverse array of architectural and sculptural styles. These range from the austere French Gothic of the nave to the stunning complexity of Henry VII's Tudor chapel and the riotous invention of the later 18th-century monuments. Many English monarchs were buried here; some of their tombs are deliberately plain, while others are lavishly decorated. At the same time, there are monuments to a number of Britain's greatest public figures – ranging from politicians to poets – crowded into the aisles and transepts.

② Lady Nightingale's Memorial
The North Transept chapels contain some of the abbey's finest monuments – this one, by Roubiliac, is for Lady Nightingale (1761).

HISTORICAL PLAN OF THE ABBEY

The first abbey church was established as early as the 10th century, when St Dunstan brought a group of Benedictine monks to the area. The present structure dates largely from the 13th century; the new, French-influenced design was begun in 1245 at the behest of Henry III. Because of its unique role as the royal coronation church, the abbey survived Henry VIII's mid-16th-century onslaught on Britain's monastic buildings.

KEY

▨	Built before 1400
▨	Added in 15th century
▨	Built in 1503–19
▨	Completed in 1745
☐	Completed after 1850

North entrance

① The Nave
Enter the abbey and proceed along the nave. At 10.5 m (35 ft) wide and 31 m (100 ft) high, it took 150 years to build.

The Choir houses a gilded 1840s screen, which contains remnants of the 13th-century original.

⑧ Cloisters
A brass rubbing centre in the cloisters invites you to create your own personal souvenir of the Abbey – perhaps a rubbing of a knight's tomb.

Main entrance

The Jerusalem Chamber has a 17th-century fireplace, fine 1540s tapestries and an interesting painted ceiling.

The Jericho Parlour, added in the early 16th century, contains some fine panelling.

The Deanery is where the monastery's abbot used to live.

CORONATION

The abbey has been the fittingly sumptuous setting for all royal coronations since 1066. The last occupant of the Coronation Chair was the present monarch, Elizabeth II. She was crowned in 1953 in the first televised coronation.

The Chapel of St John the Baptist is full of tombs dating from the 14th to the 19th centuries.

The St Faith Chapel contains works of art that date back to the 13th century.

The Pyx Chamber's gaunt columns date from the 11th century.

Dean's Yard entrance

KEY

– – – Tour route

③ St Edward's Chapel

You can see the royal Coronation Chair, the shrine of the Saxon king Edward the Confessor, and the tombs of many medieval monarchs here.

④ Tomb of Elizabeth I

Inside Henry VII's Chapel you will find Elizabeth I's (reigned 1558–1603) huge tomb. It also houses the body of her sister, "Bloody" Mary I.

⑤ Henry VII Chapel

The undersides of the choir stalls, dating from 1512, are beautifully carved with exotic and fantastic creatures.

⑥ South Ambulatory

Below Philippa of Hainault's tomb are some fine painted panels from 1270.

⑦ Poets' Corner

Take time to explore the memorials to countless literary giants, such as Shakespeare and Dickens, which are gathered here.

Banqueting House ⓫

Whitehall SW1. **Map** 13 B4.
📞 0171-839 7569. 🚇 Charing
Cross, Embankment, Westminster.
Open 10am–5pm Mon–Sat (last adm:
4.30). **Closed** 25–26 Dec, 1 Jan, for
ceremonies. **Adm charge.**
♿ 🖼 📷 📹 **Video presentations.**

Tʜɪs ᴅᴇʟɪɢʜᴛꜰᴜʟ ʙᴜɪʟᴅɪɴɢ is
of great architectural
importance. It was the first in
central London to embody
the Classical Palladian style
that designer Inigo Jones
brought back from his travels
in Italy. Completed in 1622,
its disciplined stone facade
marked a startling change
from the Elizabethans' fussy
turrets and unrestrained
external decoration. It was the
sole survivor of the fire that
destroyed most of the old
Whitehall Palace in 1698.

The ceiling paintings by
Rubens, a complex allegory
on the exaltation of James I,
were commissioned by his
son, Charles I, in 1630. This
blatant glorification of royalty
was despised by Oliver
Cromwell and the Parliamentarians, who executed King
Charles I on a scaffold
outside Banqueting House in
1649. Ironically, Charles II
celebrated his restoration to
the throne here 20 years later.
The building is occasionally
used for official functions.

**Mounted sentries stationed
outside Horse Guards**

Horse Guards ⓬

Whitehall SW1. **Map** 13 B4.
📞 0171-930 4466. 🚇 Westminster,
Charing Cross. **Closed** Sats in June.
Changing of the Guard 11am
Mon–Sat, 10am Sun. **Dismounting
Ceremony** 4pm daily. **Trooping the
Colour** see **Ceremonial London**
pp52–5.

Oɴᴄᴇ ʜᴇɴʀʏ ᴠɪɪɪ's tiltyard
(tournament ground),
the Changing of the Guard
still takes place here every
day. The elegant buildings,
completed in 1755, were
designed by William Kent.
On the left, as you pass on
to the parade ground, is the
Old Treasury, also by Kent,
and the back of Dover House,
completed in 1758 and now
used as the Scottish Office.
Nearby, in a corner of the

parade ground, is a trace of
the "real tennis" court where
Henry VIII is said to have
played the ancient precursor
of modern lawn tennis. On
the opposite side, the view is
dominated by the ivy-covered
Citadel. This is a bomb-proof
structure that was erected in
1940 beside the Admiralty.
During World War II it was
used as a communications
headquarters by the Navy.

Whitehall Theatre ⓭

Whitehall SW1. **Map** 13 B3.
📞 0171-867 1119. 🚇 Charing
Cross. **Open** for performances only.
See **Entertainment** pp326–7.

Detail of a Whitehall Theatre box

Bᴜɪʟᴛ ɪɴ 1930, the plain
white front seems to
emulate the Cenotaph (see
p74) at the other end of the
street, but, inside, the theatre
boasts some excellent Art
Deco detailing. From the 1950s
to the 1970s it was noted for
staging a wide range of farces.

Queen Anne's Gate ⓮

SW1. **Map** 13 A5. 🚇 St James's Park.

Tʜᴇ sᴘᴀᴄɪᴏᴜs terraced
houses at the west end of
this well-preserved enclave
date from 1704 and are
notable for the ornate canopies
over their front doors. At the
other end are houses built
some 70 years later, sporting
blue plaques that record
former residents, such as Lord
Palmerston, the Victorian
Prime Minister. Until recently,
the British Secret Service,
MI5, was allegedly based in
this unlikely spot. A small
statue of Queen Anne stands
in front of the wall separating
Nos. 13 and 15. To the west,
situated at the corner of Petty
France, Sir Basil Spence's
Home Office building (1976)

Panels from the Rubens ceiling, Banqueting House

is an architectural incongruity. Cockpit Steps, leading down to Birdcage Walk, mark the site of a 17th-century venue for the popular, yet blood-thirsty, sport of cockfighting.

Guards Museum ⓯

Birdcage Walk SW1. **Map** 13 A5.
📞 *0171-930 4466 x 3271.* 🚇 *St James's Park.* **Open** *10am–4pm Sat–Fri.* **Closed** *25 Dec, 1 Jan, ceremonies.* **Adm charge.** 📷 ♿

Eᴺᵀᴱᴿᴱᴰ ꜰʀᴼᴹ Birdcage Walk, the museum is under the parade ground of Wellington Barracks, head-quarters of the five Guards regiments. A must for military buffs, the museum uses tableaux and dioramas to illustrate various battles in which the Guards have taken part, from the English Civil War (1642–8) to the present. Weapons and row after row of colourful uniforms are on display, as well as a fascinating collection of models.

St James's Park Station ⓰

55 Broadway SW1. **Map** 13 A5.
🚇 *St James's Park.*

Epstein sculpture outside St James's Park Station

Tʜᴱ ꜱᵀᴬᵀᴵᴼᴺ is built into Broadway House, Charles Holden's 1929 headquarters for London Transport. It is notable for its sculptures by Jacob Epstein and reliefs by Henry Moore and Eric Gill.

Blewcoat School ⓱

23 Caxton St SW1. **Map** 13 A5.
📞 *0171-222 2877.* 🚇 *St James's Park.* **Open** *10am–5.30pm Mon–Wed, Fri, 10am–7pm Thu.*

Statue of a Blewcoat pupil above the Caxton Street entrance

A ʀᴱᴰ-ʙʀᴵᶜᴷ ɢᴱᴹ hemmed in by the office towers of Victoria Street, it was built in 1709 as a charity school to teach pupils how to "read, write, cast accounts and the catechism". It remained as a school until 1939, then became an army store during World War II and was bought by the National Trust in 1954. The beautifully proportioned interior now serves as a National Trust gift shop.

Westminster Cathedral ⓲

Ashley Place SW1. **Map** 20 F1.
📞 *0171-834 7452.* 🚇 *Victoria.* **Open** *6.45am–8pm daily.* **Adm charge** *for bell tower lift (Apr–Oct: 9am–1pm, 2–5pm).* 🔔 *5.30pm Mon–Fri, 10.30am Sat & Sun, sung Mass.* ♿ **Concerts.**

Oᴺᴱ ᴼꜰ ʟᴼᴺᴰᴼᴺ's rare Byzantine buildings, it was designed by John Francis Bentley for the Catholic diocese and completed in 1903 on the site of a former prison. Its 87-m (261-ft) high, red-brick tower, with horizontal stripes of white stone, stands out on the skyline in sharp contrast to the Abbey nearby. A restful piazza on the north side provides a good view of the

cathedral from Victoria Street. The rich interior decoration, with marble of varying colours and intricate mosaics, makes the domes above the nave seem incongruous. They were left bare because the project ran out of money before it could be completed.

Eric Gill's dramatic reliefs of the 14 Stations of the Cross, created during World War I, adorn the pier of the nave. The organ is one of the finest in Europe, and a series of concerts is held here every second Tuesday from June until September.

St John's, Smith Square ⓳

Smith Sq SW1. **Map** 21 B1.
📞 *0171-222 1061.* 🚇 *Westminster,* **Open** *10am–5pm and for evening concerts.* 🚫 🍴 ▯ **Concerts.** *See* **Entertainment** *pp330–1.*

Premiere Ensemble at St John's, Smith Square

Dᴱꜱᶜʀᴵʙᴱᴰ ʙʸ artist and art historian Sir Hugh Casson as one of the masterpieces of English Baroque architecture, Thomas Archer's plump church, with its turrets at each corner, looks as if it is trying to burst from the confines of the square, and rather over-powers the pleasing 18th-century houses on its north side. It has an accident-prone history: completed in 1728, it was burned down in 1742, struck by lightning in 1773 and destroyed again by a World War II bomb in 1941. There is a reasonably priced restaurant in the basement – a rarity in this area – that is open daily for lunch and on the evenings of concerts.

Tate Gallery ⓴

See pp82–5.

Tate Gallery ⑳

ORIGINALLY BUILT through the philanthropy of the sugar magnate Sir Henry Tate, the Tate Gallery now holds an extensive range of British works from the 16th to the 20th centuries. It is also London's leading international modern art museum. In the adjoining Clore Gallery is the magnificent Turner Bequest, left to the nation by the landscape artist J M W Turner himself.

The portico of the Tate building, which dates from 1897, overlooks the Thames.

GALLERY GUIDE

Most of the collection is housed in 30 rooms on the ground floor. Works on paper and temporary exhibitions are downstairs. The paintings are hung chronologically, tracing British art from 1550 (Room 1) to contemporary British and foreign art (Rooms 27–30). The display is changed annually, in order to emphasize different aspects of the collection. Note that not all of the works illustrated here will be on show.

Stairs to lower galleries

Stairs to lower galleries

★ **Peace – Burial at Sea**
This is J M W Turner's tribute to his friend and rival David Wilkie. It was painted in 1842, the year after Wilkie died at sea.

The Three Dancers
This large, expressive painting from 1925 was the start of a new phase of Pablo Picasso's art.

KEY TO FLOORPLAN

☐	Sculpture Gallery
☐	Temporary exhibitions
☐	Paintings
☐	Clore Gallery (Turner)
☐	Non-exhibition space

The Kiss
This sculpture (1901–4) by Auguste Rodin has become one of the Tate's most popular works.

THE ART OF GOOD FOOD

As well as a coffee bar, the Tate boasts a licensed restaurant on the lower floor decorated with a lavish mural by Rex Whistler. It tells the story of the inhabitants of the mythical Epicurania, and their pursuit of exotic foods to revive their jaded palates. The restaurant is well worth a visit for lunch, but it is not open for dinner (see pp306–7).

VISITORS' CHECKLIST

Millbank SW1. **Map** 21 B2.
☎ 0171-887 8000. ⓘ 0171-887 8008. ⊖ Pimlico. ⏛ 77a, 88, C10 or 2, 2b, 3, 36, 36b, 159, 185 (to Bessborough Gardens), 507. ⌦ Victoria, Vauxhall. **Open** 10am–5.50pm Mon–Sat, 2–5.50pm Sun. **Closed** 24–26 Dec, 1 Jan, Good Fri, May Day. **Adm charge** for major exhibitions. ⌾ ⌘ Atterbury St. ⌦ ⏛ ⌾ ⌘

Disabled entrance on ground floor ⌘

Entrance to Clore Gallery via Room 18

24
20
22
18
19
17

Stairs to lower galleries

Main entrance to Clore Gallery

Rotunda

Main entrance

★ **Whaam !**
Leading American Pop artist Roy Lichtenstein used a comic strip source for this explosive image from 1963.

★ **Three Studies for Figures at the Base of a Crucifixion** (1944)
This is the central panel of Francis Bacon's triptych.

STAR PAINTINGS

★ **Mares and Foals by George Stubbs**

★ **Burial at Sea by J M W Turner**

★ **Three Studies by Francis Bacon**

★ **Whaam! by Roy Lichtenstein**

★ **Mares and Foals**
George Stubbs's work (from 1762–8) is characterized by perfect anatomical detail.

Cossacks
Painted in 1911 by Wassily Kandinsky, it was a major step in the development of Abstract art.

Exploring the Tate's Collection

THE TATE'S COLLECTION comprises three basic elements: British art from 1550 to the present day; international 20th-century art; and the Turner Collection housed in the purpose-built Clore Gallery.

16TH- AND 17TH-CENTURY BRITISH

Endymion Porter (1643–5) by William Dobson

FORMAL PORTRAITS dominate this period of British art. The earliest painting in the Tate, *A Man in a Black Cap*, painted by John Bettes in 1545, reveals the influence of Hans Holbein, who brought Renaissance art to England. Holbein's meticulous, linear style is echoed in many works. One of England's first home-grown artistic geniuses, was the miniaturist Nicholas Hilliard. He is represented here by a rare, full-sized portrait of Elizabeth I, a typically jewelled icon of exquisite quality. In the 17th century, under the influence of Sir Anthony Van Dyck, a new grandly elegant style of portraiture emerged. Van

Dyck's *Lady of the Spencer Family* and William Dobson's *Endymion Porter* are excellent examples. Two non-portrait gems include Francis Barlow's *Monkeys and Spaniels Playing*, a charming early animal painting, and Jan Sibrecht's *Landscape with Rainbow, Henley-on-Thames* which marks the birth of the English landscape tradition.

18TH-CENTURY BRITISH

ALONG WITH the early 18th-century illustrative paintings, the collection also boasts some fine examples of "conversation pieces" (people in an informal setting). These include the elegant, doll-like *James Family* by Arthur Devis, and William Hogarth's vivid painting of *The Strode Family at Breakfast*. Hogarth, the leading figure in British art in the 18th century, is very well-known for his satirical works. From the late 18th century, the "Grand Style" of Joshua Reynolds can be compared with the feathery brushwork of portraits by his rival, Thomas Gainsborough. Richard Wilson's work from the same era shows the same Grand Style in landscape, while George Stubbs is well represented by countryside pictures and equine portraits of astonishing beauty.

19TH-CENTURY BRITISH

Satan Smiting Job with Sore Boils (c.1826) by William Blake

THE TATE HOLDS a huge number of works by the visionary genius of the 19th century, William Blake. And there are pictures by Blake's followers, including Samuel Palmer, whose intimate, pastoral scenes are imbued with mystic intensity. The two greatest landscape artists of the century are also well represented: the Turners (in the Clore) far outnumber the Constables, but a good variety of John Constable's paintings are on show, both sketches and finished works such as the famous *Flatford Mill*. Landscapes by Crome, Cotman, Bonington and others can also be seen. The collection reveals the variety of content and style found in Victorian art. It ranges from the very sentimental "subject paintings" such as *The Blind Fiddler* by Wilkie, whose death is commemorated in Turner's *Peace (see p82)*, to William Frith's view of *Derby Day* and the highly coloured, emotionally intense images of the Pre-Raphaelites.

TURNER AT THE CLORE GALLERY

When J M W Turner (1775–1851) left his works to the nation, it was on condition that they were kept together. In 1910, a suite of rooms at the Tate was given over to some of his oil paintings, but it was not until the Clore Gallery was opened in 1987 that the entire bequest, including thousands of studies, came together. The gallery also houses Turner's watercolours including *A City on a River at Sunset*, part of his *Great Rivers of Europe* project.

A City on a River at Sunset (1832)

IMPRESSIONISM AND POST-IMPRESSIONISM

The Gardener (1906) by Paul Cézanne

MANY OF THE important Impressionist and Post-Impressionist works have now been transferred over to the National Gallery *(see pp104–7)* but the Tate still maintains a selection from the major figures and these mark the beginning of modern art. Renoir, Pissarro, Sisley, Degas, Toulouse-Lautrec, Van Gogh, Gauguin and Seurat are all represented. Highlights here include Claude Monet's grid-like *Poplars on the Epte* and Cézanne's *The Gardener*, both using radically new methods of painting which led to Abstract art.

EARLY 20TH-CENTURY

THE 20TH CENTURY opens with the intimate, decorative scenes of Nabis, Vuillard and Bonnard. Then come avant-garde paintings, starting with the Fauves (the word means "wild animals"), exemplified by Henri Matisse's portrait of his fellow Fauve, Derain. All the major movements of the early century are here: the revolutionary Cubism of Picasso, Braque and Leger; the dynamic, machine-inspired Futurism of artists such as Severnini and Boccioni; the disturbing works of Munch, Kirchner, Beckman and the other German Expressionists; as well as the more traditional art styles which flourished in Britain after World War I. Most notable in this area are some works by Sir Stanley Spencer, including the massive *Resurrection, Cookham*. There are also major works by the central Abstract artists – like Kandinsky, Mondrian and Malevich – and by British Abstract artists such as Ben Nicholson. The sculpture includes major works by Rodin, Brancusi, Hepworth and Moore. The Surrealists are well in evidence – the biggest crowd-puller being the Dalis.

Madame Derain in a White Shawl (1919–20) by André Derain

LATE 20TH-CENTURY

THE RANGE OF styles and "schools" in the post World War II collection is vast, reflecting inter-national developments in Abstract and Figurative painting and sculpture. The effects of World War II can be seen directly and indirectly in the works of the 1940s and 1950s, from Paul Nash's eerie war-torn landscape *Totes Meer* (Dead Sea), to the disturbing "new images of man" created by Giacometti, Dubuffet and Bacon. Late works by Picasso, Matisse and Leger reflect the Expressionist and Abstract developments of the postwar period. One of the most magnificent images is Matisse's gigantic collage of cut-out paper, *Snail*. The Tate also contains some impressive paintings by the American Abstract Expressionists of the 1940s and 1950s: de Kooning, Newman, Pollock and Rothko. It later acquired related works, such as Morris Louis' huge drip-stained canvases.

Op (Optical) Art and Kinetic (moving) Art were two movements of the 1960s which, like Anthony Caro's amazing bright red sheet-steel sculpture *Early One Morning*, reflect a move away from the Expressionism of the 1950s. The art movement that is probably most associated with the 1960s is Pop Art. The Tate contains some key works by both American and British exponents – including Blake's *Toy Shop*, Lichtenstein's *Whaam!* and Andy Warhol's *Marilyn Diptych*.

There are many significant works of recent British figure painting: Freud, Auerbach, Kossoff, Kitaj, Hockney and Bacon can all be seen. More contentious are Minimalist works – the American Carl André's *Equivalent VIII* (made out of bricks) is an extreme example. A wide variety of Conceptual Art is on display, including Richard Long's landscape art in which maps, photos and printed words codify the artist's response to nature. The Tate's huge collection continues to grow and reflect new developments in contemporary art.

Mr and Mrs Clark and Percy (1970–1) by David Hockney

PICCADILLY AND ST JAMES'S

PICCADILLY is the main artery of the West End. Once called Portugal Street, it acquired its present name from the ruffs, or pickadills, worn by 17th-century dandies. St James's still bears traces of the 18th century, when it surrounded the royal residences, and denizens of the court and society shopped and disported

Buckingham Palace decorative lock

themselves there. Two shops in St James's Street – Lock the hatter and Berry Bros vintners – recall that era. Fortnum and Mason, on Piccadilly, has served high-quality food for nearly 300 years. Mayfair to the north is still the most fashionable address in London, while Piccadilly Circus marks the start of Soho.

SIGHTS AT A GLANCE

Historic Streets and Buildings
Piccadilly Circus ❶
Albany ❸
Burlington Arcade ❻
Ritz Hotel ❼
Spencer House ❽
St James's Palace ❾
St James's Square ❿
Royal Opera Arcade ⓫
Pall Mall ⓬
The Mall ⓯
Marlborough House ⓰
Clarence House ⓲
Lancaster House ⓳
Buckingham Palace pp94–5 ⓴
Royal Mews ㉒
Wellington Arch ㉓
Shepherd Market ㉕

Museums and Galleries
Royal Acadamy of Arts ❹
Museum of Mankind ❺
Institute of Contemporary Arts ⓭
Queen's Gallery ㉑
Royal Mews ㉒
Apsley House ㉔
Faraday Museum ㉗

Churches
St James's Church ❷
Queen's Chapel ⓱

Parks and Gardens
St James's Park ⓮
Green Park ㉖

SEE ALSO
- *Street Finder*, maps 12, 13
- *Where to Stay* pp276–7
- *Restaurants* pp292–4

GETTING THERE
The Piccadilly line serves Hyde Park Corner, Piccadilly Circus, and Green Park. The Bakerloo and Jubilee lines serve Charing Cross, which is also a major BR terminus. The area is served by buses Nos. 6, 9, 15, 23 and 139.

0 metres	500
0 yards	500

KEY
	Street-by-Street map
⊖	Underground station
⇌	British Rail station
P	Parking

Piccadilly Arcade with its many fine shops

Street-by-Street: Piccadilly and St James's

A S SOON AS HENRY VIII built St James's Palace in the 1530s, the area around it became the centre of fashionable London, and it has remained so ever since. The most influential people in the land stroll its historic streets on their way to lunch in their clubs, to shop in the capital's oldest and most exclusive stores or to visit one of the many art galleries.

★ **Museum of Mankind**
This ivory leopard is in the museum's collection of primitive art ❺

Albany
It has been one of London's smartest addresses since it opened in 1774 ❸

★ **Royal Academy of Arts**
Sir Joshua Reynolds founded the Academy in 1768. Now it mounts large popular exhibitions ❹

★ **Burlington Arcade**
Uniformed beadles discourage unruly behaviour in this 19th-century mall ❻

Fortnum and Mason
was founded in 1707 by one of Queen Anne's footmen (*see p311*).

The Ritz
Named after César Ritz, and opened in 1906, it still lives up to his name ❼

Spencer House
An ancestor of the Princess of Wales built this house in 1766 ❽

St James's Palace
This Tudor palace is still the Court's official headquarters ❾

To the Mall

Jermyn Street is one of London's most elegant streets, lined with shops for style-conscious men (*See p314*).

Piccadilly station

★ **Piccadilly Circus**
The crowds and dazzling neon lights make Piccadilly Circus the West End's focal point ❶

LOCATOR MAP
See Central London Map pp12–13

★ **St James's Church**
The organ in Christopher Wren's favourite church was brought here from White-hall Palace in 1691 ❷

Pall Mall
Its famous clubs provide a haven for businessmen (and a few women) ⓬

St James's Square
William III's statue dominates the square ❿

King Street is lined with art galleries, including Christie's, St James's.

STAR SIGHTS

★ **Museum of Mankind**

★ **Burlington Arcade**

★ **Royal Academy**

★ **St James's Church**

★ **Piccadilly Circus**

KEY

━ ━ ━   Suggested route

0 metres   100

0 yards   100

Piccadilly Circus ❶

W1. **Map** 13 A3. 🚇 *Piccadilly Circus.*

Alfred Gilbert's statue of Eros

FOR YEARS PEOPLE have congregated beneath the symbolic figure of Eros, originally intended as an angel of mercy but renamed after the Greek god of love. Poised delicately with his bow, Eros has become almost a trade mark for the capital. It was erected in 1892 as a memorial to the Earl of Shaftesbury, the Victorian philanthropist. Part of Nash's master plan for Regent's Street *(see p220)*, Piccadilly Circus has been considerably altered in recent years and consists chiefly of shopping malls. One of them can be found behind the facade of the London Pavilion (1885), once a popular music hall. The circus has London's gaudiest array of neon advertising signs marking the entrance to the city's lively entertainment district with cinemas, theatres, night clubs, restaurants and pubs.

St James's Church ❷

197 Piccadilly W1. **Map** 13 A3. 📞 *0171-734 4511.* 🚇 *Piccadilly Circus, Green Park.* **Open** *8.30am–7pm daily.* **Closed** *public hols.* **Craft market** *9.30am–6pm Thu, Fri and Sat except Easter.* 📷 *during services.* 🎫 *Concerts, lectures.*

AMONG THE many churches Wren designed *(see p47)*, this is said to be one of his favourites. It has been altered

over the years and was half-wrecked by a bomb in 1940, but it maintains its essential features from 1684 – the tall, arched windows, thin spire (a 1966 fibreglass replica of the original) and a light, dignified interior. The ornate screen behind the altar is one of the finest works of the 17th-century master carver Grinling Gibbons, who also made the exquisite marble font, with a scene depicting Adam and Eve standing by the Tree of Life. Artist and poet William Blake and Prime Minister Pitt the Elder were both baptized here. More of Gibbons's carvings can be seen above the grandiose organ, made for Whitehall Palace chapel but installed here in 1691. Today the church has a full calendar of events, and runs the vegetarian Wren Coffee House.

Albany ❸

Albany Court Yard, Piccadilly W1. **Map** 12 F3. 🚇 *Green Park, Piccadilly Circus.*

THESE DESIRABLE and discreet bachelor apartments, half hidden through an entrance off Piccadilly, were built in 1803 by Henry Holland. Notable residents have included the poet Lord Byron, novelist Graham Greene, two Prime Ministers (William Gladstone and Edward Heath) and the actor Terence Stamp. Married men were admitted in 1878 but could not bring their wives to live with them until 1919. Women are now allowed to live here in their own right.

Lord Byron lived in Albany

Royal Academy of Arts ❹

Burlington House, Piccadilly W1. **Map** 12 F3. 📞 *0171-439 7438.* 🚇 *Piccadilly Circus, Green Park.* **Open** *10am–6pm daily (last adm: 5.30pm).* **Closed** *24–26 Dec, Good Fri.* **Adm charge**. 📷 ♿ 🎫 📷 🍴 📷 **Lectures**.

Michelangelo's Madonnna and Child

THE COURTYARD in front of Burlington House, one of the West End's few surviving mansions from the early 18th century, is often crammed with people waiting to get into one of the prestigious visiting art exhibitions on show at the Royal Academy (founded 1768). The famous annual summer exhibition, which has now been held for over 200 years, comprises around 1,200 new works by both established and unknown painters, sculptors and architects. Any artist, regardless of background, can submit work.

The airy Sackler Galleries (1991), designed by Norman Foster in the former diploma galleries, show visiting exhibitions. There are permanent items in the sculpture promenade outside the galleries, notably a Michelangelo relief of the Madonna and Child (1505). The exceptional permanent collection (not all on display) includes one work by each current and former Academician. There is a good shop on the first floor which sells cards and other items that are designed by Academy members for the RA.

Museum of Mankind ⑤

6 Burlington Gdns W1. **Map** 12 F3. [0171-437 2224. ⊖ *Piccadilly Circus, Green Park.* **Open** *10am–5pm Mon–Sat, 2.30–6pm Sun.* **Closed** *24–26 Dec, 1 Jan, Good Fri, 1st Mon in May.* 🖸 🕭 🔃 🎦 🎦 🖳 🗋 **Lectures, film presentations.**

THE SMALL, well-organized ethnographic section of the British Museum *(see pp126–9)* occupies an 1860s back extension of Burlington House (the Royal Academy). Highlights of the museum's excellent collection, from both ancient and modern cultures, are displayed on the first floor. These include figures, masks, ornaments and a number of giant statues. Among the West African treasures are a pair of ivory leopards from Benin and an intricately carved Yoruba door panel. The ground floor houses changing exhibitions about particular cultures, which often include reconstructed buildings and villages.

The Colombian coffee shop provides a welcome and often uncrowded refuge for refreshments, soup and light meals. The entrance is flanked by enormous casts of two Mayan pillars.

Hawaiian war god, Museum of Mankind

Burlington Arcade ⑥

Piccadilly W1. **Map** 12 F3. ⊖ *Green Park, Piccadilly Circus. See* **Shops and Markets** *p318.*

THIS IS ONE OF three 19th-century arcades of small shops selling traditional British luxuries. (The others, Piccadilly and Princes Arcades, are on the south side of Piccadilly.) It was built for Lord Cavendish in 1819 to stop passers-by throwing rubbish into his garden. The arcade is still patrolled by beadles who ensure that decorum is maintained.

Afternoon tea served in the opulent Palm Court of the Ritz

Ritz Hotel ⑦

Piccadilly W1. **Map** 12 F3. [0171-493 8181. ⊖ *Green Park.* **Open** *to non-residents for tea or restaurant meals.* 🕭 🖸 *See* **Where to Stay** *p282 and* **Restaurants and Pubs** *p306.*

CESAR RITZ, the Swiss hotelier who inspired the word "ritzy", had virtually retired by 1906, when this hotel was built and named after him. The colonnaded front of the dominant château-style building was meant to suggest Paris, where the grandest hotels were to be found at the turn of the century. It manages to maintain its Edwardian air of opulence and is a popular stop, among those who are suitably dressed, for afternoon tea.

Spencer House ⑧

27 St James's Pl SW1. **Map** 12 F4. [0171-499 8620. ⊖ *Green Park.* **Open** *10.45am–5.30pm Sun (last adm: 4.45pm).* **Closed** *Jan & Aug.* **Adm charge. Children** *under 10 not welcome.* 🚫 🕭 🎦 *compulsory.* 🎦

THIS PALLADIAN PALACE was finished in 1766 for the first Earl Spencer, an ancestor of the Princess of Wales. Today it has been restored to its 18th-century splendour and contains fine paintings and contemporary furniture;

one of the highlights is the beautifully decorated painted room. The house is open to the public for guided tours, receptions or meetings.

St James's Palace ⑨

The Mall SW1. **Map** 12 F4. ⊖ *Green Park.* **Not open** *to the public.*

BUILT BY HENRY VIII in the late 1530s on the site of a former leper hospital, it was a primary royal residence only briefly, mainly during the reign of Elizabeth I and during the late 17th and early 18th centuries. In 1952 Queen Elizabeth II made her first speech as queen here, and foreign ambassadors are still officially accredited to the Court of St James. Its northern gatehouse, seen from St James's Street, is one of London's most evocative Tudor landmarks. Behind it the palace buildings are now occupied by privileged Crown servants.

St James's Tudor gatehouse

Royal Opera Arcade

St James's Square ⑩

SW1. **Map** 13 A3. 🚇 *Green Park, Piccadilly Circus.*

ONE OF LONDON's earliest squares, it was laid out in the 1670s and lined by exclusive houses for those whose business made it vital for them to live near St James's Palace. Many of the buildings date from the 18th and 19th centuries and have had many illustrious residents. During World War II Generals Eisenhower and de Gaulle both had headquarters here.

Today No. 10 on the north side is Chatham House (1736), home of the Royal Institute for International Affairs and, in the northeast corner, can be found the London Library (1896), a private lending library founded in 1841 by historian Thomas Carlyle *(see p192)* and others. The private gardens in the middle contain an equestrian statue of William III, here since 1808.

Royal Opera Arcade ⑪

SW1. **Map** 13 A3. 🚇 *Piccadilly Circus.*

LONDON's FIRST shopping arcade, it was designed by John Nash and completed in 1818, behind the Haymarket Opera House (now called Her Majesty's Theatre). It beat the Burlington Arcade *(see p91)* by a year or so. Farlows sell shooting equipment, fishing tackle, including the famous Hunter's green Wellington boots, and a broad range of other essentials for traditional country living, from the Pall Mall side of this arcade.

Pall Mall ⑫

SW1. **Map** 13 A4. 🚇 *Charing Cross, Green Park.*

The Duke of Wellington (1842): a frequent visitor to Pall Mall

THIS DIGNIFIED street is named from the game of *palle-maille*, a cross between croquet and golf, which was played here in the early 17th century. For more than 150 years Pall Mall has been at the heart of London's clubland. Here exclusive gentlemen's clubs were formed to provide members with a refuge from their womenfolk.

The club houses now amount to a text book of the most fashionable architects of the era. From the east end, on the left is the colonnaded entrance to No. 116, Nash's United Services Club (1827). This was the favourite club of the Duke of Wellington and now houses the Institute of Directors. Facing it, on the other side of Waterloo Place, is the Athenaeum (No. 116), designed three years later by Decimus Burton, and long the power house of the British establishment. Next door are two clubs by Sir Charles Barry, architect of the Houses of Parliament *(see pp72–3);* the Travellers' is at No. 106 and the Reform at No. 104. The clubs' stately interiors are well preserved but only members and their guests are admitted.

Institute of Contemporary Arts ⑬

The Mall SW1. **Map** 13 B3. 📞 *0171-930 3647.* 🚇 *Charing Cross, Piccadilly Circus.* **Open** *noon–1am daily.* **Closed** *Christmas week, public hols.* **Adm charge.** 🚻 *notify in advance.* 🎥 🖥 🍴 🎭 **Concerts, theatre, dance, lectures.** *See* **Entertainment** *pp332–3.*

THE INSTITUTE (ICA) was established in 1947 in an effort to offer British artists some of the facilities which were available to United States artists at the Museum of Modern Art in New York. Originally on Dover Street, it has been incongruously situated in part of John Nash's Classical Carlton House Terrace (1833) since 1968.

With its entrance on the Mall, this extensive warren contains a cinema, auditorium, bookshop, art gallery, bar and an excellent restaurant. It offers lively and often avant-garde exhibitions, talks, concerts, films and plays. Non-members pay a nominal charge.

Institute of Contemporary Arts, Carlton House Terrace

St James's Park ⑭

SW1. **Map** 13 A4. ☎ 0171-930
1793. ⊖ St James's Park. **Open**
6am–midnight daily. ▢ **Open**
10am–6pm daily. ♿ **Concerts** twice
daily in summer. **Bird collection**.

IN SUMMER office workers
sunbathe between the
dazzling flower beds of this,
the capital's most ornamental
park. In winter overcoated
civil servants discuss affairs of
state as they stroll by the lake
and eye its ducks, geese and
pelicans. Originally a marsh,
the park was drained by
Henry VIII and incorporated
into his hunting grounds.
Later Charles II redesigned it
for pedestrian pleasures, with
an aviary along its southern
edge (hence Birdcage Walk,
the street where the aviary
was). It is still a popular place
to take the air, with an
appealing view of Whitehall
rooftops. In the summer there
are concerts on the bandstand.

The Mall ⑮

SW1. **Map** 13 A4. ⊖ Charing Cross,
Green Park, Piccadilly Circus.

THIS BROAD triumphal
approach to Buckingham
Palace was created by Aston
Webb when he redesigned
the front of the palace and
the Victoria Monument in
1911 (see picture p96). It
follows the course of the old
path at the edge of St James's
Park, laid out in the reign of
Charles II when it became
London's most fashionable
promenade. On the flagpoles
down both sides of the Mall fly
national flags of foreign heads
of state during official visits.

Marlborough
House ⑯

Pall Mall SW1. **Map** 13 A4.
☎ 0171-839 3411. ⊖ St James's
Park, Green Park. **Closed** until 1995
for restoration.

MARLBOROUGH HOUSE was
designed by Christopher
Wren (see p47) for the
Duchess of Marlborough, and

finished in 1711. It was
substantially enlarged in the
19th century and used by
members of the Royal Family.
From 1863 until he became
Edward VII in 1903, it was
the home of the Prince and
Princess of Wales and the
social centre of London. An
Art Nouveau memorial in the
Marlborough Road wall of the
house commemorates
Edward's queen, Alexandra.
The building now houses the
Commonwealth Secretariat.

Queen's Chapel ⑰

Marlborough Rd SW1. **Map** 13 A4.
⊖ Green Park. **Not open** to the
public.

THIS EXQUISITE WORK of the
architect Inigo Jones was
built for Charles I's French
wife, Henrietta Maria, in 1627,
and was the first Classical
church in England. It was
initially intended to be part

Queen's Chapel

of St James's Palace but is
now separated from it by
Marlborough Gate. George III
married his queen, Charlotte
of Mecklenburg-Strelitz (who
was to bear him 15 children),
here in 1761.

The interior of the chapel,
with its wonderful Annibale
Caracci altarpiece and glorious
17th-century fittings is,
unfortunately, open only to
regular worshippers during
the spring and early summer.

Early summer in St James's Park

Buckingham Palace ⑳

BUCKINGHAM PALACE is the headquarters of the British monarchy. It doubles as an office and a home, and is also used for ceremonial state occasions such as banquets for visiting heads of state. About 300 people work at the palace. These include officers of the Royal Household, who organize the Queen's official affairs, as well as domestic staff.

John Nash converted the original Buckingham House into a palace for George IV (reigned 1820–30). Both he and his brother, William IV (reigned 1830–7), died before work was completed, and Queen Victoria was the first monarch to live at the palace. The present east front, facing the Mall, was added in 1913.

Music Room
State guests are presented and royal christenings take place in this room, which boasts a beautiful, original parquet floor by Nash.

The State Dining Room is where meals that are less formal than state banquets are held.

The Picture Gallery houses a selection of the Queen's priceless collection of paintings.

Kitchen and staff quarters

Blue Drawing Room
Imitation onyx columns, created by John Nash, decorate this room.

Private post office

Changing of the Guard
During the summer the palace guard is changed every day in a colourful ceremony. (See p52–5.)

State Ballroom
The Georgian baroque ballroom is used for state banquets and investitures.

VISITORS' CHECKLIST

SW1. **Map** 12 F5. ☎ *0171-930 5526.* ⊖ *St James's Park, Victoria.* ⊞ *2B, 11, 16, 24, 25, 36, 38, 52, 73, 135, C1.* ⊠ *Victoria.* **State rooms open** *Aug–Sept: 9.30am–5.30pm daily.* **Adm charge.** ⊘ **Changing of the Queen's Guard**: *May–Aug: 11:30am daily; Sept–April: alternate days but subject to change without notice.*

The garden is a haven for wild life and is overlooked by most of the lavishly decorated state rooms at the back of the palace.

The White Drawing Room is where the Royal Family assemble before passing into the State Dining Room or Ball Room.

A swimming pool lies in the palace grounds as does a private cinema.

The Throne Room is illuminated by seven magnificent chandeliers.

The Green Drawing Room is the first of the state rooms entered by guests at royal functions.

Queen's Audience Chamber
This is one of the Queen's 12 private rooms on the first floor of the palace.

The Royal Standard flies while the Queen is in residence.

WHO LIVES IN BUCKINGHAM PALACE?

The palace is the London residence of the Queen and her husband, the Duke of Edinburgh. Prince Edward also has an apartment here, as do Princess Anne and the Duke of York. About 50 domestic staff have rooms in the palace. There are more staff homes situated in the Royal Mews (*see p96*).

View over Mall
Traditionally, the Royal Family waves to eager crowds from the palace balcony.

Clarence House ⓲

Stable Yard SW1. **Map** 12 F4.
🚇 Green Park, St James's Park.
Not open to the public.

Overlooking the mall, it was designed in 1827 by John Nash for Queen Victoria's predecessor, William, Duke of Clarence who lived here after he became king in 1830. It is now the Queen Mother's London home.

Lancaster House ⓳

Stable Yard SW1. **Map** 12 F4.
🚇 Green Park, St James's Park.
Not open to the public.

Lancaster House

This royal residence was built for the Duke of York by Benjamin Wyatt, architect of Apsley House, in 1825. In 1848 Chopin played here for Queen Victoria, Prince Albert and the Duke of Wellington. It is now a conference centre.

Buckingham Palace ⓴

See pp94–5.

Queen's Gallery ㉑

Buckingham Palace Rd SW1.
Map 12 F5. 📞 0171-799 2331.
🚇 St James's Park, Victoria. **Open**
10am–5pm Tue–Sat, 2–5pm Sun.
Closed 25–26 Dec, 1 Jan. **Adm**
charge. ⊘ 🅿

The queen possesses one of the finest and most valuable collections of paintings in the world, rich in the work of the old masters – for instance Vermeer and Leonardo. (For 30 years her art adviser was Sir Anthony Blunt, until he was exposed as a Soviet spy in 1979 and stripped of his knighthood.)

A selection of the works is on display in this small gallery (at the side of the Palace), which was used as a conservatory until 1962. The building was once also used as a chapel, and there is still an area devoted to private worship and screened off from the public. The exhibitions here are based on a specific theme and change regularly. A shop sells a variety of royal memorabilia.

Royal Mews ㉒

Buckingham Palace Rd SW1.
Map 12 E5. 📞 0171-799 2331.
🚇 St James's Park, Victoria. **Open**
noon–4pm Wed, plus other days
during summer. Subject to closure at
short notice (phone first). **Adm**
charge. ♿ 🅿

Although open for only a few hours a week, the mews is worth catching for all lovers of horses and of royal pomp. The stables and coach houses, designed by Nash in 1825, accommodate the horses and coaches used by the Royal Family on state occasions, as well as the Rolls-Royce limousines with transparent tops that allow their royal occupants to

Fabergé egg, Queen's Gallery

be seen by bystanders. The star exhibit is the gold state coach, built for George III in 1761, with its panels painted by Giovanni Cipriani. Among the other vehicles on view are the Irish state coach, bought by Queen Victoria for the State Opening of Parliament; the open-topped royal landau; and the glass coach used for royal weddings and for transporting foreign ambassadors. The elaborate harnesses of the horses are also on display, and so are some of the splendid animals that wear them.

The mews remains open during the week of the Royal Ascot race meeting in June. For this event, however, the Mews vehicles go to the Berkshire course, where they convey the royal party past the grand-stand before the first race.

The Victoria Monument outside Buckingham Palace

Wellington Arch ㉓

SW1. **Map** 12 D4. ⊖ *Hyde Park Corner.* **Open** *5am–midnight daily.*

AFTER NEARLY A century of debate about what to do with the patch of land that lies in front of Apsley House, a vast archway, designed by Decimus Burton and called Wellington Arch, was erected in 1828. The sculpture, by Adrian Jones, was added later, in 1912. Before it was installed on the arch Jones had managed to seat eight people for dinner in the hollow, boat-shaped body of one of the horses.

Until 1992 London's second smallest police station (the smallest can be found on Trafalgar Square) used to be located inside the arch, which is sometimes referred to as Constitution Arch.

Wellington Arch

Apsley House ㉔

149 Piccadilly W1. **Map** 12 D4. 🄲 *0171-499 5676.* ⊖ *Hyde Park Corner.* **Open** *11am–5pm Tue–Sun (last adm: 4.30pm).* **Closed** *24–26 Dec, 1 Jan, Good Fri, May Day, public hols.* **Adm charge.** 🄾 🄵 *alternate Thu pm.*

APSLEY HOUSE, on the south-east corner of Hyde Park, was completed by Robert Adam for Baron Apsley in 1778. Fifty years later it was enlarged and altered by the architects Benjamin and Philip Wyatt, to provide a suitably grand home for the Duke of Wellington, hero of the Battle of Waterloo (1815) against Napoleon. Later Wellington became Prime Minister. It is now a museum of Wellington memorabilia

Interior of Apsley House

and some of his trophies, and is dominated by Canova's startling, double life-size statue of Napoleon, who was Wellington's arch-enemy, wearing only a fig leaf. This once stood in the Louvre in Paris. Most of the paintings are of Wellington's contemporaries and victories, but there are also some old masters from his collection. The few remaining Adam interiors are worth seeing.

Shepherd Market ㉕

W1. **Map** 12 E4. ⊖ *Green Park.*

THIS BIJOU pedestrianized enclave of small shops, restaurants, and outdoor cafés, between Piccadilly and Curzon Street, was named after Edward Shepherd, who built it in the mid-18th century. During the 17th century the annual 15-day May Fair (from which the area's name is derived) was held on this site, and today Shepherd Market is still very much the centre of Mayfair.

Green Park ㉖

SW1. **Map** 12 E4. 🄲 *0171-930 1793.* ⊖ *Green Park, Hyde Park Corner.* **Open** *5am–midnight daily.*

ONCE PART OF Henry VIII's hunting ground, it was, like St James's Park, adapted for public enjoyment by Charles II in the 1660s and is a natural, undulating landscape of grass and trees

(with a good spring show of daffodils). It was a favourite site for duels during the 18th century; in 1771 the poet Alfieri was wounded here by his mistress's husband, Viscount Ligonier, but then rushed back to the Haymarket Theatre still in time to catch the last act of a play. Today the park is popular with guests staying at the Mayfair hotels as a place to jog.

Faraday Museum ㉗

The Royal Institution, 21 Albemarle St W1. **Map** 12 F3. 🄲 *0171-409 2992.* ⊖ *Green Park.* **Open** *10am–6pm Mon–Fri.* **Adm charge.** 🄾 🄵 🄻.

MICHAEL FARADAY was a 19th-century pioneer of the uses of electricity. His laboratory of the 1850s has been reconstructed in the basement of the Royal Institution and is on display together with a small museum showing some of Faraday's scientific apparatus and personal effects.

Michael Faraday

SOHO AND TRAFALGAR SQUARE

SOHO HAS BEEN renowned for pleasures of the table, the flesh and the intellect ever since it was first developed in the late 17th century. For its first century the area was one of London's most fashionable, and Soho residents of the time have gone down in history for their extravagant parties.

Today the area is the capital's best-known red light district, even though most of the prostitutes were forced

Clock on Liberty department store

from the streets by legislation in 1959. There is also a fertile sub-culture of artists and writers in the scruffy pubs, clubs and cafés.

Soho is one of London's most multi-cultural districts. The first immigrants were 18th-century Huguenots from France (*see Christ Church, Spitalfields p170*). They were followed by people from all over the rest of Europe, but today Soho is famous as a Chinatown.

SIGHTS AT A GLANCE

Historic Streets and Buildings
Trafalgar Square ❶
Admiralty Arch ❷
Leicester Square ❻
Shaftesbury Avenue ❽
Chinatown ❾
Charing Cross Road ❿
Soho Square ⓬
Carnaby Street ⓮

Shops and Markets
Berwick Street Market ⓭
Liberty ⓯

Churches
St Martin-in-the-Fields ❹

Museums and Galleries
National Gallery pp104–7 ❸
National Portrait Gallery ❺
Design Council ❼

Theatres
Palace Theatre ⓫

KEY
- Street-by-Street map
- Underground station
- British Rail station
- Parking

GETTING THERE

This area is served by the Central, Piccadilly, Bakerloo, Victoria, Northern and Jubilee lines. Many buses pass through Trafalgar Square. British Rail trains run from Charing Cross.

0 metres 500
0 yards 500

SEE ALSO

The fountains of Trafalgar Square

Street-by-Street: Trafalgar Square

THEATRES, cinemas, night
clubs and restaurants
make this London's prime
area for entertainment; there
are also vast official buildings
and narrow, shop-lined
streets nearby.

**To Tottenham Court
Road station**

Charing Cross Road
*The shops here are a
feast for booklovers* **⑩**

Shaftesbury Avenue
*Theatreland's main
artery is lined with
announcements for
current shows* **⑧**

★ Chinatown
*An area of Chinese restaurants
and shops, it is home to many
Chinese-speaking people* **⑨**

The Blue Posts pub stands
on the site of a pick-up
point for sedan chairs in
the 18th century.

**Guinness World of
Records** reveals the best,
worst and most of anything
and everything *(see p340).*

Mechanized pop stars
wave from the balcony of
Rock Circus, in the former
London Pavilion.

Design Council
*The best in British
design can be seen
and bought here* **⑦**

Leicester Square
*Film pioneer Charlie
Chaplin stands in the
traffic-free square* **⑥**

The Theatre Royal, on the site
of an older theatre, is graced by
John Nash's portico.

STAR SIGHTS

★ **National Gallery**

★ **National Portrait
Gallery**

★ **St Martin-in-
the-Fields**

★ **Chinatown**

★ **Trafalgar Square**

KEY

– – – Suggested route

0 metres	100
0 yards	100

Notre Dame, once a theatre, was converted into a church in 1855. The Jean Cocteau murals inside date from 1960.

LOCATOR MAP
See Central London Map pp12–13

The Hippodrome, a disco and nightclub (see pp334–5), was once a variety theatre.

Cecil Court is lined with shops selling old books and prints (see p317).

★ **National Gallery**
The national collection of art is housed in these buildings ❸

★ **St Martin-in-the-Fields**
James Gibbs's masterpiece set the US "colonial" style ❹

★ **National Portrait Gallery**
Portraits of prominent Britons from Tudor times to the present day adorn the walls here ❺

Leicester Square station

Charing Cross station

Nelson's Column

Admiralty Arch
The Mall's regal entrance was built in 1910 ❷

★ **Trafalgar Square**
Millions of tourists come here to feed the pigeons and admire the fountains ❶

Trafalgar Square ❶

WC2. **Map** 13 B3. 🚇 *Charing Cross.*

LONDON'S MAIN venue for rallies and outdoor public meetings, the square was conceived by John Nash and was mostly constructed during the 1830s. The 50-m (165-ft) column commemorates Admiral Lord Nelson, Britain's most famous sea lord, who died heroically at the Battle of Trafalgar against Napoleon in 1805. It dates from 1842; 14 stonemasons held a dinner on its flat top before the statue of Nelson was finally installed. Edwin Landseer's four impassive lions were added to guard its base 25 years later. The north side of the square is now taken up by the National Gallery and its annexe *(see pp104–7),* with Canada House on the west side, and South Africa House on the east. The restored Grand Buildings on the south side, with their fine arcade, were built in 1880 as the Grand Hotel. Today the pigeon-filled square is a popular rallying point for demonstrations, and for raucous New Year's Eve celebrations.

Nelson's statue over-looking the square

Admiralty Arch ❷

The Mall SW1. **Map** 13 B3. 🚇 *Charing Cross.*

DESIGNED IN 1911, this triple archway was part of Aston Webb's scheme to rebuild the Mall as a grand processional route honouring Queen Victoria. The arch effectively seals the eastern end of the Mall, although traffic passes through the smaller side gates, and separates courtly London from the hurly-burly of Trafalgar Square. The central gate is opened only for royal processions, making a fine setting for the coaches and horses trotting through.

Filming *Howard's End* at Admiralty Arch

National Gallery ❸

See pp104–7.

St Martin-in-the-Fields ❹

Trafalgar Sq WC2. **Map** 13 B3. 📞 *0171-930 1862.* 🚇 *Charing Cross.* **Open** *8am–6pm daily.* ✝ *11.30 am Sun.* 🚻 ♿ 🅿 **London Brass Rubbing Centre** 📞 *0171-437 6023.* **Open** *10am–6pm Mon–Sat, noon–6pm Sun.* **Concerts** *see* **Entertainment** *pp330–1.*

THERE HAS BEEN a church on this site since the 13th century. Many famous people were buried here, including Charles II's mistress, Nell Gwynn, and the painters William Hogarth and Joshua Reynolds. The present church was designed by James Gibbs and completed in 1726. In architectural terms it was one of the most influential ever built; it was much copied in the United States where it became a model for the Colonial style of church-building. An unusual feature of St Martin's spacious interior is the royal box at gallery level on the left of the altar.

From 1914 until 1927 the crypt was opened as a shelter for homeless soldiers and down-and-outs; during World War II it was an air-raid shelter. Today it still plays a role, helping the homeless and providing a lunchtime soup kitchen for them. It also houses a café and a religious bookshop as well as the London Brass Rubbing Centre. There is a good craft market in the yard outside *(see p323)* and regular lunch-time and evening concerts are held in the church.

National Portrait Gallery ❺

2 St Martin's Place WC2. **Map** 13 B3. 📞 *0171-306 0055.* 🚇 *Leicester Sq, Charing Cross.* **Open** *10am–6pm Mon–Sat, noon–6pm Sun.* **Closed** *Good Fri, May Day, 24–25 Dec, 1 Jan.* 🚫 ♿ *limited.* 🎦 *during August.* 🎤 **Lectures.**

TOO OFTEN IGNORED in favour of the National Gallery next door, this fascinating museum recounts British history through portraits of its main characters. There are pictures of kings, queens, poets, musicians, artists, thinkers, heroes and villains from all periods since the late 14th

Rodrigo Moynihan's portrait of Margaret Thatcher (1984)

century. The oldest works, on the fourth floor, include a Hans Holbein cartoon of Henry VIII and paintings of several of his unfortunate wives. The Elizabethans, a floor higher, feature probably the only surviving portrait of Shakespeare taken from life. Lower floors continue the collection chronologically, with works from such artists as Van Dyck, Reynolds, Gainsborough and Sargent.

The 20th century is represented on the first floor where there are as many photographs as paintings. Here musicians Elton John and Mick Jagger, and fashion designers Mary Quant and Katherine Hamnett hang round the corner from the Royal Family and politicians.

The gallery also houses temporary exhibitions and has an excellent shop selling books on art and literature, as well as an extensive range of cards, prints and posters featuring pictures from the main collection.

Leicester Square 6

WC2. **Map** 13 B2. 🚇 *Leicester Sq, Piccadilly Circus.*

IT IS HARD to imagine that this, the perpetually animated heart of the West End entertainment district, was once a fashionable place to live. Laid out in 1670 south of Leicester House, a long-gone royal residence, the square's early occupants included the scientist Isaac Newton and later the artists Joshua Reynolds and William Hogarth. (Hogarth's house, in the south-east corner, became the Hôtel de la Sablionère in 1801, probably the area's first public restaurant.)

In Victorian times several of London's most popular music halls were established here, including the Empire (today the cinema on the same site perpetuates the name) and the Alhambra, replaced in 1937 by the Art Deco Odeon. The centre of the square has recently been refurbished and includes a booth selling cut-price theatre tickets (*see*

pp326–7). There is also a statue of Charlie Chaplin (by John Doubleday), unveiled in 1981. The Shakespeare fountain dates from an earlier renovation in 1874.

Design Council 7

28 Haymarket SW1. **Map** 13 A3. 📞 *0171-839 8000.* 🚇 *Leicester Sq, Piccadilly Circus.* **Open** *10am–6pm Mon–Sat.* **Closed** *public hols.* 🅿 ♿ 🅿

FOUNDED IN 1944 as the Council for Industrial Design, this centre was the only permanent showcase for modern British design until the recent opening of the Design Museum in Bermondsey (*see p179*). Its display changes periodically and winners of the Design Council's annual awards are shown in the Awards Gallery. The bookshop has books on all aspects of design.

Shaftesbury Avenue 8

W1. **Map** 13 A2. 🚇 *Piccadilly Circus, Leicester Sq.*

THE MAIN ARTERY of London's theatreland, Shaftesbury Avenue has six theatres and two cinemas, all on its north side. This street was cut through an area of terrible slums between 1877 and 1886 in order to improve communications across the city's busy West End; it follows the route of a much earlier highway. It is named after the Earl of Shaftesbury (1801–85), whose attempts to improve housing conditions had helped some of the local poor. (The Earl is also commemorated by the Eros statue in Piccadilly Circus – *see p90*.) The Lyric Theatre, which was designed by C J Phipps, has been open for almost the same length of time as the avenue.

London's West End: the Globe Theatre on Shaftesbury Avenue

National Gallery ❸

Trafalgar Square facade

THE NATIONAL GALLERY has flourished since its inception in the early 19th century. In 1824 George IV persuaded a reluctant government to buy 38 major paintings, including works by Raphael and Rembrandt, and these became the start of a national collection. The collection grew over the years as rich benefactors contributed works and money. The main gallery building was designed in Neo-Classical style by William Wilkins and built in 1834–8. To its left lies the new Sainsbury Wing, financed by the grocery family and completed in 1991. It houses some spectacular early Renaissance art.

Stairs to lower galleries

Orange St entrance ♿

Stairs to lower floor ♿ 🚹 🚹

GALLERY GUIDE

Most of the collection is housed on one floor divided into four wings. The paintings hang chronologically, with the earliest works (1260–1510) in the Sainsbury Wing. The North, West and East Wings cover 1510–1600, 1600–1700 and 1700–1920. Lesser paintings of all periods are on the lower floor.

Link to main building

Stairs to lower galleries ▢ ♿ 🚹 🚹 ℹ

★ **Leonardo Cartoon** *(1510s)*
The genius of Leonardo da Vinci glows through this chalk drawing of the Virgin and Child with St Anne and John the Baptist.

KEY TO FLOORPLAN

▨	Painting 1260–1510
▨	Painting 1510–1600
▨	Painting 1600–1700
▨	Painting 1700–1920
▨	Special exhibitions
▨	Non-exhibition space

Main entrance to Sainsbury Wing ♿

Doge Leonardo Loredan *(1501)*
Giovanni Bellini portrays this Venetian head of state as a serene father figure.

★ **Rokeby Venus** *(1649)*
*Diego Velázquez painted it
to match a lost
Venetian
nude.*

★ **The Haywain** *(1821)*
*John Constable brilliantly
caught the effect of distance
and the changing light and
shadow of a typically
English cloudy summer day
in this famous classic.*

VISITORS' CHECKLIST

Trafalgar Sq WC2. **Map** 13 B3.
📞 0171-839 3321. 📠 0171-
389 1785. 🚇 Charing Cross,
Leicester Sq, Piccadilly Circus.
🚌 3, 6, 9, 11, 12, 13, 15, 23,
24, 29, 30, 53, 77a, 88, 94, 109,
159, 176, 177, 184, 196.
🚉 Charing Cross. **Open** 10am–
6pm Mon–Sat, 2–6pm Sun.
Closed 24–26 Dec, 1 Jan, Good
Fri, May Day public hol. 🅿
♿ Orange St and Sainsbury
Wing entrances. 📷 🚻 🍴 🛍
*Lectures, film presentations,
videos, exhibitions, events.*

Bathers at Asnières *(1884)*
*Georges Seurat experiments here
with millions of little dots of colour,
to create a Neo-Classical portrayal
of modern urban life.*

**Stairs to
lower floor**
🖼 🚹 🛗

★**The Ambassadors**
*The strange shape in the
foreground of this Hans
Holbein portrait (1533)
is a foreshortened skull,
a symbol of mortality.*

**Trafalgar Square
entrance**

★ **Baptism of Christ**
*Piero della Francesca
painted this tranquil
masterpiece (1450s) of
early Renaissance
perspective for a church
in his native Umbria.*

Arnolfini Marriage
*The woman in Jan van
Eyck's famous painting
(1434) is not pregnant –
her rotund shape
conforms to contemporary
ideas of female beauty.*

STAR PICTURES

★**Baptism of Christ
by Piero della
Francesca**

★**Cartoon by
Leonardo da Vinci**

★**Rokeby Venus by
Diego Velázquez**

★**The Ambassadors
by Hans Holbein**

★**The Haywain by
John Constable**

Exploring the National Gallery

THE NATIONAL GALLERY IS London's leading art museum with over 2,200 paintings, most kept on permanent display. The collection includes everything from early works by Giotto, in the 13th century, to 20th-century Picassos, but its particular strengths are in Dutch, early Renaissance Italian and 17th-century Spanish painting. The bulk of the modern and British collections are housed in the Tate Gallery *(see pp82–5)*.

The Adoration of The Kings (1564) by Pieter Brueghel the Elder

EARLY RENAISSANCE (1260–1510): ITALIAN AND NORTHERN PAINTING

THREE LUSTROUS PANELS from the *Maestà*, Duccio's great altarpiece in Siena cathedral, are among the earliest paintings here. Other Italian works of the period include his outstanding *Madonna*.

The fine *Wilton Diptych* portraying England's Richard II is probably by a French artist. It displays the lyrical elegance of the International Gothic style that swept Europe.

Italian masters of this style include Pisanello and Gentile da Fabriano, whose *Madonna* often hangs beside another, by Masaccio – both date from 1426. Also shown are works by Masaccio's pupil, Filippo Lippi, as well as Botticelli and Uccello. Umbrian paintings include Piero della Francesca's *Nativity* and *Baptism*, and an excellent collection of Mantegna, Bellini and other works from the Venetian and Ferrarese schools. Antonello da Messina's *St Jerome in his Study* has been mistaken for a van Eyck; it is not hard to see why, when you compare it with van Eyck's *Arnolfini Marriage*. Important

Netherlandish pictures, including some by Rogier van der Weyden and his followers, are also here, in the new Sainsbury Wing.

HIGH RENAISSANCE (1520–1600): ITALIAN, NETHERLANDISH AND GERMAN PAINTING

Christ Mocked (1490–1500) by Hieronymus Bosch

SEBASTIANO DEL PIOMBO'S *The Raising of Lazarus* was painted, with Michelangelo's assistance, to rival Raphael's great *Transfiguration*, which hangs in the Vatican in Rome.

These and other well-known names of the High (or late) Renaissance are extremely well represented, often with massive works. Look out for Parmigianino's *Madonna and Child with Saints*, Leonardo da Vinci's black chalk cartoon of the *Virgin and Child* (a full-sized drawing used for copying as a painting), and his second version of the *Virgin of the Rocks*. There are also tender and amusing works by Piero di Cosimo, and several Titians, including *Bacchus and Ariadne* – which the public found too bright and garish when it was first cleaned by the gallery in the 1840s.

The Netherlandish and German collections are weaker. Even so, they include *The Ambassadors*, a fine double portrait by Holbein; and Altdorfer's superb *Christ Bidding Farewell to his Mother*, bought by the gallery in 1980. There is also an Hieronymus Bosch of *Christ Mocked* (sometimes known as *The Crowning with Thorns*), and an excellent Brueghel, *The Adoration of the Kings*.

The Annunciation (1448) by Filippo Lippi

THE SAINSBURY WING

Plans for this new wing, opened in 1991, provoked a storm of dissension. An incensed Prince Charles dubbed an early design "a monstrous carbuncle on the face of a much-loved friend". The final building, by Robert Venturi, has drawn criticism, from other quarters, for being a derivative compromise.

Inside is the Micro Gallery, a computerized database of the collection from which you can print out floorplans and illustrated information.

DUTCH, ITALIAN, FRENCH AND SPANISH PAINTING (1600–1700)

THE SUPERB DUTCH collection gives two entire rooms to Rembrandt. There are also works by Vermeer, Van Dyck (among them his equestrian portrait of King Charles I) and Rubens (including the popular *Chapeau de Paille*).

From Italy, the works of Carracci and Caravaggio are strongly represented, and Salvatore Rosa has a glowering self-portrait.

French works on show include a magnificent portrait of Cardinal Richelieu by Philippe de Champaigne. Claude's seascape, *The Embarkation of the Queen of Sheba,* hangs beside Turner's rival painting *Dido Building Carthage,* as Turner himself had instructed.

The Spanish school has works by Murillo, Velázquez, Zurbarán and others.

Young Woman Standing at a Virginal (1670) by Jan Vermeer

The Scale of Love (1715–18) by Jean Antoine Watteau

VENETIAN, FRENCH AND ENGLISH PAINTING (1700–1800)

ONE OF THE GALLERY'S most famous 18th-century works is Canaletto's *The Stone-Mason's Yard.* Other Venetians here are Longhi and Tiepolo.

The French collection includes Rococo masters such as Chardin, Watteau and Boucher, as well as landscapists and portraitists.

Gainsborough's early, gauche *Mr and Mrs Andrews* and *The Morning Walk* are favourites with visitors; his rival, Sir Joshua Reynolds, is represented by some of his most Classical work and by more informal portraits.

ENGLISH, FRENCH AND GERMAN PAINTING (1800–1900)

THE GREAT AGE OF 19th-century landscape painting is amply represented here, with fine works by Constable and Turner as well as by the French artists Corot and Daubigny.

Of Romantic art, there is Géricault's vivid work, *Horse Frightened by Lightning,* and several interesting paintings by Delacroix. In contrast, the society portrait of *Mme Moitessier* by Ingres, though still Romantic, is more restrained and Classical.

Impressionists and other French avant-garde artists are well represented. Highlights include: *Waterlilies* by Monet, Renoir's *Umbrellas,* Van Gogh's *Sunflowers,* Seurat's *Bathers at Asnières* and Rousseau's *Tropical Storm with Tiger.*

Klimt's *Hermione Gallia* is one of only four German paintings in the gallery, while most English works of the period are in the Tate Gallery (see pp82–5).

Umbrellas (1881–6) by Pierre-Auguste Renoir

Chinatown ❾

Streets around Gerrard St W1.
Map 13 A2. 🚇 *Leicester Sq,
Piccadilly Circus.*

THERE HAS BEEN a Chinese
community in London
since the 19th century.
Originally it was concentrated
around the East End docks at
Limehouse, where the opium
dens of Victorian melodrama
were sited. As the number of
immigrants increased in the
1950s, many moved into Soho
where they created an ever-
expanding Chinatown. It
contains scores of restaurants,
and mysterious aroma-filled
shops selling oriental produce.
Three Chinese arches straddle
Gerrard Street, where a vibrant,
colourful street festival, held in
late January, celebrates
Chinese New Year *(see p59).*

Charing Cross Road ❿

WC2. **Map** 13 B2. 🚇 *Leicester Sq.
See **Shops and Markets** p316.*

**Antiquarian books from the
shops on Charing Cross Road**

THE ROAD is a mecca for
book-lovers, with a row of
second-hand bookshops
south of Cambridge Circus
and, north of these, a clutch
of shops that, between them,
should be able to supply just
about any recent volume. Visit
the giants: chaotic Foyle's and
user-friendly Waterstones, and
the smaller, specialist shops:
try Zwemmer's for art books,
Silver Moon for feminism and
Books for a Change for green
issues. At the junction with
New Oxford Street rises the
1960s skyscraper, Centre
Point. It lay empty for nearly
ten years after it was built, its
owners finding this more
profitable than renting it out.

At the Palace Theatre in 1898

Palace Theatre ⓫

Shaftesbury Ave W1. **Map** 13 B2.
📞 **Box office** *0171-434 0909.*
🚇 *Leicester Sq.* **Open** *for
performances only. See
Entertainment pp326–7.*

MOST WEST END theatres
are disappointingly
unassertive. This one, which
dominates the west side
of Cambridge Circus, is a
splendid exception, with its
sparkling terracotta exterior
and opulent furnishings.
Completed as an opera house
in 1891, it became a music
hall the following year. The
ballerina Anna Pavlova made
her London debut here in
1910. Now the theatre, owned
by Andrew Lloyd Webber
whose own musicals are all
over London, stages hit
shows such as *Les Miserables.*

Soho Square ⓬

W1. **Map** 13 A1. 🚇 *Tottenham
Court Rd.*

SOON AFTER it was laid out
in 1681 this enjoyed a brief
reign as the most fashionable
address in London. Originally
it was called King Square,
after Charles II whose statue
was erected in the middle. The
square went out of fashion by
the late 18th century and is
now surrounded by bland
office buildings. The mock-
Tudor garden shed in the
centre was added much later
in Victorian times.

Berwick Street Market ⓭

W1. **Map** 13 A1. 🚇 *Piccadilly
Circus.* **Open** *9am–6pm Mon–Sat.
See **Shops and Markets** p322.*

THERE HAS BEEN a market
here since the 1840s.
Berwick Street trader Jack
Smith introduced grapefruit to
London in 1890. Today this is
the West End's best street
market, at its cheeriest and
most crowded during the
lunch hour. The freshest and
least expensive produce for
miles around is to be had
here. There are also some
interesting shops, notably
Camisa, a delectable Italian
delicatessen, and Borovick's
which sells extraordinary
fabrics. At its southern end
the street narrows into an
alley on which Raymond's
Revue Bar (the comparatively
respectable face of Soho
sleaze) has presented its
festival of erotica since 1958.

Some of London's cheapest produce at Berwick Street Market

Carnaby Street ⑭

W1. **Map** 12 F2. ⊖ *Oxford Circus.*

DURING THE 1960s this street was so much the centre of swinging London that the Oxford English Dictionary recognized the noun "Carnaby Street" as meaning "fashionable clothing for young people". Today the street is rather down-market and caters more for tourists than for the truly fashionable. England's oldest pipe maker, Inderwick's, founded in 1797, is situated at No. 45. There are some interesting young designers' shops in nearby backstreets, notably those on Newburgh Street *(see pp314–15).*

Liberty's mock-Tudor facade

Liberty ⑮

Regent St W1. **Map** 12 F2. ⊖ *Oxford Circus. See **Shops and Markets** p311.*

ARTHUR LASENBY LIBERTY opened his first shop, selling oriental silks, on Regent Street in 1875. Among his first customers were the artists Ruskin, Rossetti and Whistler. Soon Liberty prints and designs, by artists such as William Morris, influenced the Arts and Crafts movement of the late 19th and early 20th centuries. They are still very fashionable today.

The present mock-Tudor building with its country-house feel dates from 1925, and was built specifically to house the store.

Today the shop maintains its strong links with the East. The basement Oriental Bazaar and the top floor, which is crammed with period Art Nouveau and Arts and Crafts furniture, are particularly worth visiting.

The Heart of Soho

OLD COMPTON STREET is Soho's High Street. Its shops and restaurants reflect the variety of people who have lived in the area over the centuries. These include many great artists, writers and musicians.

Wheeler's opened in 1929 as part of the London-wide fish restaurant chain *(see p301).*

Ronnie Scott's opened in 1959, and nearly all the big names of jazz have played there *(see pp333–5).*

Bar Italia is a coffee shop situated under the room where John Logie Baird first demonstrated television in 1926. As a child, Mozart stayed next door with his family in 1764 and 1765.

The Coach and Horses pub has been a centre of bohemian Soho since the 1950s and is still popular.

Patisserie Valerie is a Hungarian-owned café serving delicious pastries *(see pp306–7).*

St Anne's Church Tower is all that remains after a bomb destroyed the church in 1940.

The French House was frequented by Maurice Chevalier and General de Gaulle.

The Palace Theatre has hosted many successful musicals.

COVENT GARDEN AND THE STRAND

THE OPEN-AIR cafés, street entertainers, stylish shops and markets make this area a magnet for visitors. At its centre is the Piazza, which sheltered a wholesale market until 1974. Since then, the pretty Victorian buildings here and in the surrounding streets have been converted into one of the city's liveliest districts. In medieval times the area was occupied by a convent garden which supplied Westminster Abbey with produce. Then in the 1630s, Inigo Jones laid out the Piazza as London's first square, with its west side dominated by St Paul's Church.

Dried flowers from the Piazza

The Piazza was commissioned as a residential development by the Earl of Bedford, owner of one of the mansions that lined the Strand. Before the Embankment was built, the Strand ran along the river.

SIGHTS AT A GLANCE

Historic Streets and Buildings
The Piazza and Central Market ❶
Neal Street and Neal's Yard ❼
Savoy Hotel ⓭
Somerset House ⓯
Roman Bath ⓲
Bush House ⓳
Adelphi ㉒
Charing Cross ㉓

Museums and Galleries
London Transport Museum ❸
Theatre Museum ❹
Contemporary Applied Arts ❽
Photographers' Gallery ⓫
Courtauld Institute Galleries ⓰

Churches
St Paul's Church ❷
Savoy Chapel ⓮
St Mary-le-Strand ⓱

Monuments and Statues
Seven Dials ❾
Cleopatra's Needle ⓴

Parks and Gardens
Victoria Embankment Gardens ㉑

Famous Theatres
Theatre Royal ❺
Royal Opera House ❻
Adelphi Theatre ⓬
The London Coliseum ㉔

Historic Pubs and Restaurants
Lamb and Flag ❿

0 metres	500
0 yards	500

GETTING THERE
Covent Garden, Leicester Square and Charing Cross Underground stations are all nearby. There are frequent buses: 9, 11, 15 and 30 to the Strand or 14, 19, 22b, 24, 29, 38 and 176 to Shaftesbury Avenue. Charing Cross British Rail station is a short walk.

KEY

▨	Street-by-Street map
⊖	Undergound station
⬗	British Rail station
Ⓟ	Parking

SEE ALSO
- **Street Finder**, maps 13, 14
- **Where to Stay** pp276–7
- **Restaurants** pp292–4

The old vegetable market, now converted into shops and bars

Street-by-Street: Covent Garden

ONCE AN AREA of decaying streets and warehouses, Covent Garden came alive only after dark when the fruit and vegetable market traders went about their business. Now it is completely revitalized. Day and night visitors, residents and street-entertainers of every vocation throng the Piazza, much as they would have done several centuries ago.

★ Neal Street and Neal's Yard
Shops line this traffic-free area ❼

Contemporary Applied Arts
You can buy Britain's best craftwork here ❽

Covent Garden station

Seven Dials
A replica of a 17th-century monument marks the crossroads ❾

Ching Court
is a post-modernist courtyard by architect Terry Farrell.

St Martin's Theatre
is home to the world's longest running play: *The Mousetrap.*

Stanfords,
established in 1852, is the largest map and guide retailer in the world *(see p316–17).*

Lamb and Flag
Parts of this pub, one of London's oldest, date from 1623 ❿

The Garrick Club is London's literary club.

New Row
is lined with little shops and cafés.

Goodwin's Court
was inhabited by a colony of tailors in the 18th century.

Rules
is frequented by the rich and famous for its typically English food *(see p295).*

ALL THE WORLD'S A STAGE

GARRICK CLUB

★ The Piazza and Central Market
Performers of all kinds – jugglers, clowns, acrobats and musicians – entertain the crowds in the square ❶

LOCATOR MAP
See Central London Map pp12–13

Royal Opera House
Most of the world's greatest singers and dancers have appeared on its stage ❻

Bow Street Police Station housed London's first police force, the Bow Street Runners, in the 18th century. It closed in 1992.

Floral Hall used to sell exotic fruit as well as fresh flowers.

★ Theatre Museum
A collection of theatrical memorabilia is housed here ❹

Theatre Royal
The old theatre now shows extravagant musicals ❺

Boswells, now a coffee house, is where Dr Johnson first met his biographer, Boswell.

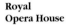

Jubilee Market sells clothes and bric-a-brac.

★ London Transport Museum
The history of the city's tube and buses is brought to life in this museum ❸

★ St Paul's Church
Despite appearances, Inigo Jones's church faces away from the Piazza – the entrance is through a churchyard ❷

STAR SIGHTS

★ **The Piazza and Central Market**

★ **St Paul's Church**

★ **London Transport Museum**

★ **Theatre Museum**

★ **Neal Street and Neal's Yard**

KEY

– – – Suggested route

0 metres	100
0 yards	100

The Piazza and Central Market ❶

Covent Garden WC2. **Map** 13 C2.
🚇 *Covent Garden.* ♿ *but cobbled streets.* **Street performers** *10am–dusk daily. See* **Shops and Markets** *p323.*

T HE 17TH-CENTURY architect Inigo Jones originally planned this area to be an elegant residential square, modelled on the piazza at Livorno, northern Italy. Today the buildings on and around the Piazza are almost entirely Victorian. The covered central market was designed by Charles Fowler in 1833 for fruit and vegetable wholesalers, the glass and iron roof anticipating the giant rail termini built later in the century – for instance, St Pancras *(see p130)* and Waterloo *(see p187)*. It now makes a magnificent shell for an array of small shops selling designer clothes, books, arts, crafts, decorative items and antiques, all surrounded by market stalls that overflow north into the adjacent streets and south into Jubilee Hall, which was built in 1903.

The colonnaded Bedford Chambers, on the north side, give a hint of Inigo Jones's plan, although even they are not original: they were rebuilt and partially modified in 1879.

Street entertainment is a tradition of the area; in 1662, diarist Samuel Pepys wrote of watching a Punch and Judy show under the portico of St Paul's Church.

West entrance to St Paul's

St Paul's Church ❷

Bedford St WC2. **Map** 13 C2.
📞 *0171-836 5221.* 🚇 *Covent Garden.* **Open** *8.30am–4.30pm Mon–Fri, 10am–1pm Sun.* ✝ *11am Sun.* 📷 ♿

I NIGO JONES built this church (completed in 1633) with the altar at the west end, so as to allow his grand portico, with its two square and two round columns, to face east into the new Piazza. Clerics objected to this unorthodox arrangement, and the altar was moved to its conventional position at the east end. Jones still went ahead with his original exterior design. Thus the church is entered from the west, and the east portico is essentially a fake door, used now as an impromptu stage for street entertainers. In 1795 the interior was destroyed by fire but was rebuilt in Jones's airy, uncomplicated style. Today the church is all that is left of Jones's original plan for the Piazza. St Paul's has long been called "the actors' church" and plaques commemorate men and women of the theatre. A 17th-century carving by Grinling Gibbons, on the west screen, is a memorial to the architect.

Punch and Judy performer

London Transport Museum ❸

The Piazza WC2. **Map** 13 C2.
📞 *0171-379 6344.* 🚇 *Covent Garden.* **Open** *10am–6pm daily (last adm: 5.15pm).* **Closed** *24–26 Dec.* **Museum closed** *Mar–Dec 1993 for refurbishment. Please ring for further details.* **Adm charge.**
📷 ♿ 🚻

London Transport Museum

Y OU DO NOT have to be a train spotter or a collector of bus numbers to enjoy this exhibition. Since 1980 the intriguing collection has been housed in the picturesque Victorian Flower Market, which was built in 1872, and features past and present public transport.

The history of London's transport is in essence a social history of the capital. Bus, tram and underground route patterns first reflected the city's growth and then promoted it: the northern and western suburbs began to develop only after their tube connections were built. The museum houses a fine collection of 20th-century commercial art. London's bus and train companies have been, and still are, prolific patrons of contemporary artists, and copies of some of the finest posters on display can be bought at the well-stocked museum shop. They include the innovative Art Deco designs of E McKnight Kauffer, as well as work by renowned artists of the 1930s, such as Graham Sutherland and Paul Nash.

This museum is excellent for children. There are plenty of hands-on exhibits, and these include the opportunity for children to put themselves in the driver's seat of a London bus, or a train from the underground system.

A mid-18th-century view of the Piazza

Theatre Museum ❹

7 Russell St WC2. **Map** 13 C2.
📞 *0171-836 7891.* 🚇 *Covent Garden.* **Open** *11am–7pm Tue–Sun.* **Closed** *25–26 Dec, 1 Jan & public hols.* **Adm charge.** 👍 ✔ 🔲
Studio theatre performances, events.

A LARGE GOLD statue of the Spirit of Gaiety, which once stood on the roof of the long-gone Gaiety variety theatre, lures you down into the museum's subterranean galleries with their fascinating collection of theatrical memorabilia. This includes playbills, programmes, props and costumes from historic productions, bits of interior decor from vanished theatres, and paintings of actors and scenes from plays. A display illustrates the development of theatre from Shakespeare's time to the present, with models of auditoriums through the ages. Exhibitions are held in the Gielgud and Irving galleries and young companies mount productions in the theatre inside.

Theatre Royal ❺

Catherine St WC2. **Map** 13 C2.
📞 *0171-494 5040.* 🚇 *Covent Garden, Holborn, Temple.* **Open** *for performances only. See* **Entertainment** *pp326–7.*

T HE FIRST THEATRE on this site was built in 1663 as one of only two venues in London where drama could legally be staged. Nell Gwynn, King Charles II's mistress, acted here. Three of the theatres built on this site since then burned down, including one designed by Sir Christopher Wren *(see p47)*. The present building, by Benjamin Wyatt, was completed in 1812 and has one of the city's largest auditoriums. In the 1800s it was famous for pantomimes – now it specializes in block-buster musicals. It is called the Theatre Royal, Drury Lane even though its entrance is on Catherine Street.

The Royal Opera House, designed by E M Barry in 1858

Royal Opera House ❻

Covent Garden WC2. **Map** 13 C2.
📞 *0171-240 1066.* 🚇 *Covent Garden.* **Open** *for performances only. See* **Entertainment** *p330.*

T HE FIRST THEATRE on this site was built in 1732, and staged plays as well as concerts. However, like its neighbour the Theatre Royal, it proved prone to fire and was destroyed in 1808 and again in 1856. The present opera house was designed in 1858 by E M Barry (son of the architect of the Houses of Parliament). John Flaxman's portico frieze, of tragedy and comedy, survived from the previous building of 1809.

The Opera House has had both high and low points during its history. In 1892, the first British performance of Wagner's *Ring* was conducted here by Gustav Mahler. Later, during World War I, the opera house was used as a storehouse by the government.

The siting of a fine opera house next to a busy produce market was exploited by George Bernard Shaw in 1913 for his *Pygmalion*, on which the musical *My Fair Lady* is based.

The building is now the home of the Royal Opera and Royal Ballet Companies – the best

tickets cost over £100 and are hard to acquire. Recently some performances have been relayed on giant screens to huge, non-paying audiences in the Piazza.

Neal Street and Neal's Yard ❼

Covent Garden WC2. **Map** 13 B1.
🚇 *Covent Garden. See* **Shops and Markets** *pp312–13.*

A specialist shop on Neal Street

I N THIS ATTRACTIVE street, former warehouses from the 19th century can be identified by the hoisting mechanisms high on their exterior walls. The buildings have been converted into a number of shops, art galleries and restaurants. Off Neal Street is Neal's Yard, a mock-rustic cornucopia for lovers of wholefoods, farmhouse cheeses and yogurts, salads, herbs and fresh-baked breads. Above the Wholefood Warehouse is a bizarre and entertaining water clock designed by Tim Hunkin.

Modern ceramics in Contemporary Applied Arts

Contemporary Applied Arts ⑧

43 Earlham St WC2. **Map** 13 B2.
📞 0171-836 6993. ⊖ Covent
Garden. **Open** 10am–6pm
Mon–Wed, Fri, Sat, 10am–7pm Thu.
Closed public hols. 🚫 ♿ ground
floor only. 🅿 **Exhibitions.** See
Shops and Markets p319.

Previously the British Craft
Centre, the ground floor
showcases the best of British
contemporary crafts including
furniture, ceramics, textiles,
glass and jewellery. The shop
sells craft works and books.

Seven Dials ⑨

Monmouth St WC2. **Map** 13 B2.
⊖ Covent Garden, Leicester Sq.

The pillar at this junction of
seven streets incorporates
six sundials (the central spike
acted as a seventh). It was

Photographers' Gallery

installed in 1989 and is a copy
of a 17th-century monument.
The original was removed in
the 19th century because it
had become a notorious
meeting place for criminals.

Lamb and Flag ⑩

33 Rose St WC2. **Map** 13 B2.
📞 0171-497 9504. ⊖ Covent
Garden, Leicester Sq. **Open**
11am–11pm Mon–Sat, noon–3pm,
7–10.30pm Sun. See **Restaurants
and Pubs** p309.

There has been an inn here
since the 16th century,
and the cramped bars are still
largely unmodernized. A
plaque commemorates the
satirist John Dryden who was
viciously attacked in the alley
outside in 1679, probably
because he lampooned the
Duchess of Portsmouth (one
of Charles II's mistresses) in
scurrilous verses.

Photographers' Gallery ⑪

5 & 8 Great Newport St WC2.
Map 13 B2. 📞 0171-831 1772.
⊖ Leicester Sq. **Open** 11am–6pm
Tue–Sat. 🅿 📷

This enterprising gallery is
London's leading venue
for photographic exhibitions,
which change periodically.
There are occasional lectures
and theatrical events and you
can also browse in the good
specialized photographic
bookshop, buy original prints
or meet fellow enthusiasts in

the café. The plaque outside
commemorates Sir Joshua
Reynolds, the founder of the
Royal Academy (see p90), who
lived here in the 18th century.

Adelphi Theatre ⑫

Strand WC2. **Map** 13 C3.
📞 0171-836 7611. ⊖ Charing
Cross, Embankment.
Open for performances only.
See **Entertainment** pp326–7.

Built in 1806, the Adelphi
was opened by John
Scott, a wealthy tradesman,
who was helping to launch
his daughter on the stage. It
was remodelled in 1930 in Art
Deco style. Note the highly
distinctive lettering on the
frontage, and the well-kept
lobby and auditorium, with
their stylized motifs.

Adelphi Theatre (1840)

Savoy Hotel ⑬

Strand WC2. **Map** 13 C2.
📞 0171-836 4343. ⊖ Charing
Cross, Embankment. See **Where to
Stay** p285.

The Savoy was opened in
1889 on the site of the
medieval Savoy Palace. One
of London's grandest hotels,
it pioneered en suite bathrooms and electric lighting.
The forecourt is the only
street in Britain where traffic
drives on the right. Attached
to the hotel are the Savoy
Theatre built for D'Oyly Carte
opera, Simpson's traditional
English restaurant specializing
in roast beef (see p295), and
the Savoy Taylor's Guild with

Front entrance to the Savoy Hotel

its Art Nouveau shop front. Next door is Shell Mex House which replaced the Cecil Hotel while keeping its Strand facade.

Savoy Chapel ⑭

Strand WC2. **Map** 13 C2.
📞 0171-836 7221. 🚇 Charing Cross, Embankment. **Open** 11.30am–3.30pm Tue–Fri. **Closed** Aug–Sep.
✝ 11am Sun. 🚫 📷

THE FIRST SAVOY CHAPEL was founded during the 16th century as the chapel for the hospital established on the site of the old Savoy Palace. Parts of the outside walls date from 1502, but most of the present building dates from the mid-19th century. In 1890 it was London's first church to be electrically lit. It became the chapel of the Royal Victorian Order in 1936, and is now a private chapel of the Queen. Nearby on Savoy Hill were the first studios of the BBC from 1922 until 1932.

Somerset House ⑮

Strand WC2. **Map** 14 D2.
📞 0171-438 6622. 🚇 Temple, Embankment, Charing Cross.
Not open to the public.

THE IMPOSING Classical compound by William Chambers was built during the 1770s on the site of the Renaissance palace of the Earls of Somerset. It was the first major building designed specifically as offices and is like four extremely grand mansions of the period grouped around a courtyard. Before the river embankment was built in the late 19th century, Somerset House stretched down to the water line. You can still see old mooring rings on the arched southern frontage. The courtyard is open to visitors but most of the interiors, still used by the Civil Service, are private. The exception is the block known as the Fine Rooms and built for the Royal Academy of Arts. It is now the Courtauld Institute.

Somerset House: Strand facade

Courtauld Institute Galleries ⑯

Somerset House, Strand WC2.
Map 14 D2. 📞 0171-873 2526.
🚇 Temple, Embankment, Charing Cross. **Open** 10am–6pm Mon–Sat, 2–6pm Sun (last adm: 5.15pm).
Closed 24–26 Dec, 1 Jan, Good Fri.
Adm charge. 🚫 ♿ 📷 📱

LONDON'S MOST spectacular small collection of paintings has been housed since 1990 in Somerset House. The Institute was established in 1931 by the textile magnate Samuel Courtauld, and its holdings are based on his collection of Impressionist and Post-Impressionist paintings. These have since been added to by donations, making the collection more representative of post-Renaissance European art.

The early galleries display work by Botticelli, Brueghel, Bellini, Rubens and Tiepolo. The Impressionists remain the chief attraction, and this collection includes Manet's *Bar at the Folies-Bergère*, one of the two versions of *Le Déjeuner sur l'Herbe*, Van Gogh's *Self-Portrait with Bandaged Ear* and works by Renoir, Monet, Degas, Gauguin, Cézanne and Toulouse-Lautrec. The gallery also houses a fine collection of 20th-century British art.

Van Gogh's *Self-Portrait with Bandaged Ear* (1889) at the Courtauld

St Mary-le-Strand ⑰

The Strand WC2. **Map** 14 D2.
📞 0171-836 3126. ⊖ Temple,
Holborn. **Open** 11am–3.30pm
Mon–Fri,10am–1pm Sun.
✝ 11am Sun. 🎥 🚻

Nᴏᴡ ʙᴇᴀᴄʜᴇᴅ on a road
island at the east end of
the Strand, this pleasing
church was completed in
1717. It was the first public
building by James Gibbs, who
designed St-Martin-in-the-
Fields *(see p102)*. Gibbs was
influenced by Christopher
Wren, but the exuberant
external decorative detail here
was inspired by the Baroque
churches of Rome, where
Gibbs studied. Its multi-
arched tower is layered like a
wedding cake, and culminates
in a cupola and lantern. St-
Mary-le-Strand is now the
official church of the Women's
Royal Naval Service.

St-Mary-le-Strand

Roman Bath ⑱

5 Strand Lane WC2. **Map** 14 D2.
📞 0171-798 2063. ⊖ Temple,
Embankment, Charing Cross. **Open**
only by prior request. 🚻 through
Temple Pl.

Tʜɪs ʟɪᴛᴛʟᴇ ʙᴀᴛʜ and its
surround may be seen
from a full-length window on
Surrey Street, by pressing a
light switch on the outside
wall. It is almost certainly not
Roman, for there is no other

Bush House from Kingsway

evidence of Roman habitation
in the immediate area. It is
more likely to have been part
of Arundel House, one of
several palaces which stood
on the Strand from Tudor
times until the 17th century,
when they were demolished
for new building. In the 19th
century the bath was open to
the public for cold plunges,
believed to be healthy.

Bush House ⑲

Aldwych WC2. **Map** 14 D2.
⊖ Temple, Holborn. **Not open** to
the public.

Sɪᴛᴜᴀᴛᴇᴅ ᴀᴛ ᴛʜᴇ ᴄᴇɴᴛʀᴇ of the
Aldwych crescent, this
Neo-Classical building was
first designed as manufacturers' showrooms by an
American, Irving T Bush, and
completed in 1935. It appears
especially imposing when
viewed from Kingsway, its
dramatic north entrance
graced with various statues
symbolizing Anglo-American
relations. Since 1940 it has
been used as radio studios,
and is the headquarters of the
BBC World Service, which is
due to be relocated to West
London within a few years.

Cleopatra's Needle ⑳

Embankment WC2. **Map** 13 C3.
⊖ Embankment, Charing Cross.

Eʀᴇᴄᴛᴇᴅ ɪɴ ʜᴇʟɪᴏᴘᴏʟɪs in
about 1500 BC, this
incongruous pink granite
monument is much older than
London itself. Its inscriptions

celebrate the deeds of the
pharaohs of ancient Egypt. It
was presented to Britain by
the then Viceroy of Egypt,
Mohammed Ali, in 1819 and
erected in 1878, shortly after
the Embankment was built. It
has a twin in New York's
Central Park, behind the
Metropolitan Museum of Art.
The bronze sphinxes, added
in 1882, are not Egyptian.
    In its base is a Victorian
time capsule of artefacts of
the day, such as the day's
newspapers, a rail timetable
and photographs of 12
contemporary beauties.

Victoria Embankment Gardens ㉑

WC2. **Map** 13 C3. ⊖ Embankment,
Charing Cross. **Open** 7.30am–dusk,
daily. 🚻 🔲

Tʜɪs ɴᴀʀʀᴏᴡ sʟɪᴠᴇʀ of a
public park, created when
the Embankment was built,
boasts well-maintained flower
beds, a clutch of statues of
British worthies (including the
Scottish poet Robert Burns)
and, in summer, a season of
concerts. Its main historical
feature is the water gate at its
north west corner, which was
built as a triumphal entry to
the Thames for the Duke of
Buckingham in 1626. It is a
relic of York House, which
used to stand on this site and
was the home first of the
Archbishops of York and then
of the Duke. It is still in its
original position and although
the water used to lap against
it, because of the Thames's
Embankment the gate is now
a good 100 m (330 ft) from
the river's edge.

Victoria Embankment Gardens

The new shopping and office block above Charing Cross

Adelphi ㉒

Strand WC2. **Map** 13 C3.
🚇 *Embankment, Charing Cross.*
Not open to the public.

John Adam Street, Adelphi

A DELPHI IS A PUN on *adelphoi*, the Greek word for brothers – this area was once an elegant riverside residential development designed in 1772 by brothers Robert and John Adam. The name now refers to the Art Deco office block, its entrance adorned with N A Trent's heroic reliefs of workers at toil, which in 1938 replaced the Adams' much admired Palladian-style apartment complex. That destruction is now viewed as one of the worst acts of 20th-century official vandalism. A number of the Adams' surrounding buildings fortunately survive, notably the ornate Royal Society for the Encouragement of Arts, Manufactures and Commerce just opposite. In the same exuberant idiom are Nos. 1–4 Robert Street, where Robert Adam lived for a time, and No. 7 Adam Street, decorated with honey-suckle reliefs.

Charing Cross ㉓

Strand WC2. **Map** 13 C3.
🚇 *Charing Cross, Embankment.*

T HE NAME DERIVES from the last of the 12 crosses erected by Edward I to mark the funeral route in 1290 of his wife, Eleanor of Castile, from Nottinghamshire to Westminster Abbey. Today a 19th-century replica stands in the forecourt of Charing Cross station. Both the cross and the Charing Cross Hotel, built into the station frontage, were designed in 1863 by E M Barry, architect of the Royal Opera House *(see p115)*.
    Above the station platforms has risen an assertive shopping centre and office block, completed in 1991. Designed by Terry Farrell it resembles a giant ocean liner, with portholes looking on to Villiers Street. The new building is best seen from the river, where it dominates its neighbours. The railway arches at the rear of the station have been modernized as a suite of small shops and cafés, as well as a new venue for the Players Theatre, the last repository of Victorian music hall entertainment.

London Coliseum ㉔

St Martin's Lane WC2. **Map** 13 B3.
📞 *0171-836 3161.* 🚇 *Leicester Sq, Charing Cross.* **Open** for performances only. 🚫 🅰 📷 📶 **Lectures.**
See **Entertainment** pp330–1.

L ONDON'S LARGEST theatre and one of its most elaborate, this flamboyant building, topped with a large globe, was designed in 1904 by Frank Matcham and was equipped with London's first revolving stage. It was also the first theatre in Europe to have lifts and has a capacity of over 2,500. Once a famous variety house, it had a brief spell as a cinema in 1961–8. Today it is the home of the English National Opera, and well worth venturing into if only for a peep at the largely unaltered Edwardian interior with its gilded cherubs and heavy scarlet curtains.

London Coliseum

BLOOMSBURY AND FITZROVIA

S INCE THE BEGINNING of the 20th century, Bloomsbury and Fitzrovia have been synonymous with litera- ture, art and learning. The Bloomsbury Group of writers and artists were active from the early 1900s until the 1930s; the name Fitzrovia was invented by writers

Carving in Russell Square

such as Dylan Thomas who drank in the Fitzroy Tavern. Bloomsbury still boasts the University of London, the British Museum and many fine Georgian squares. But it is now also noted for its Charlotte Street restau- rants and the furniture and electrical shops lining Tottenham Court Road.

SIGHTS AT A GLANCE

Historic Streets and Buildings

Bloomsbury Square **2**
Bedford Square **4**
Russell Square **5**
Queen Square **6**
St Pancras Station **9**
Woburn Walk **11**
Fitzroy Square **13**
Charlotte Street **15**

Museums

British Museum pp126–9 **1**
Dickens House Museum **7**
Thomas Coram Foundation Museum **8**

Percival David Foundation of Chinese Art **12**
Pollock's Toy Museum **16**

Churches

St George's, Bloomsbury **3**
St Pancras Parish Church **10**

Pubs

Fitzroy Tavern **14**

SEE ALSO

• *Street Finder*, maps 4, 5, 6, 13

• *Where to Stay* pp276–7

• *Restaurants* pp292–4

GETTING THERE

This area is served by the Circle, Northern, Hammer- smith and City, and Central lines. Useful buses include Nos. 8 and 98. Major BR stations are at Euston, St Pancras and King's Cross.

KEY

▨ Street-by-Street map
⊖ Underground station
⊛ British Rail station
🅿 Parking

0 metres   500
0 yards   500

A grand Georgian house in Bedford Square

Street-by-Street: Bloomsbury

THE BRITISH MUSEUM dominates Bloomsbury. Its earnestly intellectual atmosphere spills over into the surrounding streets, and to its north lies the main campus of London University. The area has been home to writers and artists, and is a traditional centre of the book trade. Most of the publishers have left, but there are still many book shops around.

The Senate House (1932) is the administrative headquarters of the University of London. It holds a priceless library.

Bedford Square
Uniform doorways in this square (1775) are fringed in artificial stone ❹

★ British Museum and Library
Designed in the mid-19th century, it is London's most popular attraction with some 5 million visitors a year ❶

STAR SIGHTS

★ British Museum and Library

★ Russell Square

KEY

━ ━ ━ Suggested route

| 0 metres | 100 |
| 0 yards | 100 |

Museum Street is lined with small cafés and shops selling old books, prints and antiques.

Pizza Express occupies a charming and little-altered Victorian dairy.

The Duke of Bedford's statue commemorates the fifth duke, Francis Russell (1765–1805). An avid farmer, he is shown with sheep and a plough.

LOCATOR MAP
See Central London Map pp12–13

★ **Russell Square**
It was once part of the Duke of Bedford's estate, and is now a shady retreat on a hot day ❺

Bloomsbury Square
Laid out in 1660, it is graced by a statue of statesman Charles James Fox (1749–1806) ❷

To Holborn station

St George's, Bloomsbury
The tower on this typically flamboyant Hawksmoor church is modelled on the tomb of King Mausolus ❸

Sicilian Avenue is a small and unexpected pedestrian precinct from 1905, where colonnades evoke Roman architecture.

British Museum ❶

See pp126–9.

Bloomsbury Square ❷

WC1. **Map** 5 C5. Ⓔ *Holborn.*

Novelist Virginia Woolf, a Bloomsbury resident

Tʜɪs ɪs ᴛʜᴇ ᴏʟᴅᴇꜱᴛ of the Bloomsbury squares. It was laid out in 1661 by the Earl of Southampton, who owned the land. None of the original buildings survive and its shaded garden is encircled by a busy one-way traffic system. (Unusually for central London, you can nearly always find a space in the car park under the square.)

The square has had many famous residents; a plaque commemorates members of the literary and artistic Bloomsbury Group, who lived in the area during the early decades of this century. The group included novelist Virginia Woolf, biographer Lytton Strachey, and artists Vanessa Bell, Duncan Grant and Dora Carrington. Look out for their individual plaques throughout the area.

St George's, Bloomsbury ❸

Bloomsbury Way WC1. **Map** 13 B1. Ⓒ 0171-405 3044.Ⓔ *Holborn, Tottenham Court Rd.* **Open** 10.30am– 3pm Mon–Fri. ✚ 10am Sun. *Recitals, exhibitions.*

A sʟɪɢʜᴛʟʏ ᴇᴄᴄᴇɴᴛʀɪᴄ church, St George's was designed by Nicholas Hawksmoor, Wren's pupil, and completed

in 1730. It was built as a place of worship for the prosperous residents of newly-developed, fashionable Bloomsbury. The layered tower, modelled on the tomb of King Mausolus (the original mausoleum in Turkey) and topped by a statue of George I, was for a long time an object of derision – the king was thought to be presented too heroically. There is some good original plasterwork, especially in the apse.

Bedford Square ❹

WC1. **Map** 5 B5. Ⓔ *Tottenham Court Rd, Goodge St.*

Bᴜɪʟᴛ ɪɴ 1775, this is one of the best-preserved of London's 18th-century squares. All the entrances to its brick houses are adorned with Coade stone, a hard-wearing artificial stone made in

A plaque in Bloomsbury Square commemorating famous residents

Lambeth (in south London) to a formula that remained secret for generations. The stately houses were once inhabited by the aristocracy. Now all are offices, many of them occupied until recently by publishers most of whom have since moved to less expensive premises. A large number of London's architects have passed through the Architectural Association at Nos. 34–36, including Richard Rogers who designed the Lloyd's Building *(see p159).*

Bedford Square's lush private gardens

Russell Square 5

WC1. **Map** 5 B5. 🚇 *Russell Sq.*
🚪 *opening hours flexible.*

O NE OF LONDON's largest
squares, the east side
boasts perhaps the best of the
Victorian grand hotels to
survive in the capital. Charles
Doll's Hotel Russell *(see p284)*,
which was opened in 1900, is
a wondrous confection of red
terracotta, with colonnaded
balconies and prancing
cherubs beneath the main
columns. The exuberance is
continued in the lobby, faced
with marble of many colours.
    The garden is open to the
public. Poet T S Eliot worked
at the west corner of the
square, from 1925 until 1965,
in what were the offices of
publishers Faber and Faber.

Queen Square 6

WC1. **Map** 5 C5. 🚇 *Russell Sq.*

I N SPITE OF being named
after Queen Anne, the
square contains a statue
of Queen Charlotte.
Her husband,
George III, stayed
at the house of a
doctor here when
he became ill with
the hereditary
disease that drove
him mad before
his death in 1820.
Today the square
is surrounded
chiefly by
hospital buildings
and there are early Georgian
houses on its west side.

The flamboyant Hotel Russell on Russell Square

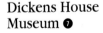
**Queen Charlotte's statue
in Queen Square**

Dickens House Museum 7

48 Doughty St WC1. **Map** 6 D4.
📞 *0171-405 2127.* 🚇 *Chancery
Lane, Russell Sq.* **Open** *10am–5pm
Mon–Sat (last adm: 4.30pm).* **Closed**
*Christmas week–New Year, public
hols.* **Adm charge.** 🚫 🚻

T HE NOVELIST Charles
Dickens lived in this
early-19th-century terraced
house for three of his most
productive years (from 1837
to 1839). The popular works

Oliver Twist and *Nicholas
Nickleby* were written here,
and *Pickwick Papers* was
finished. Although Dickens
had many London homes
throughout his lifetime, this is
the only one to have
survived. In 1923 it was
acquired by the Dickens
Fellowship and it is now
a well-conceived
museum with some of
the principal rooms
laid out exactly as
they were in
Dickens's time.
Others have been
adapted to display
a varied collection
of articles associated
with him. The
exhibits include
letters, papers,
portraits and
pieces of furniture
taken from his
other London homes as well
as first editions of many of
his best-known works.

Thomas Coram Foundation Museum 8

40 Brunswick Sq WC1. **Map** 5 C4.
📞 *0171-278 2424.* 🚇 *Russell Sq.*
Open *1.30–4.30pm Mon and Fri.*
Closed *2 weeks over Christmas,
public hols.* **Adm charge.** 🚫 🚻

T HOMAS CORAM WAS an 18th-
century sea captain who,
in 1739, was granted a charter
by King George II to establish

a hospital for the care and
education of deserted young
children. Coram asked
prominent artists to become
governors, and one of the
first to do so was the painter
William Hogarth who gave
his portrait of Thomas Coram
to the hospital.
    The foundation owns many
other treasures. In the picture
gallery are Handel's own
copy of *The Messiah* together
with the uniforms worn by
the children and some of the
mementoes left with them at
the hospital gates. The
hospital buildings were
demolished in 1926, and the
Court Room and oak staircase
are now here. The children
were moved out of London to
Hertfordshire. Today the
foundation survives – its aim
is still the care of children, in
particular the under-fives.

Hogarth's Thomas Coram portrait

British Museum and Library ❶

T HE BRITISH MUSEUM, founded in 1753, is the oldest museum in the world. Its rich collection of artefacts was started by the physician Sir Hans Sloane (1660–1753), who also helped establish the Chelsea Physic Garden

The museum's Classical Greek portico

(see p193). Over the years, Sloane's collection has been added to by gifts and purchases. It now contains treasures from all over the world – some, including many on these pages, were brought back by 18th- and 19th-century travellers and explorers. The main part of the present building (1823–50) is by Robert Smirke.

★ Egyptian Mummies

The ancient Egyptians preserved their dead in expectation of an afterlife. Animals that were believed to have sacred powers were also often mummified. This cat comes from Abydos on the Nile and dates from about 30 BC.

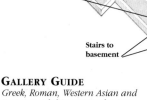

★ Elgin Marbles

Lord Elgin took these reliefs from the Parthenon in Athens. The British government bought them for the museum in 1816 (see p129).

KEY TO FLOORPLAN

- ☐ Early British collection
- ☐ Coins, medals, prints and drawings
- ☐ Medieval, Renaissance and Modern collection
- ☐ Western Asian collection
- ☐ Egyptian collection
- ☐ Greek and Roman collection
- ☐ Oriental collection
- ☐ British Library
- ☐ Temporary exhibitions
- ☐ Non-exhibition space

North stairs

North entrance

North stairs

West stairs

Stairs to basement

GALLERY GUIDE

Greek, Roman, Western Asian and Egyptian exhibits occupy the west side of the ground floor; the British Library exhibits are on the east and the rest of the floor is taken up with Library reading rooms. The collections continue on the first floor and in the basement.

Mildenhall Treasure
Thirty-four pieces of 4th-century silver tableware were ploughed up from a Suffolk field in 1942.

East stairs

British Library Reading Room

65
54
52
51
50
49
43
44
45
41
46
40 39 47 48
36 38
35
37
70
68
69
69a
32
30
31
30a
29

Main stairs

VISITORS' CHECKLIST

Great Russell St WC1.
Map 5 B5. *0171-636 1555.*
Tottenham Court Rd,
Holborn, Russell Sq. 7, 8, 10,
14, 19, 24, 25, 29, 30, 38, 55,
68, 134, 188. Euston, King's
Cross. **Open** 10am–5pm
Mon–Sat, 2.30–6pm Sun (last
adm: 15 mins before closing).
Closed 24–26 Dec, 1 Jan, Good
Fri, 8 May. *Lectures, film
presentations, exhibitions,
events.*
British Library Housed in British
Museum WC1 *0171-636
1544.* **Open** as British Museum;
individual reading rooms vary.

Lindow Man ★
The skin on this 2,000-year-old human body was preserved by the acids of a peat-bog in Cheshire. He was probably killed in an elaborate ritual.

Portland Vase
It was made in Italy or Egypt shortly before the birth of Christ. In 1845 a drunken visitor smashed it into 200 pieces. It was repaired and has been reassembled twice since then.

Main entrance

Main stairs

Lindisfarne Gospels ★
The gospels were written in Latin and illuminated in 698 by a monk called Eadfrith. Lindisfarne island is off northeast England.

STAR EXHIBITS

★ **Elgin Marbles**

★ **Lindow Man**

★ **Egyptian Mummies**

★ **Lindisfarne Gospels**

Exploring the British Museum's Collections

THE MUSEUM'S immense hoard of treasure spans two
million years of world history and civilization. There
are 94 galleries, covering 2.5 miles (4 km), which are
divided into the following specialized sections.

PREHISTORIC AND ROMAN BRITAIN

1st-century BC bronze helmet dredged up from the Thames

SIX GALLERIES cover the
period from man's first,
prehistoric, efforts at tool-
making in Africa's Olduvai
Gorge up until Christianity
overtook Britain's Roman
overlords. The first exhibit,
which stands at the top of the
main stairs, is a vast mosaic
of Christ, dating from Roman
times, which was dug up in
an English field.

The remains of an Iron Age
human sacrifice are in Room
37: "Lindow Man", probably
slain in the 1st century AD, lay
preserved in a bog until 1984.

Rooms 38 and 39 contain
superb Celtic artefacts; Room
40 houses the silver Mildenhall
Treasure and many other fine
Roman pieces, often made
by British craftsmen.

MEDIEVAL, RENAISSANCE AND MODERN OBJECTS

THE SPECTACULAR Sutton Hoo
ship treasure, the burial
hoard of a 7th-century Anglo-
Saxon king, is on display in
Room 41; this superb gold
and garnet jewellery has been
preserved unblemished.

The medieval carved walrus-
tusk chessmen from the island
of Lewis off Scotland are in
Room 42. Room 44 has a fine
collection of clocks, watches
and scientific instruments.
Timepieces have inspired the
most exquisite craftsmanship

and some grand designs – a
400-year-old table clock made
for a Holy Roman Emperor is
an ornate golden galleon that
pitched, played music and
fired a cannon. Room 45 is an
Aladdin's cave housing part of
Baron Ferdinand Rothschild's
extraordinarily diverse treasure,
all in one room. Artefacts
from the Renaissance and
later are on view in Room 47
and the museum's modern
collection is in Room 48.

Gilded brass late-16th-century ship clock from Prague

WESTERN ASIA

THERE ARE 18 galleries on
all three floors devoted to
the Western Asian collections,
which cover 7,000 years of
history from an area stretching
from Afghanistan to Phoenicia.
The most prized part of the
collection is probably the 7th-
century BC Assyrian reliefs
from King Ashurbanipal's
palace at Nineveh, in Room
21. Two large human-headed
bulls from 7th-century BC
Khorsabad are in Room 16;
there are more fine reliefs in
Rooms 17, 19, 20 and 89.
Room 19 also houses the
famous inscribed Black

Ornamental detail from a Sumerian Queen's lyre

Obelisk of King
Shalmaneser III.
Room 51 houses
part of the Oxus
Treasure, a large
hoard of gold and
silver, buried for
over 2,000 years. The
museum's collection
of clay cuneiform
tablets are in Room
55. This was the first
form of writing, developed
when civilization began 5,000
years ago. Room 56 contains
treasures from ancient Sumeria.

ANCIENT EGYPT

THE MUSEUM'S Egyptian
sculptures are in Room 25,
a giant gallery just off the front
hall. The Rosetta Stone, the
famous key to the Egyptian
hieroglyphs, is near the main
entrance. In a side gallery is
a fine New Kingdom royal
head in green schist, dated
1490 BC, with a wonderful
tomb painting of a hunt on
the far wall. Don't miss the
bronze cat with its gold
nose-ring, in the centre of the
main hall; the huge statue of
Rameses II is impossible to
miss. The amazing mummies,
jewellery and Coptic art are
in Rooms 60–66 upstairs.

Part of a colossal granite statue to Rameses II, the 13th-century BC Egyptian monarch

GREECE AND ROME

THE GREEK and Roman collections, in 30 galleries, include the museum's most famous treasure, the Elgin Marbles in Room 8. These 5th-century BC reliefs from the Parthenon once made up a marble frieze, with sculptured pediments and panels, which went right round Athena's temple on the Acropolis in Athens. Much of it was ruined in battle in 1687, and most of what survived was removed between 1801 and 1804 by British diplomat Lord Elgin, and sold to the British nation.

Ancient Greek vase illustrating the mythical hero Hercules's fight with a bull

The Greek government wants it back. However, it is still here. You can hire a recorded commentary at the entrance. Don't miss the Nereid Monument in Room 7, or, in Room 12, the 350 BC sculpture and friezes from the Mausoleum at Halicarnassus, one of the Seven Wonders of the Ancient World. The 1st-century BC Portland Vase, which was smashed by a drunken visitor in 1845 and then lovingly reassembled, is located in the Roman Empire collection upstairs in Room 70.

ORIENTAL ART

THE ORIENTAL department's magnificent Chinese collection is especially strong on fine porcelain and ancient Shang bronzes. Gallery 33, newly refurbished, features these and much other Chinese art, along with exhibits from the finest collection of South Asian sculpture outside India. Splendid Buddhist temple reliefs from Amaravati are in Room 33a. Islamic art is in Room 34, including a fine jade terrapin, found in a water tank. Room 91 houses temporary exhibitions, and

Rooms 92–4 are the new Japanese galleries, with a Classical teahouse in Room 92 and *netsuke* (small ivory carvings) in the lobby.

Statue of the Hindu God Shiva Nataraja, also known as the Lord of the Dance (11th century AD)

BRITISH LIBRARY

THE BEAUTIFUL 7th-century illuminated gospels of Lindisfarne are on display in Room 30a, and the Magna Carta is in Room 30. Fine manuscripts and bindings from many lands are on show in the magnificent King's Library, Room 32.

THE BRITISH LIBRARY READING ROOM

The British Library was established by an Act of Parliament in 1973. But though the library has only been in existence for two decades, its origins can be traced to the foundation of the British Museum in 1753. The vast Round Reading Room was designed by Sydney Smirke, architect of the museum. He based his designs on a sketch by chief librarian Sir Anthony Panizzi. Completed in 1857, it was built to give "all studious and curious persons" access to the library collections. Twenty cast-iron pillars support the great roof, and 20 tall, arched windows rise above these. Visitors are admitted from Monday to Friday at 2, 3 and 4pm. You can stand among the 30,000 reference works and think of Karl Marx, Mahatma Gandhi, or George Bernard Shaw, all of whom worked here.

The dome of the reading room is wider than that of St Peter's in Rome.

There are three levels of book-shelves up the library walls.

The massive former Midland Grand Hotel above St Pancras Station

St Pancras Station ❾

Euston Rd NW1. **Map** 5 B2.
☎ 0171-387 7070 (British Rail enquiries). ⊖ King's Cross, St Pancras. **Open** 5am–11pm daily. See **Getting to London** pp358–9.

Easily the most spectacular of the three rail termini along Euston Road, its extravagant, frontage, in redbrick gingerbread Gothic, is technically not part of the station. It was really Sir George Gilbert Scott's Midland Grand Hotel, opened in 1874 with 250 bedrooms as one of the most sumptuous and up-to-date hotels of its time. In 1890 London's first smoking room for women was opened here. From 1935 until the early 1980s the building was used

Figures on St Pancras Church

as offices; it is now being lavishly restored. The vast train shed behind is an out-standing example of Victorian engineering, with a roof that is 210 m (700 ft) long and 30 m (100 ft) high.

St Pancras Parish Church ❿

Euston Rd NW1. **Map** 5 B3.
☎ 0171-387 8250. ⊖ Euston.
Open 8am–noon Mon,
8am–6pm Wed–Sat,
8am–noon, 4–6.30pm Sun.
✝ 10am Sun ◎ ⛪
Recitals Mar–Sep: 1.15pm Thu.

This is a stately Greek revival church of 1822 by William Inwood and his son Henry, both great enthusiasts for Athenian architecture. The design is based on the Erectheum on the Acropolis in Athens, and even the wooden pulpit stands on miniature Ionic columns of its own. The long, galleried interior has a dramatic severity appropriate to the church's style. The female figures on the northern outer wall were originally taller than they are now; a chunk had to be taken out of the middle of each to make them fit under the roof they were meant to be supporting.

Woburn Walk ⓫

WC1. **Map** 5 B4. ⊖ Euston, Euston Sq.

A well-restored street of bow-fronted shops, it was designed by Thomas Cubitt in 1822. The high pavement on the east side was to protect shop fronts from the mud thrown up by carriages. The poet W B Yeats lived at No. 5 from 1895 until 1919.

Percival David Foundation of Chinese Art ⓬

53 Gordon Sq WC1. **Map** 5 B4.
☎ 0171-387 3909. ⊖ Russell Sq, Euston Sq, Goodge St. **Open** 10.30am–5pm Mon–Fri. **Closed** Christmas week–New Year, Maundy Thu–Easter Mon, public hols. ⛪ ⓘ

Particularly interesting to those with a specialized interest in Chinese porcelain, this is an important collection of exquisite wares made between the 10th and 18th centuries. Percival David presented his collection, much of it uniquely well preserved, to the University of London in 1950, and it is now administered by the School of Oriental and African Studies. The foundation includes a research library and, as well as the permanent collection, houses occasional special exhibitions of east Asian art.

Blue temple vase from David's collection

Fitzroy Square ⓭

W1. **Map** 4 F4. ⊖ Warren St, Great Portland St.

Designed by Robert Adam in 1794, the square's south and east sides survive in their original form, in dignified Portland stone. Blue plaques record the homes of many artists, writers and statesmen: George Bernard Shaw and Virginia Woolf both lived at No. 29 – although not at the same time. Shaw gave money to the artist Roger Fry to establish the Omega workshop at No. 33 in 1913. Here young artists were paid a fixed wage to produce Post-Impressionist furniture, pottery, carpets and paintings for sale to the public.

No. 29 Fitzroy Square

Fitzroy Tavern ⑭

16 Charlotte St W1. **Map** 4 F5.
📞 0171-580 3714. ⊖ Goodge St.
Open 11am–11pm Mon–Sat,
noon–3pm, 7–10.30pm Sun. ♿ See
Restaurants and Pubs pp308–9.

T HIS TRADITIONAL PUB was a meeting place between World Wars I and II for a group of writers and artists who dubbed the area around Fitzroy Square and Charlotte Street "Fitzrovia". A basement "Writers and Artists Bar" contains pictures of former customers, including the writers Dylan Thomas and George Orwell, and the artist Augustus John.

Charlotte Street ⑮

W1. **Map** 5 A5. ⊖ Goodge St.

A S THE UPPER classes moved west from Bloomsbury in the early 19th century, a flood of artists and European immigrants moved in, turning the area into a northern appendage to Soho (see pp98–109). The artist John Constable lived and worked for many years at No. 76. Some of the new residents established small workshops

to service the clothing shops on Oxford Street and the furniture stores on Tottenham Court Road. Others set up reasonably-priced restaurants. The street still boasts a great variety of eating places. It is overshadowed from the north by the 180-m (580-ft) Telecom Tower, built in 1964 as a vast TV, radio and telecommunications aerial (see p30).

Telecom Tower

Pollock's Toy Museum ⑯

1 Scala St W1. **Map** 5 A5.
📞 0171-636 3452. ⊖ Goodge St.
Open 10am–5pm Mon–Sat. **Closed**
public hols. **Adm charge.** ♿ 🎁

B ENJAMIN POLLOCK was a renowned maker of toy theatres in the late 19th and early 20th centuries – the

novelist Robert Louis Stevenson was an enthusiastic customer. The museum opened in 1956 and the final room is devoted to stages and puppets from Pollock's theatres, together with a reconstruction of his workshop. This is a child-sized museum created in two largely unaltered 18th-century houses. The small rooms have been filled with a fascinating assortment of historic toys from all over the world. There are dolls, puppets, trains, cars, construction sets, a fine rocking horse and a splendid collection of mainly Victorian dolls' houses. Toy theatre performances are held here during school holidays and children can play games with boards and pieces lent free: but parents should beware – the exit leads through a very tempting toyshop.

Pearly king and queen dolls from Pollock's Museum

HOLBORN AND THE INNS OF COURT

THIS AREA IS traditionally home to the legal and journalistic professions. The law is still here, in the Royal Courts of Justice and the Inns of Court, but most national newspapers left Fleet Street in the 1980s. Several buildings here predate the Great Fire of 1666 (see pp22–3). These

Royal crest at Lincoln's Inn

include the superb facade of Staple Inn, Prince Henry's Room, and the interior of Middle Temple Hall. Holborn used to be one of the capital's main shopping districts. Times have changed, but the jewellery and diamond dealers of Hatton Garden are still here, as well as the London Silver Vaults.

SIGHTS AT A GLANCE

Historic Buildings, Sights and Streets
Lincoln's Inn ②
Old Curiosity Shop ④
Royal Courts of Justice ⑦
Fleet Street ⑨
Prince Henry's Room ⑩
Temple ⑪
Dr Johnson's House ⑭
Holborn Viaduct ⑯
Hatton Garden ⑱
Staple Inn ⑲
Gray's Inn ㉑

Museums and Galleries
Sir John Soane's Museum ①
Public Record Office Museum ⑤

Churches
St Clement Danes ⑥

St Bride's ⑫
St Andrew, Holborn ⑮
St Etheldreda's Chapel ⑰

Monuments
Temple Bar Memorial ⑧

Parks and Gardens
Lincoln's Inn Fields ③

Pubs
Ye Olde Cheshire Cheese ⑬

Shops
London Silver Vaults ⑳

KEY

▓	Street-by-Street map
⊖	Underground station
⇌	British Rail station
P	Parking

GETTING THERE
This area is served by the Circle, Central, District, Metropolitan and Piccadilly lines. Buses 17, 18, 45, 46, 171, 243 and 259 are among many in the area, and British Rail runs from a number of mainline stations inside or close to the area.

0 metres 500
0 yards 500

SEE ALSO
- **Street Finder,** maps 6, 13, 14
- **Where to stay** pp276–7
- **Restaurants** pp292–4

The Royal Courts of Justice on the Strand

Street-by-Street: Lincoln's Inn

THIS IS CALM, dignified, legal London,
packed with history and interest.
Lincoln's Inn, adjoining one of the city's
first residential squares, has buildings
dating from the late 15th century. Dark-
suited lawyers carry bundles of briefs
between their offices here and the
Neo-Gothic Law Courts. Nearby is
the Temple, another historic legal
district with a famous 13th-century
round church.

★ Sir John Soane's Museum
The Georgian architect made this his London home and left it, with his collection, to the nation ❶

To Kingsway

★ Lincoln's Inn Fields
The mock-Tudor archway, leading to Lincoln's Inn and built in 1845, overlooks the Fields ❸

Old Curiosity Shop
It is a rare 17th-century, pre-Great Fire building which used to be a shop ❹

The Royal College of Surgeons was designed in 1836 by Sir Charles Barry. Inside there are laboratories for research and teaching as well as a museum of anatomical specimens.

STAR SIGHTS

- ★ **Sir John Soane's Museum**
- ★ **Temple**
- ★ **Lincoln's Inn Fields**
- ★ **Lincoln's Inn**

KEY

– – – Suggested route

0 metres	100
0 yards	100

Twinings have been selling tea from here since 1706. The doorway dates from 1787 when the shop was called the Golden Lion.

The Gladstone Statue was erected in 1905 to commemorate William Gladstone, the Victorian statesman who was Prime Minister four times.

★ **Lincoln's Inn**
The Court of Chancery sat here, in Old Hall, from 1835 until 1858. Sir John Taylor Coleridge was a well-known judge of the time **2**

LOCATOR MAP
See Central London Map pp12–13

Royal Courts of Justice
The country's main court for civil cases and appeals was built in 1882. It is made out of 35 million bricks faced with Portland stone **7**

Public Record Office
A display of documents here includes Shakespeare's will and the Domesday Book **5**

Fleet Street
For two centuries this was the centre of the national press. Today the newspaper offices are gone **9**

El Vino's is a venerable wine bar, where journalists still mingle with lawyers.

Prince Henry's Room
There is an authentic 17th-century room in this former gatehouse **10**

St Clement Danes
Designed by Wren (1679), it is the Royal Air Force church **6**

Temple Bar Memorial
A griffin marks where the City of London meets Westminster **8**

★ **Temple**
It was built for the Knights Templar in the 13th century, but today lawyers stroll here **11**

Wigged barristers on their way to their offices in Lincoln's Inn

Lincoln's Inn ❷

WC2. **Map** 14 D1. ☎ 0171-405 1393.
🚇 Holborn, Chancery Lane. **Grounds
open** 9am–6pm Mon–Fri. **Chapel
open** 12.30–2pm Mon–Fri. **Hall**
enquire at Porter's lodge. ☎ 0171-
405 6360. ♿ grounds only. 📷

SOME OF THE BUILDINGS in
Lincoln's Inn, the best-
preserved of London's Inns of
Court, go back to the late
15th century. The coat of
arms above the arch of the
Chancery Lane gatehouse is
Henry VIII's, and the heavy
oak door is of the same
vintage. Shakespeare's
contemporary, Ben Jonson, is
believed to have laid some of
the bricks of Lincoln's Inn
during the reign of Elizabeth I.
The chapel is early-17th-
century Gothic. Women were
not allowed to be buried here
until 1839, when the grieving
Lord Brougham petitioned to
have the rule changed so that
his beloved daughter could
be interred in the chapel, to
wait for him to join her.
    Lincoln's Inn has its share
of famous alumni. Oliver
Cromwell and John Donne,

Sir John Soane's Museum ❶

13 Lincoln's Inn Fields WC2.
Map 14 D1. ☎ 0171-430 0175.
🚇 Holborn. **Open** 10am–5pm
Tue–Sat, 6–9pm 1st Tue of month.
Closed 24–6 Dec, 1 Jan, Easter,
public hols. 📷 Sat 2.30pm.
♿ ground floor only.

ONE OF THE MOST surprising
museums in London, this
house was left to the nation
by Sir John Soane in 1837,
with a stipulation that nothing
should be changed. One of
Britain's leading 19th-century
architects, responsible for
designing the Bank of England,
Soane was the son of a brick-
layer. After marrying the niece
of a wealthy builder, whose
fortune he inherited, he bought
and reconstructed No. 12
Lincoln's Inn Fields. In 1813
he and his wife moved into
No. 13 and later, in 1824, he
rebuilt No. 14. Today, true to
Soane's wishes, the collec-

tions are much as he left
them – an eclectic gathering
of beautiful, peculiar and
often instructional objects.
    The building itself is full of
architectural surprises and
illusions. In the main ground
floor room, with its deep red
and green colouring,
cunningly placed mirrors play
tricks with light and space.
The upstairs picture gallery is
lined with layers of folding
panels to increase its capacity.
The panels open out to reveal
galleried extensions to the
room itself. Among other
works here are many of
Soanes's own exotic designs,
including those for Pitshanger
Manor (see p254) and the
Bank of England (see p147).
Here also is William Hogarth's
Rake's Progress series and
several other of his paintings.
    In the centre of the low-
ceilinged basement an atrium
stretches up to the roof. A
glass dome lights galleries, on
every floor, that are laden
with Classical statuary.

A glass dome allows
light into the basement.

A vast sarcophagus
stands on the floor of
the crypt.

the 17th-century poet, were both students here, as was William Penn, founder of the US state of Pennsylvania.

Lincoln's Inn Fields ❸

WC2. **Map** 14 D1. Ⓔ *Holborn.* **Open** *8am–dusk daily.* **Public tennis courts** Ⓒ *0171-278 4444.*

THIS USED TO BE a public execution site. Under the Tudors and the Stuarts, many religious martyrs, and those suspected of treachery to the Crown, died here.

When the developer William Newton wanted to build here in the 1640s, students at Lincoln's Inn and other residents made him undertake that the land in the centre would remain a public area for ever. Thanks to this early environmental pressure group, lawyers today play tennis here throughout the summer, or read their briefs in the fresh air. In recent years it has also become the site of a "tent city" for some of London's homeless.

Old Curiosity Shop sign

Old Curiosity Shop ❹

13–14 Portsmouth St WC2. **Map** 14 D1. Ⓔ *Holborn.* **Closed and changing ownership.**

WHETHER IT IS or is not the original for Charles Dickens's novel of the same name, this is a genuine 17th-century building and almost certainly the oldest shop in central London. With its overhanging first floor, it gives a rare impression of a London streetscape from

before the Great Fire of 1666. Recently it has sold antiques and, although it is presently unoccupied, a preservation order guarantees its future, most likely as a shop.

Public Record Office Museum ❺

Chancery Lane WC2. **Map** 14 E1. Ⓒ *0181-876 3444.* Ⓔ *Chancery Lane, Holborn, Temple.* **Open** *9.30am–5pm Mon–Fri.* **Closed** *public hols, 1st 2 weeks Oct.* Ⓟ Ⓒ Ⓘ

RECORDS OF THE official actions and decisions of central government and the law courts are kept here. There is a small changing exhibition of some of the seminal documents from all periods in British history since the Norman Conquest of 1066. The collection includes the *Domesday Book* (England's first census of land and people, made in 1086), Sir Francis Drake's report on his defeat of the Spanish Armada in 1588, Shakespeare's will, and a letter from George Washington to George III.

Every wall is covered, and every room filled, with artefacts from Soane's massive collection.

In the picture gallery, panels covered with paintings unfold to reveal more works of art behind them.

The Monk's Parlour is full of grotesque, Gothic casts.

St Clement Danes ❻

Strand WC2. **Map** 14 D2.
📞 0171-242 8282. ⊝ Temple.
Open 9am–5pm daily. **Closed** noon
25 Dec–27 Dec. ✝ 11am Sun.
See **Ceremonial London** p55.

CHRISTOPHER WREN designed this wonderful church in 1680. Its name derives from an earlier church built here by the descendants of Danish invaders whom Alfred the Great had allowed to remain in London in the 9th century.

During the 17th, 18th and 19th centuries many people were buried in the crypt. The chain now hanging on the crypt wall was probably used to secure coffin lids against body snatchers who stole fresh corpses and sold them to the teaching hospitals.

St Clement Danes sits proudly isolated on a traffic island. It is now the church of the Royal Air Force (RAF) and the interior decor is dominated by RAF symbols, memorials and monuments.

Clock at the Victorian law courts

Outside, to the east, is a statue (1910) of Dr Samuel Johnson *(see p140)* who, during the 18th century, often came to services here. The church's bells are rung to the tune of the English nursery rhyme, *Oranges and Lemons*, at 9am, noon, 3pm and 6pm daily and there is an annual oranges and lemons service.

Royal Courts of Justice (the Law Courts) ❼

Strand WC2. **Map** 14 D2.
📞 0171-936 6000. ⊝ Holborn,
Temple, Chancery Lane. **Open**
9am–4.30pm Mon–Fri. **Closed** public
hols. ♿ limited. 📷

KNOTS OF demonstrators and television cameras can often be seen outside this sprawling and fanciful Victorian Gothic building, waiting for the result of a contentious case. These are the nation's main civil courts, dealing with such matters as divorce, libel, civil liability and appeals. Criminals are dealt with at the Old Bailey *(see p147)*, ten minutes' walk to the east. The public are admitted to all the court rooms and a list tells you which case is being heard in which court.

The massive, Gothic building was completed in 1882. It is said to contain 1,000 rooms and 3.5 miles (5.6 km) of corridors.

Temple Bar Memorial ❽

Fleet St EC4. **Map** 14 D2.
⊝ Holborn, Temple, Chancery Lane.

THE MONUMENT in the middle of Fleet Street, outside the Law Courts, dates from 1880 and marks the entrance to the City of London. On state occasions the monarch traditionally has to pause here and ask permission of the Lord Mayor to enter. Temple Bar, an archway designed by Wren, used to stand here. You can see what it used to look like from one of the four reliefs that surround the base of the present monument.

Fleet Street ❾

EC4. **Map** 14 E1. ⊝ Temple, Blackfriars, St Paul's.

ENGLAND'S FIRST printing press was set up here in the late 15th century by William Caxton's assistant,

The griffon, symbol of the City, at the entrance to the City at Temple Bar

William Capon's engraving of Fleet Street in 1799

and Fleet Street has been a centre of London's publishing industry ever since. Playwrights Shakespeare and Ben Jonson were patrons of the old Mitre Tavern, now No. 37 Fleet Street. In 1702 the first newspaper, *The Daily Courant*, was issued from Fleet Street – conveniently placed for the City and Westminster, the main sources of news. Later the street became synonymous with the Press.

The printing presses underneath the newspaper offices were abandoned in 1987, when new technology made it easy to produce papers away from the centre of town in areas such as Wapping and the Docklands. Today the newspapers have left their Fleet Street offices and only the agencies, Reuters and the Press Association, remain.

El Vino's wine bar, at the western end opposite Fetter Lane, is a traditional haunt of journalists and lawyers.

Prince Henry's Room ⑩

17 Fleet St EC4. **Map** 14 E1.
【 0171-936 2710. ⊖ *Temple, Chancery Lane.* **Open** 11am–2pm Mon–Sat. **Closed** 24–26 Dec, 1 Jan, Good Fri, public hols. 🖼

B UILT IN 1610 as part of a Fleet Street tavern, this gets its name from the Prince of Wales's coat of arms and the initials PH in the centre of the ceiling. They were probably put there to mark the investiture as Prince of Wales of Henry, James I's eldest son who died before he became king. The fine half-timbered front, alongside the gateway to Inner Temple, is original and so is some of the room's oak panelling. It contains an exhibition about the diarist Samuel Pepys.

Temple ⑪

Inner Temple, King's Bench Walk EC4. **Map** 14 E2. 【 0171-353 1736. ⊖ *Temple.* **Open** 10am–4pm Wed–Sat, 12.45–4pm Sun. 🖼 &
Middle Temple Hall, Middle Temple Lane EC4. **Map** 14 E2. 【 0171-353 4355. ⊖ *Temple.* **Open** 10am–4pm Mon–Fri. **Closed** for functions.
🖼 🖼

T HIS EMBRACES TWO OF THE four Inns of Court, the Middle Temple and the Inner Temple. (The remaining two are Lincoln's and Gray's Inns – *see p136 and p141*.)

The name derives from the Knights Templar, a chivalrous order specializing in the

protection of pilgrims to the Holy Land. The order was based here from 1185 until suppressed by the Crown in 1312 because its power was viewed as a threat. Secret initiation rites into the order probably took place in the crypt of Temple Church and there are 13th-century effigies of Knights Templar in the nave.

Among other interesting and ancient buildings in this area is Middle Temple Hall. Its Elizabethan interior has survived – Shakespeare's *Twelfth Night* was performed here in 1601. Behind Temple, peaceful lawns stretch down to the Embankment.

St Bride's ⑫

Fleet St EC4. **Map** 14 F2. 【 0171-353 1301. ⊖ *Blackfriars, St Paul's.* **Open** 8.30am–5pm Mon–Fri, 9am–4.30pm Sat, 9am–7.30pm Sun. **Closed** public hols. 🖼 & ✝ 11.30am Sun. **Concerts.**

St Bride's, church of the Press

S T BRIDE'S IS ONE OF Wren's best-loved churches. Its position just off Fleet Street has made it the traditional venue for memorial services to departed journalists. Wall plaques commemorate Fleet Street journalists and printers.

The marvellous octagonal layered spire has been the model for tiered wedding cakes since shortly after it was added in 1703. Bombed in 1940, the interior was faithfully restored after World War II. The fascinating crypt contains remnants of earlier churches on the site, and a section of Roman pavement.

Effigies in Temple Church

Ye Olde Cheshire Cheese ⑬

Wine Office Court, 145 Fleet St EC4.
Map 14 E1. 📞 0171-353 6170.
⊖ Blackfriars. **Open** 11.30am–11pm
Mon–Sat, noon–3pm, 6–10pm Sun.
See **Restaurants and Pubs** pp308–9.

THERE HAS BEEN an inn here
for centuries; parts of this
building date back to 1667,
when the Cheshire Cheese
was rebuilt after the Great
Fire. The diarist Samuel Pepys
drank here in the 17th
century, but it was Dr Samuel
Johnson's association with
"the Cheese" which made it a
place of pilgrimage for 19th-
century literati. These included
novelists Mark Twain and
Charles Dickens, who was a
frequent customer.

Today it is one of the few
pubs that have kept the
comfortable 18th-century
arrangement of small rooms
with fireplaces, tables and
benches, instead of knocking
them into larger bars.

Dr Johnson's House ⑭

17 Gough Sq EC4. **Map** 14 E1.
📞 0171-353 3745. ⊖ Blackfriars,
Chancery Lane, Temple. **Open**
May–Sep: 11am–5.30pm Mon–Sat;
Oct–Apr: 11am–5pm Mon–Sat.
Closed 24–26 Dec, 1 Jan, Good Fri,
public hols. **Adm charge.** 📷 small
charge. 🚻 ♿

DR SAMUEL JOHNSON was an
18th-century scholar
famous for the many witty
(and often contentious)

19th-century St Andrew schoolgirl

remarks that his biographer,
James Boswell, recorded and
published. Johnson lived here
from 1748 to 1759. He
compiled the first definitive
English dictionary (published
in 1755) in the attic, where
six scribes and assistants
stood all day at high desks.

The house, built before
1700, is sparsely furnished
with 18th-century pieces and
a small collection of exhibits
relating to Johnson and the
times in which he lived. These
include a tea set belonging to
his friend Mrs Thrale and
pictures of the great man
himself, his contemporaries
and their houses.

Reconstructed interior of Dr Johnson's house

St Andrew, Holborn ⑮

Holborn Circus EC4. **Map** 14 E1.
📞 0171-353 3544. ⊖ Chancery
Lane. **Open** 8am–5pm Mon–Fri. 📷

THE MEDIEVAL CHURCH here
survived the Great Fire of
1666. In 1686 Christopher
Wren was, however, asked to
redesign it, and the lower
part of the tower is virtually
all that remains of the earlier
church. One of Wren's most
spacious churches, it was
gutted during World War II
but faithfully restored as the
church of the London trade
guilds. Benjamin Disraeli, the
Jewish-born Prime Minister,
was baptized here in 1817, at
the age of 12. In the 19th
century a charity school was
attached to the church.

Holborn Viaduct ⑯

EC1. **Map** 14 F1. ⊖ Farringdon, St
Paul's, Chancery Lane.

Civic symbol on Holborn Viaduct

THIS PIECE of Victorian
ironwork was erected in
the 1860s as part of a much-
needed traffic scheme. It is
best seen from Farringdon
Street which is linked to the
bridge by a staircase. Climb
up and see the statues of City
heroes and bronze images of
Commerce, Agriculture,
Science and Fine Arts.

St Etheldreda's Chapel ⑰

14 Ely Place EC1. **Map** 6 E5.
📞 0171-405 1061. ⊖ Chancery
Lane, Farringdon. **Open** 8am–6pm
daily. 📷 🎵 noon–2pm Mon–Fri.

THIS IS A RARE 13th-century
survivor, the chapel and
crypt of Ely House, where the
Bishops of Ely lived until the

Reformation. Then it was acquired by an Elizabethan courtier, Sir Christopher Hatton, whose descendants demolished the house but kept the chapel and turned it into a Protestant church. It passed through various hands and, in 1874, reverted to the Catholic faith.

Hatton Garden ⓲

EC1. **Map** 6 E5. ⊖ *Chancery Lane, Farringdon.*

BUILT ON LAND that used to be the garden of Hatton House, this is London's diamond and jewellery district. Gems ranging from the priceless to the mundane are traded from scores of small shops with sparkling window displays, and even from the pavements. One of the city's few remaining pawnbrokers is here – look for its traditional sign of three brass balls above the door.

Staple Inn ⓳

Holborn WC1. **Map** 14 E1. ℂ *0171-242 5240.* ⊖ *Chancery Lane.* **Courtyard open** *9am–5pm Mon–Fri.* 📷 🅿

ONCE THE WOOL staple, where wool was weighed and taxed, the frontage overlooks Holborn and is the only real example of Elizabethan half-timbering left in central London. Although now much restored, it would still be recognizable by someone who had known it in 1586, when it was built. The shops at street level have the feel of the 19th century, and there are some 18th-century buildings in the courtyard.

London Silver Vaults ⓴

53–64 Chancery Lane WC2. **Map** 14 D1. ⊖ *Chancery Lane. See* **Shops and Markets** *pp322–3.*

THE LONDON SILVER VAULTS originate from the Chancery Lane Safe Deposit Company, established in

Staple Inn, a survivor from 1586

1885. After descending a staircase you pass through formidable steel security doors and reach a nest of underground shops sparkling with antique and modern silverware. London silver makers have been renowned for centuries, reaching their peak in the Georgian era. The best examples sell for many thousands of pounds but most shops also offer modest pieces at realistic prices.

Coffee pot (1716): Silver Vaults

Gray's Inn ㉑

Gray's Inn Rd WC1. **Map** 6 D5. ℂ *0171-405 8164.* ⊖ *Chancery Lane, Holborn.* **Open** *10am–4pm Mon–Fri.* **Grounds open** *24 hrs daily.* 📷 ♿

THIS ANCIENT LEGAL centre and law school goes back to the 14th century. Like many of the buildings in this area, it was badly damaged by World War II bombs but much of it has been faithfully rebuilt. At least one of William Shakespeare's plays (*A Comedy of Errors*) was first performed in Gray's Inn hall in 1594. The hall's 16th-century interior screen still survives.

More recently, the young Charles Dickens was employed as a clerk here in 1827–8. Today the stately garden, once a convenient site for duels, is open to lunchtime strollers for part of the year, and typifies the cloistered calm of the four Inns of Court. The buildings may be visited only by arrangement.

THE CITY

Lᴏɴᴅᴏɴ's ꜰɪɴᴀɴᴄɪᴀʟ dis- co
trict is built on the site h
of the original Roman
settlement. Its full title is the a
City of London, but it is usu- ac
ally referred to as the City. few
Most traces of the early City since
were obliterated by the Great was ... London's main
Fire of 1666 and World War II residential centres. Today
(see pp22–3 and 31). Today only the churches, many of
glossy modern offices stand them by Christopher Wren *(see p47)*,
among a plethora of banks, with mar- are a reminder of those past times.
bled halls and stately pillars. It is the

**Traditional bank sign
on Lombard Street**

Street-by-S ...
THIS IS THE
vast
Exch
c

SIGHTS AT A GLANCE

**Historic Streets and
Buildings**
Mansion House ❶
Royal Exchange ❸
Old Bailey ❼
Apothecaries' Hall ❽
Fishmongers' Hall ❾
Tower of London pp154-7 ⓰
Tower Bridge ⓱
Lloyd's of London ㉒
Stock Exchange ㉔
Guildhall ㉕

Museums and Galleries
Bank of England Museum ❹
Tower Hill Pageant ⓳

Historic Markets
Billingsgate ⑫
Leadenhall Market ㉓

Monuments
Monument ⑪

Churches and Cathedrals
St Stephen Walbrook ❷
St Mary-le-Bow ❺
St Paul's Cathedral pp148-51 ❻
St Magnus the Martyr ⑩
St Mary-at-Hill ⑬
St Margaret Pattens ⑭
All Hallows by the Tower ⑮
St Helen's Bishopsgate ⑳
St Katharine Cree ㉑

Docks
St Katharine's Dock ⑱

GETTING THERE
The City is served by the
Circle, Central, District,
Northern and Metropolitan
lines, and bus numbers 6, 8, 9,
11, 15, 15B, 22B, 25, 133 and
501. There are many
Thameslink and mainline
British Rail stations.

KEY

▨ Street-by-Street map

⊖ Underground station

⇌ British Rail station

Ⓟ Car park

SEE ALSO

• *Street Finder,* maps 14, 15, 16

• *Where to Stay* pp276–7

• *Restaurants* pp292–4

St Paul's Cathedral with the NatWest Tower (1980) to its left

treet: The City

E BUSINESS CENTRE of London, home to
inancial institutions such as the Stock
ange and the Bank of England. But in
ntrast to these 19th- and 20th-century buildings
are the older survivors. A walk through the City
is in part a pilgrimage through the architectural
visions of Christopher Wren, England's most
sublime and probably most prolific architect.
After the Great Fire of 1666 he supervised the
rebuilding of 52 churches within the area, and
enough survive to testify to his genius.

St Mary-le-Bow
*Anyone born within earshot
of the bells of this Wren
church (the historic Bow
Bells) is said to be a true
Londoner or Cockney* ❺

The Temple of Mithras
is an important Roman
relic whose foundations
were revealed by a
World War II bomb.

★ **St Paul's**
*Wren's masterpiece
still dominates
the City skyline* ❻

St Paul's station

ST PAUL'S CHURCHYARD

NEW CHANGE

WATLING STREET

BREAD STREET

CANNON STREET

FRIDAY ST

QUEEN VICTORI

**Mansion
House
station**

COLLEGE · OF · ARMS

The College of Arms received its
royal charter in 1484 from Richard
III. Still active today, it assesses
who has a legitimate claim to a
British family coat of arms.

St Nicholas Cole was
the first church Wren
built in the City (in
1677). Like many
others, it had to be
restored after World
War II bomb damage.

St James Garlickhythe
contains unusual sword rests
and hat stands, beneath
Wren's elegant spire of 1717.

STAR SIGHTS

★ **St Paul's**

★ **St Stephen Walbrook**

★ **Bank of England
Museum**

KEY

— — — Suggested route

0 metres   100

0 yards   100

Skinners' Hall is the Italianate
18th-century guild hall for the
leather trade.

Mansion House
The official home of London's mayor, this building contains a small prison ❶

★ **Bank of England Museum**
The intriguing story of England's financial system is vividly displayed here ❹

LOCATOR MAP
See Central London Map pp12–13

Bank station

Royal Exchange
Since its foundation in Tudor times, this has been at the heart of London's commerce ❸

Lombard Street is named after Italian bankers who settled here from Lombardy in the 13th century. It is still a banking centre.

★ **St Stephen Walbrook**
Experimenting for St Paul's, Wren created its unique steeple. The interior contains original features, such as this font ❷

St Mary Abchurch owes its unusually spacious feel to Wren's large dome. The altar carving is by Grinling Gibbons.

St Mary Woolnoth is a characteristically powerful work by Wren's pupil, Nicholas Hawksmoor.

Mansion House ❶

Walbrook EC4. **Map** 15 B2
📞 0171-626 2500. 🚇 Bank, Mansion
House. **Not open** to the public.

T HE OFFICIAL RESIDENCE of the
Lord Mayor, it was
completed in 1753 to the
design of George Dance the
Elder, whose designs can now
be seen in John Soane's
Museum *(see pp136 −7)*. The
Palladian front with its six
large Corinthian columns is
one of the most familiar City
landmarks. The state rooms

are of a splendour and dignity
appropriate to the office of
mayor, one of the most
spectacular being the 27-m
(90-ft) Egyptian Hall.
    Hidden from view are 11
holding cells (10 for men and
1, "the birdcage", for women),
a reminder of the building's
other function as a magistrate's court; the Mayor is
chief magistrate of the City
during his year of office.
Emmeline Pankhurst, who
campaigned for women's
suffrage in the early 20th
century, was once held here.

Egyptian Hall in Mansion House

St Stephen Walbrook ❷

39 Walbrook EC4. **Map** 15 B2. 📞
0171-283 4444. 🚇 Bank, Cannon St.
Open 10am–4pm Mon–Thu,
10am–3pm Fri. ✝ 12.45pm Thu,
sung Mass. 📷 **Organ recitals** Fri.

T HE LORD MAYOR'S parish
church was built by
Christopher Wren in 1672–9.
Architectural writers consider
it to be the finest of his City
churches *(see p47)*. The deep,
coffered dome, with its ornate
plasterwork, was a forerunner
of St Paul's. St Stephen's airy
columned interior comes as a
surprise after its plain exterior.
The font cover and pulpit
canopy are decorated with

exquisite carved figures that
contrast strongly with the
stark simplicity of Henry
Moore's massive white stone
altar (1987).
    However, perhaps the most
moving monument of all is a
telephone in a glass box. This
is a tribute to Rector Chad
Varah who, in 1953, founded
the Samaritans, a voluntarily
staffed telephone help-line
for people in emotional need.
    *The Martyrdom of St
Stephen*, which hangs on the
north wall, is by American
painter Benjamin West, who
became a Royal Academician
(see p90) in 1768.

The spire was
added in 1717.

The dome
makes this
small church
light and airy.

Wren's
original altar
and screen
are still here.

Wren's pulpit
has a delicate
canopy.

Henry Moore's
polished stone altar
was added in 1987.

Royal Exchange ❸

EC3. **Map** 15 C2. **[** 0171-623 0444.
🚇 Bank. **Not open** to the public.

Sᴵʀ ᴛʜᴏᴍᴀs ɢʀᴇsʜᴀᴍ, the
Elizabethan merchant and
courtier, founded the Royal
Exchange in 1565 as a centre
for commerce of all kinds.
The original building was
centred on a vast courtyard
where merchants and tradesmen did business. Queen
Elizabeth I gave it its Royal
title and it is still one of the
sites from which new kings
and queens are announced.
Dating from 1844, this is the
third splendid building on the
site since Gresham's.
   Britain's first public lava-
tories (for men only) were
erected in the forecourt of the
Royal Exchange in 1855.

Bank of England Museum ❹

Bartholomew Lane EC2. **Map** 15 B1.
[0171-601 5545. **[** 0171-601
5792. 🚇 Bank. **Open** 10am–5pm
Mon–Fri. **Closed** public hols
1 Oct–Easter. 🚫 ♿ (loop
system). 📷 📱 **Filmshows,
lectures.**

**The Duke of Wellington (1884)
opposite the Bank of England**

Tʜᴇ ʙᴀɴᴋ ᴏғ ᴇɴɢʟᴀɴᴅ was
set up in 1694 to raise
money for foreign wars. It
grew to become Britain's
central bank, and also issues
currency notes.
   Sir John Soane (see pp136–7)
was the architect of the 1788
bank building on this site, but
only the exterior wall of his
design has survived. The rest
was destroyed in the 1920s
and 1930s when the Bank

The facade of William Tite's Royal Exchange of 1844

was enlarged. There is now a
reconstruction of Soane's
stock office of 1793.
   Glittering gold bars, silver
plated decoration and a Roman
mosaic floor, discovered
during the rebuilding, are
among the items on display.
The museum illustrates the
work of the Bank and the
financial system. The gift shop
sells paperweights which are
made out of used banknotes.

St Mary-le-Bow ❺

(Bow Church) Cheapside EC2.
Map 15 A2. **[** 0171-248 5139.
🚇 Mansion House. **Open** 6.30am–6pm
Mon, Wed and Fri, 6.30am–7pm Thu,
6.30am–4pm Fri. 🕀 5.45pm Thu. 🎵

Tʜᴇ ᴄʜᴜʀᴄʜ ᴛᴀᴋᴇs its name
from the bow arches in
the Norman crypt. When
Wren rebuilt the church (in
1670 – 80) after the Great Fire
(see pp22 – 3), he continued
this architectural pattern
through the graceful arches
on the steeple. The weathervane, dating from 1674, is an
enormous dragon.
   The church was destroyed
by bombs in 1941 leaving
only the steeple and two
outer walls standing. It was
restored in 1956 – 62 when
the bells were recast and
rehung. Bow bells are
important to Londoners:
traditionally only those born
within their sound can claim
to be true Cockneys.

St Paul's ❻

See pp148–51.

Old Bailey ❼

EC4. **Map** 14 F1. **[** 0171-248 3277.
🚇 St Paul's. **Open** 10.30am–1pm,
2–4.30pm Mon–Fri (but opening
hours vary from court to court).
Closed Christmas, New Year, Easter,
public hols. 🚫

Old Bailey's rooftop Justice

Tʜɪs sʜᴏʀᴛ sᴛʀᴇᴇᴛ has a long
association with crime and
punishment. The new Central
Criminal Courts opened here
in 1907 on the site of the
notorious and malodorous
Newgate prison (on special
days in the legal calendar
judges still carry small posies
to court as a reminder of
those times). Across the road,
the Magpie and Stump served
"execution breakfasts" until
1868, when mass public
hangings outside the prison
gates were stopped.
   Today, when the courts are
in session, they are open to
members of the public.

St Paul's Cathedral ❻

Following the Great Fire of London in 1666, the medieval cathedral of St Paul's was left in ruins. The authorities turned to Christopher Wren to rebuild it, but his ideas met with considerable resistance from the conservative and tightfisted Dean and Chapter. Wren's 1672 Great Model plan, which is on show in the crypt, was not at all popular, and a watered-down plan was agreed in 1675. Wren's determination paid off though, as can be seen from the grandeur of the present cathedral.

Stone statuary outside the South Transept

★ **The Inner and Outer Dome**
At 110 m (360 ft) high it is the second biggest dome in the world, after St Peter's in Rome, as spectacular from inside as outside.

The balustrade along the top was added in 1718 against Wren's wishes.

The pediment carvings, dating from 1706, show the Conversion of St Paul.

★ **The West Front and Towers**
The towers were not on Wren's original plan – he added them in 1707, when he was 75 years old. Both were designed to have clocks.

Flying buttresses support the nave walls and the dome.

The West Portico comprises two tiers of columns rather than the single colonnade that Wren intended.

The West Porch, approached from Ludgate Hill, is the main entrance to St Paul's.

STAR SIGHTS

- ★ **West Front and Towers**
- ★ **Inner and Outer Dome**
- ★ **Whispering Gallery**

Queen Anne's Statue
An 1886 copy of Francis Bird's 1712 original now stands on the forecourt.

The lantern weighs a massive 850 tonnes.

The brick cone located inside the outer dome supports the heavy lantern.

The oculus is an opening through which the lantern can be seen.

The stone gallery offers a splendid view over London.

VISITORS' CHECKLIST

Ludgate Hill EC4. **Map** 15 A2.
▐ 0171-248 2705. ⊝ St Paul's,
Mansion House. ▦ 6, 8, 11, 15,
22, 23, 25, 76. ▤ St Paul's
Thameslink. **Cathedral open**
8.30am–4pm Mon–Sat.
Galleries open 10am–4.15pm.
Crypt & ambulatory open
8.45am–4.15pm. **Closed** for
sightseeing on Sun. **Adm charge.**
✝ 10.30am Sun. ⌀ during
services. ✦ ▨ ▯ **Concerts.**

A false upper storey masks the huge flying buttresses.

★ **Whispering Gallery**
The unusual acoustics here cause whispers to echo around the dome.

The North and South Transepts cross the nave in a medieval style that contrasts with Wren's original plan *(see p150).*

South Porch
Wren took the idea of a semi-circular porch from a Baroque church in Rome.

TIMELINE

Detail on Tijou gate (see p151)

604 Bishop Mellitus built the first St Paul's. It burned down in 1087

1666 St Paul's reduced to a burnt ruin after the Great Fire

1708 Wren's son Christopher lays the last stone on the lantern

600	800	1000	1200	1400	1600	1800

1087 Bishop Maurice began Old St Paul's: a Norman cathedral of stone

1675 Foundation stone of Wren's design laid

1940–1 Slight bomb damage to the cathedral

1981 Prince Charles marries Lady Diana Spencer

A Guided Tour of St Paul's

THE VISITOR TO ST PAUL'S will be immediately impressed by its cool, beautifully ordered and extremely spacious interior. The nave, transepts and choir are arranged in the shape of a cross, as in a medieval cathedral, but Wren's Classical vision shines through this conservative floor plan, forced on him by the cathedral authorities. Aided by some of the finest craftsmen of his day, he created an interior of grand majesty and Baroque splendour, a worthy setting for the many great ceremonial events that have taken place here. These include the funeral of Winston Churchill in 1965 and the wedding of Prince Charles and Lady Diana Spencer in 1981.

The mosaics on the choir ceiling were completed in the 1890s by William Richmond.

① The Nave
Take in the full glory of the massive arches and the succession of saucer domes that open out into a huge space below the main dome.

② The North Aisle
As you walk along the North Aisle, look above: the aisles are vaulted with small domes mimicking those of the nave ceiling.

⑨ South Aisle
From here the brave can ascend the 259 steps to the Whispering Gallery and test the acoustics.

Entrance to Whispering Gallery

⑧ The Great Model
A model of Wren's original design was carved in 1672. The plan was rejected as being too revolutionary for its time.

Main entrances

The Geometrical Staircase is a spiral of 92 stone steps giving access to the cathedral library.

⑦ Wren's Tomb
Wren's burial place is marked by a slab. The inscription states: "Reader, if you seek his memorial look all around you."

KEY

- - - Tour route

③ The Crossing

The climax of Wren's interior is this great open space. The vast dome is decorated with monochrome frescoes by Sir James Thornhill, the leading architectural painter of Wren's time.

Entrance to crypt

④ The Choir

Jean Tijou, a Huguenot refugee, created much of the cathedral's fine wrought ironwork, such as these screens in the choir aisles.

John Donne's tomb, from 1631, was the only monument to survive the Great Fire of 1666. The poet posed for it in his lifetime.

⑤ The High Altar

The canopy over the altar was replaced after World War II. It is based on Wren's original Baroque drawings.

Grinling Gibbons's work can be found on the choir stalls, with typically intricate carvings of cherubs, fruits and garlands.

Lawrence of Arabia, the adventurer, is commemorated by this bust in the crypt.

⑥ The Crypt

Memorials to famous figures and popular heroes, such as Lord Nelson, can be seen in the crypt.

Apothecaries' Hall ❽

Blackfriars Lane EC4. **Map** 14 F2.
📞 0171-236 1189. 🚇 *Blackfriars.*
Courtyard open 9am–5.30pm
Mon–Fri. **Closed** public hols. **Hall
closed** to the public. ♿

Apothecaries' Hall, rebuilt in 1670

Lᴏɴᴅᴏɴ ʜᴀs had livery
companies, or guilds, to
protect and regulate specific
trades since early medieval
times. The Apothecaries'
Society was founded in 1617
for those who prepared,
prescribed or sold drugs. It
has some surprising alumni,
including Oliver Cromwell
and the poet John Keats.
Now nearly all the members
are physicians or surgeons.

Fishmongers' Hall ❾

London Bridge EC4. **Map** 15 B3.
📞 0171-626 3531. 🚇 *Monument.*
Not open to the public.

Tʜɪs ɪs ᴏɴᴇ of the oldest
livery companies, estab-
lished in 1272. Lord Mayor
Walworth, a member of the
Fishmongers' Company, killed
Wat Tyler, leader of the
Peasants' Revolt, in 1381 *(see
p162)*. Today it still fulfils its
original role; all fish sold in
the City must be inspected by
Company officials. The
building dates from 1834.

St Magnus the Martyr ❿

Lower Thames St EC3. **Map** 15 C3.
📞 0171-626 4481. 🚇 *Monument.*
🚫 ✝ 11am Sun.

Tʜᴇʀᴇ ʜᴀs ʙᴇᴇɴ a church
here for more than 1,000
years. Its patron saint, St
Magnus, was a Norwegian

Earl of the Orkney Islands off
the north coast of Scotland.
He was a highly regarded
Christian leader, murdered by
his cousin in 1110.

When Christopher Wren
built this church in 1671–6, it
was at the foot of old London
Bridge, until 1738 the only
bridge across the Thames in
London. Anyone going south
from the city would have
passed under Wren's
magnificent arched porch
spanning the flagstones
leading to the old bridge.

Highlights of the church
include the carved musical
instruments that decorate the
organ case. Wren's pulpit,
with its slender supporting
stem, was restored in 1924.

Monument ⓫

Monument St EC3. **Map** 15 C2.
📞 0171-626 2717. 🚇 *Monument.*
Open Apr–Sep: 9am–5.40pm
Mon–Fri, 2–5.40pm Sat–Sun;
Oct–Mar: 9am–3.40pm Mon–Sat.
Adm charge. 📷 **Closed** for
refurbishment until mid 1995.

Tʜᴇ ᴄᴏʟᴜᴍɴ, designed by
Christopher Wren to
commemorate the Great Fire
of London in September 1666,
is the tallest isolated stone
column in the world. It is
62 m (205 ft) high and is said
to be 62 m west of where the
fire started in Pudding Lane.
It was sited on the direct
approach to old London
Bridge, which was a few
steps downstream from the
present one. Reliefs around

The altar of St Magnus the Martyr

the column's base show
Charles II restoring the city.
The 311 steps to the top lead
to a platform with fine views.
In 1842 this was enclosed
with railings after a suicide.

Billingsgate ⓬

Lower Thames St EC3. **Map** 15 C3.
🚇 *Monument.* **Not open** to the
public.

Fish weathervane at Billingsgate

Lᴏɴᴅᴏɴ's ᴍᴀɪɴ fish market
was based here for 900
years, on one of the city's
earliest quays. During the
19th and early 20th centuries
400 tonnes of fish were sold
here every day, much of it
delivered by boat. It was
London's noisiest market,
renowned, even in
Shakespeare's day, for foul
language. In 1982 the market
moved from this building
(1877) to the Isle of Dogs.

St Mary-at-Hill ⓭

Lovat Lane EC3. **Map** 15 C2.
📞 0171-626 4184. 🚇 *Monument.*
Concerts. Open 10am–1pm Mon–Fri.

Tʜᴇ ɪɴᴛᴇʀɪᴏʀ and east end
of St Mary-at-Hill were
Wren's first church designs
(1670–6). The Greek cross
design was a prototype for
his St Paul's proposals.

Ironically, the delicate
plasterwork and rich 17th-
century fittings, which had
survived both the Victorian
mania for refurbishment and
the bombs of World War II,

were lost in a fire in 1988. The building was then restored to its original appearance, only to be damaged again, this time by an IRA bomb in 1992.

St Margaret Pattens ⑭

Rood Lane and Eastcheap EC3. **Map** 15 C2. **(** 0171-623 6630. **⊖** Monument. **Open** 8am–4pm Mon–Fri. **Closed** Christmas week, 3 weeks Aug. **✝** 1pm Wed.

WREN'S CHURCH from 1684–7 was named after a type of overshoe made near here. Its Portland stone walls are a good contrast to the Georgian stucco shopfront in the fore-court. The simple interior retains 17th-century canopied pews and an ornate font.

All Hallows by the Tower ⑮

Byward St EC3. **Map** 16 D3. **(** 0171-481 2928. **⊖** Tower Hill. **Open** 9am–6pm Mon–Fri, 10am–5pm Sun. **Closed** 26–27 Dec, 1 Jan. **&** **✝** 11am Sun. **▯**

THE FIRST CHURCH on this site was Saxon. The arch in the southwest corner, which contains Roman tiles, dates from that period and so do some crosses now in the crypt. There is also a well-preserved Roman pavement in the crypt, but this is irregularly open to the public. Most of the interior has been altered by restoration, but a limewood font cover, carved by Grinling Gibbons in 1682, still survives.

Roman tile from All Hallows

William Penn (founder of Pennsylvania) was baptized here in 1644 and John Quincy Adams married in 1797 before he was US president. Samuel Pepys watched the Great Fire from the church tower.

Tower of London ⑯

See pp154–7.

Tower Bridge ⑰

SE1. **Map** 16 D3. **(** 0171-403 3761. **⊖** Tower Hill. **Open** Apr–Oct: 10am–6.30pm daily; Nov–Mar: 10am–4.45pm daily (last adm: 45 mins before closing). **Closed** 24–26 Dec, 1 Jan, Good Fri. **Adm charge.** **▯** **&** **▯** **Video. Closed** for refurbishment Jan–Jun 1993.

COMPLETED IN 1894, this flamboyant piece of Victorian engineering quickly became a symbol of London. Its pinnacled towers and linking catwalk support the mechanism for raising the roadway when big ships have to pass through, or for special occasions, such as the return

of the *Gipsy Moth* (see p237). This is an impressive sight.

The bridge now houses a museum of its own history, with fine river views from the catwalk and a close-up look at the steam engine which powered the lifting machinery until 1976, when the system was electrified.

The catwalk, which is now open to the public, affords a beautiful view along the river.

When raised, the bridge is 40 m (135 ft) high and 60 m (200 ft) wide. In its heyday it was opened five times a day.

There are nearly 300 stairs to the top of the towers.

The Victorian winding machinery was powered by steam until 1976.

Tower of London ⑯

For much of its 900-year history the Tower was an object of fear. Those who had offended the monarch were held within its dank walls. A lucky few lived in comparative comfort, but the majority had to put up with appalling conditions. Many did not get out alive, and were tortured before meeting cruelly violent deaths on nearby Tower Hill.

★ **The White Tower**
When it was finished in 1097, it was the tallest building in London – 30 m (90 ft) high.

★ **The Jewel House** is where the magnificent English Crown Jewels are housed *(see p156)*.

"Beefeaters"
Forty-two Yeoman Warders guard the Tower and live there.

Beauchamp Tower
Many high-ranking prisoners were held here, often with their own retinues of servants.

Tower Green was where the most favoured prisoners were executed, away from the ghoulish crowds on Tower Hill. Only seven people died here – including two of Henry VIII's six wives – but hundreds had to bear more public executions.

Star Buildings

★ **White Tower**

★ **Jewel House**

★ **Chapel of St John**

★ **Martin Tower**

Main entrance

The Ravens

The Tower's most celebrated residents are a colony of eight ravens. It is not known when they first settled here, but there is a legend that should they desert the Tower, the kingdom will fall. In fact the birds have their wings clipped on one side, making flight impossible. The Ravenmaster, one of the Yeoman Warders, looks after the birds.

A memorial in the moat commemorates some of the ravens who have died at the Tower since the 1950s.

Queen's House
This is the private home of the Tower's governor.

★ Martin Tower
Instruments of torture and the executioner's axe and block are on show here.

★ Chapel of St John
The stone for this austerely beautiful Romanesque chapel was brought from France.

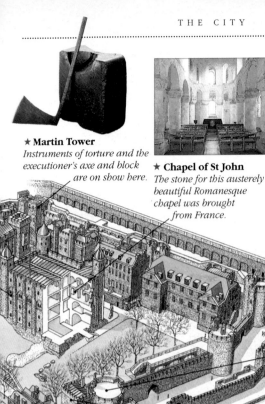

VISITORS' CHECKLIST

Tower Hill EC3. **Map** 16 D3.
📞 0171-709 0765. 🚇 Tower Hill. 🚌 15, X15, 25, 42, 78, 100. 🚊 Fenchurch Street.
Docklands Light Railway
Tower Gateway. **Open** Mar–Oct: 9.30am–6pm Mon–Sat, 10am–6pm Sun; Nov–Feb: 9.30am–5pm Mon–Sat. **Tower closed** 24–26 Dec, 1 Jan, Good Fri.
Jewel House closed Jan. **Adm charge.** ♿ except to Crown Jewels exhibition. 🚫 Ceremony of the Keys 9.30pm daily (see pp52–5). 📷 🍴

Wakefield Tower has been reconstructed to match its appearance in the 13th century.

The Bloody Tower is named after its association with the two young princes who disappeared from here in 1483 *(see p157)*.

Traitors' Gate
Prisoners, many on their way to die, entered the Tower by boat here.

TIMELINE

1078 White Tower started	**1536** Anne Boleyn executed	**1810–15** Mint moves from the Tower and arms stop being manufactured here			
	1483 Princes murdered in the Tower	**1553–4** Lady Jane Grey held and executed			
1050	1250	1450	1650	1850	1950
1066 William I erects a temporary castle	**1530s** Castle stops being a royal palace	**1671** Crown Jewels stolen by "Colonel" Blood	**1834** Menagerie moves out of Tower		
	1534–5 Thomas More imprisoned and executed	**1603–16** Walter Raleigh imprisoned in Tower	**1941** Rudolph Hess is the last prisoner held in Queen's House		

Inside the Tower

THE TOWER HAS been a tourist attraction since the reign of Charles II (1660–85), when both the Crown Jewels and the collection of armour were first shown to the public. They remain powerful reminders of royal might and wealth.

The Orb, symbolizing the power and Empire of Christ the Redeemer

THE CROWN JEWELS

THE CROWN JEWELS comprise the regalia of crowns, sceptres, orbs and swords used at coronations and other state occasions. They are impossible to price but their worth is irrelevant beside their enormous significance in the historical and religious life of the kingdom. Most of the Crown Jewels date from 1661, when a new set was made for the coronation of Charles II; Parliament had destroyed the previous crowns and sceptres after the execution of Charles I in 1649. Only a few pieces survived, hidden by the clergy of Westminster Abbey until the Restoration.

The Coronation Ceremony
Many elements in this solemn and mystical ceremony date from the days of Edward the Confessor. The king or queen proceeds to Westminster Abbey, accompanied by parts of the regalia, including the State Sword which represents the monarch's own sword. He or she is then annointed with holy oil, to signify divine approval, and invested with ornaments and royal robes. Each of the jewels represents an aspect of the monarch's role as head of the state and church. The climax comes when St Edward's Crown is placed on the sovereign's head; there is a cry of "God Save the King" (or Queen), the trumpets sound, and guns at the Tower are fired. The last coronation was Elizabeth II's in 1953.

The Imperial State Crown, made for Queen Victoria in 1837, containing 2,800 diamonds and other gems

The crowns
There are 12 crowns on display at the Tower. Many of these have not been worn for years, but the Imperial State Crown is in constant use. The Queen wears it at state events, such as the Opening of Parliament (see p73). The crown was made in 1837 for the coronation of 18-year-old Queen Victoria. The sapphire that is set in the cross is said to have been worn in a ring by Edward the Confessor (ruled 1042 – 66).

The most recent crown is not at the Tower, however. It was made for Prince Charles's investiture as Prince of Wales and is kept at Caernavon Castle in north Wales, where the ceremony took place in 1969. The Queen Mother's crown was made for the coronation of her husband, George VI, in 1937. It is made out of platinum – all the other crowns at the Tower are gold.

Other regalia
Apart from the crowns, there are other pieces of the Crown Jewels that are essential to coronations. Among these are three Swords of Justice, symbolizing mercy, spiritual and temporal justice. The orb is a hollow gold sphere encrusted with jewels and weighing about 1.3 kg (3 lbs). The Sceptre with the Cross contains the biggest cut diamond in the world, the 530-carat First Star of Africa. The rough stone it comes from weighed 3,106 carats.

The Sovereign's Ring, sometimes referred to as "the wedding ring of England"

Plate Collection
The Jewel House also holds a collection of elaborate gold and silver plate. The Maundy Dish is still used on Maundy Thursday when the monarch distributes money to selected old people. The Exeter Salt (a very grand salt cellar from the days when salt was a valuable commodity) was given by the citizens of Exeter, in west England, to Charles II; during the 1640s' Civil War Exeter was a Royalist stronghold.

The Sceptre with the Cross (1660), rebuilt in 1910 when Edward VII was presented with the First Star of Africa diamond

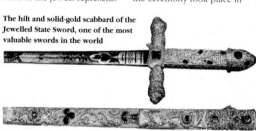

The hilt and solid-gold scabbard of the Jewelled State Sword, one of the most valuable swords in the world

ROYAL ARMOURIES

The ROYAL ARMOURIES are the nation's largest and most important collection of arms and armour. There are about 40,000 objects in the collection, including sporting pieces as well as the weapons of warfare. It was organized by Henry VIII soon after he came to the throne in 1509 and ordered the Tower arsenal to be re-equipped with the latest weapons and armour. The present collection grew over the centuries as surplus weapons and booty accumulated from Britain's imperial conquests were added.

Flintlock pistols (1695)

The earliest weaponry
All four floors of the White Tower are devoted to the collection. On the first is sporting and tournament armour. The sporting gallery contains crossbows, hunting spears and swords, and sporting guns. From about 1400 tournaments were primarily social occasions where knights sparred with one another against a background of much feasting and music, not to mention a little chivalric courting. Armour worn at tournaments was elaborately decorated but still functional. The second floor is devoted to medieval and Renaissance armour. Look out for the etched and gilt three-quarter armour made for the Earl of Southampton in 1598 and for the wonderful 15th-century armed horse and rider. The medieval, English shaffron, or head defence, that is displayed nearby is one of the the oldest pieces of horse armour in the world. It dates from about 1400.

Arms since the Tudors
Tudor and Stuart armour appears on the third floor. Among the highlights are two armours made for Henry VIII in 1520 and 1540 (observe how much weight the king put on between the two). A boy's light field armour was probably made for Edward VI, Henry's son; there is another even smaller armour, less than a metre (39 in) tall. Other treasures include richly decorated swords and a variety of pistols.

In the basement are swords, armour and cannons. Here also are the remains of the Line of Kings, established under Charles II. This was a collection of models of selected kings of England wearing 16th-century armour. Some of the horses were made by the renowned wood carver, Grinling Gibbons.

16th-century greave (leg guard) and sabaton (foot guard)

The New Armouries
Collections in the New Armouries, built as a storehouse in the 17th century, concentrate on 18th- and 19th-century weapons.

There are some early machine guns (these include a Gatling and a Maxim) and a fine pair of duelling pistols made in 1834 by Purdey, the English gunsmith. Here also are miniature guns, swords for children and the smallest automatic pistol ever made (in Germany in 1913–14).

The Martin Tower
Some of the cruellest exhibits in the armouries are on show in the Martin Tower where the instruments of torture, used to extract confessions from prisoners, are housed. Many of the victims of the rack (for stretching the body) and the scavenger's daughter (for compressing the body) suffered for religious or political beliefs at odds with those of the monarch.

Henry VIII's armour (1540)

THE PRINCES IN THE TOWER
One of the Tower's darkest mysteries concerns two boy princes, sons and heirs of Edward IV. They were put into the Tower by their uncle, Richard of Gloucester, when their father died in 1483. Neither was seen again and Richard was crowned later that year. In 1674 the skeletons of two children were found nearby.

The yacht haven of the restored St Katharine's Dock

St Katharine's Dock ⑱

E1. **Map** 16 E3. [☎] *0171-488 2400.*
[⊖] *Tower Hill.* [♿] [🍴] [⚹] [🚻]

THIS MOST CENTRAL of all London's docks was designed by Thomas Telford and opened in 1828 on the site of St Katharine's hospital. Commodities as diverse as tea, marble and live turtles (turtle soup was a Victorian delicacy) were unloaded here.

During the 19th and early 20th centuries the docks flourished, but by the mid-20th century cargo ships were delivering vast, bulky cargoes in massive containers. The old docks became too small and new ones had to be built downstream. St Katharine's closed in 1968 and the others followed within 15 years. St Katharine's is now one of London's most successful developments, with its commercial, residential and entertainment facilities, including a hotel and a yacht

St Helen's Bishopsgate

haven. Old warehouse buildings have shops and restaurants on their ground floors, and offices above.

On the north side is the London FOX (Futures and Options Exchange), trading in commodities such as coffee, sugar and oil. There is no public gallery but, if you ask at the door, you may be able to look down from the glass-walled reception area on to the frenzied trading floors. The dock is worth wandering through after visiting the Tower or Tower Bridge (*see pp154–7 and p153*).

Tower Hill Pageant ⑲

Tower Hill Terrace EC3. **Map** 16 D2.
[☎] *0171-709 0081.* [⊖] *Tower Hill.*
Open *Apr–Oct: 9.30am–5.30pm daily; Nov–Mar: 9.30am–4.30pm daily.* **Adm charge.** [♿] [⚹] [🚻]
Filmshows.

THIS UNDERGROUND ride offers a whirlwind account of London's history, with an emphasis on its role as a port. The story is told through life-sized tableaux with visual and sound effects. After the ride, the viewing cars deposit visitors in a fascinating small exhibition, organized by the Museum of London. It shows objects dug up from the river (including long-sunken boats) and explains how archae-ologists can make deductions from them about life in earlier times. In many ways, the exhibition is of more interest (for adults at least) than the ride itself. A large shop sells, among many other things, reproductions of Roman jewellery found in London.

St Helen's Bishopsgate ⑳

Great St Helen's EC3. **Map** 15 C1.
[☎] *0171-283 2810.* [⊖] *Liverpool St.*
Closed *for repairs until autumn 1995.*

THE CURIOUS, bisected appearance of this 13th-century church is due to its origins as two places of worship: one a parish church and, the other, the chapel of a long-gone nunnery next door. (The medieval nuns of St Helen's were notorious for the amount of "secular kissing" they indulged in.)

Among the church's many interesting monuments is the tomb of Sir Thomas Gresham, who founded the Royal Exchange (*see p147*).

St Katharine Cree ㉑

86 Leadenhall St EC3. **Map** 16 D1.
[☎] *0171-283 5733.* [⊖] *Aldgate, Tower Hill.* **Open** *8.30am–6pm Mon–Fri.* **Closed** *Christmas, Easter.*
[⊘] *during services.* [⚹] *1.05pm Thu.*

The organ at St Katharine Cree

A RARE PRE-WREN 17th-century church with a medieval tower, this was one of only eight churches in the City to survive the fire of 1666. Some of the elaborate plasterwork on and beneath the high ceiling of the nave portrays the coats of arms of the guilds, with which the church has special links. The 17th-century organ, supported on magnificent carved wooden columns, was played by both Purcell and Handel.

Lloyd's of London ㉒

1 Lime St EC3. **Map** 15 C2.
📞 0171-327 6210. ⊖ Bank,
Monument, Liverpool St, Aldgate.
Not open to the public.

L LOYD'S WAS FOUNDED in the late 17th century and takes its name from the coffee house where underwriters and shipowners used to meet to arrange marine insurance contracts. Lloyd's soon became the world's main insurers, issuing policies on everything from oil tankers to Betty Grable's legs.

The present building, by Richard Rogers, dates from 1986 and is one of the most interesting modern buildings in London (see p30). Its exaggerated stainless steel external piping and high-tech ducts echo Rogers's forceful Pompidou Centre in Paris. Lloyd's is a far more elegant building and particularly worth seeing floodlit at night.

Leadenhall Market ㉓

Whittington Ave EC3. **Map** 15 C2.
⊖ Bank, Monument. **Open**
7am–4pm Mon–Fri. See **Shops and Markets** pp322–3.

T THERE HAS BEEN a food market here, on the site of the Roman forum (see pp16–17), since the Middle Ages. Its name derives from a lead-roofed mansion that stood near here in the 14th century. The ornate, Victorian covered shopping precinct that is here today was designed in 1881 by Sir Horace Jones, the architect of Billingsgate fish market (see p152). The shopping precinct is at its best at Christmas time when all the stores are decorated.

Stock Exchange ㉔

Old Broad St EC4. **Map** 15 B1.
⊖ Bank. **Not open** to the public.

T THE FIRST STOCK exchange was established in Threadneedle Street in 1773. Before that, in the 17th and

Leadenhall Market in 1881

18th centuries, stockbrokers met and dealt in City coffee houses. Until 1914 the London Stock Exchange was the biggest in the world; now it is third to Tokyo and New York. The building, which dates from 1969, used to house the frenzied trading floor, but in 1986 the business was computerized and the floor effectively made redundant. The former public viewing gallery stayed open for a while, but was closed after a terrorist bomb attempt.

Guildhall ㉕

Gresham St EC2. **Map** 15 B1.
📞 0171-606 3030. ⊖ St Paul's.
Not open to the public. **Clock Museum** Aldermanbury St EC2.
Open 9.30am–5pm Mon–Sat. ♿

T THIS HAS BEEN the administrative centre of the City for at least 800 years. The crypt and great hall in the present building date from the 15th century.

For centuries the hall was used for trials and many people were condemned to death here, including Henry Garnet, one of the Gunpowder Plot conspirators (see p22). Today its role is less bloody; in November, a few days after the Lord Mayor's parade takes place (see pp54–5), the Prime Minister addresses a banquet here.

In the adjoining public library is the collection of the Clockmakers' Company. This includes some 600 watches and 30 clocks dating from the 16th to the 19th centuries. Mary Queen of Scots's skull-shaped watch is also here.

Richard Rogers's Lloyd's building illuminated at night

SMITHFIELD AND SPITALFIELDS

THE AREAS JUST north of the City walls have historically provided refuge for people and institutions that did not want to come under the City's jurisdiction, or were not welcome there. These included religious orders, dissenters, the earliest theatres, French Huguenots in the 17th century, and, in the 19th and 20th centuries, other immigrants from Europe and, later, Bengal. They established workshops and small factories and brought with them their ethnic restaurants and places of worship. The name Spitalfields derives from the medieval priory of St Mary Spital. Middlesex Street off Aldgate became known as

Tower: Smithfield Market

Petticoat Lane in the 16th century, when a market for clothing was established there; it remains the hub of a popular and crowded Sunday morning street market that spreads as far east as Brick Lane, today lined with aromatic Bengali food shops. The wholesale fruit and vegetable market at Spitalfields survived until 1991, when it moved to the eastern suburbs. The meat market at Smithfield, however, is still going strong. The area around Smithfield adjoining the City is dominated by the Barbican, a modern residential complex with an arts and conference centre.

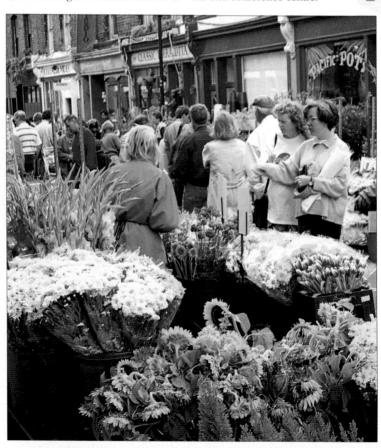

Columbia Road flower and plant market

SIGHTS AT A GLANCE

Historic Streets and Buildings
Charterhouse **5**
Cloth Fair **6**
Barbican Centre **8**
Whitbread's Brewery **10**
Wesley's House and Chapel **12**
Broadgate Centre **13**
Petticoat Lane **14**
Fournier Street **17**
Spitalfields Heritage Centre **19**
Brick Lane **20**
Dennis Severs House **21**

Museums and Galleries
National Postal Museum **2**
*Museum of London
pp166–7* **4**
Whitechapel Gallery **15**

Churches and Mosques
St Botolph, Aldersgate **3**
St Bartholomew-the-Great **7**
St Giles, Cripplegate **9**
Christ Church, Spitalfields **16**
London Jamme Masjid **18**

Cemeteries
Bunhill Fields **11**

Markets
Smithfield Market **1**
Columbia Road Market **22**

KEY

▨	Street-by-Street map
⊖	Underground station
⧦	British Rail station
P	Parking

0 metres   500

0 yards   500

SEE ALSO

- *Street Finder*, maps 6, 7, 8, 15, 16
- *Where to Stay* pp276–7
- *Restaurants* pp292–4

GETTING THERE
This area is served by the Northern, Hammersmith and City, Central and Circle Underground lines and by BR. The Nos. 8 and 15 buses run close by.

Stone dragon in Smithfield Market

Street-by-Street: Smithfield

THIS AREA IS AMONG the most historic in London. It contains one of the capital's oldest churches, some rare Jacobean houses, vestiges of the Roman wall (near the Museum of London) and central London's only surviving wholesale food market.

Smithfield's long history is also bloody. In 1381 the rebel peasant leader, Wat Tyler, was killed here by an ally of Richard III, as he presented the king with demands for lower taxes. Later, in the reign of Mary I (1553–8), scores of Protestant religious martyrs were burned at the stake here.

The Fat Boy: the Great Fire ended here

The Fox and Anchor pub is open from 7am for hearty breakfasts, washed down with ale by the market traders of Smithfield.

★ **Smithfield Market**
A contemporary print shows Horace Jones's stately building for the meat market when it was completed in 1867 ❶

SITE OF THE SARACEN'S HEAD INN DEMOLISHED 1868

Fat Boy

The Saracen's Head, an historic inn, stood on this site until the 1860s when it was demolished to make way for Holborn Viaduct *(see p140)*.

St Bartholomew-the-Less has a 15th-century tower and vestry. Its links to the hospital are shown by this early-20th-century stained glass of a nurse; a gift of the Worshipful Company of Glaziers.

St Bartholomew's Hospital has stood on this site since 1123. Some of the existing buildings date from 1759.

KEY

- - - - Suggested route

0 metres   100

0 yards   100

Charterhouse
The square contains the remnants of a medieval monastery and a school where John Wesley (see p168) studied ❺

Barbican station

LOCATOR MAP
See Central London Map pp12–13

★ Barbican Centre
World War II bombs flattened this immense site, rebuilt as a housing development in the 1960s. It has a major arts complex inside ❽

BEECH STREET

ALDERSGATE STREET

Cloth Fair
Two of its houses are survivors of the 1666 Great Fire ❻

St Bartholomew-the-Great
It has the best-preserved medieval interior of any London church ❼

LONDON WALL

MUSEUM OF LONDON

★ Museum of London
The city's history is told vividly through fascinating and colourful exhibits ❹

LITTLE BRITAIN

Christ Church tower is all that remains of one of Wren's most splendid churches (1704).

To St Paul's station

National Postal Museum
The statue of Rowland Hill, inventor of the Penny Post, is outside ❷

STAR SIGHTS

★ **Museum of London**

★ **Barbican Centre**

★ **Smithfield Market**

Smithfield Market ❶

Charterhouse St EC1. **Map** 6 F5.
⊖ *Farringdon, Barbican.* **Open** *5–9am Mon–Fri.*

LIVE CATTLE WERE sold here until the mid-19th century. Then it was the smooth field from which its name probably derives. Smithfield is still London's main meat market but, since 1855, the market has confined itself to mainly wholesale trading in dead meat and poultry. The old buildings are by Sir Horace Jones, the Victorian architect who specialized in markets, but there are 20th-century additions. Some pubs in the area keep market hours and, from dawn, serve substantial breakfasts, washed down with ale, to market traders and early-rising office workers.

Smithfield Market central tower

National Postal Museum ❷

King Edward Bldg, King Edward St EC1. **Map** 15 A1. ▐ 0171-239 5420. ⊖ *Barbican, St Paul's.* **Open** *9.30am–4.30pm Mon–Fri.* **Closed** *public hols.* 📷

THE HEADQUARTERS of the Post Office stands on the site of the old Bull and Mouth Inn, behind St Paul's, where in the 18th century the first

Stamp commemorating the 1953 Coronation: National Postal Museum

mail coaches would leave for cities across the country. The museum itself contains a comprehensive collection of British and overseas stamps, including some great rarities. There is also a collection of post office equipment which includes early letter boxes and franking machines.

St Botolph, Aldersgate ❸

Aldersgate St EC1. **Map** 15 A1. ▐ 0171-606 0684. ⊖ *St Paul's.* **Open** *11am–3pm Mon–Fri.* ✝ *1.10pm Thu.* ♿

A MODEST LATE Georgian exterior (completed 1791) conceals a flamboyant, well-preserved interior which has a finely-decorated plaster ceiling, a rich brown wooden organ case and galleries, and an oak pulpit resting on a carved palm tree. The original box pews have been kept in the galleries but not in the body of the church. Some memorials come from a 14th-century church on the site.

The former churchyard alongside was converted in 1880 into a relaxing green space known as Postman's Park, because it was used by workers from the nearby Post Office headquarters. In the late 19th century, Victorian artist G F Watts dedicated one of the walls to a quirky collection of plaques that commemorate acts of bravery and self-sacrifice by ordinary people; some of these are still there. In 1973 a powerful, modern bronze minotaur, the work of sculptor Michael Ayrton, was erected.

Museum of London ❹

See pp166–7.

Charterhouse ❺

Charterhouse Sq EC1. **Map** 6 F5. ▐ 0171-253 9503. ⊖ *Barbican.* **Open** *Apr–Jul: 2.15pm Wed.* **Adm charge.** 📷 ♿

THE 14TH-CENTURY gateway on the north side of the square leads to the site of a former Carthusian monastery dissolved under Henry VIII. In 1611 the buildings were converted into a hospital for poor pensioners, and a charity school – called Charterhouse – whose pupils included John Wesley *(see p168)*, writer William Thackeray and Robert Baden-Powell, the founder of the Boy Scouts. In 1872 the school, now a boarding school for fee-paying boys, moved to Godalming in Surrey. The site was subsequently taken over by St Bartholomew's Hospital medical school. Some of the old buildings survived, including the chapel and part of the cloisters.

Charterhouse: stone carving

Cloth Fair ⑥

EC1. **Map** 6 F5. ⊖ *Barbican*.

THIS PRETTY STREET is named after the notoriously rowdy Bartholomew Fair, which was the main cloth fair in medieval and Elizabethan England, held annually at Smithfield until 1855. Nos. 41 and 42 are fine 17th-century houses and have distinctive two-storeyed wooden bay windows, although their ground floors have since been modernized. The former poet laureate John Betjeman, who died in 1984, lived in No. 43 for most of his life. It has now been turned into a wine bar named after him.

17th-century houses: Cloth Fair

St Bartholomew-the-Great ⑦

West Smithfield EC1. **Map** 6 F5. 📞 *0171-606 5171*. ⊖ *Barbican*. **Open** *8.30am–4.30pm (4pm in winter), Mon–Fri.* ✝ *11am Sun.* 📷 ♿ 🎦 🎵 *Concerts*.

ONE OF LONDON'S OLDEST churches was founded in 1123 by a monk named Rahere whose tomb is inside. He had been Henry I's court jester until he had a dream in which St Bartholomew saved him from a winged monster.

The 13th-century arch used to be the door to the church until the nave of that earlier building was pulled down when Henry VIII dissolved the priory. Today the arch leads from Little Britain to the small burial ground – the gatehouse above it is from a later period. The present building retains the crossing and chancel of the original church, with its round arches and other fine Norman detailing. There are also some fine examples of Tudor and other monuments. The painter William Hogarth *(see p257)* was baptized in the font here in 1697.

From time to time parts of the church were used for secular purposes, including housing a blacksmith's forge and a hop store. In 1725 US statesman Benjamin Franklin worked for a printer in the Lady Chapel.

Barbican Centre ⑧

Silk St EC2. **Map** 7 A5. 📞 *0171-638 8891*. 📠 *0171-628 2295*. ⊖ *Barbican, Moorgate*. **Open** *9am–8pm Mon–Sat, noon–11pm Sun, public hols*. ♿ *induction loop*. 🎦 🖥 🍴 🎵 *Filmshows, concerts, exhibitions*. See *Entertainment pp324–37*.

AN AMBITIOUS PIECE of 1960s city planning, this large residential, commercial and arts complex was begun in 1962 on a site devastated by World War II bombs, and not completed for nearly 20 years. Tall residential tower blocks surround an arts centre, which also includes an ornamental lake, fountains and lawns.

The old city wall turned a corner here and substantial remains are still clearly visible (particularly so from the Museum of London – *see pp166–7*). The word barbican means a defensive tower over a gate – perhaps the architects

St Bartholomew's gatehouse

were trying to live up to the name when they designed this self-sufficient community with formidable defences against the outside world. Obscure entrances and raised walkways remove pedestrians from the cramped bustle of the City, but, in spite of the signposts, and yellow lines on the pavement, the centre can be difficult to navigate.

As well as two theatres and a concert hall, the Barbican includes cinemas, one of London's largest art galleries for major touring exhibitions, a convention and exhibition hall, a library and a music school (the Guildhall School of Music). There is also a surprising conservatory above the arts centre.

The well-stocked conservatory at the Barbican Centre

Museum of London ❹

Opened in 1976 on the edge of the Barbican, the museum provides a lively account of London life from prehistoric times to the present day. Reconstructed interiors and street scenes are alternated with displays of original domestic artefacts and items found in the museum's archaeological digs. Look out for the working model of the Great Fire of 1666, accompanied by readings from Samuel Pepys's eyewitness account.

GALLERY GUIDE
The chronological arrangement of the galleries creates an easy route, which takes about 90 minutes to complete.

Ramp to lower galleries

The London Plate
This early English delft plate, made in 1602 at Aldgate, in the City, bears an inscription praising Elizabeth I.

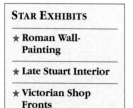

★ **Roman Wall-Painting**
The Romans left several brightly coloured wall-paintings. This fine 2nd-century example came from a Southwark bath house.

Main entrance

Lift to lower galleries

Museum entrance

ALDERSGATE STREET

LONDON WALL

To St Paul's station

ORIENTATION
The museum is in a modern building above street-level where Aldersgate Street meets London Wall. Access is by signposted steps and ramps.

KEY

☐ Museum buildings

▨ Raised walkways

☐ Roads

STAR EXHIBITS

★ Roman Wall-Painting

★ Late Stuart Interior

★ Victorian Shop Fronts

VISITORS' CHECKLIST

London Wall EC2. **Map** 15 A1.
[0171-600 3699. Barbican,
St Paul's, Moorgate. 4, 6, 8,
9, 11, 15, 22, 25, 141, 279A,
501, 513, 502. City
Thameslink. **Open** 10am–5.50pm
Tue–Sat, public hol Mon, noon–
5.50pm Sun. **Closed** 24–26 Dec,
Good Fri. **Adm charge.**
Induction loops fitted.
Lectures, film
presentations.

**Twentieth-century
London** is illustrated by
displays exploring the
major historical events of
this century. Votes for
women, World War II, the
rise of cinema and
Swinging London are
all here.

★ **Victorian Shop Fronts**
*The atmosphere of 19th-
century London is recreated
by several authentic shop
interiors, like this grocer's.*

Garden

**18th-Century
Dress**
*Luxuriously worked
Spitalfields silk was
used to make this
dress in 1753. It
was worn over light-
weight cane hoops.*

**Lift to
upper galleries**

KEY TO FLOORPLAN

☐ Prehistoric London

☐ Roman London

☐ Dark Age and Saxon London

☐ Medieval London

☐ Tudor and Early Stuart London

☐ Late Stuart London

☐ 18th-century London

☐ Victorian London and the
Imperial Capital

☐ 20th-century London

☐ Lord Mayor's coach

☐ Temporary exhibitions

☐ Non-exhibition space

★ **Late Stuart Interior**
*Outstanding features
from several grand
houses of the late 17th
century were used to
reconstruct this room.*

St Giles, Cripplegate ⑨

Fore St EC2. **Map** 7 A5.
📞 0171-606 3630. ⊖ Barbican, Moorgate. **Open** Apr–Oct: 9.30am–5.30pm daily; Nov–Mar: 9.30am–4.30pm daily. ✝ 10am Sun.
♿ ⏰

COMPLETED IN 1550, this church managed to survive the ravages of the Great Fire in 1666, but was badly damaged by a World War II bomb; only the tower survived. St Giles was refurbished during the 1950s to serve as the parish church of the Barbican development, and now stands awkwardly amid the uncompromising modernity of the Barbican.

Oliver Cromwell married Elizabeth Bourchier here in 1620 and the poet John Milton was buried here in 1674. Well-preserved remains of London's Roman and medieval walls are on view to the church's south.

Whitbread's Brewery ⑩

Chiswell St EC1. **Map** 7 B5.
⊖ Barbican, Moorgate. **Not open** to the public.

IN 1736, WHEN HE was aged just 16, Samuel Whitbread became an apprentice brewer in Bedford. By the time of his death in 1796, his Chiswell Street brewery (which he had

Blake's gravestone at Bunhill Fields

bought in 1750) was brewing 909,200 litres (200,000 gal) a year a record for London. The building has not been used as a brewery since 1976 when it was converted into rooms hired out for private functions – they are no longer open to the public. The Porter Tun room, which is now used as a banqueting suite, boasts the largest timber post roof in Europe, and has a huge span of 18 m (60 ft).

The 18th-century buildings on both sides of the street are well-preserved examples of their period, and are worth a look from the outside. A plaque on the outside of one commemorates a visit to the brewery in 1787 by George III and Queen Charlotte.

Bunhill Fields ⑪

City Rd EC1. **Map** 7 B4.
📞 0181-472 3584. ⊖ Old St.
Open noon–5.30pm Sat, Sun, public hols. **Closed** 25–26 Dec, 1 Jan.
📷 ♿

IT WAS FIRST designated a cemetery after the Great Plague of 1665 (see p23), when it was enclosed by a brick wall and gates. Twenty years later it was allocated to religious Nonconformists,

who were banned from being buried in churchyards because of their refusal to use the Church of England prayer book when carrying out their religious services. Visitors to this pleasant spot, which is situated on the edge of the bustling City, and shaded by large plane trees, can see monuments to the writers Daniel Defoe, John Bunyan and William Blake, as well as to members of the Cromwell family.

John Milton wrote his famous epic poem *Paradise Lost* while he lived in Bunhill Row, on the west side of the cemetery, in the years leading up to his death in 1674.

Wesley's House and Chapel ⑫

49 City Rd EC1. **Map** 7 B4.
📞 0171-253 2262. ⊖ Old St.
House open 10am–4pm Mon–Sat.
Adm charge. 📷 ♿ ✝ 11 am Sun.
🎬 🏠 **Films, exhibitions.**

Wesley's Chapel

JOHN WESLEY, the founder of the Methodist church, laid the chapel's foundation stone in 1777. He preached here until his death in 1791, and is buried behind the chapel. Next door is the house where he lived, and today some of his furniture, books and other assorted possessions can be seen on display there.

The chapel, adorned in a spartan style, in accordance with Wesley's austere religious principles, has columns made from ships' masts. Beneath it is a small museum that explores the history of the Methodist church. Baroness Thatcher, the first British woman Prime Minister, in office from 1979 to 1990, was married in the chapel.

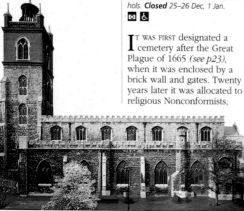

St Giles, Cripplegate

Broadgate Centre ⑬

Exchange Sq EC2. **Map** 7 C5.
📞 0171-588 6565. 🚇 Liverpool St.
♿ 🍴 🛍 🚻

Broadgate Centre skating rink

S ITUATED ABOVE and around Liverpool Street station, the terminus for trains to eastern England, this is one of the most successful recent (1985–91) shop and office developments. Each of the squares has its own distinctive character. Broadgate Arena emulates New York's Rockefeller Center, doubling as a skating rink in winter and a venue for refreshments and entertainment in summer.

Among the many sculptures dotted about the complex are George Segal's *Rush Hour Group*, and Barry Flanagan's *Leaping Hare on Crescent and Bell*. Don't miss the spectacular view of Liverpool Street station and its glass-roofed train shed, seen from Exchange Square to the north.

Petticoat Lane ⑭

Middlesex St E1. **Map** 16 D1.
🚇 Aldgate East, Aldgate, Liverpool St. **Open** 9am–2pm Sun. See **Shops and Markets** pp322–3.

I N QUEEN VICTORIA'S prudish reign the name of this street, long famous for its market, was changed to the respectable but colourless Middlesex Street. That is still its official designation, but the old name, derived from its many years as a centre of the clothing trade, has stuck, and

is now applied to the market held every Sunday morning in this and the surrounding streets. Numerous attempts have been made to stop the market, but with no success. An enormous variety of goods is sold but there is still a bias towards clothing, especially leather coats. The atmosphere is noisy and cheerful, with Cockney stall-holders making use of their wit and insolence to attract custom. There are scores of snack bars, and many of these sell traditional Jewish food such as salt beef sandwiches and bagels with smoked salmon.

Whitechapel Art Gallery ⑮

Whitechapel High St E1. **Map** 16 E1.
📞 0171-377 0107. 🚇 Aldgate East, Aldgate. **Open** 11am–5pm Tue–Sun, 11am–8pm Wed. **Closed** 25–26 Dec, 1 Jan, for exhibition installations.
Occasional adm charge. ♿ 📷 🍴
🛍 🚻 **Films, lectures.**

A STRIKING ART NOUVEAU facade by C Harrison Townsend fronts this light, airy gallery founded in 1901.

Entrance to Whitechapel Gallery

Its aim is to bring art to the people of East London. Today this independent gallery enjoys an excellent international reputation for high-quality shows of major contemporary artists; these are interspersed with exhibitions reflecting the rich cultural origins of the people in the local community. In the 1950s and 1960s the likes of Jackson Pollock, Robert Rauschenberg, Anthony Caro and John Hoyland all displayed their work here. In 1970 David Hockney's first exhibition was held here.

The gallery also has a well-stocked arts bookshop, and there is a café here, serving a range of appetizing and healthy wholefoods in a relaxed atmosphere.

Bustling Petticoat Lane Market

18th-century Fournier Street

Christat Church, Spitalfields ⓰

Commercial St E1. **Map** 8 E5.
📞 *0171-247 7202.* 🚇 *Aldgate East, Liverpool St.* **Open** *noon– 2.30pm Mon–Fri.* ✝ *10.30am Sun.*
♿ **Concerts** *in June.*

THE FINEST of Nicholas Hawksmoor's six London churches, started in 1714 and completed in 1729, was mauled by Victorian alterations started in 1866. Christ Church still dominates the surrounding narrow streets, however. Its portico and spire are best seen from the western end of Brush-field Street, showing the four Tuscan columns on pediments supporting the arched roof of the church's portico.

Christ Church was com-missioned by parliament in the Fifty New Churches Act of 1711. The act's purpose was to combat the spread of Non-conformism (to the estab-lished Church of England) and a church needed to make a strong statement here, in an area that was fast becoming a Huguenot stronghold. The Protestant Huguenots had fled from religious persecution in Catholic France and came to Spitalfields to work in the local silkweaving industry.

The church's impression of size and strength is reinforced inside by the high ceiling, the sturdy wooden canopy over the west door and the gallery. In Hawksmoor's original plan the gallery extends around the north and south sides joining the organ gallery at the west

end. The organ dates from 1735; the royal coat of arms, in Coade stone, from 1822.

During the 19th century the hand silkweaving industry declined as machinery took over and Spitalfields became too poor to maintain a church. By the early 20th century Christ Church had fallen into disrepair. In 1958 it was closed for public worship because it was dangerous. Restoration began in 1964 and the church reopened in 1987. Since 1965 the crypt has been a home for rehabilitated alcoholics.

Fournier Street ⓱

E1. **Map** 8 E5. 🚇 *Aldgate East, Liverpool Street.*

THE 18TH-CENTURY houses on the north side of this street have attics with broad windows that were designed to give maximum light to the silkweaving French Huguenot community who lived here. Even now, the textile trade lives on, in this and nearby streets, still dependent on immigrant labour. Today it is Bengalis who toil at sewing machines in workrooms that are as cramped as they were when the Huguenots used them. Working conditions are improving, however, and many of the sweatshops have been converted into show-rooms for companies which now have modern factories away from the town centre.

Christ Church, Spitalfields

Bengali sweet factory: Brick Lane

London Jamme Masjid ⓲

Brick Lane E1. **Map** 8 E5.
🚇 *Liverpool St, Aldgate East.*

LOCAL MUSLIMS NOW worship here, in a building whose life story reflects the history of immigration into the area. Built in 1743 as a Huguenot chapel, it became a synagogue in the 19th century, was used as a Methodist chapel in the early 20th century, and is now a mosque. The sundial above the entrance bears the Latin inscription *Umbra sumus* – "we are shadows".

Spitalfields Heritage Centre ⓳

19 Princelet St E1. **Map** 8 E5.
📞 *0171-377 6901.* 🚇 *Aldgate East, Liverpool St.* **Open** *10am–5pm (not guaranteed, phone first).* **Exhibitions, theatre performances.**

THIS HOUSE, built in 1719, still has a silkweavers' attic. Its most intriguing feature is a synagogue built in the garden in 1870 and used for worship until the 1960s. Its balconies are inscribed with Hebrew texts and names of benefactors.

Brick Lane ⓴

E1. **Map** 8 E5. 🚇 *Liverpool St, Aldgate East, Old St.* **Market open** *dawn–noon Sun. See* **Shops and Markets** *pp322–3.*

ONCE A LANE running through brickfields, this is now the busy centre of London's Bengali district. Its shops and

The grand bedroom of Dennis Severs House

houses, some dating from the 18th century, have seen waves of immigrants of many nationalities, and most now sell food, spices, silks and sarees. The first Bengalis to live here were sailors who came in the 19th century. In those days it was a predominantly Jewish quarter, and there are still a few Jewish shops left, including a popular 24-hour bagel shop at No. 159.

On Sundays a large market is held here and in the surrounding streets, complementing Petticoat Lane *(see p169)*. At the northern end of Brick Lane is the former Black Eagle Brewery, a medley of 18th- and 19th-century industrial architecture, now reflected in, and set off by, a sympathetic mirror-glassed extension.

Dennis Severs House ㉑

18 Folgate St E1. **Map** 8 D5.
[C] 0171-247 4013. [e] Liverpool St.
Open first Sun of month 2–5pm.
Adm charge. **Evening performances**.

A T NO. 18 Folgate Street, built in 1724, Dennis Severs, a designer and performer, has recreated an historical interior, that takes you on a journey from the 17th to the 19th centuries. It offers what he calls "an adventure of the imagination,... a visit to a time-mode rather than... merely a look at a house". The rooms are like a series of *tableaux vivants*, as if the occupants had simply left for a moment. There is broken bread on the plates, wine in the glasses, fruit in the bowl;

18th-century portrait: Dennis Severs House

the candles flicker and horses' hooves clatter on the cobbles outside. Mr Severs presents a more elaborate, three-hour version of the visit on some weekday evenings, with 18th-century music, drinks and snacks. These theatrical evenings are for groups of up to eight people, are not suitable for children under 12, and need to be booked at least three weeks in advance.

Around the corner on Elder Street are two of London's earliest surviving terraces, also built in the 1720s, where many of the orderly Georgian red-brick houses have been carefully restored.

Columbia Road Market ㉒

Columbia Rd E2. **Map** 8 D3.
[e] Liverpool St, Old St, Bethnal Green. **Open** 8.30am–1pm Sun.
See **Shops and Markets** pp322–3.

A VISIT TO this flower and plant market is one of the most delightful things to do on Sunday mornings in London, whether you want to take advantage of the exotic species on offer there or not. Set in a well-preserved street of small Victorian shops, it is a lively, sweet-smelling and colourful event. Apart from the stalls, there are several shops selling, among other things, home-made bread and farmhouse cheeses, antiques and interesting objects, many of them flower-related. There is also a Spanish delicatessen and an excellent snack bar that sells bagels and welcome mugs of hot chocolate on chilly winter mornings.

Columbia Road flower market

SOUTHWARK AND BANKSIDE

SOUTHWARK ONCE offered an escape route from the City, where many forms of pleasure were banned. Borough High Street was lined with taverns: the medieval courtyards that still run off it mark where they stood. The George survives as the only galleried London inn. Prostitution thrived in houses facing the river, and theatres and bear gardens *(see picture p178)* were established here in the

Shakespeare window at Southwark Cathedral

late 16th century. Shakespeare's company was based at the Globe Theatre and also played at the Rose nearby. The palace of the Bishops of Winchester – from which a magnificent rose window survives – was best known for its notorious Clink prison. Today the wharves are closed and the river is lined with a pleasant walkway linking its attractions and giving tremendous views over the river to the City.

SIGHTS AT A GLANCE

Historic Streets and Buildings
Hop Exchange ❷
Old St Thomas's Operating Theatre ❺
Hay's Galleria ❻
St Olave's House ❼
Cardinal's Wharf ⓫

Museums and Galleries
Clink Exhibition ❽

Shakespeare's Globe Museum ❿
Bankside Gallery ⓬
London Dungeon ⓮
Design Museum ⓯

Cathedrals
Southwark Cathedral ❶

Pubs
George Inn ❹
The Anchor ❾

Markets
Borough Market ❸
Bermondsey Antiques Market ⓭

Historic Ships
HMS Belfast ⓰

0 metres	500
0 yards	500

GETTING THERE
The Northern line runs a regular Underground service to this area. Nearly every BR train from Charing Cross or Cannon Street stops at London Bridge. Taking a bus from the city centre is very confusing as you have to change.

KEY

▨	Street-by-Street map
⊖	Underground station
⇌	British Rail station
P	Parking

View from the riverside walkway

Street-by-Street: Southwark

FROM MEDIEVAL TIMES until the 18th century Southwark was a popular venue for the pursuit of illicit pleasures – including the Elizabethan theatre. It was south of the Thames and out of the jurisdiction of the City authorities. The 18th and 19th centuries brought docks, warehouses and factories, while railways carved a swathe through the area. Today it has been developed with offices.

Southwark Bridge was opened in 1912 to replace a bridge of 1819.

★ Shakespeare's Globe Museum
A museum of Elizabethan theatres stands near the site of the Globe (shown in 1612) ❿

Hop Exchange
It used to be the main trading centre for hops used by brewers. The building is now used as offices ❷

The Anchor
For centuries it has been a favourite riverside pub with fine views ❾

Clink Exhibition
A museum on the site of the notorious old prison looks back at Southwark's colourful past ❽

Borough Market
There has been a market on or near this site since 1276. Now it sells wholesale fruit and vegetables ❸

The War Memorial, commemorating soldiers who fell in World War I, was erected in 1924 on Borough High Street where it has become a powerful landmark.

★ George Inn
It is London's only surviving traditional, galleried inn ❹

Southwark Quayside

LOCATOR MAP
See Central London Map pp12–13

London Bridge, in its various forms, was the only river crossing in London from Roman times until 1750. The present bridge, completed in 1972, replaced the one of 1831 now in Arizona, USA.

KEY

— — — Suggested route

0 metres   100

0 yards   100

★ **Southwark Cathedral**
Despite major alterations, it still contains medieval elements ❶

St Olave's House
These Art Deco offices for Hay's Wharf were built in 1932 ❼

STAR SIGHTS

★ **Southwark Cathedral**

★ **George Inn**

★ **Shakespeare's Globe Museum**

London Bridge station

Old St Thomas's Operating Theatre
The gory days of surgery without anaesthetic are reconstructed in this perfectly preserved room ❺

Southwark Cathedral ❶

Montague Close SE1. **Map** 15 B3.
📞 0171-407 2939. 🚇 *London Bridge.* **Open** 7.30am–6pm daily.
✝ 11am Sun. 🎵 **Concerts**.

THIS CHURCH DID not become a cathedral until 1905. However, some parts of the building date back to the 12th century, when it was attached to a priory, and many of its original medieval features remain. The memorials are especially interesting. The wooden effigy of a knight is late 13th-century, and another medieval gem is the tomb, dating from 1408, of John Gower, poet and contemporary of Geoffrey Chaucer *(see p39)*.

The monument to William Shakespeare, shown in front of a relief of 17th-century Southwark, was carved in 1912. Shakespeare's brother Edmond, also an actor, is buried here, and so is Philip Henslowe, who was in charge of the nearby Rose Theatre in Shakespeare's day. John Harvard, founder of Harvard University in the United States, was baptized here in 1607 and there is a chapel named after him.

Shakespeare Window in Cathedral

Hop Exchange ❷

Southwark St SE1. **Map** 15 B4. 🚇 *London Bridge.* **Not open** to the public.

SOUTHWARK, with its easy access to Kent where hops are grown, was a natural venue for brewing beer and trading hops. In 1866 this building was constructed as the centre of that trade. Now

The George Inn, now owned by the National Trust

offices, it retains its original pediment complete with carved scenes showing the hop harvest, and iron gates with a hop motif.

Borough Market ❸

Stoney St SE1. **Map** 15 B4.
🚇 *London Bridge.* **Open** midnight–10am Mon–Sat.

THIS SMALL WHOLESALE fruit and vegetable market spreads out in an L-shape beneath the railway tracks. It is the successor to a medieval market, held on London Bridge, which was moved to Borough High Street in 1276 to avoid congestion. It was moved again in 1756, for the same reason, to its present location where the buildings date from 1851. Today its future is uncertain.

George Inn ❹

77 Borough High St SE1. **Map** 15 B4.
📞 0171-407 2056. 🚇 *London Bridge, Borough.* **Open** 11am–11pm Mon–Fri, noon–3pm, 6–11pm Sat, noon–3pm, 7–10.30pm Sun. 🎵 See **Restaurants and Pubs** pp308–9.

DATING FROM THE 17th-century, this building is the only example of a traditional galleried coaching inn left in London. It was rebuilt after the Southwark fire of 1676 in a style that dates back to the Middle Ages. Originally

there would have been three wings around a courtyard where plays were staged in the 17th century. In 1889 the north and east wings were demolished to make room for the railway, so only one wing has survived.

The inn, now owned by the National Trust, still operates as a pub and restaurant. Plays, morris dancing and other entertainments are sometimes performed in the yard during the summer.

Old St Thomas's Operating Theatre ❺

9a St Thomas St SE1. **Map** 15 B4.
📞 0171-955 4791. 🚇 *London Bridge.* **Open** 10am–4pm Mon–Fri. **Closed** Christmas week–New Year, public hols. **Adm charge**.

ST THOMAS'S HOSPITAL, one of the oldest in Britain, stood here from its foundation in the 12th century until it was moved west in 1862. At this time nearly all of its buildings were demolished in order to make way for the railway.

19th-century surgical tools

The women's operating theatre survived only because it was located away from the main buildings in a garret over the hospital church (now the Chapter House of Southwark Cathedral). It lay, bricked over and forgotten, until the 1950s. It has since been fitted out exactly as it would have been in the early 19th century, before the discovery of either anaesthetics or antiseptics.

The display shows how patients were blindfolded, gagged and bound to the wooden operating table, while a box of sawdust underneath was used to catch the blood.

Hay's Galleria ➏

Tooley St SE1. **Map** 15 C3.
🚇 London Bridge.

The Galleria's atrium

T HIS IS A well-conceived development of up-market shops, restaurants, offices and private apartments on what used to be Hay's Wharf. The wharf was built by Thomas Cubitt in 1857 and was used for unloading tea and various other provisions for the London trade. It was one of the first places to use cold storage, importing New Zealand cheese and butter from 1867. Now fitted with a high glass roof on iron columns, the former warehouses are occupied by a variety of eating and drinking places, offices and some shops. There are also market

St Olave's House, Hay's Wharf: an Art Deco gem

stalls, street entertainers and, in the centre, David Kemp's intriguing moving sculpture *The Navigators*, which incorporates water jets, fountains and a glorious mish-mash of nautical symbols.

Hay's Galleria has become the focal point of London Bridge City, the name that covers all the new office developments in this area.

St Olave's House ➐

Tooley St SE1. **Map** 15 C3.
🚇 London Bridge.

W HEN IT WAS COMPLETED in 1932, H S Goodhart-Rendel's innovative Art Deco office block was considered controversial. Nowadays it is recognized as being one of the finest such buildings in London and has been carefully restored. It was the headquarters of Hay's Wharf, whose name is picked out in thick gold lettering along the top of the river front. Below this, three large bronze reliefs by sculptor Frank Dobson symbolize capital, labour and commerce. These are surrounded by smaller reliefs.

Clink Exhibition ➑

1 Clink St SE1. **Map** 15 B3.
📞 0171-403 6515. 🚇 London Bridge. **Open** 10am–6pm daily, some evenings until 9pm (phone first). **Closed** 25–26 Dec. **Adm charge.**
📷 phone first.

T HE CLINK was the popular name for the prison attached to Winchester House, a large palace which was the

home of the Bishops of Winchester from the 12th century until 1626. In the 16th century Protestant and Catholic prisoners of conscience were detained in the prison. The surrounding area was under the jurisdiction of the bishop rather than the City of London and was called "The Liberty of the Clink". It was London's red-light district, and rather than condemning prostitution, as happened in the City, the bishops licensed the brothels, regulating their opening hours.

The prison was one of five in Southwark and the first in which women were regularly confined. No doubt some of them were "Winchester geese" – prostitutes – who had broken the strict rules of their profession.

As well as displays on the history of prostitution, there are exhibits about the Clink prison. Britain's last working armoury, where arms and armour were made or mended, was also here until recently.

Also situated in the "liberty" was the Globe Theatre *(see p178)*, venue for many of William Shakespeare's plays. This was a round wooden theatre, and took its name from its sign showing Hercules carrying the world on his shoulders. Shakespeare was a shareholder and a player here. The plays written by him and performed here include *Romeo and Juliet*, *King Lear*, *Othello*, and *Macbeth*, but there is no complete record.

The only surviving part of Winchester House is a 14th-century rose window, which stands a few steps to the east of here. It was revealed when a fire broke out in 1814.

Replica of Civil War trouper's pot helmet, made in the Clink

The Anchor **9**

34 Park St SE1. **Map** 15 A3.
C 0171-407 1577. **E** London Bridge. **Open** 11.30am–11pm Mon–Sat, noon–3pm, 6.30–10.30pm Sun.

Pub sign at the Anchor Inn

T HIS IS ONE OF London's most famous riverside pubs. It dates from after the Southwark fire of 1676, which devastated the area much as the Great Fire across the river had done 10 years before (see pp22–3). The present building is 18th-century but traces of much earlier hostelries have been found beneath it. The inn was once connected with a brewery on the other side of the road that belonged to Henry Thrale, a close friend of Dr Samuel Johnson (see p140). When Thrale died in 1781, Dr Johnson went to the brewery sale and encouraged the bidders with a phrase that has passed into the English language: "The potential of

growing rich beyond the dreams of avarice".

A platform by the Thames offers patrons of the pub fine views across the river to the City as they sip their drinks on long summer evenings.

Shakespeare's Globe Museum **10**

New Globe Walk SE1. **Map** 15 A3.
C 0171-620 0202. **E** London Bridge. **Open** 10am–5pm Mon–Sun. **Closed** Christmas week–2 Jan, public hols. **Adm charge.** Ⓥ 🅿️ **Concerts, events.**

T HE MUSEUM is in a warehouse on the site of Davies Amphitheatre, a 17th-century venue for bear-baiting. Diarist Samuel Pepys saw bull-baiting here (he called it "a very rude and nasty pleasure") as well as two prize fights. The museum has exhibits on those vicious pastimes as well as on the Elizabethan theatres that thrived in the neighbourhood.

The Globe Theatre, headquarters of the band of players for whom William Shakespeare wrote his plays, is being reconstructed just east of its original site. There are interesting displays in the museum which illustrate the history of both the Globe and the Rose Theatres, where Shakespeare also acted.

The museum hosts a lively programme of lunchtime events including poetry, jazz and Elizabethan music.

Cardinal's Wharf **11**

SE1. **Map** 15 A3. **E** London Bridge.

A SMALL GROUP OF 17th-century houses today survives here in the shadow of the now abandoned power station. A plaque commemorates Christopher Wren's stay while St Paul's Cathedral (see pp148–51) was being built. He would have had a particularly fine view of the works while they were in progress just across the water.

Bankside Gallery **12**

48 Hopton St SE1. **Map** 14 F3.
C 0171-928 7521. **E** Blackfriars, Waterloo. **Open** 10am–8pm Tue, 10am–5pm Wed–Fri, 1–5pm Sun. **Closed** Christmas week–2 Jan, Easter. **Adm charge.** ♿ 🅿️ 📷 **Lectures.**

View from the Founders' Arms

T HIS MODERN RIVERSIDE gallery is the headquarters of the Royal Watercolour Society and the Royal Society of Painter-Printmakers. Its permanent collection is not on show here but there are temporary exhibitions of watercolours and engravings, many of which are for sale. There is also an excellent specialist shop that sells books and materials.

There is an unparalleled view of St Paul's Cathedral from the nearby Founders' Arms – built on the site of the foundry where St Paul's bells were cast. South of here, on Hopton Street, are some almshouses dating from 1752.

Davies Amphitheatre, on the site of Shakespeare's Globe Museum

Bermondsey Antiques Market 13

(New Caledonian Market) Long Lane and Bermondsey St SE1. **Map** 15 C5.
🚇 *London Bridge, Borough.* **Open** *5am–2pm Fri, starts closing midday. See* **Shops and Markets** *pp322–3.*

O NE OF LONDON'S main markets for antiques, Bermondsey market was established here in the 1960s when the old Caledonian Market site in Islington was redeveloped. Each Friday at dawn, serious antique dealers trade their latest acquisitions at Bermondsey. The press reports the occasional long-lost masterpiece changing hands here for a song, and early-rising optimists can try their luck and judgment. However, trading starts very early, and the best bargains go long before most tourists are likely to be awake.

Several nearby antique shops are open all week. The most interesting of these are situated in a row of old warehouses on Tower Bridge Road, piled high with furniture and knick-knacks of mixed vintage, condition and price.

London Dungeon 14

Tooley St SE1. **Map** 15 C3.
📞 *0171-403 0606.* 🚇 *London Bridge.* **Open** *Apr–Sep: 10am–6.30pm daily (last adm: 5.30pm); Oct–Mar: 10am–5.30pm daily (last adm: 4.30pm).* **Closed** *24–26 Dec.* **Adm charge.** ♿ 🖥 🚻

I N EFFECT a much expanded version of the chamber of horrors at Madame Tussaud's *(see p220)*, this museum is a great hit with ghoulish children. It illustrates the most bloodthirsty events in British history. It is played strictly for terror, and screams and moans abound as Druids perform a human sacrifice at Stonehenge, Anne Boleyn is beheaded on the orders of her husband Henry VIII, and a room full of people die in agony during the Great Plague of 1665. Torture, murder and witchcraft fill the gaps between these spectacles.

Antiques stall at Bermondsey Market

Design Museum 15

Butlers Wharf, Shad Thames SE1.
Map 16 E4. 📞 *0171-407 6261.*
🚇 *Tower Hill, London Bridge.* **Open** *11.30am–6pm Mon–Fri, 12pm–6pm Sat and Sun.* **Closed** *24–26 Dec, 1 Jan.* **Adm charge.** ♿ 🖥 🍽 🖥 🚻

T HIS MUSEUM was the first in the world to be devoted solely to the design of mass-produced everyday objects. This permanent collection offers a nostalgic look at furniture, office equipment, cars, radio and TV sets, and household utensils from the past. Temporary exhibitions of international design in

Eduardo Paolozzi sculpture (1986), outside Design Museum

the Review and Collections galleries provide a taste of what may become familiar in the future.

Located on the first floor of the museum is the Blueprint Café, a restaurant that has a wonderful view of the Thames, especially when the river is lit up at night.

HMS Belfast 16

Morgan's Lane, Tooley St SE1.
Map 16 D3. 📞 *0171-407 6434.*
🚇 *London Bridge, Tower Hill.* 🚢 *Tower Pier.* **Open** *1 Mar–31 Oct: 10am–6pm daily; 1 Nov–1 Mar: 10am–5pm daily.* **Closed** *25–26 Dec, 1 Jan.* **Adm charge.** ♿ *except for café.* 🖥 🏠 🖥 🚻

S INCE 1971, this Royal Navy cruiser has been used as a floating naval museum. Part of it has been recreated to show what the ship was like in 1943 when it participated in sinking the German cruiser *Scharnhorst.* Displays portray life on board during World War II and there are general exhibits relating to the history of the Royal Navy.

SOUTH BANK

Ｆollowing the Festival of Britain in 1951, the South Bank arts centre grew up around the newly erected Royal Festival Hall. The architecture of some buildings has been criticized, especially the chunky concrete Hayward Gallery. But the area functions well, and is crowded with culture-seekers most evenings and afternoons. The bordering areas of Waterloo and Lambeth are both down-to-earth, working class areas. Lambeth is celebrated in the song *The Lambeth Walk* from the 1930s musical *Me and My Girl*. The gatehouse of Lambeth Palace, situated on the southern edge of the area, is one of London's finest Tudor buildings.

Signpost at the South Bank Centre

SIGHTS AT A GLANCE

Historic Streets and Buildings
County Hall ❻
Lambeth Palace ❾
Waterloo Station ⓬
Gabriel's Wharf ⓮

Museums and Galleries
Museum of the Moving Image ❷
Hayward Gallery ❸
Florence Nightingale Museum ❼
Museum of Garden History ❽
Imperial War Museum ❿

Churches
St John's, Waterloo Road ⓭

Gardens
Jubilee Gardens ❺

Theatres and Concert Halls
National Theatre ❶
Royal Festival Hall ❹
Old Vic ⓫

Pubs
Doggett's Coat and Badge ⓯

GETTING THERE

The Northern and Bakerloo Underground lines pass through Waterloo station, which is also a major BR terminus. A few buses, such as Nos. 12, 53 and 176 run via Oxford Circus and Trafalgar Square, and stop south of the river a short walk from the South Bank Centre.

SEE ALSO

- **Street Finder**, maps 13, 22
- **Where to Stay** pp276–7
- **Restaurants** pp292–4

KEY

▨ Street-by-Street map
Ⓔ Underground station
🚆 British Rail station
Ⓟ Parking

Thameside promenade at the South Bank Centre

Street-by-Street: South Bank Centre

ORIGINALLY THIS WAS an area of wharves and factories which was much damaged by bombing during World War II. In 1951 it was chosen as the site of the Festival of Britain *(see p30)*, celebrating the centenary of the Great Exhibition *(see pp26–7)*. The Royal Festival Hall is the only building from 1951 to remain, but since then London's main arts centre has been created around it, including the national showplaces for theatre, music and film, and a major art gallery.

Memorial to the International Brigade of the Spanish Civil War

To the Strand

★ **Royal National Theatre**
Its three auditoriums offer a choice of plays ranging from the classics to the sharpest modern writing ❶

The National Film Theatre
was established in 1953 to show historic films *(see pp328–9)*.

Festival Pier

The Queen Elizabeth Hall
stages more intimate concerts than the Festival Hall. The adjoining Purcell Room is for chamber music *(see pp330–1)*.

Hayward Gallery
The concrete interior of this venue for important exhibitions is well suited to many modern works ❸

★ **Royal Festival Hall**
The London Philharmonic is one of many world-class orchestras to perform here in the focal point of the South Bank Centre ❹

Hungerford Bridge
was built in 1864 to carry both trains and pedestrians to Charing Cross.

★ **Museum of the Moving Image**
This all-action history of the cinema offers a lively family outing ❷

STAR SIGHTS

★ **Museum of the Moving Image**

★ **Royal National Theatre**

★ **Royal Festival Hall**

KEY

– – –   Suggested route

0 metres	100
0 yards	100

Waterloo Bridge was completed in 1945 to Sir Giles Gilbert Scott's design. It replaced Rennie's bridge of 1817.

SOHO & TRAFALGAR SQUARE

COVENT GARDEN & THE STRAND

HOLBORN & THE INNS OF COURT

PICCADILLY & ST JAMES'S

Thames

SOUTH BANK

WHITEHALL & WESTMINSTER

The Struggle is My Life is a bronze of Nelson Mandela, the South African leader. Made by Ian Walters, it was unveiled here in 1985.

The Shell Building, headquarters of the international oil company, was completed in 1963. Its architectural merit is still hotly debated.

Jubilee Gardens
Often crowded with picnickers, it was laid out in 1977 to celebrate Queen Elizabeth's silver jubilee ❺

CONCERT HALL APPROACH

BELVEDERE ROAD

CHICHELEY STREET

UPPER GROUND

WESTMINSTER BRIDGE ROAD

County Hall
A lion carved in 1837 (the date is on a paw) guards this deserted city government office ❻

To Westminster station

The stark concrete facade of the Hayward Gallery

Royal National Theatre ❶

South Bank Centre SE1. **Map** 14 D3.
📞 *0171-928 2252.* 🚇 *Waterloo.*
Open *10am–11pm Mon–Sat.* **Closed**
24–25 Dec. 🚫 *during performances.*
♿ 🍴 🖥 📷 **Concerts** *at 6pm,*
exhibitions. *See* **Entertainment**
pp326–7.

EVEN IF YOU DON'T want to see a play, this well-appointed complex is worth a visit. Sir Denys Lasdun's building was opened in 1976 after 200 years of debate about whether there should be a national theatre and where it should be sited. The company was formed in 1963, under Laurence (later Lord) Olivier, Britain's leading 20th-century actor. The largest of the three theatres is named after him – the others, the Cottesloe and the Lyttleton, commemorate administrators.

Museum of the Moving Image ❷

South Bank Centre SE1. **Map** 14 D3.
📞 *0171-401 2636.* 🚇 *Waterloo.*
Open *10am–6pm daily (last adm: 5pm).* **Closed** *24–26 Dec.* **Adm charge.** ♿ 🍴 🖥 📷 **Events, lectures, filmshows.**

MOMI is an enthralling experience for both adults and children as well as an invaluable resource for television and cinema students. The museum traces the history of film from the first experiments with zoetropes, magic lanterns, lenses and cameras. The exhibition bursts into life with the coming of silent cinema. A display devoted to Charlie Chaplin, born in nearby Kennington *(see p37),* is illustrated with clips from his films and artefacts from his era. In small viewing areas visitors watch historic scenes from films in different *genres* including French and Russian cinema, documentaries and newsreels. Actors wander round in the guise of starlets,

A "Dalek" robot: MOMI

cowboy heroes and ushers, engaging visitors in banter and luring them to take part in movie scenes. You can be interviewed on screen in a studio, draw your own cartoons, read the news from an autocue and watch yourself fly over the Thames. You should allow at least two hours for a visit here.

Hayward Gallery ❸

South Bank Centre SE1. **Map** 14 D3.
📞 *0171-928 3144.* 📠 *0171-261 0127.* 🚇 *Waterloo.* **Open** *10am–8pm Tue–Wed, 10am–6pm Thu–Mon.* **Closed** *24–26 Dec, 1 Jan, Good Fri, May Day, between exhibitions.* **Adm charge.** 📷 ♿ 🍴 🖥 📷

THE HAYWARD GALLERY is one of London's main venues for large art exhibitions. Its slabby grey concrete exterior is too starkly modern for some tastes and there has been pressure for it to be pulled down or severely modified almost ever since it opened in October 1968.
Hayward exhibitions cover classical and contemporary art, but the work of British contemporary artists is particularly well represented. You may have to queue, especially at weekends.

Royal Festival Hall ❹

South Bank Centre SE1. **Map** 14 D4.
📞 *0171-928 3191.* 🚇 *Waterloo.*
Open *10am–10pm daily.* **Closed** *25 Dec.* 🚫 *during performances.* ♿
🍴 🖥 📷 **Pre-concert talks, exhibitions, free concerts.** *See* **Entertainment** *p330.*

THIS WAS THE ONLY structure in the 1951 Festival of Britain *(see p30)* designed for permanence. Sir Robert Matthew and Sir Leslie Martin's concert hall was the first major public building in London following World War II. It has stood the test of time so well that many of the capital's major arts institutions have gathered round it. The hall's interior has always attracted much admiration; its sweeping staircases lead up majestically from the lobby to create a tremendous sense of occasion while also remaining highly functional. The stage has hosted the likes of the cellist, Jacqueline du Pré, and the conductor, Georg Solti. The organ was installed in 1954. There are a variety of cafés, bars, music and book stalls on the lower floors and backstage tours are available.

Festival of Britain: symbol of 1951

Jubilee Gardens ❺

South Bank SE1. **Map** 14 D4.
🚇 *Waterloo.*

THIS PLEASANT riverside space was laid out in 1977 to mark the Silver Jubilee of the Queen's accession to the throne. In summer it is a favourite spot for sandwich-munching office workers and a venue for concerts and festivals. Sculptures include a memorial to the International Brigade who fought in the Spanish Civil War (1936–9).

County Hall ❻

York Rd SE1. **Map** 13 C4.
🚇 *Waterloo, Westminster.* **Not open** to the public.

THIS VAST, EMPTY building used to be the headquarters of the old London County Council (LCC). It was started in 1912 but, interrupted by two World Wars, was not completed until 1958. The best views of its curved, colonnaded central section are from the river.

The LCC became the Greater London Council (GLC) in 1965, but in 1986 this London-wide authority was abolished and its powers dispersed. The future of County Hall is now uncertain.

Florence Nightingale Museum ❼

2 Lambeth Palace Rd SE1. **Map** 14 D5.
📞 *0171-620 0374.* 🚇 *Waterloo, Westminster.* **Open** 10am–4pm Tue–Sun, public hols. **Closed** 25–26 Dec, 1 Jan, Good Fri, Easter Sun. **Adm charge.** 🚫 ♿ 🖥 🎬 *Videos.*

THIS DETERMINED woman captured the nation's imagination as the "Lady of the Lamp", who nursed the wounded soldiers of the Crimea War (1853–6). She also founded Britain's first school of nursing at old St Thomas's Hospital in 1860.

Obscurely sited near the entrance to new St Thomas's Hospital, the museum is worth seeking out. It gives a

Florence Nightingale

fascinating account of Florence Nightingale's career through original documents, photographs and personal memorabilia. Vivid displays illustrate her life and the developments she continued to make in health care and sanitation, until her death in 1910, at the age of 90.

Museum of Garden History ❽

Lambeth Palace Rd SE1. **Map** 21 C1.
📞 *0171-261 1891.* 📠 *0171-373 4030.* 🚇 *Waterloo, Vauxhall, Lambeth North, Westminster.* **Open** 11am–3pm Mon–Fri, 10.30am–5pm Sun. **Closed** 2nd Sun Dec–1st Sun Mar. 📷 *small charge.* ♿ 🍴 🖥 🎬 *Lectures, filmshows.*

HOUSED IN AND AROUND the 14th-century tower of St Mary's Church, this museum opened in 1979. In the church-yard is the tomb of a father and son both called John Tradescant. The Tradescants were gardeners to the 17th-century monarchs and were also pioneer plant hunters in the Americas, Russia and Europe. Their collection of rarities formed the basis of the Ashmolean Museum, Oxford.

The museum here consists of a history of gardening in Britain, illustrated by ancient implements, plans and documents. A knot garden outside is devoted to plants from the Tradescants' era. There is a shop with a stock of garden-related items.

County Hall: seeking a new role

The Tudor gatehouse

Lambeth Palace ⓿

SE1. **Map** 21 C1. ⊖ *Lambeth North, Westminster, Waterloo, Vauxhall*. **Not open** *to the public.*

THIS HAS BEEN the London base of the Archbishop of Canterbury, the senior cleric in the Church of England, for 800 years. The chapel and its undercroft contain elements from the 13th century, but a large part of the rest of the building is far more recent. It has been frequently restored, most recently by Edward Blore in 1828–34. The Tudor gatehouse dates from 1485 and is one of London's most pleasing and familiar riverside landmarks.

Until the first Westminster Bridge was built, the horse ferry that operated between here and Millbank was a principal river crossing. The revenues from it went to the Archbishop, who received compensation for loss of business when the bridge opened in 1750.

Imperial War Museum ⓿

Lambeth Rd SE1. **Map** 22 E1.
📞 *0171-416 5000*. 📠 *0171-820 1683*. ⊖ *Lambeth North, Elephant & Castle*. **Open** *10am–6pm daily.* **Closed** *24–26 Dec, 1 Jan.* **Adm charge.** 📷 ♿ 🍴 🔲 🚻 *Filmshows, lectures.*

IN SPITE OF THE TWO colossal guns that point up the drive from the main entrance, this is not just a display of the engines of modern warfare. Massive tanks, artillery, bombs and aircraft *are* on show, yet some of the most fascinating exhibits in the museum relate more to the social effects of 20th-century wars and their impact on the lives of people at home than to the actual business of fighting. There are displays about food rationing, air raid precautions, censorship and morale-boosting.

The arts are well represented, with extracts from wartime films, radio programmes and literature, plus many hundreds of photographs, paintings by Graham Sutherland and Paul Nash, and sculpture by Jacob Epstein. Henry Moore did some evocative drawings of life during the Blitz of 1940, when many Londoners slept in underground stations in order to protect themselves from falling bombs.

The museum is kept up to date with exhibits relating to recent military engagements of British forces, including the

Gulf War of 1991. It is housed in part of what used to be Bethlehem Hospital for the Insane ("Bedlam"), built in 1811. In the 19th century, visitors would come for the afternoon to enjoy the antics of the patients. The hospital moved out to new premises in Surrey in 1930, leaving this vast building empty. Its two large, flanking wings were pulled down and this central block converted into the museum which moved here from its former South Kensington site in 1936.

Old Vic ⓿

Waterloo Rd SE1. **Map** 14 E5.
📞 *0171-928 7616*. 📠 *0171-928 7618*. ⊖ *Waterloo*. **Open** *for performances and guided tours only.* 🔲 *See* **Entertainment** *pp326–7.*

The Old Vic's facade from 1816

THIS SPLENDID building dates from 1816, when it was opened as the Royal Coburg Theatre. In 1833 the name was changed to the Royal Victoria in honour of the future queen. Shortly after this the theatre became a centre for "music hall", the immensely popular Victorian entertainment in which singers, comedians and other acts were introduced by a chairman, who needed a booming voice to control unruly audiences.

In 1912 Lillian Baylis took over as manager and in 1914 introduced Shakespearean plays to the Old Vic. Between 1963 and 1976 it was the first home of the National Theatre *(see p184)*. In 1983 it was restored, since when it has operated as a conventional West End theatre.

The machinery of war through the ages

Waterloo Station ⑫

York Rd SE1. **Map** 14 D4.
📞 0171-928 5100 🚇 Waterloo.
See **Getting to London** pp358–9.

THE TERMINUS FOR trains to southwest England, it is being enlarged to become London's main link to the Channel Tunnel. It was originally built in 1848 but completely remodelled in the early 20th century, with a grand formal entrance on the northeast corner. Today the spacious concourse, lined with shops, makes it one of the most practical of the London rail termini.

St John's, Waterloo Road ⑬

SE1. **Map** 14 E4. 📞 0171-633 9819.
🚇 Waterloo. **Open** 11.45am–1pm
Mon–Fri, 10am–noon Sat; at other
times phone first. ✝ 10.30am Sun.

ST JOHN'S IS ONE of four "Waterloo churches" that were commissioned in 1818, after the Napoleonic Wars. They are often thought to have been built as a thanksgiving for Britain's victory in these wars, but it is more likely that they were built to serve Lambeth's rapidly growing population. The church's portico, with its six Doric columns supporting a pediment, is in the Greek Revival style that was then popular. Damaged by wartime bombing, it was restored in time to become the official church for the Festival of Britain in 1951
(see p30).

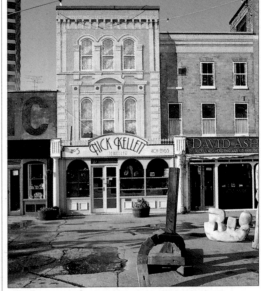

Illusionistic painting on the buildings around Gabriel's Wharf

Gabriel's Wharf ⑭

56 Upper Ground SE1. **Map** 14 E3.
🚇 Waterloo. See **Shops and Markets** pp322–3.

THIS PLEASANT enclave of boutiques, craft shops and cafés was the product of a long and stormy debate over the future of what was once an industrial riverside area. Residents of Waterloo strongly opposed various schemes for office developments before a community association was able to acquire the site in 1984 and build co-operative housing around the wharf. Adjoining the market is a small garden and a riverside walkway with marvellous views to the north of the City. The tower to the east, built in 1928, highlights an ingenious way of avoiding advertising restrictions. Its windows spell Oxo, the brand name of a popular meat extract.

Doggett's Coat and Badge ⑮

1 Blackfriars Bridge SE1. **Map** 14 F3.
📞 0171-633 9081. 🚇 Blackfriars.
Open normal licensing hours Mon–Sat. **Closed** 25 Dec. 🍽 See
Ceremonial London p55.

A MODERN RIVERSIDE pub next to Blackfriars Bridge, it is named after an historic annual boat race. The race was instituted in 1716 for the boatmen who used to row passengers across the river. Its patron was Thomas Doggett, an actor who was grateful for the services of the watermen; they were held in low esteem because of their vulgarity and coarse language.

The coat and ceremonial arm badge are still competed for today in a boat race between London Bridge and Cadogan Pier, Chelsea.

The memorial to the dead of World War I at Waterloo Station

CHELSEA

THE SHOWY young shoppers who paraded along the King's Road from the 1960s until the 1980s have more or less gone, along with Chelsea's reputation for extreme behaviour established by the bohemian

Cow's head outside the Old Dairy on Old Church Street

Chelsea Set of writers and artists in the 19th century. Formerly a riverside village, Chelsea became fashionable in Tudor times. Henry VIII liked it so much that he built a small palace (long vanished) here. Artists, including Turner, Whistler and Rossetti, were attracted by the river views from

Cheyne Walk. The historian Thomas Carlyle and the essayist Leigh Hunt arrived in the 1830s and began a literary tradition continued by writers such as the poet Swinburne. Yet Chelsea has always had a raffish element, too: in the 18th century the pleasure gardens were noted for beautiful courtesans and the Chelsea Arts Club has had riotous balls for nearly a century. Chelsea is too expensive for most artists now, but the artistic connection is maintained by many galleries and antique shops.

SIGHTS AT A GLANCE

Historic Streets and Buildings
King's Road ❶
Carlyle's House ❷
Cheyne Walk ❺
Royal Hospital ❽
Sloane Square ❾

Museums
National Army Museum ❼

Churches
Chelsea Old Church ❸

Gardens
Roper's Garden ❹
Chelsea Physic Garden ❻

GETTING THERE
The District and Circle Underground lines serve Sloane Square; the Piccadilly line passes just outside this area, through South Kensington. Buses 11, 19 and 22 all stop on the King's Road.

SEE ALSO

• *Street Finder*, maps 19, 20

• *Where to Stay* pp276–7

• *Restaurants* pp292–4

• *Chelsea and Battersea Walk* pp266–7

No. 56 Oakley Street, where the polar explorer, R F Scott, once lived

KEY
Street-by-Street map
🄴 Underground station
🄿 Parking

0 metres   500
0 yards   500

Picturesque Chelsea residences in a cul-de-sac off the King's Road

Street-by-Street: Chelsea

O NCE A PEACEFUL riverside village,
Chelsea has been fashionable since
Tudor times when Sir Thomas More,
Henry VIII's Lord Chancellor, lived here.
Artists, including Turner, Whistler and
Rossetti, were attracted by the views
from Cheyne Walk, before a busy main
road disturbed its peace. Chelsea's

King's Road
*In the 1960s and
1970s it was the
boutique-lined
centre of fashionable
London and is still
a main shopping
street* ❶

artistic connection
is maintained by
its galleries and
antique shops,
while enclaves of
18th-century
houses preserve
its old village
atmosphere.

**To Kings
Road**

The Old Dairy, at 46 Old
Church Street, was built in
1796, when cows still
grazed in the surrounding
fields. The tiling is original.

Carlyle's House
*The historian and philosopher
lived here from 1834 until his
death in 1882* ❷

Chelsea Old Church
*Although severely
damaged during
World War II, it still
holds some fine Tudor
monuments* ❸

Roper's Garden
*It includes a sculpture
by Jacob Epstein who
had a studio here* ❹

Thomas More, sculpted in 1969
by L Cubitt Bevis, gazes
calmly across the river near
where he lived.

Thomas More

STAR SIGHT

★ **Chelsea Physic
Garden**

KEY

– – –   Suggested route

0 metres	100
0 yards	100

Chelsea Town Hall was built in the late 19th century and is now a venue for exhibitions and antique fairs.

LOCATOR MAP
See Central London Map pp12–13

To Sloane Square station

★ **Chelsea Physic Garden**
The statue is of Sir Hans Sloane, benefactor of this historic herb garden ❻

Cadogan Pier

Albert Bridge, completed in 1873, is the most elegant of the Thames Bridges, especially at night when it is illuminated by hundreds of light bulbs.

Boy and Dolphin, the vigorous sculpture (1975) by David Wynne, enlivens the Albert Bridge junction.

Cheyne Walk
Once favoured by artists, it boasts some of London's finest houses and has had many famous residents. Look out for the plaques ❺

The Pheasantry, King's Road

King's Road ①

SW3 and SW10. **Map** 19 B3.
🔵 *Sloane Square. See* **Shops and Markets** *pp310–23.*

THIS IS CHELSEA's central artery, with its wealth of small fashion shops packed with young people looking for avant-garde fashions. The mini-skirt revolution of the 1960s began here and so have many subsequent style trends, perhaps the most famous of them being punk.

Look out for the Pheasantry at No. 152, with its columns and statuary. It was built in 1881 as the shop-front of a furniture maker's premises but now conceals a modern restaurant. Antique-lovers will find three warrens of stalls on the south side of the King's Road: Antiquarius at No. 137, the Chenil Galleries at Nos. 181–3 and the Chelsea Antiques Market at No. 253.

Carlyle's House ②

24 Cheyne Row SW3. **Map** 19 B4.
📞 *0171-352 7087.* 🔵 *Sloane Square, South Kensington.* **Open** *Apr–Oct: 11am–5pm Wed–Sun, public hols (last adm: 4.30pm).* **Closed** *Good Fri.*
Adm charge. 🚫

THE HISTORIAN, and founder of the London Library *(see St James's Square p96),* Thomas Carlyle moved into this modest 18th-century house in 1834, and wrote many of his best-known books here, most notably *The French Revolution*

and *Frederick the Great.* His presence made Chelsea more fashionable and the house became a mecca for some of the great literary figures of the 19th century. The novelists Charles Dickens and William Thackeray, poet Alfred Lord Tennyson, naturalist Charles Darwin and philosopher John Stuart Mill were all regular visitors here. The house has been restored so that it looks as it did during Carlyle's lifetime, and is now a museum dedicated to his life and work.

Chelsea Old Church ③

Cheyne Walk SW3. **Map** 19 A4.
📞 *0171-352 7978.* 🔵 *Sloane Square, South Kensington.* **Open** *10am–1pm, 2–5pm daily (phone first).* 🚫 ♿ 📷 *most days.* ✝ *11am Sun.*

Chelsea Old Church in 1860

REBUILT AFTER World War II, this square-towered building does not look old from the outside. However, early prints confirm that it is a careful replica of the medieval church that was destroyed by World War II bombs.

The glory of this church are its Tudor monuments. One to Sir Thomas More, who built a chapel here in 1528, contains an inscription he wrote (in Latin), asking to be buried next to his wife. Among other monuments is a chapel to Sir Thomas Lawrence, who was an Elizabethan merchant, and a 17th-century memorial to Lady Jane Cheyne, after whose husband Cheyne Walk was named. Outside the church is a statue in memory of Sir Thomas More, "statesman, scholar, saint", gazing piously across the river.

Roper's Garden ④

Cheyne Walk SW3. **Map** 19 A4.
🔵 *Sloane Square, South Kensington.*

THIS IS A SMALL PARK outside Chelsea Old Church. It is named after Margaret Roper, Sir Thomas More's daughter, and her husband William, who wrote More's biography. The sculptor Sir Jacob Epstein worked at a studio on the site between 1909 and 1914, and there is a stone carving by him commemorating the fact. The park also contains a figure of a nude woman by Gilbert Carter.

Cheyne Walk ⑤

SW3. **Map** 19 B4. 🔵 *Sloane Square, South Kensington.*

UNTIL CHELSEA Embankment was constructed in 1874, Cheyne Walk was a pleasant riverside promenade. Now it overlooks a busy road that has destroyed much of its charm. Many of the 18th-century houses remain, though, bristling with blue plaques celebrating some of the famous people who have lived in them. Most were writers and artists, including J M W Turner who lived incognito at No. 119, George Eliot who died at No. 4 and a clutch of writers (Henry James, T S Eliot and Ian Fleming) in Carlyle Mansions.

Thomas More on Cheyne Walk

Chelsea Physic Garden ❻

Swan Walk SW3. **Map** 19 C4.
☎ 0171-352 5646. ⊖ Sloane Square. **Open** Apr–Oct: 2–5pm Wed, Sun. **Adm charge**.
♿ 🖥 3.15–4.45pm. 🎫 **Annual exhibition** during Chelsea Flower Show, see p56.

ESTABLISHED BY the Society of Apothecaries in 1673 to study plants for medicinal use, this garden has survived to the present day. It was saved from closure in 1722 by a gift from Sir Hans Sloane, whose statue adorns it. The garden has since broadened its range of plants but parts of it would be recognizable to Sir Hans today.

Many new varieties have been nurtured in its glasshouses, including cotton sent to the plantations of the southern United States. Today, visitors can see ancient trees, an historical walk and one of Britain's first rock gardens, installed in 1772.

Chelsea Physic Garden in spring

National Army Museum ❼

Royal Hospital Rd SW3. **Map** 19 C4.
☎ 0171-730 0717. ⊖ Sloane Square. **Open** 10am–5.30pm daily.
Closed 24–26 Dec, 1 Jan, Good Fri, May Day. ♿ 🖥 🎫

A VIVID AND LIVELY account of the history of British land forces from 1485 to the present day can be found here. Tableaux, dioramas and archive film clips illustrate major engagements and give a taste of what life behind the lines was like. There are fine paintings of battle scenes as well as portraits of soldiers. The attached museum shop offers a good range of military books and model soldiers.

Royal Hospital ❽

Royal Hospital Rd SW3. **Map** 20 D3.
☎ 0171-730 0161. ⊖ Sloane Square. **Open** 10am–noon, 2–4pm Mon–Sat, 2–4pm Sun.

T HIS GRACEFUL COMPLEX was commissioned by Charles II from Christopher Wren in 1682 as a retirement home for old or wounded soldiers, who have been known as Chelsea Pensioners ever since. The hospital opened ten years later and is still home to about 400 retired soldiers, who are instantly recognizable in their scarlet coats and tricorne hats, a distinctive uniform which dates from the 17th century.

A Chelsea Pensioner in uniform

Flanking the northern entrance are Wren's two main public rooms: the chapel, which is notable for its wonderful simplicity, and the panelled Great Hall, still used today as the dining room. A small museum explains the history of the Pensioners.

A statue of Charles II by Grinling Gibbons is to be found on the terrace outside, and there is a fine view of the remains of Battersea Power Station across the river.

Sloane Square ❾

SW1. **Map** 20 D2. ⊖ Sloane Square.

Sloane Square fountain

T HIS PLEASANT SMALL square (rectangle to be precise) has a paved centre with a flower stall and fountain depicting Venus. Laid out in the late 18th century, it was named after Sir Hans Sloane, the wealthy physician and collector who bought the manor of Chelsea in 1712. Opposite Peter Jones, the 1936 department store on the square's west side, is the Royal Court Theatre, which for over a century has fostered new drama.

SOUTH KENSINGTON AND KNIGHTSBRIDGE

BRISTLING WITH embassies and consulates, South Kensington and Knightsbridge remain among London's most desirable and salubrious areas. The proximity of Kensington Palace, still a royal residence, means the area has remained relatively unchanged. It vies with Mayfair as the most expensive place to live in London. The elite shops of Knightsbridge, led by Harrod's, serve its wealthy residents. With Hyde Park to the north and the museums that once celebrated Victorian learning and self-confidence at its heart, visitors to this part of London can expect to find a unique combination of the serene and the grandiose.

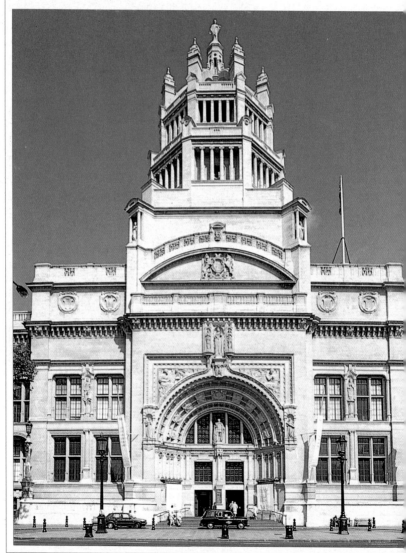

Facade of the Victoria and Albert Museum

Statue of Peter Pan in
Kensington Gardens

Decorative relief outside
the Natural History Museum

Historic Streets and Buildings
Royal College of Music ❺
National Sound Archive ❻
Royal College of Art ❽
Kensington Palace ⓫
Speakers' Corner ⓮

Churches
Brompton Oratory ❹

Museums and Galleries
Natural History Museum pp204–5 ❶
Science Museum pp208–9 ❷
Victoria and Albert Museum pp198–201 ❸
Serpentine Gallery ❿

Parks and Gardens
Kensington Gardens ⓬
Hyde Park ⓭

Monuments
Albert Memorial ❾
Marble Arch ⓯

Concert Halls
Royal Albert Hall ❼

Shops
Harrod's ⓰

GETTING THERE
South Kensington station is on the Piccadilly, Circle and District lines; only the Piccadilly line passes through Knightsbridge. The No. 14 bus runs direct from Piccadilly Circus to South Kensington, via Green Park and Knightsbridge.

KEY

▨ Street-by-Street map

🅴 Underground station

🅿 Parking

Street-by-Street: South Kensington

A CLUTCH OF MUSEUMS and colleges
provide this area with its dignified
character. The Great Exhibition of 1851
in Hyde Park was so successful that in
the following years smaller exhibitions
were held here, just to its south. By the
end of the 19th century some of these
had become permanent museums,
housed in grandiose buildings
celebrating Victorian self-confidence.

Royal College of Art
*David Hockney and Peter
Blake are among the great
artists who trained here* **8**

**The Royal College
of Organists** was
decorated by F W
Moody in 1876.

★ **Royal Albert Hall**
*Opened in 1870, the
Hall was partly
funded by selling
seats on a 999-
year lease* **7**

Royal College of Music
*Historic musical instruments, like this
harpsichord (1531) are
exhibited here* **5**

★ **Natural
History Museum**
*The dinosaur exhibits
are one of the museum's
most popular attractions* **1**

★ **Science Museum**
*Visitors here can
experiment with the
interactive displays* **2**

★ **Victoria and Albert Museum**
*A vast range of objects illustrate the nation's
history of design and decoration* **3**

Albert Memorial
This memorial was built to commemorate Queen Victoria's consort **9**

The Albert Hall Mansions, built by Norman Shaw in 1879, started a fashion for red brick.

LOCATOR MAP
See Central London Map pp12–13

KEY

— — — Suggested route

| 0 metres | 100 |
| 0 yards | 100 |

The Royal Geographical Society was founded in 1830. Scottish missionary and explorer David Livingstone (1813–73) was a member.

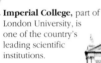

National Sound Archive
You can listen to a recording of Queen Victoria's voice here **6**

Imperial College, part of London University, is one of the country's leading scientific institutions.

Brompton Oratory
The Oratory was built during the 19th-century Catholic revival **4**

Brompton Square, begun in 1821, established this as a fashionable residential area.

Holy Trinity church dates from the 19th-century and is located in a calm backwater among cottages.

To Knightsbridge station

STAR SIGHTS

★ **Victoria and Albert Museum**

★ **Natural History Museum**

★ **Science Museum**

★ **Royal Albert Hall**

Victoria and Albert Museum ❸

Main entrance

T HE VICTORIA AND ALBERT (or V&A)
contains one of the world's widest
collections of fine and applied arts. The
exhibits range from early Christian
devotional objects
to Doc Marten
boots, from the
paintings of John
Constable to the
mystical art of
southeast Asia.
The V&A also houses collections of
sculpture, watercolours, jewellery and
musical instruments. The building was
originally opened in 1857 after nearly 25
years of planning and construction.

★ **Twentieth-
Century Gallery**
*This gallery shows
modern design like
Daniel Weil's* Radio
in a Bag *(1983).*

GALLERY GUIDE
*The V&A consists of 7 miles
(11 km) of galleries which
occupy four main floor levels.
The key to understanding the
labyrinthine layout is in the
division of galleries devoted to
art and design and those concentrating on materials and
techniques. In the former,
many different kinds of
artefacts are assembled to
illustrate the art and design of
a particular period or place –
for example Europe 1600–
1800. The materials and
techniques galleries contain
collections of particular forms
of art – porcelain, tapestries
and so on. The art and design
galleries occupy most of the
ground floor, with British arts
situated on the first floor. The
Henry Cole Wing is situated
on the northwest side of the
main building, and contains
the museum's collections of
paintings, drawings, prints
and photographs. It also
houses the new Frank Lloyd
Wright Gallery.*

European Ornament Gallery
*Over 500 years of decorative art is
shown here. This sculpture, made for
Marie Antoinette, represents the five
orders of Classical architecture.*

**Henry Cole
Wing**

**Exhibition Road
entrance**

KEY TO FLOORPLAN
☐	Lower ground floor
☐	Ground floor
☐	Upper ground floor
☐	First floor
☐	Upper first floor
☐	Second floor
☐	Henry Cole Wing

Constable Collection
*John Constable (1776–
1837) vividly captured the
East Anglian landscape.
This painting is called* A
Windmill Among Houses.

STAR EXHIBITS

★ Medieval Treasury

★ Nehru Gallery of Indian Art

★ Dress Collection

★ Morris and Gamble Rooms

★ Twentieth-Century Gallery

★ Morris and Gamble Rooms
The Victorian decorations here draw on past styles and the modern materials of an industrial age.

VISITORS' CHECKLIST

Cromwell Rd SW7. **Map** 19 A1.
📞 0171-938 8500. 📠 0171-938 8441. 🚇 *South Kensington.*
🚌 *14, 45A, 49, 74, 349, C1.*
Open *noon–5.50pm Mon, 10am–5.50pm Tue–Sun.* **Closed**
24–26 Dec, 1 Jan, Good Fri, May Day hol. ♿ 🎫 🍴 📷 🎁
Lectures, film shows, presentations, concerts, exhibitions, events.

T T Tsui Gallery of Chinese Art
This ancestor portrait, in watercolour on silk, is from the Qing Dynasty (1644–1912).

Pirelli Garden

★ Medieval Treasury
The Eltenberg Reliquary (c.1180) is one of the museum's masterpieces of medieval craftsmanship.

★ Nehru Gallery of Indian Art
Much of this collection dates from when Britain ruled India. The Emperor Shah Jehan's jade wine cup was made in 1657.

Main entrance

★ Dress Collection
Clothing here dates from 1600 to the present. This dress is from the 1880s.

Exploring the V&A's Collections

THE V&A WAS FOUNDED in 1852 as a Museum of Manufactures to inspire students of design. It was renamed by Queen Victoria, in memory of Prince Albert, in 1899. Many of the exhibits originate from parts of the British Empire, and among the wealth of artefacts is the greatest collection of Indian art outside India. The museum houses the National Art Library, which contains works on aspects of art and design, items illustrating the art of book production from the Middle Ages onwards, and artists' diaries and correspondence.

German Castle
Cup (15th
century)

SCULPTURE

THERE ARE 26 galleries devoted to Post-Classical sculpture, alabasters and ivories, bronzes and casts. The superb Renaissance collection includes a marble relief of *The Ascension* by Donatello. At the museum's Exhibition Road entrance stand 17 pieces by Auguste Rodin, presented by the sculptor in 1914. There are also collections of sculpture from India, the Middle East and the Far East.

CERAMICS AND GLASS

EXAMPLES OF 2,000 years of crafts-manship in pottery, porcelain and glass from Europe and the Near and Far East are exhibited across 21 galleries. These contain superb porcelain from all the major European china factories such as Meissen, Sèvres, Royal Copenhagen and Royal Worcester; stained glass, including some lovely medieval "Labours of the Months"; studio

pottery, with rare pieces by masters such as William de Morgan, Picasso and Bernard Leach; rich and intricately patterned Persian and Turkish tiles; and a wide selection of Chinese pieces.

FURNITURE AND DESIGN

THERE ARE 37 galleries containing a vast array of furniture and interior design, with especially outstanding collections of 18th-century French and English pieces. Fully furnished interiors offer a vivid re-creation of social life through their displays of furniture, paintings, pottery and other domestic objects – one fine example is a room from La Tournerie, near Alençon, in France (Room 3A). The V&A also has a wide collection of musical instruments including virginals, lutes, flutes, barytons, musical boxes, harps and a Dutch "giraffe" piano with six percussion pedals that ring bells, drum and buzz.

Russian porcelain (1862)

METALWORK

INTRICATELY WROUGHT CUPS and decanters, medals, snuff-boxes, arms and armour, hunting horns, watches and clocks are among more than 35,000 objects from Europe and the Near East which are on display across 22 of the museum's galleries. Highlights include the 16th-century Burghley Nef (Room 26), a great silver salt cellar which was used to indicate the position of the host at the dinner table; the 15th-century German Castle Cup (Room 27), a castellated, turreted copper gilt extravaganza; and the Ashburnham Centrepiece, an 18th-century silver tureen in Rococo style.

THE GREAT BED OF WARE

Made in about 1590 of oak with inlaid and painted decoration, the Great Bed of Ware measures some 3.6 by 3.6 m (12 by 12 ft) and is 2.6 m (8 ft 9 inches) high. It is the V&A's most celebrated piece of furniture. Elaborately carved and decorated, the bed is a superb example of the art of the English wood-worker. Its name derives from the town of Ware in Hertfordshire, about a day's ride north of London, where it resided in a number of inns. The Great Bed's enormous size made it an early tourist attraction, and no doubt interest in it was boosted by Shakespeare's reference to it in *Twelfth Night*, which he wrote in 1601.

The bed was draped with curtains when in use.

Tippoo's Tiger, carved in wood for the Sultan of Mysore in about 1790, is depicted mauling an Englishman.

INDIAN ART

THE NEHRU GALLERY of Indian Art forms the centrepiece of the museum's extensive collection of Indian art from 1550 to 1900, a period that includes the opulent Mughal Empire and the India of the British Raj. Textiles, weapons, jewellery, metalwork, glass and paintings, both secular and religious, are on display. Highlights of the collection include a Mughal tent of hanging painted cotton (1640) decorated with birds, trees and a double-headed eagle (Room 41). Also look out for an 11th-century bronze depicting the Hindu deity Shiva as Lord of the Eternal Dance (Room 47B).

Indian panel of painted and dyed cotton from the 18th century

TEXTILES AND DRESS

THE WORLD-RENOWNED Dress Collection, displayed in Room 40, is devoted to fashionable clothing from about 1600 to the present day. The figures are fully dressed, complete with accessories; in addition, small cases display collections of such items as buttons, shoes, hats and parasols. The scope of the textile collection, displayed in 18 galleries, is worldwide,

starting with ancient Egypt. English textiles of the last three centuries are particularly well represented.

The four great medieval tapestries in Room 94, from the collection of the Duke of Devonshire, depict fascinating scenes of courtly pastimes, while the Syon Cope, from 1300–20, is an exquisite example of *opus anglicanum*, a type of English embroidery which was popular in Europe during the Middle Ages.

FAR EASTERN ART

EIGHT GALLERIES are devoted to the arts of China, Japan, Korea and other Far Eastern countries. Under a dramatic arc of burnished steel fins representing the spine of a Chinese dragon, the T T Tsui Gallery of Chinese Art shows how the artefacts displayed would have been used in everyday life. Among the highlights of the collection are a giant Buddha's head from 700–900 AD, a huge Ming canopied bed, and rare jade and ceramics (Room 44). Japanese art is concentrated in the Toshiba Gallery, which is particularly notable for lacquer, ceramics, textiles,

Mantle for Buddhist priest from the mid-19th century

Samurai armour and woodblock prints. Especially fine exhibits include a 17th-century wooden writing table inlaid with gold and silver lacquer and the Akita Armour, dating from 1714, both in Room 38A.

PAINTINGS, PRINTS, DRAWINGS AND PHOTOGRAPHS

THESE COLLECTIONS are housed in the Henry Cole Wing. The highlights include British paintings from 1700 to 1900, some wonderful English portrait miniatures, European paintings between 1500 and 1900, and the largest collection of paintings and drawings by John Constable. The Print Room is a public study room for the museum's collection of more than half a million watercolours, engravings, etchings and even playing cards and wallpapers.

Nicholas Hilliard's *A Young Man Among Roses* **(1588)**

Natural History Museum ❶

See pp204–5.

Relief: Natural History Museum

Science Museum ❷

See pp208–9.

Victoria and Albert Museum ❸

See pp198–201.

Brompton Oratory ❹

Brompton Rd SW7. **Map** 19 A1.
📞 0171-589 4811. 🚇 South
Kensington. **Open** 6.30am–8pm daily.
✝ 11am Sun sung Latin Mass. ♿

THE ITALIANATE Oratory is a
rich (some think too rich)
monument to the English
Catholic revival of the late
19th century. The Oratory
was established by John
Henry Newman (who later
became Cardinal Newman).
Father Frederick William
Faber (1814–63) had founded
a London community of
priests at Charing Cross. The
community had moved to
Brompton, then an outlying
London district, and this was
to be its oratory. Newman
and Faber (both Anglican
converts to Catholicism) were
following the example of St
Philip Neri, who established a
community of secular priests
living without vows and
based in large cities.

The present church was
opened in 1884. Its facade
and dome were added in
the 1890s, and the interior
has been progressively
enriched ever since. Herbert
Gribble, the architect, yet
another convert to
Catholicism, was 29 when
he won the competition
to design it.

Inside, the most
important treasures
predate the church –
many of them were
bought from churches
in Italy. Giuseppe
Mazzuoli carved the
huge marble figures
of the 12 apostles for
Siena Cathedral in the
late 17th century. The
elaborate Lady Altar was
created in 1693 for the
Dominican church in Brescia,
and the 18th-century altar in
St Wilfrid's Chapel is from
Rochefort in Belgium.

The Oratory has always
been famous for its splendid
musical tradition.

The sumptuous interior of Brompton Oratory

Royal College of Music ❺

Prince Consort Rd SW7. **Map** 10 F5.
📞 0171-589 3643. 🚇 High St
Kensington, Knightsbridge, South
Kensington. **Museum of Musical
Instruments open** 2–4.30pm Wed in
term time. **Adm charge**. 🚫 ▯

SIR ARTHUR BLOMFIELD
designed the turretted
Gothic palace, with Bavarian
overtones, that has housed
this distinguished institution
since 1894. The college was
founded in 1882 by George
Grove, who also compiled
the famous *Dictionary of
Music*; famous pupils have
included English composers
Benjamin Britten and Ralph
Vaughan Williams.

You have to be smart to
catch the Museum of
Musical Instruments, which
is rarely open; but, if
you do manage to get
in, you will see
instruments dating
from the earliest times
and from many parts of
the world. Some of
the exhibits were
played by great
musicians such as
Handel and Haydn.

**17th-century viol at the
Royal College of Music**

National Sound Archive ❻

29 Exhibition Rd SW7. **Map** 11 A5.
📞 0171-589 6603. 🚇 South
Kensington. **Open** 10am–5pm
Mon–Fri, 10am–9pm Thu (last adm:
4.45pm). **Closed** public hols. 📷

THIS BRANCH OF the British
Library contains 900,000
discs, some dating from the
very start of recording in the
1890s. The 80,000 hours of
tape and 6,000 videos include
an 1880s recording of Queen
Victoria. The archive has a
reference library, and anything in the collection can be
heard by prior appointment.
There is a small exhibition of
early gramophones, phon-
ographs and other objects
including a German machine
for children that played
chocolate records (1903).

Joseph Durham's statue of Prince Albert (1858) by the Royal Albert Hall

Royal Albert Hall ●

Kensington Gore SW7. **Map** 10 F5.
☎ 0171-589 3203. ⊖ *High St
Kensington, South Kensington
Knightsbridge.* **Open** *for
performances and guided tours*
☎ 0171-589 8212. ⏊ ⚫ ▣ *See
Entertainment pp330–1.*

Designed by an engineer,
Francis Fowke, and
completed in 1871, this huge
concert hall was modelled on
Roman amphitheatres and is
easier on the eye than most
Victorian structures. On the
red-brick exterior the only
ostentation is a pretty frieze
symbolizing the triumph of
arts and science. In plans the
building was called the Hall
of Arts and Science but
Queen Victoria changed it to
the Albert Hall, in memory of
her husband, when she laid
the foundation stone in 1868.
   The hall is often used for
Classical concerts, most
famously the "Proms", but it
also accommodates every
other kind of large gathering
from boxing matches (first
held here in 1919) to major
business conferences.

Royal College of Art ●

Kensington Gore SW7. **Map** 10 F5.
☎ 0171-584 5020. ⊖ *High St
Kensington, South Kensington,
Knightsbridge.* **Open** *8.30am–10pm,
Mon–Fri (phone first).* ▣ ▣
*Lectures, events, film
presentations, exhibitions.*

Sir Hugh Casson's mainly
glass-fronted building
(1973) is in stark contrast to
the Victoriana around it. The
college was founded in 1837
as a school of design and
practical art for the manufacturing industries. It became
noted for modern art in the
1950s and 1960s when David
Hockney, Peter Blake and
Eduardo Paolozzi were there.

Albert Memorial ●

South Carriage Drive, Kensington
Gdns SW7. **Map** 10 F5. ⊖ *High St
Kensington, Knightsbridge, South
Kensington. Undergoing restoration
until 1995.*

This grandiose memorial to
Queen Victoria's beloved
consort was completed in
1876. Albert was a German
prince and a cousin of Queen
Victoria's. When he died from
typhoid in 1861 he was 41
and they had been happily
married for 21 years with nine
children. It is fitting that the
monument is near the site of
the 1851 Exhibition *(see
pp26–7),* for Prince Albert was
closely identified with it and
with the scientific advances it
celebrated. The larger than
life statue, by John Foley,
shows him with an exhibition
catalogue on his knee.
   The desolate Queen chose
Sir George Gilbert Scott to
design the monument which
stands 55 m (175 ft) high. It is
loosely based on a medieval
market cross – although many
times more elaborate, with a
black and gilded spire, multi-
coloured marble canopy,
stones, mosaics, enamels,
wrought iron and nearly 200
sculpted figures. The steps
around it are guarded by four
groups symbolizing Europe,
Africa, America and Asia. In
the corners Engineering,
Agriculture, Manufacturing
and Commerce are shown.

Victoria and Albert at the Great
Exhibition opening (1851)

Natural History Museum ❶

Museum's main entrance

L IFE ON EARTH and the Earth itself are vividly explained at the Natural History Museum. Combining the latest interactive techniques with traditional displays, the exhibits tackle some fundamental issues, such as the delicate ecology of our planet and its gradual evolution over millions of years, the origin of species and how humans beings evolved. The vast, cathedral-like museum building is a masterpiece in itself. It opened in 1881 and was designed by Alfred Waterhouse using revolutionary Victorian building techniques. It is built on an iron and steel framework concealed behind arches and columns, richly decorated with sculptures of plants and animals.

★ **Creepy Crawlies**
Eight out of ten animal species are arthropods from the world of insects and spiders, like this tarantula.

First floor

Ground floor

★ **New Dinosaur Exhibition**
The killer dinosaur Deinonychus is one of the life-size robotic models in the display, opened in 1992.

GALLERY GUIDE

*The museum is divided into Life and Earth Galleries, with the Life Gallery housed in the main body of the building. A 26-m (85-ft) skeleton of the dinosaur Diplodocus dominates the entrance hall (**10**). Left are Dinosaurs; Human Biology (**22**), Marine Invertebrates (**23**); and Discovering Mammals (**24**). To the right are Ecology (**32**) and Creepy Crawlies (**33**). Reptiles and Fish (**12**) are behind the main hall. The basement houses a Discovery Centre for children.*

*On the first floor are found Origin of Species (**105**), and the Mammal Balcony (**107**). British Natural History (**202**) is on the second floor.*

*The Earth Galleries are to the right of the entrance hall in a separate wing, and house Treasures of the Earth (**73**) and The Story of the Earth (**71**).*

Main entrance

Access to basement

★ **Ecology Gallery**
A moonlit rainforest buzzing with the sounds of life begins an exploration of the complex web of the natural world and man's role in it.

Mammal Balcony
An Indian elephant, a rare white rhino and a dugong, almost as rare, are among the wide variety of mammals on display in this gallery.

VISITORS' CHECKLIST

Cromwell Rd SW7. **Map** 19 A1.
0171-938 9123.
0426 927654 South Kensington. 14, 30, 45A, 49, 74, 264, 349, C1.
Open 10am–5.50pm Mon–Sat, 11am–5.50pm Sun. **Closed** 24–26 Dec, 1 Jan. **Adm charge** but free 4.30–6pm Mon–Fri, 5–6pm Sat, Sun, public hols.
 Lectures, film presentations.

Second floor Earth Galleries

Second floor

First floor Earth Galleries

General Library

Access to Earth Galleries

British Natural History
Detailed displays show animal, insect and plant life in characteristic habitats throughout the British Isles. This butterfly is one of many surprisingly exotic creatures exhibited here.

Earth Galleries
Three galleries explore the story of our planet and its wealth of natural resources. This malachite is one of thousands of mineral and gem specimens.

Exhibition Road entrance to Earth Galleries

Bird Gallery
This traditional display, with many species in glass cases, includes the extinct dodo.

KEY TO FLOORPLAN

☐ Life Galleries
☐ Earth Galleries

STAR EXHIBITS

★ **New Dinosaur Exhibition**

★ **Creepy Crawlies**

★ **Ecology Gallery**

Statue of young Queen Victoria by her daughter Princess Louise outside Kensington Palace

Serpentine Gallery ⑩

Kensington Gdns W2. **Map** 10 F4.
📞 0171-402 6075. ⊖ *Lancaster Gate, South Kensington.* **Open** 10am–6pm daily. **Closed** for exhibition installations, Christmas week. ♿ 📖 **Lectures** on current exhibition 3pm Sun.

IN THE SOUTHEAST corner of Kensington Gardens is the Serpentine Gallery, which houses temporary exhibitions of contemporary painting and sculpture. The building is a former tea pavilion built in 1912; exhibits often spill out into the surrounding park. Its tiny bookshop has a remarkable stock of art books.

Kensington Palace ⑪

Kensington Palace Gdns W8.
Map 10 D4. 📞 0171-937 9561.
⊖ *High St Kensington, Queensway.* **Open** 9am–5pm Mon–Sat, 11am–5pm Sun (last adm: 4.15pm). **Closed** 24–26 Dec, 1 Jan, Good Fri. **Adm charge.** 🚫 ♿ ground floor only. 📷 📖 **Exhibitions, holiday activities.**

HALF OF THIS SPACIOUS palace is used as lavish royal apartments: Princess Margaret has a base here. The other half, which includes the 18th-century state rooms, is open to the public. When William III and his wife Mary came to the throne in 1689 they bought a mansion, dating from 1605,

and commissioned Christopher Wren to convert it into a royal palace. He created separate suites of rooms for the king and queen, and today visiting members of public use the queen's entrance – note the William and Mary monogram over the door.

The palace has seen some important royal events. In 1714 Queen Anne died here from a fit of apoplexy brought on by over-eating and, on 20 June 1837, Princess Victoria of Kent was woken at 5am to be told that her uncle William IV had died and she was now queen – the start of her 64-year reign.

Highlights of the palace are the finely decorated state rooms and, on the ground floor, a fascinating exhibition of court dress from 1760 to the present, culminating in the Princess of Wales's wedding dress from 1981.

Detail of the Coalbrookdale gate, Kensington Gardens

Henry Moore's *Arch* (1979), Kensington Gardens

Kensington Gardens ⑫

W8. **Map** 10 E4. 📞 0171-262 5484.
⊖ *Bayswater, High St Kensington, Queensway, Lancaster Gate.* **Open** 5am–midnight daily.

THE FORMER GROUNDS of Kensington Palace became a public park in 1841 and now merge imperceptibly into Hyde Park to the east. The gardens are full of charm, starting with Sir George Frampton's statue (1912) of J M Barrie's fictional Peter Pan, the boy who never grew up, playing his pipes to the bronze fairies and animals that cling to the column below him. Often surrounded by parents, nannies and their charges, the statue stands near the west bank of the Serpentine, not far from where Harriet, wife of the poet Percy Bysshe Shelley drowned herself in 1816.

Just north of here are the ornamental fountains and statues, including Jacob Epstein's *Rima*, at the lake's head. George Frederick Watts's statue of a muscular horse and rider, *Physical Energy*, stands to the south. Not far away are a summer house designed by William Kent in 1735 and the Serpentine Gallery.

The Round Pond, created in 1728 just east of the palace, is often packed with model boats navigated by children and older enthusiasts. In winter it is occasionally fit for skating. In the north, near Lancaster Gate, is a dogs' cemetery, started in 1880 by the Duke of Cambridge while mourning one of his pets.

Hyde Park ⓭

W2. **Map** 11 B3. **⌂** *0171-262 5484.* **⊖** *Hyde Park Corner, Knightsbridge, Lancaster Gate, Marble Arch.* **Open** *5am–midnight daily.* **□** ***Sporting facilities***. *See also **Five Guided Walks** pp 260–1.*

Riding on Rotten Row, Hyde Park

Tʜᴇ ᴀɴᴄɪᴇɴᴛ ᴍᴀɴᴏʀ of Hyde was part of the lands of Westminster Abbey seized by Henry VIII at the Dissolution of the Monasteries in 1536. It has remained a royal park ever since. Henry used it for hunting but James I opened it to the public in the early 17th century, and it became one of the city's most prized public spaces. The Serpentine, an artificial lake used for boating and bathing, was created when Caroline, George II's queen, dammed the flow of the Westbourne River in 1730.

In its time the park has been a venue for duelling, horse racing, highwaymen, political demonstrations, music (Mick Jagger and Luciano Pavarotti have each had a concert here) and parades. The 1851 Exhibition was held here in a vast glass palace *(see pp26–7)*. The aristocracy drove their carriages on the outer roads.

Speakers' Corner ⓮

Hyde Park W2. **Map** 11 C2. **⊖** *Marble Arch.*

Aɴ 1872 ʟᴀᴡ made it legal to assemble an audience and address them on whatever topic you chose; since then this corner of Hyde Park has become the established venue for budding orators and a fair number of eccentrics. It is well worth spending time here on a Sunday: speakers from fringe groups and one-member political parties reveal their plans for the betterment of mankind while the assembled onlookers heckle them without mercy.

Marble Arch ⓯

Park Lane W1. **Map** 11 C2. **⊖** *Marble Arch.*

Jᴏʜɴ ɴᴀsʜ designed the arch in 1827 as the main entrance to Buckingham Palace. It was, however, too narrow for the grandest coaches and was moved here in 1851. Now, only senior members of the Royal Family and one of the royal artillery regiments are allowed to pass under it.

The arch stands near the site of the old Tyburn gallows (marked by a plaque), where until 1783 the city's most notorious criminals were hanged in front of crowds of bloodthirsty spectators.

An orator at Speakers' Corner

Harrod's ⓰

Knightsbridge SW1. **Map** 11 C5. **⌂** *0171-730 1234.* **⊖** *Knightsbridge.* **Open** *10am–6pm Mon–Tue, 10am–7pm Wed–Sat.* **⌀ ⛾ ⑪ □** *See **Shops and Markets** p311.*

Lᴏɴᴅᴏɴ's ᴍᴏsᴛ ꜰᴀᴍᴏᴜs department store had beginnings in 1849 when Henry Charles Harrod opened a small grocery shop nearby on Brompton Road. By concentrating on good quality and impeccable service (rather than on low prices) the store was soon popular enough to expand over the surrounding area.

It used to be claimed that Harrod's could supply anything from a packet of pins to an elephant – not quite true today, but the range of stock is still phenomenal.

Harrod's at night, lit by 11,500 lights

Science Museum ❷

Cᴇɴᴛᴜʀɪᴇꜱ ᴏꜰ ᴄᴏɴᴛɪɴᴜɪɴɢ scientific and technological development lie at the heart of the Science Museum's massive collections. The hardware on show is magnificent: steam engines, the earliest and the latest computers, spacecraft – the list is endless. Equally important is the social context of science – what discoveries and inventions mean for day-to-day life – and the process of discovery itself. Exciting interactive displays enable visitors to take part in scientific enquiry themselves.

Science Museum facade

★ Launch Pad
A plasma ball is one of many hands-on exhibits for children in this first-floor gallery where basic scientific principles are demonstrated.

★ Glimpses of Medical History
A 17th-century Italian vase for storing snake bite potion is part of this fascinating collection.

Computing Then and Now
reveals the history of counting machines and computers from the abacus onwards.

GALLERY GUIDE
There are five floors. In the basement is the Children's Gallery, with many working demonstrations; there are also displays of domestic appliances through the ages. Big machines – steam engines, locomotives, cars – dominate the ground floor; here too are displays on space exploration and fire-fighting. The first floor has exhibits on telecommunications, iron and steel, gas and food. On the second floor are such diverse galleries as nuclear power, ships, printing and computing. On the third floor is the new flight gallery which opened in 1992, along with photography, optics and electricity. The smaller fourth and fifth floors house the medical galleries, featuring many fascinating full-scale reconstructions.

★ The Exploration of Space
Apollo 10 took US astronauts around the moon in May 1969, and now forms part of an exhibition on people and space.

Main entrance

VISITORS' CHECKLIST

Exhibition Rd SW7. **Map** 19 A1.
0171-938 8000. South
Kensington. 14, 45A, 49, 74,
349, C1. **Open** 10am–6pm Mon–
Sat, 11am–6pm Sun. **Closed**
24–26 Dec. **Adm charge.**
Lectures, film shows,
activity workshops,
demonstrations.

★ Flight
A replica of one of Otto Lilienthal's gliders (1895) is one of the displays that range from man's early dreams of flight to today's jets.

Navigation and Surveying
The display of navigational and surveying aids includes this ornately decorated circumferentor (1676) by the architect Joannes Macarius.

Food for Thought
The science of food is explored through demonstrations and historic reconstructions, such as this 18th-century kitchen.

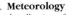

Meteorology
There is a rich collection of weather instruments and other exhibits, like this 16th-century watercolour of a comet.

KEY TO FLOORPLAN

- Basement
- Ground floor
- First floor
- Second floor
- Third floor
- Fourth floor
- Fifth floor

★ Land Transport
Exhibits here include early cars, motorbikes, a tram and this prototype British Deltic locomotive (1956).

STAR EXHIBITS

- ★ Launch Pad
- ★ The Exploration of Space
- ★ Land Transport
- ★ Flight
- ★ Glimpses of Medical History

KENSINGTON AND HOLLAND PARK

THE WESTERN and northern perimeters of Kensington Gardens are a rich residential area including many foreign embassies. Here, the shops on Kensington High Street are almost as smart as the ones on Knightsbridge, and Kensington Church Street is a good source of quality antiques. Around Holland Park are some magnificent late Victorian houses, two of them open to the public. But as you cross into Bayswater and Notting Hill you enter a more vibrant, cosmopolitan part of London. Its stucco terraces are lined with medium-priced hotels and a huge number of inexpensive restaurants. There has always been

Tiled crest from Holland House

something rather furtive about Bayswater. Victorian men would keep mistresses in its terraces; the Profumo sex scandal (1963) that toppled a government occurred here and today prostitution remains a major, if discreet, local industry. Its high street, Queensway, is a centre of club life and café society, while further west Portobello Road is a popular street market. Many West Indians settled in Notting Hill in the 1950s and for three days every August its streets are home to a lively Caribbean carnival *(see p57).*

SIGHTS AT A GLANCE

Historic Streets and Buildings
Holland House ❷
Leighton House ❸
Commonwealth Institute ❹
Linley Sambourne House ❺
Kensington Square ❻
Kensington Palace Gardens ❼
Queensway ❽

Parks and Gardens
Holland Park ❶

Markets
Portobello Road ❾

Historic Areas
Notting Hill ❿

GETTING THERE
The District, Circle and Central lines serve the area. Bus numbers 9, 10, 73, 27, 28, 49, 52, 70, C1, 31 stop on Kensington High Street; 12, 27, 28, 31, 52, 70, 94, go to Notting Hill Gate; and 70, 7, 15, 23, 27, 36, 12, 94 cross Bayswater.

KEY
- Street-by-Street map
- ⊖ Underground station

SEE ALSO
- **Street Finder**, maps 9, 17
- **Where to Stay** pp276–7
- **Restaurants** pp292–4

0 metres   500
0 yards   500

Entrance to a house in Edwardes Square, Kensington

Street-by-Street: Kensington and Holland Park

ALTHOUGH NOW PART OF central London, as recently as the 1830s this was a country village of market gardens and mansions. Outstanding among these was Holland House; part of its grounds are now Holland Park. The area grew up rapidly in the mid-19th century and most of its buildings date from then – mainly expensive apartments, mansion flats and fashionable shops.

Holland House
The rambling Jacobean mansion, started in 1605 and pictured here in 1795, was largely demolished in the 1950s ❷

★ **Holland Park**
Parts of the old formal gardens of Holland House have been retained to grace this delightful public park ❶

The Orangery, now a restaurant, has parts that date from the 1630s when it was in the grounds of Holland House.

Melbury Road is lined with large, Victorian houses. Many were built for fashionable artists of the time.

Commonwealth Institute
Exhibits capture the exotic flavour of the countries that were once British colonies ❹

The Victorian letter box on the High Street is one of the oldest in London.

★ **Leighton House**
It is preserved as it was when the Victorian painter, Lord Leighton, lived here. He had a passion for Middle Eastern tiles ❸

**No. 16
Phillimore Place** was home to the author of the children's classic *The Wind in the Willows,* from 1901 until 1908.

Church Walk leads to Church Street, which is lined with antique shops *(see p321).*

LOCATOR MAP
See Central London Map pp12–13

Kensington High Street station

Kensington Civic Centre, an assertive modern building by Sir Basil Spence, was completed in 1976.

Linley Sambourne House
Its carefully preserved late Victorian interior remains intact, complete with original furnishings and draperies ❺

Drayson Mews is one of the quaint alleys that were built behind large town houses for the stabling of horses and coaches. Today most have been converted into small houses.

Sticky Fingers, a lively café on the corner of Phillimore Gardens, is owned by Bill Wyman, former guitarist with the *Rolling Stones* rock group.

STAR SIGHTS
★ **Holland Park**
★ **Leighton House**

KEY

— — — Suggested route

0 metres — 100
0 yards — 100

Holland Park **1**

Abbotsbury Rd W14. **Map** 9 B4.
📞 *0171-602 9487.* 🚇 *Holland Park,
High St Kensington, Notting Hill Gate.*
Open *Apr–late Oct: 7.30am–10pm
daily (but flexible); late Oct–Mar:
7.30am–4.30pm (11pm floodlit areas).*
🍴 🎭 *Open-air opera, theatre,
dance. **Art exhibitions** Apr–Oct.
See **Entertainment** pp326–7.*

Tʜɪs sᴍᴀʟʟ but delightful
park, more wooded and
intimate than the large royal
parks to its east (Hyde Park
and Kensington Gardens,
see pp206–7), was opened in
1952 on what remained of the
grounds of Holland House –
the rest had been sold off in
the late 19th century for the
construction of large houses
and terraces to the north and
west. The park still contains
some of the formal gardens,
laid out in the early 19th
century for Holland House.
There is also a Japanese
garden, created for the 1991
London Festival of Japan. The
park has an abundance of
wildlife, including peacocks.

Holland House **2**

Holland Park W8. **Map** 9 B5. **Youth
Hostel** 📞 *0171-937 0748.* 🚇
*Holland Park, High St Kensington. See
Where to Stay p275.* ♿

Original tiling in Holland House

Dᴜʀɪɴɢ ɪᴛs ʜᴇʏᴅᴀʏ in the
19th century, this was a
noted centre of social and
political intrigue. Statesmen
such as Lord Palmerston
mixed here with the likes of
the poet Byron. The remains
of the house are now used as
a youth hostel.
    The outhouses are put to
various uses: exhibitions are
held in the orangery and the
ice house (a forerunner of the
fridge), and the old Garden
Ballroom is now a restaurant.

The café in Holland Park

Leighton House **3**

12 Holland Park Rd W14. **Map** 17 B1.
📞 *0171-602 3316.* 🚇 *High St
Kensington.* **Open** *11am–5.30pm
Mon–Sat.* **Closed** *public hols.*
📷 🎫 🚻 *Concerts, exhibitions.*

Bᴜɪʟᴛ ғᴏʀ Pre-Raphaelite
painter Lord Leighton in
1866, the house has been
preserved, with its opulent
decoration almost intact, as
an extraordinary monument
to the Victorian Aesthetic
movement. The highlight is
the Arab hall, which Leighton
added in 1879 to house his
stupendous collection of
Islamic tiles, some of which
are inscribed with quotations
from the Koran. The best
paintings, including some by
Edward Burne-Jones, John
Millais and Lord Leighton
himself, can be seen in the
downstairs reception rooms.

Commonwealth Institute **4**

Kensington High St W8. **Map** 9 C5.
📞 *0171-603 4535.* 🚇 *High St
Kensington.* **Open** *10am–5pm
Mon–Sat, 2–5pm Sun.* **Closed** *24–26
Dec, 1 Jan, Good Fri, May Day.*
♿ *phone first.* 🍴 🚻 📷 🎫
Lectures, concerts, workshops.

Iɴ 1962, the Commonwealth
Institute replaced the old
Imperial Institute (founded in
1887). It is housed in a tent-
like building, erected in 1962,
and includes displays on the
history, industries and culture
of the 50 member nations of
the Commonwealth. As well

as the permanent displays
there are temporary art
exhibitions and live music
from Commonwealth grou

Linley Sambourn House **5**

18 Stafford Terrace W8. **Map** 9 C
📞 *0181-994 1019.* 🚇 *High St
Kensington.* **Open** *1 Mar–31 Oct.
10am–4pm Wed, 2–5pm Sun.* **Clo**
1 Nov–28 Feb. **Adm charge.** 🚫

Tʜᴇ ʜᴏᴜsᴇ, built in about
1870, has hardly change
since Linley Sambourne
furnished it in the cluttered
Victorian manner, with chi
ornaments and heavy velve
drapes. Sambourne was a
cartoonist for the satirical
magazine *Punch* and drawin
including some of his own
cram the walls. Some room
have William Morris wallpa
(see p245), and even the
lavatory is a Victorian gem

**Logo for
Punch
magazine
(1841–1992)**

Kensington Square ❻

W8. **Map** 10 D5. ⊖ *High St Kensington.*

THIS IS ONE of London's oldest squares. It was laid out in the 1680s, and a few early 18th-century houses remain. (Nos. 11 and 12 are the oldest.) The renowned philosopher John Stuart Mill lived at No. 18, and the Pre-Raphaelite painter and illustrator Edward Burne-Jones at No. 41.

JOHN STUART MILL
1806-1873
Philosopher
Lived Here

Resident's plaque in Kensington Square

Kensington Palace Gardens ❼

W8. **Map** 10 D3. ⊖ *High St Kensington, Notting Hill Gate, Queensway.*

THIS PRIVATE ROAD of luxury mansions is on the site of the former kitchen gardens of Kensington Palace *(see p206)*.

It changes its name half-way down; the southern part is known as Palace Green. It is open to pedestrians but closed to cars, unless they have specific business here. Most of the houses are occupied by embassies and their staff. At the cocktail hour, watch the black limousines with their diplomatic number plates sweep beneath the raised barriers at each end of the road.

Queensway ❽

W2. **Map** 10 D2. ⊖ *Queensway, Bayswater.*

ONE OF LONDON'S most cosmopolitan streets, Queensway has the heaviest concentration of eating places anywhere except Soho. At newsagents, you may see more Arabic and European than British newspapers on sale. At the northern end is the domed Whiteley's shopping centre. Founded by

Queensway shopfront

William Whiteley, who was born in Yorkshire in 1863, it was probably the world's first department store. The present building dates from 1911.

The street is named after Queen Victoria, who rode here as a princess.

Portobello Road ❾

W11. **Map** 9 C3. ⊖ *Notting Hill Gate, Ladbroke Grove.* **Antiques market open** *9.30am–4pm Fri, 8am–5pm Sat. See also **Shops and Markets** p323.*

THERE HAS been a market here since 1837. The southern end today consists almost exclusively of stalls selling antiques, jewellery, souvenirs and many other collectables popular with tourists. The market is crowded on summer weekends, but is worth visiting for its bustling and cheerful atmosphere even if you don't intend to buy. If you do, you are unlikely to get a real bargain, since the stallholders have a sound idea of the value of what they sell.

Notting Hill ❿

W11. **Map** 9 C3. ⊖ *Notting Hill Gate.*

NOW THE HOME of Europe's biggest street carnival, most of this area was farmland until the 19th century.

In the 1950s and 1960s Notting Hill became a centre for the Caribbean community, many of whom lived here when they first arrived in Britain. The carnival started in 1966 and takes over the area every August over the holiday weekend *(see p57)* when costumed parades flood through the streets.

Antique shop on Portobello Road

REGENT'S PARK AND MARYLEBONE

THE AREA south of Regent's Park, incorporating the medieval village of Marylebone, has London's highest concentration of quality Georgian housing. It was developed by Robert Harley, Earl of Oxford, as London shifted west in the 18th century. Terraces by John Nash adorn the southern edge of Regent's Park, the busiest of the royal parks, while to its northwest lies St John's Wood, a smart inner suburb.

GETTING THERE

Regent's Park and Great Portland Street are the nearest tube stations. Marylebone is served by tube and British Rail. Buses 13, 139 and 159 run from Trafalgar Square to near Baker Street, and numerous buses run along Oxford Street.

SIGHTS AT A GLANCE

Historic Streets and Buildings

Harley Street ④
Portland Place ⑤
Broadcasting House ⑥
Cumberland Terrace ⑮

Museums and Galleries

Wallace Collection ⑩
Sherlock Holmes Museum ⑪

Churches and Mosques

St Marylebone Parish Church ③
All Souls, Langham Place ⑦
London Central Mosque ⑫

Parks and Gardens

Regent's Park ②

Entertainment

Madame Tussauds and the Planetarium ①
Wigmore Hall ⑨
London Zoo ⑭

Historic Hotels

Langham Hilton Hotel ⑧

Historic Waterways

Regent's Canal ⑬

KEY

Street-by-Street map

⊖ Underground station

P Parking

0 metres   500
0 yards   500

SEE ALSO

- **Street Finder**, maps 3, 4, 12
- **Where to Stay** pp276–7
- **Restaurants** pp292–4
- **Regent's Canal Walk** pp262–3

St Andrew's Place, Regent's Park

Street-by-Street: Marylebone

Sⁿᵗ SOUTH OF REGENT'S PARK, the medieval village of
Marylebone (originally Maryburne, the stream by
St Mary's church) has London's highest concentration of genteel Georgian housing. Until the 18th
century it was surrounded by fields and a pleasure
garden, but these were built over as fashionable
London drifted west. In the mid-19th century,
professional people, especially doctors,
used the spacious houses to receive
wealthy clients. The area has maintained
both its medical connection and its elegance.

**Tiananmen
Square
memorial:
Portland Place**

★ Regent's Park
*John Nash laid out the
royal park in 1812 as
a setting for Classically
designed villas and
terraces* ❷

**The Royal Academy of
Music,** England's first
music academy, was
founded in 1774. The
present brick building,
with its own concert
hall, is from 1911.

**★ Madame Tussauds and the
Planetarium**
*The wax museum of famous people,
historical and contemporary, is one
of London's most popular attractions.
Next door, a planetarium shows
models of the sky at night* ❶

**To Regent's
Park**

**St Marylebone Parish
Church**
*Poets Robert Browning
and Elizabeth Barrett
married in this church* ❸

KEY

- - - Suggested route

**Baker Street
station**

| 0 metres | 100 |
| 0 yards | 100 |

Park Crescent's breathtaking facades by Nash have been preserved, although the interiors were rebuilt as offices in the 1960s. The crescent seals the north end of Nash's ceremonial route from St James's to Regent's Park, via Regent Street and Portland Place.

LOCATOR MAP
See Central London Map pp12–13

The London Clinic is one of the best-known private hospitals in this medical district.

Regent's Park station

Portland Place
In the centre of this broad street stands a statue of Field Marshal Sir George Stuart White, who won the Victoria Cross for gallantry in the Afghan War of 1879 **5**

The Royal Institute of British Architects is housed in a controversial Art Deco building designed by Grey Wornum in 1934.

Harley Street
Consulting rooms of eminent medical specialists have been here for more than a century **4**

STAR SIGHTS

★ Madame Tussauds and the Planetarium

★ Regent's Park

Mme Tussauds and the Planetarium ❶

Marylebone Rd NW1. **Map** 4 D5.
☎ 0171-935 6861. ⊖ Baker St.
Open 9.30am–5.30 pm daily.
Closed 25 Dec. **Adm charge.**
♿ phone first. 📷 🖥 🚻

MADAME TUSSAUD began her wax-modelling career taking death masks of many of the best-known victims of the French Revolution. In 1835 she set up an exhibition of her work in Baker Street, not far from the collection's present site.

The 1990s collection still relies upon traditional wax-modelling techniques to recreate the razzmatazz of politicians, film and television actors, rock stars and sporting heroes.

The main sections of the exhibition are the "Garden Party", where visitors mingle with extraordinarily lifelike models of celebrities; "Super Stars", devoted to the giants of the entertainment world;

Traditional wax-modelling at Madame Tussauds

and the "Grand Hall", containing a collection of royalty, statesmen and world leaders, writers and artists. Where else do Lenin, Martin Luther King and William Shakespeare all rub shoulders?

The Chamber of Horrors is the most renowned part of Madame Tussauds. It includes recreations of the most gruesome episodes in the grim catalogue of crime and punishment: the murderers Dr Crippen and Ethel le Nève;

Gary Gilmore facing a firing squad; and the chill gloom of a Victorian street in Jack the Ripper's London.

The "Spirit of London" is the finale. Visitors travel in stylized London taxi-cabs and participate in momentous events of the city, from the Great Fire of 1666 to 1960s Swinging London.

Situated next door, and part of the same great complex, is the London Planetarium, where a spectacular star show explores and reveals some of the mysteries of the planets and the solar system. The interactive Space Trail exhibition contains many detailed models of the planets, satellites and spacecraft.

Waxwork of Elizabeth II

Tulip time at Queen Mary's Gardens in Regent's Park

Regent's Park ❷

NW1. **Map** 3 C2. ☎ 0171-486 7905.
⊖ Regent's Park, Baker St, Great Portland St. **Open** 5am–dusk daily.
♿ 📷 **Open air theatre.** See **Entertainment** pp326–8.

THIS AREA OF land became enclosed as a park in 1812. John Nash designed the scheme and originally envisaged a kind of garden suburb, dotted with 56 villas in a variety of Classical styles,

with a pleasure palace for the Prince Regent. At the end of the day only eight villas – but no palace – were built inside the park (three survive round the edge of the Inner Circle).

The boating lake, which has many varieties of water birds, is marvellously romantic, especially when music drifts across from the bandstand in the distance. Queen Mary's Gardens are a mass of wonderful sights and smells in summer, when visitors

can enjoy Shakespeare productions at the Open Air Theatre nearby. Broad Walk provides a picturesque stroll north from Park Square.

Nash's master plan for Regent's Park continues just beyond its north-eastern edge in Park Village East and West. These captivating buildings in elegant stucco were completed in 1828, some adorned with Wedgwood-style medallions.

St Marylebone Parish Church ❸

Marylebone Rd NW1. **Map** 4 D5.
☎ 0171-935 7315. ⊖ Regent's Park.
Open 12.30–1.30pm Mon–Fri, Sun mornings. ♿ 📷 ✝ 11am Sun. 🍴

THIS IS WHERE the poets Robert Browning and Elizabeth Barrett were married in 1846 after eloping from her strict family home on nearby Wimpole Street. The large, stately church by Thomas Hardwick was consecrated in 1817 after the former church, where Lord Byron was christened in 1778, had become too small. Hardwick was determined that the same should not happen to his new church – so everything is on a grand scale.

Commemorative window in St Marylebone Parish Church

Harley Street ❹

W1. **Map** 4 E5. ❺ *Regent's Park, Oxford Circus, Bond St, Great Portland St.*

THE LARGE HOUSES on this late 18th-century street were popular with successful doctors and specialists in the middle of the 19th century when it was a rich residential area. The doctors' practices stayed and lend the street an air of hushed order, unusual in central London. There are very few private houses or apartments here now, but William Gladstone lived at No. 73 from 1876 to 1882.

Portland Place ❺

W1. **Map** 4 E5. ❺ *Regent's Park.*

THE ADAM BROTHERS, Robert and James, originally laid this street out in 1773. Only a few of their original houses remain, the best being Nos. 27 to 47 on the west side, south of Devonshire Street. John Nash added the street to his processional route that ran from Carlton House to Regent's Park and sealed its northern end with the Park Crescent.
    The building of the Royal Institute of British Architects (1934) at No. 66 is adorned with symbolic statues and reliefs. Its bronze front doors depict London's buildings and the River Thames.

Broadcasting House ❻

Portland Place W1. **Map** 12 E1. ❺ *Oxford Circus.* **Not open** to the public.

THIS IS THE HEADQUARTERS of the BBC's national radio services and of its senior management; the television service is located in west London, at White City. It was constructed in 1931 as a suitably modern Art Deco headquarters for the brand-new medium of broadcasting. Its front, curving with the street, is dominated by sculptor Eric Gill's stylized relief of *Prospero and Ariel*, and more Gill ornament can be seen higher up. The lobby has been carefully restored to something close to its 1930s' appearance.

All Souls, Langham Place ❼

Langham Place W1. **Map** 12 F1. ❒ *0171-580 3522.* ❺ *Oxford Circus.* **Open** *9.30am–6pm Mon–Fri, 9am–9pm Sun.* ❒ *11am Sun.* ❒

JOHN NASH designed this church in 1824. Its quirky round frontage is best seen from Regent Street. When it was first built, the spire was ridiculed as it appeared too slender and flimsy. The only Nash church in London, it has

Relief on the Royal Institute of British Architects on Portland Place

close links with the BBC opposite, at Broadcasting House, and often doubles as a recording studio, for the daily broadcast service.

Langham Hilton Hotel ❽

1 Portland Place W1. **Map** 12 E1. ❒ *0171-636 1000.* ❺ *Oxford Circus. See* **Where to Stay** *p284.*

THIS WAS LONDON'S grandest hotel after it was opened in 1865. The writers Oscar Wilde and Mark Twain and composer Antonin Dvořák were among its many distinguished guests. The hotel was, for a time, used by the BBC, but since then has been restored behind its original facade. Its marble-lined entrance hall leads into the Palm Court, where there is piano music at tea-time. Colonial days are recalled in the Memories of the Empire restaurant and the Chukka bar whose theme is the game of polo.

All Souls, Langham Place (1824)

Wigmore Hall ❾

36 Wigmore St W1. **Map** 12 E1.
【 *0171-935 2141.* ⊖ *Bond St.*
See **Entertainment** *p331.*

T HIS APPEALING little concert
hall for chamber music
was designed by T E Collcutt,
architect of the Savoy Hotel
(see p285), in 1900. At first it
was called Bechstein Hall
because it was attached to the
Bechstein piano showroom:
the area used to be the heart
of London's piano trade.
Opposite is the white-tiled Art
Nouveau emporium built in
1907 as Debenham and
Freebody's department store –
the forerunner of today's
Debenham's on Oxford Street.

Wallace Collection ❿

Hertford House, Manchester Square
W1. **Map** 12 D1. 【 *0171-935 0687.*
⊖ *Bond St.* **Open** *10am–5pm
Mon–Sat, 2–5pm Sun.* **Closed** *24–26
Dec, 1 Jan, Good Fri, May Day.* 🚫
♿ 🎥 🎧 **Lectures.**

**16th-century Italian dish from
the Wallace Collectiom**

T HIS IS ONE of the world's
finest private collections
of art. It has remained intact
since it was bequeathed to
the government in 1897 with
the stipulation that it should
go on permanent public
display with nothing added or
taken away. The product of
passionate collecting for four
generations of the Hertford
family, it is a must for anyone
with even a passing interest
in the progress of European
art up to the late 19th century.
   Most of its highlights are in
gallery 22, which contains
some 70 master works. Frans
Hals's *The Laughing Cavalier*

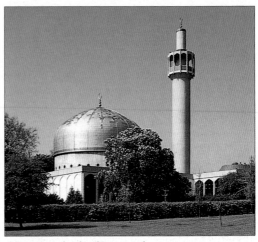

The Mosque on the edge of Regent's Park

is here, and Rembrandt's
Titus, along with Titian's
Perseus and Andromeda and
Nicolas Poussin's *A Dance to
the Music of Time.* There are
also superb English portraits
by Reynolds, Gainsborough
and Romney. The 25 galleries
contain fine Sèvres porcelain
and sculpture by Houdon,
Roubiliac and Rysbrack. There
is also an armour collection.

Sherlock Holmes Museum ⓫

221b Baker St NW1. **Map** 3 C5.
【 *0171-935 8866.* ⊖ *Baker St.*
Open *10am–6pm daily.* **Closed** *25
Dec.* **Adm charge.** 📷 🎥 🖥 🎧

S IR ARTHUR CONAN DOYLE'S
fictional detective was
supposed to have lived at
221b Baker Street – this

Conan Doyle's Sherlock Holmes

museum, which boasts the
right number, actually sits
between Nos. 237 and 239.
Visitors are greeted by
Holmes's "housekeeper" and
shown to his recreated rooms
on the first floor. The fourth
floor shop sells copies of the
stories and deerstalker hats.

London Central Mosque ⓬

146 Park Rd NW8. **Map** 3 B3.
【 *0171-724 3363.* ⊖ *Marylebone,
St John's Wood, Baker St.* **Open**
dawn–dusk daily. ♿ 🎧 **Lectures.**

S URROUNDED BY TREES on the
edge of Regent's Park, this
large, golden-domed mosque
was designed by Sir Frederick
Gibberd and completed in
1978. It was built to cater for
the increasing number of
Muslim residents and visitors
in London. The mosque's
main hall of worship, which
is capable of holding 1,800
people, is a plain square
chamber with a domed roof.
It is sparsely furnished apart
from a magnificent carpet and
a colossal chandelier. The
dome is lined in a traditional
Islamic pattern of broken
shapes, predominantly blue.
Visitors must remove their
shoes before entering the
mosque, and women, for
whom there is a separate
gallery, should also remember
to cover their heads.

Regent's Canal ⑬

NW1 & NW8. **Map** 3 C1. 📞 0171-482 0523. 🚇 Camden Town, St John's Wood, Warwick Ave. **Canal towpaths open** dawn – dusk daily. See **Five Guided Walks** pp262–3.

A boat trip on Regent's Canal

JOHN NASH was extremely enthusiastic about this waterway, opened in 1820 to link the Grand Junction Canal, which ended at Little Venice in Paddington in the west, with the London docks at Limehouse in the east. He saw it as an added attraction for his new Regent's Park, and originally wanted the canal to run through the middle of that park. He was persuaded out of that by those who thought that the bargees' bad language would offend the genteel residents of the area. Perhaps this was just as well – the steam tugs that hauled the barges were dirty and sometimes dangerous.

In 1874 a barge carrying gunpowder blew up in the cutting by London Zoo, killing the crew, destroying a bridge and terrifying the populace, and the animals. After an initial period of prosperity the canal began to be hit by increasing competition from the new railways and so gradually slipped into decline.

Today it has been revived as a leisure amenity; the towpath is paved as a pleasant walkway and short boat trips are offered between Little Venice and Camden Lock, where there is a thriving crafts market. Visitors to the zoo can use the landing stage that is situated alongside it.

London Zoo ⑭

Regent's Park NW1. **Map** 4 D2. 📞 0171-722 3333. 🚇 Camden Town. **Open** 10am – 5.30pm daily. **Adm charge**. 🍴 ▯ 📷 **Filmshows** in summer.

OPENED IN 1828, the zoo has been one of London's biggest tourist attractions ever since, and is also a major research centre. However, spectacular TV programmes on wildlife, and doubts about the ethics of keeping animals in cages, have caused attendances at the zoo to drop from their

London Zoo's aviary designed by Lord Snowdon (1964)

1950s peak of 3 million visitors a year. In recent years the future of London zoo has been subject to a great deal of uncertainty.

Cumberland Terrace ⑮

NW1. **Map** 4 E2. 🚇 Great Portland St, Regent's Park.

JAMES THOMSON is credited with the detailed design of this, the longest and most elaborate of the Nash terraces around Regent's Park. Its imposing central block of raised Ionic columns is topped with a decorated triangular pediment. Completed in 1828, it was designed to be visible from the palace Nash planned for the Prince Regent (later George IV). The palace was never built because the Prince was too busy with his plans for Buckingham Palace (see pp94–5).

Nash's Cumberland Terrace, dating from 1828

HAMPSTEAD

HAMPSTEAD HAS ALWAYS stayed aloof from London, looking down from its site on the high ridge north of the metropolis. Today it is essentially a Georgian village. The heath separating Hampstead from Highgate reinforces its appeal, isolating it further from the hurly-burly of the modern city. A stroll around the charming village streets, followed by a tramp across the heath, makes for one of the finest walks in London.

SIGHTS AT A GLANCE

Historic Streets and Buildings
Flask Walk and Well Walk **1**
Church Row **5**
Downshire Hill **6**
Vale of Health **13**

Museums and Galleries
Burgh House **2**
Fenton House **4**
Keats House **7**
Kenwood House **10**

Parks and Gardens
Hampstead Heath **8**
Parliament Hill **9**
The Hill **12**

Pubs and Restaurants
Jack Straw's Castle **3**
Spaniards Inn **11**

HAMPSTEAD HEATH

GETTING THERE
Hampstead Underground station lies on the Edgware branch of the Northern line, and there is a BR service, which stops at Hampstead Heath. Bus No. 24 operates a daily service from Victoria to Hampstead Heath, via Trafalgar Square and Tottenham Court Road.

SEE ALSO
- *Street Finder*, maps 1, 2
- *Where to Stay* pp276–7
- *Restaurants* pp292–4

KEY

▨	Street-by-Street map
⊖	Underground station
⊟	British Rail station

0 metres   500
0 yards   500

View across Hampstead Heath from Holly Hill

Street-by-Street: Hampstead

Perched awkwardly on a hilltop, with its broad heath to the north, Hampstead has kept its villagey atmosphere and sense of being aloof from urban pressures. This has attracted artists and writers since Georgian times and made it one of London's most desirable residential areas. Its mansions and town houses are perfectly maintained and a stroll through Hampstead's narrow streets is one of London's quieter pleasures.

Jack Straw's Castle
The pub on the edge of the Heath is named after a 14th-century rebel ❸

★ Hampstead Heath
A welcome retreat from the city, its broad open spaces include bathing ponds, meadows and lakes ❽

Whitestone Pond takes its name from the old white milestone nearby. It is 4.5 miles (7 km) from Holborn (*see pp132–41*).

Grove Lodge was home to novelist John Galsworthy (1867–1933), author of the *Forsyte Saga*, for the last 15 years of his life.

Admiral's House dates from about 1700. Built for a sea captain, its name derives from its external maritime motifs. No admiral ever actually lived in it.

Star Sights

- ★ **Burgh House**
- ★ **Hampstead Heath**
- ★ **Fenton House**
- ★ **Church Row**

Key

- – – – Suggested route

| 0 metres | 100 |
| 0 yards | 100 |

★ Fenton House
Summer visitors should seek out this late 17th-century house and its exquisite walled garden, which are well hidden in the jumble of streets near the heath ❹

★ **Burgh House**
*Built in 1702 but much
altered since, the house
contains an intriguing
local history museum and
a café overlooking the
small garden* ❷

LOCATOR MAP
See Greater London Map pp10–11

The New End Theatre
produces rare but significant
work. The building used to
be a morgue.

No. 40 Well Walk is where
artist John Constable lived
while working on his many
Hampstead pictures.

Flask Walk and Well Walk
*An alley of charming
specialist shops broadens
into a residential village
street* ❶

**Hampstead
station**

**The
Everyman
Cinema**
has been an
art cinema
since 1933.

★ **Church Row**
*The tall houses are
rich in original detail.
Notice the superb iron-
work on what is probably
London's finest
Georgian street* ❺

Jack Straw's Castle in the 19th century

Flask Walk and Well Walk ❶

NW3. **Map** 1 B5. ⊖ *Hampstead.*

FLASK WALK IS named after the Flask pub. Here, in the 18th century, therapeutic spa water from what was then the separate village of Hampstead was put into flasks and sold to visitors or sent to London. The water, rich in iron salts, came from nearby Well Walk where a disused fountain now marks the site of the well. The Wells Tavern, almost opposite the spring, used to be a hostelry that specialized in accommodating those who engaged in the illicit liaisons for which the spa became notorious.

In later times, there have been many notable residents of Well Walk including artist John Constable (at No. 40), novelists D H Lawrence and J B Priestley and the poet John Keats, before he moved to his better-known house in what is now Keats Grove.

Site of the well on Well Walk

At the High Street end, Flask Walk is narrow and lined with old shops. Beyond the pub (note the Victorian tiled panels outside) it broadens into a row of Regency houses, one of which used to belong to the novelist Kingsley Amis.

Burgh House ❷

New End Sq NW3. **Map** 1 B4. 🄲 *0171-431 0144.* ⊖ *Hampstead.* **Open** *noon–5pm Wed–Sun, 2–5pm public hols.* **Closed** *Christmas week, Good Fri.* 🄾 🍴 🄰. **Music recitals.**

THE LAST PRIVATE tenant of Burgh House was the son-in-law of the writer Rudyard Kipling, who visited here occasionally in the last years of his life until 1936. After a period under the ownership of Hampstead Borough Council, the house was let to the independent Burgh House Trust. Since 1979 the Trust has run it as the Hampstead Museum, which illustrates the history of the area and concentrates on some of its most celebrated residents.

One room is devoted entirely to the life of John Constable, who painted an extraordinary series of studies of clouds from Hampstead Heath. The house also has sections on Lawrence, Keats, the artist Stanley Spencer and others who lived and worked in the area. There is a display about Hampstead as a spa in the 18th and 19th centuries, which is also well worth a visit. Burgh House regularly accomodates exhibitions by contemporary local artists. The house itself was built in

1703 but is named after a 19th-century resident, the Reverend Allatson Burgh. It has been much altered inside, and today the marvellously carved staircase is a highlight of the interior. Also worth seeing is the music room which was reconstructed in 1920, but contains good 18th-century pine panelling from another house. In the 1720s Dr William Gibbons, chief physician to the then thriving Hampstead spa, lived here.

There is a moderately priced café in the basement, with a terrace that overlooks the house's pretty garden.

Burgh House staircase

Jack Straw's Castle ❸

12 North End Way NW3. **Map** 1 A3. 🄲 *0171-435 8374* ⊖ *Hampstead.* **Open** *licensing hours (see p308).* ♿ 🍴

THIS PUB IS NAMED after one of Wat Tyler's lieutenants in the Peasants' Revolt of 1381 *(see p162).* Jack Straw is believed to have built an encampment here, from which he planned to march on London. Instead, he was captured and hanged by the king's men. There has certainly been a pub here for many years – Charles Dickens was a customer – but the present building, a mock castle, dates only from 1962. It is a huge place, and there are good views across the Heath from the restaurant and Turret Bar on the second floor.

Fenton House ○4

20 Hampstead Grove NW3.
Map 1 A4. ☎ *0171-435 3471.*
⊖ *Hampstead.* **Open** *1–5.30pm
Mon–Wed, 11am–5.30pm Sat, Sun,
public hols.* **Closed** *Nov–Feb.* **Adm
charge**. ✍ **Summer concerts**
8pm Wed.

BUILT IN 1693, this splendid
William and Mary house is
the oldest mansion in
Hampstead. It contains two
specialized exhibitions that
are open to the public during
the summer: the Benton-
Fletcher collection of early
keyboard instruments, which
includes a harpsichord dating
from 1612, said to have been
played by Handel; and a fine
collection of porcelain. The
instruments are kept in full
working order and are
actually used for concerts held
in the house. The porcelain
collection was largely
accumulated by Lady
Binning, who, in 1952,
bequeathed the house
and all of its contents
to the National Trust.

Church Row ○5

NW3. **Map** 1 A5. ⊖ *Hampstead.*

THE ROW IS ONE of the most
complete Georgian streets
in London. Much of its
original detail has survived,
notably the ironwork.
   At the west end is St John's,
Hampstead's parish church,
built in 1745. The iron gates
are earlier and come from
Canons Park in Edgware.
Inside the church is a bust of
John Keats. John Constable's
grave is in the churchyard,
and many Hampstead
luminaries are buried in the
adjoining cemetery.

Downshire Hill ○6

NW3. **Map** 1 C5. ⊖ *Hampstead.*

A BEAUTIFUL STREET of mainly
Regency houses, it lent its
name to a group of artists,
including Stanley Spencer and
Mark Gertler, who would
gather at No. 47 between the
two World Wars. That same

house had been the meeting-
place of Pre-Raphaelite artists,
among them Dante Gabriel
Rossetti and Edward Burne-
Jones. A more recent resident,
at No. 5, was Jim Henson, the
creator of the television
puppets, *The Muppets*.
   The church on the corner
(the second Hampstead church
to be called St John's) was
built in 1823 to serve the
Hill's residents. Inside, it still
has its original box pews.

Keats House ○7

Keats Grove NW3. **Map** 1 C5.
☎ *0171-435 2062.* ⊖ *Hampstead,
Belsize Park.* **Open** *Apr–Oct: 10am–
1pm, 2–6pm Mon–Fri; Nov–Mar:
1–5pm Mon–Fri; all year: 10am–1pm,
2–5pm Sat; 2–5pm Sun, public hols.*
Closed *24–26 Dec, 1 Jan, Easter, May
Day.* 🎧 **Poetry readings, talks**.

Lock of John Keats's hair

ORIGINALLY TWO semi-
detached houses built in
1816, Keats was persuaded to
move into the smaller one in
1818 by his friend, Charles

St John's, Downshire Hill

Armitage Brown. Keats spent
two productive years here:
Ode to a Nightingale, perhaps
his most celebrated poem,
was written under a plum
tree in the garden. The
Brawne family moved into
the larger house a year later
and Keats became engaged to
their daughter, Fanny.
However, the marriage never
took place because Keats
died of consumption in Rome
before two years had passed.
He was only 25 years old.
   One of Keats's love letters
to Fanny, the engagement
ring he offered her, and a
lock of her hair are among
the mementoes that are now
exhibited at the house – it
was first opened to the public
in 1925. Visitors are also able
to see some of Keats's original
manuscripts and books, part
of a collection that serves as
an evocative and memorable
tribute to his life and work.

Fenton House's 17th-century facade

View over London from Hampstead Heath

Hampstead Heath ⑧

NW3. **Map** 1 C2. 📞 0181-348 9945.
⊖ Belsize Park, Hampstead. **Open**
24hrs daily. **Special walks** on
Sundays. **Concerts, poetry readings,
children's activities** in summer.
**Sports facilities, bathing ponds.
Sports bookings** 📞 0181-458 4548.

THE BEST TIME to stride
across these broad 3 sq
miles (8 sq km) is Sunday
afternoon, when the local
residents walk off their roast
beef lunches, discussing the
contents of the Sunday
papers. Separating the hilltop
villages of Hampstead and

Highgate *(see p242)*, the Heath
was made from the grounds
of several, formerly separate,
properties and embraces a
variety of landscapes –
woods, meadows, hills, ponds
and lakes. It remains
uncluttered by the haphazard
buildings and statues that
embellish the central London
parks, and its open spaces
have become increasingly
precious to Londoners as
the areas around it get more
crowded. There are ponds for
bathing and fishing and, on
three holiday weekends –
Easter, late spring and late
summer – the southern part of
the Heath is taken over by a
popular funfair *(see pp56–9)*.

Parliament Hill ⑨

NW3. **Map** 2 E4. 📞 0171-485 4491.
⊖ Belsize Park, Hampstead.
🎵 **Concerts, children's activities** in
summer. **Sporting facilities**. 📷

AN UNLIKELY BUT romantic
explanation for the area's
name is that it is where Guy
Fawkes's fellow-plotters
gathered on 5 November 1605
in the vain hope of watching
the Houses of Parliament
blow up after they had
planted gunpowder there *(see
p22)*. More probably it was a
gun emplacement for the
Parliamentary side during the
Civil War 40 years later. The
gunners would have enjoyed

Kenwood House ⑩

Hampstead Lane NW3. **Map** 1 C1.
📞 0181-348 1286. 📞 0171-973
3427. ⊖ Highgate, Archway. **Open**
Apr–Sep: 10am–6pm daily; Oct–Mar:
10am–4pm daily. **Closed** 24–25 Dec.
♿ ⌀ 🅿 **Lakeside concerts** in
summer. **Exhibitions, poetry
readings, recitals.** 🍴 📷 📷
See **Entertainment** pp330–31.

THIS IS A MAGNIFICENT Adam
mansion, filled with Old
Master paintings, including
works by Vermeer, Turner
and Romney (who lived in
Hampstead). It is situated in
landscaped grounds high on
the edge of Hampstead Heath.
There has been a house here
since 1616 – the present one

was remodelled by Robert
Adam in 1764 for the Earl of
Mansfield, the Lord Chancellor.
Adam refitted existing rooms
and added to the original
building. Most of his interiors
have survived, the highlight
being the library. A Rembrandt
self-portrait is the star attraction
of the collection, and there
are also works by Van Dyck,
Hals, Reynolds and others.

The orangery is
now used for
occasional concerts
and recitals.

a broad view across London: even today, when many tall buildings have intervened, it provides one of the most spectacular views over the capital. From here the dome of St Paul's is prominent.

Parliament Hill is also a popular place for flying kites or sailing model boats.

Spaniards Inn ⓫

Spaniards Rd NW3. **Map** 1 B1. *0181-455 3276.* ⊖ *Hampstead, Golders Green.* **Open** *11am–11pm Mon–Sat, noon–3pm, 7–10pm Sun.* ⛓ *See* **Restaurants and Pubs** *pp308–9.*

The historic Spaniards Inn

Dᴵᴄᴋ Tᴜʀᴘᴵɴ, the notorious 18th-century highwayman, is said to have frequented this pub. When he wasn't holding up stage coaches on their way to and from London, he stabled his horse, Black Bess, at the stables nearby. The building certainly dates from Turpin's

time and, although the bar downstairs has been altered frequently, the small upstairs Turpin Bar is original. A pair of guns over the bar were reputedly taken from anti-Catholic rioters, who came to Hampstead to burn the Lord Chancellor's house at Kenwood during the Gordon Riots of 1780. The landlord detained them by offering pint after pint of free beer and, when they were drunk, disarmed them.

Among the pub's noted patrons have been the poets Shelley, Keats and Byron, the actor David Garrick and the artist Sir Joshua Reynolds.

The toll house has been restored; it juts into the road so that, in the days when tolls were levied, traffic could not race past without paying.

The Hill ⓬

North End Way NW3. **Map** 1 A2. *0181-455 5183.* ⊖ *Hampstead, Golders Green.* **Open** *9am–dusk daily.*

Tʜᴵs ᴄʜᴀʀᴍᴵɴɢ garden was created by the Edwardian soap manufacturer and patron of the arts, Lord Leverhulme. It was originally the grounds to his house, now a hospital, and is now part of Hampstead Heath. Its highlight is a pergola walkway, best seen in summer when many of the plants are in flower; the garden also has a beautiful formal pond.

The pergola walk at The Hill

Vale of Health ⓭

NW3. **Map** 1 B4. ⊖ *Hampstead.*

Tʜᴵs ᴀʀᴇᴀ was famous as a distinctly unhealthy swamp before it was drained in 1770; until then it was known as Hatches Bottom. Its newer name may derive from people fleeing here from cholera in London at the end of the 18th century. Alternatively, the name could have been the hype of a property developer, when it was first recorded in 1801.

The poet James Henry Leigh Hunt put it on the literary map when he moved here in 1815, and played host to Coleridge, Byron Shelley and Keats. D H Lawrence lived here and Stanley Spencer painted in a room above the Vale of Health Hotel, demolished in 1964.

Adam added a floor to the old building.

Adam furnished these older rooms.

Lord Mansfield, who lived here from 1754 until 1793, had his dressing room here.

The ante-room was designed at the same time as the library.

The Adam library has a spectacularly curved, painted ceiling.

GREENWICH AND BLACKHEATH

BEST KNOWN AS the place from which the world's time is measured, Greenwich marks the historic eastern approach to London by land and water. Home to the National Maritime Museum and the exquisite Queen's House, Greenwich avoided the industrialization of its neighbours in the 19th century and today remains an elegant oasis of bookshops, antique shops and markets. Blackheath lies just to its south.

SIGHTS AT A GLANCE

Historic Streets and Buildings
Queen's House ❷
Royal Naval College ❼
Old Royal Observatory ❾
Croom's Hill ⓬

Museums
National Maritime Museum ❶
Fan Museum ⓭

Churches
St Alfege Church ❸

Parks and Gardens
Greenwich Park ❿
Blackheath ⓫

Walkway
Greenwich Foot Tunnel ❻

Pubs and Restaurants
Trafalgar Tavern ❽

Ships
Gipsy Moth IV ❹
Cutty Sark ❺

GETTING THERE
The best way is by BR from Charing Cross, Cannon Street or London Bridge stations. The 188 bus goes five times an hour to Greenwich from Euston. There are also numerous river boats *(pp60–5).*

SEE ALSO
- *Street Finder*, maps 23, 24
- *Where to Stay* pp276–7
- *Restaurants* pp292–4

KEY
▧	Street-by-Street map
⇥	British Rail station
P	Parking

View across the Thames from Greenwich Park, overlooking Queen's House

Street-by-Street: Greenwich

Tis HISTORIC TOWN marks the eastern approach to London and is best visited by river *(see pp60–5)*. In Tudor times it was the site of a palace much enjoyed by Henry VIII, near a fine hunting ground and his naval base. He and his daughters Elizabeth I and Mary were born here but the old palace is gone, leaving Inigo Jones's exquisite Queen's House, built for James I's wife. Museums, book and antique shops, markets, Wren's architecture and the magnificent park make Greenwich an enjoyable day's excursion.

Greenwich Foot Tunnel
Leading to the Isle of Dogs, this is the only Thames tunnel built solely for pedestrians **6**

Greenwich Pier provides a boarding point for boat services to Westminster and the Thames Barrier.

Gipsy Moth IV
Sir Francis Chichester sailed single-handedly round the world in this little yacht **4**

Cutty Sark
Majestic clipper ships, such as this, once traded across the oceans **5**

Goddard's Pie and Eel House is a rare survivor of a London tradition *(see p307).*

Greenwich Market sells crafts, antiques and books at weekends. It is especially popular on Sundays.

St Alfege Church
There has been a church here since 1012 **3**

Spread Eagle Yard was a stopping point for horse-drawn carriages. The ticket office is now a second-hand book shop.

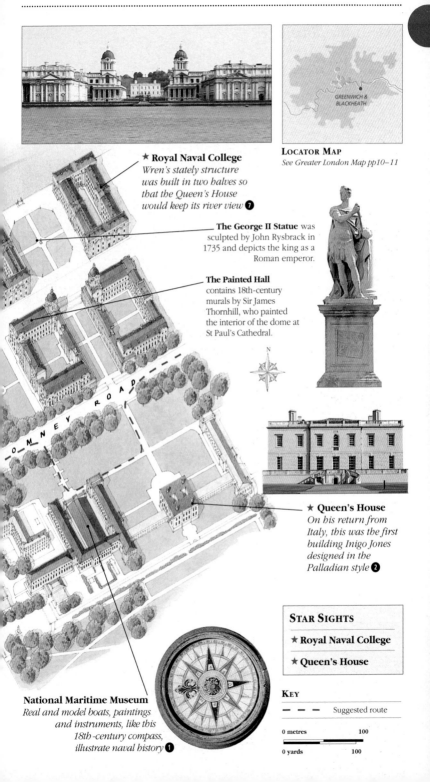

LOCATOR MAP
See Greater London Map pp10–11

★ Royal Naval College
Wren's stately structure was built in two halves so that the Queen's House would keep its river view ❼

The George II Statue was sculpted by John Rysbrack in 1735 and depicts the king as a Roman emperor.

The Painted Hall contains 18th-century murals by Sir James Thornhill, who painted the interior of the dome at St Paul's Cathedral.

★ Queen's House
On his return from Italy, this was the first building Inigo Jones designed in the Palladian style ❷

National Maritime Museum
Real and model boats, paintings and instruments, like this 18th-century compass, illustrate naval history ❶

STAR SIGHTS

★ Royal Naval College

★ Queen's House

KEY

－ － － Suggested route

0 metres   100

0 yards   100

National Maritime Museum ❶

Romney Rd SE10. **Map** 23 C2.
🌣 0181-858 4422. 🚊 Maze Hill.
Open Apr–Sep: 10am–6pm Mon–Sat,
noon–6pm Sun; Oct–Mar: 10am–5pm
Mon–Sat, noon–5pm Sun (last adm:
30 mins before closing). **Closed**
24–26 Dec. **Adm charge**. 📷
♿ to most of museum. **Lectures,
exhibitions**. 📱 🚹

THE SEA HAS ALWAYS played an extremely important role in British history, and this extensive museum celebrates the "island nation's" seafaring heritage. Exhibits include everything from the earliest coracles (primitive hollow canoes) made from wood and leather, through early models of Elizabethan galleons to modern cargo, passenger and naval ships. There are sections devoted to trade and empire, the exploratory expeditions of Captain Cook and others, and the Napoleonic Wars.

One of the star exhibits is the uniform that Lord Nelson was wearing when he was shot at the Battle of Trafalgar in October 1805: you can easily see the bullet hole and the bloodstains. Rather more spectacular, however, are the royal barges in the basement, most notably one that was built for Prince Frederick in 1732, elaborately decorated with gilded mermaids, shells, garlands and his Prince of Wales's feathers on the stern. Throughout the museum, which was built in the 19th century as a school for sailors' children, are scores of exquisitely crafted models of ships and historic paintings.

**Prince Frederick's barge at the
National Maritime Museum**

St Alfege's altar with rails by Jean Tijou

Queen's House ❷

Romney Rd SE10. **Map** 23 C2.
🌣 0181-858 4422. 🚊 Maze Hill,
Greenwich. **Open** Apr–Sep:
10am–6pm Mon–Sat, noon–6pm
Sun; Oct–Mar: 10am–5pm Mon–Sat,
noon–5pm Sun (last adm: 30 mins
before closing). **Adm charge**. 📷 🚹
🍴 📱 🚹 **Lectures,
concerts, exhibitions**.

THE HOUSE WAS designed by Inigo Jones after his return from Italy and completed in 1637. It was originally meant as the home of Anne of Denmark, wife of James I, but she died while it was being built and it was finished for Charles I's queen, Henrietta Maria. She loved it and called it her house of delights. After the Civil War it was briefly occupied by Henrietta as dowager queen, but was not much used by the royal family after that.

It has recently been restored and furnished as it would have been in the late 17th century, with brightly coloured wallhangings and fabrics. The house was built as two halves, with one on each side of the road from Woolwich to Deptford, and linked by a bridge. Later the road was diverted; its former course is marked by cobbles in the courtyard. The main hall is a perfect cube, 12 m (40 ft) in all three dimensions. Another feature is the spiral "tulip staircase" (named after the design on its balustrades), curving sinuously upwards without a central support.

St Alfege Church ❸

Greenwich Church St SE10.
Map 23 B2. 🌣 0181-853 0687.
🚊 Greenwich. **Open** 12.30–4.30pm
daily. 🕆 9.30am Sun. 📷 ♿ 🎦
Concerts, exhibitions.

THIS IS ONE OF Nicholas Hawksmoor's distinctive and powerful designs, with its gigantic columns and pediments topped by urns. It was completed in 1714 on the site of an older church which marked the martyrdom of St Alfege, the then Archbishop of Canterbury, killed on this spot by Danish invaders in 1012.

Some of the carved wood inside is by Grinling Gibbons, but much of it was badly damaged by a World War II bomb and has been restored. The wrought iron of the altar and gallery rails is original, attributed to Jean Tijou. There is a reproduction of the register entry recording the baptism of Henry VIII in the former church, and a brass plate denoting the tomb of General Wolfe, who died fighting the French in Quebec in 1759. A window commemorates Thomas Tallis, the 16th-century composer and organist, who is buried here.

Gipsy Moth IV ❹

King William Walk SE10. **Map** 23 B2.
📞 0181-858 2698. 🚊 Greenwich, Maze Hill. 🚢 Greenwich Pier. **Open** Apr–Sep: 10am–6pm Mon–Sat, noon–6pm Sun. **Closed** Nov–Mar. **Adm charge.** 📷 ♿

Gipsy Moth IV

Sᴵᴿ ꜰᴿᴀɴᴄɪꜱ ᴄʜɪᴄʜᴇꜱᴛᴇᴿ sailed single-handed around the world in this little yacht. The journey, in 1966–7, took 226 lonely days to cover the 30,000 miles (48,000 km). He had to endure very cramped conditions on this 16-m (54-ft) vessel. The Queen knighted him on board using the sword with which Elizabeth I had knighted that earlier English seaman, Sir Francis Drake.

The domed terminal of the Greenwich Foot Tunnel

Cutty Sark ❺

King William Walk SE10. **Map** 23 B2.
📞 0181-858 2698. 📠 0181-853 3589. 🚊 Greenwich, Maze Hill. 🚢 Greenwich Pier. **Open** Apr–Sep: 10am–6pm Mon–Sat, noon–6pm Sun; Oct–Mar: 10am–5pm Mon–Sat, noon–5pm Sun, public hols (last adm: 30 mins before closing). **Closed** 24–26 Dec. **Adm charge.** 📷 ♿ restricted. 🎥 📽 **Filmshows, videos**.

Tʜɪꜱ ᴍᴀᴊᴇꜱᴛɪᴄ vessel is a survivor of the clippers that crossed the Atlantic and Pacific Oceans in the 19th century. Launched in 1869 as a tea carrier, it won the annual clippers' race from China to London in 1871, taking 107 days. It made its last sea voyage in 1938 and was put on display here in 1957. On board you can see where the merchant seamen slept, ate and lived. Exhibits illustrate the history of sail and the Pacific trade, and there is a tremendous collection of carved ships' figureheads.

Greenwich Foot Tunnel ❻

Between Greenwich Pier SE10 and Isle of Dogs E14. **Map** 23 B1. 🚊 Maze Hill, Greenwich. **Docklands Light Railway** Island Gardens. 🚢 Greenwich Pier. **Open** 24hrs daily. **Lifts open** 5am–9pm daily. 📷 ♿ when lifts open.

Tʜɪꜱ 370-ᴍ (1,200-ꜰᴛ) long tunnel was opened in 1902 to allow south London labourers to walk to work in

Millwall Docks. Today it is worth crossing for the wonderful views, across the river, of Christopher Wren's Royal Naval College and Inigo Jones's Queen's House.

Matching round red-brick terminals, with glass domes, mark the top of the lift shafts on either side of the river. The tunnel is about 2.5 m (9 ft) high and is lined with 200,000 tiles. The north end, on the southern tip of the Isle of Dogs, is close to the terminus of the Docklands Light Railway, with trains to Canary Wharf (see p245), Limehouse, East London and the City. Although there are security cameras, the tunnel can be eerie at night.

A late 19th-century figurehead in the Cutty Sark

Royal Naval College ❼

Greenwich SE10. **Map** 23 C2.
📞 0181-858 2154. 🚊 Greenwich, Maze Hill. **Open** 2.30pm–5pm Fri–Wed. 🚫

THESE AMBITIOUS buildings by Sir Christopher Wren were built on the site of the old 15th-century royal palace, where Henry VIII, Mary I and Elizabeth I lived. The chapel and hall are the only parts of the college that are open to the public. The west front was completed by Vanbrugh.

The chapel, by Wren, was destroyed by fire in 1779. The present Rococo interior, designed by James Stuart, is marvellously light and airy, and has dainty plasterwork decorations on the ceilings and walls. The altar rail and communion table, as well as the candelabra, are gilded.

The Painted Hall was opulently decorated by Sir James Thornhill in the first quarter of the 18th century. The magnificent ceiling paintings are supported by his illusionistic pillars and friezes. At the foot of one of his paintings on the west wall, the artist himself is shown, apparently extending his hand for more money.

Trafalgar Tavern ❽

Park Row SE10. **Map** 23 C1.
📞 0181-858 2437. See **Restaurants and Pubs** pp308–9.

THIS CHARMING panelled pub was built in 1837 and quickly became established, along with other waterside

Thornhill's painting of King William in the Hall of the Naval College

inns in Greenwich, as a venue for "whitebait dinners". Government ministers, legal luminaries and the like would arrive from Westminster and Charing Cross by water on celebratory occasions and feast on the tiny fish, which could in those days be caught locally. The last such meeting of government ministers was held here in 1885. Whitebait still features, when in season, on the menu at the pub's restaurant, though they no longer come from the now polluted Thames.

This is another of Charles Dickens's haunts. He drank here with one of his novels' most famous illustrators, the engraver George Cruickshank.

In 1915 the pub became an institution for old merchant seamen. It was restored in 1965 after a spell when it was used as a club for working men.

Old Royal Observatory ❾

Greenwich Park SE10. **Map** 23 C3.
📞 0181-858 4422. 🚊 Maze Hill, Greenwich. **Open** Apr–Sep: 10am–6pm Mon–Sat, noon–6pm Sun; Oct–Mar: 10am–5pm Mon–Sat, 2–5pm Sun. **Adm charge.** 📷 🚻

THE MERIDIAN (0° longtitude) that divides the earth's eastern and western hemispheres passes through here, and millions of visitors have been photographed standing with a foot on either side of it. In 1884, Greenwich Mean Time became the basis of time measurement for most of the world following an important international agreement.

The original building, still standing, is Flamsteed House, designed by Wren. It has a distinctive octagonal room at the top, hidden by square outer walls and crowned with two turrets. Above one of them is a ball on a rod which has dropped at 1pm every day since 1833, so that sailors on ships on the Thames, and makers of chronometers (navigators' clocks), could set their clocks by it.

Flamsteed was the first Astronomer Royal, appointed by Charles II, and this was the official government observatory from 1675 until 1948, when the lights of

Trafalgar Tavern viewed from the Thames

London became too bright and the astronomers moved to darker Sussex. Today the Astronomer Royal is based in Cambridge and in the old Observatory there is housed an intriguing exhibition of astronomical instruments, chronometers and clocks.

A rare 24–hour clock at the Old Royal Observatory

Greenwich Park ⑩

SE10. **Map** 23 C3. **[** 0181-858 2608. ⇌ Greenwich, Blackheath, Maze Hill. **Open** 6am–dusk daily, pedestrians. **☐** *Children's shows, music, sports.* **Ranger's House,** Chesterfield Walk, Greenwich Park SE10. **Map** 23 C4. **[** 0181-853 0035. **Open** Good Fri–30 Sep: 10am–1pm, 2–6pm Wed–Sun; 31 Oct–Maundy Thu: 10am–1pm, 2–4pm Wed–Sun. **Closed** 24–25 Dec. **&** ground floor only.

ORIGINALLY THE GROUNDS of a royal palace and still owned by the Crown, the park was enclosed in 1433 and its brick wall built in the reign of James I. Later, in the 17th century, the French royal landscape gardener André Le Nôtre, who laid out the gardens at Versailles, was invited to design one at Greenwich. The broad avenue, rising south up the hill, was part of his plan. There are great river views from the hilltop and on a fine day most of London can be seen. On the south-east edge of the park is the Ranger's House (1688), allotted in 1815 to the Park Ranger, but today housing the fine Suffolk Collection of 17th-century English portraits by William Larkin, Sir Peter Lely and others, as well as a display of historic musical instruments.

Ranger's House in Greenwich Park

Blackheath ⑪

SE3. **Map** 24 D5. ⇌ Blackheath.

THIS OPEN HEATH used to be a rallying point for large groups entering London from the east, including Wat Tyler's band of rebels at the time of the Peasants' Revolt in 1381. It is also the place where James I introduced the game of golf, from his native Scotland, to the then largely sceptical English.

Today the heath is well worth exploring for the stately Georgian houses and terraces that surround it. In the prettily-named Tranquil Vale to the south, there are shops selling books, prints and antiques.

Croom's Hill ⑫

SE10. **Map** 23 C3. ⇌ Greenwich.

THIS IS ONE of the best kept 17th- to early 19th-century streets in London. The oldest buildings are at the southern end, near Blackheath: the Manor House of 1695; near it, No. 68, from about the same date; and No. 66 the oldest of all.

Famous residents of Croom's Hill have included General James Wolfe (buried in St Alfege), and the English actor Daniel Day Lewis.

Fan Museum ⑬

12 Croom's Hill SE10. **Map** 23 B3. **[** 0181-858 7879. ⇌ Greenwich. **Open** 11am–4.30pm Tue–Sat, noon–4.30pm Sun. **Adm charge** but free to pensioners and disabled 2–4.30pm Tue. **⊙ & ⬛ ⬛** *Lectures, fan-making workshops.*

ONE OF LONDON'S most unlikely museums – the only one of its kind in the world – was opened here in 1989. It owes its existence and appeal to the enthusiasm of Helene Alexander, whose personal collection of 2,000 fans from the 17th century onwards has been augmented by gifts from others, including several fans that were made for the stage. The exhibitions are changed regularly in order to highlight a wide-ranging craft which embraces design, miniature painting, carving and embroidery. If there, Ms Alexander will guide you around the exhibits.

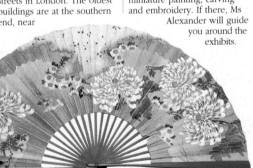

Stage fan used in a D'Oyly Carte operetta

FURTHER AFIELD

MANY OF THE GREAT houses originally built as country retreats
for London's high and mighty
were overrun by sprawling suburbs
in the Victorian era. Fortunately several have survived as museums in
these now less-rustic surroundings.
Most are less than an hour's journey
from central London. Richmond Park
and Wimbledon Common give a
taste of the country, while a trip to
Canary Wharf is an adventure.

SIGHTS AT A GLANCE

Historic Streets and Buildings
Sutton House ⑪
Charlton House ⑱
Eltham Palace ⑲
Ham House ㉘
Hampton Court pp250–3 ㉗
Marble Hill House ㉚
Syon House ㉜
Osterley Park House ㉞
Pitshanger Manor Museum ㉟
Strand on the Green ㊳
Chiswick House ㊴
Fulham Palace ㊶

Churches
St Mary, Rotherhithe ⑬
St Mary's, Battersea ㉓
St Anne's, Limehouse ⑭

Museums and Galleries
Lord's Cricket Ground ①
Saatchi Collection ②
Freud Museum ③
St John's Gate ⑦
Crafts Council Gallery ⑧
Geffrye Museum ⑩
Bethnal Green Museum of Childhood ⑫
William Morris Gallery ⑯
Horniman Museum ⑳
Dulwich Picture Gallery ㉑
Wimbledon Lawn Tennis Museum ㉔
Wimbledon Windmill Museum ㉕
Musical Museum ㉝
Kew Bridge Steam Museum ㊱
Hogarth's House ㊵
London Toy and Model Museum ㊸

Parks and Gardens
Battersea Park ㉒
Richmond Park ㉖
Kew Gardens pp256–7 ㊲

Cemeteries
Highgate Cemetery ⑤

Modern Architecture
Canary Wharf ⑮
Chelsea Harbour ㊷

Historic Districts
Highgate ④
Clerkenwell ⑥
Islington ⑨
Richmond ㉛

Modern Technology
Thames Barrier ⑰

All the sights in this section lie inside the M25 motorway *(see pp10–11)*.

KEY
▨ Main sightseeing areas
═ Motorway

North of the Centre

Lord's Cricket Ground ❶

NW8. **Map** 3 A3. 【 *0171-289 1611.*
🚇 *St John's Wood.* **Open** *summer:*
10am–5pm match days; winter: tours
only. **Closed** *25 Dec.* **Adm charge.**
🔲 ♿ 🎥 *noon, 2pm daily.* 🎦
See **Entertainment** *pp336–7.*

T HE HEADQUARTERS of
Britain's chief summer
sport contains a suitably
eccentric museum, including
a stuffed sparrow killed by a
cricket ball in play and the
Ashes (burned wood in an
urn), the object of ferocious
competition between the
English and Australian
national teams. The museum
explains the history of the
game, while paintings and
mementos of notable
cricketers make it a
place of pilgrimage for
devotees of the sport.
   Cricket pioneer
Thomas Lord moved
his ground to this site
in 1814. The Pavilion
(1890), with its weather
vane depicting Old
Father Time, is a late
Victorian confection.
There are guided tours
of Lord's even when
there is no game
being played.

The Ashes at Lord's

Saatchi Collection ❷

98a Boundary Rd NW8. 【 *0171-624*
8299. 🚇 *St John's Wood, Swiss*
Cottage. **Open** *noon–6pm Fri, Sat &*
Sun. 🎦 **Lectures.**

C HARLES SAATCHI, who is an
advertising executive, and
his former wife established
this gallery of contemporary
art in a converted warehouse.
(There is no sign outside so
take care not to miss it.) He
owns approximately 600 works
by renowned artists such as
Andy Warhol, Carl André and
Frank Stella, and selections of
these are put on display in
exhibitions that are changed
every few months.

Sigmund Freud's famous couch

Freud Museum ❸

20 Maresfield Gdns NW3.
【 *0171-435 2002.* 🚇 *Finchley Rd.*
Open *noon–5pm Wed–Sun.* **Adm**
charge. 🔲 ♿ 🎦 **Lectures,**
videos, evening classes.

I N 1938 SIGMUND FREUD, the
founder of psychoanalysis,
fled from Nazi persecution in
Vienna to this Hampstead
house. Making use of the
possessions he brought
with him, his family
recreated the atmos-
phere of his Vienna
consulting rooms. After
Freud died in 1939 his
daughter Anna (who
was a pioneer of child
psychoanalysis) kept the
house as it was. In 1986,
four years after Anna's
death, the house was
opened as a museum
dedicated to Freud.
The most famous
item is the couch
on which patients
lay for analysis. A compil-
ation of 1930s home movies
shows cheerful moments with
his dog as well as scenes of
Nazi attacks on his apartment.
The museum's bookshop has
a large collection of his works.

Highgate ❹

N6. 🚇 *Highgate.*

T HERE HAS BEEN a settlement
here since at least the
early Middle Ages, when an
important staging post on the
Great North Road from London
was established here with a
gate to control access. Like
Hampstead across the Heath
(see pp228–31), it soon
became fashionable for its
unpolluted air, and noblemen

built country houses here. It
still has an exclusive feel,
with a Georgian High Street
and expensive houses. On
Highgate Hill, a statue of a
black cat marks the spot
where a dejected Richard
Whittington and his pet are
said to have paused. He was
about to leave London, when
he heard the sound of Bow
Bells telling him to turn
back – to become Lord Mayor
three times *(see p39).*

Highgate Cemetery ❺

Swain's Lane N6. 【 *0181-340 1834.*
🚇 *Archway.* **Eastern Cemetery**
open *Apr–Oct: 10am–5pm daily;*
Nov–Mar: 10am–4pm daily. **Western**
Cemetery open 🎥 *only Apr–Oct:*
noon, 2pm, 4pm Mon–Fri,
11am–4pm Sat, Sun; Nov–Mar: noon,
2pm, 3pm Mon–Fri, 11am–3pm Sat,
Sun. **Closed** *25–26 Dec, during*
funerals. **Adm charge.** ♿

T HE WESTERN part of this early
Victorian delight opened
in 1839. Its graves and tombs
perfectly reflect high Victorian
taste. For many years it lay
neglected until a voluntary
group, called the Friends of
Highgate Cemetery stepped
in. They have restored the
Egyptian Avenue, a street of
family vaults, built in a style
based on that of ancient
Egyptian tombs, and the
Circle of Lebanon, more
vaults in a ring, topped by a
cedar tree. In the eastern
section lies Karl Marx, beneath
a gigantic black bust of himself. The novelist George Eliot
(real name, Mary Anne Cross)
is also buried here.

George Wombwell's Memorial at
Highgate Cemetery

St John's Priory: today, only the gatehouse remains intact

Clerkenwell **6**

EC1. **Map** 6 D4. ⊖ *Farringdon. See* **Entertainment** *p332.*

Sadler's Wells poster

THE CLERKS IN the name were parish clerks from the City. St John's Priory dominated the area until Henry VIII dissolved the monasteries in 1536. It became a fashionable suburb, but declined after the Plague of 1665 *(see p22).* Then French Huguenot refugees moved in, establishing jewellery and silver workshops. Later it became a centre for clockmaking. In Victorian times Clerkenwell had some of London's worst slums, described by Dickens in *Oliver Twist.* More recently, the area became known as Little Italy, after the Italian immigrants who moved here from the late 19th century up until the 1930s.

On Rosebery Avenue is Sadler's Wells Theatre, where Thomas Sadler built a "musick house" in 1683, next to a well that was said to have healthful properties. It was rebuilt in 1927 by Lilian Baylis, who was also a benefactor of the Old Vic *(see p186),* and was home to the Sadler's Wells Royal Ballet Company until 1990.

St John's Gate **7**

St John's Square EC1. **Map** 6 F4.
📞 *0171-253 6644.* ⊖ *Farringdon.*
Museum open *10am–5pm Mon–Fri, 10am–4pm Sat.* **Closed** *25 Dec, Easter, public hols.* **Adm charge.** 📷
📹 *11am, 2.30pm Tue, Fri, Sat.* 📱

THE TUDOR GATEHOUSE and parts of the 12th-century church are all that remain of the priory of the Knights of St John, which flourished here for 400 years and was the precursor of the St John Ambulance. Over the years, the priory buildings have had many uses. These include times as offices for Elizabeth I's Master of the Revels, a pub, a coffee shop run by artist William Hogarth's father, and the offices of Edward Cave's *Gentlemen's Magazine* (1731–54). A museum of the order's history is open daily, but to see the rest of the building, join a guided tour.

Crafts Council Gallery **8**

44a Pentonville Rd N1. **Map** 6 D2.
📞 *0171-278 7700.* ⊖ *Angel.*
Open *11am–6pm Tue–Sat, 2–6pm Sun.* ♿ 💻 📱 **Lectures.**

THE COUNCIL is the national body for promoting the creation and appreciation of crafts in Britain. It has a collection of contemporary British crafts, some of which are displayed here, along with special exhibitions. There is a reference library and information service and a well-stocked bookshop which also sells good examples of modern crafts.

Islington **9**

N1. **Map** 6 E1. ⊖ *Angel, Highbury & Islington.*

ISLINGTON WAS ONCE a highly fashionable spa, but the rich began to move out in the late 18th century, and the area deteriorated rapidly. During the 20th century, writers such as Evelyn Waugh, George Orwell and Joe Orton lived here. Now Islington has again returned to fashion as one of London's first areas to become "gentrified", with many young professionals buying and refurbishing old houses.

An older relic is Canonbury Tower, the remains of a medieval manor house converted into apartments in the 18th century. Writers such as Washington Irving and Oliver Goldsmith lived here and today it houses the Tower Theatre. On Islington Green there is a statue of Sir Hugh Myddleton, who built a canal through Islington in 1613 to bring water to London from Hertfordshire; today a pleasant landscaped walk along its banks runs between Essex Road and Canonbury British Rail stations *(see pp264–5).* There are two markets close to the Angel station *(see p322):* Chapel Road selling fresh food and cheap clothing, and the nearby Camden Passage, selling expensive antiques.

The Crafts Council Gallery

East of the Centre

Geffrye Museum's Victorian Room

Geffrye Museum ⑩

Kingsland Rd E2. **[** 0171-739 9893.
⊖ Liverpool St, Old St. **Open**
10am–5pm Tue–Sat, 2–5pm Sun,
Mon & public hols. **Closed** 24–26
Dec, 1 Jan, Good Fri. **♿ ♺ ▯ ▯**
Exhibitions, lectures, events.

THIS COMPACT MUSEUM is
housed in an attractive set
of almshouses built in 1715
on land bequeathed by Sir
Robert Geffrye, a 17th-century
Lord Mayor of London who
made his fortune through
trade, including the slave
trade. The almshouses (built
for ironworkers and their
widows) have been adapted
into typical room settings of
specific periods, and provide
an insight into the history of
family life and the evolution
of interior design. The historic
room settings begin with
Elizabethan (which contains
magnificent panelling) and
run through various major
styles finishing with Art
Nouveau and the 1950s.

Each room contains splendid
examples of the furniture of
the period collected from all
over Britain. In the middle,
the chapel has not been
altered significantly from its
original appearance, with
box pews: the Creed, the
Commandments and the
Lord's Prayer are inscribed
on the alcove wall. There are
attractive gardens outside the
museum, which include a
walled herb garden.

Sutton House ⑪

2–4 Homerton High St E9.
[0181-986 2264. **⊖** Bethnal
Green then bus 253. **Open** 11.30am–
5.30pm Wed, Sun. **Closed** Dec, Jan,
Good Fri. **Adm charge**. **♺ ♿ ▯**
▯ ▯ Concerts, lectures, films.

ONE OF THE FEW London
Tudor merchants' houses
to survive in something like
its original form, it is now
being restored. Built in 1535
for Ralph Sadleir, a courtier to
Henry VIII, it was owned by
several wealthy families before
becoming a girls' school in
the 17th century. In the 18th
century the front was altered,
but the Tudor fabric remains
surprisingly intact, with much
original brickwork, large fireplaces and linenfold panelling.

Bethnal Green Museum of Childhood ⑫

Cambridge Heath Rd E2.
[0181-980 3204. **⊖** Bethnal
Green. **Open** 10am–5.50pm
Mon–Thu, Sat, 2.30–5.50pm Sun.
Closed 24–26 Dec, 1 Jan, May Day.
▯ ♿ ▯ Workshop, children's
activities.

THIS BRANCH of the Victoria
and Albert Museum (see
pp198–201) is more usefully
described as a toy museum,
although there are plans to
broaden its range by showing
exhibits on the social history
of childhood. Its array of
dolls, lavish dolls' houses
(some donated by royalty),

Tate "Baby" house made in 1760

games, model trains, theatres,
puppets and some large play
equipment are well explained
and enticingly displayed.

The purpose-built museum
building was erected on the
V&A site. In 1872, when the
V&A was extended, it was
dismantled and reassembled
here to bring the light of
learning to the East End. The
toy collection began early this
century and Bethnal Green
became a dedicated toy
museum in 1974.

St Mary, Rotherhithe ⑬

St Marychurch St SE16.
[0171-231 2465. **⊖** Rotherhithe.
Open 7am–6pm daily. **♱** 9.30am,
6pm Sun. **♺ ♿** restricted.
Concerts, exhibitions.

St Mary, Rotherhithe

THIS BRIGHT CHURCH was
built in 1715 on the site of
a medieval church, traces of
which remain in the tower. It
has nautical connotations,
most notably a memorial to
Christopher Jones, captain of
the *Mayflower* on which the
Founding Fathers sailed to
North America. The barrel
roof resembles an inverted
hull. The communion table
is made from the timbers of
the *Temeraire*, a warship
whose final journey to the
breaker's yard at Rotherhithe
was evocatively recorded in
Turner's painting at the
National Gallery (see pp104–7).

William Morris tapestry (1885)

St Anne's, Limehouse ⓮

Commercial Rd E14.
[0171-987 1502. **Docklands Light Railway** Westferry. **Open** 3–4.30pm Sun, key from rectory at other times, 5 Newell St, E14. **♦** 10.30am Sun.
⚑ ⚑ Concerts, lectures.

THIS IS ONE of the group of East End churches that were designed by Nicholas Hawksmoor. It was completed in 1724. Its 40-m (130-ft) tower soon became a landmark for ships using the East End docks – St Anne's still has the highest church clock in London. The church was badly damaged by fire in 1850 and, while it was being restored, the architect Philip Hardwick Victorianized its interior. It was bombed in World War II and is today in need of further restoration.

Canary Wharf ⓯

E14. **Docklands Light Railway** Canary Wharf. **♦ ⓫ ⚑ ⚑**
Information centre, concerts, exhibitions. See **The History of London** pp30–1.

LONDON'S MOST ambitious commercial development opened in 1991, when the first tenants moved into the

50-storey Canada Tower, designed by US architect Cesar Pelli. At 250 m (800 ft) it dominates the city's eastern skyline and is the tallest office building in Europe. It stands on what was the West India Dock, closed, like all the London docks, between the 1960s and the 1980s, when trade moved to the modern container port down river at Tilbury. When completed, Canary Wharf will have 21 office buildings plus shops and leisure facilities. However, it underwent serious financial difficulties in 1992 and its future is uncertain.

William Morris Gallery ⓰

Forest Rd E17. **[** 0181-527 3782.
⊖ Walthamstow Central. **Open** 10am–1pm, 2–5pm Tue–Sat, 10am–1pm, 2–5pm first Sun each month. **♦ ⚑ Lectures.**

THE MOST influential designer of the Victorian era, born in 1834, lived in this imposing 18th-century house as a youth. It is now a beguiling and well-presented museum giving a full account of William Morris the artist, designer, writer, craftsman and pioneer socialist. It has choice examples of his work and that of various other members of the Arts and Crafts movement that he inspired – furniture by A H Mackmurdo, Kelmscott Press books, tiles by de Morgan, pottery by the Martin brothers, and paintings by the Pre-Raphaelites.

Thames Barrier ⓱

Unity Way SE18. **[** 0181-854 1373.
⚑ Charlton. **Open** 10am–5pm Mon–Fri, 10.30am–5.30pm Sat, Sun.
Closed 25 Dec, 1 Jan.
Adm charge. **⚑ ♦ ⚑ ⚑**
Multi-media show, exhibition.

Thames Barrier

IN 1236 THE THAMES rose so high that people rowed across Westminster Hall in boats; London was flooded again in 1663 and 1928. A tidal surge in 1953 caused great damage in the estuary below London. Something had to be done, and in 1965 the Greater London Council (see County Hall p183) invited proposals – nine years later work began on the barrier. It is 520 m (1,700 ft) across, and its 10 gates, which pivot from their normal position flat on the river bed, swing up to 1.6 m (6 ft) above the level reached by the tide in 1953. The barrier was opened in 1984 and seldom has to be raised more than once or twice a year. It is best visited by boat (see pp60–65).

Canada Tower at Canary Wharf

South of the Centre

A Jacobean fireplace at Charlton House

Charlton House 🔞

Charlton Rd SE7. 🎧 0181-856 3951.
🚊 Charlton. **Open** 9am–11pm daily.
Closed public hols. 🎥 ♿ 🎁 🖥

THE HOUSE was completed in 1612 for Adam Newton, tutor to Prince Henry, the eldest son of James I. It has good river views and is the best-preserved Jacobean mansion in the London area. The house is now used as a community centre. Inside,
many of the original ceilings and fireplaces survive, as does the carved main staircase, all with an astonishing quantity of ornament. Some parts of the wood panelling, too, are original. The ceilings have been restored by using the original moulds, which were found in the basement. In the grounds there is a summer house that may possibly have been designed by Inigo Jones, and a mulberry tree (probably the oldest in England) planted by James I in 1608.

Rembrandt's *Jacob II de Gheyn* at Dulwich Picture Gallery

Eltham Palace 🔞

Court Yard SE9. 🎧 0181-781 4232.
🚊 Eltham. **Open** Oct–Mar:
10am–4pm Thu, Sun; Apr–Sep:
10am–6pm Thu, Sun. 🎥 🎁

IN THE 14TH CENTURY, kings traditionally spent Christmas here. The Tudors used the palace as a base to hunt deer but it fell to ruin after the Civil War (1642–60). In 1934 Stephen Courtauld, from the
textile family, restored the hall which, apart from the bridge over the moat, was the only part to survive. Near the moat is the 15th-century house of Cardinal Wolsey (*see p253*).

Horniman Museum 🔞

100 London Rd SE23. 🎧 0181-699 2339. 🚊 Forest Hill. **Gardens open** 8am–dusk daily. **Museum open** 10.30am–5.30pm Mon–Sat, 2–5.30pm Sun. **Closed** 24–26 Dec.
♿ 🎥 🎁 🍴 🖥 📷
Concerts, lectures, events.

FREDERICK HORNIMAN, the tea merchant, had this museum built in 1901 to house the curios he had collected on his travels. It has a distinctly Victorian feel, from the inspirational mosaic on the front (representing Humanity in the House of Circumstance) to the overstuffed walrus inside. As you would expect, there is also an exhibition of tea-making paraphernalia.

Dulwich Picture Gallery 🔞

College Rd SE21. 🎧 0181-693 5254.
🚊 West Dulwich, North Dulwich.
Open 10am–1pm, 2–5pm Tue–Fri, 11am–5pm Sat, 2–5pm Sun (last adm: 4.45pm). **Closed** public hols.
Adm charge. 📷 ♿ 🎥 3pm Sat, Sun. 🎁 **Concerts, events.**

ENGLAND'S OLDEST public art gallery, it was opened in 1817 and designed by Sir John Soane (*see pp136–7*). Its imaginative use of skylights

Actor's mask (Java late 19th-century), Horniman Museum

made it the prototype of most art galleries built since. The gallery was commissioned to house the collection of nearby Dulwich College. (The College, by Charles Barry, was opened in 1870.)

This superb collection has works by Rembrandt (whose *Jacob II de Gheyn* has been stolen from here four times), Canaletto, Poussin, Watteau, Claude, Murillo and Raphael.

The building houses Soane's mausoleum to Desenfans and Bourgeouis, original founders of the collection. Dulwich Park is across the road.

Battersea Park ㉒

Albert Bridge Rd SW11. **Map** 19 C5. 0181-871 7530. *Sloane Square then bus 137.* Battersea Park. **Open** *dawn–dusk daily.* **Horticultural Therapy Garden** 0171-720 2212. **Events.** See **Five Guided Walks** pp266–7.

Peace Pagoda, Battersea Park

THIS WAS THE second public park created to relieve the growing urban stresses on Victorian Londoners (the first was Victoria Park in the East End). It opened in 1858 on the former Battersea Fields – a swampy area notorious for every kind of vice, centred around the Old Red House, a disreputable pub.

The new park immediately became popular, especially for its man-made boating lake, with its romantic rocks, gardens and waterfalls. Later it became a great site for the new craze of cycling.

In 1985 a peace pagoda – one of more than 70 built throughout the world – was opened in the park. Buddhist nuns and monks took 11 months to complete the 35-m (100-ft) high monument.

Tennis racket and net from 1888, Wimbledon Lawn Tennis Museum

St Mary's, Battersea ㉓

Battersea Church Rd SW11. 0171-228 9648. *Sloane Square then bus 19 or 219.* **Open** *noon–4pm Tue & Wed, otherwise key available from Vicarage, 32 Vicarage Crescent SW11.* 11am Sun. **Concerts.**

THERE HAS BEEN a church here since at least the 10th century. The present brick building dates from 1775; but the 17th-century stained glass, commemorating Tudor monarchs, comes from the former church.

In 1782 the poet and artist William Blake was married in the church to the daughter of a Battersea market gardener. Later J M W Turner was to paint some of his marvellous views of the Thames from the church tower. Nearby is Old Battersea House (1699).

Wimbledon Lawn Tennis Museum ㉔

Church Rd SW19. 0181-946 6131. *Southfields.* **Open** *10.30am–5pm Tue–Sat, 2–5pm Sun.* **Adm charge.** **Exhibitions.**

EVEN THOSE with only a passing interest in the sport will find plenty to enjoy at this lively museum, on the site of the international tennis tournament. It traces tennis's development from its invention in the 1860s as a diversion for country house parties, to the wealthy professional sport it is today. Alongside strange 19th-century equipment are

film clips showing great players of the past. More recent matches may be viewed in the video theatre.

Wimbledon Windmill Museum ㉕

Windmill Rd SW19. 0181-947 2825. *Wimbledon & then a 30-minute walk.* **Open** *Easter–31 Oct: 2–5pm Sat–Sun.* **Closed** *1 Nov–Easter.* **Adm charge.**

THE MILL on Wimbledon Common was built in 1817 and modified in 1893. The building at its base was converted into cottages in 1864. Lord Baden-Powell, founder of the Boy Scout movement, lived in the mill house. Now the site is a windmill museum.

St Mary's, Battersea

West of the Centre

Ham House

Richmond Park ㉖

Kingston Vale SW15.
📞 0181-940 0654. 🚇 🚉 Richmond then bus 65 or 71. **Open** Oct–Mar: 7.30am–dusk daily; Apr–Sep: 7am–dusk daily. **Fishing, golf.**

Deer in Richmond Park

CHARLES I, WHEN he was Prince of Wales in 1637, built a wall 8 miles (13 km) round to enclose the royal park as a hunting ground. Deer still graze warily among the chestnuts, birches and oaks, no longer hunted but still discreetly culled. They have learned to co-exist with the many thousands of human visitors who stroll here on fine weekends.

In late spring the highlight is the Isabella Plantation with its spectacular display of rhododendrons, while the nearby Pen Ponds are very popular with optimistic anglers. (Adam's Pond is for model boats.) The rest of the park is heath, bracken and trees. Richmond Gate, in the northwest corner, was designed by the landscape gardener Capability Brown in 1798. Nearby is Henry VIII Mound, where in 1536 the

king, staying in Richmond Palace, awaited the signal that his former wife, Anne Boleyn, had been executed. The Palladian White Lodge, built for George II in 1729, is home to the Royal Ballet School.

Hampton Court ㉗

See pp250–3.

Ham House ㉘

Ham St, Richmond. 📞 0181-940 1950. 🚇 🚉 Richmond then bus 65 or 371. **Open** 1–5pm Mon–Wed, 1–5.30pm Sat, 11.30am–5.30pm Sun.

THIS MAGNIFICENT HOUSE by the Thames was built in 1610 but had its heyday later that century, when it became the home of the Duke of Lauderdale, confidant to Charles II and Secretary of State for Scotland. His wife,

Marble Hill House

the Countess of Dysart, inherited the house from her father who, as a child, had been Charles I's "whipping boy" – meaning that he was punished for the future king's misdemeanours. From 1672 the Duke and Countess modernized the house and grounds until it was regarded as one of the finest in Britain. The diarist John Evelyn admired the Lauderdales' garden, which has now been restored to its 17th-century form.

On some days in summer, a foot passenger ferry runs from here to Marble Hill House and Orleans House at Twickenham.

Orleans House ㉙

Orleans Rd, Twickenham.
📞 0181-892 0221. 🚇 🚉 Richmond then bus 33, 90, 290, R68 or R70. **Open** Apr–Sep: 1–5.30pm Tue–Sat, 2–5.30pm Sun, public hols. Oct–Mar: 1–4.30pm Tue–Sat, 2–4.30pm Sun, public hols. **Closed** 24–26 Dec, Good Fri. 🕭 restricted. 🎭 **Concerts, lectures.**

ONLY THE OCTAGON, designed by James Gibbs for James Johnson in 1720, remains of this early 18th-century house. It is named after Louis Philippe, the exiled Duke of Orleans, who lived here between 1800 and 1817, before becoming king of France in 1830. The lively interior plasterwork of the Octagon still remains intact. The adjacent gallery shows temporary exhibitions, and these include some local history displays of the area.

Marble Hill House ㉚

Richmond Rd, Twickenham.
📞 0181-892 5115. 🚇 🚉 Richmond then bus 33, 90, 290, R68 or R70. **Open** Apr–Sep: 10am–6pm daily; Oct–Mar: 10am–4pm daily. **Closed** 24–25 Dec. 🚫 🕭 restricted. 🎭 🎫 🎇 **Concerts, fireworks** on summer weekends.
See **Entertainment** p331.

BUILT IN 1729 for George II's mistress, the house and its grounds have been open to the public since 1903. It has now been largely restored to its

Georgian appearance, but is not yet fully furnished. There are paintings by William Hogarth and a view of the river and house in 1762 by Richard Wilson, who is regarded as the father of English landscape painting.

Richmond ㉛

SW15. ⊖ ⇄ Richmond.

Richmond side street

THIS ATTRACTIVE London village took its name from the palace that Henry VII built here in 1500. Many early 18th-century houses survive near the river and off Richmond Hill, notably Maids of Honour Row, which was built in 1724. The classic view of the river from the top of the hill, that has been painted by numerous landscape artists, remains even now largely unspoiled.

Syon House ㉜

London Rd, Brentford. ☎ 0181-560 0881. ⊖ Gunnersbury then bus 237 or 267. **House open** Apr–Sep: 11am–5pm Sat, Sun, public hols and by arrangement. **House closed** Oct–Mar. **Gardens open** 10am–dusk daily. **Adm charge.** ⌀ ♿ to gardens only. ⎗ ⌂ ⏹ ⊟ ⏹

THE EARLS and Dukes of Northumberland have lived here for 400 years – it is the only large mansion in the London area still in its

hereditary ownership. The outbuildings accommodate a museum of 120 historic cars, a butterfly house, an art centre, a garden centre, a National Trust gift shop and two restaurants. However, the house itself remains the star exhibit with lavish interiors created by Robert Adam. Some rooms have Spitalfields silk wall-hangings and there are many fine pictures. The gardens include a rose garden and a spectacular conservatory built in 1830.

Musical Museum ㉝

368 High St, Brentford. ☎ 0181-560 8108. ⊖ Gunnersbury, South Ealing then bus 65, 237 or 267. **Open** Apr–Jun, Sep–Oct: 2–5pm Sat & Sun; Jul & Aug: 2–4pm Wed–Fri, Sat & Sun 2–5pm. **Closed** Nov–Mar. **Adm charge.** ⏹ ♿ ⎗ ⏹

THE COLLECTION comprises chiefly large instruments, including player (or automatic) pianos and organs, miniature and cinema pianos, and what is thought to be the only surviving self-playing Wurlitzer organ in Europe.

Drawing room: Osterley Park House

Osterley Park House ㉞

Isleworth. ☎ 0181-560 3918. ⊖ Osterley. **Open** 1 Apr–31 Oct: 1–5pm Wed–Sat, 11am–5pm Sun, public hols. **Closed** 1 Nov–31 Mar, Good Fri. ⏹

OSTERLEY is ranked among Robert Adam's finest works, especially for its colonnaded portico and multi-coloured library ceiling. Much of the furniture was designed by Adam. The garden and its temple are by William Chambers, architect of Somerset House (see p117). The greenhouse is by Adam.

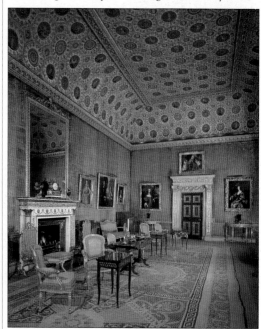

Robert Adam's red drawing room at Syon House

Hampton Court ㉗

Ceiling decoration from the Queen's drawing room

CARDINAL WOLSEY, powerful Archbishop of York to Henry VIII, began building Hampton Court in 1514. Originally it was not a royal palace, but was intended as Wolsey's riverside country residence. Later, in 1525, in the hope of retaining royal favour, Wolsey offered it to the king. After the royal takeover, Hampton Court was twice rebuilt and extended, first by Henry himself and then, in the 1690s, by William and Mary, who employed Christopher Wren as architect.

There is a striking contrast between Wren's Classical royal apartments and the Tudor turrets, gables and chimneys elsewhere. The inspiration for the gardens as they are today comes largely from the time of William and Mary, for whom Wren created a vast, formal Baroque landscape, with radiating avenues of majestic limes and many collections of exotic plants.

★ **The Maze**
Lose yourself in one of the garden's surviving Tudor features.

Royal tennis court

Main entrance

River Thames

★ **The Great Vine**
The vine was planted in 1768, and, in the 19th century, produced up to 910 kg (2,000 lbs) of black grapes.

The Pond Garden
This sunken water garden was part of Henry VIII's elaborate designs.

River boat pier

★ **The Mantegna Gallery**
Andrea Mantegna's nine canvases depicting The Triumph of Julius Caesar *(1490s) are housed here.*

VISITORS' CHECKLIST

East Molesey, Surrey. **C** 0181-
977 8441. **=** 111, 131, 216,
267. **≠** Hampton Court.
≈ Hampton Court pier. **Open**
Apr–Oct: 9.30am–6pm Tue–Sun,
10.15am–6pm Mon; Nov–Mar:
9.30am–4.30pm Tue–Sun,
10.15am–4.30pm Mon. **Closed**
24–26 Dec, 1 Jan, Good Fri. **Adm
charge.** & ⚑ ▣ ⛔ ⛔
See **Where to Stay** p274.

Broad Walk
*A contemporary print shows the
east front and the Broad Walk
during the reign of George II
(1714–27).*

Long Water
*A man-made lake runs
parallel to the Thames,
from the Fountain Garden
across the Home Park.*

Fountain Garden
*A few of the clipped yews
here were planted in the
reign of William and Mary.*

The East Front
*The windows of the
Queen's Drawing
Room, designed by
Wren, overlook the
central avenue of the
Fountain Garden.*

STAR FEATURES

★ **The Great Vine**

★ **The Mantegna
Gallery**

★ **The Maze**

Exploring the Palace

Carving on the roof of the Great Hall

AS AN HISTORIC royal palace, Hampton Court bears traces of all the kings and queens of England from Henry VIII to the present day. From the outside the palace is an harmonious blend of Tudor and English Baroque architecture. Inside, visitors can see the Great Hall, built by Henry VIII, as well as state apartments of the Tudor court. Many of the state apartments, including those above Fountain Court by Christopher Wren, are decorated with furniture, tapestries and old masters from the Royal Collection.

Queen's State Bedroom
William III bought the crimson bed from his Lord Chamberlain.

Queen's Presence Chamber

Queen's Guard Chamber

★ Chapel Royal
The Tudor chapel was redecorated by Wren except for the carved and gilded vaulted ceiling.

Haunted gallery

★ Great Hall
The stained-glass window in the Tudor Great Hall shows Henry VIII flanked by the coats of arms of his six wives.

★ Clock Court
Anne Boleyn's Gateway is at the entrance to Clock Court. The Astronomical Clock, created for Henry VIII in 1540, is also located here.

STAR FEATURES
★ **Great Hall**
★ **Fountain Court**
★ **Clock Court**
★ **Chapel Royal**

Queen's Gallery
This marble chimneypiece by John Nost adorns the Queen's Gallery, where entertainments were often staged.

Wren's east facade

N

Tudor Chimneys
Ornate chimneys, some original, some careful restorations, adorn the roof of the Tudor palace.

CARDINAL WOLSEY

Thomas Wolsey (c.1475–1530), simultaneously a cardinal, Archbishop of York and chancellor, was, after the king, the most powerful man in England. However, when he was unable to persuade the pope to allow Henry VIII to divorce his first wife, Catherine of Aragon, Wolsey fell from royal favour. He died while making his way to face trial for treason.

★ **Fountain Court**
The windows of state apartments are visible above the cloisters of Fountain Court.

King's Staircase
Leading to the royal apartments, the King's Staircase has wall paintings by Antonio Verrio.

TIMELINE

1514 Construction of palace

1532 Henry starts new hall

1529 Wolsey gives the palace to Henry VIII

Henry VIII painted by Hans Holbein

1647 Charles I imprisoned by Cromwell

1689 William and Mary move to Hampton Court

1734 William Kent decorates the Queen's Staircase

1716–18 Queen's apartments are finally completed

1770 Great Gatehouse reduced by two storeys

1838 Public first admitted to the palace

1986 State apartments partly damaged by fire

1992 Damaged apartments are reopened

| 1500 | 1600 | 1700 | 1800 | 1900 |

Pitshanger Manor Museum ⑤

Mattock Lane W5. **[** 0181-567 1227.
🚇 Ealing Broadway. **Open** 10am–
5pm Tue–Sat. **Closed** some public
hols. 🅿 & ▢ **Exhibitions,
concerts, lectures**.

SIR JOHN SOANE, architect of
the Bank of England (see
p147), designed this house
on the site of an earlier one.
Completed in 1803 it was to
become his own country
residence. There are clear
echoes of his elaborately
constructed town house in
Lincoln's Inn Fields (see
pp136–7), especially in the
library, with its
imaginative use of
mirrors, in the darkly-
painted breakfast room
opposite and in the
"monk's dining room"
which is located on the
basement level.

Soane retained two
of the principal formal
rooms: the drawing room
and the dining room. These
were designed in 1768 by
George Dance the
Younger, with whom
Soane had worked
before establishing
his own reputation.
The eating room has
been extended
sympathetically and serves as
a venue for concerts and
poetry readings.

The house also contains a
small exhibition of Martinware, highly decorated glazed
pottery made in nearby
Southall between 1877 and
1915 and fashionable in late

**Martinware bird at
Pitshanger Manor**

Victorian times. The gardens
of Pitshanger Manor now
make a pleasant public park
and provide a welcome
contrast to the busy shopping
centre of nearby Ealing.

Kew Bridge Steam Museum ⑥

Green Dragon Lane, Brentford.
[0181-568 4757. 🚇 Kew Bridge,
Gunnersbury then bus 237 or 267.
Open 11am–5pm daily. **Closed** week
before Christmas, Good Fri. **Adm
charge**. 🅿 & 🚻 ▢ 🅱

THE 19TH-CENTURY water
pumping station, near
the north end of Kew
Bridge, has now been
opened as a museum of
steam power. Its chief
exhibits are five giant
Cornish beam engines
which used to pump
the water here from
the river, to be
distributed through
London. The earliest
engines, which date
from 1820, were
designed to pump
water out of the
Cornish tin and
copper mines. An
exhibition relates to
the water supply.

Kew Gardens ⑦

See pp256–7.

City Barge: Strand on the Green

Strand on the Green ⑧

W4. 🚇 Gunnersbury then bus 237
or 267.

THIS CHARMING Thames-side
walk passes some fine
18th-century houses as well
as rows of more modest
cottages once inhabited by
fishermen. The oldest of its
three pubs is the City Barge
(see pp308–9), parts of which
date from the 15th century:
the name is older and derives
from when the Lord Mayor's
barge was moored on the
Thames outside.

Chiswick House ⑨

Burlington Lane W4. **[** 0181-995
0508. 🚇 Chiswick. **Open** Apr–Sep:
10am–6pm daily; Oct–Mar: 10am–
4pm Wed–Sun. **Closed** 1–2pm some
days. **Adm charge**. 🚫 ▢ 🅱

COMPLETED IN 1729 to the
design of the third Earl of
Burlington, this is a textbook
example of a Palladian villa.
Burlington revered both
Palladio and his disciple Inigo

**Chiswick
House**

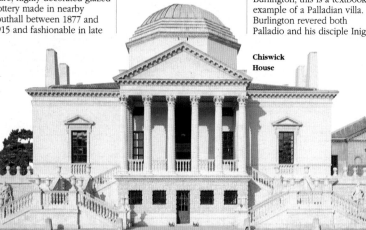

Jones, and their statues stand outside. Built round a central octagonal room, the house is packed with references to ancient Rome and Palladian devices, such as rooms whose dimensions form perfect cubes.

Chiswick was Burlington's country residence and this house was built as an annexe to a larger, older house, which was later demolished. It was designed for recreation and entertaining – Lord Hervey, Burlington's enemy, dismissed it as "too little to live in and too big to hang on a watch chain". Some of the ceiling paintings are by William Kent, who also laid out the gardens.

The house was a private mental home from 1892 until 1928 when a long process of restoration began. The restorers are still searching for pieces of its original furniture, but the layout of the garden, now a public park, is much as Kent designed it.

Hogarth's House 40

Hogarth Lane, W4. **(** 0181-994 6757. **⊖** Turnham Green. **Open** Apr–Sep: 11am–6pm Wed–Mon, 2–6pm Sun; Oct–Mar: 11am–4pm Wed–Mon, 2–4pm Sun. **Closed** first 2 wks in Sep, last 3 wks in Dec. **⊘ ⊙ ⑤** ground floor only. **⑤**

WHEN THE PAINTER William Hogarth lived here from 1749 until his death in 1764, he called it "a little country box by the Thames" and painted bucolic views from its windows – he had moved

Tudor entrance to Fulham Palace

from Leicester Square *(see p103)*. Today heavy traffic roars by along the Great West Road, on its way to and from Heathrow Airport – rush hour traffic is also notoriously bad here. In an environment as hostile as this, and following years of neglect and then bombing during World War II, the house has done well to survive. It has now been turned into a small museum and gallery, which is filled mostly with a collection of engraved copies of the moralistic cartoon-style pictures with which Hogarth made his name. Salutary tales, such as *The Rake's Progress* (in Sir John Soane's Museum – *see pp136–7)*, *Marriage à la Mode, An Election Entertainment* and many others, can all be seen here.

Plaque on Hogarth's House

Fulham Palace 41

Bishops Ave SW6. **(** 0171-736 3233. **⊖** Putney Bridge. **Open** Wed–Sun, public hol Mon, Mar–Oct: 2–5pm; Nov–Mar: 1–4pm Thu–Sun. **Closed** 25–26 Dec. **Park open** daylight hours. **Adm charge. ⑤ ⊘ ⑦ ⑤** Events, concerts, lectures.

THE HOME of the Bishops of London from the 8th century until 1973, the oldest parts of Fulham Palace date from the 15th century. The rest of the building has been embellished in a mixture of styles by successive bishops. The palace stands in its own gardens in Bishop's Park west and north of Putney Bridge, where the annual Oxford versus Cambridge Boat Race begins *(see p56)*.

1940s wind-up cycle, London Toy and Model Museum

Chelsea Harbour 42

SW10. **⊖** Fulham Broadway. **⑤** **Exhibitions. ⑤ ⑦**

THIS IS AN impressive development of modern apartments, shops, offices, restaurants, a hotel and a marina. It is near the site of Cremorne Pleasure Gardens, which closed in 1877 after more than 40 years as a venue for dances and circuses. The centrepiece is the Belvedere, a 20-storey apartment tower with an external glass lift and pyramid roof, topped with a golden ball on a rod that rises and falls with the tide.

London Toy And Model Museum 43

21–23 Craven Hill W2. **Map** 10 E2. **(** 0171-402 5222. **⊖** Paddington. **Open** 10am–5.30pm Mon–Sat, 11am–5.30pm Sun (last adm: 4.30pm). **Adm charge. ⊙ ⑤ ⑤** **⑦** Annual exhibitions.

AN ENORMOUS NUMBER of toys models and dolls, dating from the 18th century up to the present, are crammed into this house near Paddington station. There is a room of model trains and another of cars; a teddy bears' picnic; and dolls' houses, the biggest of which is 2.4 m (8 ft) long and has 16 rooms. In the garden are a carousel and two model railways, one of which offers rides. The museum provides many delights and activities for children, and much nostalgia for adults.

Kew Gardens ㊲

THE ROYAL BOTANIC GARDENS at Kew are the most complete public gardens in the world. Their reputation was first established by Sir Joseph Banks, the British naturalist and plant hunter, who worked here in the late 18th century. In 1841 the former royal gardens were given to the nation and now display about 40,000 different kinds of plant. Kew is also a centre for scholarly research into horticulture and botany and garden enthusiasts will want a full day for their visit.

Princess Augusta
King George III's mother established the first garden on a nine-acre (3.6 ha) site here in 1759.

Queen's Cottage

★ Temperate House
The building dates from 1899. Delicate woody plants are arranged here according to their geographical origins.

★ Pagoda
Britain's fascination with the Orient influenced William Chambers's pagoda, built in 1762.

HIGHLIGHTS

Spring
Flowering cherries ①
Crocus "carpet" ②

Summer
Rock Garden ③
Rose Garden ④

Autumn
Autumn foliage ⑤

Winter
Alpine House ⑥
Witch Hazels ⑦

Lion Gate entrance

Flagpole

Marianne North Gallery
The Victorian flower painter, Marianne North, gave her works to Kew and paid for this gallery of 1882.

★ Palm House
Designed by Decimus
Burton in the 1840s, this
recently restored jewel of
Victorian engineering offers
a warm winter refuge.

River
Thames

VISITORS' CHECKLIST

Royal Botanic Gdns, Richmond,
Kew. **(0181-940 1171.**
Kew Gdns. **65, 391, from**
Richmond. **Kew Bridge, Kew
Gdns. Open daylight hours.
Closed 25 Dec, 1 Jan. Adm
charge.**

★ Kew Palace
Known as the Dutch House
because of its distinctive
gables, this building, dating
from 1631, was used as a
royal palace by George III.
It is now open to the public
from April to October.

Brentford Gate
entrance

Nash Conservatory

Sir Joseph Banks
Building

Main gate
entrance

Orangery

Cottage Garden

Temple of
Bellona

Campanile

Victoria Gate
entrance

Cumberland Gate
entrance

STAR SIGHTS

★ Kew Palace

★ Temperate House

★ Pagoda

★ Palm House

Aquatic Garden
The water lilies here
are spectacular between
July and September.

**Princess of Wales
Conservatory**
It houses cacti in ten
enclosures, each with
its own micro-climate.

FIVE GUIDED WALKS

LONDON IS AN EXCELLENT city for walkers. Although it is much more spread out than most European capitals, many of the main tourist attractions are fairly close to each other (see pp12–13). Central London is full of parks and gardens (see pp48–51), and there are also several walk routes planned by the tourist board and local history societies. These include footpaths along canals and the Thames, and the Silver Jubilee Walk. Planned in 1977 to commemorate the Queen's Silver Jubilee, the walk runs for 12 miles (19 km) between Lambeth Bridge in the west and Tower Bridge in the east; the London Tourist Board (see p345) has maps of the route, which is marked by silver-coloured plaques placed at intervals on the pavement.

Statue of boy and dolphin in Regent's Park

Each of the 16 areas described in the *Area-by-Area* section of this book has a short walk marked on its *Street-by-Street* map. These walks will take you past many of the most interesting sights in that area. On the following ten pages are routes for five walks that take you through areas of London not covered in detail elsewhere. These range from the crowded 18th-century streets of Mayfair (see pp260–1) to the wide open spaces of riverside. Richmond and Kew (see pp268–9).

Several companies offer guided walks (see below). Most of these have themes, such as ghosts or Shakespeare's London. Look in listings magazines (see p324) for details.

Useful numbers The Original London Walks 【 0171-624 3978. City Walks 【 0171-700 6931.

CHOOSING A WALK

The Five Walks
This map shows the location of the five guided walks in relation to the main sightseeing areas of London.

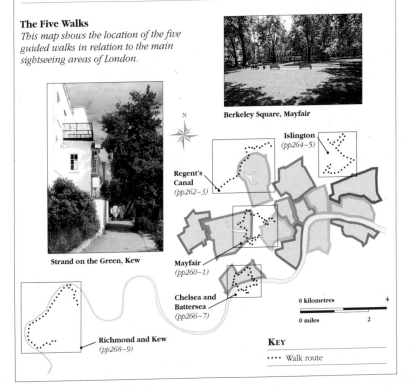

Berkeley Square, Mayfair

Strand on the Green, Kew

Islington
(pp264–5)

Regent's
Canal
(pp262–3)

Mayfair
(pp260–1)

Chelsea and
Battersea
(pp266–7)

Richmond and Kew
(pp268–9)

N

0 kilometres 4

0 miles 2

KEY

•••• Walk route

Houseboats on Regent's Canal, Little Venice

A Two-Hour Walk through Mayfair

THIS WALK PENETRATES the heart of Mayfair and Knightsbridge, London's most elegant Georgian residential districts. It includes a bracing stroll through the green elegance of Hyde Park and, if you wish, a row on the grey waters of the Serpentine.

L'Artiste Musclé, Shepherd Market ⑦

Green Park to Berkeley Square

Leave Green Park station ① by the signs for Piccadilly North Side. With Green Park opposite you, turn left. You now pass Devonshire House ②, a 1920s office block that replaced William Kent's 18th-century mansion for the dukes of Devonshire – only Kent's gates survive, now at the entrance to the park across Piccadilly. Turn left up Berkeley Street to Berkeley Square ③. To the south, Lansdowne House by Robert

Nymph on Berkeley Square ③

Adam has been replaced by the headquarters of an advertising agency ④. There are still some splendid 18th-century houses on the west side, including No. 45 ⑤ where the soldier and governor, Clive of India, lived.

Mayfair

Keep to the south of the square and turn left into Charles Street, noting the evocative lamp-holders at Nos. 40 and 41 ⑥. Turn left into Queen Street and cross Curzon Street to enter Shepherd Market ⑦ *(see p97)* through Curzonfield House alleyway. Turning right up the pedestrianized street you come to Tiddy Dols Eating House ⑧. Turn right into Hertford Street, passing the Curzon Cinema ⑨ on the corner of Curzon Street. Here you are almost facing Crewe House ⑩, built in 1730 by the Edward Shepherd who laid out the market.

Turn left up Curzon Street, then right into Chesterfield Street. Another left turn at Charles Street brings you to Red Lion Yard ⑪, where a pub stands opposite one of the few weather-boarded buildings in the West End. Turn right into Hay's Mews and left up Chesterfield Hill. Cross Hill Street and then South Street and head slightly left until you reach an alley leading to

Houses on Berkeley Square ③

0 metres		500
0 yards		500

Memorial on Grosvenor Square ⑭

the peaceful haven of Mount Street Gardens ⑫. It backs on to the Church of the Immaculate Conception ⑬.

Cross the garden and turn left into Mount Street; then right into South Audley Street

South Audley Street

TIPS FOR WALKERS

Starting point: Green Park Underground station.
Length: 3 miles (5 km).
Getting there: Green Park, Marble Arch, Hyde Park Corner and Knightsbridge Underground stations are all on the route. Bus Nos. 9, 14, 19, 22, 25 and 38 go to Green Park.
Stopping-off points: There are numerous pubs, cafés and restaurants in the area. The Dell Café on the Serpentine is open 8am–8pm.

and left at Grosvenor Square ⑭ into Upper Grosvenor Street, passing to the left of the US Embassy (1961). Turn right up Park Lane and go past the remnants of the houses ⑮ that lined what used to be London's most desirable residential street before the traffic got so heavy.

Hyde Park

Enter the pedestrian subway ⑯ at exit No. 6 and follow signs for Park Lane West Side, exit No. 5. You will emerge at Speakers' Corner ⑰ (see p207). Cross Hyde Park (see p207) south-southwest, making for the boat house ⑱ of the Serpentine, an artificial lake created by Queen Caroline in 1730. You could hire a boat, or turn left and follow the path to the Dell Café ⑲. From there, cross a stone bridge ⑳ and cross Rotten Row ㉑, where the most fashionable riders exercise their horses. Leave the park at Edinburgh Gate ㉒, where the road tunnels through Bowater House.

Speakers' Corner ⑰

far side, turning left in Motcomb Street. On your left is the Pantechnicon, an eccentric structure fronted by colossal Doric columns, built in 1830. A path beside it leads to Halkin Arcade ㉕, adorned by Geoffrey Wickham's fountain (1971).

Belgravia

Turn left out of the arcade into Kinnerton Street, which boasts one of London's smallest pubs, the Nag's Head ㉖. Pretty mews run off the left of this street at its northern end: look for Ann's Close and Kinnerton Place North. Almost opposite the latter, the street makes a sharp right turn to emerge into Wilton Place opposite St Paul's church (1843). Turn right here and follow Wilton Crescent around to the left before turning left into Wilton Row where there is another miniature pub, the Grenadier ㉗, once the officers' mess of the Guards' barracks and reputedly frequented by the Duke of Wellington. Up Old Barracks Yard to its right are some old officers' billets and a worn stone said to have been used by the duke for mounting his horses. The alley leads to a T-junction. Turn right into Grosvenor Crescent Mews, then left into Grosvenor Crescent, which leads you to Hyde Park Corner Underground station.

Serpentine Lake ⑱

KEY

— Walk route

☙ Good viewing point

Ⓔ Underground station

Knightsbridge

Resisting the temptations of two of London's great department stores – Harvey Nichols ㉓ on your left and Harrod's ㉔ (see p207) 90 m (100 yd) to your right – cross Knightsbridge and head down Sloane Street to turn left at Harriet Street. At Lowndes Square turn right and leave the square on the

Grenadier Pub ㉗

A Two-Hour Walk along the Regent's Canal

MASTER BUILDER John Nash wanted the Regent's Canal to pass through Regent's Park, but instead it circles north of the park. Opened in 1820, it is long defunct as a commercial waterway but is today a valuable leisure amenity. This walk starts at Little Venice and ends at Camden Lock market, diverting briefly to take in the view from Primrose Hill. For more details on the sights near the Regent's Canal, see pages 216–23.

Houseboat on the canal ③

From Little Venice to Lisson Grove

At Warwick Avenue station ① take the left-hand exit and walk straight to the traffic lights by the canal bridge at Blomfield Road. Turn right and descend to the canal through an iron gate ② opposite No. 42, marked "Lady Rose of Regent". The pretty basin with moored narrow boats is Little Venice ③. At the foot of the steps turn left to walk back beneath the blue iron bridge ④. You soon have to climb up to street level again because this stretch of the towpath is reserved for access to the

The Warwick Castle, near Warwick Avenue

barges. Cross Edgware Road and walk down Aberdeen Place. When the road turns to the left by a pub, Crockers ⑤, follow the signposted Canal Way down to the right of some modern flats. A short stretch of towpath is closed for repair, but you can walk above the canal before rejoining it down a ramp by a bus stop. The scenery here is unremarkable until a splash of green on the right announces that you are alongside Regent's Park ⑥.

Houseboats moored at Little Venice ③

TIPS FOR WALKERS

Starting point: Warwick Avenue Underground station.
Length: 3 miles (5 km).
Getting there: Warwick Avenue and Camden Town Underground stations are at either end of the walk. Buses 16, 16A and 98 go to Warwick Avenue; 24, 29 and 31 go to Camden Town.
Stopping-off points: Crockers, Queens and The Princess of Wales (corner of Fitzroy and Chalcot Roads) are good pubs. At the junction of Edgware Road and Aberdeen Place is Café La Ville. Camden Town has many cafés, restaurants and sandwich shops.

KEY

— Walk route
⁂ Good viewing point
Ⓔ Underground station
🚉 British rail

Regent's Park

Soon you see four mansions ⑦. A bridge on huge pillars marked "Coalbrookdale" ⑧ carries Avenue Road into the park. Cross the next bridge, with London Zoo ⑨ on your right, then turn left up a slope. A few steps later, take the right fork, and turn left to cross Prince Albert Road. Turn right before entering Primrose Hill through a gate ⑩ on your left.

Mansion with riverside gardens ⑦

Primrose Lodge, Primrose Hill ⑩

Primrose Hill
From here there is a view of the zoo aviary ⑪, designed by Lord Snowdon and opened in 1965. Inside the park, keep to the left-hand path that climbs to the top of the hill. Soon you fork right to the summit, which offers a fine view of the city skyline. A viewing panel ⑫ helps identify the landmarks but it does not include the 1990 skyscraper at Canary Wharf, with its pyramid crown, on the left. Descend on the left, making for the park gate at the junction of Regent's Park Road and Primrose Hill Road.

Indoor market, Camden Lock ⑲

Towards Camden
Almost opposite the gate is the Queens ⑬, a Victorian pub and, just to the left, is No. 122 Regent's Park Road ⑭. This was for 24 years the home of the communist philosopher Friedrich Engels; he was often visited there by his friend Karl Marx.

Turn right and walk down Regent's Park Road for 135 m (150 yd) then turn left up Fitzroy Road. On the right, between Nos. 41 and 39, is the entrance to Primrose Hill Studios ⑮, built in 1882. Residents have included the musician Sir Henry Wood and illustrator Arthur Rackham, famous for his fairy pictures.

Continue down Fitzroy Road past No. 23 ⑯, once home to the poet W B Yeats, then go right into Chalcot Road and left down Princess Road, past a Victorian board school ⑰. Turn right and rejoin the canal down steps across Gloucester Avenue. Turn left under the railway bridge and past the Pirate Castle ⑱, a water sports centre. Cross a hump bridge and enter Camden Lock Market ⑲ *(see p322)* through an arch on your left. After browsing there you can take the water bus ⑳ back to Little Venice or turn right into Chalk Farm Road and walk up to Camden Town Underground station.

Pedestrian bridge over the canal at Camden Lock ⑲

A Two-Hour Walk in Islington

THIS WALK OF CONTRASTS starts in the quiet streets of Canonbury, which have intriguing literary associations. It traces the route of a 17th-century man-made river, visits a canalside pub and ends among London's most concentrated array of antique shops.

Canonbury Grove houses

Canonbury Square

Turn right on leaving Highbury and Islington station ① and head southeast down Canonbury Road. The road soon dissects Canonbury Square ②, laid out in 1800. If you turn left into the eastern half, you can walk through the garden to admire the flower beds and statue. The novelist Evelyn Waugh lived at No. 17a ③ in 1928, while the writer George Orwell lived at No. 27a ④ in 1945.

Canonbury

Leaving the square at the northeast corner, you face the late 18th-century Canonbury House ⑤. Other charming houses from the same period line the cul-de-sac to its right. Next to it is the historic Canonbury Tower ⑥, which is mainly 16th-century although parts date from the 13th century when the de Berners family built their

Statue in Canonbury Square

manor house here, in what was then countryside. Later it was occupied by the canons of St Bartholomew, hence the name Canonbury. The tower, now the home of a theatre company, served as an apartment house in the 18th century; the writers Oliver Goldsmith and Washington Irving were among its residents. Beyond the Tower, fork left into Canonbury Park North ⑦. Where the street meets St Paul's Road, opposite the New Crown pub ⑧, turn right and, after a few paces, right again along a paved lane between trees. After 25 m (30 yd) a gate on the right leads you into the New River Walk ⑨.

New River Walk

The New River was a real feat of engineering for its day. In the 17th century Sir Hugh Myddleton, a Welsh jeweller, cut a 40-mile (65-km) channel to bring water from Hertfordshire. Today, a landscaped park lines part of its course.

Keep to the path until you go over a stone bridge ⑩ and reach Willow Bridge Road. Cross the road and turn left, re-entering the river walk through a gate ⑪ in Canonbury Grove. You pass a round brick hut ⑫ just before exiting on Canonbury

View along the towpath of the Grand Union Canal ⑮

The river walk at Canonbury Grove ⑨–⑫

Grove. The final stretch of the path ⑬ is in a park just across Canonbury Road. Head southeast down Canonbury Road and into New North Road; after 450 m (500 yds) turn left into Shepperton Road ⑭. At the junction with Baring Street, a gate leads to steps down to the towpath of the Grand Union Canal ⑮.

Along the Grand Union Canal

At the foot of the steps go straight ahead, with the canal on your left. This is a very different waterside walk from the bucolic New River; here the canal is lined with old industrial buildings and new housing estates. At weekends fishermen sit silently in hope, not

Narrow Boat pub ⑱

seeming to catch much. Soon Sturt's Lock ⑯ comes into view, and beyond it a few houseboats moored near the entrance to Wenlock Basin ⑰. On the right, the Narrow Boat Pub ⑱ is ideal for a refreshment stop.

Beyond the City Road Lock and Basin ⑲ the right of way switches to the opposite bank – this route must be taken to avoid a dead-end. Leave the towpath on Danbury Street and cross the bridge ⑳ to descend on the other side. You finally leave the canal at the entrance to the 730-m (800-yd) Islington Tunnel ㉑, climbing steps up to Colebrooke Row.

Camden Passage antique shop

Islington

Turn right here, past some fine Georgian terraces ㉒, then go left at the Market Tavern into St Peter's Street and left again at Islington Green ㉓, in Victorian times renowned as the site of the lively Collins' Music Hall. Just past the petrol station on your left you can enter Camden Passage, the heart of a network of antiques shops, indoor markets and excellent restaurants.

After you have passed the Camden Head pub ㉔ you will see, on the south end of the green, a statue of Sir Hugh Myddleton ㉕, whose river you explored earlier. Follow Islington High Street south and on the left, just before the junction with City Road, is the Angel Underground station, named after the coaching inn that used to stand nearby.

Sir Hugh Myddleton ㉕

KEY

— Walk route

� Good viewing point

Ⓔ Underground station

Ⓑ British Rail

TIPS FOR WALKERS

Starting point: *Highbury and Islington Underground station.*
Length: *3 miles (5 km).*
Getting there: *Highbury and Islington tube or Canonbury British Rail are the nearest stations. Buses 4, 30 and 43 go to Highbury; 19 and 73 to Angel.*
Stopping-off points: *There are sandwich bars and pubs at the Highbury end of the walk; the Narrow Boat pub is on the canal; and there are a number of pubs, cafés and restaurants clustered around the Angel.*

0 metres   250

0 yards   250

A Three-Hour Walk in Chelsea and Battersea

THIS DELIGHTFUL CIRCULAR WALK ambles through the grounds of the Royal Hospital and across the river to Battersea Park, with its romantic Victorian landscaping. It then returns to the narrow village streets of Chelsea and the stylish shops on the King's Road. For more details on the sights in Chelsea see pages 188–93.

Royal Hospital ③

Sloane Square to Battersea Park

From the station ①, turn left and walk down Holbein Place. The Renaissance painter's connection with Chelsea stems from his friendship with Sir Thomas More who lived nearby. Pass the cluster of good antique shops ② as you turn on to Royal Hospital Road. Enter the grounds of the Royal Hospital ③, designed by Christopher Wren, and turn left into the informal Ranelagh Gardens ④. The small pavilion by John Soane ⑤ displays a history of the gardens as a Georgian pleasure resort – it was the most fashionable meeting place for London society.

Galleon on Chelsea Bridge

Leave the gardens for fine views of the hospital and Grinling Gibbons's bronze of Charles II ⑥. The granite obelisk ⑦ commemorates the 1849 battle at Chilianwalla, in what is now Pakistan, and forms the centrepiece of the main marquee at the Chelsea Flower Show (see p56).

Battersea Park

When crossing the Chelsea Bridge ⑧ (1937), look up at the four gilded galleons on top of the pillars at each end. Turn into Battersea Park ⑨ (see p247), one of London's liveliest, and follow the main path along the river to enjoy the excellent views of Chelsea. Turn left at the exotic Buddhist Peace Pagoda ⑩ to the main part of the park.

Past the bowling greens lies Henry Moore's carving of *Three Standing Figures* ⑪ (1948) and the lake, a favoured spot for wildfowl. (There are boats for hire.) Just beyond the sculpture head northwest and, after crossing the central avenue, fork right and make for the wooden gate into the rustic Old English Garden ⑫. Leave the garden by the metal gate and return to Chelsea via the Victorian Albert Bridge ⑬.

Charles II statue in Royal Hospital ⑥

Three Standing Figures by Henry Moore ⑪

KEY

—— Walk route

☆ Good viewing point

e Underground station

TIPS FOR WALKERS

Starting point: *Sloane Square.*
Length: *4 miles (6.5 km).*
Getting there: *Sloane Square is the nearest tube. There are frequent buses 11, 19, 22 and 349 to Sloane Square and along the King's Road.*
Royal Hospital Grounds are open only *10am–6pm Mon–Sat, 2–6pm Sun.*
Stopping-off points: *There is a café in Battersea Park, by the lake. The King's Head and Eight Bells, on Cheyne Walk, is a well known local pub. There are several other pubs, restaurants and sandwich shops to be found along the King's Road. The Chelsea Farmers' Market on Sydney Street has several cafés.*

Old English Garden in Battersea Park ⑫

Albert Bridge ⑬

much of its original character. Where Glebe Place meets the King's Road are three pretty, early 18th-century houses ㉓. Cross Dovehouse Green opposite (it used to be a burial ground), to Chelsea Farmers' Market ㉔, an enclave of cafés and craft shops.

The King's Road

Leave the market on Sydney Street and cross into the garden of St Luke's Church ㉕, where the writer Charles Dickens was married. The walk then winds through pretty back streets until it rejoins the King's Road ㉖ (see p192), which was very fashionable in the 1960s. On the left is The Pheasantry ㉗. Look down the side streets on both left and right to see the squares and terraces: Wellington Square ㉘, then Royal Avenue ㉙, intended as a triumphal way to the Royal Hospital, and Blacklands Terrace ㉚, where book-lovers will want to visit John Sandoe's shop. The Duke of York's Territorial Head-quarters ㉛ (1803) on the right marks the approach to Sloane Square ㉜ and the Royal Court Theatre (see Sloane Square p193).

Thomas Carlyle statue ⑮

its carving by Jacob Epstein. Just beyond these is the old, medieval

The Back Streets of Chelsea

Over the bridge is David Wynne's sculpture of a boy and dolphin ⑭ (1975). Pass the sought-after residences on Cheyne Walk and the statues of historian Thomas Carlyle ⑮, and Sir Thomas More ⑯. The area was renowned for gatherings of intellectuals. Past Chelsea Old Church ⑰ is Roper's Gardens ⑱ with

Crosby Hall ⑲. Justice Walk ⑳ has a nice view of two early Georgian houses – Duke's House and Monmouth House. Turn left to pass the site of the Chelsea porcelain factory ㉑, which used to make highly fashionable (and today very highly collectable) wares in the late 18th century. Glebe Place ㉒ has retained

Royal Court Theatre ㉜

A 90-Minute Walk around Richmond and Kew

THIS DELIGHTFUL RIVERSIDE walk begins in historic Richmond by the remains of Henry VII's once-splendid palace and ends at Kew, Britain's premier botanic garden. For more details on the sights in Richmond and Kew, turn to pages 248–54.

The river at low tide

Richmond Green

From Richmond station ①, proceed to Oriel House ②, which is practically opposite. Take the alleyway beneath it, and turn left towards the red-brick and terracotta Richmond Theatre ③, built in 1899. The remarkable Edmund Kean, whose brief, meteoric career in the early 19th century had a lasting impact on English acting, was closely associated with the previous theatre on the site. Opposite is Richmond Green ④. Cross it diagonally and go through the entrance arch ⑤ of the old Tudor palace, which is adorned with the arms of Henry VII.

Old Palace: carving over entrance ⑤

remnants, much modified, of the 16th-century buildings.

Leave Old Palace Yard at the right-hand corner ⑥, following a sign "To the River", and turn left to pass the White Swan pub ⑦. At the river, go right along the towpath under the iron railway bridge and then the concrete Twickenham Bridge ⑧, completed in 1933, to reach Richmond Lock ⑨, with its cast-iron footbridge built in 1894. The Thames is tidal as far as Teddington, some 3 miles (5 km) upstream, and the lock is used to make the river continuously navigable.

Richmond Theatre ③

Richmond

Richmond owes much of its importance – as well as its name – to Henry, victor of the Wars of the Roses and the first Tudor monarch. On becoming king in 1485 he spent a lot of time at an earlier residence on this site, Sheen Palace, dating from the 12th century. The palace burned down in 1499 and Henry had it rebuilt, naming it Richmond after the town in Yorkshire where he held an earldom. In 1603 Henry's daughter, Elizabeth I, died here. The houses inside the archway on the left contain

The Riverside

Do not cross the bridge but continue along the wooded path by the river to Isleworth Ait ⑩, a large island where herons may be standing warily on the river bank. Just beyond it, on the far shore, is All Saints' Church ⑪, where the 15th-century tower has survived several rebuildings, most recently in the 1960s. Further round the inlet, Isleworth ⑫, once a small riverside village with a busy harbour, is now a dormitory for central London. Here there will be river traffic to watch: barges, yachts and, in summer, the passenger boats that ply up-river to Hampton Court (see pp60–1). Rowers are out at most times of year, training for races and regattas. The most prestigious occasions are the Henley Regatta in July and the Oxford v Cambridge boat race, every spring from Putney to Mortlake (see p56).

Herons fish the river

KEY

—	Walk route
⁂	Good viewing point
⊖	Underground station
⇋	British rail

Kew

After a while the appearance of iron railings on your right marks where Old Deer Park ⑬ turns into Kew Gardens ⑭ (more correctly the Royal Botanic Gardens – *see pp256–7*). There used to be a riverside entrance for visitors arriving on foot or by water, but the gate ⑮ is now

Kew Palace in Kew Gardens ⑲

Just beyond are modern waterside apartments at Brentford ⑰. This was originally an industrial suburb, sited where the Grand Union Canal runs into the Thames, and its residential potential has only recently been exploited. You can pick out the tall chimney of the waterworks ⑱, now a museum dedicated to steam power. On the right, behind the Kew Gardens car park, there is soon a view of Kew Palace ⑲, a gloomy edifice in red brick built in 1631.

Beyond the car park, leave the river by Ferry Lane on to Kew Green ⑳. Now you could spend the rest of the day in Kew Gardens or cross Kew Bridge and turn right on to Strand on the Green ㉑, a fine riverside walkway with atmospheric pubs, the oldest of them the City Barge ㉒ *(see p256)*. Head south down Kew Road if you need to get back, then turn left at Kew Gardens Road to depart from Kew Gardens underground station (District line).

Steam Museum ⑱

closed and the nearest entrance is to the north, near the car park.

Across the river, there are magnificent views of Syon House ⑯, seat of the Dukes of Northumberland since 1594. Part of the present house dates from the 16th century but it was largely redesigned by Robert Adam in the 1760s. You are looking at it across the garden Capability Brown laid out in the 18th century.

TIPS FOR WALKERS

Starting point: *Richmond station.*

Length: *3 miles (5 km).*

Getting there: *Richmond Underground or British Rail station. Bus 415 comes from Victoria; 391 and R68 from Kew.*

Stopping-off points: *There are many cafés, pubs and tearooms in Richmond. The famous Maids of Honour tearoom is at Kew, as is Jasper's Bun in the Oven, a good restaurant.*

| 0 metres | 500 |
| 0 yards | 500 |

The river bank between Richmond and Kew

TRAVELLERS' NEEDS

WHERE TO STAY

L ONDON'S HOTELS have had one of the worst reputations for value in Europe, but things are improving rapidly. At the top end of the market, there are the reliable, if expensive, international establishments and the pedigree hotels, such as the Savoy and the Ritz, for which London is renowned. Many of the mid-range hotels offer better value for money, although they tend to be slightly further out of the centre of town. There is, however, a distinct lack of appealing hotels at the lower end of the market, and budget hotels can be rather seedy and run down.

Hilton doorman

We have inspected more than 200 hotels across a wide range of price brackets and have selected 84 of them as offering visitors particularly good value for money. *Choosing a Hotel* on pages 276–7 will help you to narrow down your choice of hotel; for further details on each of the hotels turn to the listings found on pages 278–85.

Apart from hotels, there are other options worth considering. Self-catering apartments and private homes *(see pp274–5)* are available at a wide range of prices, and there are camping sites, halls or hostels for students and budget travellers *(see p275)*.

WHERE TO LOOK

T HE MOST EXPENSIVE hotels tend to be in smart West End areas such as Mayfair and Belgravia. Often large and opulent, with uniformed flunkies, they are not always the most relaxing places to stay. For smaller, but still luxurious hotels, head for South Kensington or Holland Park.

The streets off Earl's Court Road are full of hotels at the bottom of the price range. Several of the big railway stations are well served with smaller hotels too. Try Ebury Street near Victoria, or Sussex Gardens near Paddington. From Euston, head for Bloomsbury (avoiding the insalubrious area behind King's Cross), where several modern hotels offer sensibly priced accommodation.

There are inexpensive hotels in the suburbs, such as Ealing, Hendon, Wembley or Harrow, where you can leave your car, and get into town easily on public transport (although it may take an hour or more to do so).

If you get stranded at an airport or have to catch a very early morning flight, consult the list on pages 356–7.

For further information, advice and booking services, contact the **London Tourist Board** which offers useful leaflets about all sorts of accommodation in central and Greater London.

DISCOUNT RATES

P RICES TEND to be high all year round, but there are usually bargains to be had. Many hotels, including the big groups, reduce their rates at weekends and for special breaks *(see p274)*. Others work on a more ad hoc basis, depending on how busy they are. If a hotel isn't full, it is always worth trying to negotiate a discount.

Hotels in the lower price brackets often offer rooms without attached showers or bathrooms. These cost about 20% less than the full tariff.

HIDDEN EXTRAS

T HERE IS A tendency to quote tariffs exclusive of VAT (currently 17.5% – *see p310*), and the final bill can come as a shock. Read the small print carefully. Most hotels give room rates rather than rates per person, but check. You should also check the service charge, which is usually included in the quoted price but in some cases is added on. Beware of extras, such as a mark-up on telephone calls.

The Tearoom at the Waldorf Hotel (*see p284*)

The Hampshire Hotel *(see p283)*

Breakfast is likely to be charged on top of the room rate in more expensive hotels, but tends to be included in the price in cheaper ones. Continental breakfast usually consists of coffee, fruit juice and a roll, toast or croissants with jam. English (or full) breakfast will see you through the busiest mornings of sightseeing. At its most basic it consists of cereal and fruit juice, followed by bacon, eggs and toast *(see p288)*.

Tipping is expected in the more expensive hotels. There is generally no need to tip staff other than porters, the exception being the concierge if, for example, he or she books theatre tickets for you.

Single travellers are usually charged a "supplement" and end up paying about 80% of the double room rate, even if they are occupying a "single" room – so make sure you get a good one.

The elegant hallway of the Gore Hotel in Kensington *(see p279)*

FACILITIES

Rooms at all prices can be small (see the chart on pages 276–7 for hotels with larger than average rooms), but all except the most basic provide at least a telephone and television. In general, recently modernized hotels provide the most facilities at any price level, although in some small and very smart hotels you pay for atmosphere and pampering rather than for mini-bars and electronic gadgetry.

Whatever the hotel, you will be expected to vacate your room by noon on the day you leave, and sometimes even earlier.

HOW TO BOOK

It is always advisable to book well in advance, as room availability fluctuates. Booking directly with the hotel can be done by letter, phone or fax, and usually entails giving some kind of guarantee: either a credit card number from which a cancellation fee can be deducted, or a one-night deposit (some hotels will expect more for longer stays).

The **London Tourist Board** provides a free booking service. To take advantage of this, write, at least six weeks in advance, to the Accommodation Service's Advance Booking Office stating how much you want to spend. Remember to confirm any bookings they make for you. If you give less than six weeks notice, a small booking fee is charged, plus a deposit for your stay which is deducted from the final bill. You can book by credit card over the phone, or turn up at an LTB Tourist Information Centre in Victoria or Liverpool Street stations or at Heathrow (on the underground station concourse for terminals 1, 2 and 3). The LTB also has branches at Harrods, Selfridges and the Tower of London.

Accommodation booking services are also available at the **British Travel Centre** on Regent Street. A number of non-LTB booking agencies

Hotel 167 *(see p278)*

operate from booths in the major railway stations too. Unidentified touts, who hang around at railway and coach stations offering cheap accommodation to tourists, should be avoided.

USEFUL BOOKING ADDRESSES

British Hotel Reservation Centre
10 Buckingham Palace Rd,
SW1 0QP.
📞 0171-828 2425.

British Travel Centre
4–12 Lower Regent St,
SW1Y 4PQ.
📞 0171-930 0572.

Central London Accommodation System and Service
83 Addison Gdns, W14 0DT.
📞 0171-602 9668.

Concordia Hotel Tourist Bookings Europoint
5–11 Lavington St, SE1 0NZ.
📞 0171-945 6000.

London Accommodation Centre
22 Wardour St, W1V 3HH.
📞 0171-287 6315.

London Tourist Board (LTB)
Accommodation Service's Advance Booking Office
26 Grosvenor Gdns, SW1W 0DU.
📞 0171-730 3488.
Credit Card Reservation Line
📞 0171-824 8844 *(for bookings with less than six weeks notice).*

SPECIAL BREAKS

MANY TRAVEL agencies carry brochures from the major hotel chains listing special offers, which are usually costed on a minimum two-night stay. Some are extraordinarily good value compared to the usual tariff. For most travellers, this is the best way to take advantage of London hotels.

Other brochures are produced by specialist city-break operators, not tied to a single chain, and many privately owned hotels produce their own special-break brochures. Ferry companies and airlines offer packages including hotel breaks. Sometimes the same hotel may be featured in several brochures at widely differing prices and with different perks. It's worth asking the hotel directly what special rates they offer.

1920s Savoy poster

DISABLED TRAVELLERS

OUR INFORMATION about wheelchair access to hotels was gathered by questionnaire and depends on the hotels' own assessment of their suitability. The **LTB** provide two useful leaflets: *Accessible Accommodation in London* and *London for All*. A booklet, *Access in London*, can be obtained from RADAR, 25 Mortimer Street W1N 8AB (0171-637 5400).

TRAVELLING WITH CHILDREN

LONDON HOTELS have long been notorious child-free zones, but some of them now try to accommodate children's needs. It is worth asking about deals for children; some hotels have special rates, or allow children to stay free in their parents' rooms. See *Choosing a Hotel* on pages 276–7 for hotels with facilities for children.

SELF-CATERING FLATS

MANY AGENCIES offer self-catering accommodation in flats, usually for stays of a week or more. Prices, depending on size and location, start at about £300 per week.

The **Landmark Trust** rents apartments in historic or unusual buildings. These include rooms in Hampton Court *(see pp250–3)* and flats in a pretty 18th-century terrace in the City: one of them was the home of the late poet laureate, Sir John Betjeman. A handbook of Landmark properties is available from them for a small charge.

SELF-CATERING AGENCIES

Ashburn Gardens Apartments
3 Ashburn Gdns, SW7 4DG.
℡ 0171-370 2663.

Astons Budget Studios/ Luxury Apartments
39 Rosary Gdns, SW7 4NQ.
℡ 0171-370 0737.

Ealing Tourist Flats
94 Gordon Rd, W13 8PT.
℡ 0181-566 8187.

The Landmark Trust
Shottesbrooke, Maidenhead, Berkshire, SL6 3SW.
℡ 01628-825925.

Service Suites
42 Lower Sloane St, SW1W 8BP.
℡ 0171-730 5766.

STAYING IN PRIVATE HOMES

A NUMBER OF agencies organize stays in private homes, several are registered with the **LTB**. Prices depend on the location, and range from £15 to £60 per person per night. Sometimes you will stay with the family, but this isn't guaranteed, so it's as well to make your preference clear when you book. Even though you are not making a hotel booking, the same rules about deposits and cancellation fees may apply. Reservations can be made by credit card through LTB's telephone booking service *(see p273)*, or through any of the information centres listed under Self-Catering. Several agencies have minimum stays of anything up to a week.

Wolsey Lodges, a consortium of private homes, offers interesting hospitality and often a good dinner. It has four London properties.

AGENCIES FOR STAYS IN PRIVATE HOMES

Alma Tourist Services
21 Griffiths Rd, SW19 1SP.
℡ 0181-542 3771.

Anglo World Travel
123 Shaftesbury Ave, WC2H 8AD.
℡ 0171-379 7477.

At Home in London
70 Black Lion Lane, W6 9BE.
℡ 0181-748-1943.

Host and Guest Service
Harwood House, 27 Effie Rd, SW6 1EN.
℡ 0171-731 5340.

Classical opulence at Claridge's Hotel *(see p282)*

London Home to Home
19 Mount Park Crescent, W5 2RN.
[C] & [FAX] *0181-566 7976.*

Welcome Homes
6 Turnpin Lane, SE10 9JA.
[C] *0181-853 2706.*

Wolsey Lodges
17 Chapel Street, Bildeston,
Suffolk, IP7 7EP.
[C] *01449 741297.*

BUDGET ACCOMMODATION

DESPITE THE generally high cost of staying in London, budget possibilities do exist, and not only for the young.

Dormitory accommodation and youth hostels
These can be booked through LTB's information centre at Victoria *(see p273)* for a small fee plus a refundable deposit. There are private hostels near Earl's Court, where a dormitory bed with breakfast can cost as little as £10 a night. Don't expect anything fancy for prices like this. More upmarket is the **Central Club**, a Lutyens building run by the YWCA but open to all. Single rooms here cost about £30, much less if you share.

There are seven **Youth Hostels Association** hostels in London. Despite the name, there is no age limit on staying in these. One of the most interesting is Holland House, a Jacobean mansion in Holland Park *(see p214)*. Book well in advance, as it is deservedly popular.

HOSTEL ADDRESSES

Central Club
16–22 Great Russell St, WC1B 3LR.
[C] *0171-636 7512.*

Central London Hostel
28 Lancaster Gate, W2 3LP.
[C] *0171-706 1916. An independent hostel.*

London Hostel Association
54 Eccleston Sq, SW1V 1PG.
[C] *0171-828 3263.*

Youth Hostels Association
Trevelyan House, 8 St Stephen's Hill,
St Albans, Herts, AL1 2DY.
[C] *017278 55215.*

City of London Youth Hostel

Camping Sites
Tent City in East Acton (open June-September) is close to the underground, has basic facilities and a 400-bed tented hostel but can't take caravans. Hackney, Edmonton, Leyton, Chingford, Abbey Wood and Crystal Palace sites are further from transport, but have more facilities and caravan spaces. The **LTB** has a camping leaflet.

CAMPING SITES

Tent City
Old Oak Common Lane, W3 7DP.
[C] *0181-749 9074.*

Halls of residence
Student rooms are available from July to September at very reasonable prices. Some of these are in central locations such as South Kensington. It is best to book in advance, but **King's College** or **Imperial College** can sometimes find a place at short notice.

BOOKING ADDRESSES FOR RESIDENCE HALLS

City University Accommodation and Conference Service
Northampton Sq, EC1V 0HB.
[C] *0171-477 8037.*

Imperial College Summer Accommodation Centre
Room 170, Sherfield Building,
Exhibition Rd, SW7 2AZ.
[C] *0171-594 9507.*

King's Campus Vacation Bureau
King's College London, 552 King's Rd,
SW10 0UA.
[C] *0171-351 6011.*

USING THE LISTINGS

The hotels on pages 278–85 are listed according to area and price category. The symbols summarize the facilities at each hotel.

🛁 all rooms have bath and/or shower unless otherwise indicated
[1] single-rate rooms available
🛏 rooms for more than two people available, or an extra bed can be put in a double room
[24] 24-hour room service
[TV] television in all rooms
[Y] minibar in all rooms
🚭 non-smoking rooms available
🌇 rooms with good views
▤ air-conditioning in all rooms
[Y] gym/fitness facilities
🏊 swimming pool in hotel
[B] business facilities: message-taking service, fax machine for guests, desk and telephone in all rooms and a meeting room within the hotel
👶 children's facilities *(see p277).*
[&] wheelchair access
[⇑] lift
🐕 pets allowed in bedrooms (confirm with the management). Most hotels accept guide dogs regardless of rulings on pets. NB: Animals brought into the UK are subject to six months quarantine.
[P] hotel parking available
[⊕] garden or terrace open to guests
[Y] bar
[¶] restaurant
[i] tourist information point
🖅 credit and charge cards accepted:
AE American Express
DC Diners Club
MC Mastercard/Access
V Visa
JCB Japanese Credit Bureau
Price categories for a standard double room per night, including breakfast, tax and service:
Ⓔ under £70
ⒺⒺ £70–£100
ⒺⒺⒺ £100–£140
ⒺⒺⒺⒺ £140–£190
ⒺⒺⒺⒺⒺ over £190

Choosing a Hotel

THE 84 HOTELS listed in the following pages have all been inspected and assessed. This choosing chart shows a selection of factors affecting the choice of hotel. For more information on each hotel see pages 278–85. The hotels are listed by area and alphabetically within their price categories.

Hotel	Price	Number of Rooms	Large Rooms	Business Facilities	Children's Facilities	Recommended Restaurant	Close to Shops and Restaurants	Quiet Location	24-Hour Room Service
BAYSWATER, PADDINGTON *(see p278)*									
Byron	££	42		■	●			■	●
Delmere	££	38							
Mornington	££	68			●			■	
Whites	££££	54	●	■	●				●
KENSINGTON, HOLLAND PARK, NOTTING HILL *(see p278)*									
Abbey House	£	15						●	
Pembridge Court	££	21			●			●	
Portobello	££	25							
Abbey Court	£££	22		■				■	●
Copthorne Tara	£££	825		■			●		●
Halcyon	£££££	44		■	●	■		■	●
SOUTH KENSINGTON, GLOUCESTER ROAD *(see pp278–9)*									
Hotel 167	£	19							
Swiss House	£	16		■					
Aster House	££	12			●			■	
Five Sumner Place	££	13						■	●
Number Sixteen	££	36			●			■	
Cranley	£££	36						■	●
Gore	£££	54		■		■		■	
Pelham	£££	37		■	●				●
Rembrandt	£££	195	●	■	●				●
Sydney House	£££	21					●	■	●
Blakes	£££££	52	●	■		■	●	■	●
KNIGHTSBRIDGE, BROMPTON, BELGRAVIA *(see pp279–81)*									
Executive	££	29					●		
Knightsbridge Green	££	24			●		●		
Beaufort	£££	28		■	●		●	■	
Basil Street	££££	96		■	●		●		●
Draycott	££££	25		■	●		●	■	●
Egerton House	££££	28		■			●		●
Eleven Cadogan Gardens	££££	61					●		●
Fenja	££££	13		■	●		●		●
Berkeley	£££££	160	●	■			●		●
Capital	£££££	48			●	■		■	●
Halkin	£££££	41	●	■		■		■	●
Hyatt Carlton Tower	£££££	224	●	■	●	■	●		●
Lowndes	£££££	78		■			●	■	●
WESTMINSTER, VICTORIA *(see p281)*									
Collin House	£	13							
Elizabeth	£	42			●			■	
Windermere	£	23							●
Woodville House	£	12							
Ebury Court	££	42		■					●
Royal Horseguards	£££	376		■				■	●
Stakis London St Ermins	£££	290		■	●			■	●
Goring	££££	80	●					■	●
Scandic Crown	££££	210	●		●				●

Price categories for a standard double room per night including breakfast, tax and service:
£ under £70
££ £70–£100
£££ £100–£140
££££ £140–£190
£££££ over £190

CLOSE TO SHOPS AND RESTAURANTS Within a 5-minute walk of a good centre for shops and restaurants.

CHILDREN'S FACILITIES Family rooms and/or an extra bed in a double room, child cots, a baby-sitting service and children's portions and high chairs in the breakfast room or restaurant.

BUSINESS FACILITIES Message-taking service, fax machine for guests, desk and telephone in each room and a meeting room within the hotel.

	Price	Number of Rooms	Large Rooms	Business Facilities	Children's Facilities	Recommended Restaurant	Close to Shops and Restaurants	Quiet Location	24-Hour Room Service
PICCADILLY, MAYFAIR (see pp281–2)									
Athenaeum	££££	112	●	●	●		●		●
Inn on the Park	££££	227		●	●	●	●		●
Twenty-two Jermyn St	££££	18	●	●	●		●	●	●
Brown's	£££££	120	●	●					●
Claridge's	£££££	190	●	●	●				●
Connaught	£££££	90	●			●	●		●
Dorchester	£££££	252	●	●	●	●			●
Dukes	£££££	64	●	●	●		●	●	●
Fortyseven Park Street	£££££	52	●	●		●	●	●	●
Grosvenor House	£££££	454	●	●	●	●	●		●
Ritz	£££££	129	●	●	●		●		●
SOHO, LEICESTER SQUARE, OXFORD STREET (see p283)									
Concorde	£	27			●		●		●
Edward Lear	£	31			●		●		
Parkwood	£	18			●		●	●	●
Bryanston Court	££	56		●			●		●
Durrants	£££	96		●				●	●
Hazlitt's	£££	23					●		
Marble Arch Marriott	££££	239	●	●	●				●
Hampshire	££££	124	●	●	●		●		●
REGENT'S PARK, MARYLEBONE (see pp283–4)									
Blandford	££	33						●	
La Place	££	23		●	●			●	●
Dorset Square	£££	37	●		●			●	●
White House	£££	576		●	●			●	●
Langham Hilton	£££££	387	●	●	●		●		●
BLOOMSBURY, FITZROVIA, COVENT GARDEN, STRAND (see pp284–5)									
Mabledon Court	£	33							
Academy	££	33			●				●
Fielding	££	26		●			●	●	●
Bonnington	£££	215			●				●
Russell	£££	328	●	●	●				●
Mountbatten	££££	127	●	●	●		●		●
Waldorf	££££	292		●	●		●		●
Howard	£££££	135	●	●	●				●
Savoy	£££££	200	●	●	●	●	●		●
THE CITY (see p285)									
Great Eastern	£££	161		●					●
Tower Thistle	££££	808		●				●	●
FURTHER AFIELD (see p285)									
Chase Lodge	£	9			●			●	
La Reserve	££	40		●					●
Swiss Cottage	££	80		●	●			●	
Cannizaro House	£££	46	●	●				●	
Kingston Lodge	£££	62		●	●				
Sheraton Skyline	£££	354	●	●	●				●

BAYSWATER
PADDINGTON

Byron

36–38 Queensborough Terrace,
W2 3SH. **Map** 10 E2. **(** 0171-243
0987. **FAX** 0171-792 1957.
TX 263431 BYRON G. **Rooms:** 42.
🛏 1 ⏰ 24 TV ⚡ ▤ 🔊 🚹
🔊 📺 🗂 AE, DC, MC, V. **££**

The decor is generally pleasant,
ranging from traditional country
house style in the small cosy
lounge to unfussy neutrality in
the bedrooms. Staff are young
and unstarchy, and the setting
is peaceful. A few scuffs are
forgivable in such a friendly,
unpretentious hotel.

Delmere

130 Sussex Gdns, W2 1UB.
Map 11 A2. **(** 0171-706 3344.
FAX 0171-262 1863. **TX** 8953857.
Rooms: 38. 🛏 1 ⏰ 🗂 🔊 🖥
📺 🍴 🗂 DC, MC, V, JCB. **££**

This well-kept building stands
out amid a line of lack-lustre
neighbours. Furnishings can be
pretentious in places, and some
bedrooms have been shoe-horned
into spaces scarcely adequate.
Nonetheless, the hotel is well-run
and civilized. The comfortable
sitting room downstairs has a gas
powered coal fire and supplies of
daily newspapers.

Mornington

12 Lancaster Gate, W2 3LG.
Map 10 F2. **(** 0171-262 7361.
FAX 0171-706 1028. **TX** 24281.
Rooms: 68. 🛏 1 ⏰ 🗂 🚹 🔊
🖥 📺 🗂 AE, DC, MC, V. **££**

This quiet hotel is run with
courteous efficiency. The clubby
intimacy of the book-lined library
lounge provides a good contrast
to the almost chilly Scandinavian
austerity of the bedrooms. The
sauna and smorgasbord buffet
breakfast underline the hotel's
Swedish parentage.

Whites

90 Lancaster Gate, W2 3NR.
Map 10 F2. **(** 0171-262 2711.
FAX 0171-262 2147. **TX** 24771.
Rooms: 54. 🛏 1 ⏰ 24 🗂 📺
⚡ 🔊 ▤ 🔊 🖥 📺 🍴
🗂 AE, DC, MC, V. **££££**

This large 19th-century hotel
overlooking Kensington Gardens
has an almost seaside feel to its
wedding-cake exterior. Inside,
pretty chandeliers give the
attractive public areas a festive
and cheering air. The crystal look

even extends to the bedrooms,
where the decor is a mixture of
Oriental, Louis XV and Belle
Epoque themes. The historic
appearance of these rooms is
preserved by having hidden
television sets that rise magically
from cupboards at the press of a
button when required.

KENSINGTON
HOLLAND PARK
NOTTING HILL

Abbey House

11 Vicarage Gate, W8 4AG.
Map 10 D4. **(** 0171-727 2594.
Rooms: 15. 1 🚹 🗂 **£**

The outside of this attractively
located, Victorian family home
looks charming, and the
proportions of the plant-filled
stairwell hint at gracious living.
But no-frills bed and breakfast is
what Abbey House offers.
Bedrooms, though spacious, are
very simply furnished, without en-
suite bathrooms. The only public
area is a bright, cheerful breakfast
room in the basement.

Portobello

22 Stanley Gdns, W11 2NG.
Map 9 B2. **(** 0171-727 2777.
FAX 0171-792 9641. **Rooms:** 25. 🛏
1 🚹 🗂 📺 🖥 🔊 🔊 🍴 📺 🍴
🗂 AE, DC, MC, V. **££**

This eccentric place around the
corner from Portobello Road has
a darkish and sophisticated decor
which is a mix of Victorian Gothic
and Edwardian. The tiniest single
rooms have box-like beds and
minute, spartan bathrooms. Larger
rooms are available, and for an
exotic touch there is the Round
Room (a round bed beneath free-
flying drapes). A casually chic
restaurant is downstairs.

Abbey Court

20 Pembridge Gdns, W2 4DU.
Map 9 C3. **(** 0171-221 7518.
FAX 0171-727 8166. **TX** 262167
ABBYCT. **Rooms:** 22. 🛏 1 🚹 24
🗂 🔊 🖥 📺 🗂 AE, DC, MC, V.
£££

This lavishly decorated and well-
kept town house provides a
successful brand of luxury bed
and breakfast. An elegant reception
lounge and a conservatory breakfast form the public areas.
Bedrooms vary, but all include
handsome Victorian-style
bathroom fittings and antiques. An
unusually high proportion are
singles – handy for lone travellers.
Children over 12 catered for.

Copthorne Tara

Scarsdale Pl, Wright's Lane, W8 5SR.
Map 8 D1. **(** 0171-937 7211.
FAX 0171-937 7100. **TX** 918834
TARAHL G. **Rooms:** 825. 🛏 1 24
🗂 📺 ⚡ 🔊 🔊 🔊 🚹 📺
🍴 🗂 AE, DC, MC, V, JCB. **£££**

The location, in a quiet sidestreet
just off Kensington High Street, is
a strong point. Inside, the style and
facilities of this modern chain hotel
are predictably comfortable and
include a number of themed bars.

Pembridge Court

34 Pembridge Gdns, W2 4DX.
Map 9 C3. **(** 0171-229 9977.
FAX 0171-727 4982. **TX** 298363.
Rooms: 21. 🛏 1 🚹 24 🗂
🔊 📺 🍴 🗂 AE, DC, MC, V, JCB.
£££

This elegant town house hotel in a
smart quiet street close to Notting
Hill Gate is privately owned.
Throughout, it is comfortable and
civilized, not indigestibly ornate,
but made interesting by displays
of costume accessories: gloves,
fans, purses, in all the rooms.
Caps Restaurant downstairs is an
evening-only wine-bar.

Halcyon

81 Holland Park, W11 3RZ.
Map 9 A4. **(** 0171-727 7288.
FAX 0171-229 8516. **TX** 266721.
Rooms: 44. 🛏 1 🚹 24 🗂 📺
🔊 🚹 📺 📺 🍴 🗂 AE, DC,
MC, V. **£££££**

This is a luxurious hotel in the
heart of Holland Park. Within the
splendid Belle Epoque exterior,
the beautifully proportioned
reception rooms retain all their
original features. The bedrooms
are hedonistic fantasies filled with
canopies, swags and drapes of
fabric. Bathrooms have whirlpool
baths and bidets. The hotel can
not, in all honesty, be described as
good value, but it does provide a
feeling of comfortable opulence.

SOUTH KENSINGTON
GLOUCESTER ROAD

Hotel 167

167 Old Brompton Rd, SW5 0AN.
Map 18 E3. **(** 0171-373 3221.
FAX 0171-373 3360. **Rooms:** 19. 🛏
1 🚹 🗂 📺 🗂 AE, DC, MC, V.
£

Simple but refreshingly different,
this little gem dispenses a unique
brand of bed and breakfast. Large
modern paintings catch the visitor's
eye in the breakfast room and the
reception area, which doubles as

daytime lounge (one cushion-piled sofa). The bedrooms are stylishly practical, with their small fridges, Venetian blinds, pleasant furnishings and good bathrooms.

Swiss House

171 Old Brompton Rd, SW5 0AN.
Map 18 E3. 0171-373 2769.
FAX 0171-373 4983. **Rooms:** 16.
11. MC, V.

Trailing plants at the entrance give this tall, terraced guesthouse an immediately welcoming look. Inside, the impression is reinforced by the cheerful, cottagey breakfast room – pine dresser with china and dried flower arrangements – and neat bedrooms, some of which are surprisingly spacious.

Aster House

3 Sumner Pl, SW7 3EE. **Map** 19 A2.
0171-581 5888. FAX 0171-584 4925. **Rooms:** 12. AE, DC, MC, V, JCB.

Several houses in this elegant South Kensington terrace are discreet, upmarket hotels, but few have such reasonable tariffs. L'Orangerie, the hotel's stylish conservatory restaurant, serves health-conscious breakfasts. The bedrooms, all non-smoking, are individually decorated in varying degrees of sumptuousness. Children over 12 catered for.

Five Sumner Place

5 Sumner Pl, SW7 3EE. **Map** 19 A2.
0171-584 7586. FAX 0171-823 9962. **Rooms:** 13. AE, DC, MC, V.

Smart enough to win the British Tourist Association's Best Bed and Breakfast Award in 1991, this Victorian terraced town house is elegant and stylish. An eye-catching conservatory set with blue-skirted breakfast tables and fresh flowers overlooks a pretty patio garden. Upstairs, 13 bedrooms, all individually decorated, provide quiet, civilized havens from the bustle and noise of central London.

Number Sixteen

16 Sumner Pl, SW7 3EG. **Map** 19 A2.
0171-589 5232. FAX 0171-584 8615. TX 266638. **Rooms:** 36.
34. AE, DC, MC, V.

The unmarked entrance is typical of the classy little hotels along this smart, white-painted Victorian street. Inside, the ambience is understated but luxurious.

Number Sixteen scores over its neighbours with better facilities and more extensive public areas, including a conservatory leading on to a charming garden of dribbling fountains. The bedrooms are surprisingly spacious and imaginatively decorated, while the bathrooms are in the process of being upgraded. Children over 12 catered for.

Cranley

10–12 Bina Gdns, SW5 0LA.
Map 18 E2. 0171-373 0123.
FAX 0171-373 9497. TX 991503.
Rooms: 36. AE, DC, MC, V, JCB.

Antiques and designer fabrics abound in this grand American-owned town house hotel, although not all of the rooms are particularly large. Discreetly concealed kitchenettes with fridge and microwave are an unusual and practical feature of the bedrooms. The drawing room is exceptionally attractive.

Gore

189 Queen's Gate, SW7 5EX.
Map 10 F5. 0171-584 6601.
FAX 0171-589 8127. TX 296244.
Rooms: 54. AE, DC, MC, V, JCB.

This idiosyncratic Victorian hotel is a sister to Hazlitt's (see p283). The trendy Kensington crowd hustle for tables at the chic Bistrot 190. Its Restaurant 190 is presided over by one of London's top chefs, Antony Worrall-Thompson. Bedrooms vary from tiny singles with pine washstands to Tudor fantasies complete with their own minstrel's galleries; many bathrooms have Victorian and Edwardian furniture. Service is endearingly laid-back but always charming, and the tariff need not make you gasp.

Pelham

15 Cromwell Pl, SW7 2LA. **Map** 19 A1.
0171-589 8288. FAX 0171-584 8444. TX 881 4714 TUDOR G.
Rooms: 37. AE, MC, V.

Less than a minute from South Kensington tube, the Pelham looks straight from the pages of a glossy magazine. From the 18th-century panelling in the drawing room to the flowers in the bedrooms, everything shows perfect house-keeping and exquisite (if opulent) taste. The restaurant (which also functions as lounge and bar) is particularly comfortable.

Rembrandt

11 Thurloe Pl, SW7 2RS. **Map** 19 A1.
0171-589 8100. FAX 0171-225 3363.
TX 295828. **Rooms:** 195. AE, DC, MC, V, JCB.

The corporate style of this large hotel opposite the Victoria and Albert Museum does not preclude the restful atmosphere throughout its refurbished interior. There is a pool downstairs.

Sydney House

9–11 Sydney St, SW3 6PU.
Map 19 A1. 0171-376 7111. FAX 0171-376 4233. **Rooms:** 21. AE, DC, MC, V, JCB.

The palazzo wall treatments, Bugatti furniture, and Baccarat chandeliers of the foyer set the tone here. Each room is a self-contained mini-world: Biedermeier here, Paris fabrics there. The dining room is deep sunshine and navy wicker. For this kind of style, the tariff is remarkably reasonable.

Blakes

33 Roland Gdns, SW7 3PF. **Map** 18 F3.
0171-370 6701. FAX 0171-373 0442. TX 8813500. **Rooms:** 52.
AE, DC, MC, V, JCB.

Designer Anouska Hempel's dashing establishment is a London legend. The racing green facade distinguishes it instantly, and one glimpse of the exotic, scented interior declares this is no ordinary hotel. Each bedroom is a unique, extravaganza of deep colours, rich silks, and opulent furnishings such as brocaded four-posters and antique lacquered chests.

KNIGHTSBRIDGE

BROMPTON

BELGRAVIA

Executive

57 Pont St, SW1X 0BD. **Map** 19 C1.
0171-581 2424. FAX 0171-589 9456. TX 9413498 EXECUT G.
Rooms: 29. AE, DC, MC, V.

This unobtrusive listed town house lies a short stroll from some of London's most exclusive shops. Beyond the gracious entrance hall, bedrooms are modern and agreeably furnished, if not strong on personality. Downstairs, buffet breakfast is served in a room of pink Chinese Chippendale.

Knightsbridge Green

159 Knightsbridge, SW1X 7PD.
Map 11 C5. [0171-584 6274.
FAX 0171-225 1635. *Closed 24–27
Dec. Rooms:* 24. 🛏 1 🎼 ✗ ⚡
🕭 🔧 🌂 *AE, MC, V.* ££

Its proximity to Harrods, coupled
with its reassuring ambiance,
makes this long-established, upmarket bed and breakfast popular
with women. Tea and coffee are
available all day long in the Club
Room, where magazines lie on the
large central coffee table. Most
bedrooms have attached sitting
rooms where breakfast is served.
Decor is restful, and the practical
details of lighting, sound-proofing,
and storage space are considered.

Beaufort

33 Beaufort Gdns, SW3 1PP.
Map 19 B1. [0171-584 5252.
FAX 0171-589 2834. TX 929200.
Rooms: 28. 🛏 1 ✗ 🎼 🕭 🔧
🕭 🌂 🌂 *AE, DC, MC, V, JCB.*
£££

Sheer elegance at least partially
excuses the high tariffs of this
classy little place tucked away in a
leafy cul-de-sac near Harrods.
Fresh flowers, stylish fabrics and
floral watercolours characterize its
delightful bedrooms. Downstairs,
Harry (the hedonistic resident cat)
may monopolize one of the
luxurious sofas. Personal service
and pampering are what you pay
for, and neither is in short supply.
Children over 10 catered for.

Basil Street

Basil St, SW3 1AH. **Map** 11 C5.
[0171-581 3311. FAX 0171-581
3693. TX 28379. *Rooms:* 96. 🛏 73.
1 🎼 24 ✗ 🕭 🔧 🕭 🔧 🌂
🍴 🌂 *AE, DC, MC, V.* ££££

The civilized but unintimidating
atmosphere of this old-fashioned,
privately owned hotel with an
unpretentious Edwardian air
explains its enduring popularity.
The comfortable lounge bar is a
perfect place to relax for
afternoon tea. Its wine-bar and
upper carvery are excellent value
for the area, and the unique Parrot
Club for women (which men can
visit by invitation only) is an
interesting riposte to the leathery
male bastions found elsewhere in
London's hotels. Many of the
regular "Basilites" are women.

Draycott

24–26 Cadogan Gdns, SW3 2RP.
Map 19 C2. [0171-730 6466. FAX
0171-730 0236. *Rooms:* 25. 🛏 1
🎼 24 ✗ 🕭 🍴 🕭 🔧 🌂 🌂
🍴 🌂 *AE, DC, MC, V.* £££££

This unobtrusive Knightsbridge
mansion is more like a residential
club than an hotel. Downstairs by
the entrance, is a small panelled
"smoking room", where blazing
fires are lit in winter and newspapers are available all year
round, as though you're in some
well-mannered private country
house. Plants, antiques, prints, and
marble baths furnish the varying
bedrooms, many of which have
garden views.

Egerton House

17–19 Egerton Terrace, SW3 2BX.
Map 19 B1. [0171-589 2412.
FAX 0171-584 6540. *Rooms:* 28.
🛏 1 🎼 24 ✗ 🕭 🍴 🕭 🔧 P
🍴 🌂 *AE, DC, MC, V.* ££££

This smart, recently decorated
town house provides high
standards of both service and
comfort. The style is urbane and
professional. Although some of
the furnishings have not yet
achieved the patina of age, they
certainly look good enough to
stand alongside what are
obviously genuine antiques.

Eleven Cadogan Gardens

11 Cadogan Gdns, SW3 2RJ.
Map 19 C2. [0171-730 3426.
FAX 0171-730 5217. TX 8813318.
Rooms: 61. 🛏 1 🎼 24 ✗
🕭 🌂 🌂 *AE, MC, V.* ££££

From the outside you would never
guess that this redbrick mansion is
a hotel. Perhaps it explains why
so many famous people retreat
here for peace and privacy when
they become tired of being
lionized by the public. An
atmosphere of quiet good taste
and unobtrusive service matches
the panelling on the walls and the
crisp sheets on the beds. Furnished
with dignity and conservative
elegance, the more mundane of
hotel-type trappings are largely
absent from this establishment.

Fenja

69 Cadogan Gdns, SW3 2RB.
Map 19 C2. [0171-589 7333.
FAX 0171-581 4958. *Rooms:* 13.
🛏 1 🎼 24 ✗ 🕭 🍴 🕭 🔧
🌂 *AE, DC, MC, V.* ££££

Hidden in a maze of Victorian
mansions, this quietly grand bed
and breakfast has the air of a
private home. Paintings, antique
busts and fine china fill the house,
and many of the building's original features remain – including
fireplaces, cornices, and huge
windows. Breakfast is served in
the peaceful and comfortable
bedrooms, and light meals can be
ordered at other times of the day.

Berkeley

Wilton Pl, SW1X 7RL. **Map** 12 D5.
[0171-235 6000. FAX 0171-235
4330. TX 919252. *Rooms:* 160. 🛏
1 24 ✗ 🌿 🍴 🕭 🎼 🕭 🔧
P 🍴 🌂 🌂 *AE, DC, MC, V, JCB.*
£££££

The discreet main entrance to this
august member of the Savoy
Group of hotels leads to a
dignified hallway of marble and
Lutyens panelling. The Buttery
and Bar downstairs are slightly
less formal, while bedrooms
display unusual individuality.

Capital

22–24 Basil St, SW3 1AT. **Map** 11 C5.
[0171-589 5171. FAX 0171-225
0011. *Rooms:* 48. 🛏 1 24 ✗
🍴 🕭 🔧 🕭 🔧 P 🍴 🍴 🌂 ££££
AE, DC, MC, V. £££££

The Capital is a small and
distinctly luxurious hotel with a
noted restaurant. Furnishings are
imaginative and elaborate in a
French *fin de siècle* mode. Its
sister next door at No. 28, the
equally stylish L'Hôtel (0171-589
6286), offers less expensive rooms
but has fewer facilities and no
room service.

Halkin

5 Halkin St, SW1X 7DJ. **Map** 12 D5.
[0171-333 1000. FAX 0171-333
1100. *Rooms:* 41. 🛏 🎼 24 ✗ 🍴
🕭 🍴 🕭 🔧 🌂 *AE, DC, MC,*
V, JCB. £££££

For those weary of artificial period
charm, the minimalism of the
Halkin will come as a breath of
fresh air. A restrained palette of
blue and grey, black and white
creates a cool, sophisticated and
utterly contemporary look. The
bedrooms luxuriate in tawny
marble, state-of-the-art bedside
consoles, and fitted furniture in
coppery veneers.

Hyatt Carlton Tower

Cadogan Pl, SW1X 9PY. **Map** 19 C1.
[0171-235 1234. FAX 0171-245
6570. TX 21944. *Rooms:* 224.
🛏 🎼 24 ✗ 🍴 🌿 🍴 🍴 🕭
🔧 🕭 🔧 P 🍴 🍴 🌂 *AE, DC,*
MC, V, JCB. £££££

This large chain hotel avoids the
usual soullessness of its type.
The staff are well-trained and
friendly. In some places the
furnishings are too predictable,
but the Chinoiserie Lounge, where
a harpist plays, is a wonderful
place to rest weary feet after
battling round shops or museums.
After tasting the wicked
patisseries, there's a health club
upstairs to restore muscle tone.

Lowndes

Lowndes St, SW1X 9ES. **Map** 20 D1.
[*0171-823 1234*. FAX *0171-235 1154*. TX *919065*. **Rooms:** 78. ▦
1 ⊞ 24 ✕ Y ⯑ ▤ ⯑ ⯑
Y ⯑ ⯑ *AE, DC, MC, V, JCB.*
€€€€€

This little sister of the Hyatt Carlton Tower just round the corner has a pleasant, small-scale feel, and guests can use the larger hotel's excellent facilities at no extra cost. The designer country-house reception lounge provides a relaxing place to read papers over coffee. Bedrooms contain a panoply of excellent facilities amid smart contemporary decor. The Biedermeier Suite is top of the range, with high-quality reproduction furnishings.

WESTMINSTER
VICTORIA

Collin House

104 Ebury St, SW1W 9QD.
Map 20 E2. [*0171-730 8031.*
Closed 2 weeks at Christmas.
Rooms: 13. ▦ 8. 1 ⊞ €

This small guesthouse distinguishes itself from many similar neighbours by its pleasant welcome, and if decor is scarcely fashionable the rooms are fresh and clean. A minute breakfast room downstairs, cheered up by landscape photographs and honey pine, is the only public room.

Elizabeth

37 Eccleston Sq, SW1V 1PB.
Map 20 F2. [*0171-828 6812.*
FAX *0171-828 6814*. **Rooms:** 42.
▦ 25. 1 ⊞ ⯑ ⯑ ⯑ €

Recent refurbishment has made the Elizabeth even better value for money than in the past – and the price has always been surprisingly low for the area. As a bonus, guests also have access to the pleasant, leafy gardens and the tennis courts of Eccleston Square.

Windermere

142–144 Warwick Way, SW1V 4JE.
Map 20 E2. [*0171-834 5163.*
FAX *0171-630 8831*. TX *94017182*
WIRE G. **Rooms:** 23. ▦ 19. 1 ⊞
24 ✕ ⯑ *AE, MC, V, JCB.* €

The well-kept Victorian exterior of this inexpensive, friendly hotel stands out on a desolate and busy road. Inside the illusion is not broken: it is as neat as a pin, with a pleasant breakfast room, that doubles as a coffee shop, downstairs where snacks and

drinks are available all day. Light, clean bedrooms have curtains of heavy glazed chintz and modern, practical fittings.

Woodville House

107 Ebury St, SW1W 9QU.
Map 20 E2. [*0171-730 1048.*
FAX *0717-730 2574*. **Rooms:** 12.
1 ⊞ ✕ ▤ ⯑ ⯑ €

Though neither spacious nor luxurious, this guesthouse, in a Georgian building, is civilized, personal and much frequented by budget-conscious visitors. The breakfast room is screened off into intimate spaces; the bedrooms have tiny armchairs and other neat fittings.

Ebury Court

28 Ebury St, SW1W 0LU. **Map** 20 E1.
[*0171-730 8147.* FAX *0171-823 5966*. **Rooms:** 42. ▦ 21. 1 ⊞ 24
✕ ⯑ ⯑ Y ⯑ ⯑ ⯑ *AE, DC, MC, V.* €€

Several adjacent town houses make up this classy, privately owned hotel. Family heirlooms and pictures deck cosy public rooms. Labyrinthine passages and stairways connect the rooms, most of which are small and plain. The price is very good for the area.

Royal Horseguards Thistle

2 Whitehall Court, SW1A 2EJ.
Map 13 C4. [*0171-839 3400.*
FAX *0171-925 2263*. TX *917096.*
Rooms: 376. ▦ 1 ⊞ 24 ✕ Y ⯑
▤ ⯑ ⯑ Y ⯑ ⯑ *AE, DC, MC, V, JCB.* €€€

This grand 19th-century hotel overlooks the river not far from the Houses of Parliament. Potted palms, chandeliers and ornate plasterwork fill the lobby. Beyond, the comfortable public rooms include Granby's Restaurant, smart and formal in green leather, and a haunt of well-known political faces. The style of the bedrooms varies from Classical opulence to contemporary smartness.

Stakis London St Ermin's

Caxton St, SW1H 0QW. **Map** 13 A5.
[*0171-222 7888.* FAX *0171-222 6914.*
TX *917731*. **Rooms:** 290. ▦ 1 ⊞
24 ✕ ⯑ ⯑ ⯑ Y ⯑ ⯑ ⯑
⯑ *AE, DC, MC, V, JCB.* €€€

This institutional-looking, late-Victorian hotel is close enough to Westminster to have once had its own tunnel-link to the House of Commons. The most striking interior feature is a grand Baroque staircase rearing from the main

lounge up towards the glittering chandeliers, curving balustrades, and ornate plaster ceilings. The bedrooms are comfortably furnished in a less overbearing style than the rest of the hotel.

Goring

Beeston Pl, Grosvenor Gdns, SW1W
0JW. **Map** 20 E1. [*0171-396 9000.*
FAX *0171-834 4393*. TX *919166.*
Rooms: 80. ▦ 1 ⊞ 24 ✕ ▤ ⯑
⯑ P Y ⯑ ⯑ *AE, DC, MC, V.*
€€€€

This imposing Edwardian building is a rare beast – a central London hotel that is both grand and family-run. The third-generation Gorings maintain immaculate standards, with meticulous attention to every detail. The hotel exudes an air of understated elegance. Exceptional points include the bar-lounge and a delightful formal garden, which is, alas, only for looking at.

Scandic Crown

2 Bridge Pl, SW1V 1QA. **Map** 20 F2.
[*0171-834 8123.* FAX *0171-828 1099*. TX *914973*. **Rooms:** 210. ▦
1 ⊞ 24 ✕ Y ⯑ ⯑ ⯑ ⯑ ⯑ ▤ ⯑ Y ⯑ ⯑ *AE, DC, MC, V, JCB.* €€€€

This uncompromising modern block, that overlooks the train marshalling yards of nearby Victoria station, is Swedish-owned. The slight starkness of its chrome, glass and plastic coffee shop is more than offset by the friendly, efficient Scandinavian welcome and the stylish, well-equipped bedrooms. One of the hotel's special attractions is the panoply of health facilities that are made available to residents.

PICCADILLY
MAYFAIR

Athenaeum

116 Piccadilly, W1V 0BJ. **Map** 12 E4.
[*0171-499 3464.* FAX *0171-493 1860*. TX *261589*. **Rooms:** 112. ▦
1 ⊞ 24 ✕ Y ⯑ ⯑ ▤ ⯑ ⯑
⯑ Y ⯑ ⯑ ⯑ *AE, DC, MC, V, JCB.* €€€€€

Despite the prestigious Mayfair location of this smart hotel, the welcome is friendly, personal and unforbidding. Tea or coffee in the relaxing Windsor lounge is a particular strong point. So, too, is the vast range of malt Scotch whiskies in the clubby cocktail bar. Some bedrooms are a little insipid, but all are extremely comfortable and well-furnished.

The Four Seasons

Hamilton Pl, Park Lane, W1A 1AZ.
Map 12 D4. **(** 0171-499 0888.
FAX 0171-493 6629. TX 227711.
Rooms: 227. AE, DC, MC, V, JCB. ££££

The Four Seasons prides itself on individual service and understated luxury, and the overall effect is firmly traditional. In the opulent, well-equipped rooms, quieter styles are gradually replacing the Oriental birds and heavy chintzes, and the foyer and lounge areas glitter with Venetian crystal. Up the grand staircase the elegant Four Seasons Restaurant and the less formal Lanes buffet provide worthy arenas for splendid food.

Twenty-Two Jermyn Street

22 Jermyn St, St James's, SW1Y 6HL.
Map 12 F3. **(** 0171-734 2353. FAX 0171-734 0750. **Rooms:** 18. AE, DC, MC, V, JCB. ££££

An unobtrusive entrance leads to a warren of luxurious suites and studios, perfectly kitted out for the business visitor. They are very comfortable for anyone else, too, lavishly decorated and beautifully maintained. Round-the-clock room service, use of a nearby health club and an emphasis on security and privacy justify the hotel's apparently steep tariffs.

Brown's

Albemarle and Dover Sts, W1A 4SW.
Map 12 F3. **(** 0171-493 6020.
FAX 0171-493 9381. TX 28686.
Rooms: 120. AE, DC, MC, V, JCB. ££££ See **Restaurants and Pubs** pp306–7.

Some of the urbane charm of the original Mr Brown (who must have been the perfect gentleman's gentleman) still lingers here in one of London's oldest and most traditional hotels. The legendary afternoon teas are served in the chintzy lounge. Bedrooms are mostly large, with charming, slightly outmoded decor.

Claridge's

Brook St, W1A 2JQ. **Map** 12 E2.
(0171-629 8860. FAX 0171-499 2210. TX 218762 CLRDGS G.
Rooms: 190. AE, DC, MC, V, JCB. £££££

So much part of the establishment that it functions virtually as an annexe to Buckingham Palace, Claridge's favours the traditional approach – yet the atmosphere is surprisingly unstarchy. Art Deco blends with the Classical grandeur of marble mosaic, chandeliers, and a staircase wide enough for two full ballgowns to pass unhindered. Hungarian musicians play in the foyer; waiters, valets and maids can be summoned to the vast, bedrooms at the touch of a button.

Connaught

16 Carlos Pl, W1Y 6AL. **Map** 12 E3.
(0171-499 7070. FAX 0171-495 3262. **Rooms:** 90. MC, V. £££££

So self-confident is this famous hotel that it provides neither brochure nor tariff. (Terms – not the highest in Mayfair – are available "on application".) The hotel is not large and its decor is unshowy. Utter discretion is the watchword: guests' privacy is jealously guarded and every last whim is noted for future reference. Those outside the charmed circle may feel they are being exluded from the club of Connaught residents. Many are gently informed that the hotel is quite, quite full . . . To book, don't ring up – and don't dream of just turning up! Write, courteously, well in advance.

Dorchester

53 Park Lane, W1A 2HJ. **Map** 12 D3.
(0171-629 8888. FAX 0171-495 7342. TX 887704 DORCH G. **Rooms:** 252. AE, DC, MC, V, JCB. £££££

Soft, pale gold gleams on marble pillars and scalloped ceiling domes, towering arrangements of flowers deck the Promenade where teas are served, and all is conspicuous, flamboyant grandeur in this old hotel. Eating places include the famous Grill Room, the calmer Terrace, and the exotically themed Oriental restaurants. Suites and bedrooms, which have triple-glazing on the Park Lane side, are – needless to say – sybaritic.

Dukes

35 St James's Pl, SW1A 1NY.
Map 12 F4. **(** 0171-491 4840.
FAX 0171-493 1264. TX 28283.
Rooms: 64. AE, DC, MC, V.
£££££

This fine Edwardian building is wedged into a tiny secluded courtyard where the gas-lamps are still lit by hand. Though expensive and exclusive, Dukes is notably friendly and cheering. The bar has a masculine look: monumentally priced cognacs are dispensed beneath the stern gaze of three ducal portraits (Wellington, Marlborough, Norfolk). Children over 5 catered for.

Forty-Seven Park Street

47 Park St, W1Y 4EB. **Map** 12 D2.
(0171-491 7282. FAX 0171-491 7281. TX 22116 LUXURY. **Rooms:** 52. AE, DC, MC, V, JCB. £££££

Many have heard of the Roux's celebrated restaurant, Le Gavroche. Fewer realize that you can, if you are wealthy enough, stagger just next door to recover from gastronomic excess. Here 52 luxurious suites, each one different, feature French-style clocks and bronzes on fireplaces, finely crafted furniture, downy duvets, and thick fluffy towels. Room service from the restaurant is also available.

Grosvenor House

86–90 Park Lane, W1A 3AA. **Map** 12 D3. **(** 0171-499 6363. FAX 0171-493 3341. TX 24871. **Rooms:** 454. AE, DC, MC, V, JCB. £££££

This establishment is perhaps most famous as host to grand occasions. The Great Room is the largest banqueting room in Europe, with space for 2,000. Behind the Lutyens facade overlooking Hyde Park, the hotel is formal and luxurious but thoroughly comfortable. Several very different restaurants include the suavely elegant Nico at 90 (see p296).

Ritz

Piccadilly, W1V 9DG. **Map** 12 F3.
(0171-493 8181. FAX 0171-493 2687. TX 267200. **Rooms:** 129. AE, DC, MC, V. £££££ See p91.

Cunard's flagship still draws the crowds, especially for afternoon teas in the Palm Court – perhaps the closest most of us can get to sampling Life at the Top. The Ritz's marbled, Frenchified rooms are undeniably grand – especially the restaurant, where gilded chandeliers are suspended from a fresco of clouds above the diners' heads. If you don't look up, look out over the attractive Italian Garden towards the tree-filled oasis of Green Park.

SOHO
LEICESTER SQUARE
OXFORD STREET

Concorde

50 Great Cumberland Pl, W1H 7FD.
Map 11 C1. [C] 0171-402 6169.
[FAX] 0171-724 1184. [TX] 262076.
Rooms: 27. 🛏 1 ▦ ✕ ⛎ 🕭
🛏 📺 £ AE, DC, MC, V. £

This hotel shares the pleasantly
bygone but cared-for ambience
of its bigger sister next door (see
Bryanston Court). Facilities,
however, are simpler, and the
tariff is correspondingly lower –
representing remarkably good
value this close to Oxford Street.

Edward Lear

28–30 Seymour St, W1H 5WD.
Map 11 C2. [C] 0171-402 5401.
[FAX] 0171-706 3766. *Rooms: 31.*
4. 1 ▦ ✕ ⛎ 🛏 £ MC, V. £

Once the home of humourist
Edward Lear, this clean, simple
bed and breakfast is not too far
from Oxford Street. It caters for
single people and families as well
as for the orderly couples most
hotels seem meant for. There are
two small lounges (one full of
Edward Lear books and limericks),
and a light breakfast room. Rear
rooms are free of traffic noise.

Parkwood

4 Stanhope Pl, W2 2HB. **Map** 11 B2.
[C] 0171-402 2241. [FAX] 0171-402
1574. *Rooms: 18.* 🛏 12. 1 ▦ ✕
£ MC, V. £

This friendly, family bed and
breakfast is in a tidy house, with
Classical portico and black
railings, just a block from Marble
Arch. The lounge-cum-reception
has a gracious air, but bedrooms
are not at all luxurious and show
some signs of wear. Downstairs is
a small, cheerful breakfast room
with simple bentwood chairs.

Bryanston Court

56–60 Great Cumberland Pl, W1H 7FD.
Map 11 C1. [C] 0171-262 3141.
[FAX] 0171-262 7248. *Rooms: 56.* 🛏
1 ▦ ✕ ⛎ 🛏 📺
£ AE, DC, MC, V. ££

Blue awnings add a continental
jauntiness to this well-kept hotel.
Inside, soft lighting gleams on oil
portraits and gently battered
brown leather. The atmosphere is
civilized and old-fashioned, but
personal – as few West End hotels
are these days. Bedrooms are
simple, smallish, and functional.

Durrants

George St, W1H 6BJ. **Map** 11 B1.
[C] 0171-935 8131. [FAX] 0171-57487
3510. *Rooms:* 96. 🛏 86 1 ▦ 24
✕ 🛏 ⛎ 📺 📺 ▮1 £ AE,
MC, V. £££

This well-loved Georgian hotel
still has the feel of the old country
coaching inn it once was. The
restaurant is a place of crisp linen
and silver domed tureens. Bars
and sitting rooms full of leather
and oak panelling reinforce the
impression of old-fashioned,
masculine taste. Bedrooms are
unfussy and smallish at the rear.

Hazlitt's

6 Frith St, W1V 5TZ. **Map** 13 A2.
[C] 0171-434 1771. [FAX] 0171-439
1524. *Closed* 24–26 Dec. *Rooms:*
23. 🛏 1 ▦ ✕ £ AE, DC, MC,
V. £££

One of London's most beguiling
and individual hotels is set in
three 18th-century houses – the
critic and essayist William Hazlitt
(1778–1830) once lived in one of
them. Although not luxurious, it is
resoundingly civilized. Pictures
deck every wall, but bedrooms
are restfully plain in greens and
creams, with solid, interesting
antiques. Palms and ferns, and
sometimes a Classical bust, perch
on Victorian baths with huge claw
feet. Apart from a small fire-lit
sitting-room behind reception,
there are no public areas.

Marble Arch Marriott

134 George St, W1H 6DN.
Map 11 B1. [C] 0171-723 1277.
[FAX] 0171-402 0666. [TX] 27983.
Rooms: 239. 🛏 1 ▦ 24 ✕
📺 🛏 📺 ▮1 £ ⛎ 🛏
📺 📺 ▮1 £ AE, DC, MC, V, JCB.
££££

This modern box just off Edgware
Road has remarkably good
facilities and a cared-for, relaxing
atmosphere. Rooms contain one
or two comfortable queen-sized
beds, American-style. There is also
a health club with gym and
swimming pool, and – unusual for
the centre of town – free parking.

Hampshire

Leicester Sq, WC2H 7LH. **Map** 13 B3.
[C] 0171-839 9399. [FAX] 0171-930
8122. [TX] 814848 HAMPS G.
Rooms: 124. 🛏 1 ▦ 24 ✕ 📺
⛎ 🖥 🛏 ⛎ 📺 ▮1 ▮1
£ AE, DC, MC, V, JCB. ££££

Few suspect such lavishness could
possibly be concealed on one of
London's seedier squares in the
unlikely setting of the former
Dental Hospital. Inside, this

imposing brick building is plush
enough to please the most
exacting of American executives
(the core of its trade). It is a chain
hotel (part of the Edwardian
group), and stylishly immaculate.
A slightly colonial air prevails
among the Hampshire's ceiling
fans and vast Chinese jars.

REGENT'S PARK
MARYLEBONE

Blandford

80 Chiltern Street, W1M 1PS.
Map 4 D5. [C] 0171-486 3103.
[FAX] 0171-487 2786. [TX] 262594
BLANFD G. *Rooms* 33. 🛏 1 ▦
✕ 🛏 📺 £ AE, DC, MC, V.
££

The Blandford has won numerous
awards for its welcoming brand of
inexpensive bed and breakfast. It
is a family-run establishment
offering simple, unassuming, and
practical accommodation, and a
lavish breakfast, in a quiet side-
street near Baker Street station.

La Place

17 Nottingham Pl, W1M 3FB.
Map 4 D5. [C] 0171-486 2323.
[FAX] 0171-486 4335. *Rooms:* 23. 🛏
1 ▦ 24 ✕ 📺 🛏 ⛎ 🛏
▮1 £ DC, MC, V. ££

Just a stone's throw from Madame
Tussauds, this is a rare commodity
in central London: a pleasant,
affordable bed and breakfast. In
fact, La Place is rather more than
that, also producing simple meals
in its basement restaurant. A plant-
filled bar of blonde bentwood and
rattan skilfully suggests a garden
setting. Bedrooms are well-
furnished and equipped with
many more features than you
would expect for these prices. The
care that is taken about security
makes this an attractive hotel for
women travelling alone.

Dorset Square

39–40 Dorset Sq, NW1 6QN.
Map 3 C5. [C] 0171-723 7874.
[FAX] 0171-724 3328. [TX] 263964.
Rooms: 37. 🛏 1 ▦ 24 ✕ 📺
⛎ 🛏 🛏 📺 ▮1 £ AE,
MC, V. £££

This beautifully restored Regency
building has enormous panache:
antiques, bold fabrics, *objets d'art*,
and interesting paintings happily
mingle. Each room is different.
Downstairs, a restaurant and bar,
with games like backgammon in
progress, provide a relaxed
alternative to the carefully
plumped sitting rooms.

For key to symbols *see p275*

White House

Albany St, NW1 3UP. **Map** 4 E4.
█ 0171-387 1200. **FAX** 0171-388
0091. **TX** 24111. **Rooms:** 576. ▮
🖼 🛏 24 ✖ 🍽 🛗 🐕 ▮
🅿 ▮ ▮ ▮ 🅿 ▮ ▮ 🍽 *AE, DC, MC,*
V, JCB. ⓔⓔⓔ

Once touched by the Profumo
Affair (a political sex scandal of
the 1960s), this large complex of
suites and apartments today
provides high standards of
accommodation and a varied
range of public rooms. The smart,
classic restaurant and comfortably
chintzy cocktail lounge are
complemented by a popular
basement wine bar with beams
and copper knickknacks, and the
spacious Garden Café. An extra
advantage is the hotel's proximity
to Euston mainline railway station
(*see p358–9*).

Langham Hilton

1 Portland Pl, W1N 3AA. **Map** 4 E5.
█ 0171-636 1000. **FAX** 0171-323
2340. **Rooms:** 387. ▮ 1 🖼 24
✖ ▮ ▮ 🍽 🛗 🐕 🅿 ▮
🅿 ▮ ▮ *AE, DC, MC, V, JCB.*
ⓔⓔⓔⓔⓔ *See p221.*

Reopened as a hotel in 1991,
after long tenure by the BBC
who used it for radio broadcasting, the Langham offers a
lavish, Hilton-style re-creation of
its former Victorian splendour, in
addition to all the contemporary
"mod cons" anyone could possibly
wish for. The public rooms reflect
a fashionable nostalgia for the
days of the British Empire. The
spacious bedrooms are
sumptuous, as is the famous
ballroom, decked with glittering
Italian chandeliers and pompously
ornate plasterwork.

BLOOMSBURY
FITZROVIA
COVENT GARDEN
THE STRAND

Mabledon Court

10–11 Mabledon Pl, WC1H 9BA.
Map 5 B3. █ 0171-388 3866.
FAX 0171-387 5686. **Rooms:** 33.
▮ 1 ✖ ▮ 🍽 *MC, V.* ⓔ

There's nothing fancy about this
rather plain building, or its
surroundings, but the tariff doesn't
give itself airs either, and the hotel
is handily placed for both King's
Cross and St Pancras railway
stations. The small rooms are
clean and neat, with a tiny lounge
and a stylishly modern breakfast
room in the basement.

Academy

17–21 Gower St, WC1E 6HG.
Map 5 A5. █ 0171-631 4115.
FAX 0171-636 3442. **Rooms:** 33. ▮
25. 1 🖼 24 ✖ 🐕 🛗 ▮ ▮
🍽 *AE, DC, MC, V, JCB.* ⓔⓔⓔ

Sentinel bay trees mark these
three Georgian town houses near
the heart of London University.
Inside the Academy, the ambience
is sophisticated without excess.
French windows by the book-
shelves of a cosy sitting room
lead to an inviting patio garden.
A basement restaurant offers
interesting food in intimate
surroundings, sometimes
accompanied by live music.

Fielding

4 Broad Court, Bow St, WC2B 5QZ.
Map 13 C2. █ 0171-836 8305.
FAX 0171-497 0064. **Rooms:** 26.
▮ 24. 1 🖼 24 ✖ ▮ 🐕 ▮
AE, DC, MC, V. ⓔⓔ

As an inexpensive, personally
run bed and breakfast in a
fascinating part of London, the
Fielding is hard to beat. Smoky the
parrot may well be the first to
greet you in a small bar of pink
plush. Upstairs, a miscellany of
bedrooms rambles in all
directions, some split-level and
oddly shaped, all small, none
luxurious. Several have useful
desks for working visitors; shower-
rooms with minuscule basins are
ingeniously squeezed into
impossible spaces.

Bonnington

92 Southampton Row, WC1B 4BH.
Map 5 C5. █ 0171-242 2828.
FAX 0171-831 9170. **TX** 261591.
Rooms: 215. ▮ 1 🖼 24 ✖ ▮
🐕 🛗 ▮ 🐕 ▮ ▮ 🍽 *AE, DC,*
MC, V. ⓔⓔⓔ

This family-run hotel is one
of the most useful in Bloomsbury.
The furnishings are mostly
unremarkable, but the managerial
style is personal and quietly
assured. The lounge-bar and
restaurant are pleasant and
modern. Weekend deals are
excellent value for families.

Russell

Russell Sq, WC1B 5BE. **Map** 5 B5.
█ 0171-837 6470. **FAX** 0171-837
2857. **TX** 24615. **Rooms:** 328. ▮
1 🖼 24 ✖ ▮ ▮ 🐕 🛗 ▮
▮ 🍽 *AE, DC, MC, V, JCB.* ⓔⓔⓔ

The portentous exterior of this
grand, late-Victorian pile is
matched by the foyer, a maze of
tawny marble with an imposing
stairway leading off it. Wood
panelling, leather chesterfields,

rich dark fabrics, and chandeliers
set the tone elsewhere. The nicest
rooms overlook the gardens. The
Virginia Woolf brasserie serves
pre-theatre dinners.

Mountbatten

20 Monmouth St, WC2H 9HD.
Map 13 B2. █ 0171-836 4300.
FAX 0171-240 3540. **TX** 298087.
Rooms: 127. ▮ 🖼 24 ✖ ▮ ▮
🐕 ▮ ▮ 🍽 🍽 *AE, MC, V, JCB.*
ⓔⓔⓔⓔ

Well-located for theatreland or
Covent Garden, the hotel is filled
with memorabilia of World War II
veteran, Lord Mountbatten. Public
areas have the ease and style of
Edwardian drawing rooms and
are pleasantly decked out with
colonial and Oriental touches:
ceiling fans, rugs, huge potted
palms. The popular wine bar
downstairs serves a very good
range of snacks in pleasing
surroundings, and pre-theatre
dinners can also be arranged.

Waldorf

Aldwych, WC2B 4DD. **Map** 14 D2.
█ 0171-836 2400. **FAX** 0171-836
7244. **TX** 24574. **Rooms:** 292. ▮
1 24 ✖ ▮ ▮ 🐕 🛗 🐕 ▮
▮ ▮ 🍽 *AE, DC, MC, V, JCB.*
ⓔⓔⓔ

Still smart, this superior Forte hotel
is no longer quite the exclusive
haunt of its heyday. However, the
tea dances for which it was once
so famous still take place at
weekends, and afternoon tea
beneath the famous scrolled
balcony where the band plays is
a popular pastime. The Aldwych
Brasserie offers a less formal
setting for pre-theatre dinners.
Some of the bedrooms are a bit
glum, but they are gradually
being refurbished.

Howard

Temple Pl, Strand, WC2R 2PR.
Map 14 D2. █ 0171-836 3555.
FAX 0171-379 4547. **TX** 268047.
Rooms: 135. ▮ 1 🖼 24 ✖ ▮
▮ 🐕 🛗 🐕 ▮ 🅿 ▮ ▮
🍽 *AE, DC, MC, V, JCB.*
ⓔⓔⓔⓔⓔ

The building is unmistakably
modern, but the authoritative
polish of the hotel's staff soon
transports you to a bygone era.
The foyer is an ornate Classical
pastiche, with *diamanté*
chandeliers and riotous plasterwork painted in ice-cream shades.
Other notable features are a
landscaped interior garden visible
from restaurant and bar, and
splendid river views from many
of the pleasant, traditionally
furnished bedrooms.

Savoy

Strand, WC2R 0EU. **Map** 13 C2.
[0171-836 4343. FAX 0171-240
6040. TX 24234. **Rooms:** 200. 🛏
1 ❖ ✕ 🍽 ✿ 🎦 ⛱ 🏊
🎯 ⛴ 📶 P 📺 🍸 ‖ 🏋
MC, V, JCB. ⓔⓔⓔⓔⓔ
See p116.

On its dais above the Thames,
Richard D'Oyly Carte's dream
hotel still lords it over this part
of London. Inside, the Savoy Grill
is a time-honoured institution for
political and journalistic *tête-à-
têtes*, and piano-accompanied tea
in the lovely Thames Foyer is
ever-popular. Art Deco features
give the Savoy much of its
distinctive elegance. Many of the
bedrooms have old-fashioned
bathrooms with enormous
watering-can shower-heads. Some
particularly appealing balconied
singles have views upriver. But it
is the little touches that give the
Savoy its excellent reputation:
those mattresses with 836 springs,
the bells by the beds for instant
service, and the managing
director's quaint belief that
"standardization is not part of
hotel-keeping". The skylighted
rooftop swimming pool and the
fitness centre are as stylish as
one would expect.

THE CITY

Great Eastern

Liverpool St, EC2M 7QN. **Map** 15 C1.
[0171-283 4363. FAX 0171-283
4897. TX 886812. **Rooms:** 161. 🛏
126. 1 ❖ 24 ✕ ⛱ 🎦
🍸 ‖ 🎯 AE, DC, MC, V. ⓔⓔⓔ

This old Victorian railway hotel
next to Liverpool Street railway
station is, amazingly, the only
hotel within the old City area. Its
good points include several
restaurants: Café Pierre, a French-
style sandwich bar; L'Entrecôte, a
windowless sanctum where
businessmen meet; and Bowlers
in the City, with Classical columns
and a stained-glass saucer dome.
Food in all these comforts to
conservative City norms, and
bedrooms spring no surprises.

Tower Thistle

St Katherine's Way, E1 9LD.
Map 16 E3. [0171-481 2575.
FAX 0171-481 3799. TX 885934.
Rooms: 808. 🛏 1 ❖ 24 ✕
🎯 📶 P 📺 🍸 ‖
🎯 AE, DC, MC, V, JCB.
ⓔⓔⓔⓔ

This 1970s concrete ziggurat
commands a splendid piece of
river frontage, just below Tower

Bridge and looking across to
Butler's Wharf. Inside, the foyer is
cool and spacious, with running
water and plants. Restaurants
range from the expensive Princes
and a hearty Carvery to the chic
Which Way West, which
transforms into a nightclub.
Bedrooms are not very large, but
all have good views, modern
decor and excellent facilities.

FURTHER AFIELD

Chase Lodge

10 Park Rd, Hampton Wick, KT1 4AS.
[0181-943 1862. **Rooms:** 9. 🛏 7.
1 ❖ ✕ ⛱ 🎦 🏊 P 🍸 ‖
🎯 AE, DC, MC, V. ⓔ

This modest Victorian house
has an airy conservatory where
excellent breakfasts and dinners
are served. There is also a small,
smart bar and sitting room. The
bedrooms, though small, are
prettily done out in cottagey
styles with pine or Victorian
furnishings, and bathrooms are
fitted in where possible.

La Reserve

422–428 Fulham Rd, SW6 1DU.
Map 18 D5. [0171-385 8561.
FAX 0171-385 7662. **Rooms:** 40. 🛏
1 ❖ 24 ✕ ⛱ 🏊 🎯
🍸 ‖ 🎯 AE, DC, MC, V. ⓔⓔ

Although the frontage is Classical,
the hotel is determinedly different
inside. The austere, ultra-modern
furnishings may not appeal to
everyone, but the minimalist
bedrooms have smart bedspreads
and good bathrooms. The
restaurant serves a short but
spirited menu of ethnic specialities
all day long.

Swiss Cottage

4 Adamson Rd, NW3 3HP.
[0171-722 2281. FAX 0171-483
4588. TX 297232 SWISSCO G.
Rooms: 80. 🛏 76. 1 ❖ 24 ✕
🎯 🏊 🍸 ‖ 🎯 AE, DC, MC,
V. ⓔⓔ

This well-kept Victorian house
in a quiet street not far from
Swiss Cottage underground
station offers a pleasantly old-
fashioned stay. Antiques and a
grand piano mingle with the
reproduction furniture and an
interestingly unusual collection
of paintings and antiquated
wallpapers. Bedrooms are
spacious and comfortable, the
more expensive rooms boasting
velvet sofas or *chaises longues*.
The restaurant's short menu is
supplemented by sandwiches
and simple snacks served in the
bar and lounge.

Cannizaro House

West Side, Wimbledon Common,
SW19 4UF. [0181-879 1464.
FAX 0181-879 7338. TX 941 3837.
Rooms: 46. 🛏 1 ❖ 24 ✕ 🎦
🎯 ⛴ 🏊 P 📺 🍸 ‖
AE, DC, MC, V, JCB. ⓔⓔⓔ

King George III (reigned
1760–1820) once breakfasted in
this merchant's mansion, originally
dating from 1705, and the hotel
has an ostentatious style that is
appropriate to its royal
connection. Plaster ceilings,
imposing fireplaces, huge flower
arrangements, and windows
ornamented with swagged curtains
all add to an air of grandeur. The
splendour continues upstairs in
the bedrooms. But the best feature
of Cannizaro House is its splendid
secluded gardens, which give it
the feel of a country house.

Kingston Lodge

Kingston Hill, Kingston-upon-Thames,
KT2 7NP. [0181-541 4481. FAX 0181-
547 1013. TX 936034. **Rooms:** 62.
🛏 1 ❖ 24 ✕ ⛱ 🏊 ⛴ 🍽 P
📺 🍸 🎯 AE, DC, MC, V. ⓔⓔⓔ

This small-scale, suburban hotel,
which is part of the Forte chain, is
light and homely. It is on a fairly
busy road, but there are plenty of
quieter rooms at the rear. The
open-plan but nicely intimate,
split-level public areas ramble
from the reception desk. A gas
coal fire burns cheerfully in a
wooden Adam-look surround,
and billowy blinds shield diners
from the sun in the glass-walled
restaurant. There are a few signs
of wear and tear, but generally
the comfortable effects are
sustained and successful.

Sheraton Skyline,
Heathrow Airport

Bath Rd, Hayes, Middlesex, UB3 5BP.
[0181-759 2535. FAX 0181-750
9150. TX 934254. **Rooms:** 354. 🛏
1 ❖ 24 ✕ ⛱ 🎦 ⛴ 🏊 🏋
🎯 🍽 P 📺 🍸 ‖ 🎯 AE, DC,
MC, V, JCB. ⓔⓔⓔⓔⓔ

If you are looking for something
in the vicinity of Heathrow Airport
which is more than just an air-
conditioned, soundproofed box,
try the Sheraton Skyline. One of
its main attractions is the Patio
Caribe, an extraordinary indoor
pool amid a jungle of tropical
foliage, which makes a nice
setting for cocktails or buffet
lunch. Other features conform to
the smart chain hotel pattern.
Courtesy transport to the airport
and free parking are provided.
*For a list of other hotels that are
close to Gatwick or Heathrow
airports see pages 356–7.*

For key to symbols *see p275*

RESTAURANTS AND PUBS

A pre-theatre menu board

ATING OUT IN London is like taking a gastronomic world tour. In the space of just a few days you can travel from America to Africa, taking in all the European countries, and the Near, Middle and Far East on the way. Over the past 30 years, and particularly the last decade, London has been transformed into a veritable United Nations of cuisine.

afield have also been included. *Choosing a Restaurant* on pages 292–4 summarizes key features of the restaurants, and is organized by area so that you can locate one close by. More details can be found in the individual listings on pages 295–305, grouped according to the type of cuisine.

CHOOSING YOUR TABLE

The restaurants listed in this book offer a high standard of cooking, value for money and an enjoyable evening out, and represent a huge range of styles and prices. They are spread across the main tourist areas; a few that merit a special trip further

In recent years, London's cafés have taken on a new look and are among the most lively places in town. As for pubs, for which Britain is famed, many now serve tasty meals, ranging from simple snacks to popular ethnic dishes. Some mainly more informal places to eat and drink, including pubs, are on pages 306–9.

LONDON RESTAURANTS

COVENT GARDEN, Piccadilly Circus, Soho and Leicester Square are the areas where you will find the widest choice of eating places. Kensington and Chelsea also boast a good range of restaurants, and the Docklands area, east of the City, has spawned some stylish establishments.

You can still get traditional British roast beef and stodgy puddings at the likes of Simpson's *(see p295),* but the most significant trend is a new style of British cooking which marries a lighter approach to

a variety of culinary influences. Home-grown chefs like Sally Clarke (of Clarke's, *see p297),* Gary Rhodes (The Greenhouse, *see p295)* and Marco Pierre White (The Restaurant, *see p298)* lead the way.

London is a real paradise for lovers of Indian food, with countless tandoori, balti and bhel poori houses serving cheap food. Two very popular cuisines are Thai and Italian; Soho has a couple of the best-known Thai venues, alongside Japanese, Indonesian, and some of the best Chinese chefs and restaurants outside Hong Kong. Some modern Italian restaurants, epitomised by Riva *(see p299)* and the River Café *(see p299),* offer a lighter style of cooking than the traditional trattorias. French cooking, the longest-established "guest" cuisine in the city, accounts for a sizeable percentage of the high-class establishments in The City and around Mayfair.

Most restaurants, notably Leith's *(see p 298),* provide a vegetarian option and some offer a separate vegetarian menu. A number of specialist vegetarian restaurants offer more adventurous dishes, such as The Place Below *(see p302).* Seafood is a London speciality, with both new-style and traditional fish restaurants being well represented.

La Famiglia *(see p299)*

OTHER PLACES TO EAT

MANY LONDON hotels have excellent restaurants open to non-residents. Some hotel restaurants can be stuffy and rather over-priced, but others offer top-quality food prepared by star chefs.

Several pizza and pasta chains serve decent meals in branches across the city, and some pubs now rival wine bars, serving a range of food from standard British dishes to exotic curries, quiches and lasagne – though the best pub lunches are not to be found in central London. French-style café-brasseries are catching on and a number of coffee houses-pâtisseries are worth a visit. Otherwise, you can grab a quick, cheap snack from a sandwich bar, pizza stand or all-night bagel bakery.

Commissionaire at the Hard Rock Café *(see p302)*

Bibendum *(see p297)*

TIPS ON EATING OUT

MOST LONDON restaurants serve lunch between 12.30pm and 2.30pm and dinner from 7pm until 11pm. Last orders are usually at 10.30pm. Ethnic restaurants usually stay open longer; often until midnight or even later. Many restaurants close on Sunday and Monday. All-day café-brasseries (11am–11pm) may be allowed to serve alcohol only at certain times or with a meal. The traditional British Sunday lunch *(see p289)* appears in almost every pub and many restaurants – always check first, unless that's what you want, as even high-class restaurants may suspend their normal menu on Sundays.

Only the most expensive spots demand a collar and tie; the preferred dress is usually "smart casual". Booking is advisable, especially at places like the Connaught *(see p295)* and Bibendum *(see p297)*.

PRICE AND SERVICE

AN AVERAGE three-course meal with wine at a medium-priced restaurant in central London can be had for between £25 and £35 per head. Lower prices (£5–£15 a head) prevail at small ethnic and vegetarian cafés, wine bars and pubs. Many smarter restaurants have brasseries where you can sample similar fare to the main restaurant, but at a cheaper rate and in more informal circumstances.

Before ordering, check the small print at the bottom of the menu. Prices should include Value Added Tax (VAT) but not necessarily the service charge (between 10 and 15%). In addition, some restaurants impose a cover charge (£1–£2 a head); some have a minimum charge during their busiest periods, and some refuse to take certain credit cards. Beware of the old trick where service is included in the bill but staff leave the "total" box on your credit slip blank, hoping you will add another 10%.

Expect different types of service in different types of restaurant: cheerful and breezy in fast-food joints; discreet yet attentive in high-class places. At peak times you will have to wait longer, though some restaurants offer special pre-theatre meals geared for quick service.

EATING WITH CHILDREN

EXCEPT IN ITALIAN restaurants, fast-food places and a few other places, children are generally tolerated rather than warmly welcomed in London restaurants. However, many do offer a special children's menu, small portions and high chairs *(see pp292–4)* and some actively encourage children and teenagers with entertainments, music and activities. Turn to page 339 for a list of places that cater particularly well to children of various ages.

USING THE LISTINGS
Key to symbols in the listings on pp295–305.

🍴 fixed-price menu
🚭 no-smoking area
Ⓥ vegetarian specialities
🚹 children's portions and high chairs
♿ wheelchair access
👔 jacket and tie required
🎵 live music
🍽 tables outside
🍷 particularly good wine list
★ highly recommended
💳 credit cards accepted:
AE American Express
DC Diners Club
MC Mastercard/Access
V Visa
JCB Japanese Credit Bureau

Price categories for a three-course meal for one including a half-bottle of house wine and all unavoidable extra charges (eg cover, service, VAT):
ⓔ under £12
ⓔⓔ £12–£20
ⓔⓔⓔ £20–£30
ⓔⓔⓔⓔ £30–£40
ⓔⓔⓔⓔⓔ over £40

Clarke's Restaurant *(see p297)*

London's top Hungarian restaurant *(see p300)*

What to Eat in London

THE TRADITIONAL SUNDAY lunch displays what is best about British food – good ingredients prepared simply but well. A joint of roast meat (usually lamb or beef) served with appropriate accompaniments (mint sauce or redcurrant jelly for lamb, mustard or horseradish sauce for beef) is the centrepiece of the meal; wonderful homely puddings and fine British cheeses served with cheese biscuits are obligatory "afters". Sunday lunch is still an institution for Londoners and you will find versions of it in many restaurants and cafés as well as in hotels and pubs all over the capital. The legendary English breakfast may be less ambitious than the five-course feast enjoyed by the Victorians, but it is still a hearty meal and the perfect start to a hard day's sightseeing. Afternoon tea (which is usually taken at around 4pm) is another treat, when the British genius for cakes and their fondness for tea-drinking come together. The smell of fish and chips will often greet you as you wander around the city, and this classic British meal is best eaten in the open air, direct from its paper wrapping.

Fish and Chips
The battered fish (usually haddock or cod) and chips are deep fried.

Full English Breakfast
This favourite meal consists of bacon, egg, tomato, fried bread and a variety of sausages.

Toast and Marmalade
Breakfast is usually finished off with slices of toast spread with orange marmalade.

Ploughman's Lunch
Crusty bread, cheese and sweet pickle are at the heart of this simple pub lunch.

Cheeses
British cheeses are mostly hard or semi-hard, such as Cheshire, Leicester and the most famous of all, Cheddar. Stilton is blue-veined.

Cheddar

Sage Derby

Cheshire

Stilton

Red Leicester

Bread and Butter Pudding
Served hot, the layers of bread and dried fruit are baked in a creamy custard.

Strawberries and Cream
Strawberries served with sugar and cream are a favourite summer dessert.

Summer Pudding
The outer bread lining is soaked in the juice of the many soft fruits inside.

Cucumber Sandwiches
Wafer-thin cucumber sandwiches are a traditional part of an English tea.

Jam and Cream Scones
Halfway between a cake and a bun, scones are served with cream and jam.

Tea
A cup of tea, served with milk or lemon, is still the British national drink.

Meat dishes are usually served with at least one green vegetable.

Horseradish sauce

Yorkshire pudding

Roast beef

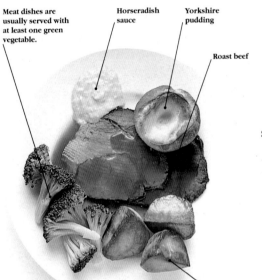

Roast potatoes

Roast Beef and Yorkshire Pudding
Yorkshire pudding, a savoury batter baked in the oven, is the traditional accompaniment to roast beef along with horseradish sauce, roast potatoes and a meat gravy.

Steak and Kidney Pie
Chunks of beef and pigs' kidneys are braised in a thick gravy and topped off with a browned pastry crust.

Shepherd's Pie
This is made with stewed minced lamb, vegetables and a mashed potato topping.

What to Drink
Beer is the British drink. The many different kinds (see p308) range from light lager to stout and bitter. Gin originally came from London. Pimms, usually mixed with lemonade, fruit and mint, is a cooling drink on those hot summer days.

Stout (Guinness)   Bitter   Lager

Pimms   Gin and tonic

London's Best: Restaurants and Pubs

The SHEER VARIETY OF eating and drinking places in London is overwhelming. There are elegant high-class restaurants offering the most *haute* of *haute cuisine*, exotic ethnic specialists (from the Indian sub-continent to the Caribbean), cheap and cheerful cafés, friendly neighbourhood pubs, and fish and chip shops. There is something for every taste, pocket and occasion. See pages 295–305 for the full restaurant listings, pages 306–7 for more informal eating places and pages 308–9 for pubs.

Chutneys
Eat as much as you like, for a few pounds, from a superb lunchtime buffet in this vegetarian Indian restaurant. (See p303.)

Sea Shell
One of the best fish and chip shops in London, this busy restaurant and take-away has customers who come from far and wide. (See pp306–7.)

Regent's Park and Marylebone

Kensington and Holland Park

South Kensington and Knightsbridge

Veronica's
This award-winning rest-aurant serves an intriguing blend of British regional and traditional dishes. (See p296.)

Chelsea

Brown's
Afternoon tea is a speciality of this traditional hotel. (See pp306–7.)

Le Gavroche
The famous Roux brothers' restaurant is a temple of French haute cuisine. (See p296.)

Bibendum
In the restored Michelin building diners enjoy sophi-sticated creations by chef Simon Hopkin-son, and a superb wine list. (See p297.)

Valerie's

The Sun
This traditional London pub in the heart of Bloomsbury has one of the widest ranges of "real ales" in the capital. (See pp308–9.)

Pâtisserie Valerie
This busy, old-fashioned pâtisserie serves cakes, coffee and croissants to an arty clientele. (See pp306–7.)

Bloomsbury and Fitzrovia

Smithfield and Spitalfields

Holborn and the Inns of Court

Covent Garden and the Strand

and Trafalgar re

The City

0 kilometres 1

0 miles 0.5

dilly
1 St
es's

South Bank

RIVER THAMES

Southwark and Bankside

itehall and stminster

The Place Below
Vegetarian food is exquisitely prepared and presented in St Mary-le-Bow's crypt. (See p302.)

New World
Diners hail passing trolleys laden with lunchtime dim sum at this huge, cheap, restaurant in China-town. (See p305.)

The George Inn
Plays are sometimes performed in the courtyard of London's only surviving coaching inn, now a popular pub. (See pp308–9.)

Choosing a Restaurant

THE RESTAURANTS IN this section have been selected for their good value or exceptional food. This chart highlights some of the main factors which may influence your choice. For more details about the restaurants see pages 295–305; light meals and snack places are on pages 306–7; and pubs on pages 308–9.

	Page Number	Seafood Specialities	Fixed-Price Menu	Late Opening	Children's Facilities	Tables Outside	Quiet Restaurant	Vegetarian Specialities
BAYSWATER, PADDINGTON								
Magic Wok (Chinese) ★ ££	305	●	■					
Mega Kalamaras (Greek) ££	300		■	●	■			●
L'Accento Italiano (Italian) £££	299		■		■	●		
Veronica's (British) £££	296		■		■			●
KENSINGTON, HOLLAND PARK, NOTTING HILL								
Malabar (Indian) ££	303		■		■			
L'Altro (Fish) £££	301	●	■		■	●		
Boyd's (Modern/International) £££	297							
Kensington Place (Modern/International) ★ £££	298			●	■			
Wodka (Polish) £££	301							
Clarke's (Modern/International) ££££	297		■				■	
The Halcyon (Modern/International) ££££	297				■	●		
Leith's (Modern/International) ★ £££££	298		■				■	●
SOUTH KENSINGTON, GLOUCESTER ROAD								
St Quentin (French) £££	297		■					
Bibendum (Modern/International) ★ £££££	297	●	■	●				
Hilaire (Modern/International) £££££	298		■	●	■			
KNIGHTSBRIDGE, BROMPTON, BELGRAVIA								
Ognisko Polskie (Polish) ££	301					■		
Bill Bentley's (Fish) £££	301	●						
Caravela (Portuguese) £££	300	●		●				
Khun Akorn (Thai) ★ £££	304	●			■			●
Le Suquet (Fish) £££	301	●		●				
Tui (Thai) £££	304	●						
Bombay Brasserie (Indian) ££££	303		■	●				●
The English House (British) ££££	295		■				■	
L'Incontro (Italian) ££££	299	●		●	■			●
Memories of China (Chinese) ££££	305	●	■					
Poissonnerie de L'Avenue (Fish) ££££	301	●		●	■	●	■	
Salloos (Indian) ★ ££££	303		■				■	
The Restaurant (Modern/International) £££££	298	●	■				■	
Turner's (Modern/International) £££££	298		■				■	
CHELSEA, FULHAM								
Chutney Mary (Indian) £££	303		■					●
Eleven Park Walk (Italian) £££	299		■	■				
La Famiglia (Italian) £££	299			●	■	●		●
Nikita's (Russian) ££££	301		■					
La Tante Claire (French) ★ £££££	297	●	■				■	
WESTMINSTER, VICTORIA								
Tate Gallery Restaurant (British) £££	295				■			
Auberge de Provence (French) £££££	296	●	■				■	
Mijanou (Modern/International) £££££	298		■				●	■

RESTAURANTS AND PUBS 293

Price categories include a three-course meal for one, half a bottle of house wine, and all unavoidable extra charges such as cover, service, VAT.
£ under £12
££ £12–£20
£££ £20–£30
££££ £30–£40
£££££ over £40.

★ Means highly recommended.

SEAFOOD SPECIALITIES Seafood or fish restaurant, or restaurant with good seafood selection.
LATE OPENING Last orders taken at or after 11.30pm excluding Sunday.
CHILDREN'S FACILITIES Children's portions and/or high chairs.
QUIET RESTAURANT No piped music; intimate atmosphere.
VEGETARIAN SPECIALITIES Vegetarian restaurant, or restaurant with at least one vegetarian main course.

Restaurant	Price	Page Number	Seafood Specialities	Fixed-Price Menu	Late Opening	Children's Facilities	Tables Outside	Quiet Restaurant	Vegetarian Specialities
PICCADILLY, MAYFAIR, BAKER STREET									
Down Mexico Way (Mexican)	££	302			●	■			
Hard Rock Café (American)	££	302			●	■	●		●
Sofra (Turkish)	££	300	●	■	●				●
Stephen Bull (Modern/International)	£££	298				■			
Al Hamra (Lebanese)	£££	300			●	■	●		
Le Caprice (Modern/International)	££££	297			●				
The Greenhouse (British)	££££	295							
Ikeda (Japanese)	££££	304	●	■					
Mulligan's of Mayfair (Irish)	££££	298							
Miyama (Japanese)	££££	304	●			■			
Quaglino's (Modern/International)	££££	298	●	■	●				
The Connaught (British) ★	£££££	295						■	
Le Gavroche (French) ★	£££££	296	●	■					
Nico at Ninety (French) ★	£££££	296							
The Oriental (Chinese)	£££££	305	●	■		■			
Suntory (Japanese) ★	£££££	304	●	■				■	
SOHO									
Mildred's (Vegetarian)	£	302							●
Tokyo Diner (Japanese)	£	305			●	■			
Deal's (American)	££	302				■	●		
Fung Shing (Chinese)	££	305	●	■	●				
Harbour City (Chinese) ★	££	305	●	■	●	■			
Melati (Indonesian)	££	304	●	■	●				●
New World (Chinese)	££	305		■		■			
Jade Garden (Chinese)	££	305				■			
Bahn Thai (Thai)	£££	304	●			■			●
Bistrot Bruno (Modern/International) ★	£££	297	●		●				
Café Fish (Fish)	£££	301	●		●				
Chiang Mai (Thai)	£££	304	●	■					●
The Gay Hussar (Hungarian) ★	£££	300						■	
Gopal's (Indian)	£££	303		■	●				
Grahame's Seafare (Fish)	£££	301	●	■		■			
Ming (Chinese)	£££	305		■	●				●
Sri Siam (Thai) ★	£££	304	●	■					●
Wheeler's (Fish)	£££	301	●			■			
Alastair Little (Modern/International)	£££	297		■	●				
COVENT GARDEN, THE STRAND									
Food for Thought (Vegetarian)	£	302						●	●
Calabash (African)	££	302							
Plummers (British)	££	295		■	●				
Alfred (British) ★	£££	295	●	■	●	■	●	■	
Joe Allen (American)	£££	302			●				
Bertorelli's (Italian)	£££	299							●
Café des Amis du Vin (French)	£££	296				■	●		
Manzi's (Fish)	£££	301	●		●				

Price categories include a three-course meal for one, half a bottle of house wine, and all unavoidable extra charges such as cover, service, VAT.
£ under £12
££ £12–£20
£££ £20–£30
££££ £30–£40
£££££ over £40.

★ Means highly recommended.

SEAFOOD SPECIALITIES
Seafood or fish restaurant, or restaurant with good seafood selection.
LATE OPENING
Last orders taken at or after 11.30pm excluding Sunday.
CHILDREN'S FACILITIES
Children's portions and/or high chairs.
QUIET RESTAURANT
No piped music; intimate atmosphere.
VEGETARIAN SPECIALITIES
Vegetarian restaurant, or restaurant with at least one vegetarian main course.

Restaurant	Price	Page Number	Seafood Specialities	Fixed-Price Menu	Late Opening	Children's Facilities	Tables Outside	Quiet Restaurant	Vegetarian Specialities
Mon Plaisir *(French)*	£££	296		■					
Orso *(Italian)*	£££	299			●				●
Rules *(British)*	£££	295							
Simpson's *(British)*	£££	295		■					
The Ivy *(Modern/International)* ★	££££	298			●			■	
The Neal Street Restaurant *(Italian)*	£££££	299						■	
BLOOMSBURY, FITZROVIA									
Chutneys *(Indian)*	£	303		■					●
Ravi Shankar *(Indian)*	£	303		■		■			●
Wagamama *(Japanese)* ★	£	305							●
Mandeer *(Indian)*	££	303		■					●
Museum Street Café *(Modern/International)*	£££	298		■					
Pied-à-Terre *(French)*	£££££	296	●	■					
CAMDEN TOWN, HAMPSTEAD									
Cottons *(Caribbean)*	££	303			●				
Daphne *(Greek)*	££	300			●	■	●		●
Lemonia *(Greek)*	££	300		■	●	■			●
ISLINGTON									
Anna's Place *(Swedish)*	£££	300	●			■	●	■	
SPITALFIELDS, CLERKENWELL									
Nazrul *(Indian)*	£	303			●				●
Bloom's *(Jewish)*	££	300				■			
The Alba *(Italian)*	£££	299							●
The Peasant *(Italian)* ★	£££	299	●			●			
Quality Chop House *(British)*	£££	295			●	■			
Tatsuso *(Japanese)*	££££	305	●	■		■			
THE CITY, SOUTH BANK									
The Place Below *(Vegetarian)* ★	££	302		■					●
RSJ *(French)*	£££	297		■				■	
Le Pont de la Tour *(French)*	£££££	296	●		●		●		
FURTHER AFIELD									
The Abacus *(Chinese)*	££	305		■	●	■			●
Istanbul Iskembecisi, N16 *(Turkish)*	££	300			●	●			
Madhu's Brilliant, Southall *(Indian)*	££	303		■	●				
Osteria Antica Bologna, SW11 *(Italian)*	££	299				■	●		●
The Brixtonian, SW9 *(Caribbean)*	£££	302		■					
Riva, SW13 *(Italian)* ★	£££	299		■		■		■	●
Spread Eagle, SE10 *(French)*	£££	297				■			
Wilson's, W14 *(Scottish)*	£££	296	■			■			
Cibo, W14 *(Italian)*	££££	299	■			■			
River Café, W6 *(Italian)* ★	££££	299				■	●		

BRITISH

British food has an unenviable reputation and is increasingly irrelevant to the British daily diet, which has become a medley of ingredients and styles from around the world. However, there are restaurants which take pride in producing authentic British food at its best *(see pp288–9)*, and these have a very loyal following.

Alfred

245 Shaftesbury Avenue WC2. **Map** 13 B1. (0171-240 2566. **Open** noon–3.30pm, 6–11.30pm Mon–Sat. **Closed** 24 Dec–2 Jan. ⑩ 🍴 🔊 ★ 🥂 AE, DC, MC, V. €€€

Opened in 1994, this is one of a new breed of restaurants that avoids the "starch and two veg" formula of many traditional British restaurants. The minimal decor is retro, reminiscent of a post-war café, tastefully decorated with carefully-chosen details in Bakelite and Formica. The menu changes seasonally to make the best use of market produce. Simple classics and imaginative modern dishes are immaculately prepared and presented. Staff are polite and purposeful, and there's a useful bar downstairs in the evening with an excellent list of beers, ciders and English country wines.

The Connaught

Carlos Pl W1. **Map** 12 E3. (0171-499 7070. **Open** 12.30–2.30pm, 6–10.45pm daily. **Grill open** 12.30–2.30pm, 6–10.45pm Mon–Fri. **Grill closed** public hols. 🚹 🍴 🍷 ★ 🥂 AE, MC. €€€€€

The Connaught Hotel possesses London's grandest old-fashioned dining room. Here French flair is seamlessly joined with British formality, both in the food and the surroundings. Immaculate staff serve indigenous specialities like fillet steak, mixed grill and bread and butter pudding; or Gallic treats like *feuilleté d'oeufs brouillés aux truffes* (pastries filled with scrambled eggs and truffles), *homard grillé aux herbes* (grilled lobster with herbs) and crème brûlée. The same menu is served in the Grill Room during the week, and you need to book well in advance for both restaurants.

The English House

3 Milner St SW3. **Map** 19 C1. (0171-584 3002. **Open** 12.30–2.30pm, 7.30–11.15pm Mon–Sat, 12.30–2pm, 7.30–10pm Sun. **Closed** 25–26 Dec. ⑩ 🍴 🥂 AE, DC, MC. €€€€€

Homely British food is served at this pretty, chintzy little house in a quiet street close to Harrod's. Recommended starters are crab cakes and the soup of the day. Best main courses are the traditional roasts (rack of lamb, beef, duck); for pudding, try the steamed sponge if available. This restaurant is particularly good for Sunday lunch, when you get the real flavour of a British domestic occasion.

The Greenhouse

27a Hay's Mews W1. **Map** 12 E3. (0171-499 3331. **Open** 7–10pm Sun, 7–11pm Mon–Sat. 🥂 AE, DC, MC, V. €€€€

Worth seeking out, in a quiet Mayfair mews, is this elegant, low-ceilinged restaurant, serving British food with confidence. Dishes such as boiled bacon with lentils, faggots in gravy or cod in batter with mushy peas are raised by celebrity chef Gary Rhodes from their lowly status to the level of smart, dinner-party fare. The atmosphere buzzes, the lighting glows warmly, and the steamed sultana, ginger and syrup sponge never ceases to amaze.

Plummers

33 King St WC2. **Map** 13 C2. (0171-240 2534. **Open** noon–2.30pm, 5.30–11.30pm Mon–Fri, noon–2.30pm, 5.30–11.30pm Sat, 6.00–10pm Sun. **Closed** public hols. 🔊 ⑩ 🥂 AE, DC, MC, V. €€

In an area full of transient restaurants, Plummers has stayed in business by serving good food in sizeable portions, from a menu which offers set prices for one, two or three courses. Diners can choose from a menu that has changed little over the past 15 years: chunky British food like steak and kidney pie and pork and apple casserole, alongside equally chunky American dishes such as clam chowder, Cajun meatloaf, and hamburgers with a choice of sauces.

Quality Chop House

94 Farringdon Road EC1. **Map** 6 E4. (0171-837 5093. **Open** noon–3pm, 6.30pm–11.30pm Mon–Sat, noon–4pm, 7–11.30pm Sun. **Closed** Christmas week. 🚹 €€€€

"Progressive working class caterer" says the sign on the etched glass window of this beautiful Victorian diner with its original 1869 fittings wonderfully intact. But the workers these days are more likely to hail from the City than the factory. Sausages and mash may still appear on the bill of fare, but the sausages are meaty veal and the mash is perfectly fluffy and creamy. Other upgraded stalwarts of British cuisine include salmon fishcakes (with sorrel sauce), liver and bacon, scrambled egg and smoked salmon, and, of course, chops. If you're a small party you may have to share one of the six-seater booths; if smoke bothers you, this can be a problem.

Rules

35 Maiden La WC2. **Map** 13 C2. (0171-836 5314. **Open** noon–midnight daily. **Closed** 24–25 Dec. 🥂 AE, DC, MC. €€€

London's oldest surviving restaurant has been serving staunchly traditional British food since 1798. Long a haunt of actors and aristocrats (historical cartoons and photographs signed by the great luminaries of British theatre cover the walls), it now attracts tourists, businessmen, and a few "hunting-shooting-fishing" types visiting town. Specialities include beef, venison and feathered game (grouse, woodcock, partridge). *(See also p112.)*

Simpson's

110 Strand WC2. **Map** 13 C2. (0171-836 9112. **Open** noon–2.30pm, 6–11pm Mon–Sat, noon–2.30pm, 6–9pm Sun. **Closed** public hols. 🚹 🔊 🍴 🎵 🥂 AE, DC, MC, V, JCB. €€€

This is a vast, open dining hall, with more than a hint of British public school (men must wear jackets and ties). Go there to have the roast beef, carved in thick slices from giant, silver-domed trolleys. A recommended starter is the quail's eggs in haddock and cheese sauce, and, for the truly British experience, finish with bread and butter pudding or spotted dick. You'll hardly be able to get up from the table.

Tate Gallery Restaurant

Tate Gallery, Millbank SW1. **Map** 21 B2. (0171-887 8877. **Open** noon–3pm Mon–Sat. **Closed** Christmas, public hols. 🔊 🚹 🔊 🍷 🥂 MC, V. €€€€

The food is an interesting mix of traditional old English cooking (roast beef, steak and kidney pie) and the very new (scallop mousse with pink grapefruit sauce, veal and apricot galantine). A main attraction, apart from the excellent wine list, is the opportunity of dining amid the impressive and unusual setting of the Rex Whistler mural, *Expedition in Pursuit of Rare Meats. (See also p82.)*

Veronica's

3 Hereford Rd W2. **Map** 10 D2.
[0171-229 5079. **Open** noon–3pm,
7pm–midnight. **Closed** Sat lunch,
Sun, public hols. ¶●¶ V ⚡ ⚡ ⚡
⚡ AE, DC, MC, V. £££

Veronica's specializes in a style of
British regional and historical
cooking that is unique among
London restaurants. Dishes might
include calves' liver and beetroot
(1940), spring lamb with crabmeat
(19th-century) or Hannah Woolley
chicken and mustard (1644). Every
couple of months, proprietress
Veronica Shaw changes both the
menu and the decor to tie in with
a different theme (such as Scottish
or Tudor food, the Middle Ages or
World War II).

Wilson's

236 Blythe Road, W14. **Map** 17 A1.
[0171-603 7267. **Open** 12.30–
2.30pm Sun-Fri, 7.30–10.30pm Mon-
Sat. **Closed** Christmas week, public
hols. ¶●¶ ⚡ ⚡ ⚡ MC, V.
£££

Bob Wilson runs the best "Scottish"
restaurant in London. It's not a
theme park though; dishes from
the daily-changing menu are
mostly Anglo-Gallic, though there
are a few Scottish dishes such as
haggis, Athol brose (a dessert of
cream with oats, whisky and
honey), plus of course Scotch beef
and salmon. There are also half a
dozen malt whiskies to choose
from. After dinner Mr Wilson will
play the bagpipes, if requested.

FRENCH

As London's longest established
"guest" cuisine, French food is
readily available throughout the
capital, and the quality can be
superb. La Tante Claire and Nico
at Ninety Park Lane (three
Michelin stars) and Le Gavroche
(two), are legendary names on the
London restaurant scene, and
prices are commensurately high.
You'll find most types of French
food well represented in London,
from *haute cuisine*, through the
modern, lighter style, to
traditional, regional cuisines.

Auberge de Provence

41 Buckingham Gate SW1.
Map 12 F5. [0171-821 1899.
Open 12.30–2.30pm Mon–Fri,
7.30–11pm Mon–Sat. ¶●¶ ⚡
⚡ AE, DC, MC, V, JCB.
£££££

This white-painted, cavernous-
but-cosy restaurant is attached to
the St James Court Hotel, near
Victoria Station. The combinations
of lightly cooked meats, and

especially fish, with imaginatively
flavoured sauces and fresh fruits
and vegetables are inspired. This
is the best place in London for a
taste of Provence.

Café des Amis du Vin

11–14 Hanover Place WC2.
Map 13 C2. [0171-379 3444.
Open noon–2.30pm, 6–11.30pm
Mon–Sat, noon–10.30pm Sun. ¶●¶
⚡ ⚡ ⚡ AE, DC, MC, V, JCB. £££

This popular brasserie, just across
the road from the Royal Opera
House, is usually thronging with
customers. The food can be
simple – omelettes, or meaty
Toulouse sausages in the bar – or
more elaborate, ranging from trout
stuffed with spinach and turkey
brochettes in the café, to fish
terrine, pan-fried calves' liver with
lime and char-grilled steaks with
piquant sauces, in the restaurant.

Le Gavroche

43 Upper Brook St W1. **Map** 12 D2.
[0171-408 0881or 0171-499 1826.
Open noon–2pm, 7–11pm Mon–Fri.
Closed public hols. ¶●¶ ⚡ ⚡ ★
⚡ AE, DC, MC, V. £££££

This is the high temple of *haute
cuisine*, with prices to match.
However, the standard of cooking
set by the Roux brothers is
consistently superb. The Roux
philosophy is to create a perfect
marriage between ingredients,
cooking methods and flavourings
– for example, sautéed scallops
in a soy and spice sauce, served
with crisp, fried vegetable strips.
Décor, like the food, is tasteful
and firmly traditional. The service
is relentlessly formal, the menu
written entirely in French, and the
wine list vast and daunting (800
wines). If you want to experience
Le Gavroche on a budget, there
are set meals which work out half
the price of going *à la carte* –
two people might even get some
change from a hundred quid.

Mon Plaisir

21 Monmouth St WC2. **Map** 13 B2.
[0171-836 7243. **Open** noon–
2.15pm, 6–11.15pm daily. ¶●¶
⚡ AE, DC, MC, V, JCB. £££

A long-standing fixture of Covent
Garden's theatreland, Mon Plaisir
retains its reputation for reliable,
unpretentious French provincial
food, cooked and served with
care and courtesy. The menu
changes, but you will usually find
the likes of fish soup, goat's
cheese salad, snails in garlic, *coq
au vin*, *daube de boeuf* and a
marvellous array of cheeses. The
pre-theatre fixed-price menu is
particularly convenient.

Nico at Ninety

90 Park La W1. **Map** 12 D3.
[0171-409 1290. **Open** noon–2pm,
7–11pm Mon–Fri, 7–11pm Sat.
Closed public hol eves, 10 days
Christmas. ¶●¶ ⚡ ⚡ ★ ⚡ AE,
DC, MC, V. £££££

Nico at Ninety is the three-star
Michelin headquarters of volatile
superstar chef Nico Ladenis. In
these spacious surroundings,
Nico's artistry runs riot. *Foie gras*
is a recurring theme, adding a
richness and strength of flavour
that is balanced by painstakingly
delicate touches. Nico's other
restaurants, Nico Central on
Great Portland Street (0171-436
8846) and Simply Nico near
Victoria Station (0171-630 8061),
allow you to enjoy less complicated creations in more cramped
surroundings. Here, the Provençal
influence is more peasant- than
prince-orientated; dishes might be
fish soup, squid salad or duck
confit with herb dumplings.

Pied-à-Terre

34 Charlotte St W1. **Map** 13 A1.
[0171-636 1178. **Open** 12.15–
2.30pm Mon–Fri, 7.15–10.15pm
Mon–Sat. **Closed** last week Dec-1st
week Jan, last 2 weeks Aug. ¶●¶
⚡ AE, DC, MC, V. £££££

In the shadow of the Telecom
Tower, this rather serious French
restaurant is a beacon of quality in
a street of mainly cheap-and-
cheerful eating houses. Both decor
and menu are on the stark side,
but the food is sybaritic in the
extreme. Starters favour seafood
(tagliatelle of langoustines, roasted
scallops with coriander, crab
galette); main courses are meat-
orientated – pigeon, lamb, even
pig's head. Wines start expensive
and go upwards.

Le Pont de la Tour

Butlers Wharf SE1. **Map** 16 E4.
[0171-403 8403. **Bar and grill
open** noon–midnight daily.
Restaurant open noon–3pm daily,
6pm–midnight Mon–Sat, 6–11pm
Sun. ¶●¶ ⚡ ⚡ ⚡ ⚡ ⚡ AE,
MC, V. £££££

This riverside creation of design
mogul Terence Conran boasts,
among other things, wonderful
views of Tower Bridge. Set in a
converted warehouse, the interior
of the restaurant has the stylish
look of an ocean liner, and
the food is equally bold and
streamlined: pea risotto with mint,
scallops with garlic butter, calves'
liver with red onions, grilled tuna
with coriander. There is also a bar,
and a grill serving seafood, steaks,
and salads. Bread comes from
their own bakery.

RSJ

13a Coin St SE1. **Map** 14 E3.
[0171-928 4554. **Open** noon–2pm
Mon–Fri, 6–11pm Mon–Sat. **Closed**
public hols. ¶ | & ⚑ ☕ AE, MC,
V. €€€

RSJ serves a mixture of unspec-
tacular but well-executed dishes.
Salmon, lamb, duck and chicken
are the most commonly featured,
served both plain and with sauces.
An extraordinarily good wine list
specializes in wines of the Loire
region of France.

St Quentin Restaurant

243 Brompton Rd SW3. **Map** 19 B1.
[0171-581 8377. **Open** noon–3pm,
7–11.30pm Mon–Sat, noon–3.30pm,
6.30–10.30pm Sun. ¶ | ☕ AE, DC,
MC, V. €€€

In this many-mirrored meeting
place of well-to-do local residents,
the decor is matched by the rich
food: *foie gras*, confit of duck,
chicken in cream. It can be
expensive, but the set menus
provide an escape. The Grill St
Quentin (0171-581 8377), just
round the corner, specializes in
seafood and is more child-friendly
than most London restaurants. The
pâtisserie at both St Quentin
restaurants is superb.

Spread Eagle

1–2 Stockwell St SE10. **Map** 23 B2.
[0181-853 2333. **Open** 6.30–
10.30pm Mon–Sat, noon–3.30pm
Sun. ¶ | & 🎠 ☕ AE, DC, MC, V.
€€€

If you're visiting Greenwich, eat at
the Spread Eagle, one of the few
reliable and reasonably-priced
restaurants in the area. Set meals
of hearty, no-nonsense food are
served in this dark and rather
quaint 17th-century coaching inn:
generous mussel soup, seafood
sausage, veal kidneys in mussel
sauce and the excellent lamb
with tomatoes and black olives.

La Tante Claire

68 Royal Hospital Rd SW3.
Map 19 C3. [0171-351 0227 or
0171-352 6045. **Open** 12.30–2pm,
7–11pm Mon–Fri. **Closed** public hols.
¶ | & 🍽 🍸 ★ ☕ AE, DC, MC,
V, JCB. €€€€€

You have to book well ahead at
this small, smart, top-notch,
expensive establishment.
Gascon owner-chef, Pierre
Koffman, likes to cook rich dishes,
using goose fat and *foie gras*
liberally. Stuffed pig's trotter,
tournedos Rossini and kid with
chocolate and raspberry vinegar
sauce give an idea of the style.

MODERN INTERNATIONAL

These restaurants represent an
approach to cooking that has
evolved quite recently. Its main
feature is a willingness to borrow
ingredients and styles from various
cuisines all over the world and to
create something new: a dish might
include a cut of British lamb, some
Oriental herbs, and a few sun-dried
tomatoes from Italy. The lightness
of touch and innovative use of
fresh ingredients is much favoured
by adventurous new chefs such as
Sally Clarke and Alastair Little.

Alastair Little

49 Frith St W1. **Map** 13 A2.
[0171-734 5183. **Open** noon–3pm
Mon–Fri, 6–11.30pm Mon–Sat.
Closed public hols. ¶ | &
☕ AE, MC, V. €€€€

This bastion of innovation in the
heart of Soho serves always
interesting food in a rather spartan
restaurant that perpetually treads
the line between lively and plain
noisy. Star dishes are fish soup,
tournedos with *polenta*, oysters
with Thai sausages, plus anything
else that sports Alastair Little's
brilliant relishes or garnishes.

Bibendum

Michelin House, 81 Fulham Road
SW3. **Map** 19 A2. [0171-581 5817.
Open 12.30–2.30pm Mon–Fri,
7–11.30pm Mon–Sat, 12.30–3pm,
Sat & Sun, 7–10.30pm Sun. **Closed**
Easter Mon, 4 days Christmas. ¶ |
& 🍽 ★ ☕ MC, V. €€€€€

In the glorious, stained-glass
setting of the restored Michelin
building, well-heeled diners feast
on the sophisticated creations of
top chef Simon Hopkinson.
Calves' kidneys are matched with
anchovy butter, poached veal with
watercress purée; bacon is used to
wrap a host of meats. There are
sensational risottos, and you can
choose from a splendid wine list.
Book well in advance.

Bistrot Bruno

63 Frith Street W1. [0171-734
4545. **Open** 12.15–2.30pm Mon-Fri,
6.15–11.30pm Mon-Sat. ★ ☕ AE,
DC, MC, V. €€€

This bare but comfortable canteen
serves Bruno Loubet's eclectic but
uncommonly successful dishes.
The combinations in main courses
might include duck confit on
chestnut and celeriac with a red
onion gravy, or jugged hare with
split pea ravioli. Starters and
desserts are equally improbable,
but the overall effect is satisfying.

Boyd's

135 Kensington Church St W8.
Map 10 D4. [0171-727 5452.
Open 12.30–2.30pm, 7–11pm Mon–
Sat. ¶ | ☕ AE, MC, V. €€€

The calling card of chef-owner
Boyd Gilmour is his ability with
sauces: wholegrain mustard sauce
(calves' liver), béarnaise (beef),
pink peppercorn (venison). He
also dots around the world for his
flavours – lime juice, soy sauce,
ginger and sesame oil. Puddings
have a tendency to incorporate
chocolate and cream.

Le Caprice

Arlington House, Arlington St SW1.
Map 12 F3. [0171-629 2239.
Open noon–3pm, 6pm–midnight
daily. **Closed** 24 Dec–2 Jan. & 🎵
☕ AE, DC, MC, V. €€€€

This stylish, elder sister of The Ivy
(see p298) attracts the same kind
of elegant and celebrity-studded
clientele. The food is simple,
modern and uses influences and
ingredients from all corners of the
globe, with the emphasis on grills
(tuna, rabbit and squid). Gravy
and thick sauces are taboo – clean
lines and clean shirt fronts are
essential in such a high-profile
eaterie. Book well ahead.

Clarke's

124 Kensington Church St W8.
Map 10 D4. [0171-221 9225.
Open 12.30–2pm, 7–10pm Mon–Fri.
Closed 2 weeks summer, Christmas,
Easter, public hols. ¶ | & ⚑
☕ MC, V. €€€€

Britain, California and Italy meet
over a char-grill in the kitchens of
talented chef-proprietress Sally
Clarke. There is a no-choice set
dinner menu that changes daily
and is always superb. Food is light
but incredibly tasty; recurring ingredients are Mediterranean vegetables,
corn-fed chicken, salmon, bream,
fresh herbs and wild plants like
dandelion and elderflower.

The Halcyon

129 Holland Park Ave W11.
Map 9 A4. [0171-727 7288.
Open 7–10.30am, noon–2.30pm,
7–10.30pm daily. ¶ | 🎠 🍽 ☕ AE,
DC, MC, V. €€€€

Housed at the back of the Halcyon
Hotel (see p278), this is a frequent
stopping-place of the stars. The
menu changes frequently, but you
will find successful exotica such as
marinated scallops or *foie gras* with
brioche. The main courses are
always interesting – chicken with
aubergine and mint, duck with
honey and almonds, for example.

Hilaire

68 Old Brompton Rd SW7.
Map 18 F2. [0171-584 8993. **Open**
12.30–2.30pm, 6.30–11.30pm Mon–
Fri, 6.30–11.30pm Sat. [icons]
[icons] AE, DC, MC, V. ££££

Thick drapes and a sweeping glass
frontage welcome diners to this
rather boudoir-like restaurant,
serving similarly sumptuous food.
Rather than use conventional
sauces, owner-chef Bryan Webb
flavours meat and fish with pesto,
chutney, foie gras or herbed or
spiced lentils. His supper menu
(after 9.30pm) is the cheapest way
to get the best out of this most
original of eating places.

The Ivy

1 West St WC2. **Map** 13 B2.
[0171-836 4751. **Open** noon–3pm,
5.30–12pm daily. [icons] ★ [icons] AE, DC,
MC, V. ££££

The Ivy has long been a landmark of the theatre district and
traditional venue for first-night
parties. Stars cluster in the oak-
panelled, leather-benched interior
to dine on fashionable fare like
salmon fishcakes with rocket and
shaved Parmesan salad.

Kensington Place

201–205 Kensington Church St W8.
Map 9 C3. [0171-727 3184.
Open noon–3pm, 6.30–11.45pm daily.
Closed Christmas, Aug public hol.
★ [icons] MC. ££££

This austerely decorated restaurant
attracts a noisy, vibrant crowd. It
combines conventional fare like
Parma ham with melon, steak au
poivre and grilled salmon with the
unusual – braised squid with peas,
pigeon crostini (on toasted or
fried bread) with truffle paste,
boiled ox tongue with lentils and
salsa verde, raspberries with
mascarpone cheese.

Leith's

92 Kensington Park Road W11.
Map 9 B2. [0171-229 4481.
Open 7.30–11.30pm daily. [icons]
[icons] ★ AE, DC, MC, V.
£££££

Hushed diners explore gourmet
offerings at this elegant restaurant
run by good-food apostle Prue
Leith, proprietor of Leith's School
of Food and Wine. British
specialities include rib of beef and
ox tongue, and there is an all-
British cheeseboard. Small, filled
savoury tartlets are a recurring
feature, along with monkfish,
scallops and guinea fowl. An
outstanding vegetarian menu
offers imaginative dishes and is
very popular with omnivores too.

Mijanou

143 Ebury St SW1. **Map** 20 E2.
[0171-730 4099. **Open** noon–2pm,
7–11pm Mon–Fri. **Closed** 2 weeks
Christmas, 1 week Easter, 3 weeks
Aug, public hols. [icons] [icons]
[icons] AE, MC, V. £££££

Owners Mr (wine) and Mrs (food)
Blech pair ingredients and wine
with great care and ingenuity:
quail slices in a foie gras mousse
beside an orange and passion fruit
jelly, or a mousseline of melon
with raisin-stuffed ham slices. The
wine list is one of London's best.

Mulligan's of Mayfair

13–14 Cork St W1. **Map** 12 F3.
[0171-409 1370. **Open** noon–
2.15pm Mon–Fri, 6.30–11pm
Mon–Sat. **Closed** public hols. [icons] AE,
DC, MC, V. ££££

Dishes tend to be hearty at this
Irish basement restaurant – turnip
and brown bread soup, black
pudding, ox tongue, and a good
range of fish dishes. Sample
specialities such as colcannon
(mashed cabbage and potatoes)
and boxty (potato pancake).

Museum Street Café

47 Museum St WC1. **Map** 13 B1.
[0171-405 3211. **Open** 12.30–
2.30pm, 6.30–9.30pm Mon–Fri.
[icons] [icons] £££

The plain and simple decor and
the blackboard menu are more
than made up for by the excellent
cooking, which makes good use
of Californian char-grilling and
trendy Italian ingredients such as
bresaola, arugula (rocket) and
pesto. Bring your own alcohol.

Quaglino's

16 Bury Street SW1. **Map** 12 F3.
[0171-930 6767. **Open**
noon–3pm daily;, 5.30–midnight
Mon–Thur, 5.30pm–1am Fri–Sun.
Closed Christmas, New Year. [icons]
[icons] AE, DC, MC, V. ££££

Terence Conran's flagship in the
centre of town has great elegance
and attention to detail. This is a
bustling barn of a place though,
and not the place for a discreet
and relaxing meal. The seafood is
particularly recommended; the
service can be brusque.

The Restaurant

Hyde Park Hotel, 66 Knightsbridge
SW1. **Map** 11 C5. [0171-259
5380. **Open** noon–2.15pm Mon–Fri,
7–11pm Mon–Sat.. **Closed** public
hols, Christmas–New Year.
[icons] AE, DC, MC, V. £££££

Food critics have showered praise
and awards on the talented and
temperamental chef Marco Pierre
White. White moved to these new
premises from the less imposing
Harvey's in Wandsworth during
1994 – and has added his third
Michelin star. His sauces travel
from the subtle to the exquisite,
ranging from Sauternes to soy-
based, with foie gras and truffles
featuring prominently. Fish and
seafood are particular strengths,
and his desserts are sublime.
There's a three course set lunch
costing under £30, but dinner will
cost more than double this.

Stephen Bull

5–7 Blandford St W1. **Map** 12 D1.
[0171-486 9696. **Open** 12.15–
2.30pm Mon–Fri, 6.30–10.30pm
Mon–Sat. [icons] [icons] MC, V.
£££

This immaculate and stylish
modern restaurant offers delicate,
rather than sturdy, fare: crab and
orange ravioli with basil cream,
cuttlefish risotto with saffron and
lemon, grilled baby chicken with
citrus fruit. The fish dishes are
particularly well executed, and an
interesting wine list offers good
value. There's a bistro and bar
(0171-490 1750) near Smithfield
Market (see p164), offering
cheaper food in a striking setting.

Turner's

87–89 Walton St SW3. **Map** 19 B2.
[0171-584 6711. **Open** 12.30–
2.30pm, 7.30–11pm Sun–Fri,
7.30–11pm Sat. **Closed** 25–
31 Dec. [icons] AE, DC, MC.
£££££

This highly acclaimed restaurant
serves clever but unpretentious
food to its fashionable clientele:
guinea fowl terrine with pistachio
nuts, roast turbot with butter bean
ragout, grilled beef with bone
marrow sauce, lamb with duck
liver in black olive sauce. Other
distinctive features are a long
Chablis list (there are 15 types)
and burly owner-chef Brian
Turner, who is often to be seen
out among the diners.

ITALIAN

Italian cuisine in London is
undergoing a renaissance. A
move away from the pizza, pasta,
and veal standards, towards a
style that combines traditional
home cooking with a modern
lightness of touch, has captivated
the capital's restaurant-goers.
Seafood, beans, mixed-leaf salads,
char-grilled vegetables and pan-
roasted meats, stuffed breads,
polenta and wild mushrooms
feature strongly.

L'Accento Italiano

16 Garway Rd W2. **Map** 10 D2.
[0171-243 2201. **Open** 12.30–
2.30pm, 6.30–11.30pm daily. |◉|
🚶 ♿ 🍴 🎵 MC, V. €€€

This popular restaurant offers
stylish new-wave Italian food. It
has a good value set menus in
town which might feature saffron
risotto with sausages, followed by
a warm salad of octopus and
potato. A typical dessert is sweet
fritters with a fruit sauce. The
menu changes frequently, but
standards remain high. Book
ahead.

The Alba

107 Whitecross St EC1. **Map** 7 A4.
[0171-588 1798. **Open** noon–3pm,
6–11pm Mon–Fri. **Closed** public
hols. Ⓥ 🎵 AE, DC, MC, V, JCB.
€€€

Stark and clean, this offers an
interesting range of meat, fish and
vegetable dishes. Italian cheeses,
wild mushrooms and fresh herbs
feature strongly and the pasta and
sausages – both home-made – are
particularly good. Eat in the wine
bar if you don't want a full meal.

Bertorelli's

44a Floral St WC2. **Map** 13 C2.
[0171-836 3969. **Open** noon–3pm,
5.30–11.30pm Mon–Sat. Ⓥ ♿
restaurant only. 🎵 AE, DC, MC, V,
JCB. €€€

This slick operation near the
Opera House is used to dealing
with rushed pre-theatre diners.
Upstairs there is a grander
restaurant, while downstairs a
simpler café concentrates on
reliable pasta and pizza dishes.
Booking is essential.

Cibo

3 Russell Gdns W14. **Map** 9 A5.
[0171-371 2085. **Open** noon–3pm
Sun–Fri, 7–11pm Mon–Sat. |◉|
🚶 ♿ 🎵 AE, DC, MC, V.
€€€€

This was one of the leaders in the
move towards traditional Italian
home cooking. Pasta here is
stuffed with wild mushrooms,
broad beans or sea bass and
spinach. Salads are red, green and
orange and there are char-grilled
lamb cutlets and sautéed calves'
liver. Noisy, trendy and bright.

Eleven Park Walk

11 Park Walk SW10. **Map** 18 F4.
[0171-352 3449. **Open** noon–
3pm daily, 7pm–11pm Mon–Sat.
Closed public hols. |◉| 🚶 ♿ 🎵
🎵 AE, MC, V, JCB. €€€

With well-spaced tables, mirrors
and potted plants, this reliable, if
somewhat conventional, restaurant
is patronized by a band of local
devotees. Go for standards like
ravioli with tomato and basil,
scallops with wine sauce and
spaghetti with fresh lobster.

La Famiglia

7 Langton St SW7. **Map** 18 F4.
[0171-351 0761. **Open** noon–3pm,
7pm–midnight daily. **Closed**
Christmas, Easter. Ⓥ ♿ 🍴
🎵 AE, DC, MC, V. €€€

This bright, noisy, for-all-the-family
place has a fresh blue and white
tiled interior and large awnings in
the back garden – eating outside is
a particular treat. The grilled and
baked fish and traditional starters
such as mozzarella salad and
pasta e fagioli (pasta with white
beans) are highly recommended.

L'Incontro

87 Pimlico Road SW1. **Map** 20 D2.
[0171-730 6327 or 0171-730 3663.
Open 12.30–11.30pm Mon–Fri, 7–
11.30pm Sat, Sun. Ⓥ 🚶 ♿ 🎵 🎵
🎵 AE, DC, MC, V, JCB. €€€€

Clean and gleaming, there is a
distinct leaning towards Venetian
food – fish in particular – in this
startlingly designed establishment.
Try the salt cod with olive oil and
milk or the squid-in-its-own-ink.
The fresh pasta is legendary.

Neal Street Restaurant

26 Neal St WC2. **Map** 13 B1.
[0171-836 8368. **Open** 12.30–
2.30pm, 7.30 11pm Mon–Sat.
Closed public hols, 1 week Christmas,
New Year. |◉| ♿ 🍴 🎵 AE,
DC, MC, V €€€€€

Famed for his passion for fungi,
owner Antonio Carluccio makes
sure a mushroomy theme runs
through the menu at this stylish
eating place. There's wild
mushroom soup, warm mushroom
and bacon salad, venison with
morels and beef medallions with
wild mushrooms. Make sure to ask
how much the seasonal mushroom
special costs before you order it:
the prices can be astronomical.

Orso

27 Wellington St WC2. **Map** 13 C2.
[0171-240 5269. **Open** noon–
midnight daily. **Closed** Christmas,
public hols. 🎵 €€€

At this gathering point for media
and theatre types, the food is
modern and constantly changing.
It is particularly noted for
innovative pasta and meat and fish
in bold sauces. The interior is
attractive but noisy; service is brisk.

Osteria Antica Bologna

23 Northcote Rd SW11.
[0171-978 4771. **Open** 6–11pm
Mon–Tue, noon–11pm Wed–Sat,
12.30–10.30pm Sun. |◉| Ⓥ
🚶 ♿ 🍴 🎵 AE, MC, V.
€€

This is an ideal venue for parties;
friends can enjoy a cheap but
satisfying meal by sharing a
selection of small dishes *(assagi)* –
delicious vegetable and fish
combinations for a few pounds.
Otherwise, there's an impressive
selection of innovative salads,
pastas and meat and fish.

The Peasant

240 St John Street EC1.
Map 6 F3. [0171-336 7726.
Open 12.30–2.30pm Mon–Fri,
6.30–10.45pm Mon–Sat. **Closed**
public hols, 24 December–3 January.
★ Ⓥ 🚶 ♿ 🎵 MC, V. €€€

This converted pub produces
modern Italianate meals that puts
many grander Italian restaurants to
shame. Fresh ingredients are
cooked without cream or alcohol
sauces to produce simple, robust
dishes served in generous portions.
The bottled beers are interesting
too. Prices seem high for a pub,
but this is pub grub like no other.

River Café

Thames Wharf Studios, Rainville Rd W6.
[0171-381 8824. **Open** 12.30–
2.30pm, 7.30–11pm Mon–Fri,
1–2.30pm, 7.30–11pm Sat,
1–2.30pm Sun. **Closed** public hols.
🚶 ♿ 🍴 🎵 ★ 🎵 MC, V.
€€€€

Praise has been heaped on this
headquarters of the Italian new-
wave movement. Both the food
and the surroundings are clean,
light and crisp. Mozzarella, sage,
sun-dried tomatoes, Parmesan,
pine nuts, basil, thyme and garlic
are the recurring flavours that
accompany delicious char-
grilled fish and meats.

Riva

169 Church Road SW13.
[0181-748 0434. **Open**
12–2.30pm Sun–Fri, 7–11pm
Mon–Sat. **Open** 7–9.30pm Sun.
Ⓥ 🚶 ♿ ★ 🎵 MC, V. €€€

Barnes is a long way out from the
centre of town, but residents of
southwest London are devoted to
the regional Italian cooking served
here. The emphasis is on top-
quality ingredients combined in
imaginative ways. Seafood and fish
are always well-represented on the
menu, which changes regularly.
Quiet, civilized, and great value.

For key to symbols *see p287*

GREEK
MIDDLE EASTERN

Cuisines from all over the Middle East (Greece, Turkey, Lebanon and North Africa) have a lot in common. Dishes tend to be lightly rather than heavily spiced – barbecued meats, herby stews, salads and vegetable dips such as *taramasalata* (cod's roe), *houmous* (chick pea) and *tzatziki* (yoghurt and cucumber) feature strongly. The cheapest way to eat is with a set-price *meze* – a selection of such dishes: it's a sociable affair and particularly good for those new to this food.

Daphne

83 Bayham St NW1. **Map** 4 F1.
[0171-267 7322. **Open** noon–2.30pm, 6–11.30pm daily. **Closed** 25–26 Dec, 1 Jan. V ⚑ ⚑ ⚑ ⚑ MC, V. ££

Daphne is a welcoming and friendly place. It offers all that's best about good Greek food: simple and fresh ingredients, carefully flavoured with herbs and at a reasonable price. Good meat and fish dishes predominate but there is also a changing list of vegetarian specials. The meze is good value.

Al Hamra

31–33 Shepherd Market W1.
Map 12 E4. [0171-493 1954.
Open noon–11.45pm daily. V ⚑ ⚑ ⚑ AE, DC, MC, V. £££

On arrival at this smart Lebanese restaurant you will be brought a plate of olives, fresh Middle Eastern bread and raw vegetables to accompany the meze dishes, of which there are over 40. Try the *moutabal*, made with aubergine and sesame, or for a warm dish, the *houmous kawarmah* (chick pea paste topped with lamb and pine nuts). The service is formal.

Istanbul Iskembecisi

9 Stoke Newington Road N16.
[0171-254 7291. **Open** 5pm–5am Mon–Sat, 2pm–5am Sun. ⚑ ⚑ ⚑ MC, V. ££

Istanbul Iskembecisi is one of several cheap Turkish restaurants in this part of Dalston. It serves offal dishes such as grilled lamb intestines and boiled brains with salad. It also serves excellent dishes for the fainter of heart, such as char-grilled meats. It's lively, with charming staff and low prices.

Lemonia

89 Regent's Park Road NW1.
Map 3 C1. [0171-586 7454. **Open** noon–3pm Sun–Fri, 6–11.30pm Mon–Sat. V ⚑ ⚑ ££

This enormously popular Greek restaurant serves beautifully prepared food in a bustling atmosphere. The menu includes good vegetarian options such as stuffed vegetables and bean and lentil dishes; the meze dishes include a fine *tabouleh* (a bulgar wheat salad) and an aubergine dip. Book evenings well in advance.

Mega Kalamaras

76 Inverness Mews W2. **Map** 10 E2.
[0171-727 9122. **Open** 7pm–midnight Mon–Sat. **Closed** public hols. ⚑ V ⚑ ⚑ ⚑ on request. ⚑ AE, DC, MC, V. ££

This is the best Greek cooking in London, served in spacious surroundings with a pleasantly laid-back atmosphere. The menu includes a wide and creative choice of vegetarian dishes. Seafood and casserole dishes are also well represented, but a selection of the meze often makes the most interesting meal. Micro Kalamaras next door is a bring-your-own-booze basement taverna which packs out with merry bargain-hunters.

Sofra

18 Shepherd St W1. **Map** 12 E4.
[0171-493 3320. **Open** noon–midnight daily. ⚑ V ⚑ AE, DC, MC. £££

Sofra is one of the best-known and most expensive Turkish restaurants in London. The meat grills are good, but the real attraction is the delicious but tiny meze dishes: *kisir* (a crushed wheat salad), *imam biyaldi* (stuffed aubergine), *böreks* (filled pastries) and so on.

OTHER
EUROPEAN

Although most international cuisine can be found in London, some are restricted to only one or two establishments of any note. The British generally favour food from climates more southern and exotic than their own, but there are a few Northern and Eastern European restaurants well worth a visit.

Anna's Place

90 Mildmay Pk N1. [0171-249 9379. **Open** 12.15–2.15pm, 7.15–10.30pm Tue–Sat. **Closed** 2 weeks Christmas, 2 wks Easter, Aug. ⚑ ⚑ £££

Virtually everything in this airy Swedish restaurant is home-made, including the bread and the

sorbets. With the attentive service, and Anna herself as often as not stopping by your table for a chat, it is like eating in a friend's kitchen. The menu is short, with marinated fish and meat featuring strongly. The main courses include some quite simple dishes – roast lamb in a herb crust, grilled fish and more traditional Swedish specialities. The puddings, in particular, are unmissable. Booking in advance is essential, especially if you want to sit outside on the very pretty terrace.

Bloom's

90 Whitechapel High St E1.
Map 16 E1. [0171-247 6001 or 0171-247 6835. **Open** 11am–9.30pm Mon–Thu, 11am–3pm Fri. **Closed** 25 Dec, Jewish hols. ⚑ ⚑ ⚑ AE, DC, MC, V. ££

After a Sunday morning spent bargain-hunting among the stalls of nearby Petticoat Lane, you can have lunch at London's most famous Jewish eating house. The food and decor are a throwback to the city's old East End. Start with a good, thick beetroot, barley or butter-bean soup and continue with the chopped liver or the salt beef. The traditional accompaniments to these are fried potato latkes and dill pickles.

Caravela

39 Beauchamp Place SW3.
Map 19 B1. [0171-581 2366.
Open noon–3pm Mon–Sat, 7pm–1am daily. ⚑ ⚑ AE, DC, MC, V. £££

In the evenings a serenading guitarist and *fado* singer add to the holiday atmosphere in this lively Portuguese restaurant. The food draws on a tradition of simple peasant cooking dominated by seafood – salt cod, grilled fish and shellfish – but also soups, marinated meats and fresh vegetables and salads.

The Gay Hussar

2 Greek St W1. **Map** 13 B2.
[0171-437 0973. **Open** 12.30–2.30pm, 5.30–11pm Mon–Sat. **Closed** public hols. ⚑ ★ ⚑ AE. £££

The atmosphere in the city's only Hungarian restaurant is masculine and library-like. For many years politicians and literary figures have gathered in the wood-panelled and velvet-upholstered interior to feast on specialities such as the renowned chilled wild cherry soup, stuffed cabbage, pork schnitzel with smoked sausage, cold pike and of course the rich goulash with egg dumplings, spiked with Hungarian paprika.

Nikita's

65 Ifield Rd SW10. **Map** 18 E4.
[0171-352 6326. **Open** 7.30–
11.30pm Mon–Sat. **Closed** public
hols. 🍴 🍷 AE, MC, V. ££££

This exotic basement restaurant
serves excellent Russian food:
borscht (beetroot soup), *pirozhki*
(meat pastries), *blinis* (yeast
pancakes) with smoked salmon
and sour cream, chicken Kiev,
beef stroganoff and salmon
coulibiac (stuffed with rice and
egg and encased in pastry). Stars
of the show are the vodkas in
17 different flavours, such as
pepper, lemon and tarragon; the
carafes come spectacularly
encased in ice.

Ognisko Polskie

55 Prince's Gate, SW7.
Map 11 A5. [0171-589 4635.
Open noon–3pm, 6–11pm daily.
🚹 ♿ ££

This Polish restaurant and bar are
set together in a rather grand old
Knightsbridge building. The Polish
dishes consist of the usual hearty
combinations of heavy dumplings,
sauerkraut and bits and pieces of
meat, but cooked more deftly than
you'll find in Warsaw. The bar is
open all afternoon and serves a
good selection of vodkas, popular
with the many Polish regulars.

Wodka

12 St Albans Gro W8. **Map** 10 E5.
[0171-937 6513. **Open** 12.30–
2.30pm, 7–11.15pm Mon–Fri,
7–11pm Sun, 1–3.30pm Sun. ♿ AE,
MC, V. £££

A mixture of heavy traditional and
light modern Polish food is served
in a small, bare, but friendly
setting. Alongside the bulky
standards – meat-stuffed cabbage
(*golabki*) and olive-stuffed beef
(*zrazy*) – you can find vegetable
timbale with couscous, blinis with
aubergine mousse and chicken
with lentils and mustard sauce.

FISH AND SEAFOOD

London boasts a thriving, though
fairly small, collection of fish
restaurants, the best of which get
their produce fresh every morning
from local markets. Solid, old-
fashioned establishments like
Manzi's and Wheeler's serve a
traditional mix of grilled, poached,
fried and steamed plaice, cod,
haddock, sole and salmon, and
richer dishes with cream and
butter sauces. Others have a
range of allegiances from Kosher
(Grahame's) to French (Le Suquet)
and Italian (L'Altro).

L'Altro

210 Kensington Park Road W11.
Map 9 B2. [0171-792 1066 or
0171-792 1077. **Open** noon–2.30pm,
7–11pm Mon–Thu, noon–2.30pm,
7–11.30pm Fri, Sat, noon–3pm Sun.
🍴 🚹 ♿ 🔲 🅿 ♿ AE, DC, MC.
£££

In this busy spin-off of Cibo (*see
p299*) highlights include seafood
risotto, octopus and rocket salad,
roast sea bass with rosemary-
dotted potatoes and *gratinata di
mare* (shellfish in olive oil, lemon
and breadcrumbs). The wine list is
informative and friendly.

Bill Bentley's

31 Beauchamp Pl SW3. **Map** 19 B1.
[0171-589 5080. **Open** 11.30am–
2.30pm, 6–10.30pm Mon–Sat. 🔲
♿ MC. £££

Standing in Knightsbridge's main
restaurant street, this small, busy
eating place has a pleasant open-
air patio. The short, Anglo-French
menu includes traditional dishes
like oysters, smoked salmon and
Dover sole, alongside up-to-date,
more adventurous offerings such
as cod in a herb crust and grilled
red mullet with balsamic vinegar
and coriander.

Café Fish

39 Panton St SW1. **Map** 13 A3.
[0171-930 3999. **Open** noon–3pm
Mon–Fri, 5.45–11.30pm Mon–Sat.
Wine bar open 11.30am–11pm
Mon–Sat. 🍸 ♿ restaurant only. 🎵
🔲 ♿ AE, DC, MC, JCB. £££

This large, bustling, seagreen-
coloured restaurant and wine bar
is a convenient two-minute walk
from Piccadilly. Starters are
straightforward (oysters, whitebait,
smoked salmon, fish soup), but
the main courses lean towards
cream and butter sauces. A short
wine list has one of the cheapest
house Champagnes in London.

Grahame's Seafare

38 Poland St W1. **Map** 12 F1.
[0171-437 0975 or 0171-437 3788.
Open noon–2.45pm, 5.30–9pm
Sun–Thu, noon–2.45pm, 5.30–8pm
Fri, Sat. **Closed** public hols, 2 weeks
Christmas. 🍸 🍴 🚹 ♿ ♿ AE,
DC, MC. £££

This Jewish restaurant serves
kosher specialities such as gefilte
fish, followed by gigantic portions
of plainly grilled, steamed or
deep-fried fish. Tables are packed
at lunchtime, but evening trade is
slower (note the early closing
times). The decor is minimal and
the cooking unsophisticated, but
the fish is fresh every day.

Manzi's

1–2 Leicester St WC2. **Map** 13 A2.
[0171-734 0224. **Open** noon–
2.30pm Mon–Sat, 5.30–11.30pm
daily. **Closed** 25–26 Dec. ♿ AE, DC,
MC, V, JCB. £££

This grand, old-fashioned, family-
run (since 1928) restaurant is
situated near Leicester Square. You
can ask for your fish poached or
grilled and your eels jellied,
smoked or served in a parsley
sauce. It can be expensive unless
you stick to house wine and mid-
priced dishes.

Poissonnerie de L'Avenue

82 Sloane Ave SW3. **Map** 19 B2.
[0171-589 5774 or 0171-589 2457.
Open 12.30–3pm, 7–11.30pm
Mon–Sat. **Closed** public hols. 🚹 ♿
🔲 ♿ AE, DC, V. ££££

At this smart, oak-panelled,
avuncular establishment there are
some plain dishes (oysters, grilled
sole or scallops), but rich dishes
involving cream, butter and
mayonnnaise are more common,
flavoured with ingredients such as
tarragon, fennel and Pernod. Its
restful, old-world atmosphere
makes it an ideal place for a
discreet lunch.

Le Suquet

104 Draycott Ave SW3. **Map** 19 B2.
[0171-581 1785. **Open** noon–
2.30pm, 7–11.30pm daily. ♿ AE, DC,
MC, V. £££

Le Suquet is a lively but relaxed
French hang-out. It is at its best on
summer nights, when the
windows open out onto Draycott
Avenue. Highlights are foil-
wrapped sea bream, scallops in
garlic and the spectacular seafood
platter – a seaweed-fronded
cornucopia of marine life.

Wheeler's

19–21 Old Compton St W1.
Map 13 A2. [0171-437 2706.
Open 12.30–2.30pm, 6–11.15pm
Mon–Sat, 12.30–2.30pm, 7–10.30pm
Sun. **Closed** 25 Dec. 🍸 🍴 🚹
♿ ♿ AE, DC, MC, V, JCB.
£££

The accent at Wheeler's is on large
helpings of plain, traditional fish
dishes served in old-fashioned,
comfortable surroundings. Oysters
are a speciality starter, as are fried
sole and lobster thermidor for
the main course. Wheeler's
has been a London institution for
decades, and there are several
branches throughout the London
area. (Look in the phone directory
for details.)

For key to symbols *see p287*

VEGETARIAN

Vegetarians can eat well at many London restaurants, but there are still relatively few places that offer a completely vegetarian menu. The restaurants in this section specialize in food without meat or fish, though Mildred's sneaks in the occasional seafood dish. Menus often indicate which dishes are suitable for vegans.

Food for Thought

31 Neal St WC2. **Map** 13 B2.
[0171-836 0239 or 9072. **Open** noon–8pm Mon–Sat, noon–4pm Sun. 🍴 V 🍴 ⓔ

The short but imaginative menu features stir-fries, Japanese tofu dishes and European casseroles and soups, plus interesting quiches (leek, cauliflower) and indulgent puddings and cakes (raspberry scrunch, apple crumble, orange and coconut scones with whipped cream). It's very cheap for Covent Garden, which partly explains the crowds, especially at lunchtimes.

Mildred's

58 Greek St W1. **Map** 13 B2.
[0171-494 1634. **Open** noon–11pm Mon–Sat. 🍴 V 🍴 ⓔ

This is one of the few vegetarian restaurants that offers a range of dishes to match its meat-serving rivals. Soups range from Japanese miso to Polish vegetable and barley (krupnik), main courses from Brazilian vegetable and coconut casserole to Chinese black bean vegetables with fresh pineapple and noodles. Small, cramped surroundings mean you may be asked to share tables; staff are happy to collect you from the pub opposite if you want to have a drink while you wait.

The Place Below

St Mary-Le-Bow Church EC2.
Map 15 A2. [0171-329 0789.
Open 7.30am–2.30pm Mon–Fri, 6.30–9.30pm Thu, Fri. 🍴 only.
🍴 V ★ ⓔⓔ

At lunchtimes, city workers pack the crypt of Wren's famous "Bow Bells" church (see p147) for tasty soups, quiches and hot dishes. After olive bread, there might be red pepper and almond soup, then courgette, fetta and mint tartlets with tomato gravy and an avocado and plum tomato salad. This can be followed by a dessert of seasonal fruits, home-made ice-cream or something indulgent like dark and white chocolate truffle cake. You can bring your own wine (free corkage) or sample the delicious home-made lemonade.

AMERICAN
MEXICAN

Apart from the long-standing flood of burger bars (see pp306–7), American food – especially of a reasonable standard – is comparatively new to London. Joints like the Hard Rock Café make some concessions to the healthy-eating trend, but as a rule big is beautiful. Standard fare is hamburgers, fried chicken, BBQ spare ribs and BLTs (bacon, lettuce and tomato sandwiches), all under a mountain of French fries and followed by rich cakes and ice-cream sundaes. Most of the restaurants throw in a few dishes from Mexico and Louisiana.

Deal's

14–16 Fouberts Pl W1. **Map** 12 F2.
[0171-287 1001. **Open** noon–11pm Mon–Sat, 12–4pm Sun. 🍴
🍴 🍴 🍴 🍴 AE, MC, V. ⓔⓔ

The young clientele at this lively eating place are served typically American food (burgers, spare ribs, T-Bone steaks) with a strong Oriental slant (Thai curries, steak teriyaki, delicious seafood spring rolls). The Chelsea Harbour branch (0171-352 5887) is also worth a visit.

Down Mexico Way

25 Swallow St W1. **Map** 12 F3.
[0171-437 9895. **Open** noon–midnight Mon–Sat, noon–10.30pm Sun. **Closed** 25–26 Dec. 🍴 groups of six or more. 🍴 🍴 🍴 AE, DC, MC, V, JCB. ⓔⓔ

The most attractive Mexican restaurant in London has a menu that is much less orientated to fast food than most. It has all the standard nachos (tortilla chips with various toppings and sauces) and empanaditas (pasties with corn or spiced meat fillings), but it's also got the more interesting possibilities of fish in chilli and almond sauce, lime-cooked chicken, stuffed courgettes and shark with tabasco butter.

Hard Rock Café

150 Old Park Lane W1. **Map** 12 E4.
[0171-629 0382. **Open** 11.30am–12.30am Sun–Thu, 11.30am–1am Fri, Sat. **Closed** 25–26 Dec. 🍴 V
🍴 🍴 🍴 AE, MC, V. ⓔⓔ

This is the only eating place in London where a queue is a permanent feature. Rock fans flock from all over the planet to eat burgers here beneath Jimi Hendrix's old guitar, or beside Ozzie Osborne's white leather shoes. A rock museum, a place of pilgrimage, a marketing outlet –

this is a place people either love or hate. There is a surprisingly good selection of vegetarian dishes – devised by Linda McCartney, of course.

Joe Allen

13 Exeter St WC2. **Map** 13 C2.
[0171-836 0651. **Open** noon–1am Mon–Sat, noon–midnight Sun.
Closed 24–25 Dec. V ⓔⓔⓔ

Hard-nosed haunt of the famous, Joe Allen's menu used to be all-American chopped steak and cold shoulder, but now has a strong Italian influence. Recommended are the spaghetti with prawns, tomato, garlic and red pepper; the baked John Dory with tomato, capers, black olives and garlic; and pasta with roast chicken and peppers. Book ahead.

AFRO-CARIBBEAN

Given London's multi-ethnic population, there are fewer Afro-Caribbean restaurants than you might expect; the style of cooking has not caught on like Indian and Chinese. African and Caribbean cooking have basic foods in common – fibrous root vegetables like sweet potato and cassava, rice and flat breads, pumpkin, beans and peas and sweet, fleshy fruits like guava and mango. Common dishes are fried plantain (a type of banana) with a hot sauce, spicy stews and soups and curried goat.

The Brixtonian

11 Dorrell Place SW9.
[0171-978 8870. **Open** 7–11pm Tue–Sat, 6pm–midnight Mon. 🍴
🍴 🍴 MC, V. ⓔⓔⓔ

This coolly sophisticated Caribbean specialist features dishes from different Antillean islands each month. Everything is immaculately prepared and presented, albeit rather expensive. The atmosphere is enhanced by the sound of live jazz escaping from the downstairs bar, which serves lunches and is popular for the widest selection of rum in London. A sister restaurant, the Brixtonian Backyard, is in Covent Garden (0171-240 2769).

Calabash

The Africa Centre, 38 King St WC2.
Map 13 C2. [0171-836 1976.
Open 12.30–3pm Mon–Fri, 6–11.30pm Mon–Sat. **Closed** public hols. 🍴 🍴 AE, DC, MC, V. ⓔⓔ

On a side-street just off Covent Garden's Piazza, one of London's premier African restaurants is hidden down a flight of stairs.

By day, its soothing lunchtime atmosphere comes as a relief from the market's crowds. By night, especially at weekends, the place comes alive. A carefully explained menu demystifies the exotic dishes like *yassa* – Senegalese chicken cooked with onions in a lemon sauce.

Cottons Rhum Shop, Bar and Restaurant

55 Chalk Farm Road NW1.
(*0171-482 1096.* **Open** *noon–midnight daily.* **Closed** *25–26 Dec.*
⬜ *MC, V.* **£££**

The loud reggae music announcing Cottons' presence doesn't bother the smart young crowd that flocks to this intimately lit bar-restaurant for cocktails every night. On the menu, jokily named dishes such as "rasta pasta" and "ragga prawns" sit beside such staples of Jamaican cooking as curried goat and fried chicken. The desserts are positively wicked.

INDIAN

Indian food is a true delight of eating out in London. There is a vast number of Indian restaurants, and many of them specialize in specific styles of food. Dishes range from mildly spicy *(korma)* through medium-hot *(bhuna, dansak, dopiaza)* to very hot *(madras, vindaloo)*. Indian meals in the West may begin with soup or a starter and main course dishes (with rice or flat breads such as *chapati* or *nan*) are often shared. 'Balti' dishes, fast-cooked dishes served in a small wok, are recent import from the Midlands.

Bombay Brasserie

Courtfield Cl, Courtfield Rd SW7
Map *18 E2.* **(** *0171-370 4040.*
Open *noon–3pm, 7pm–midnight daily.* **Closed** *25–26 Dec.* **⬜** **V**
⬜ *DC, MC, V.* **££££**

This is one of the most acclaimed Indian restaurants outside Asia. It has an impressive colonial atmosphere, redolent of the Raj. The mainly North Indian menu includes some unusual regional specialities. The execution of the regional dishes (including Parsi and Goan) is second to none. If you visit at lunchtime, there's a much less expensive buffet.

Chutney Mary

Plaza 535, Kings Rd SW10.
Map *18 E5.* **(** *0171-351 3113.*
Open *12.30–2.30pm, 7–11.30pm Mon–Sat, 12.30–3.30pm (buffet), 7–10.30pm Sun.* **⬜** **V** **⬜** *AE, DC, MC, V.* **£££**

"Chutney Mary" is an Indian term used to describe women who straddle two cultures: Indian and British. It neatly sums up the cookery of this smart restaurant. There are standard Indian staples such as *rogan josh* (lamb braised in yoghurt or cream and coloured with beetroot or tomato) and *chicken tikka* (cubed, marinated and baked), but the majority of the cooking is a unique – and very successful – blend of Indian and Western tastes.

Chutneys

124 Drummond St NW1. **Map** *4 F4.*
(*0171-388 0604.* **Open** *noon–2.45pm, 6–11.30pm daily.* **Closed** *Christmas.* **⬜** **V** **⬜** *MC.* **£**

Pale and cool, this is the smartest of the clutch of Indian vegetarian restaurants that line Drummond Street and are all great value. At the buffet lunches you can help yourself to as much as you like from a table groaning with *dals* (lentils), vegetable curries, rice, chutneys, breads and a sweet – all for about £4.

Gopal's

12 Bateman St W1. **Map** *13 A2.*
(*0171-434 1621 or 0840.* **Open** *noon–3pm, 6–11.30pm daily.* **Closed** *25–26 Dec.* **⬜** **⬜** **⬜** **⬜** *AE, DC, MC, V.* **£££**

This is one of the best "new wave" Indian restaurants, with dishes freshly prepared for the serious tandoori and curry lover. There are a few unusual dishes on the menu such as a *meenu* fish curry from Karnataka.

Madhu's Brilliant

39 South Rd, Southall, Middx UB1.
(*0181-574 1897 or 0181-571 6380.*
Open *12.30–3pm, 6–11.30pm Mon–Fri, 6–11.30pm Sat, Sun.*
Closed *Tue.* **⬜** **⬜** **⬜** *AE, DC, MC, V.* **£**

Madhu's Brilliant may not look like much, but the cooking is authentic and outstanding value for money – half the price (or less) than you might expect. The accent is on strongly flavoured Indian and Pakistani meat dishes and it is well worth the effort of making the trip to this peripheral location.

Malabar

27 Uxbridge St W8. **Map** *9 C3.*
(*0171-727 8800.* **Open** *noon–3pm, 6–11.30pm daily.* **Closed** *1 week following Aug public hol, 4 days Christmas.* **⬜** **⬜** **⬜** *MC, V.* **££**

A stylish little place situated in a quiet mews, the Malabar is one of very few Indian restaurants in the area which offers outstanding North-Indian/Pakistani style cookery. Try, for example, the venison or char-grilled chicken livers – both marinated.

Mandeer

21 Hanway Place W1 **Map** *13 A1.*
(*0171-323 0660 or 0171-580 3470.* **Open** *noon–3pm, 5.30–10pm Mon–Sat.* **Closed** *public hols.* **⬜**
V **⬜** **⬜** *AE, DC, MC, V.* **££**

Easily the most elegant Indian vegetarian restaurant in London, and also the priciest, it serves a good selection of dishes, from run-of-the-mill South Indian fare to less common Gujarati-inspired dishes (puffed lotus seeds, a yellow pea dal, even tofu curry).

Nazrul

130 Brick Lane E1. **Map** *8 E5.*
(*0171-247 2505.* **Open** *noon–3pm, 5.30pm–midnight Mon–Thu, noon–3pm, 5.30pm–1am Fri, Sat, noon–midnight Sun.* **V** **£**

Nazrul is one of the scores of cheap Bangladeshi-run cafés and restaurants in the Brick Lane area. Decor and furnishings are very basic, prices very low and the atmosphere lively. Portions sizes can be big, so take it easy when ordering. It's unlicensed, but you can bring your own alcohol.

Ravi Shankar

133–135 Drummond St NW1:
Map *4 F4.* **(** *0171-388 6458.*
Open *noon–10.45pm daily.* **⬜** **V**
⬜ **⬜** **⬜** *MC, V.* **£**

This South Indian restaurant serves vegetarian *bhel poori* (South Indian) fare from the kitchens of Chutneys *(see above).* The *dosas* (pancakes) and *thalis* (set meals) are especially good and the fresh carrot juice is wonderful. There is also a branch on St John Street (0171-833 5897), handy for Sadler's Wells *(see p243).*

Salloos

62–64 Kinnerton St SW1. **Map** *11 C5.*
(*0171-235 4444.* **Open** *noon–2.30pm, 7–11.15pm Mon–Sat.*
Closed *public hols.* **⬜** **★** **⬜** *AE, DC, MC, V.* **££££**

Almost certainly the best Indian restaurant in town isn't Indian at all – it's Pakistani. There's a predominance of meat (lamb, chicken, quails) grilled, baked in the tandoori oven and curried. The wine list is impressive and the cooking is precise and fresh, but the prices reflect this. Try the bargain set lunch. The atmosphere here is upmarket and almost sombre and the service is faultlessly professional.

For key to symbols *see p287*

SOUTHEAST ASIAN

Southeast Asian food, especially
Thai, has made a distinctive mark
on the London restaurant scene.
The majority of restaurants in this
section tend to emphasize Thai,
Singaporean, Malaysian or
Indonesian cuisine but also offer a
combination of all of them. A
sharp, tangy taste comes from lime
juice, kaffir lime leaves and lemongrass; a sour note from tamarind;
ginger and garlic; a variety of
chillies provide the fire; coconut
milk the coolant. Rice or noodles
are the basis of any Southeast
Asian meal, the preferred cooking
methods are steaming and stir-
frying, and the food is usually
served lukewarm.

Bahn Thai

21a Frith St W1. **Map** 13 A2.
[0171-437 8504. **Open** noon–
2.45pm, 6–11.15pm Mon–Sat,
11am–1.30pm, 6.30–10.30pm Sun.
Closed Christmas, Easter, public hols.
V ♿ 🅱 🍴 AE, DC, MC, V.
€€€

Bahn Thai offers many dishes
which are rarely found outside
Thailand. Thai-style pigs' trotters,
frogs' legs and chicken liver
appear on the menu, but the more
mainstream dishes are also
excellent; try the *tom yum* (hot
soup spiced with lemongrass) or
the *kwaitiew pad Thai* (a quickly
fried noodle dish). Vegetarian
dishes are clearly marked on the
menu and so is the heat (chilli) of
dishes. The wine list is unusually
good, but Singha beer tends to
complement the food better.

Chiang Mai

48 Frith St W1. **Map** 13 A2.
[0171-437 7444. **Open** noon–3pm
Mon–Sat, 6–11pm daily. **Closed**
public hols. 🍴 V ♿ 🅱 AE,
MC, V. €€€€

This prominent Thai restaurant has
an airy dining room and separate
vegetarian menu, which helps it
stand apart from others of its kind
It is particularly renowned for its
delicious noodles and unusual
yams (spicy salads). The *som tam*
(fresh papaya salad) and *kow soy*
(chicken noodle dish), both very
popular dishes from northern
Thailand, are faithfully reproduced
at this restaurant.

Khun Akorn

136 Brompton Rd SW3. **Map** 11 C5.
[0171-225 2688. **Open** noon–3pm
daily, 6.30–11pm, Mon–Sat. ✈
V 🅱 ★ 🍴 AE, DC, MC, V.
€€€

Diagonally across the road from
Harrods, Khun Akorn is an
elegant, calm and comfortable
dining room. Most dishes are Thai
classics – aromatic curries, stir-
fried noodles, and plenty of
seafood, chicken and beef dishes.
The flavours and scents of
lemongrass, holy basil, coconut,
coriander chilli and fish sauce
predominate. Both cooking and
presentation are immaculate. The
set lunches are outstanding value.

Melati

21 Gt Windmill St W1. **Map** 13 A2.
[0171-734 6964 or 0171-437 2745.
Open noon–11.30pm Sun–Thu,
noon–12.30am Fri, Sat. **Closed**
Christmas. 🍴 V ♿ 🎵 🍴 AE,
DC, MC, V, JCB. €€

Booking is advisable in this
bustling Indonesian restaurant if
you don't want to queue. The
service is swift and polite but a
little rushed and the preparation
of dishes very authentic. The
Singapore *laksa* – an aromatic
vermicelli noodle soup – is
particularly good, the *satés* (small
spicy kebabs) are moist and tasty
and desserts such as *kue dadar* (a
green pancake roll stuffed with
coconut) are unmissable.

Sri Siam

14 Old Compton St W1. **Map** 13 A2.
[0171-434 3544. **Open** noon–
3pm, 6–11.15pm Mon–Sat,
6–10.30pm Sun. **Closed** 24–26 Dec,
1 Jan. 🍴 V ★ 🍴 AE, DC, MC,
V. €€€

This stylish restaurant is a perfect
place for your first taste of Thai
food; the heat is toned down, but
the flavours aren't. Try the mixed
starters, and any of the seafood
dishes. There is an extensive
vegetarian menu, which contains
exquisite hot and sour soups and
salads, as well as *saté*, curries,
deep-fried beancurd, and more.
The set lunch menu is good value.

Tui

19 Exhibition Rd SW10. **Map** 19 A1.
[0171-584 8359. **Open** noon–
2.30pm, 6.30–11pm Mon–Sat,
12.30–3pm, 7–10.30pm Sun.
Closed public hols. 🅱 🍴 AE, DC,
MC, V. €€€

Tui looks cool and modern in
contrast to the neo-Gothic facade
of the Victoria and Albert Museum
just opposite. The menu is
conservative and a bit pricey,but
the Thai staples are reliable and
portions of the expertly prepared
soups (such as seafood *pob tak*,
which simmers at your table) are
more generous than usual.

JAPANESE

Japanese restaurants are renowned
for being simply but stylishly
decorated. Some have *teppan-yaki*
tables (where diners surround a
chef who cooks on a hotplate)
and a bar where you can snack on
sushi – raw fish or vegetable on
vinegared rice. The most expensive
places have *tatami* rooms, where
parties eat seated on straw mats.

Ikeda

30 Brook St W1. **Map** 12 E2.
[0171-629 2730. **Open** 12.30–
2.30pm Mon–Fri, 6.30–10pm daily.
🅱 🍴 🍴 AE, DC, MC, V, JCB.
€€€€

Prices are reasonable and the
food delicious at this small but
comfortable *yakitori* and *sushi* bar.
The reasonably priced set lunches
are particularly appealing; the
chicken *yakitori* meal is centred
on bamboo skewers of grilled
chicken, while the *sashimi* (raw
fish) is prepared as you wait. A
seaweed appetizer, miso soup,
fresh orange dessert and green tea
are also all included in the price.

Miyama

38 Clarges St W1. **Map** 12 E3.
[0171-499 2443. **Open** noon–
2.30pm Mon–Fri, 6–10.30pm daily.
🍴 🍴 🅱 🍴 AE, DC, MC,
V, JCB. €€€€

Close to the Japanese Embassy
just off Piccadilly, Miyama is an
elegant place for meticulously
prepared and presented Japanese
food. Besides *sushi* and *sashimi*
meals, the *teppan-yaki* counter is
popular for meats and seafood
grilled as you watch.

Suntory

72–73 St James's St SW1. **Map** 12 F3.
[0171-409 0201. **Open**
noon–2pm, 6–9.30pm Mon–Sat.
Closed public hols. 🍴 🍴 ★ 🍴
AE, DC, MC, V, JCB. €€€€€

Britain's top Japanese restaurant
with a much-deserved Michelin
star is as professionally run as you
might expect. It has several dining
areas, including private *tatami*
rooms, *teppan-yaki* tables and a
simply decorated main dining
area. The atmosphere is only as
formal as you want it to be and
the presentation is immaculate.

Tatsuso

32 Broadgate Circle, Broadgate EC2.
Map 7 C5. [0171-256 9304.
Open 11.30am–2.30pm, 6.30–
9.30pm Mon–Fri. **Closed** public hols.
🍴 🍴 🅱 🍴 AE, DC, MC, V, JCB.
€€€€€

Tatsuso is discreetly tucked under the sweeping curves of the Broadgate Circle. The quality is superb, but be warned that the prices are strictly expense-account territory.

Tokyo Diner

2 Newport Place, WC1. **Map** 13 B2.
🄲 *0171-287 8777.* **Open** *noon–midnight daily.* 🚭 🆅 🚹 👶 *MC, V.* Ⓔ

The handy location (just behind Leicester Square) and the low prices make this restaurant a very useful bolt-hole. In true Japanese fashion, the door is electric, the taps in the restrooms automatic, and tips are not expected or accepted. The menu is extensive and clearly annotated, covering sushi, sashimi, noodle soups, and Japanese curries; accompany these with Japanese lager. The cooking may not be first-rate, but the bill is a pleasant surprise.

Wagamama

4 Streatham St, off Coptic St WC1.
Map 13 B1. 🄲 *0171-323 9223.*
Open *noon–2.30pm, 5.45–11pm Mon–Sat, 12.30–3pm, 6–10pm Sun.*
🚭 *only.* 🆅 ★ Ⓔ

This basement noodle bar near the British Museum is immensely popular. The bustling interior is decorated in a minimalist style. The food is cheap, filling and interesting: large bowls of soup, or pan-fried noodles or rice with seafood and vegetables. Studiously cool waiting staff take orders on handsets which resemble Nintendo Game Boys. The queue looks very daunting as it can stretch out into the street, but it's fast-moving.

CHINESE

The cuisine most common to London's Chinese restaurants is Cantonese, which has rice as its staple food and favours steaming or light frying. However, most also offer Peking dishes, which rely more on deep-fried crispiness and may replace rice with bread, and Shanghai dishes, which have more starch, fat and spices and may be noodle-based. The highly spiced Szechuan or Hunan food is popular here, too. At lunchtime in many Cantonese restaurants you can eat *dim sum*, a series of delicious snacks, mostly steamed or deep-fried dumplings, which you choose from heated trolleys wheeled from table to table.

The Abacus

38 Clapham High St SW4. . 🄲 *0171-497 0376.* **Open** *noon–2.30pm, 6pm–midnight Mon–Sat; 6pm–midnight Sun.*
🍴 🆅 🚹 👶 🍽 *AE, DC, MC, V.* Ⓔ Ⓔ

This is one of the best Chinese restaurants south of the Thames, but is very reasonably priced. It specializes in Peking dishes, such as duck served with pancakes and plum sauce. For those who prefer spicier food, there are Szechuan standards like twice-cooked beef or pork, or kung-po king prawns. From the large choice of starters, try the deep-fried shredded smoked chicken. And don't miss the ginseng beer, served ice cold.

Fung Shing

15 Lisle St WC2. **Map** 13 A2.
🄲 *0171-437 1539.* **Open** *noon–11.30pm daily.* **Closed** *24–25 Dec.*
🍴 🍽 *AE, DC, MC, V.* Ⓔ Ⓔ

For many, Fung Shing is Chinatown's best restaurant. Furnishings are markedly more elegant than many you'll find in the vicinity and food from the breadth of the Cantonese repertoire is on the menu. The hot-pot dishes (hearty stews in delicious stock) are recommended.

Harbour City

46 Gerrard Street W1. **Map** 13 A2.
🄲 *0171-439 7859.* **Open** *noon–11.30pm Mon–Thurs, noon–midnight Fri, Sat, 11am–10.30pm Sun.* 🍴 🚹 ★ 🍽 *AE, DC, MC, V.* Ⓔ Ⓔ

One of many establishments on Gerrard Street serving an extensive *dim sum* selection, Harbour City stands out because the *dim sum* menu is carefully translated into English, and because the staff are very gracious. As with all Chinese food vegetarian dishes are limited, but all the dishes taste superb.

Jade Garden

15 Wardour St W1. **Map** 13 A2.
🄲 *0171-437 5065.* **Open** *noon–11.45pm Mon–Sat, 11.30am–10.45pm Sun.* **Closed** *Christmas.*
🍴 🚹 🍽 *AE, MC, V.* Ⓔ Ⓔ

The Jade Garden has long been a favourite *dim sum* venue for London's Cantonese. Well-spaced, round tables lend themselves to communal feasting, service is patient and the *dim sum* are of top quality and include elaborate delicacies such as quail's eggs with prawn dumplings. Try the fish dishes on the à la carte menu.

Magic Wok

100 Queensway W2. **Map** 10 D2.
🄲 *0171-792 9767 or 0171-221 9953.*
Open *noon–11pm daily.* 🆅 ★ 🍽 *lunch only.* 🆅 ★ 🍽 *AE, DC, MC, V.* Ⓔ Ⓔ

Magic Wok is one of the finest of Queensway's many Chinese restaurants. The list of specials changes regularly, yet invariably

contains the most interesting Cantonese dishes. Deep-fried soft-shell crab with garlic and spicy chilli makes an excellent starter.

Memories of China

67–69 Ebury St SW1. **Map** 20 E1.
🄲 *0171-730 7734.* **Open** *noon–2.15pm, 7–10.45pm Mon–Sat.*
Closed *public hols.* 🍴 👶 🍽 *AE, DC, MC, V, JCB.* Ⓔ Ⓔ Ⓔ

At this restaurant decorated in a light, minimalist style, the menu aims to guide Western diners through China's major cuisines. Set meals provide a sound (if expensive) introduction to regional food, tailored to Western tastes.

Ming

35–36 Greek St W1. **Map** 13 A1.
🄲 *0171-734 0292.* **Open** *noon–11.45pm Mon–Sat, Chinese New Year (Sun).* **Closed** *24–25 Dec.* 🚭 🍴 🆅 🍽 *AE, DC, MC, V, JCB.* Ⓔ Ⓔ Ⓔ

Ming offers a soothing alternative to the bustle of nearby Chinatown. Food includes interesting dishes from north China; try *ta tsai mi*, lamb cooked to an 18th-century recipe. Unusually for a Chinese restaurant, vegetarians have been thoughtfully considered.

New World

1 Gerrard Pl W1. **Map** 13 B2.
🄲 *0171-434 2508.* **Open** *11am–12.30am daily, 11am–11pm Sun.*
Closed *25–26 Dec.* 🍴 🚹 👶 🍽 *AE, DC, MC, V, JCB.* Ⓔ Ⓔ

This is one of the most authentic, restaurants serving *dim sum* in Chinatown. Flag down a trolley and take your pick. Many staff have shaky English, so there's an element of chance in what you'll receive and it adds to the fun. The full menu is as long as the Great Wall, accommodating both the meek and the daring diner.

The Oriental

The Dorchester Hotel, Park La W1.
Map 12 D4. 🄲 *0171-629 8888.*
Open *noon–2.30pm Mon–Fri, 7–11pm Mon–Sat.* 🍴 🚹 👶 🆅 🍽 *AE, DC, MC, V, JCB.*
Ⓔ Ⓔ Ⓔ Ⓔ Ⓔ

The Dorchester Hotel unveiled its Chinese restaurant with much aplomb in 1991. Battalions of skilful chefs were shipped in to prepare the Cantonese food meticulously. The expensive ingredients and exquisite presentation find favour with the business and social elite that gather here. Don't miss the full Chinese tea service. Parties of up to 12 can hire the sumptuous private rooms.

For key to symbols *see p287*

Light Meals and Snacks

Sometimes you have neither the time nor the money to sit down for a full meal. Fortunately, London has a wonderful range of places offering simple, quick and sometimes cheap food. The places listed here are ideal for hungry tourists on a tight sightseeing schedule.

BREAKFAST

A GOOD BREAKFAST IS essential preparation for a hard day's sightseeing. Many hotels *(see pp272–85)* will serve breakfast to non-residents, and you can get a taste of luxury by breakfasting in one, such as the **Savoy** *(see p285)*. Here wonderful English breakfasts *(see pp288–9)* are served from silver trays and tureens for £10 to £20. If a mug of tea with eggs and baked beans on toast is more your scene, there are "greasy spoons" all over the city. A more cosmopolitan option is a pastry and a cappuccino from a café. If you're late to bed or early to rise, **Harry's** is open from 11pm to 6am, and several pubs around Smithfield market, including the **Cock Tavern**, serve good-value fare from 5.30am.

COFFEE AND TEA

I F YOU'RE OUT SHOPPING, many of London's department stores have their own cafés, the most stylish being the new-wave Italian **Emporio Armani Express**. There are also some good coffee houses; **Bar Italia** stays open over the weekend. Patisseries such as **Patisserie Valerie** and **Maison Bertaux** are a particular delight and also have mouthwatering window displays. Afternoon tea is an English institution not to be missed. Top hotels like the **Ritz** and **Brown's** *(see p282)* offer pots of tea, scones with jam and cream, delicious, thin cucumber sandwiches and cakes galore. **Fortnum and Mason** *(see p311)* serves both afternoon and high teas (a more substantial meal). In Greenwich, try **Peter de Wit's**, a toyshop which serves tea-time treats. On the other side of London, the **Kew Greenhouse** serves

homely food, and the **Maids of Honour** tea-room offers pastries, reputedly enjoyed here by King Henry VIII.

GALLERY AND THEATRE CAFÉS

M OST GALLERIES HAVE cafés: the one at **Whitechapel Art Gallery** *(see p169)* has lots of vegetarian dishes; the **Café de Colombia** at the Museum of Mankind *(see p91)* offers excellent coffee accompanied by chocolate coffee beans. At the **Tate Gallery** there is a splendid restaurant *(see pp82–5)* as well as a café. If you intend seeing a film at the **Everyman** cinema *(see pp328–9)*, visit the delightful basement café. If you're visiting the Institute of Contemporary Arts *(see p92)*, enjoy the ambience of the trendy **ICAfé**. The **Arts Theatre Café** and the lively **Almeida Theatre** café bar also serve excellent food.

DINERS

L ONDON IS LITTERED with burger bars, where the food consists of burgers, fries, fried chicken, apple pie, milk shakes and cola. **Fatboy's Diner** is an authentic 1940s trailer brought from the USA, and at the **Rock Island Diner** staff leap on to tables for rock 'n' roll routines. Try the tasty burgers and fun atmosphere at the branches of **Ed's Easy Diner**.

PIZZA AND PASTA

I TALIAN FAST FOOD IS sold all over London. The best pizza chain is **Pizza Express**; try its branches in a converted dairy *(see p122)* as well as at the elegant **Kettners**. For pasta, go for family-run trattorias like **Centrale, Lorelei** and **Pollo**; these have character and are very good value.

VEGETARIAN

T HERE ARE quite a number of vegetarian cafés in London selling tasty food in informal settings. Increasingly, they are run by special interest groups: sample **Country Life**, a self-service café run by Seventh-Day Adventists; a curry that has been cooked by Radha Krishnas at **Govinda's**; or a healthy salad and a wicked dessert served by Buddhist women at **Cherry Orchard**. Neal's Yard *(see p115)* is home to several vegetarian restaurants and takeaways.

FISH AND CHIPS

F ISH AND CHIPS is a British experience you should not miss. Visit local "chippies" for fish deep-fried in batter, with thick potato chips, smothered in salt and vinegar. Traditional accompaniments are bread baps and pickled onions. For a higher-class supper, try a sit-down restaurant that offers a range of fresh fish such as lemon sole, skate and cod. The best are the **Sea Shell**, **Faulkner's** and the **Upper Street Fish Shop**.

BARS

I F YOU FANCY A drink, the obvious venue is a pub *(see pp308–9)*. A more elegant option is to visit a hotel like **Claridge's** and relax in a comfortable armchair in the foyer while a waiter brings the drinks. Wine bars are good if you want a choice of snack, meal or just a glass of wine. The **Cork and Bottle** is popular and always full, and the **Brackenbury** serves a variety of outstanding international food. Bar-brasseries are convenient places to drop in for food and drink at any time. The **Dôme** chain of cafés emphasizes a European style. If rum is a passion, then Afro-Caribbean **Cottons** *(see p303)* and the **Brixtonian** *(see p302)* both have large selections. *Tapas* bars are also fun. Drink Spanish beer and wine and eat tasty snacks while enjoying live flamenco music. West London's Spanish community has spawned some of the best – try **Galicia** or **Los Remos**, and for after pub hours the basement **Bar Sol Ona** stays open until 2am – but be prepared for a crush.

STREET FOOD

Hot roasted chestnuts are an autumnal delight. Shellfish stalls, which sell ready-to-eat potted shrimps, crab, whelks and jellied eels are a feature of every street market. At Camden Lock and Spitalfields you can wander from stall to stall choosing between falafels, satay chicken, vegeburgers, Chinese noodles and honey balls. If you're in the East End, Jewish bakeries such as **Brick Lane Beigel Bake** and **Ridley Bagel Bakery** are open 24 hours a day; they're great fun and very cheap. London is not generally geared towards hot weather, but try **Marine Ices**, which serves some of the best ice cream in town.

PIE AND MASH

You won't find pie and mash shops in smart areas, but they are worth trying for a true Cockney experience. Have eels and potatoes, or meat pie with mashed potato and liquor (green parsley sauce) for only a few pounds. They should be eaten with vinegar and washed down with tea. Worth a visit is **F Cooke and Sons**.

DIRECTORY

BREAKFAST

Cock Tavern
East Poultry Market, Smithfield Market EC1.
Map 6 F5.

Harry's Bar
19 Kingly St W1.
Map 12 F2.

Savoy Hotel
Strand WC2. **Map** 13 C2.

COFFEE AND TEA

Bar Italia
22 Frith St W1.
Map 13 A2.

Brown's Hotel
Albermarle St W1.
Map 12 F3.

Emporio Armani Express
191 Brompton Rd SW3.
Map 19 B1.

Fortnum and Mason
181 Piccadilly W1.
Map 12 F3.

Kew Greenhouse
1 Station Parade, Richmond.

Maids of Honour
288 Kew Rd, Richmond.

Maison Bertaux
28 Greek St W1.
Map 13 A1.

Patisserie Valerie
215 Brompton Rd SW3.
Map 19 B1.

Peter de Wit
21 Greenwich Church St SE10. **Map** 23 B2.

Ritz
Piccadilly W1. Palm Court. Ritz Bar. **Map** 12 F3.

GALLERY AND THEATRE CAFÉS

Almeida Theatre Wine Bar
1 Almeida St N1.

Arts Theatre Café
6 Great Newport St WC2.
Map 13 B2.

Café de Colombia
Museum of Mankind, 6 Burlington Gardens W1.
Map 12 F3.

Everyman Café
Holly Bush Vale NW3.
Map 1 A5.

ICAfé
The Mall SW1. **Map** 13 A4.

Tate Gallery Coffee Shop
Millbank SW1. **Map** 21 B2.

Whitechapel Café
Whitechapel Gallery, 80 Whitechapel High St E1.
Map 16 E1.

DINERS

Ed's Easy Diner
12 Moor St W1. **Map** 13 B2.
One of several branches.

Fatboy's Diner
21–22 Maiden La WC2.
Map 13 C2.

Rock Island Diner
2nd Floor, London Pavilion, Piccadilly Circus W1.
Map 13 A3.

PIZZA AND PASTA

Centrale
16 Moor St W1.
Map 13 B2.

Kettners
(Pizza Express) 29 Romilly St W1. **Map** 13 A2.

Lorelei
21 Bateman St W1.
Map 13 A2.

Pizza Express
30 Coptic St WC1.
Map 13 B1.
One of several branches.

Pollo
20 Old Compton St W1.
Map 13 A2.

VEGETARIAN

Cherry Orchard
241–245 Globe Rd E2.

Country Life
1b Heddon St W1. **Map** 12 F2.

Govinda's
9–10 Soho St W1.
Map 13 A1.

FISH AND CHIPS

Faulkner's
424–426 Kingsland Rd E8.

Sea Shell
49–51 Lisson Grove NW1.
Map 3 B5.

Upper St Fish Shop
324 Upper St N1.
Map 6 F1.

BARS

Bar Sol Ona
17 Old Compton St W1.
Map 13 A2.

Brackenbury
129 Brackenbury Rd W6.

Brixtonian
11 Dorrell Pl, off Nursery Rd SW9.

Claridge's
Brook St W1.
Map 12 E2.

Cork and Bottle
44–46 Cranbourn St WC2. **Map** 13 B2.

Cottons Rhum Shop, Bar and Restaurant
55 Chalk Farm Rd NW1.

Dôme
38 Long Acre WC2.
Map 13 C2.
One of several branches.

Galicia
323 Portobello Rd W10.
Map 9 B2.

Los Remos
38a Southwick St W2.
Map 11 A1.

STREET FOOD

Brick Lane Beigel Bake
159 Brick La E1.
Map 8 E5.

Marine Ices
8 Haverstock Hill NW3.

Ridley Bagel Bakery
13–15 Ridley Rd E8.

PIE AND MASH

F Cooke and Sons
41 Kingsland High St E8.

London Pubs

Pᴜʙʟɪᴄ ʜᴏᴜsᴇs ᴏʀ ᴘᴜʙs were originally just that – houses where the public could eat, drink, and stay the night. Large inns with courtyards, like the **George Inn** *(see p176)*, were the interchanges for horse-drawn coach services. Some pubs stand on age-old ale-house sites, like the **Ship**, the **Lamb and Flag** *(see p116)*, and the **City Barge** *(see p254)*. But many of the finest pubs date from the emergence in the late 1800s of "gin palaces", where Londoners escaped from the misery of the slums into lavish interiors, often with stunning mirrors (the **Salisbury**) and elaborate decoration (the **Tottenham** and the **Princess Louise**). Near Little Venice *(see pp262–3)* you will find **Crockers**, probably the finest of London's surviving gin palaces.

Rᴜʟᴇs ᴀɴᴅ Cᴏɴᴠᴇɴᴛɪᴏɴs

Iɴ ᴛʜᴇᴏʀʏ, ᴘᴜʙs are open 11am–11pm Monday to Saturday and noon–3pm and 7–10.30pm Sunday, but some close in the afternoon or early evening and also at weekends. You must be at least 18 to buy or drink alcohol, and at least 14 to enter a pub without an adult. Children can be taken into pubs that serve food, or can use outside areas. Order at the bar, and pay when you are served; tips are not usual unless you are served food and drink at a table. "Last orders" are usually called five minutes before closing, then "time" is called, and a further 10 minutes are then allowed for finishing up drinks.

Bʀɪᴛɪsʜ Bᴇᴇʀ

Tʜᴇ ᴍᴏsᴛ ᴛʀᴀᴅɪᴛɪᴏɴᴀʟ British beers come in many different strengths and tastes, are flat (not fizzy), and are only lightly cooled. The spectrum of bottled beers goes from "light" ale, through "pale", "brown" and "old", up to the particularly potent "barley wine". A sweeter, lower alcohol alternative is shandy, a mixture of draught beer or lager with lemonade.

Many traditional methods of brewing and serving beer have been preserved over the years, and there is a great variety of "real ale" in London pubs. Some real ale pubs, such as the **Sun** in Bloomsbury, pride themselves on a

gimmick-free atmosphere, with bare wooden floors and tables. The Sun serves 20 different beers – one of the widest ranges in London. Serious beer drinkers should also try the **Princess Louise**, the **Anglesea Arms**, or pubs run by local brewers like Young's (try the very strong "Winter Warmer" beer) or Fuller's, who produce a beer called London Pride. "Free Houses" are pubs that are not tied to any particular brewery.

Oᴛʜᴇʀ Dʀɪɴᴋs

Aɴᴏᴛʜᴇʀ ᴛʀᴀᴅɪᴛɪᴏɴᴀʟ English drink found in every London pub is cider. Made from apples, it comes in a range of strengths and levels of dryness. A truly local London spirit is gin, usually drunk with tonic water. In winter, mulled wine (warm and spicy) or hot toddies (brandy or whisky with hot water and sugar) may be served. Non-alcoholic drinks like mineral water and fruit juices are always available, too.

Fᴏᴏᴅ ɪɴ Pᴜʙs

Pᴜʙ ꜰᴏᴏᴅ is at its best at lunchtime (though some pubs serve meals in the evenings). Many still offer traditional fare *(see pp288–9)*, such as Ploughman's Lunch (cheese, salad and bread), Shepherd's Pie, and roast beef lunch on Sundays. Others now offer newer, more adventurous food. The beautiful **Warrington**, for example, has a Thai restaurant.

Tʏᴘᴇs ᴏꜰ Pᴜʙs

Oʟᴅ-ꜰᴀsʜɪᴏɴᴇᴅ London pubs still exist in a few places (try the **White Lion**), but they are rare. Today, pubs cater for many different tastes. Plain but stylish, with a better choice of wine and excellent food, are the **Eagle** and the **Crown and Goose**. Team darts are still played at the **Angel** and **City Darts**. Pool tables can be found in some pubs, including **Jack Straw's Castle** *(see p228)*, and the **Freemasons' Arms** has a traditional skittle alley and lawn billiards.

Hɪsᴛᴏʀɪᴄ Pᴜʙs

Nᴇᴀʀʟʏ ᴇᴠᴇʀʏ ᴘᴜʙ in London has a fascinating history. The buildings might contain beamed medieval snugs, extravagant Victorian fantasies, or the stunning Arts and Crafts style interior of the **Black Friar**. At the **Bunch of Grapes** (SW3), the bar is divided by "snobscreens", a feature once found in many pubs that allowed the upper classes to enjoy a drink without having to mix with their servants. The 16th-century **King's Head and Eight Bells** has a display of antiques. Many pubs have strong literary associations, such as the **Fitzroy Tavern** (a meeting place for writers and artists: *see p131*), **Ye Olde Cheshire Cheese** (associated with Dr Johnson: *see p140*) and the **Trafalgar Tavern** *(see p238)* where Charles Dickens was a regular customer. On a less literary note, the **Bull and Bush** in North London was the subject of an old music-hall song.

Other pubs have more violent associations – victims of Jack the Ripper were found near the **Roebuck** and the **Ten Bells**. The 18th-century highwayman Dick Turpin refreshed himself between robberies at **Spaniards Inn** in north London *(see p231)*, and the **French House** *(see p109)* in Soho was once a meeting point for the French Resistance in World War II.

Outdoor Drinking

THERE ARE FEW pubs in the centre of London with outdoor areas; the better choices tend to be further out of town. The **Freemasons Arms** has a pleasant garden; the **Bunch of Grapes** in Southwark welcomes families. Some pubs enjoy riverside locations with fine views. From the **Grapes** down in Limehouse to the **White Cross** in Richmond, there are many choices along the length of the Thames in London.

Pubs With Entertainment

ENTERTAINMENT is on offer in many London pubs. There are theatre productions at the **King's Head**, the **Bush**, the **Latchmere**, and the **Prince Albert**. Other pubs have live music (*see pp333–5*): rock at the **Half Moon**, country at the **Prospect of Whitby**, English folk at the **Archway Tavern** and modern jazz at the **Bulls Head**; the **Mean Fiddler** draws full houses for a wide variety of styles.

Pub Names

Signs have hung outside public houses since 1393, when King Richard II decided they should replace the older practice of having a bush outside the door. Most people were illiterate, so names were chosen that could easily be pictured: coats of arms (Freemasons' Arms), historical figures (Princess Louise) or heraldic animals (White Lion).

DIRECTORY

Key to symbols:
🎭 stage in bar area or special room for live performers (phone for details)
🍴 offers more than standard bar snacks
🎵 regular live music (phone for details)
🪑 outside drinking area

SOHO, TRAFALGAR SQUARE

French House
49 Dean St W1.
Map 13 A2. 🍴

Tottenham
6 Oxford St W1.
Map 13 A1.

COVENT GARDEN, STRAND

Lamb and Flag
33 Rose St WC2.
Map 13 B2. 🍴

Angel
61 St Giles High St WC2.
Map 13 B1.

Salisbury
90 St Martin's Lane
WC2. **Map** 13 B2.

BLOOMSBURY, FITZROVIA

Fitzroy Tavern
16 Charlotte St W1.
Map 13 A1. 🍴

Sun
63 Lamb's Conduit St WC1.
Map 5 C4. 🍴

HOLBORN, FLEET STREET

Princess Louise
208 High Holborn WC1.
Map 13 C1. 🍴

Ye Olde Cheshire Cheese
145 Fleet St EC4.
Map 14 E1. 🍴

THE CITY, CLERKENWELL

Black Friar
174 Queen Victoria St EC4.
Map 14 F2.

City Darts
40 Commercial St E1.
Map 16 E1.

Eagle
159 Farringdon Rd EC1.
Map 6 E4. 🍴

Ship
23 Lime St EC3. **Map** 15 C2.

Ten Bells
84 Commercial St E1.
Map 16 E1.

White Lion
37 Central St EC1.
Map 7 A3.

SOUTHWARK

Bunch of Grapes
St Thomas St SE1.
Map 15 C4. 🪑 🍴

George Inn
77 Borough High St SE1.
Map 15 B4. 🪑 🍴

CHELSEA, SOUTH KENSINGTON

Anglesea Arms
15 Selwood Ter SW7.
Map 18 F3.

Bunch of Grapes
207 Brompton Rd SW3.
Map 19 B1.

King's Head and Eight Bells
50 Cheyne Walk SW3.
Map 19 A5. 🍴

CAMDEN TOWN, HAMPSTEAD

Crown and Goose
100 Arlington Rd NW1.
Map 4 F1. 🍴

Freemasons Arms
32 Downshire Hill NW3.
Map 1 C5. 🪑

Jack Straw's Castle
North End Way NW3.
Map 1 A3. 🍴

Bull and Bush
North End Way NW3.
Map 1 A3.

Spaniards Inn
Spaniards Rd NW3.
Map 1 A3. 🪑

NOTTING HILL, MAIDA VALE

Crockers
24 Aberdeen Pl NW8.

Prince Albert
11 Pembridge Rd W11.
Map 9 C3. Gate Theatre:
📞 0171-229 0706. 🎭

Warrington
93 Warrington Cres W9. 🍴

GREENWICH

Trafalgar Tavern
Park Row SE10.
Map 23 C1. 🎵 🍴

FURTHER AFIELD

Archway Tavern
1 Archway Close N19. 🎵

Bull's Head
373 Lonsdale Rd SW13.
🎵

Bush
Shepherd's Bush Green
W12. Theatre: 📞 0181-743 3388. 🎭

City Barge
27 Strand-on-the-Green
W4. 🪑 🍴

Grapes
76 Narrow St E14. 🪑

Half Moon
93 Lower Richmond Rd
SW15. 🎵

King's Head
115 Upper St N1. **Map** 6
F1. Theatre 📞 0171-226 1916. 🎭 🎵 🍴

Latchmere
503 Battersea Park Rd
SW11. Grace Theatre
📞 0171-228 2620. 🎭

Mean Fiddler
28a High St NW10. 🎵

Prospect of Whitby
57 Wapping Wall E1.
🎵 🍴

Roebuck
27 Brady St E1.

White Cross
Cholmondeley Walk,
Richmond. 🪑 🍴

SHOPS AND MARKETS

LONDON IS STILL one of the most lively shopping cities in the world. Within just a few minutes' walk you can find both vast department stores, with glittering window displays, and tiny, cluttered rooms where one customer almost fills the entire shop. Many of the most famous London shops are in Knightsbridge or Regent Street, where prices can be steep, but Oxford Street, which is packed with a huge number of shops offering quality

Bags from two of the most famous West End shops

goods at a range of prices, is also worth a visit. All over London, there are plenty of places tucked away down side-streets – and don't forget to try the markets for antiques, crafts, household goods, food and clothing. You can buy virtually anything in London; specialities include clothes (from Burberry raincoats and traditional tweeds to "street fashion"); floral scents and soaps; art and antiques; and craft goods such as jewellery, ceramics and leather.

WHEN TO SHOP

IN CENTRAL LONDON, most shops open somewhere between 9am and 10am and close between 5pm and 6pm on weekdays; some earlier on Saturdays. The "late night" shopping (until 7pm or 8pm) is on Thursdays in Oxford Street and the rest of the West End, and on Wednesdays in Knightsbridge and Chelsea; some shops in tourist areas, such as Covent Garden *(see pp110–19)* and the Trocadero, are open until 7pm or later every day, including Sundays. A few street markets *(see pp322–3)* and a slowly growing number of other shops are also open on Sundays.

HOW TO PAY

MOST SHOPS WILL accept the following major credit cards: Access (Mastercard), American Express, Diners Club, Japanese Credit Bureau and Visa. Some, however, do not, notably the John Lewis stores and Marks and Spencer, as well as street markets and some smaller shops. Some of the stores do accept traveller's cheques, especially if they're in sterling; for other currencies the rate of exchange is less favourable than in a bank. You need your passport with you. Very few shops accept personal cheques drawn against foreign banks, unless they are Eurocheques.

RIGHTS AND SERVICES

IF YOUR PURCHASE is defective you are usually entitled to a refund if you have proof of purchase and return the goods. This isn't always the case with sales goods, so inspect them carefully before you buy.

Most large stores, and some small ones, will pack goods up for you and also send them anywhere in the world.

VAT EXEMPTION

VAT (VALUE ADDED tax) is a sales tax of 17.5% which is charged on virtually all goods sold in Britain (the notable exceptions are books, food and all children's clothes). VAT is nearly always included in the advertised or marked price, although often business suppliers, including some stationers and electrical goods shops, charge it separately.

Non-European Community visitors to Britain who stay no longer than three months may claim back VAT. If you plan to do this, make sure you take along your passport when shopping. You must complete a form in the store when you buy the goods and then give a copy to customs when you leave the country. (You may have to show your purchases to customs, so do pack them somewhere accessible.) The tax refund may be returned to you by cheque or attributed to your credit card, but then a service charge will usually be

Harrod's elaborate Edwardian tiled food halls

deducted and most stores have a minimum purchase threshold (often £50 or £75). If you arrange to have your goods shipped directly home from the store, VAT should be deducted before you pay.

TWICE-YEARLY SALES

THE TRADITIONAL sale season is from January to February and June to July, when virtually every shop cuts its prices and sells off imperfect or unwanted stock. The department stores have some of the best reductions; one of the most famous sales is at **Harrod's** *(see p207)* where queues start to form outside long before opening.

BEST OF THE DEPARTMENT STORES

THE KING OF London's department stores, by tradition, is **Harrod's**, with its 300 departments and staff of 4,000. Prices are not always as high as you may well expect. The spectacular food hall, decorated with Edwardian tiles, has splendid displays of fish, cheese, fruit and vegetables; other specialities include fashions for all ages, china and glass, electronics and kitchenware. Though Harrod's is still just as popular, especially with well-heeled visitors, Londoners often head instead for nearby **Harvey Nichols**, which aims to stock the best of everything with the price tags to match. Clothes are particularly strong, with the emphasis firmly on very high fashion, with many talented British, European and American names represented. There is also an impressive menswear section. The food hall, opened in 1992, is one of the most stylish in London.

Selfridge's vast building on Oxford Street houses everything from Gucci bags and Hermès scarves to household gadgets and bed-linen. **Miss Selfridge**, the popular high street fashion chain, also has a branch in the store.

The original **John Lewis** was a draper and his shop still has a gorgeous selection of fabrics and haberdashery. Its china, glass and household items make John Lewis, and its well-known Sloane Square partner, Peter Jones, equally popular with Londoners.

Liberty *(see p109),* the last privately owned department store in London, still sells the hand-blocked silks and other oriental goods it was famed for when it opened in 1875. Look out for the famous scarf department.

Fortnum and Mason's ground floor provisions department is so engrossing that the upper floors of classic fashion remain peaceful. The food section stocks everything from baked beans to the beautifully prepared hampers.

Some of the best-known names in British clothes design today

DEPARTMENT STORES

Fortnum and Mason
181 Piccadilly W1. **Map** 12 F3.
[C] *0171-734 8040.*

Harrod's
87–135 Brompton Rd SW1.
Map 11 C5.
[C] *0171-730 1234.*

Harvey Nichols
109–125 Knightsbridge SW1.
Map 11 C5.
[C] *0171-235 5000.*

John Lewis
278–306 Oxford St W1. **Map** 12 E1.
[C] *0171-629 7711.*

Liberty
210–220 Regent St W1. **Map** 12 F2.
[C] *0171-734 1234.*

Selfridge's
400 Oxford St W1. **Map** 12 D2.
[C] *0171-629 1234.*

Doorman at Fortnum and Mason

MARKS AND SPENCER

MARKS AND SPENCER has come a long way since 1882 when Russian emigré Michael Marks had a stall in Leeds's Kirkgate market under the sign, "Don't ask the price – it's a penny!" It now has over 680 stores worldwide and everything in them is "own label". It stocks reliable versions of more expensive clothes – Marks and Spencer's underwear in particular is a staple of the British wardrobe. The food department concentrates entirely on upmarket convenience foods. The main Oxford Street branches at the Pantheon (near Oxford Circus) and Marble Arch are the most interesting and well stocked.

Penhaligon's for scents *(see p318)*

London's Best: Shopping Streets and Markets

LONDON'S BEST shopping areas range from the elegance of Knightsbridge, where porcelain, jewellery and *couture* clothes come at the highest prices, to colourful markets such as Brick Lane and Portobello Road. Meccas for those who enjoy searching for a bargain, London's markets also reflect the vibrant street life engendered by its enterprising multi-racial community. The city is fertile ground for specialist shoppers: there are streets crammed with antique shops, antiquarian booksellers and art galleries. Turn to pages 316–23 for more details of shops, grouped according to category.

Kensington Church Street
The small book and furniture shops on this winding street still provide old-fashioned service. (See p321.)

Regent's Park and Marylebone

PORTOBELLO ROAD. W.11.
The Royal Borough of Kensington and Chelsea

Portobello Road Market
Over 200 stalls sell objets d'art, *jewellery, medals, paintings and silverware – plus fresh fruit and vegetables.* (See p323.)

Kensington and Holland Park

South Kensington and Knightsbridge

See inset map

Piccadilly and St James's

Knightsbridge
Exclusive designer-wear is on sale here, at Harrod's as well as smaller stores. (See p207.)

Chelsea

King's Road
A centre for avant-garde fashion in the 1960s and 1970s, the street is still popular with West London shoppers. There is also a good antiques market. (See p192.)

LONDON'S WEST END SHOPS

Oxford Street is sometimes called London's
High Street and many of the shops that line it are
branches of national or international chains. The
big department stores such as Selfridge's and John
Lewis also loom along this street, as do smaller
shops selling clothes and tourist souvenirs. South
of Oxford Street, on Regent Street, Piccadilly and Bond
Street, prices rise and shoppers search for specialized
purchases among the designer clothes and accessories
shops, jewellers and art and antique dealers.

**Brick Lane
Market**
*In this East End
street, everything
from old books to
new trainers is on
sale.* (See p322.)

Gabriel's Wharf
*The wharf has been con-
verted into small shops
selling art, jewellery and
crafts.* (See p187.)

Petticoat Lane
*London's most famous
market has leather,
clothes, watches,
jewellery and toys.*
(See p323.)

Charing Cross Road
*Crammed shops selling
old and new books
line this long street.*
(See p316.)

Covent Garden
and Neal Street
*Street enter-
tainers perform
in this lively and
historic market.
The specialist
shops of Neal
Street are nearby.*
(See p115.)

Clothes

LONDON OFFERS the clothes-shopper a seemingly inexhaustible range of styles, price levels, quality and areas to shop in. The world's top designers are here, clustered around Knightsbridge, Bond Street and Chelsea, as are familiar chains such as Benetton and The Gap. But it is the wealth of home-based style that makes London such an exciting place to buy clothes. British designers excel in the opposite extremes of the market – traditional tailoring and street fashions.

TRADITIONAL CLOTHING

THE RUGGED country look is best found in the Regent Street/Piccadilly area. Waxed Barbour jackets are available from Farlow's *(see Royal Opera Arcade p92)* of Pall Mall and riding accessories from **Swaine Adeney**. **Kent and Curwen** is the place for cricket jumpers and **Captain Watts**, guernsey sweaters and oilskins. Try the Knightsbridge branch of **The Scotch House** for traditional tartan clothing, cashmere, Aran jerseys and Shetland shawls.

Classic town and business wear is another speciality of this area. **Burberry** sells the famous trenchcoats as well as checked clothing and some distinctive luggage from their shop on Haymarket. **Hackett** stocks traditionally tailored men's clothing. For shirts visit Jermyn Street, where you can order them made-to-measure or choose the more reasonably priced off-the-shelf ones. Many manufacturers now also sell classic women's blouses.

Liberty *(see p109)* use their famous patterned prints to make scarves, ties, blouses, pretty English rose dresses and some unusual trimmed denim jackets. **Laura Ashley** is also well renowned for its floral print dresses and frilly blouses.

For the ultimate in luxury, visit Savile Row, home of the top few tailors, including the famous **Gieves and Hawkes**.

MODERN BRITISH DESIGN AND STREET FASHION

LONDON IS one of the world's capitals for street fashion – designer **Jean Paul Gaultier** prefers it to Paris because, he says, the street fashion is "free from the constraints of good taste". In Britain, quirky

Vivienne Westwood won the Fashion Designer of the Year Award (1991). Other over-the-top British designers can be found in **Browns**. For more wearable styles, try the shops around Newburgh Street, West Soho. Most are predominantly for women, but **The Duffer of St George** is among the trailblazers for men. New designers often start with a small stall at **Hyper Hyper**, **Kensington Market** or **The Garage** – all good for whacky or unusual clothing. Nowadays Oxford Street shops like **Top Shop** and **Mash** excel at copying street fashions at very low prices. For British high fashion, **Paul Smith** is one of the best shops for men. For women, try **Browns**, **Whistles**, **Jasper Conran**, **Katharine Hamnett** and finally **Caroline Charles**.

KNITWEAR

FROM Fair Isle jumpers to Aran knits, the traditional British knitwear is famous. The best places for these are in Piccadilly – where you will find **N Peal** – and in Regent Street and Knightsbridge. Top designers such as **Patricia Roberts** and **Joseph Tricot**, and small shops such as **Jane and Dada**, stock a range of quite unusual and innovative machine- and hand-knits.

CHILDREN'S CLOTHES

YOU can get traditional hand-smocked dresses and romper suits from Liberty, **Young England** and **The White House**, which stock

SIZE CHART
For Australian sizes follow British and American convention

Children's clothing

British	2–3	4–5	6–7	8–9	10–11	12	14	14+ (years)
American	2–3	4–5	6–6X	7–8	10	12	14	16 (size)
Continental	2–3	4–5	6–7	8–9	10–11	12	14	14+ (years)

Children's shoes

British	7¹⁄	8	9	10	11	12	13	1	2
American	7½	8½	9½	10½	11½	12½	13½	1½	2½
Continental	24	25½	27	28	29	30	32	33	34

Women's dresses coats and skirts

British	6	8	10	12	14	16	18	20
American	4	6	8	10	12	14	16	18
Continental	38	40	42	44	46	48	50	52

Women's blouses and sweaters

British	30	32	34	36	38	40	42
American	6	8	10	12	14	16	18
Continental	40	42	44	46	48	50	52

Women's shoes

British	3	4	5	6	7	8
American	5	6	7	8	9	10
Continental	36	37	38	39	40	41

Men's suits

British	34	36	38	40	42	44	46	48
American	34	36	38	40	42	44	46	48
Continental	44	46	48	50	52	54	56	58

Men's shirts

British	14	15	15½	16	16½	17	17½	18
American	14	15	15½	16	16½	17	17½	18
Continental	36	38	39	41	42	43	44	45

Men's shoes

British	7	7½	8	9	10	11	12
American	7½	8	8½	9½	10½	11	11½
Continental	40	41	42	43	44	45	46

nostalgically styled clothes such as smocks, gowns, and tweed coats with smart velvet collars. **Trotters**, just behind Sloane Square, offers everything from shoes to haircuts.

SHOES

WITH SHOES, again it's the very traditional or the very trendy British designers and manufacturers who excel.

Their ready-made traditional brogues and Oxfords are the mainstay of **Church's Shoes**. For hand-made, classic footwear, try the Royal Family's shoe-maker **John Lobb**. At the other end of the scale, **Shelly's** sells the utilitarian, trendy Dr Martens, originally designed as hard-wearing work boots but now the shoe to be seen in. **Red or Dead** designs and produces some

really extravagant designs in shoes as well as clothes, while for something a little more elegant, try **Johnny Moke** of the King's Road or **Emma Hope** in east London. If you are on the look-out for more exquisite women's shoes visit **Manolo Blahnik**. Cheaper and less exclusive, but often equally original, designs can be found either in **Hobbs** or **Pied à Terre.**

Specialist Shops

LONDON MAY BE famed for the grand department stores such as Harrod's, but there are many specialist shops which should also figure on the visitor's itinerary. Some have expertise built up over a century or more, while others cater for the new and fashionable.

FOODS

BRITISH FOOD may be much maligned but there are many specialities that are well worth sampling, such as teas, cheeses, chocolates, biscuits and preserves *(see pp288–9)*. The food halls of Fortnum and Mason, Harrod's and Selfridge's are good for all of these. Otherwise, head for **Paxton and Whitfield**, a delightful shop dating from 1830 and stocking over 300 cheeses, including baby Stiltons and Cheshire truckles, along with pork pies, elegant biscuits, oils and preserves.

For chocolates, the ultimate extravagance is **Charbonnel et Walker**. Despite the name it is an English manufacturer, and the chocolates are all handmade. **Bendicks** on Curzon Street stands 50 yards from the original 1921 premises. They make dark chocolates in Winchester by hand, and the classic dessert mint is still the speciality.

TEAS

THAT MOST famous of British drinks comes in all kinds of flavours, from the delicate gunpowder green to the rich, strong and dark English breakfast types. An interesting selection, including fruit-flavoured teas, is available at the **Tea House** in Covent Garden. Jolly tea pots are also stocked here. The **Algerian Coffee Stores** sells more tea than coffee, including herbal and fruity ones. The selection of coffees is still excellent, however, and there are many luxury grocery items in stock.

ONE-OFFS

THERE ARE hundreds of odd shops in London that specialize in just one sort of thing. **The Bead Shop**, for example, sells a massive selection of beads, and also stocks the equipment for making them into jewellery. **The Candle Shop** supplies candles of every imaginable shape and size, along with candle holders and candle-making equipment. Demonstrations of the art take place outside. **Halcyon Days** specializes in little enamelled copper boxes, a revived English 18th-century craft.

Astleys sells pipes but not tobacco; the range is quite bewildering, from simple handturned straightgrains to weird-looking slope-domed calabashes and Sherlock Holmesian meerschaums. For serious collectors of antique scientific instruments, **Arthur Middleton** has a fascinatingly cluttered shop full of ancient globes and early microscopes. For equally serious collectors of dolls' houses, the **Singing Tree** has the ultimate in English dolls' houses, and many beautifully crafted tiny things to put inside them, all replicated to precise scale in accurate period style.

Finally, at the **Left-Handed Shop** in Soho, everything is designed to make life easier for the left-hander. Scissors, corkscrews, cutlery, pens and kitchen and garden tools are the main sellers.

BOOKS AND MAGAZINES

BOOKSHOPS ARE high among London's specialities. Charing Cross Road *(see p108)* is the focal point for those searching for new, antiquarian and second-hand volumes, and is the home of **Foyle's**, with its massive but notoriously badly organized stock. Large branches of chains such as **Books Etc** and **Waterstone's** are also here; so are many specialists, such as **Murder One** for crime books, **Silver Moon** for women's and feminist writing, **Books for a Change** for green politics, and **Zwemmer** for art books.

Stanford's *(see p112)*, with maps and guides to cover the globe, is in Long Acre; more travel books can be found at the **Travel Bookshop**. Nearby is **Books for Cooks**, complete with café and demonstration kitchen. Adult comics are the speciality at **Comic Showcase** in Neal Street, while fantasy, science fiction and graphic novels abound at **Forbidden Planet**. For gay writing, visit the pioneering **Gay's The Word**, near Russell Square. The best selection of books on movies is found at the **Cinema Bookshop**.

The **PC Bookshop** sells a huge range of books on all aspects of computers, while its sister shop nearby stocks multimedia packages.

Two of the best general bookshops are **Hatchard's** in Piccadilly and the flagship **Dillons** store in Gower Street, both of which offer a well-organized and extensive choice. **Compendium**, an alternative bookstore near Camden Market, features interesting and hard-to-obtain titles, while the **Penguin Bookshop** and its children's wing, the **Puffin Bookshop**, despite their names, stock a discerning choice from a wide range of publishers.

The Charing Cross Road area is the best hunting ground for antiquarian books. Many shops offer a book-finding service if the title you want is no longer in print.

If you're looking for news-papers and magazines from abroad, the basement of **Tower Records** has the best selection of US newspapers, while **Capital Newsagents** stocks (among others) Italian, French, Spanish and Middle Eastern publications. **Gray's Inn News** is also worth a visit for publications from overseas *(see pp352–3)*.

RECORDS AND MUSIC

AS ONE OF the world's greatest centres of recorded music, London has a huge and excellent selection of record shops catering to all manner of musical styles. The **Music Discount Centre** has a very good range of classical music, as do the mega-stores such as **HMV**, **Virgin** and **Tower Records**, which are best for mainstream adult-orientated rock and easy listening. The small specialist shops tend to cater to the more esoteric tastes. For jazz try **Ray's Jazz** and **Honest Jon's**, while reggae fans should jam down to **Daddy Kool**. **HMV** has a good selection of world music, and **Stern's** has no competition when it comes to African music. For 12-inch singles, the medium of club and dance music, **Trax** and **Black Market** are two of the most central places to look.

DIRECTORY

FOODS

Bendicks of Mayfair
7 Aldwych WC2.
Map 13 C2.
[0171-836 1846.

Charbonnel et Walker
1 Royal Arcade, 28 Old Bond St W1. **Map** 12 F3.
[0171-491 0939.

Paxton and Whitfield
93 Jermyn St SW1.
Map 12 F3.
[0171-930 0250.

TEAS

Algerian Coffee Stores
52 Old Compton St W1.
Map 13 A2.
[0171-437 2480.

The Tea House
15 Neal St WC2.
Map 13 B2.
[0171-240 7539.

ONE-OFFS

Astleys
16 Piccadilly Arcade SW1.
Map 13 A3.
[0171-499 9950.

Arthur Middleton
12 New Row, Covent Garden WC2.
Map 13 B2.
[0171-836 7042.

The Bead Shop
43 Neal Street WC2.
Map 13 B1.
[0171-240 0931.

The Candle Shop
30 The Market, Covent Garden Piazza WC2.
Map 13 C2.
[0171-836 9815.

Halcyon Days
14 Brook St W1.
Map 12 E2.
[0171-629 8811.

The Left-Handed Shop
57 Brewer St W1.
Map 13 A2.
[0171-437 3910.

The Singing Tree
69 New King's Rd SW6.
[0171-736 4527.

BOOKS AND MAGAZINES

Books Etc
120 Charing Cross Rd WC2.
Map 13 B1.
[0171-379 6838.

Books for a Change
52 Charing Cross Rd WC2.
Map 13 B2.
[0171-836 2315.

Books for Cooks
4 Blenheim Crescent W11.
Map 9 B2.
[0171-221 1992.

Capital Newsagents
48 Old Compton St W1.
Map 13 A2.
[0171-437 2479.

Cinema Bookshop
13–14 Great Russell St WC1. **Map** 13 B1.
[0171-637 0206.

Comic Showcase
76 Neal St WC2. **Map** 13 B1.
[0171-240 3664.

Compendium
234 Camden High St NW1.
[0171-485 8944.

Dillons
82 Gower St WC1.
Map 5 A5.
[0171-636 1577.

Forbidden Planet
71 New Oxford St WC1.
Map 13 B1.
[0171-836 4179.

Foyle's
113–119 Charing Cross Rd WC2. **Map** 13 B1.
[0171-437 5660.

Gay's The Word
66 Marchmont St WC1.
Map 5 B4.
[0171-278 7654.

Gray's Inn News
50 Theobald's Rd WC1.
Map 6 D5.
[0171-405 5241.

Hatchard's
187 Piccadilly W1.
Map 12 F3.
[0171-439 9921.

Murder One
71 Charing Cross Rd WC2.
Map 13 B2.
[0171-734 3485.

PC Bookshop
11 Sicilian Ave WC1.
Map 13 1C.
[0171-831 0022.
(Multimedia at No. 25)

Penguin/Puffin Bookshop
10 The Market, Covent Garden Piazza WC2.
Map 13 C2.
[0171-379 7650.

Silver Moon
64–68 Charing Cross Rd WC2. **Map** 13 B2.
[0171-836 7906.

Stanford's
12–14 Long Acre WC2.
Map 13 B2.
[0171-836 1321.

Travel Bookshop
13 Blenheim Crescent W11. **Map** 9 B2.
[0171-229 5260.

Waterstone's
121–125 Charing Cross Rd WC2. **Map** 13 B1.
[0171-434 4291.

The Women's Book Club
45–6 Poland St W1.
Map 13 A2.
[0171-437 1019.

Zwemmer
26 Litchfield St WC2.
Map 13 B2.
[0171-379 7886.

RECORDS AND MUSIC

Black Market
25 D'Arblay St W1.
Map 13 A2.
[0171-437 0478.

Daddy Kool Music
12 Berwick St W1.
Map 13 A2.
[0171-437 3535.

HMV
150 Oxford St W1.
Map 13 A1.
[0171-631 3423.

Honest Jon's Records
278 Portobello Rd W10.
Map 9 A1.
[0181-969 9822.

The Music Discount Centre
33–34 Rathbone Pl W1.
Map 13 A1.
[0171-637 4700.

Ray's Jazz
180 Shaftesbury Ave WC2. **Map** 13 B1.
[0171-240 3969.

Rough Trade
130 Talbot Rd W11.
Map 9 C1.
[0171-229 8541.

Stern's
116 Whitfield St W1.
Map 4 F4.
[0171-387 5550.

Tower Records
1 Piccadilly Circus W1.
Map 13 A3.
[0171-439 2500.

Trax
55 Greek St W1.
Map 13 A2.
[0171-734 0795.

Virgin Megastore
14–30 Oxford St W1.
Map 13 A1.
[0171-631 1234.

Gifts and Souvenirs

Lᴏɴᴅᴏɴ ɪs ᴀ ᴡᴏɴᴅᴇʀꜰᴜʟ ᴘʟᴀᴄᴇ to shop for presents. As well as an impressive array of original ceramics, jewellery, perfume and glassware, there is exotic merchandise from around the world, including jewellery from India and Africa, stationery from Europe and kitchenware from France and Italy. The elegant, Regency-period Burlington Arcade (see p91) is a popular shopping destination selling high-quality gifts, clothes, art and crafts, many of which are made in the UK.

The shops at big museums, such as the Victoria and Albert (see p198–201), the Natural History (see p204–5) and the Science Museum (see p208–9) often have unusual and original items to take home as mementoes of your visit, while **Contemporary Applied Arts** and the market in Covent Garden Piazza (see p114) have a range of British pottery, jewellery, knitwear and other crafts. If you want to buy all your presents under one roof, go to Liberty (see p311), where beautiful stock from all over the globe fills every department.

Jᴇᴡᴇʟʟᴇʀʏ

Jᴇᴡᴇʟʟᴇʀʏ shops in London range from the extremely traditional to the tiny shops and stalls that huddle in areas like Covent Garden (see pp110–19), Gabriel's Wharf (see p187), and Camden Lock (see p322), which specialize in unusual pieces. **Butler and Wilson** has some of the most eye-catching costume jewellery in town, while next door **Electrum** keeps less bold but equally innovative pieces.

Past Times sells modern reproductions of ancient British designs, including Celtic, Roman and Tudor, as do the shops at the British Museum (see p126–9) and the V&A. The **Leslie Craze Gallery** sells new designs, while **Contemporary Applied Arts** has stylish craft jewellery. The essential place for Gothic jewellery is **The Great Frog** on Carnaby Street. Liberty stocks spectacular ethnic, costume and fashion jewellery. **Manquette** is also worth visiting, for its elegant, one-off pieces in lapis lazuli, amber, coral, gold and silver.

Hᴀᴛs ᴀɴᴅ Aᴄᴄᴇssᴏʀɪᴇs

Tʀᴀᴅɪᴛɪᴏɴᴀʟ ᴍᴇɴ's hats, from flat caps to trilbies and pith helmets, can be found at **Edward Bates** and **Herbert Johnson**. For women, truly distinctive creations come from **Herald and Heart Hatters**, while **Stephen Jones** has a wide range of designs from the everyday to the extravagant and will make hats to match any outfit if you supply your own fabric.

For a selection of the best in British accessories, try the shops on Jermyn Street or in the arcades off Piccadilly. Elsewhere, **James Smith & Sons** produces wonderful umbrellas, ideal for wet London weather. For walking sticks, canes and riding crops, pay a visit to Swaine Adeney (see p315).

Mulberry Company stocks classically English luggage, as well as accessories such as belts, purses and wallets, and **Janet Fitch** sells a wide range of bags, belts, jewellery, hats and other essential accessories.

At the cheaper end of the market, the **Accessorize** chain sells all manner of beads and baubles, grouped by colour to help co-ordinate your outfit.

Pᴇʀꜰᴜᴍᴇs ᴀɴᴅ Tᴏɪʟᴇᴛʀɪᴇs

Mᴀɴʏ ʙʀɪᴛɪsʜ perfumeries use recipes that are hundreds of years old. **Floris** and **Penhaligon's**, for example, still manufacture the same flower-based scents and toiletries for men and women that they sold in the 19th century. The same goes for **Czech and Speake**, and for men's specialists **Truefitt and Hill** and **George F Trumper**, where you can buy some wonderful reproductions of antique shaving equipment as well. Both **Culpeper** and **Neal's Yard Remedies** employ traditional herbal and floral remedies as bases for their natural, therapeutic toiletries.

Other manufacturers have a more contemporary approach to their wares; the **Body Shop**, for example, uses recyclable plastic packaging for its natural cosmetics and toiletries and encourages staff and customers alike to take an interest in environmental issues. **Molton Brown** sells a range of natural cosmetics, body and haircare products, from both its own shops in South Molton Street and Hampstead and from other outlets.

Sᴛᴀᴛɪᴏɴᴇʀʏ

Sᴏᴍᴇ ᴏꜰ ᴛʜᴇ most interesting wrapping paper on sale in London is designed by **Tessa Fantoni**, whose paper-covered boxes, photo frames and albums are sold in several specialist stationery and gift shops, as well as the Conran Shop and her own shop in Clapham. **Falkiner Fine Papers** stocks a range of handmade and decorative papers. Their marbled paper makes glorious giftwrapping for a very special gift. To find luxurious writing paper, pens, pencils and desk accessories, try the Queen's stationer, **Smythson** of Bond Street. Fortnum and Mason (see p311) does handsome leather-bound diaries, blotters and pencil holders, while Liberty embellishes desk accessories with its famous Art Deco prints. For personal organizers covered in anything from vinyl to iguana skin there's the **Filofax Centre** or the more original **Lefax**. The minuscule shop **Pencraft** is the place for pens by Mont Blanc, Watermans, Parker, or Sheaffer. Finally, for cards, pens, wrapping paper and stationery, pop into one of the branches of **Paperchase**.

INTERIORS

Wedgwood still makes the famous pale blue Jasper china that Josiah Wedgwood designed in the 18th century. You can buy it, as well as Irish Waterford crystal and Coalport bone china, at **Waterford Wedgwood** on Piccadilly. Adventurous contemporary tableware is available at **Anta**, which produces stoneware handpainted in various colourful Scottish tartans. For a fine selection of original pottery, visit the **Craftsmen Potters Association** of Great Britain and **Contemporary Applied Arts**. Quirky ceramics are the speciality of **Mildred Pearce**, offering a trendy new slant on everything from candlesticks to clocks. Personalized gifts are also available. **Heal's**, the **Conran Shop**, **Gore Booker** and **Freud's** all offer a great selection of stylish, well-designed accessories for the home. For good-quality kitchen and household items, **Divertimenti** and **David Mellor** are the places to go.

DIRECTORY

JEWELLERY

Butler & Wilson
20 South Molton St W1.
Map 12 E2.
[0171-409 2955.

Contemporary Applied Arts
43 Earlham St WC2.
Map 13 B2.
[0171-836 6993.

Electrum Gallery
21 South Molton St W1.
Map 12 E2.
[0171-629 6325.

The Great Frog
51 Carnaby St W1.
Map 12 F2.
[0171-734 1900.

Leslie Craze Gallery
34 Clerkenwell Green
EC1. **Map** 6 E4.
[0171-608 0393.

Manquette
20a Kensington Church
Walk W8. **Map** 10 D5.
[0171-937 2897.

Past Times
146 Brompton Rd SW3.
Map 11 C5.
[0171-581 7616.

HATS AND ACCESSORIES

Accessorize
42 Carnaby St W1.
Map 12 F2.
[0171-437 4766.

Edward Bates
21a Jermyn St SW1.
Map 13 A3.
[0171-734 2722.

Herald & Heart Hatters
131 St Philip St SW8.
[0171-627 2414.

Herbert Johnson
30 New Bond St W1.
Map 12 F2.
[0171-408 1174.

James Smith & Sons
53 New Oxford St WC1.
Map 13 C1.
[0171-836 4731.

Janet Fitch
2 Percy St, W1. **Map** 13 A1.
[0171-580 8710.

Mulberry Company
11–12 Gees Court, St
Christopher's Pl W1.
Map 12 D1.
[0171-493 2546.

Stephen Jones
29 Heddon St, W1.
Map 12 F2.
[0171-734 9666.

PERFUMES AND TOILETRIES

The Body Shop
32–34 Great Marlborough
St W1. **Map** 12 F2. Branches
throughout London.
[0171-437 5137.

Culpeper Ltd
21 Bruton St W1.
Map 12 E3.
[0171-629 4559.

Czech & Speake
39c Jermyn St SW1.
Map 13 A3.
[0171-439 0216.

Floris
89 Jermyn St SW1.
Map 13 A3.
[0171-930 2885.

Molton Brown
58 South Molton St W1.
Map 12 E2.
[0171-629 1872.

Neal's Yard Remedies
15 Neal's Yard WC2.
Map 13 B1.
[0171-379 7222.

Penhaligon's
41 Wellington St WC2.
Map 13 C2.
[0171-836 2150.

Truefitt & Hill
71 St James's St SW1.
Map 12 F3.
[0171-493 2961.

George F Trumper
9 Curzon St W1.
Map 12 E3.
[0171-499 1850.

STATIONERY

Falkiner Fine Papers
76 Southampton Row
WC1. **Map** 5 C5.
[0171-831 1157.

The Filofax Centre
21 Conduit St W1.
Map 12 F2.
[0171-499 0457.

Lefax
69 Neal St WC2.
Map 13 B2.
[0171-836 1977.

Paperchase
213 Tottenham Court Rd
W1. **Map** 5 A5.
[0171-580 8496.

Pencraft
91 Kingsway WC2.
Map 13 C1.
[0171-405 3639.

Smythson of Bond Street
44 New Bond St W1.
Map 12 E2.
[0171-629 8558.

Tessa Fantoni
77 Abbeville Rd SW4.
[0181-673 1253.

INTERIORS

Anta
46 Crispin St E1.
Map 8 D5.
[0171-247 1634.

Conran Shop
Michelin House, 81
Fulham Rd SW3.
Map 19 A2.
[0171-589 7401.

Craftsmen Potters Association of Great Britain
7 Marshall St W1.
Map 12 F2.
[0171-437 7605.

David Mellor
4 Sloane Sq W1.
Map 20 D2.
[0171-730 4259.

Divertimenti
45–47 Wigmore St W1.
Map 12 E1.
[0171-935 0689.

Freud's
198 Shaftesbury Ave
WC2. **Map** 13 B1.
[0171-831 1071.

The Glasshouse
21 St Albans Place N1.

Gore Booker
41 Bedford St WC2.
Map 13 C3.
[0171-497 1254.

Heal's
196 Tottenham Court Rd
W1. **Map** 5 A5.
[0171-636 1666.

Mildred Pearce
33 Earlham St WC2.
Map 13 B2.
[0171-738 0055 .

Waterford Wedgwood
173 Piccadilly W1.
Map 12 F3.
[0171-629 2614.

Art and Antiques

L ONDON'S ART AND antique shops are spread across the capital. While the more fashionable (and more expensive) dealers are concentrated in a relatively small area bounded by Mayfair and St James's, other shops and galleries catering to a more modest budget are scattered over the rest of the city. Whether your taste is for Old Masters or young modern artists, Boule or Bauhaus, you are bound to find something of beauty in London that is within your financial means.

MAYFAIR

C ORK STREET is the centre of the British contemporary art world. Walk up from Piccadilly and pass, on your left, the **Piccadilly Gallery**, which sells modern British pictures. Next come several galleries, including **Raab** and **Salama-Caro**, offering contemporary art in varying degrees of the avant-garde. The biggest name to look out for is **Waddington**, and if you want to discover the flavour of the month a stop here is a must. However, purchasing is only for the serious (and rich) collector. **Chat Noir** in nearby Albemarle Street is committed to selling contemporary work at a more affordable price. Before retracing your steps down Cork Street, look into Clifford Street, where **Jeremy Maas** excels in Victorian masters. Return via a wide variety of artistic styles, from traditional British sporting pictures and sculpture at **Tryon and Morland** and the Scottish themes of **William Jackson** to **Mayor's** Surrealism and mainstream art at **Redfern**.

Nearby, Old Bond Street is the centre of the fine antiques trade in London. If it's Turner watercolours or Louis XV furniture you're after, this is the place. A walk up from Piccadilly takes you past the lush portals of **Richard Green** and the **Fine Art Society**, among other extremely smart galleries. For furniture and decorative arts visit **Bond Street Antiques Centre** and **Asprey**; for silver go to **S J Phillips**; and for Victorian art try **Christopher Wood's** gallery. Even if you are not a buyer these galleries are fascinating places to visit,

so don't be afraid to walk in – you can learn more from an hour spent here than you can from weeks of studying text books. Also on Old Bond Street are two of the big four London auction houses, **Phillips** and **Sotheby's**.

ST JAMES'S

S OUTH OF Piccadilly lies a maze of 18th-century streets. This is gentlemen's club country *(see Pall Mall p92)* and the galleries mostly reflect the traditional nature of the area. The centre is Duke Street, home of Old Master dealers **Johnny van Haeften** and **Harari and Johns**. At the bottom is King Street, with that leviathan of antiques dealers, **Spink**. A few doors down you will find the main salerooms of **Christie's**, the well-known auction house where Van Goghs and Picassos sell for millions.

Walk back up Bury Street past several interesting galleries and duck into Ryder Street to visit **Chris Beetle's** gallery of works by illustrators and caricaturists.

WALTON STREET

C LOSE TO fashionable and expensive Knightsbridge, the art galleries and antique shops along this elegant little street have prices to match. Here the well-heeled visit galleries such as **Malcolm Innes**, where there are sporting watercolours on show. A short walk away in nearby Montpelier Street is **Bonham's** the auctioneers, fourth in line of the big four and recently redecorated in chic style. You may be lucky enough to find a bargain here.

PIMLICO ROAD

T HE ANTIQUE shops that line this road tend to cater predominantly for the pricey requirements of the interior decorator – this is where to come if you are searching for an Italian leather screen or a silver-encrusted ram's skull. Of particular interest is **Westenholz**. Nearby, **Henry Sotheran** offers fine prints.

BELGRAVIA

T HIS AREA HAS a reputation for good British pictures. The hub of art activity is Motcomb Street, which caters for most tastes. Those seeking fine but well-priced British pictures should visit **Michael Parkin's** gallery, while Oriental-art enthusiasts will revel in the **Mathaf Gallery**, with its 19th-century British and European paintings of the Arab world.

AFFORDABLE ART

T HE HUGELY popular Contemporary Art Society's market takes place every autumn at **Smith's Galleries** in Covent Garden, with work on sale from £100. The three galleries here also show (and sell) excellent work throughout the year. London's East End, a growth area for contemporary art, is home to a host of small galleries as well as the magnificent **Flowers East**, which is strong on work by young artists. For sometimes brilliant shows of contemporary art, step along to Portobello and the **East-West Gallery**. A lot of the work here is reasonably-priced, too.

PHOTOGRAPHY

T HE LARGEST collection of original photographs for sale in the country is at the **Photographers' Gallery**. The **Special Photographers' Company** is well known for selling top-quality work – by unknown artists as well as famous photographic names. **Hamilton's** is worth visiting during its major exhibitions.

BRIC-A-BRAC AND COLLECTABLES

For smaller, more affordable pieces, it's worth going to one of the markets, such as Camden Lock (see p322), Camden Passage (p322) or Bermondsey (p322), which is the main antiques market, catering to the trade. Many high streets out of the centre of town have covered markets of specialist stalls. Finally, a browse along Kensington Church Street in west London will reveal everything from Arts and Crafts furniture to Staffordshire dogs in a concentration of small emporia.

AUCTIONS

If you are confident enough, auctions are a cheaper way to buy art or antiques but be sure to read the small print in the catalogue (which usually costs around £15). Bidding is simple – you simply register, take a number, then raise your hand when the lot you want comes up. The auctioneer will see your bid. It's as easy as that, and can be great fun. The main auction houses are Christie's, Sotheby's, Phillips and Bonham's. Don't forget Christie's saleroom in South Kensington, which offers art and antiques for the more modest budget.

DIRECTORY

MAYFAIR

Asprey
165–169 New Bond St W1. **Map** 12 E2.
[0171-493 6767.

Bond Street Antiques Centre
124 New Bond St W1.
Map 12 F3.
[0171-351 5353.

Chat Noir
35 Albemarle St W1.
Map 12 F3.
[0171-495 6710.

Christopher Wood Gallery
141 New Bond St W1.
Map 12 E2.
[0171 499 7411.

Fine Art Society
148 New Bond St W1.
Map 12 E2.
[0171-629 5116.

Jeremy Maas & Son
15a Clifford St W1.
Map 12 F3.
[0171-734 2302.

Mayor Gallery
22a Cork St W1.
Map 12 F3.
[0171-734 3558.

Piccadilly Gallery
16 Cork Street W1.
Map 12 F3.
[0171-629 2875.

Raab Gallery
9 Cork St W1. **Map** 12 F3.
[0171-734 6444.

Redfern Art Gallery
20 Cork St W1.
Map 12 F3.
[0171-734 1732.

Richard Green
4 New Bond St W1.
Map 12 E2.
[0171-493 3939.

Salama-Caro Gallery
5–6 Cork St W1.
Map 12 F3.
[0171-734 9179.

S J Phillips
139 New Bond St W1.
Map 12 E2.
[0171-629 6261.

Tryon and Morland
23 Cork St W1.
Map 12 F3.
[0171-734 6961.

Waddington Galleries
11, 12, 34 Cork St W1.
Map 12 F3.
[0171-437 8611.

William Jackson Gallery
4 New Burlington St W1.
Map 12 F3.
[0171-287 2121.

ST JAMES'S

Chris Beetle
8 & 10 Ryder St SW1.
Map 12 F3.
[0171-839 7429.

Harari and Johns
12 Duke St SW1.
Map 12 F3.
[0171-839 7671.

Johnny van Haeften
13 Duke St SW1.
Map 12 F3.
[0171-930 3062.

Spink & Son
5 King St SW1. **Map** 12 F4.
[0171-930 7888.

WALTON STREET

Malcolm Innes Gallery
172 Walton St SW3.
Map 19 B2.
[0171-584 0575.

PIMLICO ROAD

Henry Sotheran Ltd
80 Pimlico Rd SW1.
Map 20 D3.
[0171-730 8756.

Westenholz
76 Pimlico Rd SW1.
Map 20 D2.
[0171-824 8090.

BELGRAVIA

Mathaf Gallery
24 Motcomb St SW1.
Map 12 D5.
[0171-235 0010.

Michael Parkin Gallery
11 Motcomb St SW1.
Map 12 D5.
[0171-235 8144.

AFFORDABLE ART

East-West Gallery
8 Blenheim Cres W11.
Map 9 A2.
[0171-229 7981.

Flowers East
199–205 Richmond Rd E8.
[0181 985 3333.

Smith's Galleries
56 Earlham St WC2.
Map 13 B2.
[0171-836 9701.

PHOTOGRAPHY

Hamiltons
13 Carlos Place W1.
Map 12 E3.
[0171-499 9493.

Photographers' Gallery
5 & 8 Great Newport St WC2. **Map** 13 B2.
[0171-831 1772.

Special Photographers Company
21 Kensington Park Rd W11. **Map** 9 B2.
[0171-221 3489.

AUCTIONS

Bonhams, W & F C, Auctioneers
Montpelier St SW7.
Map 11 B5.
[0171-584 9161
Also: Chelsea Galleries, 65–69 Lots Road SW10.
Map 18 F5.
[0171-351 7111.

Christie's Fine Art Auctioneers
8 King St SW1.
Map 12 F4.
[0171-839 9060.
Also: 85 Old Brompton Road SW7. **Map** 18 F2.
[0171-581 7611.

Sotheby's Auctioneers
34–35 New Bond St W1.
Map 12 E2.
[0171-493 8080.

Phillips Auctioneers & Valuers
101 New Bond St W1.
Map 12 E2.
[0171-629 6602.

Markets

LONDON STREET MARKETS have an air of exuberant
irreverence which in itself provides sufficient reason
to pay them a visit. At many you'll also find some of
the keenest prices in the capital. Keep your wits about
you and your hand on your purse and join in the fun.

Bermondsey Market (New Caledonian Market)

Long Lane and Bermondsey St SE1.
Map 15 C5. ⊖ *London Bridge,
Borough.* **Open** *5am–2pm Fri.* **Starts
closing** *midday. See p179.*

Bermondsey is the gathering point
for London's antique traders every
Friday. Serious collectors start
early and scrutinize the paintings,
the silver and the vast array of old
jewellery. Browsers might uncover
some interesting curiosities but
most bargains go before 9am.

Berwick Street Market

Berwick St W1. **Map** 13 A1.
⊖ *Piccadilly Circus, Leicester Sq.*
Open *9am–6pm Mon–Sat. See p108.*

The spirited costermongers of
Soho's Berwick Street sell the
cheapest and most attractive fruit
and vegetables in the West End.
Spanish black radish, star fruit and
Italian plum tomatoes are among
the produce you might find here;
Dennis's vegetable stall sells a
massive range of interesting edible
fungi, all immaculately presented.
The market is good for fabrics and
cheap household goods too, as
well as for leather handbags and
delicatessen. Separated from
Berwick Street by a seedy passage-
way is Rupert Street market,
where prices tend to be higher
and the traders quieter.

Brick Lane Market

Brick Lane E1. **Map** 8 E5.
⊖ *Shoreditch, Liverpool St, Aldgate
East.* **Open** *daybreak to 1pm Sun. See
pp170–1.*

This massively popular East End
jamboree is at its best around its
gloriously frayed edges. Explore
the Cheshire Street lock-ups,
packed with tatty furniture and old
books, or the mish-mash of junk
sold on Bethnal Green Road. East
End spivs huddle together on
Bacon Street proffering gold rings
and watches, while much of
Sclater Street is given over to pet
foods and provisions. On the
wasteland off Cygnet Street, new
bicycles, fresh meat and frozen
food are among the myriad of
goods up for grabs. Brick Lane
itself is rather more prosaic, with
new goods such as handbags,

sports shoes and jeans on sale, but
look out too for the wonderful
range of spice shops and curry
restaurants in this centre for
London's Bangladeshi community.

Brixton Market

Electric Ave SW9. ⊖ *Brixton.*
Open *8.30am–5.30pm Mon, Tue,
Thu–Sat; 8.30am–1pm Wed.*

This market offers a wonderful
assortment of Afro-Caribbean
food, from goats' meat, pigs' tails
and salt fish to plantain, yams and
breadfruit. The best food is to be
found in the old Granville and
Market Row arcades, where exotic
fish are a highlight. Afro style
wigs, strange herbs and potions,
religious tracts sold by Rastafarian
priests and, on Brixton Station
Road, cheap second-hand clothes
are also to be had. From record
stalls, the bass of raw reggae
pounds through this cosmopolitan
market like a heartbeat.

Camden Lock Market

Buck St NW1. ⊖ *Camden Town.*
Open *9am–5pm Thu and Fri,
10am–6pm Sat and Sun.*

Camden Lock Market has grown
swiftly since its opening in 1974.
Handmade crafts, new and second-
hand street fashions, wholefoods,
books, records and antiques form
the bulk of the goods that are on
sale, although thousands of young
people come here simply for the
atmosphere, especially at weekends.
This is enhanced by the buskers
and street performers who draw
the crowds to the attractive
cobbled area around the canal.

Camden Passage Market

Camden Passage N1. **Map** 6 F1.
⊖ *Angel.* **Open** *10am–2pm Wed,
10am–5pm Sat.*

Camden Passage is a quiet walkway where bookshops and
restaurants nestle among bijou
antique shops. Prints, silverware,
19th-century magazines, jewellery
and toys are among the many
collectables that are on show.
There aren't very many bargains to
be picked up here, as most of the
traders tend to be specialists.
However, it is an ideal market for
those who want to indulge in
some genteel browsing.

Chapel Market

Chapel Market N1. **Map** 6 E2.
⊖ *Angel.* **Open** *9am–3.30pm Tue,
Wed, Fri, Sat; 9am–1pm Thu, Sun.*

This is one of London's most
traditional and exuberant street
markets. Weekends are best; the
fruit and vegetables are varied and
cheap, the fish stalls are the finest
in the area, and there's a wealth
of bargain household goods and
clothing to be had.

Church Street and Bell Street Markets

Church St NW8 and Bell St NW1.
Map 3 A5. ⊖ *Edgware Rd.*
Open *8.30am–4pm Mon–Thu,
8.30am–5pm Fri, Sat.*

Like many of London's markets,
Church Street reaches a crescendo
at the weekend. On Friday, stalls
selling electrical goods, cheap
clothes, household goods, fish,
cheese and antiques join the
everyday fruit and vegetable stalls.
Alfie's Antique Market at Nos.
13–25 houses over 300 small stalls
selling anything from jewellery to
old radios and gramophones. Bell
Street, running parallel, has its
own market where second-hand
clothes, records and antiquated
electrical goods are sold for a
song on Saturdays.

Columbia Road Market

Columbia Rd E2. **Map** 8 D3.
⊖ *Shoreditch, Old St.* **Open** *8am–
12.30pm Sun. See p171.*

This is the place to come to buy
greenery and blossoms or just to
enjoy the fragrances and colours.
Cut flowers, plants, shrubs,
seedlings and pots are all sold at
about half normal prices in this
charming Victorian street on a
Sunday morning.

East Street Market

East St SE17. ⊖ *Elephant and Castle.*
Open *8am–5pm Tue, Wed, Fri, Sat;
8am–2pm Thu, Sun.*

East Street Market's high spot is
Sunday, when over 250 stalls fill
the narrow street and a small
plant and flower market is set up
on Blackwood Street. Fruit and
vegetable stalls are in a minority
as traders of clothes (mainly new),
electrical and household goods
swing into action, while furtive
street-hawkers proffer shoelaces
and razor blades from old
suitcases. Many locals come here
more for the entertainment than to
buy, as did the young Charlie
Chaplin *(see p37)* at the beginning
of the century.

Gabriel's Wharf and Riverside Walk Markets

56 Upper Ground and Riverside Walk SE1. **Map** 14 E3. ⊖ *Waterloo.* **Gabriel's Wharf open** *9.30am–6pm Fri–Sun; Riverside Walk open 10am–5pm Sat, Sun and irregular weekdays. See p187.*

Little shops filled with ceramics, paintings and jewellery surround a bandstand in Gabriel's Wharf where jazz groups sometimes play in the summer. A few stalls are set up around the courtyard, selling ethnic clothing and handmade jewellery and pottery. The nearby book market, to be found under Waterloo Bridge, includes a good selection of new and old Penguin paperbacks, as well as new and second-hand hardbacks.

Greenwich Market

College Approach SE10. **Map** 23 B2. ⊝ *Greenwich.* **Open** *9am–6pm Sat, Sun.*

At weekends, the area west of the Hotel Ibis accommodates dozens of trestle tables piled with coins, medals and banknotes, second-hand books, Art Deco furniture, and assorted bric-a-brac. The covered crafts market specializes in wooden toys, clothes made by young designers, handmade jewellery and accessories.

Jubilee and Apple Markets

Covent Gdn Piazza WC2. **Map** 13 C2. ⊖ *Covent Gdn.* **Open** *9am–5pm daily.*

Covent Garden has become the centre of London street-life, with some of the capital's best busking. Both these markets sell lots of interesting crafts and designs. The Apple Market, inside the Piazza where the famous fruit and vegetable market was housed *(see p114)* has chunky knitwear, leather jewellery and novelty goods; a nearby open-air section has cheap army-surplus clothes, old prints and more jewellery. Jubilee Hall sells antiques on Monday, crafts at the weekend, and a large selection of clothes, handbags, cosmetics and tacky mementoes in between.

Leadenhall Market

Whittington Ave EC3. **Map** 15 C2. ⊖ *Bank, Monument.* **Open** *7am–4pm Mon–Fri. See p159.*

Leadenhall Market is a welcome culinary oasis in the City and houses some of the best food shops in the capital. The market's traditional strengths of poultry and game have been well maintained: mallard, teal, partridge and woodcock are all available when in season. There is also a fabulous display of sea food, including excellent oysters, at Ashdown. Other stores stock high-class delicatessen, cheeses and chocolate – an expensive but mouth-watering display of goods that is hard to beat.

Leather Lane Market

Leather Lane EC1. **Map** 6 E5. ⊖ *Chancery Lane.* **Open** *10.30am–2pm Mon–Fri.*

This ancient street has played host to a market for over 300 years. The history of the Lane has nothing to do with leather (it was originally called Le Vrune Lane), but it is in this commodity that some of the best buys are to be had in modern times. The stalls selling electrical goods, cheap tapes and CDs, clothes and toiletries are also worth having a browse through.

Petticoat Lane Market

Middlesex St E1. **Map** 16 D1. ⊖ *Liverpool St, Aldgate, Aldgate East.* **Open** *9am–2pm Sun (Wentworth St 10am–2.30pm Mon–Fri). See p169.*

Probably the most famous of all London's street markets, Petticoat Lane continues to attract many thousands of visitors and traders every Sunday. The prices may not be as cheap as some of those to be found elsewhere, but the sheer volume of leather goods, clothes (the Lane's traditional strong point), watches, cheap jewellery and toys more than makes up for that. A variety of fast-food sellers do a brisk trade catering for the bustling crowds.

Piccadilly Crafts Market

St James's Church, Piccadilly W1. **Map** 13 A3. ⊖ *Piccadilly Circus, Green Park.* **Open** *10am–5pm Thu–Sat.*

Many of the markets in the Middle Ages were held in churchyards and Piccadilly Crafts Market is rekindling that ancient tradition. It is aimed mostly at visitors to London rather than locals, and the merchandise on display ranges from tacky T-shirts to genuine 19th-century prints. Warm Aran woollens, handmade greetings cards and, on a few of the stalls, antiques also compete for custom and attention. All are spread out in the shadow of Wren's beautiful church *(see p90)*.

Portobello Road Market

Portobello Rd W10. **Map** 9 C3. ⊖ *Notting Hill Gate, Ladbroke Grove.* **Open** *antiques and junk: 7am–5.30pm Sat. General market: 9am–5pm Mon–Wed, Fri, Sat; 9am–1pm Thu. See p215.*

Portobello Road is really three or four markets rolled into one. The Notting Hill end has over 2000 stalls displaying a compendium of objets d'art, jewellery, old medals, paintings and silverware. Most are managed by experts, so bargains are rare. Further down the gentle hill, antiques give way to fruit and vegetables. The next transformation comes under the Westway flyover, where cheap clothes, bric-a-brac and tacky jewellery take over. From this point on the market becomes increasingly shabby.

Ridley Road Market

Ridley Rd E8. ≠ *Dalston.* **Open** *9am–3pm Mon–Wed. 9am–noon Thu. 9am–5pm Fri, Sat.*

Early this century Ridley Road was a centre of the Jewish community. Since then, Asians, Greeks, Turks and West Indians have also settled in the area and the market is a lively celebration of this cultural mix. Highlights include the 24-hour bagel bakery, the shanty-town shacks selling green bananas and reggae records, the colourful drapery stalls and the very cheap fruit and vegetables.

St Martin-in-the-Fields Market

St Martin-in-the-Fields Churchyard WC2. **Map** 13 B3. ⊖ *Charing Cross.* **Open** *11am–5pm Mon–Sat; noon–5pm Sun. See p102.*

This crafts market was started in the late 1980s. T-shirts and football scarves are among the unremarkable selection of London mementoes; more interesting are the Russian dolls, the South American handicrafts and the assorted knitwear.

Shepherd's Bush Market

Goldhawk Rd W12. ⊖ *Goldhawk Road, Shepherd's Bush.* **Open** *9.30am–5pm Mon–Wed, Fri, Sat. 9.30am–2.30pm Thu.*

Like Ridley Road and Brixton, Shepherd's Bush Market is a focal point for many of the local ethnic communities. West Indian food, Afro wigs, Asian spices and cheap household and electrical goods are just some of the attractions.

ENTERTAINMENT IN LONDON

Café sign advertising free live music

LONDON HAS THE ENORMOUS, multi-layered variety of entertainment that only the great cities of the world can provide, and, as always, the city's historical backdrop adds depth to the experience. While few things could be more contemporary than dancing the night away in style at a famed disco such as Stringfellows or Heaven, you could also choose to spend the evening picturing the ghosts of long-dead Hamlets pacing ancient boards in the shadow of one of the living legends that grace the West End theatres today. There's a healthy, innovative fringe theatre scene too, plus world-class ballet and opera in fabled venues such as Sadler's Wells, the Royal Opera House and the Coliseum. In London you'll be able to hear the best music, ranging from classical, jazz and rock to rhythm and blues, while dedicated movie buffs can choose from hundreds of different films each night, both in large, multi-screen complexes and excellent small independent cinemas. Sports fans can watch a game of cricket at Lords, cheer on oarsmen on the Thames or eat strawberries and cream at Wimbledon. Should you be feeling adventurous and sporty yourself, you could try going for a horse ride along Rotten Row in Hyde Park. There are festivals, celebrations and sports to attend, and there's plenty for children to do, too – in fact, there's plenty for everyone to do. Whatever you want, you'll be sure to find it on offer in London; it's just a question of knowing where to look.

Cultural classics: a concert at Kenwood House *(top)*; open-air theatre at Regent's Park *(above left)*; *The Mikado* at the Coliseum *(above right)*

Independent has daily listings and also reviews a different arts sector every day; the *Guardian* has arts reviews in its G2 section every day and weekly listings on Saturday; the *Independent*, *Guardian* and *The Times* all have lists of ticket availability.

Specialized news sheets, brochures and advance listings are distributed free in the foyers of theatres, concert halls, cinemas and arts complexes such as the South Bank and Barbican. Tourist information offices and hotel foyers often have the same publications. Fly posters advertise forthcoming events on billboards everywhere.

The Society of West End Theatres (SWET) publishes an informative free broadsheet every fortnight, available in many theatre foyers. It tends to concentrate on mainstream theatres, but does provide invaluable information about what's on. The National Theatre and the Royal Shakespeare Company also publish free broadsheets detailing future performances, distributed at the theatres.

Each SWET theatre has a phone-in "Theatreline" with details of seat availability

INFORMATION SOURCES

FOR DETAILS OF events in London, check the comprehensive weekly listings and review magazine *Time Out* (published every Wednesday), sold at most newsagents and many bookshops; the magazine also carries news, features and adverts, including a travel section and some interesting personal columns. The weekly *What's On and Where to Go In London* (Wednesdays) is also useful, and London's evening newspaper, the *Evening Standard*, gives daily listings (less comprehensive). The updated daily. Note that these calls cost three times as much as a standard local call, and five times as much in peak hours. The general SWET line (0171-836 0971) provides daily updates on seat availability as well as more general information on choice of shows.

BOOKING TICKETS

SOME OF THE more popular shows and plays in London's West End – the latest Lloyd Webber musical for instance – can be totally booked out for weeks and even months ahead and you will find it impossible to purchase any tickets. This is not the norm, though, and most tickets will be available on the night, especially if you would be prepared to queue in front of the theatre for returns. However, for a stress-free holiday it helps to book tickets in advance; this will ensure that you get the day, time and seats that you want. You can book tickets from the box office in person, by telephone or by post. Quite a few hotels have concierges or porters who will give advice on where to go and arrange tickets for you.

Box offices are usually open from about 10am–8pm, and accept payment by cash, credit card, traveller's cheque or else a personal UK cheque

Line-up from the Royal Ballet, on stage at Covent Garden

when supported by a cheque guarantee card. Many venues will now sell unclaimed or returned tickets just before the performance; ask at the box office for the queuing times. To reserve seats by telephone, call the box office and either pay on arrival or send payment – seats are usually held for three days. Some venues now have separate phone numbers for your credit card bookings – check before you call. Reserve your seat, and always take your credit card with you when you collect your ticket. Some smaller venues do not accept credit cards.

Palace Theatre plaque

DISABLED VISITORS

MANY LONDON venues are old buildings and were not originally designed with disabled visitors in mind, but

recently many facilities have been updated, particularly to give access to those using wheelchairs, or for those with hearing difficulties.

Telephone the box office prior to your visit to reserve the special seating places or equipment, which are often limited. It is also worth your while enquiring about any special discounts that might be available for disabled people and for their party.

TRANSPORT

NIGHT BUSES are now the preferred late-night mode of transport, or phone for a cab from the venue. If you find yourself outside the city centre late at night, do not rely on being able to hail a taxi quickly in the street. The Underground usually runs until just after midnight but the times of last trains vary according to the lines. Check timetables in the stations (see p362–3).

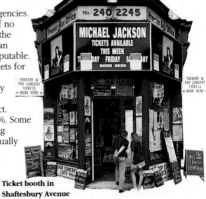

BOOKING AGENCIES

Tickets are also available from agencies. Try the theatre box office first; if no seats are available there, find out the standard prices before going to an agency. Most, but not all, are reputable. Agencies advertising top show tickets for "tonight" may really have them, and they may be a fair price. If you order by phone, tickets will be posted to you or sent to the theatre for you to collect. Commission should be a standard 22%. Some shows waive the agency fee by paying the commission themselves; this is usually advertised, and agencies should then charge standard box office prices. Always compare prices, try to avoid agencies in bureaux de change, and buy from ticket touts in the street only in desperation.

The major listings magazines

Ticket booth in Shaftesbury Avenue

London's Theatres

LONDON OFFERS AN extraordinary range of theatrical entertainment – this is one of the world's great stages, and, at its best, standards of quality are extremely high. Despite their legendary reputation for reserve, the British are passionate about theatre and London's theatres reflect every nuance of this passion. You can stroll along a street of West End theatres and find a sombre Samuel Beckett, Brecht or Chekhov play showing next door to some absurdly frothy farce like *No Sex Please, We're British!* Amid such diversity there is always something to appeal to everyone.

WEST END THEATRE

THERE IS A distinct glamour to the West End theatres. Perhaps it is the glittering lights of the foyer and the impressively ornate interiors, or maybe it is their hallowed reputations – but whatever it is, the old theatres retain a magic all of their own.

The West End billboards always feature a generous sprinkling of world-famous performers such as Judi Dench, Vanessa Redgrave, John Malkovich, Richard Harris and Peter O'Toole.

The major commercial theatres cluster along Shaftesbury Avenue and the Haymarket and around Covent Garden and Charing Cross Road. Unlike the national theatres, most West End theatres survive only on profits; and do not receive any state subsidy. They rely on an army of ever-hopeful "angels" (financial backers) and producers to keep the old traditions alive.

Many theatres are historical landmarks, such as the classic **Theatre Royal Drury Lane**, established in 1663 *(see p115)*, and the elegant **Theatre Royal Haymarket** – both superb examples of early 19th-century buildings. Another to note is the **Palace** *(see p108)*, with its terracotta exterior and imposing position right on Cambridge Circus.

NATIONAL THEATRE

THE **Royal National Theatre** is based in the South Bank Centre *(see p330)*. Here, the large, open-staged Olivier, the proscenium-staged Lyttelton and the

small, flexible Cottesloe offer a range of size and style, making it possible to produce every kind of theatre from large, extravagant works to miniature masterpieces. The complex is also a lively social centre. Enjoy a drink with your friends before your play begins; watch the crowds and the river drift by; wander around the many free art exhibitions; relax during the free early evening concerts in the foyer or browse through the theatre bookshop.

The **Royal Shakespeare Company**, Britain's national theatre company, has its London home at the Barbican Centre. While this unique company centres its work mainly on Shakespeare's many plays its repertoire also includes some classic Greek tragedies, gems of the Restoration theatre and a multitude of modern works. Vast productions of superb quality are staged in the magnificent Barbican Theatre, and smaller performances can be seen on the more intimate stage of The Pit, which is contained in the same complex. The centre's layout is known to be somewhat confusing so go a little early to ensure you arrive before the performance. Use any spare time to enjoy the free art and craft exhibitions in the foyer, often complementary to the plays being staged at the time, and the free musical entertainments which range from classical opera to chamber music, samba to the sound of the big brass band.

The Barbican can also supply information about RSC productions at their theatres in Stratford-upon-Avon.

NATIONAL THEATRE BOOKING ADDRESSES

Royal National Theatre
(Lyttelton, Cottesloe, Olivier) South Bank SE1. **Map** 14 D3.
📞 *0171-928 2252.*

Royal Shakespeare Company
Barbican Centre, Silk St EC2.
Map 7 A5.
📞 *0171-638 8891.*

PANTOMIME

SHOULD YOU HAPPEN to be visiting London between December and February, one unmissable experience for the whole family is pantomime. Part of nearly every British child's upbringing, "panto" is an absurd tradition in which major female characters are played by men and principal male roles are played by women and the audience has to participate, shouting encouragement and stage directions to a set formula. Adults may find the whole experience rather strange, but most children love the experience.

OPEN-AIR THEATRE

A PERFORMANCE OF one of Shakespeare's airier creations such as *Comedy of Errors, As You Like It* or *A Midsummer Night's Dream*, takes on an atmosphere of pure enchantment and magic among the green vistas of Regent's Park *(see p220)* or Holland Park *(see p214)*. Be sure to take a blanket and, to be safe, an umbrella.

Refreshments are available, or you can take a picnic.

OPEN-AIR THEATRE BOOKING ADDRESSES

Holland Park Theatre
Holland Park. **Map** 9 B4.
📞 *0171-602 7856.*
Open *Jun–Aug.*

Open-Air Theatre
Inner Circle, Regent's Park NW1.
Map 4 D3.
📞 *0171-486 2431.*
📠 *0171-486 1933.*
Open *May–Sep.*

WEST END THEATRES

Adelphi ⓲
Strand WC2.
📞 0171-344 0055.

Albery ❶
St Martin's Lane WC2.
📞 0171-867 1115.

Aldwych ⓱
Aldwych WC2.
📞 0171-836 6404.

Ambassadors ⓴
West St WC2.
📞 0171-836 6111.

Apollo ㉚
Shaftesbury Ave W1.
📞 0171-494 5070.

Cambridge ㉒
Earlham St WC2.
📞 0171-379 5299.

Comedy ❽
Panton St SW1.
📞 0171-867 1045.

Criterion ❼
Piccadilly Circus W1.
📞 0171-839 4488.

Duchess ⓯
Catherine St WC2.
📞 0171-494 5075.

Duke of York's ❹
St Martin's Lane WC2.
📞 0171-836 5122.

Fortune ⓳
Russell St WC2.
📞 0171-836 2238.

Garrick ❺
Charing Cross Rd WC2.
📞 0171-494 5085.

Globe ㉙
Shaftesbury Ave W1.
📞 0171-494 5065.

Her Majesty's ❿
Haymarket SW1.
📞 0171-494 5050.

Lyric ㉛
Shaftesbury Ave W1.
📞 0171-494 5045.

New London ⓴
Drury Lane WC2.
📞 0171-405 0072.

Palace ㉖
Shaftesbury Ave W1.
📞 0171-434 0909.

Phoenix ㉕
Charing Cross Rd WC2.
📞 0171-867 1044 .

Piccadilly ㉜
Denman St W1.
📞 0171-867 1118.

Playhouse ⓬
Northumberland Ave WC2.
📞 0171-839 4401.

Prince Edward ㉗
Old Compton St W1.
📞 0171-734 8951.

Prince of Wales ❻
Coventry St W1.
📞 0171-839 5972.

Queen's ㉘
Shaftesbury Ave W1.
📞 0171-494 5040.

Shaftesbury ㉑
Shaftesbury Ave WC2.
📞 0171-379 5399.

Strand ⓰
Aldwych WC2.
📞 0171-930 8800.

St Martin's ㉓
West St WC2.
📞 0171-836 1443.

Theatre Royal:
–Drury Lane ⓲
Catherine St WC2.
📞 0171-494 5062.
–Haymarket ❾
Haymarket SW1.
📞 0171-930 8800.

Vaudeville ⓮
Strand WC2.
📞 0171-836 9987.

Whitehall ⓫
Whitehall SW1.
📞 0171-867 1119.

Wyndham's ❸
Charing Cross Rd WC2.
📞 0171-867 1116.

WEST END THEATRES

Lyric Theatre

Palace Theatre

Vaudeville Theatre

Theatre Royal, Haymarket

Leicester Square half-price ticket booth (see p328)

FRINGE THEATRE

LONDON'S FRINGE theatre acts as an outlet for new, adventurous writing and for writers from other cultures and lifestyles – works by Irish writers appear regularly, as do plays by Caribbean and Latin American authors and feminist and gay writers.

The plays are usually staged in tiny theatres based in pubs, such as the **Gate Theatre** above the Prince Albert pub in Notting Hill, the **King's Head** in Islington and the **Grace** in the Latchmere pub in Battersea (*see p309*), or in warehouses and spare space in larger theatres, such as the **Studio** in the Lyric.

Venues like the **Bush**, the **Almeida** and the **Theatre Upstairs** at the Royal Court have earned their reputations for discovering outstanding new works, some of which have subsequently transferred to the West End.

Foreign-language plays are sometimes performed at national cultural institutes; for example you might be able to catch Molière at the **French Institute** or Brecht at the **Goethe Institute**; check the listings magazines.

For alternative stand-up comedy and cabaret, where you can encounter the sharp edge of satire with its brash, newsy style, try the **Comedy Store**, the birthplace of so-called "alternative" comedy, the **Hackney Empire** (a former Victorian music hall well worth visiting for its magnificent well-preserved interior), and also the **Canal Café Theatre** in Little Venice.

BUDGET TICKETS

THERE IS A wide range of prices for seats in London theatres. The cheaper West End tickets, for example, can cost under £10, whereas the best seats for musicals hover around the £30 mark. However, it is quite possible to obtain cheaper tickets.

The Leicester Square Half Price Ticket Booth (*see p327*) sells tickets on the day of the performance for a wide range of mainstream shows. Situated in Leicester Square, the booth is open Monday to Saturday, from noon for matinees and from 2.30–6.30pm for evening performances. Payment is by cash and there is a strict limit of only four tickets for each purchaser. There is also a small service charge to pay.

You can sometimes get reduced price seats for matinee performances, press and preview nights – it is always worth checking with the box office to see what they currently have on offer.

CHOOSING SEATS

IF YOU GO TO the theatre in person, you will be able to see its seating plan and note where you can get a good view at an affordable price. If you book by telephone, you should note the following: stalls are in front of the stage and expensive. The back stalls are slightly cheaper; dress, grand or royal circles are above the stalls and cheaper again; the upper circle or balcony are the cheapest seats but you will have to climb several flights of stairs; the slips are seats that run along the very edges of the theatre; boxes are the most expensive option.

It is also well to remember that some of the cheapest seats may have a restricted view of the stage.

THEATRE-RELATED ACTIVITIES

IF YOU ARE curious about how the mechanics of the theatre work, you would probably enjoy a back-stage tour. The National Theatre and the RSC both organize these tours (contact the box office – *see p326* – for details). If you enjoy a good walk, London Theatre Walks (0171-839 7438) may interest you. The Theatre Museum (*see p115*) is well worth a visit.

IRATE GHOSTS

Many London theatres are reputed to have ghosts; however, the two most famous spectres haunt the environs of the Garrick and the Duke of York's (*see p327*). The Garrick is heavily atmospheric and the ghost of Arthur Bourchier, a manager at the turn of the century, is reputed to make fairly regular appearances. He hated critics and many believe he is still trying to frighten them away. The ghost occupying the Duke of York's theatre was Violet Melnotte, an actress manager during the 1890s, who was famed for her extremely fiery temper.

FRINGE THEATRE

Almeida
Almeida St N1.
【 0171-359 4404.

Bush
Shepherds Bush Green W12.
【 0181-743 3388.

Canal Café Theatre
The Bridge House
Delamere Ter W2.
【 0171-289 6054.

Comedy Store
28a Leicester Sq WC2.
Map 13 B3.
【 0171-839 6642.

French Institute
17 Queensberry Pl SW7.
Map 18 F2.
【 0171-589 6211.

Gate Theatre
The Prince Albert,
11 Pembridge Rd W11.
Map 9 C3.
【 0171-229 0706.

Goethe Institute
50 Prince's Gate, Exhibition Rd SW7. **Map** 11 A5.
【 0171-411 3400.

Grace
503 Battersea Park Rd SW11.
【 0171-228 2620.

Hackney Empire
291 Mare St E8.
【 0181-985 2424.

King's Head
115 Upper St N1.
Map 6 F1.

【 0171-226 8561.
Ⓕ 0171-226 1916.

Studio
Lyric, Hammersmith,
King St W6.
【 0181-741 8701.
【 0181-836 3464.

Theatre Upstairs
Royal Court,
Sloane Sq SW1.
Map 19 C2.
【 0171-730 2554.
【 0171-836 2428.

Cinemas

I F YOU CAN'T FIND a movie you like in London, then you don't like movies. The huge choice of British, American, foreign-language, new, classic, popular and special-interest films makes London a major international film centre, with about 250 different films showing at any one time. There are about 50 cinemas in the central district of London alone, many of them ultra-modern multi-screened complexes. The big commercial chains show current smash-hits and a healthy number of independent cinemas offer some inventive programmes drawing on the whole history of film. London's listings magazines carry full details of what's on, where.

WEST END CINEMAS

W EST END is a loose term for the main cinemas in the West End of London which show new releases, such as the **Odeon Leicester Square** and the **MGM** Shaftesbury Avenue, but it also includes the cinemas found in Chelsea, Fulham and Notting Hill. Programmes normally begin around midday and are then repeated every two or three hours, with the last show around 8.30pm; there are late-night screenings on Fridays and Saturdays at most of the central cinemas.

West End cinemas are very expensive and a seat in front of the best screens will cost you twice what you would pay to see the same film at a local cinema outside central London. The price of admission is often cheaper for the afternoon performances or on Mondays. It is a good idea to reserve your seats well in advance for screenings of the more popular films on Friday and Saturday evenings and Sunday afternoon. Most of the larger cinemas now take credit card reservations for seats over the telephone.

REPERTORY CINEMAS

T HESE CINEMAS OFTEN show foreign-language and slightly more "off-beat" art films and sometimes change programmes daily or even several times each day. Some cinemas show two or three films, often on the same theme, for one entrance charge.

These include the **Prince Charles**, which is situated centrally, close to Leicester Square, the **Everyman** in north London, the ICA in the Mall, the **Electric** in west London, the **Ritzy** and the National Film Theatre.

NATIONAL FILM THEATRE

T HE NATIONAL FILM Theatre (NFT) *(see p182)* and the Museum of the Moving Image (MOMI) *(see p184)* are both located in the South Bank Arts Complex, near Waterloo Station. The NFT has two cinemas of its own, both of which offer a huge and diverse selection of films. The NFT also holds regular screenings of rare and restored films and television programmes taken from the National Film Archive. A must for movie buffs.

FOREIGN-LANGUAGE FILMS

T HESE ARE screened at the repertory and independent cinemas, including the **Renoir**, the **Prince Charles**, the **Lumière**, the Curzon in Shaftsbury Avenue, the **Minema** and the **Screen** cinemas. Films are shown in original language, with English subtitles.

FILM CERTIFICATES

C HILDREN ARE ALLOWED to go to a cinema unaccompanied by an adult to films which have been awarded either a U (universal) or a PG (parental guidance advised) certificate for viewing.

With other films, the numbers 12, 15 or 18 quite simply denote the minimum ages allowed for admission to the cinema. These classifications are always clearly advertised in the publicity for the film.

LONDON FILM FESTIVAL

T HE MOST important cinema event in Britain is held every November, when over 100 films – some of which will have already won awards abroad – from a number of countries are screened. The NFT, several of the repertory cinemas and some of the big West End cinemas will have special showings of these films. Details are published in the listings magazines. Tickets are quite hard to come by but some "standby" tickets will generally be available to the public 30 minutes before the start of a performance.

CINEMA ADDRESSES

Electric
191 Portobello Road
W11.
0171-792 2020.
0171-792 0328.

Everyman
Hollybush Vale NW3.
Map 1 A5.
0171-435 1525.

Lumière
49 St Martin's Lane WC2.
Map 13 B2.
0171-836 0691.
0171-379 3014.

MGM
135 Shaftesbury Ave WC2.
Map 13 B2.
0171-836 6279.

Minema
45 Knightsbridge SW1.

Map 12 D5.
0171-235 4225.

Odeon Leicester Sq
Leicester Sq WC2.
Map 13 B2.
0171-930 3232.
01426-915 683.

Prince Charles
Leicester Pl WC2.
Map 13 B2
0171-437 8181.

Renoir
Brunswick Sq WC1.
Map 5 C4.
0171-837 8402.

Ritzy
Brixton Rd SW2.
0171-737 2121.

Screen Cinemas
96 Baker St NW1
Map 3 C5.
0171-935 2772.

Opera, Classical and Contemporary Music

Until recently, opera enjoyed a somewhat elitist reputation. However, televised concerts and free outdoor concerts in Hyde Park and the Piazza, Covent Garden, have greatly increased its popularity. London is home to five world-class orchestras and a veritable host of smaller music companies and contemporary music ensembles; it also houses three permanent opera companies and numerous smaller opera groups and leads the world with its period orchestras. It is a major centre for the classical recording industry, which helps to support a large community of musicians and singers. Mainstream, obscure, traditional and innovative music are all to be found in profusion. *Time Out* magazine *(see p324)* has the most comprehensive listings of the classical music on offer around the capital.

Royal Opera House

Floral Street WC2. **Map** 13 C2.
[C] 0171-240 1066. See p115.

The building, with its opulent, elaborate red, white and gold interior, is very glamorous; it looks, and is, expensive. It is the home of the Royal Opera, but very often visiting opera and ballet companies also perform here. Many productions are shared with foreign opera houses, so if you are a visitor to England check that you haven't already seen the same production at home. Works are always performed in the original language, but English translations are flashed up above the stage.

Seats are usually booked well in advance, particularly if major stars such as Placido Domingo, Luciano Pavarotti or Kiri Te Kanawa are performing. The sound is best in the seats centre of stage, right in the front. Tickets range from about £5 to £200 or more for a world-class star. The cheapest seats tend to be bought first, although a number of these tickets are reserved for sale on the day. (Remember some of the cheaper seats in the Royal Opera House have extremely restricted views of the stage.) Standing passes can often be obtained right up to the time of a performance. Standby information is available on the day of the performance on 0171-836 6903 and there are often concessions on tickets. It is also worthwhile queuing for last-minute returns.

London Coliseum

St Martin's Lane WC2. **Map** 13 B3.
[C] 0171-836 3161.
[E] 0171-240 5258. See p119.

The Coliseum, home of the English National Opera (ENO), has rather faded decor but the musical standards are extremely high. The company trains its own singers for its productions and they rehearse in the setting in which they will perform. ENO productions of the classics are nearly all sung in English. The productions are often adventurous and critics have been known to complain that the clarity of the storyline is impaired. The audiences tend to be younger than at the Royal Opera House, the seats are much cheaper and there is less corporate entertaining. The cheapest seats are infamous for being real backbreakers.

Sadler's Wells

Rosebery Ave EC1. **Map** 6 E3.
[C] 0171-278 8916.

Less glamorous, expensive and central than the other opera houses, Sadler's Wells does not have its own company but it provides a useful venue for many visiting companies. Among these, three have a regular season here, each presenting two works: the D'Oyly Carte company, formed in 1875 specifically to perform works by Gilbert and Sullivan, has its season in April and May; Opera 80, with a cast of 22 singers and an orchestra of 27, offers opera in English at a reasonable price in the last two weeks of May; and the British Youth Opera performs here each year in early September.

South Bank Centre

South Bank Centre SE1. **Map** 14 D4.
[C] 0171-928 8800. See p182.

The South Bank Centre houses the Royal Festival Hall (RFH), the Queen Elizabeth Hall and the Purcell Room. There are nightly performances, mostly of classical music, interspersed with opera, ballet and modern dance seasons, jazz, festivals of contemporary and ethnic music and other one-off events running throughout the year. The largest concert hall on the South Bank is the RFH, which is ideal for the major national and

LONDON MUSIC FESTIVALS

The London Opera Festival takes place in June. Venues include the Place Theatre, the Lilian Baylis Theatre (Sadler's Wells), the Purcell Room, St John's Smith Square and the Royalty Theatre. Singers and companies from all over the world come to London to perform in this festival. For tickets and general information, contact the individual theatres.

The City of London Festival is held annually in July, when churches and public buildings in the City host a range of varied musical events. Venues such as the Tower of London *(see p154)* and Goldsmiths' Hall can themselves lend much atmosphere to the events. Many concerts are free. For more details, apply to the box office (0171-248 4260) from May onwards.

international orchestras and large-scale choral works. The Purcell Room is comparatively small and tends to host string quartets and contemporary music in addition to many debut recitals of young artists. The Queen Elizabeth Hall lies somewhere in between. It stages medium-sized ensembles whose audiences, while too large for the Purcell Room, would not fill the Festival Hall. Jazz and ethnic music are performed here and the very innovative and often controversial Opera Factory makes several appearances throughout the year. It performs a range of modern interpretations of the classics, and often also commissions and performs new works. The acoustics are very good throughout the complex.

The London Philharmonic Orchestra is resident at the South Bank. The Royal Philharmonic, the Philharmonia and the BBC Symphony Orchestra are frequent visitors, along with leading ensembles and soloists such as Shura Cherkassky, Stephen Kovacevich and Anne-Sofie von Otter.

The Academy of St Martin-in-the-Fields, the London Festival Orchestra, Opera Factory, the London Classical Players and the

London Mozart Players all have regular seasons. There are also frequent free foyer concerts, and throughout the summer the centre is well worth visiting as musical events take place on the terraces when the weather permits.

Barbican Concert Hall

Silk Street EC2. **Map** 7 A5.
[0171-638 8891. See p165.

This stark concrete building is the permanent home of the London Symphony Orchestra, (LSO), which concentrates on the work of one composer each season. The LSO Summer Pops features an impressive line-up of stars from stage, television, film and the recording world, which in the past has included famous artists such as Victor Borge and the jazz singer Barbara Cook.

The English National Opera makes regular appearances, and the Royal Philharmonic Orchestra has a spring season.

The Barbican is also renowned for its concerts of contemporary music: the BBC Symphony Orchestra holds an annual festival of 20th-century composers here and the London Sinfonietta, which specializes in 20th-century music, performs most of its London concerts at the same venue. There are free foyer concerts too.

Royal Albert Hall

Kensington Gore SW7. **Map** 10 F5.
[0171-589 8212. See p203.

The beautiful Royal Albert Hall is the venue for a wide variety of events from fashion and pop shows to wrestling. However, from mid-July to mid-September it is devoted solely to the Henry Wood Promenade Concerts, the "Proms". Organized by the BBC, the season features the BBC Philharmonic Orchestra, which performs some modern symphonic music as well as classics. Visiting orchestras from around the United Kingdom and worldwide, such as the City of Birmingham Orchestra, the Chicago Symphony Orchestra and the Boston Symphony Orchestra, make up a very varied programme. Tickets for the Proms can be bought on the day of performance but long queues build up early in the day so experienced Promenaders take cushions to sit on. Tickets sell out weeks ahead for the "Last Night of the Proms", which has become a national institution. The audience wave flags and sing. Some people may consider it an evening of nationalistic fervour, although the majority just like singing the traditional *Land of Hope and Glory* without giving much thought to the jingoistic words.

OUTDOOR MUSIC

London has many outdoor musical events in summer. At Kenwood House on Hampstead Heath *(see p230)*, a grassy hill leads down to a lake, beyond which is the concert platform. Arrive early as the concerts are popular, particularly if fireworks are to accompany the music. Deck-chairs tend to be booked up early, so most people sit on the grass. Take a sweater and a picnic. Purists beware – people walk around, eat and talk throughout and the music is amplified so it can be a little distorted. You don't get your money back if it rains, as they have never abandoned a performance yet.

Other venues include Marble Hill House in Twickenham *(see p248)*, with practices similar to Kenwood, Crystal Palace Park and Holland Park.

Wigmore Hall

36 Wigmore St W1. **Map** 12 E1.
[0171-935 2141. See p222.

Because of its excellent acoustics the Wigmore Hall is a favourite with visiting artists, and attracts international names such as Jessye Norman and Julian Bream for a very wide-ranging programme of events. It presents seven evening concerts a week, and a Sunday morning concert from September through to July.

St Martin-in-the-Fields

Trafalgar Sq WC2. **Map** 13 B3.
[0171-930 1862. See p102.

This elegant Gibbs church is home to the Academy of St Martin-in-the-Fields and the famous choir of the same name. These and orchestras as disparate as the Henry Wood Chamber Orchestra, the Penguin Café Orchestra and the St Martin-in-the-Fields Sinfonia provide evening concerts. The choice of each programme is, to a degree, dictated by the religious year; for example, Bach's *St John Passion* is played at Ascensiontide and Handel's *Messiah* at Christmas.

Free lunchtime concerts are given on Mondays, Tuesdays and Fridays by young artists.

St John's, Smith Square

Smith Sq SW1. **Map** 21 B1.
[0171-222 1061. See p81.

This converted Baroque church has good acoustics and provides comfortable seating, making it a marvellous setting. It hosts varied concerts and recitals by groups such as the Wren Orchestra, the Vanbrugh String Quartet and the London Sonata Group. A daily series of BBC Radio lunchtime concerts covers the music and song recitals.

Broadgate Arena

3 Broadgate EC2. **Map** 7 C5.
[0171-588 6565. See p169.

This is the new City-based venue for a summer season of lunchtime concerts offering varied programmes, often from up-and-coming musicians.

MUSIC VENUES

Orchestral
Barbican Concert Hall
Broadgate Arena
Queen Elizabeth Hall
Royal Albert Hall
Royal Festival Hall
St Martin-in-the-Fields
St John's, Smith Square

Chamber and Ensemble
Barbican Concert Hall
Broadgate Arena
Purcell Room
Royal Festival Hall foyer
St Martin-in-the-Fields
St John's, Smith Square
Wigmore Hall

Soloists and Recitals
Barbican Concert Hall
Purcell Room
Royal Albert Hall
St Martin-in-the-Fields
St John's, Smith Square
Wigmore Hall

Children's
Barbican Concert Hall
Royal Festival Hall

Free
Barbican Concert Hall
National Theatre foyer *(see p326)*
Royal Festival Hall foyer
St Martin-in-the-Fields (lunchtime)

Early Music
Purcell Room
Wigmore Hall

Contemporary Music
Barbican Concert Hall
South Bank Complex

Dance

LONDON-BASED DANCE companies present a range of styles from classical ballet to mime, jazz, experimental and ethnic dance. London is also host to visiting companies as diverse as the classic Bolshoi Ballet and the innovative Jaleo Flamenco. Most dance companies (with the exception of the resident ballets) have short seasons that seldom last longer than a fortnight and often less than a week – check the listings magazines for details (*see pp324*). Theatres that regularly feature dance are the **Royal Opera House**, the **London Coliseum**, **Sadler's Wells** and **The Place Theatre**. There are also performances at the **South Bank Centre** and other arts centres throughout the city.

BALLET

THE **Royal Opera House** (*see p115*) and the **London Coliseum** in St Martin's Lane are by far the best venues for classical ballet; providing the stage for foreign companies when they visit London. The Opera House is home to the Royal Ballet, which usually invites major international guest artists to take up residence. Book well in advance for classics such as *Swan Lake* and *Giselle*. The company also has an unusual repertoire of modern ballet; triple bills provide a mixture of new and old and seats are normally readily available.

The English National Ballet holds its summer season at the **London Coliseum**. It has a similar repertoire to the Royal Ballet and stages some very popular productions.

Visiting companies also perform at **Sadler's Wells** (*see p243*), where the London City Ballet has its annual season during December and January. This company has a mainly classical repertoire.

CONTEMPORARY

A PLETHORA OF new and young companies is flourishing in London, each with its own distinctive style. **Sadler's Wells** is one of the main venues, with short seasons featuring visiting and local companies. Attached to Sadler's Wells is the Lilian Baylis Studio, a venue for smaller and often more experimental productions.

The Place Theatre is the home of contemporary and ethnic dance companies and has a year-round programme of performances from these and visiting dancers. The London Contemporary Dance Theatre, the largest of Britain's contemporary dance companies, is based here.

The **Island Theatre** was designed as a theatre/cinema and has only recently been used for dance. During the summer, Rambert Dance performs its season of works by internationally acclaimed choreographers. Rambert has another short season and runs a week of choreographic

workshops in April at the **Riverside Studios**. Other venues that are sometimes used include the **Institute of Contemporary Arts** (ICA) (*see p92*) and the **Shaw Theatre** as well as a new East End venue, the **Chisenhale Dance Space**, a centre for small and independent companies currently regarded as on the experimental fringe of contemporary dance.

ETHNIC

THERE IS A constant stream of visiting groups coming to perform traditional dance from all over the world. Both **Sadler's Wells** and the **Riverside Studios** are major venues, while classical ethnic dance companies, including Indian and Far Eastern, have seasons at the South Bank Centre, often in the **Queen Elizabeth Hall**. Check the listings magazines for details.

DANCE FESTIVALS

THERE ARE TWO major contemporary dance festivals each year in London, featuring many different companies. Spring Loaded runs from February to April, while Dance Umbrella runs from early October to early November. The listings magazines carry all details.

Other smaller festivals include Almeida Dance, from the end of April to the first week of May at the **Almeida Theatre**, and The Turning World, a festival running in April and May offering dance from all over the world.

DANCE VENUES

Almeida Theatre
Almeida St N1.
📞 0171-359 4404.

Chisenhale Dance Space
64 Chisenhale Rd E3.
📞 0181-981 6617.

ICA
Nash House,
Carlton House Terrace,
The Mall SW1.
Map 13 A4.
📞 0171-930 3647.

Island Theatre
Portugal St WC2.
Map 14 D1.
📞 0171-494 5090.

London Coliseum
St Martin's Lane WC2.
Map 13 B3.
📞 0171-836 3161.
📠 0171-240 5258.

The Place Theatre
17 Duke's Rd WC1.
Map 5 B3.
📞 0171-387 0031.

Riverside Studios
Crisp Rd W6.
📞 0181-741 2255.

Queen Elizabeth Hall
South Bank Centre SE1.
Map 14 D4.
📞 0171-928 8800.

Royal Opera House
Floral St WC2. **Map** 13 C2.
📞 0171-240 1066 or
0171-240 1911.

Sadler's Wells
Rosebery Ave EC1.
Map 6 E3.
📞 0171-278 8916.

Shaw Theatre
100 Euston Rd NW1.
Map 5 B3.
📞 0171-388 1394.

Rock, Pop, Jazz and Ethnic Music

YOU WILL FIND THE WHOLE range of popular music being strummed and hummed, howled, growled or synthesized in London. There may be as many as 80 listed concerts on an ordinary weeknight, featuring rock, reggae, soul, folk, country, jazz, Latin and world music. In addition to the gigs, there are music festivals in the summer at parks, pubs, halls and stadiums throughout the capital *(see p335)*. Check the listings magazines and publicity posters *(see p324)*.

MAJOR VENUES

THE LARGEST venues in London are host to an extraordinary variety of music. Stars who are guaranteed to fill thousands of seats play **Wembley Stadium** in the summer when the football season is over. In winter, the pop idols tend to prefer the cavernous indoor **Wembley Arena**, the **Hammersmith Odeon**, or, if they take themselves rather seriously, the **Royal Albert Hall**.

The **Brixton Academy** and the **Town and Country Club** are next in prominence and size. Each can take well over 1,000 people, and for many Londoners these former cinemas are the capital's best venues, with seating upstairs, large dance-floors downstairs and accessible bars.

ROCK AND POP

INDIE MUSIC is one of the mainstays of London's live music scene. It has also now encompassed goth rock, where pallid fans in black clothing gaze at bands playing ponderous power chords (Kentish Town's **Bull and Gate** and the **Powerhaus** in Islington are the places for this). The newer Manchester Sound, popular with latter-day psychedelics (try the **Astoria** in the West End and the **National Ballroom Kilburn**, among many others). The **Marquee** in Charing Cross Road has long been a major rock and pop venue. The **Grand** in Clapham, a former music hall, has recently been renovated as a rock venue, run by the same management as the **Mean Fiddler** in Harlesden, one of the best of the mid-sized venues.

London is the home of pub-rock, which is an odd blend of rhythm and blues, heavy rock and punk that has been developing since the 1960s. The **Station Tavern** in West London holds many of the best pub-rock bands around; and while there's usually no entrance charge, drinks are surcharged. The **Sir George Robey** near Finsbury Park and dozens of other pubs across the city follow suit.

New bands have a popular showcase at the **Rock Garden** in Covent Garden most nights of the week, while **Borderline,** near to Leicester Square, is known to be often frequented by record company talent scouts.

Subterania in Ladbroke Grove holds new songwriter nights, often with some session musicians backing. The **Camden Palace** is very good value for money, especially on Tuesdays, with the finest indie pop both before and after live performances from up-and-coming indie bands.

JAZZ

THE NUMBER of jazz venues in London has grown in the last few years. **Ronnie Scott's** in the West End is still the pick of the old crop: and since the 1950s the finest performers in the world have played here. The **100 Club** in Oxford Street is another very popular venue for jazz lovers.

The **Bass Clef** in Hoxton was a great success in the 1980s and gets very crowded at weekends. A sister club located in the same building, called the **Tenor Clef**, stages Latin and African jazz in smaller and more upmarket surroundings. Jazz and food have formed a partnership at

many venues such as the **Palookaville** in Covent Garden, the **Dover Street Wine Bar** and the largely vegetarian **Jazz Café** which are among the best; others include the **Pizza Express** on Dean Street and also the **Pizza on the Park** which is by Hyde Park Corner.

The **South Bank Centre** *(see p182)* and also the **Barbican** *(see p165)* feature formal jazz concerts and free jazz in the foyers.

REGGAE

LONDON'S LARGE West Indian community has made the city the European reggae capital. At the **Notting Hill Carnival** *(see p57)*, late in August, many top bands perform free.

Reggae has now become integrated with the mainstream rock music scene, and bands appear at most of London's rock venues.

WORLD MUSIC

MUSICIANS FROM every corner of the globe live in London. "World music" includes African, Latin, South American, anything exotic, and its popularity has sparked a revitalization of British and Irish folk music. **Cecil Sharp House** has regular shows for folk purists, while the **ICA** *(see p92)* hosts innovative acts. Many pubs in Kilburn and Willesden now have regular nights for Irish folk music, as does the Acoustic Room at the **Mean Fiddler.**

The **Weavers Arms,** near Newington Green, has a reputation for Cajun, African and Latin American music. Hot Latin nights can be found at **Down Mexico Way** near Piccadilly and at **Cuba Libre** in Islington. For all French Caribbean and African sounds you could check **Le Café de Piaf** inside Waterloo Station; and for the widest selection of African sounds and food in town, try visiting the **Africa Centre** in Covent Garden.

Clubs

THE OLD CLICHÉ that London dies when the pubs shut no longer holds true. Europe has long scoffed at Londoners going to bed at 11pm when the night is only just beginning in Paris, Madrid and Rome, but London has caught on at last and you can revel all night if you want to. The best clubs are not all confined to the city's centre – initial disappointment that your hotel is a half-hour tube-ride from Leicester Square can be offset by the discovery of a trendy club right on your doorstep.

ETIQUETTE

FASHIONS and club nights change very rapidly and nightspots open and close down all the time. Some of the best club nights are one-nighters – check the listings magazines (see p324). Style magazines like *The Face* can help you avoid humiliating comments from bouncers who don't like your appearance. Some clubs change the dress policy with each evening, so it is best to check in advance.

A few clubs require that you arrange membership 48 hours in advance, and you may also find that you have to be introduced by a member. Again, check these details in the listings magazines. Groups of men may not be welcome, so split up and find a woman to go in with; expect to queue to get in. Entrance fees may seem reasonable, but drinks tend to be over-priced.

Opening times are usually 10pm–3am Monday to Saturday, although many clubs stay open until 6am at the weekend and some open on Sunday from about 8pm to midnight.

MAINSTREAM

LONDON IS HOME to one of the best-known discos in the world: **Stringfellows** is as much a part of the tourist circuit as Madame Tussaud's. It's glitzy and expensive so jeans are out of the question. The nearby **Hippodrome** is similar. One of the world's largest discos, it has stunning lighting, several bars and also serves food.

Most of the more upmarket nightclubs in London, for example, **Annabel's**, have a strict members-only policy; they require nominations by

current members and have long waiting lists, so unless you mix in privileged circles you are unlikely to get in.

Traditional West End disco-type clubs which are easier to enter include **Limelight**, the sleek club **Legends** and **Café de Paris**, where you can waltz and foxtrot all night.

Further north, the **Forum** hosts popular club nights, which feature classic soul, funk and rhythm and blues. Similar clubs are **Equinox** in Leicester Square and the **Tattershall Castle**, a disco boat moored on the Thames.

FASHIONABLE VENUES AND CLUB NIGHTS

OVER THE LAST few years London has become one of the most innovative club capitals in the world, a major stage where trends are set. **Heaven** hosts England's premier "house" night. With its huge dance floor, excellent lasers, sound systems and lightshows it's very popular, so start queuing early. The **Ministry of Sound** is a New York-style club that set the pattern for others to follow, but it has no alcohol licence and is very hard to get into. House nights are also run at **Maximus** (cheaper and wilder after 3am), the **Gardening Club** and **Woody's**, home to garage as well as hardcore house and the young and trendy **Wag Club**. **LA2** hosts an alternative dance night with "Popscene" for "indie" music sounds.

"Talkin' Loud" club night at the **Fridge** offers some of the funkiest jazz-based sounds. **Turnmills** is London's first 24-hour club; it's cheap, plays funky jazz and also boasts a decent restaurant.

For fans of 1970s nostalgia, **Le Scandale** hosts "Carwash" – disco was never so trashy or fun. There is also cheaper admission for those who dress up in seventies style. For more Earth, Wind and Fire, head for "Boogie Wonderland" at **79 Club** in Oxford Street.

There are surprisingly few regular reggae nights. **Gossips** has the best dance reggae on Saturday and ska, classic soul and R and B on Thursday.

GAY

LONDON HAS a number of gay nightclubs. The best-known and most popular is **Heaven**, with its huge dance floor and bar and video lounge upstairs. Islington's **Paradise** hosts a men-only leather and rubber night and has transvestite floorshows as well as games rooms and two discos. **Club Copa** in Earl's Court is a relaxed club for gay men and is consistently popular. The **Fridge** and the **Gardening Club** host mixed gay nights, and the Fridge holds women-only nights.

TRANSVESTITE

WATCH for the occasional "Kinky Gerlinky" night in the listings magazines, an outrageously kitsch collection of drag queens and assorted exotica. In Soho, **Madame Jojo**'s revue is a fabulous whirl of glittering colour and extreme high camp.

CASINOS

TO GAMBLE in London you must be a member, or at least the guest of a member, of a licensed gambling club. Most clubs are happy to let you join but membership must be arranged 48 hours in advance. Many will let you in to use facilities other than the gambling tables until about 4am, when most close. Try the excellent restaurants and bars, which are often subject to the usual licensing laws (see p308). Many clubs also have "hostesses" – beware the cost of their company.

DIRECTORY

MAJOR MUSIC VENUES

Brixton Academy
211 Stockwell Rd SW9.
0171-924 9999.

Hammersmith Odeon
Queen Caroline St W6.
0181-741 4868.

Royal Albert Hall
See p203.

Forum
9–17 Highgate Rd NW5.
0171-284 1001.
0171-284 2200.

Wembley Arena and Stadium
Empire Way, Wembley, Middlesex.
0181-900 1234.

ROCK AND POP VENUES

Astoria
157 Charing Cross Rd WC2. Map 13 B1.
0171-434 0403.

Borderline
Orange Yard, Manette St WC2. Map 13 B1.
0171-734 2095.

Bull and Gate
389 Kentish Town Rd NW5. 0171-485 5358.

Camden Palace
1a Camden High St NW1. Map 4 F2.
0171-387 0428.

Grand
Clapham Junction, St John's Hill SW11.
0171-738 9000.

LA2
157 Charing Cross Rd WC2. Map 13 B2.
0171-734 6963.

Limelight
136 Shaftesbury Ave WC2. Map 13 B2.
0171-434 0572.

Marquee
105 Charing Cross Rd WC2. Map 13 B2.
0171-437 6601.

Mean Fiddler
24–28a High St NW10.
0181-961 5490.
0181-963 0940.

National Ballroom Kilburn
234 Kilburn High Rd NW6.
0171-328 3141.

Powerhaus N1
1 Liverpool Rd N1.
Map 6 E2.
0171-837 3218.
0171-284 2200.

Rock Garden
6–7 The Piazza, Covent Garden WC2. Map 13 C2.
0171-240 3961.

79 Club
79 Oxford St W1.
Map 13 A1.
0171-439 7250.

Sir George Robey
240 Seven Sisters Rd N4.
0171-263 4581.

Station Tavern
41 Bramley Rd W10.
0171-727 4053.

Subterania
12 Acklam Rd W10.
0181-960 4590.
0181-284 2200.

Woody's
41–43 Woodfield Rd W9.
0171-286 5574.

JAZZ VENUES

100 Club
100 Oxford St W1.
Map 13 A1.
0171-636 0933.

Barbican Hall
See p165.

Bass Clef
35 Coronet St N1.
Map 7 C3.
0171-729 2476.

Dover Street Wine Bar
8 Dover St W1. Map 12 F3.
0171-629 9813.

Jazz Café
5 Parkway NW1. Map 4 E1.
0171-916 6000.

Pizza Express
10 Dean St W1. Map 13 A1.
0171-437 9595.

Pizza on the Park
11 Knightsbridge SW1.
Map 12 D5.
0171-235 5550.

Ronnie Scott's
47 Frith St W1.
Map 13 A2.
0171-439 0747

Royal Festival Hall
See p184.

Tenor Clef
1 Hoxton Sq N1.
Map 7 C3.
0171-729 2440.

Vortex
Stoke Newington Church St N16. 0171-254 6516.

WORLD MUSIC VENUES

Africa Centre
38 King St WC2.
Map 13 C2.
0171-836 1973.

Cecil Sharp House
2 Regent's Park Rd NW1.
Map 4 D1.
0171-485 2206.

Cuba Libre
72 Upper St N1. Map 6 F1.
0171-354 9998.

Down Mexico Way
25 Swallow St W1.
Map 12 F3.
0171-437 9895.

ICA
See p92.

Mean Fiddler
24-28A High St NW10.
0181-961 5490.

Weavers Arms
98 Newington Green Rd N1.
0171-226 6911.

CLUBS

Annabel's
44 Berkeley Sq W1.
Map 12 E3.
0171-629 1096.

Café de Paris
3 Coventry St W1.
Map 13 A3.
0171-287 3481.

Club Copa
180 Earl's Court Rd SW5.
Map 18 D2.
0171-373 3407.

Equinox
Leicester Sq WC2.
Map 13 B2.
0171-437 1446

Fridge
Town Hall Parade, Brixton Hill SW2.
0171-326 5100.

Gardening Club
4 The Piazza, Covent Garden WC2.
Map 13 C2.
0171-497 3154.

Gossips
69 Dean St W1.
Map 13 A2.
0171-434 4480.

Heaven
Under the Arches, Villiers St WC2. Map 13 C3.
0171-839 3852.

Hippodrome
Cranbourn St WC2.
Map 13 B2.
0171-437 4311.

Legends
29 Old Burlington St W1.
Map 12 F3.
0171-437 9933.

Madame Jojo
8–10 Brewer St W1.
Map 13 A2.
0171-734 2473.

Maximus
14 Leicester Sq WC2.
Map 13 B2.
0171-734 4111.

Ministry of Sound
103 Gaunt St SE1.
0171-378 6528.

Paradise Club
1–5 Parkfield St N1.
Map 6 E2.
0171-354 9993.

Scandale
53–54 Berwick St W1.
Map 13 A1.
0171-437 6830.

Stringfellows
16 Upper St Martin's Lane WC2. Map 13 B2.
0171-240 5534.

Tattershall Castle
Victoria Embankment, SW1. Map 13 C3.
0171-839 6548.

Turnmills
63 Clerkenwell Road EC1
Map 6 E5.
0171-250 3409.

Wag Club
35 Wardour St W1.
Map 13 A2.
0171-437 5534.

Sport

THE RANGE OF SPORTS on offer in London is quite phenomenal. Should you feel the urge to watch a game of medieval tennis or go scuba-diving in the city centre, you've come to the right place. More likely, you'll just want to watch a football or rugby match, or play a set of tennis in a park. With far more public facilities than most European capitals, London is the place to enjoy cheap, accessible sport.

AMERICAN FOOTBALL

THE LONDON MONARCHS play teams from Europe and America in March and April. The NFL Bowl, in which two top American football teams compete in an exhibition match, is held in August, also at Wembley.

ATHLETICS

ATHLETES WILL find a good choice of running tracks, often with free admission. **West London Stadium** has good facilities; **Regent's Park** is free; try also **Parliament Hill Fields**. For a sociable jog, meet the Bow Street Runners at **Jubilee Hall** on Tuesdays at 6pm.

CRICKET

TEST CRICKET is played in the summer at **Lord's** *(see p242)* and the **Oval**. Tickets have to be booked well in advance, though tickets for one-day internationals are easier to come by. Middlesex and Surrey play first-class county matches at Lord's and the Oval. You can also take a tour of the Long Room and Pavilion at Lord's.

FOOTBALL

THE MOST popular spectator sport in Britain is football. The season runs from August to May, and matches start at 3pm on Saturdays. Although the FA Cup Final at **Wembley** sells out in advance, tickets for international matches are usually available from the box office. The biggest London football clubs are **Arsenal** and **Tottenham Hotspur** and, unless the match is all-ticket, admission on the day should not be a problem.

GOLF

THERE ARE NO golf courses in Central London, but a few are scattered around the outskirts. The most accessible public courses are **Hounslow Heath**, **Chessington** (nine holes, train from Waterloo) and **Richmond Park** (two courses, computerized indoor teaching room). If you didn't pack your clubs, sets can be hired at a reasonable price.

GREYHOUND RACING

AT A NIGHT "down the dogs" you can follow the races on a screen in the bar, stand by the track or watch from the restaurant (book in advance) at **Walthamstow Stadium**, **The Embassy London Stadium** or **Wimbledon Stadium**.

HORSE-RIDING

FOR CENTURIES, fashionable riders have exercised their steeds in Hyde Park; **Ross Nye** will provide you with a horse so that you can follow a long tradition.

ICE-SKATING

ICE-SKATERS SHOULD head for London's best-known rink, **Queens**, where you can hire skates. The most attractive ice rink, open only in winter, is in the **Broadgate** complex in the heart of the City.

RUGBY

THE PROFESSIONAL Rugby League has 13 players a side and plays cup final matches at **Wembley** stadium; Rugby Union, or rugger, is a 15-a-side amateur game, and its international matches are played at **Twickenham Rugby Football Ground**. The season runs from September to April and you can watch "friendly" weekend games at local sports grounds. Top London teams **Saracens** and **Rosslyn Park** can be seen at their own sports grounds outside the centre of town.

SQUASH

SQUASH COURTS tend to be busy, so try to book at least two days ahead. Many sports centres have squash facilities and will hire out equipment, including **Swiss Cottage Sports Centre** and **Saddlers Sports Centre**.

STOCK CAR RACING

STOCK CAR RACING can be found at **Wimbledon Stadium**. It is an extremely noisy sport, but spectators can always forsake the row, the wrecks and the fumes for the calm of the restaurant.

SWIMMING

BEST INDOOR pools include **Chelsea Sports Centre** and **Porchester Baths**; for outdoor, try **Highgate** (men), **Kenwood** (women) and **Hampstead** (mixed bathing).

TENNIS

THERE ARE hundreds of tennis courts in London's public parks, most of them cheap and easily reserved. It can be busy in the summer, so book your court two or three days ahead. You must supply your own racquet and balls. Good public tennis courts include the following: **Holland Park**, **Parliament Hill** and **Swiss Cottage**.

Tickets for the Centre Court of the **All England Lawn Tennis Club** at Wimbledon are hard to obtain – it is possibly easier to enter the tournament as a player than to obtain tickets for Centre Court; try queueing overnight, or queue for return tickets after lunch on the day – for a bargain price, you can still enjoy a good four hours of tennis. *(See p247.)*

TRADITIONAL SPORTS

AN OLD LONDON tradition is the University Boat Race, held in March or April, when Oxford and Cambridge row from Putney to Mortlake (see p56); a newer tradition is the Marathon, which is run from Greenwich to Big Ben at Westminster (see p56) on an April Sunday. You can watch croquet at the **Hurlingham Club**, polo at the **Guards Polo Club** and medieval tennis at **Queen's Club**.

WATER SPORTS

THERE ARE FACILITIES for a wide variety of water sports at the **Docklands Sailing and Water Sports Centre** (windsurfing, dinghy sailing, powerboating and canoeing), **Docklands Water Sports Club**, **Peter Chilvers Windsurfing School** and **Royal Docks Waterski Club**. Boats are also available for hire on the calmer waters of the **Serpentine** in Hyde Park and **Regent's Park Lake**.

WORKING OUT

MOST SPORTS centres have gymnasiums, work-out studios and health clubs. If you are a member of the YMCA, you'll be able to use the excellent facilities at the **Central YMCA**. **Jubilee Hall** and **Swiss Cottage Sports Centre** both offer a variety of aerobic classes, keep-fit and weight training. For those who have overdone it, the **Chelsea Sports Centre** has a sports injury clinic.

DIRECTORY

General Sports Information Line
☎ 0171-222 8000.

Greater London Sports Council
☎ 0181-778 8600.

All England Lawn Tennis and Croquet Club
Church Rd, Wimbledon SW19. ☎ 0181-946 2244.

Arsenal
Avenell Rd, Highbury N5.
☎ 0171-359 0131.

Broadgate Ice Rink
Eldon St EC2. **Map** 7 C5.
☎ 0171-588 6565.

Central YMCA
112 Great Russell St WC1. **Map** 13 B1.
☎ 0171-637 8131.

Chelsea Sports Centre
Chelsea Manor St SW3.
Map 19 B3.
☎ 0171-352 6985.

Chessington Golf Course
Garrison Lane, Surrey.
☎ 0181-391 0948.

Docklands Sailing and Watersports Centre
235a Westferry Rd, E14.
☎ 0171-537 2626.

Docklands Water Sports Club
King George V Dock, Woolwich Manor Way E16. ☎ 0171-511 5000.

The Embassy London Stadium
Waterden Rd, E15 2EQ.
☎ 0181-986 3511.

Guards Polo Club
Windsor Great Park, Englefield Green, Egham, Surrey.
☎ 0784-434212.

Hampstead Ponds
off East Heath Rd NW3.
Map 1 C4.
☎ 0171-435 2366.

Holland Park Lawn Tennis Courts
Kensington High St W8.
Map 9 B5.
☎ 0171-602 2226.

Hounslow Heath Golf
Staines Rd, Hounslow, Middlesex.
☎ 0181-570 5271.

Hurlingham Club
Ranelagh Gdns SW6.
☎ 0171-736 3148.

Jubilee Hall Sports Centre
30 The Piazza, Covent Garden WC2. **Map** 13 C2.
☎ 0171-836 4835.

Kenwood and Highgate Ponds
off Millfield Lane N6.
Map 2 E3.
☎ 0181-340 4044.

Lord's Cricket Ground
St John's Wood NW8.
Map 3 A3.
☎ 0171-289 1611.

Oval Cricket Ground
Kennington Oval SE11.
Map 22 D4.
☎ 0171-582 6660.

Parliament Hill
Highgate Rd NW5.
Map 2 E4.

☎ 0171-435 8998 (athletics).
☎ 0171-485 4491 (tennis).

Peter Chilvers Windsurfing Centre
Gate 6, Tidal Basin, Royal Victoria Docks E16.
☎ 0171-474 2500.

Porchester Centre
Queensway W2.
Map 10 D1.
☎ 0171-792 2919.

Queen's Club Real Tennis
Palliser Rd W14.
Map 17 A3.
☎ 0171-385 3421.

Queens Ice Skating Club
17 Queensway W2.
Map 10 E2.
☎ 0171-229 0172.

Regent's Park Lake
Regent's Park NW1.
Map 3 C3.
☎ 0171-486 4759.

Richmond Park Golf
Roehampton Gate, Priory Lane SW15.
☎ 0181-876 3205.

Rosslyn Park Rugby
Priory Lane, Upper Richmond Rd SW15.
☎ 0181-876 1879.

Ross Nye
8 Bathurst Mews W2. **Map** 11 A2.
☎ 0171-262 3791.

Royal Docks Waterski Club
Gate 16, King George V Dock, Woolwich Manor Way E16.
☎ 0171-511 2000.

Saddlers Sports Centre
Goswell Rd EC1.
Map 6 F3.
☎ 0171-253 9285.

Saracens Rugby
Dale Green Rd N14.
☎ 0181-449 3770.

Serpentine
Hyde Park W2.
Map 11 B4.
☎ 0171-262 3751.

Swiss Cottage Sports Centre
Winchester Rd NW3.
☎ 0171-413 6490.

Tottenham Hotspur
White Hart Lane, 748 High Rd N17.
☎ 0171-396 4567.

Twickenham Rugby Ground
Whitton Rd, Twickenham, Middlesex.
☎ 0181-892 8161.

Walthamstow Stadium
Chingford Rd E4.
☎ 0181-531 4255.

Wembley Stadium
Wembley, Middlesex.
☎ 0181-900 1234.

Linford Christie Stadium
Du Cane Rd W12.
☎ 0181-749 5505.

Wimbledon Stadium
Plough Lane SW19.
☎ 0181-946 5361.

CHILDREN'S LONDON

LONDON OFFERS children a potential goldmine of fun, excitement and adventure. Each year finds new attractions and sights opening up and older ones being updated.

First-time visitors may want to watch traditional ceremonies (see pp52–5) or visit famous buildings (see p35), but these are merely the tip of the iceberg. While London's parks, zoos and

Humpty Dumpty doll

adventure playgrounds provide outdoor activities there are also loads of workshops, activity centres and museums providing quizzes, hands-on experiments and interactive displays. A day out needn't be costly: children are entitled to reduced fares on London Transport and lower admission prices at museums. Some of London's star attractions, for instance all the ceremonies, are free.

PRACTICAL ADVICE

A LITTLE PLANNING is the key to a successful outing. You may want to check the opening hours of the places you plan to visit in advance, by telephone. Work out your journey thoroughly using the tube map at the end of this book. If you are travelling with very young children remember that there will be queues at the Underground stations or bus stops near popular sights. These will be long during peak hours, so buy your tickets or a Travelcard in advance (see p360).

Children under 5 can travel free on buses and tubes and child fares operate for all children between the ages of 5 and 15. (Children of 14 and 15, and those who look older than they are, need to have a Photocard.) Children very often enjoy using public transport, especially when it's

Punch and Judy show in the Piazza, Covent Garden

a novelty, so plan your outing carefully using one form of transport for the outward journey and another for the journey home. You can get around London easily by bus, Underground, taxi, train and riverboat (see pp 360–7). Visiting all the exhibitions and museums as a family doesn't have to be

Covent Garden clowns

as expensive as it sounds. An annual family season ticket, usually for two adults and up to four children, is available at many of the museums and often costs only marginally more than the initial visit. In some cases you can buy a family ticket that covers a group of museums; for instance the Science, Natural History and Victoria and Albert Museums in South Kensington (see pp194–209). Being able to visit a sight more than once means that you won't exhaust your children and put them off museums for life by trying to see absolutely everything over one long, tiring day.

If your children want a break from sightseeing, most borough councils provide information on activities for children such as playgroups, theatres, fun fairs and activity centres in their area. Leaflets are usually available from libraries and leisure centres, as well as local town halls. During the long summer school holidays (July to the beginning of September) there are organized activity programmes all over London.

CHILDREN AND THE LAW

CHILDREN UNDER 14 are not allowed into British pubs and wine bars (unless there is a special family room or garden) and only people over 18 can drink or buy any alcohol. In restaurants, only those over 16 can drink wine and beer with their meal (over 18 for spirits).

EATING OUT WITH CHILDREN

The choosing chart *(see pp292–4)* in the front of the restaurants section of this book shows establishments that welcome children. But as long as your offspring are reasonably well-behaved, most of London's more informal and ethnic restaurants will be happy to serve a family. Some can also provide highchairs and booster cushions, as well as colouring mats to keep children quiet while waiting for their food to arrive.

Many will also offer special children's menus with small helpings which, although fairly unadventurous, will cut the cost of your meal.

Over the weekend some restaurants (such as **Smollensky's Balloon** and **Sweeny Todds**) provide live entertainment for children in the form of clowns, storytellers and magicians. A number accept bookings for children's parties. It is always worth trying to book in advance (especially for Sunday lunch), so that you don't have to hang around waiting with tired and hungry children.

London has a number of restaurants ideal for older children. Among these are the Rock Island Diner *(see p306)* and the **Hard Rock Café** on Old Park Lane. For budget eating, try the Café in the Crypt, St Martin-in-the-Fields *(see p102).*

Coming up for air at Smollensky's Balloon

Colourful service at the Rock Island Diner

USEFUL ADDRESSES

Haagen-Dazs
14 Leicester Square WC2. **Map** 13 B2.
0171-287 9577.

Hard Rock Café
150 Old Park Lane W1. **Map** 12 E4.
0171-629 0382.

Smollensky's Balloon
1 Dover St W1. **Map** 12 F3.
0171-491 1199.

Sweeny Todds
3–5 Tooley St SE1. **Map** 15 C3.
0171-407 5267.

Some films are classed as unsuitable for children *(see p329)*, and young children are rarely welcome anywhere they might create a nuisance.

If you want to take your children by car, you must use seat belts wherever they are provided. Babies will need a special child seat. If you are in doubt, ask at any police station.

GETTING THEM OFF YOUR HANDS

MANY OF London's great museums *(see pp40–3)* and theatres *(see pp326–8)* provide weekend and holiday activities and workshops where you can leave children for a few hours or even for a whole day, and the children's theatres are a great way to spend a rainy afternoon. A day at the fair is always a success – try Hampstead fair on summer bank holidays.

London has a great many sports centres *(see pp336–7)*, which usually open daily and

often have special clubs and activities to occupy children of every age.

From 4pm to 6pm Kids Line (0171-222 8070) details children's events in London.

If you want a total break, contact **Childminders**, **Babysitters Unlimited**, **Universal Aunts** or **Pippa Pop-Ins**, London's hotel for children between 2 and 12.

CHILDMINDING

Babysitters Unlimited
2 Napoleon Road, Twickenham.
0181-892 8888.

Childminders
9 Paddington Street W1.
Map 4 D5.
0171-487 5040.

Pippa Pop-Ins
430 Fulham Road SW6.
Map 18 D5.
0171-385 2458.

Universal Aunts
PO Box 304, SW4.
0171-738 8937.

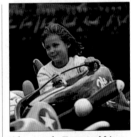

Airborne at the Hampstead fair

Bathtime fun at Pippa Pop-Ins

SHOPPING

All children love a visit to **Hamleys** toy shop or Harrod's toy department *(see p311)*. **Davenport's Magic Shop** and **The Doll's House** are smaller and more specialized.

The **Early Learning Centre**, the **Children's Book Centre** and the **Puffin Book Shop** all have good selections of books. Some bookshops organize readings and signings by children's authors, especially during Children's Book Week which is held in October.

Useful numbers Children's Book Centre 0171-937 7497; Davenport's Magic Shop 0171-836 0408; The Doll's House 0171-379 7243; Early Learning Centre 0171-937 0419; Hamleys 0171-734 3161; Puffin Book Shop 0171-379 7650.

Bears at Hamleys toy shop

MUSEUMS AND GALLERIES

LONDON HAS a wealth of museums, exhibitions and galleries; more information on those listed here is to be found on pages 40–43. Most have been updated over the last few years to incorporate some exciting modern display techniques. It's unlikely that you'll have to drag reluctant children around an assortment of lifeless and stuffy exhibits.

The Bethnal Green Museum of Childhood (the children's branch of the Victoria and Albert Museum), the London Toy and Model Museum, with its garden and steam railway, and Pollock's Toy Museum are especially good for young children.

For older children try one of London's Brass Rubbing Centres: the great Brass Rubbing Centre in the Crypt of St Martin-in-the-Fields *(p102)*, Westminster Abbey *(pp76–9)* or St James's Church, Piccadilly *(p90)*. The Guinness World of Records Exhibitions *(p100)* at the Trocadero, the Museum of the Moving Image *(p184)*, Madame Tussauds *(p220)* or Tower Bridge *(p153)* are all firm favourites with children too.

The British Museum has fabulous treasures from all over the world, and the Commonwealth Institute, Horniman Museum and Museum of Mankind have colourful displays from many different cultures. The Science Museum, with over 600 working exhibits, is one of London's best attractions for children – its Launch Pad gallery will help keep them amused for hours. If you have the stamina, the Natural History Museum next door contains hundreds of amazing objects and animals from the world of nature, including a new Dinosaur Exhibition

Shirley Temple doll at Bethnal Green Museum

complete with sound effects. Suits of armour built for knights and monarchs can be seen at the Tower of London. More up-to-date armoury and weapons, including aircraft and the tools of modern warfare, can be seen at the National Army Museum, and the Imperial War Museum. Also worth a visit is the Guards' Museum located on Birdcage Walk. London's colourful past is brought alive at the Museum of London. Its new offshoot, the Tower Hill Pageant, manages to cover 2,000 years of the capital's history, complete with some realistic sights, sounds and smells.

THE GREAT OUTDOORS

LONDON IS FORTUNATE in having many parks and open spaces *(see pp48–51)*. Most local parks contain conventional playgrounds for children, many with modern, safe equipment. Some parks also have One O'Clock Clubs (specially enclosed areas for children under 5 with activities supervised by playworkers) as well as adventure

Puppets at the Little Angel Marionette Theatre, Highbury

Playground at Gunnersbury Park

playgrounds, nature trails, boating ponds and athletic tracks for older children and energetic adults.

Kite-flying on Blackheath *(p239)*, Hampstead Heath or Parliament Hill can be great fun, as can boating in Regent's Park. A trip to Primrose Hill *(pp262–3)* can be combined with a visit to London Zoo and Regent's Canal *(p223)*.

The large parks are one of London's greatest assets for parents who have energetic children. For a good walk or cycle ride, there is quite an abundance of parks all over London. For instance, there's Hyde Park in the city centre; Hampstead Heath up in the north; Wimbledon Common in southwest London; and Gunnersbury Park in west London. Cyclists should be sure to watch out for pedestrians and remember that some paths may be out of bounds.

Battersea Park has a children's zoo and Crystal Palace Park (Thicket Rd, Penge SE20) has a children's farm. Greenwich and Richmond Parks have herds of deer. If you want a relaxing trip, why not go and feed the ducks on the pond in St James's Park?

Tuojiangasaurus skeleton at the Natural History Museum

CHILDREN'S THEATRE

Introducing children to the theatre can be great fun for adults too. Grab the nearest tot and trot along to the **Little Angel Marionette Theatre**, or the floating fantasy of the **Puppet Theatre Barge** in Little Venice. **The Unicorn Theatre** offers the best range of children's theatre and the **Polka Children's Theatre** has some good shows.
Useful numbers Little Angel Marionette Theatre 【 *0171-226 1787;* Polka Children's Theatre 【 *0181-543 4888;* Puppet Theatre Barge 【 *0171-249 6876;* The Unicorn Theatre 【 *0171-836 3334.*

Deer at Richmond Park

SIGHTSEEING

For seeing the sights of London you can't beat the top of a double-decker bus *(see pp364–5)*. It's a cheap and easy way of entertaining children, and if they get restless you can always jump off the bus at the next stop. London's colourful ceremonies are detailed on pages 52–5.

Children will also enjoy such spectacles as the summer fun fairs in London's parks, the firework displays throughout London on

Boating lake near Winfield House in Regent's Park

Guy Fawkes Night (every 5 November) and the Christmas decorations in Regent Street and Trafalgar Square.

BEHIND THE SCENES

Older children in particular will love the opportunity to look "behind the scenes" and see how famous events or institutions are run.

If you have a brood of sports enthusiasts, you should visit the impressive Wembley Stadium, Twickenham Rugby Football Ground *(see p337)*, Lord's Cricket Ground *(p242)*, or the Wimbledon Lawn Tennis Museum *(p247)*.

For budding theatre buffs, the Royal National Theatre *(p184)*, the Royal Opera House *(p115)*, and Sadler's Wells *(p243)* all offer tours.

Other good buildings to visit include the Tower of London *(pp154–7)*, the Old Bailey law courts *(p147)* and the Houses of Parliament *(pp72–3)*.

If none of the above satisfy the children, the London Fire Brigade (0171-587 4063) and the London Diamond Centre (0171-629 5511) offer more unusual guided tours.

SURVIVAL
GUIDE

PRACTICAL INFORMATION

L ONDON HAS RESPONDED well to the demands of tourism. The range of facilities on offer to travellers, from cashpoint machines and bureaux de change to medical care and late-night transport, has expanded very quickly over the last few years. Whether or not you find London an expensive city will depend on the prevailing exchange rate between the pound and your own currency. It is known for its high hotel prices but even here there are budget options *(see pp272–5)*. Nor need you spend a lot on food if you choose carefully: for the price of a single meal at some Mayfair restaurants you could feed yourself, albeit modestly, for several days *(see pp306–7)*. The following tips will help you to make the most of your visit.

A walking tour of the City

AVOIDING THE CROWDS

M USEUMS AND GALLERIES can be crowded with school parties, particularly at the end of terms, so it might be best to plan your visit to start after 2.30pm during term-time. At other times of the year, visit early in the day and try and avoid weekends if you can.

Coach parties are another source of congestion. They do, however, tend to follow a predictable path. To miss them, it is wise to steer well clear of Westminster Abbey in the morning, and St Paul's around the afternoon. The Tower of London is usually busy all day.

A lot of London can be seen on foot. Brown signs indicate sights and facilities of interest to tourists. Look out, too, for the blue plaques attached to many buildings *(see p39)* showing where famous citizens have lived in the past.

GUIDED TOURS

A GOOD WAY to enjoy London, weather permitting, is from the top of a traditional open-topped double-decker bus. The **London Transport Sightseeing Tour** lasts around 90 minutes, and leaves every half-hour or so (10am–6pm) from various central locations. Commercial rivals, including **Frames Rickards**, **Harrod's** and **Cityrama**, offer tours lasting anything from an hour to a full day. You can buy your tickets just before boarding, or in advance (sometimes more cheaply) at Tourist Information Centres. Private tours can also be arranged with many companies, for instance **Tour Guides Ltd** or **British Tours.** The best tour guides receive a Blue Badge qualification from the London Tourist Board.

You can also explore London by joining a walking tour *(see p259)*. Themed tours range from pub crawls to a jaunt in the steps of Charles Dickens. Check for details of the walks at tourist offices, or in listings magazines *(see p324)*.

Cruise boats operate on the River Thames – an excellent way of travelling the breadth of London *(see pp60–5)*.

Useful numbers British Tours (0171-629 5267; Cityrama (0171-720 6663; Frames Rickards (0171-837 3111; Harrod's (0171-581 3603; London Transport Sightseeing Tour (0171-828 7395; Tour Guides Ltd (0171-495 5504; information for the disabled: (0171-495 5504.

OPENING HOURS

O PENING TIMES for sights have been listed in the *Area by Area* section of this book. Core visiting times in London are 10am–5pm daily, though many places stay open longer, especially in summer. Some major sights, like the British Museum, also stay open late on certain evenings. There are variations at weekends and public holidays. Opening times on Sundays are often restricted and a few museums close on Mondays.

Double-decker sightseeing bus with an open top

Queueing for a bus

ADMISSION CHARGES

MANY MAJOR sights, including London's cathedrals and some churches, have recently started either to charge for admission or to ask for a voluntary contribution upon entry. Charges vary greatly, from the cheap (only a few pounds for the Florence Nightingale Museum, *see p185*) to the more expensive (over £6.00 for the Tower of London, *see pp154–7*). The *Area by Area* listings tell you which museums charge for admission.

Some sights have reduced-price visiting times and offer concessions. It is best to telephone if you think you might be eligible.

Signposted information for tourists

ETIQUETTE

SMOKING IS NOW forbidden in many of London's public places. These include the bus and Underground transport systems, taxis, some British Rail stations, all theatres and most cinemas. Many London restaurants now have no-smoking sections. The great exception to the anti-smoking trend is pubs. ASH (Action on Smoking and Health) can give advice on smoke-free venues (0171-935 3519). Consult the Hotels and Restaurants listings (*pp278–85* and *pp295–305*) for details of places that cater for non-smokers.

Londoners queue for anything from shops, buses and post offices to theatre tickets, takeaway food and taxis. Anyone barging in will encounter frosty glares and acid comments. The exceptions are commuter rail and rush-hour tube services, when the laws of the jungle prevail.

The words "please", "thank you" and "sorry" are used regularly in London; people sometimes apologize if you step on their feet. It may seem unnecessary to thank a barman for simply doing his job, but it should improve your chances of decent service.

Like any big city, London can seem alienating to newcomers, but Londoners are usually helpful, and most will respond generously to your request for directions. The stalwart British bobby (police constable on the beat) is also always patiently ready to help stranded tourists (*see p346*).

DISABLED VISITORS

MOST SIGHTS HAVE access for wheelchairs. Again, this information is listed in the *Area by Area* section of this book, but phone first to check that your special needs are catered for. Useful guides to buy include *Access in London*, published by Nicholson, *London for All*, published by the London Tourist Board, and a booklet from London Transport called *Access to the Underground*, available at main tube stations. **Artsline** gives free information on facilities for disabled people at cultural events and venues. **Holiday Care Service** offers many facts on hotel facilities for the disabled. **Tripscope** provides free information on transport for the elderly and the disabled.

Useful numbers Artsline (0171-388 2227; Holiday Care Service (01293 774535; Tripscope (0181-994 9294.

Box for voluntary contributions in lieu of admission charges

TOURIST INFORMATION CENTRES

THESE OFFER ADVICE on anything from day trips and guided tours to accommodation.

Tourist information symbol

If you need tourist information, including free leaflets on current events, look for the large blue symbol at the following locations:

Heathrow Airport
Location The Underground station. Heathrow, 1, 2, 3. **Open** 8am–6pm daily.

Liverpool Street Station
EC2. **Map** 7 C5.
Location The Underground station. Liverpool Street. **Open** 8.15am–7pm Mon, 8.15am–6pm Tue–Sat, 8.15am–4.45pm Sun.

Selfridge's
400 Oxford St W1. **Map** 12 D2.
Location The basement.
Bond Street. **Open** 9.30am–7pm Fri–Wed, 9.30–8pm Thu.

Victoria Station
SW1. **Map** 20 F1.
Location The railway station forecourt. Victoria. **Open** 8am–7pm daily.

You can also telephone the London Tourist Board on (0171-971 0026.

Another service exists for information about the City of London area only (see pp143–59):

City of London Information Centre
St Paul's Churchyard EC4.
Map 15 A1. (0171-606 3030.
St Paul's. **Open** Apr–Oct: 9.30am–5pm daily; Nov–Mar: 9.30am–12.30pm Sat only.

Personal Security and Health

LONDON IS A LARGE city which, like any other, has had its recent share of urban problems. It has also often been a terrorist target, and London life is sometimes disrupted by security alerts. Nearly all of these turn out to be false alarms, but they should always still be taken seriously. Never hesitate to approach one of London's many police constables for assistance – they are trained to help the public with any of their problems.

SUITABLE PRECAUTIONS

THERE IS LITTLE likelihood that your stay in London will be blighted at all by the spectre of violent crime. Even in the run-down and rougher parts of the town, the risk of having your pocket picked, or your bag stolen, is not very great. It is far more likely to happen right in the middle of heaving shopping crowds in areas like Oxford Street or Camden Lock, or perhaps on a very busy tube platform.

Muggers and rapists prefer poorly lit or isolated places like back-streets, parks and unmanned railway stations. If you avoid these, especially at night, or travel round in a group, you should manage to stay out of danger.

Pickpockets and thieves pose a much more immediate problem. Keep your valuables securely concealed. If you carry a handbag or a case, never let it out of your sight – particularly in restaurants, theatres and cinemas, where it is not unknown for bags to vanish from between the feet of their owners.

Although London has a small population of homeless people, they do not present a threat. The very worst they are likely to trouble you with is a request for spare change.

WOMEN TRAVELLING ALONE

UNLIKE SOME European cities, it is considered quite normal in London for women to eat out on their own or go out in a group, perhaps to a pub or a bar. However, risks do exist, and caution is essential. Stick to well-lit streets with plenty of traffic. Many women avoid travelling on the tube late at

Mounted police

night, and it is best not to travel alone on trains. If you have no companions, try to find an occupied carriage – preferably with more than one group of people. Best of all, take a taxi *(see p367)*.

Many forms of self-defence are restricted in the UK, and it is illegal for anyone to carry various offensive weapons in public places. These include knives, coshes, guns and tear-gas canisters, all of which are strictly prohibited. Personal alarm systems are permitted.

PERSONAL PROPERTY

TAKE SENSIBLE precautions with personal property at all times. Make sure that your possessions are adequately insured before you arrive, since it is difficult for visitors to arrange once in the UK.

Don't carry your valuables around with you; take just as much cash as you need, and leave the rest in a hotel safe or lock it up in your suitcase. Traveller's cheques are the safest method of carrying large amounts of money *(see p349)*. Never leave bags or briefcases unattended in tube or train stations – they will either be stolen or suspected of being bombs and therefore cause a security alert.

Report all lost items to the nearest police station (get the necessary paperwork if you plan an insurance claim). Each of the main rail stations has a lost property office on the premises. If you do leave something on a bus or tube, it may be better to call in at the address given below rather than to telephone.

Lost Property

Lost Property Offices
London Transport Lost Property Office, 200 Baker Street W1. *Open weekday mornings only.* 0171-486 2496, enquiries should be made in person; Black Cab Lost Property Office. 0171-833 0996.

Woman Police Constable

Traffic Police Officer

Police Constable

Typical London police car

London ambulance

London fire engine

EMERGENCIES

LONDON'S EMERGENCY police, ambulance and fire services are on call 24 hours a day. These, like the London hospital casualty services, are strictly for emergencies only.

Services are also available to offer help in emergencies, for instance in case of rape. If there is no appropriate number in the Crisis Information box *(see right)* you may be able to obtain one from the directory enquiries service (dial 142 or 192). Police stations and also hospitals with casualty wards are shown on the Street Finder maps *(see pp368–9)*.

MEDICAL TREATMENT

VISITORS TO LONDON from all countries outside the European Community (EC) are strongly advised to take out medical insurance against the cost of any emergency hospital care, specialists' fees and repatriation. Emergency treatment in a British casualty ward is free, but additional medical care may be costly.

Residents of the EC and nationals of other European and Commonwealth countries are entitled to receive free medical treatment under the National Health Service (NHS). Before travelling, you should obtain a form confirming that your country of origin has adequate reciprocal health arrangements with Britain. Even without this form, free medical treatment can still be obtained if you offer proof of nationality, but there are exceptions for certain kinds of treatment and medical insurance is always advisable.

If you need to see a dentist while staying in London, you will have to pay at least a small amount. This will vary, depending on your entitlement to NHS treatment, and whether you can find an NHS dentist. Various institutions offer 24-hour dental treatment *(see addresses right)*, but if you wish to visit a private dental surgeon, try looking in the Yellow Pages *(see p352)*.

MEDICINES

YOU CAN BUY most medical supplies from chemists and supermarkets throughout London. However, many medicines are available only with a doctor's prescription. If you are likely to require drugs, either bring your own supplies or get your doctor to write out the generic name of the drug, as opposed to the brand name. If you are not eligible to receive NHS treatment, you will be charged at the medicine's cost price; remember to get a receipt to support any medical insurance claim you may wish to make.

Boots, a chain of chemists' shops

CRISIS INFORMATION

Police, fire and ambulance services
Dial 999 or 112. Calls are free.

Emergency Dental Care
0171-837 3646 (24-hour phoneline).

London Rape Crisis Centre
0171-837 1600 (24-hour phoneline).

Samaritans
0171-734 2800 (24-hour helpline). For all emotional problems. Check in local telephone directory for nearest branch.

Chelsea and Westminster Hospital
369 Fulham Rd SW10. **Map** 18 F4.
0181-746 8000.

St Thomas's Hospital
Lambeth Palace Rd SE1.
Map 13 C5. 0171-928 9292.

University College Hospital
Gower St WC1. **Map** 5 A4.
0171-387 9300.

Medical Express (Private Casualty Clinic)
117A Harley St W1.
Map 4 E5. 0171-499 1991.
Treatment guaranteed within 30 minutes, but a fee is charged for consultations and tests.

Eastman Dental School
256 Gray's Inn Rd WC1.
Map 6 D4. 0171-837 3646.
Private and NHS dental care.

Guy's Hospital Dental School
St Thomas's St SE1. **Map** 15 B4.
0171-955 5000.

Late-opening chemists
Contact your local London police station for a comprehensive list.

Bliss Chemist
5 Marble Arch W1. **Map** 11 C2.
0171-723 6116.
Open until midnight daily.

Boots the Chemist
Piccadilly Circus W1. **Map** 13 A3.
0171-734 6126. **Open** 8.30am–8pm Mon–Fri, 9am–8pm Sat, noon–6pm Sun.

Banking and Local Currency

V ISITORS TO LONDON will find that banks usually
offer them the best rates of exchange. Privately
owned bureaux de change have variable exchange
rates, and care should be taken to check the small
print details relating to commission and minimum
charges before completing any transaction. Bureaux
de change do, however, have the advantage of
staying open long after the banks have closed.

Cashpoint machine

BANKING

B ANKING HOURS vary in
London. The minimum
opening hours are, without
exception, 9.30am–3.30pm
Mon–Fri, but many stay open
longer than this, especially
those in the centre of London.
Saturday morning opening is
also more common now. All
banks are closed on public
holidays (known as bank
holidays in the UK, *see p59*),
and some may close early on
the day before a holiday.

Many major banks in London
have cashpoint machines that
will allow you to obtain money
by using your credit card and
a PIN (personal identification
number); some machines have
clear computerized instructions
in several languages. American
Express cards may be used
in 24-hour Lloyds Bank and
Royal Bank of Scotland cash
machines in London, but you
must arrange to have your
PIN linked by code to your
personal account before you
leave home. There is a 2%
charge for each transaction.
Besides the main clearing
banks, good places to change
your traveller's cheques are
Thomas Cook and **American
Express** offices, or the bank-
operated bureaux de change,
which can usually be found
at airports and major railway
stations. Don't forget to bring
along a passport if you want
to change cheques.

BUREAUX DE CHANGE

American Express
6 Haymarket SW1. **Map** 13 A3.
█ *0171-930 4411.*

Chequepoint
13–15 Davies St W1.
Map 12 E2. █ *0171-409 1122.*

**Exchange
International**
Victoria Station SW1.
Map 20 E1. █ *0171-630 1107.*

**Thomas
Cook**
45 Berkeley St
W1. **Map** 12 F3.
█ *0171-408
4179.*

**Ways of paying
accepted at
bureaux
de change**

You can find facilities for
changing money all over the
city centre, at main stations
and tourist information offices,
and in most large stores.
Chequepoint is one of the
largest bureaux de change
in Britain; **Exchange International** has a number of
useful late-opening branches.
Since, in London, there is no
consumer organization to
regulate the activities of the
privately run bureaux de
change, their prices need
to be examined carefully.

CREDIT CARDS

I T IS WORTH bringing a credit
card with you, particularly
for hotel and restaurant bills,
shopping, car hire and booking tickets by telephone. Visa
is the most widely accepted
card in London, followed by
Mastercard (its local name is
Access), American Express,
Diners Club and JCB.
It is possible to obtain cash
advances (up to your credit
limit) with an internationally
recognized credit card at any
London bank displaying the
appropriate card sign. You
will be charged the credit card
company's interest rate, which
appears on your statement
with the amount advanced.

MAIN BANKS IN LONDON

England's main clearing banks (those whose dealings are
processed through a single clearing house) are Barclays,
Lloyds, Midland and National Westminster (NatWest). Each
bank can be easily identified by a distinctively styled sign
bearing its name. The Royal Bank of Scotland also has a
number of branches in London with exchange facilities.
Commissions charged by each bank for changing money
vary, so check before going ahead with your transaction.

CASH AND TRAVELLER'S CHEQUES

BRITAIN'S CURRENCY is the pound sterling (£), which is divided into 100 pence (p). Since there are no exchange controls in Britain, there is no limit to how much cash you may import or export.

Traveller's cheques are the safest alternative to carrying large amounts of cash. Keep receipts from your traveller's cheques separately, and also make a note of offices where you will be able to obtain a refund if the cheques are lost or stolen. Some banks issue traveller's cheques free of commission to established customers, but the normal rate is about 1%. It is sensible to change some money into sterling before arriving in Britain, as queues at airport exchange offices can be very long. Do obtain some smaller denominations: shopkeepers may refuse to accept £20 notes for small purchases.

English bank notes of all denominations always feature the Queen's head on one side.

Bank Notes

English notes used in the UK are £5, £10, £20 and £50. Scotland has its own notes which, despite being legal tender throughout the UK, are not always accepted.

£50 note

£20 note

£10 note

£5 note

Coins of the Realm

Coins in circulation are £1, 50p, 20p, 10p, 5p, 2p and 1p (shown here at actual sizes). They all have the Queen's head on one side. Some, such as the 10p and 5p, have recently been changed.

1 pound (£1)

50 pence (50p)

20 pence (20p)

10 pence (10p)

5 pence (5p)

2 pence (2p)

1 penny (1p)

Using London's Phones

Y OU WILL FIND A PHONEBOX on many street corners in central London and in every British Rail station. Rather than searching your pockets to find loose change to make a call, you can buy prepaid phonecards. British Telecom (BT) and Mercury phonecards both come in £2, £4 and £10 denominations and can be purchased from some newsagents and post offices.

Old BT phonebox

New BT phonebox

Phoneboxes
There are three different types of phonebox in London: old and new BT phoneboxes, and Mercury phoneboxes. All Mercury public phones will accept Mercury phonecards and credit cards but not coins. Some BT phones accept BT phonecards and credit cards, some only BT phonecards, and some are solely coin-operated.

Mercury phonebox

USING A BT CARD PHONE

1 Lift the receiver and wait for a dialling tone.

2 Insert a BT phonecard, green side up and in the direction of the arrows on the card.

3 The display shows how many units are left. The minimum charge is one unit.

4 Some BT phones accept credit cards as well as phonecards. Insert, with the black stripe to the right and away from you, and slide through.

5 Dial the number and wait to be connected.

6 When your phonecard runs out you will hear a rapid bleeping noise. To continue, press the button and the old card will come out. Remove it and put a new card in.

7 If you want to make a further call, do not replace the receiver, press the follow-on call button.

USING A MERCURY PHONE

1 Lift the receiver and wait for a dialling tone.

2 Insert a Mercury phonecard, with the picture face up, in the direction of the arrows on the card.

Credit card slot

3 The display shows how much credit is left.

4 Mercury phones accept credit cards as well as phonecards. Insert a credit card, with black stripe face up on the left, and slide through.

5 Dial the number and wait to be connected.

Mercury card slot

6 When the phonecard runs out, it automatically ejects.

7 If you want to make a further call, do not replace the receiver, press the follow-on call button.

BT phonecards come from shops with this sign.

Some Mercury cards are now collectors' items.

Reaching the Right Number

• Central London areas use the prefix 0171.
• Outer areas use 0181.

To ring Greenwich from Covent Garden, for example, you must first dial 0181; for Covent Garden from Greenwich, dial 0171.

• Internal directory enquiries are on 192.
• If you have any problems contacting a number, call the operator on 100.

Inland calls are charged according to the time of day. They are most expensive from 9am to 1pm on weekdays. Cheap rate applies before 8am or after 6pm on weekdays, and all day at weekends.

• To make an international call, dial 00 followed by the country code (USA and Canada: 1; Australia: 61; New Zealand: 64), area code and the number.
• The international operator is on 155.
• International directory enquiries are on 153. You need a phonecard with at least £2 credit to make an international call.

Cheap times for overseas calls vary from country to country, but in general they tend to be at weekends and in evenings.

• **In an emergency, dial 999 or 112.**

Using a BT Coin Phone

1 Lift the receiver and wait for a dialling tone.

2 Insert any combination of the coins below (the illuminated display shows the minimum amount you must put in).

3 Dial the number and wait to be connected.

4 The display indicates how much money you have put in and the credit left. A rapid bleeping noise means your money has run out. Insert more coins.

5 If you want to make a further call, do not replace the receiver, press the follow-on call button.

6 When you've finished speaking, replace the receiver. Any coins that were not used will be in the chute. Pay phones do not give change, so use 10p and 20p coins.

£1   50p   20p   10p

Sending a Letter

Post Office sign

BESIDES MAIN post offices, London has many sub post offices, which often double as newsagents. These are open from 9am until 5.30pm on weekdays, and 9am–12.30pm on Saturdays. London's most central post office is in King Edward Street EC1A 1AA (Map 9 A3), where there is a *poste restante*. Stamps can be bought from outlets with the "stamps sold here" sign. First-class

Shops sell stamps

stamps can be used for letters and cards to the European Community. Always include the post code when writing to a UK address. Main post offices are shown on the *Street Finder* maps (see pp368–9).

Books of 10 stamps

UK Post

Letters within the UK can be sent first or second class. First class is more expensive, but most first class letters reach their UK destinations the following day (except Sunday).

**Second class   First class
stamp   stamp**

Aerogrammes go first class anywhere in the world. They cost the same regardless of destination.

New-style post box

First class and overseas mail has its own slot on many post boxes.

Initials show who was monarch when the post box was built.

EXTRA INFORMATION

SHOULD YOU require any services that are not listed in this guide, try consulting one of London's telephone directories. The Yellow Pages comprehensively lists services throughout London, and should be available at your hotel. **Talking Pages** is a telephone service operated by British Telecom. It gives you the telephone number of someone who offers the service you want in any part of London (or the UK) that you specify.

Directory enquiries (dial 192) can be dialled free from payphones and will give you any telephone number in the directory. You need to know the name and address of the person or business.

CUSTOMS AND IMMIGRATION

A VALID PASSPORT is needed to enter the UK. Visitors from the EC, the US, Canada, Australia and New Zealand do not require a visa to enter, nor are any inoculations or vaccinations necessary.

When you arrive at one of Britain's airports or seaports you will find separate queues at immigration control – one for European Community (EC) nationals, several others for everyone else.

European union has led to changes in UK customs and immigration policy. Travellers entering the UK from outside the EC still have to pass through customs channels: red exit routes for people carrying goods on which a duty has to be paid; green routes for those with no payment to make (nothing to "declare"). If, however, you are travelling from within the EC you will find that these have been replaced by a blue channel – EC residents no longer have to "declare" goods. Random checks will still be made to guard against the likes of drug traffickers.

EC residents are no longer entitled to a VAT (Value Added Tax) refund on goods bought in the UK. Travellers from outside the EC can obtain one if they leave the UK within three months of the purchase date *(see p310).*

STUDENT TRAVELLERS

AN ISIC CARD (International Student Identity Card) entitles full-time students to discounts on things from travel to sports events. For students from the US, the ISIC also includes some medical cover,

though this may not be sufficient on its own. If you don't have an ISIC, it can be obtained (with proof of student status) from the **University of London Union** (ULU) or branches of **STA Travel**. ULU offers many social and sports facilities to valid union card holders and reciprocating educational establishments. **International Youth Hostel Federation** membership is also worth having for cheap accommodation in London.

EC nationals do not require a permit to work in the UK. Commonwealth citizens under the age of 27 are allowed to do part-time work in the UK for up to two years. Visiting students from the US can get a blue card which enables them to work for up to six months (you must get this before you arrive). **BUNAC** is a student club organizing work exchange schemes for students from Australia, the United States, Canada and Jamaica.

International Student Identity Card

USEFUL ADDRESSES AND TELEPHONE NUMBERS

BUNAC
16 Bowling Green Lane EC1.
Map 6 E4. (0171-251 3472.

International Youth Hostel Federation
(0707-332 487.

STA Travel
74 and 86 Old Brompton Rd SW7.
Map 18 F2. (0171-937 9962.

Talking Pages
(0800-600 9000.

University of London Union
Malet St WC1. **Map** 5 A5.
(0171-580 9551.

NEWSPAPERS, TELEVISION AND RADIO

LONDON'S PRINCIPAL news-paper is the *Evening Standard*, available from about midday, Monday to Friday.

PUBLIC TOILETS

Although many older-style, supervised public conveniences still exist, these have largely been replaced by coin-operated "Superloos". Young children should never use these devices on their own – they will find it almost impossible to operate the inner door handle.

1 If the green "vacant" light is shown, insert the required fee. The door located on your left will slide open.

"Vacant" light   Coin slot

2 Once inside, the door slides closed and locks.

3 To exit, pull down the inner door handle.

London newspaper stand

The Friday edition is worth getting for its listings section and reviews. International newspapers are sold in many newsagents. The *International Herald Tribune* is available on the day of issue; others may appear a day or more later. Four television channels can be seen with conventional receiving equipment: two run by the BBC (called BBC1 and BBC2), and two independent (ITV and Channel 4). Satellite and cable networks are both available in the UK, and some hotels have installed these facilities for their guests.

The BBC's local and national radio stations are supplemented by many independent local companies, like London's Capital Radio (194m/1548kHz MW; 95.8mHz FM), a pop music station.

INTERNATIONAL NEWSAGENTS

Gray's Inn News
50 Theobald's Rd WC1. **Map** 5 C5.
[0171-405 5241.

A Moroni and Son
68 Old Compton Street W1.
Map 13 A2. [0171-437 2847.

D S Radford
61 Fleet St EC4. **Map** 14 E1.
[0171-583 7166.

ELECTRICAL ADAPTORS

T HE ELECTRICAL supply in London is 240V AC. Plugs have three square pins and take fuses of 3, 5 and 13 amps. Visitors will need an adaptor for appliances; this is best bought before leaving home. Most hotels have two-pronged European-style sockets for shavers only.

Standard British plug

LONDON TIME

D IAL 123 TO CHECK the time on London's 24-hour **Speaking Clock** service. Clocks change for summer and winter time.

CONVERSION CHART

O FFICIALLY THE metric system is used, but imperial measures are still common.

Imperial to metric
1 inch = 2.5 centimetres
1 foot = 30 centimetres
1 mile = 1.6 kilometres
1 ounce = 28 grams
1 pound = 454 grams
1 pint = 0.6 litre
1 gallon = 4.6 litres

Metric to imperial
1 millimetre = 0.04 inch
1 centimetre = 0.4 inch
1 metre = 3 feet 3 inches
1 kilometre = 0.6 mile
1 gram = 0.04 ounce
1 kilogram = 2.2 pounds

EMBASSIES AND CONSULATES

Australian High Commission
Australia House, The Strand WC2. **Map** 13 C2.
[0171-379 4334.

Canadian High Commission
Haut Commissariat du Canada, Macdonald House,1 Grosvenor Square W1. **Map** 12 D2.
[0171-258 6600.

New Zealand High Commission
New Zealand House,
80 Haymarket SW1. **Map** 13 A3.
[0171-930 8422.

United States Embassy
24 Grosvenor Square W1.
Map 12 D2. [0171-499 9000.

RELIGIOUS SERVICES

T HE FOLLOWING organizations can help you find a place to worship.

Church of England
St Paul's Cathedral EC4.
Map 15 A2. [0171-248 2705.

Roman Catholic
Westminster Cathedral,
Victoria St SW1. **Map** 20 F1.
[0171-834 7452.

Jewish
Liberal Jewish Synagogue,
28 St John's Wood Rd NW8.
Map 3 A3. [0171-286 5181.
United Synagogue (Orthodox)
Woburn House, Tavistock Square WC1. **Map** 5 B4.
[0171-387 4300.

Moslem
Islamic Cultural Centre,
146 Park Rd NW8. **Map** 3 B3.
[0171-724 3363.

Baptist
London Baptist Association,
1 Merchant St E3.
[0181-980 6818.

Quakers
Religious Society of Friends,
173–7 Euston Rd NW1.
Map 5 A4. [0171-387 3601.

Evangelical
Whitefield House, 186
Kennington Park Rd SE11.
Map 22 E4. [0171-582 0228.

Buddhist
The Buddhist Society,
58 Eccleston Sq SW1.
Map 20 F2. [0171-834 5858.

**St Martin-in-the-Fields,
Trafalgar Square *(see p102)***

GETTING TO LONDON

L ONDON IS ONE of Europe's central routing points for international air and sea travel. By air, travellers face a bewildering choice of carriers serving North America, Europe and Australasia. Stiff competition on some routes means that low fares are occasionally introduced to attract new passengers. British Airways has a Concorde service, boasting the fastest flights in the world, between London and New York or Washington. Long-distance sea travel is, however, a different proposition as few transatlantic liners operate these days.

Cunard offers the only regular services and doubt looms even over these. There are efficient and regular ferry services from Europe, but these too will be subject to change once the Channel Tunnel opens. About 20 passenger and car ferry routes, served by large ferries, hovercrafts, jetfoils and catamarans, cross the North Sea and the English Channel to Britain. When it is eventually operating at full capacity the Channel Tunnel will provide a new, efficient high-speed train link running between Europe and the UK.

Concorde

AIR TRAVEL

T HE MAIN United States airlines offering scheduled flights to London include Delta, United, American Airlines and USAir. Two major British operators are **British Airways** and **Virgin Atlantic**. From Canada, the main carriers are Canadian Airlines (now incorporating WardAir) and Air Canada. Fierce competition for these prestigious transatlantic routes means that there are some excellent deals available. The flight time from New York is about six and a half hours (less on Concorde), and from Los Angeles about 10 hours.

There are regular scheduled flights to London from all the major European cities, as well as from numerous other parts of the UK itself, including northern England, Scotland and Northern Ireland.

The choice of carriers from Australasia is enormous. Well over 20 airlines share around two dozen different routes. Journey times can vary from just over 20 hours on a big modern jet to over 100 hours via China. The more indirect your route, the cheaper the fare; but remember that three days' jet travel is bound to be stressful. **Qantas**, **Air New Zealand** and **British Airways** may be your first thoughts for comfort and speed, but all the Far Eastern operators and several European airlines offer interesting alternatives.

Getting a good deal
Cheap deals are available from good travel agents and package operators, and are advertised in newspapers and travel magazines. Airlines will quote you the regular price, but they often reduce this if seats are unsold. Students, senior citizens and regular or business travellers may well be able to obtain a discount. Children under two (who do not occupy a separate seat) pay 10% of the adult fare; older children up to 12 also travel at lower fares.

Ticket types
APEX (Advanced purchase) tickets can be good buys, but they need to be booked up to a month in advance. They are subject to restrictions and cannot be changed without penalty. There are usually

minimum (and maximum) length of stay requirements. Fares on scheduled flights are available through specialist agents at much lower rates. Charter flights offer even cheaper seats, but have less flexible departure times and can be less punctual.

If you book a cheap deal with a discount agent, check whether you will get a refund if the agent or operator ceases trading, and don't part with the full fare until you see the ticket. You will have to pay a deposit. Check with the relevant airline to ensure that your seat has been confirmed.

AIRLINE NUMBERS

Major Carriers

Air New Zealand
📞 *0181-741 2299.*

British Airways
📞 *0181-897 4000.*

Qantas
📞 *0181-846 0321.*

Virgin Atlantic
📞 *0293 747747.*

Discount ticket agents

ATAB (Air Travel Advisory Bureau)
This regulatory organization will recommend a discount agency.
📞 *0171-636 5000.*

Lukas Travel *(European travel)*
📞 *0171-734 9174.*

Major Travel *(worldwide travel)*
📞 *0171-485 7017.*

Passenger jet landing at Heathrow

TRAVELLING BY RAIL

LONDON HAS EIGHT main rail stations at which InterCity express trains terminate (for information, call: 0171-928 5100). These are scattered in a ring around the city centre *(see pp358–9)*. Paddington in west London serves the West Country, Wales and the South Midlands; Liverpool Street in the City covers East Anglia and Essex. In north London, Euston, St Pancras and King's Cross serve northern and central Britain. In the south, Charing Cross, Victoria and Waterloo serve the whole of southern England and are also the termini for travel by ferry and train from Europe.

All these stations have had recent facelifts and are now smart and modern with many facilities for the traveller, such as bureaux de change and shops selling books and

Station concourse at Liverpool Street

BR information point *(see p345)*

confectionery. There are bars and cafés serving a range of refreshments but, like the buffet service on some long-distance trains, these can be very expensive.

Information about British Rail (BR) services is now easy to find; most rail stations have an information point detailing times, prices and destinations.

In addition, constantly updated details of services are either screened on to monitors scattered around the stations or written up on information boards located at platform entrances. BR staff are usually helpful and courteous.

If your ferry ticket does not include the price of rail travel to the centre of London, tickets can be bought at the clearly signposted ticket offices or automatic machines *(see p366)*. You may decide to buy a Travelcard from the first day you are in London *(see p360)*.

COACH SERVICES

THE MAIN COACH station in London is on Buckingham Palace Road (about 10 minutes' walk from Victoria railway station). You can travel to London by coach from many European cities, but the majority of services travelling through London are from within the UK. National Express run to about 1,000 British destinations, but other companies depart from this station, too. Coach travel is cheaper than the railway, but journeys are longer and arrival times can be unpredictable if there are problems on the roads. National Express Rapide coaches can be very comfortable and normally have sophisticated facilities. Green Line buses operate within 40 miles (64 km) of London.

Coach numbers Green Line 【 *0181-668 7261*; Rapide 【 *0171-730 0202*.

CROSSING THE CHANNEL BY SEA

Britain's sea links with Europe were finally joined by a landlink in late 1994 when the Channel Tunnel opened. At present a net-work of ferry services operates between 13 British ports and over 20 Continental ports. Many of the vessels on these routes have recently been refitted. The ferry services presently on offer may change dramatically, depending on the impact of the tunnel. Ferry crossings from the Continent are operated by **Sealink Stena**, **P&O European Ferries**, **Sally Line**, the **Olau Line** and **Brittany Ferries**. Fast hovercraft services between Dover and Calais or Boulogne are run by **Hoverspeed**. A **Seacat** service crosses between Folkestone and Boulogne *(see pp358–9)*. From 1995 another will operate between Newhaven and Dieppe. The shortest crossings are not necessarily

Cross-channel ferry

the cheapest – you pay for both the speed of your journey and the convenience. If you are travelling with your car you will need to check out the terms of your insurance cover.

Useful numbers Brittany Ferries 【 *01705 827701*; Hoverspeed 【 *01304 240241*; P&O European Ferries 【 *0181-575 8555*; Sally Line 【 *01843 595522*; Seacat 【 *01304 240241*; Sealink Stena 【 *01233 647047*.

London's Airports

Passenger jet

L ONDON'S TWO MAIN airports, Heathrow and Gatwick, are supported by Luton, Stansted and London City airport *(see pp358–9)*. Heathrow and Gatwick are both well connected with the city centre and have a range of facilities, from banks and bureaux de change to hotels, shops and restaurants. Find out which airport you'll be landing at so you can plan the last stages of your journey.

Customs channels at Heathrow

HEATHROW (LHR)

H EATHROW IN WEST London (airport information 0181-759 4321) is the world's busiest international airport. Mainly scheduled long-haul aircraft land there, and a fifth terminal is being planned to cope with the rising levels of air traffic to the UK. Money exchanging facilities are also found in all terminals.

All of the four terminals are linked to the Underground system by a variety of moving walkways, passageways and lifts. Just follow the clearly marked directions posted throughout the terminals and

you can't go wrong. London Underground runs a regular service on the Piccadilly line. The tube journey into central London normally takes about 40 minutes (add 10 minutes more from terminal 4).

Regular Airbus services travel from Heathrow into the

Signs for exits in Heathrow

centre of London. Services stop outside each terminal. The Airbus costs more than the Underground, but it involves less struggling with luggage. A taxi into central London takes about 45 minutes and costs about £25.

AIRPORT HOTELS

Forte Crest
(0181-759 2323.

Holiday Inn
(01895-445555.

Sheraton Skyline
See p285.

London Heathrow Hilton
(0181-759 7755.

Terminal 3, for long-haul flights (apart from British Airways) and SAS flights to Scandinavia, has 24-hour exchange facilities.

To M4 and A4 roads for London

Terminal 1 deals with British airlines' flights to Europe and within Britain.

PLAN OF HEATHROW AIRPORT
When leaving London be sure to check which terminal you need. Terminal 4 is some way from the others and therefore has its own Underground station.

Heathrow terminals 1, 2 and 3 station

Terminal 2 handles most European services of non-British airlines.

Heathrow terminal 4 station

Terminal 3 Departures

KEY

- ⊖ Underground station
- 🚌 Bus terminal (local services)
- Coach station
- P Short-term parking
- ⇥ Direction of traffic flow

Terminal 4 serves Concorde, British Airways intercontinental flights, and some flights to Paris, Athens and Amsterdam.

A30 road

Sterling Hotel

GATWICK (LGW)

GATWICK AIRPORT (airport information: 0293-535 353) is located south of London, on the Surrey–Sussex border. Unlike Heathrow, it handles scheduled and charter flights.

A large volume of package holiday traffic passes through Gatwick. This can cause long queues at immigration desks and security checks, so make sure to leave plenty of time in which to check in on your return journey if you want to avoid being rushed. Make

PLAN OF GATWICK AIRPORT

There are two terminals at Gatwick: north and south. They are linked by a free monorail service, and the journey between them takes only a couple of minutes. Near the British Rail station entrance (which, if you are not arriving by rail, is clearly marked) you will find boards that state which terminal serves your carrier.

Gatwick Express

Trains to London

Services to Victoria Station every 15 minutes; hourly throughout the night

Platform indicator for express railway service to London

certain, too, that you know which terminal your flight home leaves from.

Gatwick has fewer business facilities than Heathrow. On the positive side, however, it has a number of 24-hour restaurants, banks, exchange

KEY

⬛	British Rail station
🚌	Coach station
P	Short-term parking
🚔	Police station
➡	Direction of traffic flow

facilities and duty-free shops located in both the north and south terminals.

Gatwick has convenient rail links with the capital, including BR's Thameslink. The Gatwick Express train provides a fast, regular service into Victoria station. Allow about half an hour for the journey, but check *(see p366)* to find out off-peak variations.

Driving from Gatwick to central London can take a couple of hours. A taxi will cost from £50 to £60.

AIRPORT HOTELS

Chequers Thistle
📞 *0293-786992.*

Forte Crest
📞 *0293-567070.*

Hilton International
📞 *0293-518080.*

(Map labels: To A23 and M23 roads for London; Hilton International; To A23 and M23 roads for London; Railway line; A23 road; Inter-terminal monorail link; Forte Crest Hotel; Taxi rank; Arrivals pick-up (lower level); Coach station and arrivals pick-up (lower level); North terminal; South terminal)

OTHER AIRPORTS SERVING LONDON

Luton and Stansted airports, both located to the north of London, are at present used principally by charter flights. Both airports have future plans for expansion. From Luton, connecting buses take passengers to the rail station, and from there trains run to King's Cross station. Alternatively, take a coach to Victoria. The half-hourly Stansted Express train terminates at Liverpool Street station and there is a regular and efficient coach service to Victoria.

The relatively new London City Airport, in Docklands, is designed mainly for business travellers and operates short flights to Europe. It has particularly good business facilities and is only a short taxi (or helicopter) journey from the City.

One of two large hotels at Gatwick

Arriving in London

THIS MAP SHOWS the bus, rail and Underground links between London's airports and its mainline railway stations. It also shows rail connections not only between these stations and the southeastern seaports, but those linking London with the rest of the UK. Travel information, including journey times for rail, bus and coach services, is listed in each information box. Details of how to reach London by car from the seaports are also given.

KEY

✈ Airport see pp356–7

⛴ Seaport see p355

🚄 British Rail see p366

🚌 Coach link see p355

🚍 Bus service see pp364–5

🔵 Underground link see pp362–3

— British Rail link see p355

— British Rail Thameslink see p366

— Piccadilly line see p356

— Bus link see p355

🚄 **East Midlands**
Links with St Pancras station.
Leicester (1 hr 10 mins),
Nottingham (1 hr 45 mins),
Sheffield (2 hrs 20 mins).

🚄 **West Midlands, the North West and West Scotland**
Links with Euston station.
Birmingham (1 hr 40 mins),
Glasgow (5 hrs),
Liverpool (2 hrs 40mins),
Manchester (2 hrs 30 mins).

🚄 **The West and South Wales**
Links with Paddington station.
Bristol (1 hr 45 mins), **Cardiff** (2 hrs), **Oxford** (55 mins), **Plymouth** (3 hrs 30 mins).

✈ **HEATHROW**
Underground service to the city centre every 5 minutes. Bus services to the city centre.
🔵 **Piccadilly line** through city centre (40 mins).
🚍 **Airbus** A1 to **Victoria** (1 hr).
🚍 **Airbus** A2 to **Russell Sq** (1 hr).

🚄 **The South**
Links with Waterloo station.
Winchester (1 hr 5 mins).

⛴ **SOUTHAMPTON**
Ferry links with **Cherbourg**.
Take M3 motorway for the city centre.

⛴ **PORTSMOUTH**
Ferry links with **Caen, St Malo, Le Havre** and **Cherbourg**.
Take A3 trunk road for the city centre.

N

0 kilometres 1

0 miles 0.5

Regent's Park and Marylebone

Euston 🚄

Soho and Trafalgar Square

Paddington 🚄 🔵

Piccadilly Circus 🔵

Kensington and Holland Park

South Kensington and Knightsbridge

Piccadilly and St James's

Victoria 🚄 🔵

Chelsea

Victoria Coach Station

National Express operates regular coach services throughout the UK.

✈ The North East and Scotland
Links with King's Cross station.
Aberdeen (7 hrs), **Durham**
(3 hrs), **Edinburgh** (4 hrs 30 mins),
Leeds (2 hrs 30 mins),
York (2 hrs).

✈ STANSTED
Bus and train services to the city
centre every 30 mins. Underground from **Tottenham Hale**.
🚄 to **Liverpool Street** (45 mins).
🚌 **National Express** to Victoria
(1 hr 25 mins).

✈ LUTON
Direct bus services. Train services
from **Luton town** to the centre of
London every 15–30 mins. Bus
services to **Luton railway
station**.
🚄 to **King's Cross** (30 mins).
🚌 **Greenline** to **Victoria**
(1 hr 15 mins).

**Tottenham
Hale** 🚄 ⊖

London's airports have bus, coach
and rail links with the capital.

King's Cross 🚄 ⊖

🚄 The East
Links with Liverpool Street station.
Colchester (1 hr), **Norwich** (2 hrs).

Pancras 🚄 ⊖

*omsbury
d Fitzrovia*

*Holborn
and the
Inns of Court*

*Smithfield
and
Spitalfields*

🚢 FELIXSTOWE
Ferry links with **Zeebrugge**. Take
A45 and A12 trunk roads
for the city centre.

🚢 HARWICH
Ferry links with **Hook of Holland**.
Take A120 and A12 trunk roads
for the city centre.

*ent Garden
and
e Strand*

Liverpool Street 🚄 ⊖

The City

Blackfriars 🚄 ⊖

Charing Cross 🚄 ⊖

*South
Bank*

*Southwark
and
Bankside*

Hovercraft crossing the Channel

*iitehall
and
minster*

Waterloo 🚄 ⊖

🚄 The South East
Links with Charing Cross station.
Canterbury West (1 hr 40 mins).

🚢 RAMSGATE
Ferry services to **Dunkirk**. Take
A253 and A299 trunk roads,
then M2 motorway for
the city centre.

🚢 DOVER
Ferry, catamaran and hovercraft
(summer only) links with **Calais**,
jetfoil links with **Ostend**.
Take A2 (M2) motorway
for the city centre.

✈ GATWICK
Bus and train services to the city
centre every 15–30 mins.
🚄 to **Victoria** (30–35 mins).
🚌 **Flightline** to **Victoria** (2 hrs).

🚄 The South and South East
Links with Victoria station.
Brighton (55 mins), **Canterbury
East** (1 hr 30 mins).

🚢 NEWHAVEN
Ferry links with **Dieppe**.
Take A22 trunk road for the
city centre.

🚢 FOLKESTONE
Catamaran links with **Boulogne**.
Take M20 motorway for the
city centre.

GETTING AROUND LONDON

Londons's public transport system is one of the busiest and largest in Europe, and has all the over-crowding problems to match. The worst and busiest times to travel are in the two rush hours, between 8am and 9.30am or later, from 4.30pm to 6.30pm. Within London and its suburbs, most of the public transport is organized by London Regional Transport (LRT). This consists of various types of bus, the

Routemaster bus

Underground system, and Network SouthEast (an overland train system which is operated by British Rail). For any information you require about fares, routes and timings of the various transport services, ring 0171-222 1234 *(see p345)*, or visit one of the LRT Travel Information Centres which are to be found at Euston, King's Cross and Victoria main-line stations as well as at Oxford Circus, Piccadilly Circus and Heathrow Airport.

THE TRANSPORT SYSTEM

The underground (the "tube") is usually by far the quickest way of travelling around London. Services are, however, prone to delays and the trains are often crowded. Changing lines may involve a longish walk at some stations.

London is so large that some sights are a long way, even a bus journey, from any Underground station. There are also areas, often in the south, with no Underground service. Bus travel can be slow, and walking may be quicker.

Photocard and Weekly Travelcard

TRAVELCARDS

Public transport in London is expensive compared with many cities in Europe because levels of government subsidy are low, and the distances are great. Short trips are relatively more expensive than the longer journeys; it is rarely worthwhile getting on a tube to travel just one stop.

By far the most economical tickets are Travelcards – daily, weekly or monthly passes that allow unlimited travel on all forms of transport in the zones you require. (Six

bands, called travel zones, extend from the city centre into the outer suburbs; most of London's main sights are located in zone one.)

Travelcards are bought in train or Underground stations *(see p362)* and at newsagents displaying a red "pass agent" sign. For weekly and monthly tickets you have to provide a passport-sized photo for a

Photocard. One-day Travel-cards (no photo needed) cannot be used before 9.30am from Monday to Friday. There are, however, no restrictions when you use your weekly or monthly Travelcards. If you are in London for four days or more, a one- or two-zone weekly Travelcard is probably the most economical and convenient pass to buy.

LONDON ON FOOT

Once you get used to traffic driving on the left, London can be safely explored on foot but take care when crossing the road. There are two types of pedestrian crossing in London: striped zebra crossings marked by beacons, and push-button crossings at traffic lights. Traffic should stop for you if you are waiting at a zebra crossing, but at push-button crossings cars will not stop until the green man lights up. Look out for instructions written on the road; these tell you from which direction you can expect the traffic to come.

Zebra crossing

Beacons mark London's older-style zebra crossings.

Pushing the button makes the red man, located on a pillar across the road, turn into a green man.

Push-button control

Do not cross   **Cross the road**

Driving a Car in London

Sign for a car park

MOST VISITORS ARE better off not driving in central London. Traffic moves at an average speed of about 11 mph (18 km/h) during the rush hour, and parking is hard to find. Many Londoners only take their car out at weekends and after 6.30pm on weekdays, when you are allowed to park on some single yellow lines and at parking meters free of charge. Remember that you must drive on the left.

Double yellow lines on road, meaning no parking at any time

PARKING REGULATIONS

PARKING IN London is scarce, and you should look closely at any restrictions (usually attached to lampposts). Meters close to the centre are expensive during working hours (usually 8.00am–6.30pm Mon–Sat). You will also need plenty of coins *(see p349)* to feed them. Two hours is usually the maximum time you can stay at any meter. National Car Parks (marked with the logo NCP) are available in central areas and are easy to find. NCP produces a free London Parking Guide showing its parks; write to 21 Bryanston Street, W1A 4NH or call 0171-499 7050.

Parking meter

You are not allowed to park along red routes or on double yellow lines at any time. Parking on single yellow lines is prohibited during working hours but you can park on them during the evenings or on Sundays provided you are not causing an obstruction. Resident permit zones are unenforceable outside office hours, but remove your car before 8am. Steer clear of any parking areas marked "cardholders only". Parking on pedestrian crossings is always forbidden. In Pay-and-Display areas, you should buy a ticket for the appropriate time span to display on your windscreen.

CLAMPING AND TOWING

IF YOU PARK illegally or allow a meter to run out, you may well find your car has been clamped. A large notice

slapped across your windscreen will inform you which Payment Centre you need to visit to get your car released (after paying a hefty fine). If you can't find your car at all, it is quite likely to have been removed by a team of London's feared and hated car impounders. Their speed and efficiency are remarkable, the cost and inconvenience to drivers enormous: it is rarely worth taking the risk. The main car pounds are at Hyde Park, Kensington and Camden Town. Ring 0171-747 7474 and you will be told if they do have your car and whereabouts it is being held.

TRAFFIC SIGNS

Every driver should read the UK Highway Code *manual (available from bookshops) and familiarize themselves with London's traffic signs.*

Illegally parked car immobilized by wheel clamp

CAR HIRE AGENCIES

Avis
 0171-917 6700.

Eurodollar
0171-278 2273.

Europcar
0171-387 2276.

Hertz
0171-278 1588.

No stopping

30 mph (48 km/h) speed limit

No entry

Give way to all vehicles

One-way traffic

No right turn allowed

CYCLING AROUND LONDON

London's busy roads can be quite hazardous for cyclists, but the parks and quieter districts make excellent cycling routes. Use a solid lock to deter thieves, and wear weatherproof reflective clothing. Cycle helmets are not compulsory but are strongly recommended. Bikes can be hired from **On Your Bike** and **Portobello Cycles**.
Hire shop numbers and adresses On Your Bike, 52–54 Tooley St SE1. 0171-357 6958. Portobello Cycles, 69 Golborne Rd W10. 0181-960 0444.

Travelling by Underground

London Underground train

THE UNDERGROUND system, known as the "tube" to Londoners, has 273 stations, each clearly marked with the Underground logo. Tube trains run every day, except Christmas Day, from about 5.30am until just after midnight, but a few lines or sections of lines have an irregular service. Check when the last train leaves if you are relying on it after 11.30pm. Fewer trains run on Sundays. It can occasionally be unpleasant travelling on the tube late at night.

Underground sign outside a station

Reading the Underground Map

The 11 Underground lines are colour-coded and maps (see inside cover) called Journey Planners are posted at every station. Maps of the central section are displayed in the trains. The map shows how to change lines to travel from where you are to any station on the Underground system. Some lines, such as the Victoria and Jubilee, are simple single-branch routes; others, such as the Northern line, have more than one branch. The Circle line is a continuous loop around central London. Distances shown on the map are not to scale and the routes that lines are seen to take should not be relied upon for directions.

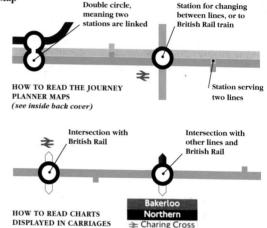

Double circle, meaning two stations are linked

Station for changing between lines, or to British Rail train

HOW TO READ THE JOURNEY PLANNER MAPS
(see inside back cover)

Station serving two lines

Intersection with British Rail

Intersection with other lines and British Rail

HOW TO READ CHARTS DISPLAYED IN CARRIAGES

Bakerloo
Northern
⇌ Charing Cross

BUYING A TICKET

If you are likely to be making more than two journeys a day on London's Underground, the best ticket to buy is a Travelcard *(see p360)*. You can also buy single tickets or return tickets either from the ticket office in each station or from one of the two types of automatic machines that are found in most stations. The large machines *(see below)* take coins and £5 or £10 notes, and normally give change. You select the ticket type you need, then the station you are travelling to, and the cost of the fare is automatically displayed. The smaller machines only show a choice of fare prices from which you select the correct one for your journey. They do not take notes, seldom give change, and are geared towards regular Underground travellers, who know the cost of their journey in advance.

1 Select the type of ticket you need from those shown: adult or child, single, return, or one-day Travelcard.

2 Press the button for the station you want to travel to.

3 The fare is shown here. Also indicated is whether you need to give exact money or if change can be given.

4 Insert either coins or a bank note. The machine will give you change if it has enough coins.

5 Collect your tickets and any change.

Tickets
Keep your ticket – you will need it at the end of your journey.

MAKING A JOURNEY BY UNDERGROUND

1 When you first enter the station, check which line, or lines, you will need to take. If you have any difficulty planning your route, ask the clerk at the ticket office for help.

⊖ **Journey planner**

Feed your ticket or Travelcard into the slot found at the front of the machine.

2 Buy your ticket or Travelcard from one of the automatic machines *(see facing page)* or the ticket office located in each station. If you wish to make a return journey by Underground, you will normally be given one ticket which you must keep until you have completed both journeys.

As soon as your ticket emerges, withdraw it and the gate will open.

3 The platforms are on the other side of the ticket barriers. These are easy to use if you follow the correct procedure.

The ticket office is near the ticket barriers in most stations.

Central line →

4 Follow the directions to the line on which you need to travel. In some cases this can be a complicated route, so keep your eyes open.

Central line
Westbound platform 5 →

5 You will eventually find yourself with a choice of platforms for the line you want. Look at the list of stations if you are not sure which direction to take.

6 Most platforms now have electronic indicators displaying the destination of the next two or three trains and the length of time that you will have to wait before they arrive.

1 HAINAULT via Newbury Park
2 EPPING   5 mins

On some trains, you must push a button to open the carriage doors.

7 Once you have boarded the train and begun your journey, you can check on your progress using the line chart displayed in every carriage. As you pull into each station, you will see its name posted along the length of the walls.

Way out →
⇌ British Rail

Hammersmith & City →
Metropolitan and Circle lines

8 After leaving the train, look for signs giving directions to exits or to platforms for any connecting lines.

London's Buses

ONE OF LONDON'S most recognizable symbols is the old-fashioned, red double-decker Routemaster bus, but it is a less common sight than it once was. As a result of deregulation and privatization of the city's bus system, there are now many

London Regional Transport symbol

smaller modern buses, some single-decker and some not even red, carrying passengers on London's streets. If you are able to get a seat, a bus journey is an undemanding and enjoyable way of seeing London. If you are in a hurry, however, it can be frustrating. London's traffic is notoriously congested and slow-moving and bus journeys can take a long time, especially during rush hours (8–9.30am and 4.30–6.30pm).

FINDING THE RIGHT BUS

EACH BUS STOP in central London has a list of main destinations showing which bus routes you need. There may also be a local street plan with each nearby bus stop letter-coded. Make sure you catch a bus going in the right direction; if in doubt, check with the driver.

USING LONDON'S BUSES

BUSES PAUSE, even if nobody wants to get on or off, at stops marked with the LRT symbol *(see above)*, unless they are labelled "request" stops. Route numbers and destinations are displayed clearly on the front and rear of the bus. The newer buses have only a driver, who takes fares as passengers board. Routemaster services have both a driver and a conductor who collects fares during the journey. The driver or conductor will tell you the fare for your destination and give change (but not for large notes). You will be given a ticket valid only for that journey – if you change buses you have to pay again. Keep your ticket until the end of your journey

Bus Conductor
Conductors sell tickets on London's Routemaster buses.

in case an inspector boards. Buying a Travelcard *(see p360)* is more convenient especially if you are making several journeys.

When you want to get off the bus, ring the bell as the bus approaches the stop you require; on Routemasters the conductor will do this for you. Never get on or off a bus unless it is standing at a bus stop. If you are not sure which stop you need, ask the conductor or driver.

Bus Stops
Buses always pause at stops marked with the LRT symbol (far left). At request stops (below), hail the driver by raising your arm. In practice it pays to do this at any stop.

Tickets on Routemasters
The conductor will issue you with the right ticket for your journey. Try not to pay with a large note.

USEFUL BUS ROUTES

Several of London's bus routes are convenient for many of the capital's main sights and shops. If you arm yourself with a Travelcard and are in no particular hurry, sightseeing or shopping by bus can be great fun. The cost of a journey by public transport is far less than any of the charges levied by tour operators, but you won't have the commentary that tour companies give you as you pass sights *(see p344)*.

There are also some sights or areas in London that are inaccessible by Underground. Buses run regularly from the city centre to, for instance, the Albert Hall *(see p203)*, Chelsea *(see pp188–93)*, and Clerkenwell *(see p243)*.

Harrod's

Marble Arch

Knightsbridge

Hyde Park Corner

Natural History Museum
South Kensington

Sloane Square

Victoria and Albert Museum

To stop the bus, press the bell located by the doors or near the stairs, just once.

Destinations are shown on the front and rear of buses.

To buy a ticket, have your money ready before you board.

Routemaster Bus
Board these buses at the rear. The conductor asks for your fare after you have boarded and found a seat.

Night Buses
These services run through the night from stops with this logo. One-day Travelcards are not valid on them.

New-Style Bus
These buses are controlled by the driver and do not have a conductor. The driver collects fares as passengers board.

NIGHT BUSES

LONDON'S NIGHT-TIME services run on several popular routes from 11pm until 6am. The routes are prefixed with the letter "N" before blue or yellow numbers. All these services pass through Trafalgar Square, so if you are out late, head there to get a ride at least part of the way home. Be sure to plan your journey carefully; London is so big that even if you board a bus going in the right direction you could end up completely lost, or a long walk from your accommodation. As always, make sure that you employ a little common sense when travelling on a night bus. Sitting all alone on the top deck is not a good idea; night buses never have a conductor. Travel information centres can supply you with details of routes and time-tables for night buses, which are also posted at bus stops.

Seeing London by British Rail

British Rail station sign

BRITISH RAIL'S train service is used by many hundreds of thousands of commuters each day. As far as visitors to London are concerned, BR services are useful for trips to the outskirts of the capital, especially south of the river where the Underground hardly extends. You may also decide to take a train for much longer excursions around Britain (*see pp358–9*).

USEFUL ROUTES

PERHAPS THE MOST useful BR line for visitors to London is the one that starts off from Charing Cross or Cannon Street stations (services from here only run on weekdays) and goes via London Bridge to Greenwich (*see pp232–9*).

The Thameslink service also connects Luton Airport with south London, Gatwick Airport and Brighton via West Hampstead and Blackfriars.

USING THE TRAINS

LONDON HAS EIGHT main railway stations serving the whole of the southeast and beyond (*see pp358–9*). BR

services travel overground and vary between slow stopping trains, express services to major towns and Intercity trains which travel throughout the UK. Make sure that you study the platform indicators carefully so that you get on the most direct train to the correct destination.

Some train doors will open automatically, others at the touch of a button or else by means of a handle. To open the older-style manual doors from inside, you need to pull down the window and reach outside. Keep well away from the doors while the train is travelling, and if you have to stand, make sure you hold on firmly to a strap or hand-rail.

BR TICKETS

All tickets must be bought in person, either from a travel agent or from a BR station. Most credit cards are accepted. Queues for ticket offices can often be long, so use the automatic machines that operate similarly to those on the Underground (*see p362*).

A bewildering range of train tickets exists, but two main options stand out: for travel within Greater London, Travelcards (*see p360*) offer the most flexibility, while for longer journeys, Cheap Day Return tickets offer excellent value compared to the standard return fares. However, these are both only obtainable and usable after 9.30am.

**Cheap Day
Return tickets**

DAY TRIPS

Southeast England has a lot more besides the capital to offer visitors. Getting out of London is fast and very easy with British Rail. For details of sights ring the English Tourist Board (*see p345*). BR Passenger Enquiries (0171-928 5100) will give you details of all their services.

Boating on the River Thames at Windsor Castle

Audley End
Village with a stunning Jacobean mansion nearby.
🚊 *from Liverpool Street. 40 miles (64 km); 1 hr.*

Bath
Beautiful Georgian city which has escaped redevelopment. It also has Roman remains.
🚊 *from Paddington. 107 miles (172 km); 1 hr 25 mins.*

Brighton
Lively and attractive seaside resort. See the Royal Pavilion.
🚊 *from Victoria. 53 miles (85 km); 1 hr.*

Cambridge
University city with fine art gallery and ancient colleges.
🚊 *from Liverpool Street or King's Cross. 54 miles (86 km); 1 hr.*

Canterbury
Its cathedral is one of England's oldest and greatest sights.
🚊 *from Victoria. 84 miles (98 km); 1 hr 25 mins.*

Hatfield House
Elizabethan palace with remarkable contents.
🚊 *from King's Cross or Moorgate. 21 miles (33 km); 20 mins.*

Oxford
Like Cambridge, famous for its ancient university.
🚊 *from Paddington. 56 miles (86 km); 1 hr.*

Salisbury
Famous for its cathedral, Salisbury is within driving distance of Stonehenge.
🚊 *from Waterloo. 84 miles (135 km); 1 hr 40 mins.*

St Albans
Once a great Roman city.
🚊 *from King's Cross or Moorgate. 25 miles (40km); 30 mins.*

Windsor
Riverside town; royal castle damaged by fire in 1992.
🚊 *from Paddington, change Slough. 20 miles (32 km); 30 mins.*

Getting a Taxi

Lolondon's well-known black cabs are almost as much of an institution as its red buses. But they, too, are being modernized, and you may well see blue, green, red or even white cabs, with some carrying advertising. Black-cab drivers have to take a stringent test on their knowledge of London's streets and its quickest traffic routes before they are awarded a licence. Contrary to popular opinion, they are also among London's safest drivers, if only because they are forbidden to drive a cab with damaged bodywork.

London taxi rank

FINDING A CAB

Licensed cabs must carry a "For Hire" sign, which is lit up whenever they are free. You can ring for them, hail them on the streets or find them at ranks, especially near large stations and some major hotels. Raise your arm and wave purposefully. The cab will stop and you simply tell the driver your destination. If a cab stops, it must take you anywhere within a radius of 6 miles (9.6 km) as long as it is

in the Metropolitan Police district, which includes most of the Greater London area and Heathrow Airport.

An alternative to black cabs are mini-cabs, saloon cars summoned by ringing a firm or going into one of their offices, which are usually open 24 hours a day. Do not take a mini-cab in the street as they often operate illegally, without proper insurance, and can be dangerous. Negotiate your fare before setting off. Mini-cab firms are listed in the Yellow Pages (see p352).

TAXI FARES

All licensed cabs have meters which will start ticking at around £1 as soon as the taxidriver accepts your custom. The fare increases by minute or for each 311 m (340 yds) travelled. Surcharges are then added for every piece of luggage, each extra passenger

The modern colours of traditional London cabs

and unsocial hours such as late at night. Fares should be displayed in the vehicle.

USEFUL NUMBERS

Computer Cabs (licensed)
0171-286 0286.

Radio Taxis (licensed)
0171-272 0272.

Ladycabs (women-only drivers) 0171-254 3501.

My Fare Lady (women-only drivers) 0181-458 9200.

Lost property
0171-833 0996.
Open 9am–4pm Mon–Fri.

Complaints
0171-230 1631
You will need to know the cab's serial number.

The light, when lit, shows the cab is available and whether there is wheelchair access.

The meter displays your fare as it increases, and surcharges for extra passengers, luggage or unsocial hours. Fares are the same in all licensed cabs.

Fare / Surcharges /

Licensed Cabs
London's cabs are a safe way of travelling around the capital. They have two fold-down seats, can carry a maximum of five passengers and have ample luggage space.

H301XYW

STREET FINDER

THE MAP REFERENCES given with all sights, hotels, restaurants, shops and entertainment venues described in this book refer to the maps in this section (*see* How Map References Work *opposite*). A complete index of street names and all the places of interest marked on the maps can be found on the following pages.

The key map shows the area of London covered by the *Street Finder*, with the postal codes of all the various districts. The maps include the sightseeing areas (which are colour-coded), as well as the whole of central London with all the districts important for hotels, restaurants, pubs and entertainment venues.

Postal districts are labelled and outlined in orange.

KEY

-- Postal district boundary

HOW THE MAP REFERENCES WORK

The first figure tells you which Street Finder map to turn to.

Wesley's House and Chapel ⑫

49 City Rd EC1. **Map** 7 B4.
📞 0171-253 2262. ⊖ Old St.
House open 10am–4pm Mon–Sat.
Adm charge. 📷 ♿ ✝ 11 am Sun.
🎦 📷 **Films, exhibitions.**

A letter and number give the grid reference. Letters go across the map's top and bottom; figures on its sides.

The map continues on map 15 of the Street Finder.

KEY TO STREET FINDER

🟦	Major sight
⬜	Other sight
🟦	Other building
⊖	Underground station
🚉	Railway station
🚌	Coach station
⛴	River boats boarding point
ℹ	Tourist information office
➕	Hospital with casualty unit
🚔	Police station
✝	Church
✡	Synagogue
☒	Post office
=	Railway line
▬	Motorway
—	One-way street
▬	Pedestrian street
«130	House number (main street)

SCALE OF MAP PAGES

0 metres   200

0 yards   200

1:12, 000

Street Finder Index

Each place name is followed by its postal district, and then by its Street Finder reference

Each place name is followed by its postal district, and then by its Street Finder reference

Each place name is followed by its postal district, and then by its Street Finder reference

Each place name is followed by its postal district, and then by its Street Finder reference

General Index

Acknowledgments

DORLING KINDERSLEY would like to thank the following people whose help and assistance contributed to the preparation of this book.

MAIN CONTRIBUTOR

Michael Leapman was born in London in 1938 and has been a professional journalist since he was 20. He has worked for most British national newspapers and now writes about travel and other subjects for several publications, among them *The Independent, Independent on Sunday, The Economist* and *Country Life*. He has written ten books, including *London's River* (published 1991) and the award-winning *Companion Guide to New York* (1983, revised 1991). In 1989 he edited the widely praised *Book of London*.

CONTRIBUTORS

Yvonne Deutch, Guy Dimond, George Foster, Iain Gale, Fiona Holman, Phil Harris, Christopher Middleton, Steven Parissien, Bazyli Solowij, Mark Wareham, Jude Welton.

DORLING KINDERSLEY wishes to thank the following editors and researchers at Webster's International Publishers: Sandy Carr, Matthew Barrell, Siobhan Bremner, Serena Cross, Annie Galpin, Miriam Lloyd, Ava-Lee Tanner.

ADDITIONAL PHOTOGRAPHY

Max Alexander, Peter Anderson, June Buck, Peter Chadwick, Michael Dent, Philip Dowell, Mike Dunning, Andreas Einsiedel, Steve Gorton, Christi Graham, Alison Harris, Peter Hayman, Stephen Hayward, Roger Hilton, Ed Ironside, Colin Keates, Dave King, Neil Mersh, Nick Nichols, Robert O'Dea, Vincent Oliver, John Parker, Tim Ridley, Kim Sayer, Chris Stevens, James Stevenson, James Strachan, Doug Traverso, David Ward, Mathew Ward, Steven Wooster and Nick Wright.

ADDITIONAL ILLUSTRATIONS

Ann Child, Tim Hayward, Fiona M Macpherson, Janos Marffy, David More, Chris D Orr, Richard Phipps, Michelle Ross, John Woodcock.

CARTOGRAPHY

Advanced Illustration (Cheshire), Contour Publishing (Derby), Euromap Limited (Berkshire). Street Finder maps: ERA Maptec Ltd (Dublin) adapted with permission from original survey and mapping from Shobunsha (Japan).

CARTOGRAPHIC RESEARCH

James Anderson, Roger Bullen, Tony Chambers, Ruth Duxbury, Jason Gough, Ailsa Heritage, Jayne Parsons, Donna Rispoli, Jill Tinsley, Andrew Thompson, Iorwerth Watkins.

RESEARCH ASSISTANCE

Chris Lascelles, Kathryn Steve.

DESIGN AND EDITORIAL ASSISTANCE

Keith Addison, Oliver Bennett, Michelle Clark, Carey Combe, Vanessa Courtier, Lorna Damms, Simon Farbrother, Marcus Hardy, Sasha Heseltine, Stephanie Jackson, Stephen Knowlden, Jeanette Leung, Jane Middleton, Fiona Morgan, Louise Parsons, Leigh Priest, Liz Rowe, Simon Ryder, Susannah Steel, Anna Streiffert, Andrew Szudek, Diana Vowles, Andy Wilkinson.

SPECIAL ASSISTANCE

Christine Brandt at Kew Gardens, Shelia Brown at The Bank of England, John Cattermole at London Buses Northern, the DK picture department, especially Jenny Rayner, Pippa Grimes at the V & A, Emma Healy at Bethnal Green Museum of Childhood, Alan Hills at the British Museum, Emma Hutton and Cooling Brown Partnership, Gavin Morgan at the Musuem of London, Clare Murphy at Historic Royal Palaces, Ali Naqei at the Science Museum, Patrizio Semproni, Caroline Shaw at the Natural History Museum, Gary Smith at British Rail, Monica Thurnauer at The Tate and Alistair Wardle.

PHOTOGRAPHIC REFERENCE

The London Aerial Photo Library, and P and P F James.

PHOTOGRAPHY PERMISSIONS

DORLING KINDERSLEY would like to thank the following for their kind permission to photograph at their establishments: All Souls Church, Banqueting House (Crown Copyright by kind permission of Historic Royal Palaces), Barbican Centre, Burgh

House Trust, Cabinet War Rooms, Chapter House (English Heritage), Charlton House, Chelsea Physic Garden, Clink Exhibition, Maritime Trust (Cutty Sark), Design Museum, Gatwick Airport Ltd, Geffrye Museum, Hamleys and Merrythought, Heathrow Airport Ltd, Imperial War Museum, Dr Johnson's House, Keats House (the London Borough of Camden), London Underground Ltd, Madame Tussaud's, Old St Thomas's Operating Theatre, Patisserie Valerie, Place Below Vegetarian Restaurant, Royal Naval College, St Alfege's, St Bartholomew-the-Great, St Bartholomew-the-Less, St Botolph's Aldersgate, St James's, St John's Smith Square, The Rector and Churchwardens of St Magnus the Martyr, St Mary le Strand, St Marylebone Parish Church, St Paul's Cathedral, the Master and Wardens of the Worshipful Company of Skinners, Smollensky's Restaurants, Southbank Centre, Provost and Chapter of Southwark Cathedral, HM Tower of London, Wellington Museum, Wesley Chapel, the Dean and Chapter of Westminster, Westminster Cathedral, and Hugh Hales, General Manager of the Whitehall Theatre (part of the Maybox Theatre group). Dorling Kindersley would also like to thank all the other museums, galleries, churches, restaurants, shops, and other sights who aided us with photography at their establishments. These are too numerous to thank individually.

PICTURE CREDITS

t = top; tl = top left; tc = top centre;
tr = top right; cla = centre left above;
ca = centre above; cra = centre right above;
cl = centre left; c = centre; cr = centre right;
clb = centre left below; cb = centre below;
crb = centre right below; bl = bottom left;
b = bottom; bc = bottom centre;
br = bottom right.

Every effort has been made to trace the copyright holders and we apologise in advance for any unintentional omissions. We would be pleased to insert the appropriate acknowledgments in any subsequent edition of this publication.

Works of art have been reproduced with the permission of the following copyright holders:
© ADAGP, Paris and DACS, London 1993: 83br, 85c; © DACS 1993: 82cr; © D. HOCKNEY 1970 1: 85b; © the family of ERIC H. KENNINGTON,

RA: 151bl; © ROY LICHTENSTEIN DACS 1993: 83ca. The works illustrated on pages 45c, 206b, 266cb have been reproduced by kind permission of the HENRY MOORE FOUNDATION.

The Publishers are grateful to the following individuals, companies and picture libraries for permission to reproduce their photographs:

Printed by kind permission of MOHAMED AL FAYED: 310b; GOVERNOR AND COMPANY OF THE BANK OF ENGLAND: 145tr; BRIDGEMAN ART LIBRARY, London: 21t, 28t; British Library, London 14, 19tr, (detail) 21br, 24cb, (detail) 32tl, 32bl; Courtesy of the Institute of Directors, London 29cla; Guildhall Art Gallery, Corporation of London (detail) 26t; Guildhall Library, Corporation of London 24br, 76c; ML Holmes Jamestown – Yorktown Educational Trust, VA (detail) 17bc; Master and Fellows, Magdalene College, Cambridge (detail) 23clb; Marylebone Cricket Club, London 242c; William Morris Gallery, Walthamstow 19tl, 247tl; Museum of London 22–3; O'Shea Gallery, London (detail) 22cl; Royal Holloway & Bedford New College 157bl; Russell Cotes Art Gallery and Museum, Bournemouth 38tr; Thyssen-Bornemisza Collection, Lugano Casta 253b; Westminster Abbey, London (detail) 32bc; White House, Bond Street, London 28cb.

BRITISH AIRWAYS: 354t, 356tl, 359t; reproduced with permission of the BRITISH LIBRARY BOARD: 127b; © THE BRITISH MUSEUM: 16t, 16ca, 17tl, 40t, 91c, 126–7 all pics except 126t & 127b, 128–9 all pics.

CAMERA PRESS, London: P. Abbey - LNS 73cb; Cecil Beaton 79tl; HRH Prince Andrew 95bl; Allan Warren 31cb; COLORIFIC!: Steve Benbow 55t; David Levenson 66–7; THOMAS CORAM FOUNDATION FOR CHILDREN: 125b; Courtesy of the CORPORATION OF LONDON: 55c, 146t; COURTAULD INSTITUTE GALLERIES, London: 41c, 117b.

PERCIVAL DAVID FOUNDATION OF CHINESE ART: 130c; DEPARTMENT OF TRANSPORT (Crown Copyright): 361b; Courtesy of the GOVERNORS AND THE DIRECTORS DULWICH PICTURE GALLERY: 43bl, 248bl.

ENGLISH HERITAGE: 254b, 256b; ENGLISH LIFE PUBLICATIONS LTD: 255b; PHILIP ENTICKNAP:

247tr; ET ARCHIVE: 19bl, 26c, 26bc, 27bl, 28br, 29cra, 29clb, 33tc, 33cr, 36bl, 185tl; British Library, London 18cr; Imperial War Museum, London 30bc; Museum of London 15b, 27br, 28bl; Science Museum, London 27cla; Stoke Museum Staffordshire Polytechnic 23bl, 25cl, 33bc; Victoria and Albert Museum, London 20c, 21bc, 25tr; MARY EVANS PICTURE LIBRARY: 16bl, 16br, 17bl, 17br, 20bl, 22bl, 24t, 25bc, 25br, 27t, 27cb, 27bc, 30bl, 32br, 33tl, 33cl, 33bl, 33br, 36t, 36c, 38tl, 39bl, 72cb, 72b, 90b, 112b, 114b, 116c, 135t, 139t, 155bl, 159t, 162ca, 174ca, 178b, 203b, 212t, 222b.

Courtesy of the FAN MUSEUM (The Helene Alexander Collection) 239b; FREUD MUSEUM, London: 242t.

THE GORE HOTEL, London: 273.

ROBERT HARDING PICTURE LIBRARY: 31ca, 42c, 52ca, 169tl, 325t, 347cb, 366b; Philip Craven 206t; Brian Hawkes 21clb; Michael Jenner 21cra, 238t; 58t, 223t; HEATHROW AIRPORT LTD: 356tr; Reproduced with permission of HER MAJESTY'S STATIONARY OFFICE (Crown Copyright): 156 all pics; JOHN HESELTINE: 12tr, 13tl, 13tr, 13cb, 13br, 51tr, 63br, 98, 124b, 132, 142, 172, 216; FRIENDS OF HIGHGATE CEMETERY: 37tr, 240, 242b; HISTORIC ROYAL PALACES (Crown Copyright): 5t, 35tc, 250–1 all except 250br, 252–3 all except 253b; THE HORNIMAN MUSEUM, London: 248br; HOVERSPEED LTD: 359b; HULTON-DEUTSCH COLLECTION: 24bl, 124tl, 228t.

THE IMAGE BANK, London: Gio Barto 55b; Derek Berwin 31t, 272t; Romilly Lockyer 72t, 94br; Leo Mason 56t; Simon Wilkinson 197t; Terry Williams 139b; Courtesy of ISIC, UK: 352t.

PETER JACKSON COLLECTION: 24–5.

ROYAL BOTANIC GARDENS, KEW: Andrew McRob 48cl, 56b, 244–5 all pics except 245t & 245br.

LEIGHTON HOUSE, ROYAL BOROUGH OF KENSINGTON: 212b; LITTLE ANGEL MARIONETTE THEATRE: 341tl; LONDON AMBULANCE SERVICE: 347ca; LONDON TOY AND MODEL MUSEUM: 257t; LONDON TRANSPORT MUSEUM: 28ca; 362–3 all maps and tickets.

MADAME TUSSAUD'S: 218c, 220t; MANSELL COLLECTION: 19br, 20t, 20br, 21bl, 22t, 22cl, 23br, 27ca, 32tr; METROPOLITAN POLICE SERVICE: 346t, 347t; MUSEUM OF LONDON: 16cb, 17tr, 17cb, 18t, 21crb, 41tc, 166–7 all pics.

NATIONAL EXPRESS LTD: 358; Reproduced by courtesy of the TRUSTEES, THE NATIONAL GALLERY, London: (detail) 35c, 104–5 all except 104t, 106–7 all except 107t; NATIONAL PORTRAIT GALLERY, London: 4t, 41tl, 101cb, (detail) 102b; NATIONAL POSTAL MUSEUM, London: 26bl, 164t; By permission of the KEEPER OF THE NATIONAL RAILWAY MUSEUM, York: 28–9; NATIONAL SOUND ARCHIVE, London – The trademark HIS MASTER'S VOICE is reproduced with the kind permission of EMI RECORDS LIMITED: 197cl; NATIONAL TRUST PHOTOGRAPHIC LIBRARY: Wendy Aldiss 23ca; John Bethal 254t, 255t; Michael Boys 38b; NATURAL HISTORY MUSEUM, LONDON: 205t; Derek Adams 204b; John Downs 204c; NEW SHAKESPEARE THEATRE CO: 324bl.

PALACE THEATRE ARCHIVE: 108t; PICTOR INTERNATIONAL, London: 61t; PIPPA POP-INS CHILDREN'S HOTEL, London: 339b.

PITSHANGER MANOR MUSEUM: 256c; POPPERFOTO: 29tl, 29crb, 30tl, 30tr, 30c, 33tr, 39br; PRESS ASSOCIATION LTD: 29bl, 29br; PUBLIC RECORD OFFICE (Crown Copyright): 18b.

BILL RAFFERTY: 324br; REX FEATURES LTD: 53tl; Peter Brooker 53tr; Andrew Laenen 54c; THE RITZ, London: 91t; ROCK CIRCUS: 100cb; ROCK ISLAND DINER: 339ca; ROYAL ACADEMY OF ARTS, London: 90tr; THE BOARD OF TRUSTEES OF THE ROYAL ARMOURIES: 41tr, 155tl, 157tl, 157c, 157br; ROYAL COLLECTION, ST JAMES'S PALACE © HM THE QUEEN: 8–9, 53b, 88t, 93t, 94–5 all pics except 94br & 95bl, 96t, 250br; ROYAL COLLEGE OF MUSIC, London: 196c, 202c.

THE SAVOY GROUP: 274t, 274b; SCIENCE MUSEUM, London: 208cr, 208b, 209cla, 209cb; SCIENCE PHOTO LIBRARY: Maptec International Ltd 10b; SEALINK PLC: 355b; SPENCER HOUSE LTD: 88b; SOUTHBANK PRESS OFFICE: 182bl; SYNDICATION INTERNATIONAL: 31bl, 35tr, 52cb, 53c, 58bl, 59t, 136; Library of Congress 25bl.

TATE GALLERY: 43br, 82–3 all pics except 82t & 83t, 84–5 all pics.

Courtesy of the BOARD OF TRUSTEES OF THE VICTORIA AND ALBERT MUSEUM: 35br, 40b, 198–9 all except 198t, 200–1 all pics, 246b, 340t.

THE WALDORF, London: 272b; THE WALLACE COLLECTION, London: 40ca, 222c; Courtesy of the TRUSTEES OF THE WEDGWOOD MUSEUM, Barlaston, Stoke-on-Trent, Staffs, England: 26br; VIVIENNE WESTWOOD: Patrick Fetherstonhaugh 31br; THE WIMBLEDON LAWN TENNIS MUSEUM: Micky White 249t; Photo © WOODMANSTERNE: Jeremy Marks 35tl, 149t.

YOUTH HOSTEL ASSOCIATION: 275.

ZEFA: 10t, 52b, 54br, 324c; Bob Croxford 57t; Clive Sawyer 57b.

Front Endpaper: all special or additional photography except THE IMAGE BANK, London: Romilly Lockyer bl, crb; MUSEUM OF LONDON: bcr; NATURAL HISTORY MUSEUM: John Downs cl; TATE GALLERY: bcl; Courtesy of the BOARD OF TRUSTEES OF THE VICTORIA AND ALBERT MUSEUM: cla.

The London Underground

O   Interchange stations

⇌   Connections with British Rail

⇌   Connections with British Rail within
     walking distance

★   Closed Sundays

⊠   Closed Saturdays and Sundays

▲   Served by Piccadilly line trains all day Sundays
     and early morning and late evening Mondays to
     Saturdays

†   For opening times see poster journey planners
     Certain stations are closed during public holidays

© Copyright London Regional Transport

UNDERGROUND

Travel Information 071-222 1234
Travelcheck 071-222-1200